AND TRY THESE FEATURES...

Making Relationship Choices	Skills Practice	Self-Reflection	Focus on Culture	Pop Quiz
Read about a misunderstanding between friends on pages 34-35	Learn to convey information about an interpersonal relationship on page 25	Think about the influence of interpersonal communication on your conversations on page 20		
	Practice overcoming negative self-fulfilling prophecies on page 47		Read about appearance cultures and self-esteem on page 50	Test your self-esteem on page 51
Learn how to deal with change in intimate relationships on pages 108-109	Learn how to make better attributions online on page 87	Analyze how you perceive others based on personality traits on page 96	Think about how your race effects your perception of others on page 92	Find out how you perceive gender differences on page 93
Read about providing support while angry on pages 144-145	Improve how you manage anger while using e-mail or instant-messaging on page 140	Assess your use of emotional management strategies on page 132		Find out your hostility level on page 131
		Assess how you communicate with people whose beliefs, attitudes, and values differ from yours on page 175	Learn how to communicate better with people of different ages on page 160	Test your intercultural competence on page 175
Learn how to competently listen during difficult situations on pages 210-211	Boost your recall of information exchanged during online encounters on page 197	Examine how to avoid listening for the wrong purposes on page 201		Assess your ability to adapt your listening to different situations on page 201
Examine how honesty works in verbal communication on pages 250-251	Discover how to avoid unintentional miscommunication online on page 246		Learn how using insults conveys prejudice on page 232	Test when you think deception is acceptable on page 247
Learn how to deal with mixed messages from a possible romantic partner on pages 286-287		Understand how nonverbal communication defines relationships on page 284	Read about how the use of touch varies in different cultures on page 276	
Consider how to deal with family conflicts on pages 322-323	Create better conflict resolutions on page 317	Try to identify the causes of a conflict on page 314	Learn about Radical Pacifism as a way to approach conflict on page 308	Learn how you approach conflict on page 307
Analyze how to deal with infidelity on pages 370-371		Assess your views on types of betrayal on page 368		Think about how often you betray romantic partners on page 367
	Learn to maintain long-distance friendships on page 409	Think about how you follow friendship rules on page 408		Discover what kind of friend you are on page 401
Examine what to do when a friend gets promoted on pages 444-445	Learn how to sharpen your advocacy skills on page 436	Assess your relationships with people at work on page 421	Confront the model minority myth on page 438	Test your peer relationship maintenance on page 433

Reflect & Relate

An Introduction
to Interpersonal Communication

Reflect & Relate

An Introduction
to Interpersonal Communication

Steven McCornack

Michigan State University

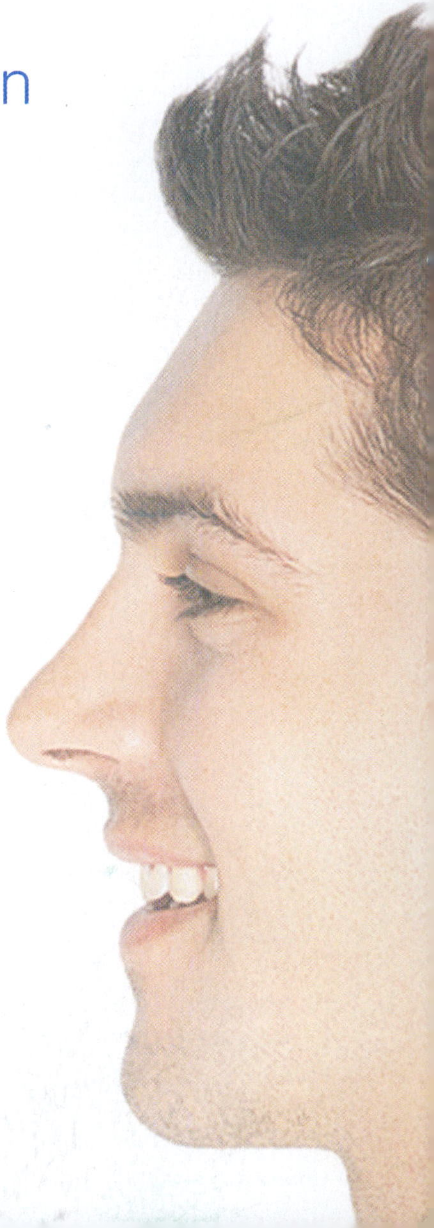

BEDFORD/ST. MARTIN'S

Boston ◆ New York

For Bedford/St. Martin's

Executive Editor for Communication: Erika Gutierrez
Developmental Editor: Vikram Mukhija
Associate Editor: Noel Hohnstine
Senior Production Editor: Harold Chester
Senior Production Supervisor: Joe Ford
Executive Marketing Manager: Rachel Falk
Art Director: Lucy Krikorian
Text Design: Anna Palchik
Copy Editor: Pat Herbst
Photo Research: Sue McDermott
Cover Design: Donna Lee Dennison and Billy Boardman
Cover Art: Front left: *Side view of a businesswoman* © Mash/ GettyImages. Front right: *Young man's profile* © Joe Kingleigh/GettyImages. Back left: *Businessman* © LaCoppola-Meier/ GettyImages. Back right: *Profile of woman* © Russell Monk/ Masterfile
Composition: Techbooks
Printing and Binding: R.R. Donnelley & Sons Company

President: Joan E. Feinberg
Editorial Director: Denise B. Wydra
Director of Development: Erica T. Appel
Director of Marketing: Karen Melton Soeltz
Director of Editing, Design, and Production: Marcia Cohen
Managing Editor: Shuli Traub

Library of Congress Control Number: 2006935060

Manufactured in the United States of America.
2   1   0   9   8   7
f   e   d   c   b   a

For information, write: Bedford/St. Martin's, 75 Arlington Street, Boston, MA 02116 (617-399-4000)

ISBN-10: 0-312-25949-2
ISBN-13: 978-0-312-25949-5

Acknowledgments

Acknowledgments and copyrights appear at the back of the book on pages C-1–C-3, which constitute an extension of the copyright page.

Preface

I still remember the first introductory interpersonal communication class I taught as a graduate student at the University of Illinois. I recall the layout of the classroom, my nervousness, and how I arrived early to set the desks in a circle. I can even remember some of my students' faces and names: Andrew the social activist, Kelly the cynical genius, Randy the handsome charmer—people whose lives I would come to know well in the weeks that followed. But what I recall most about teaching my first interpersonal communication class are the questions that dominated my thoughts, questions whose answers I ultimately encoded into the design of the course. What impact do I want to have on my students? What concepts do I want them to learn? How do I want them to make use of these concepts?

These questions face every instructor teaching an introductory interpersonal communication class, whether for the first or the forty-first time. My answers to them still guide my approach to teaching: I want to provide students with the best scholarship, help them improve their communication skills, and empower them to build and maintain healthy interpersonal relationships. While my goals for the course have not changed over the years, the field of interpersonal communication, its students, and the world have. Textbooks have tried to adapt by adding on content and have had varying success. But only a new book can truly address the world we live in now. I believe the time has come for that new text, one that provides a fresh synthesis of the field of interpersonal communication in a way specifically designed to help students meet the challenges they currently face.

The ideal textbook for today's student and today's world would be rock-solid in content, represent the finest of new and classic scholarship in our discipline, and provide a clear sense of the field as a domain of scientific endeavor, not just "common sense." At the same time, it would be accessible, welcoming, and friendly—never intimidating. It should be a great read, leading students to complete entire chapters before they realize they have done so. The examples would hook students' interest, clearly illustrate the concepts being discussed, and help students relate theory and research to real-life situations. Everything in my new textbook, *Reflect & Relate: An Introduction to Interpersonal Communication*—its content, its writing, its pedagogy, its examples, and even its design—is created to achieve these objectives.

Reflect & Relate arms students with the best coverage our field has to offer, including topics that were almost unknown a few years ago but are now heavily studied. Whether it's a discussion of managing challenging emotions, family communication patterns, or workplace relationships, you will find them framed with accessible language and engaging examples.

And, in an era saturated with pop culture advice about interpersonal behavior, *Reflect & Relate* provides students with trustworthy, useful, and practical information about how to improve their communication skills and their relationships.

The book also takes into account that students' perspectives on many topics have radically shifted. For example, online communication is so naturally integrated into students' lives that they perceive little difference between it and face-to-face communication. For this reason, *Reflect & Relate* integrates coverage of online communication throughout the text showing students how everyday technologies such as e-mail, instant messaging, and social networking Web sites can be used to better connect them with others. Although students live in an increasingly diverse world and are familiar with differences in gender, culture, sexual orientation, and class, they often don't realize how such differences shape communication. Every chapter in *Reflect & Relate* helps sensitize students to the many communication differences—and similarities—that exist and explains how they can manage them in their own communication practices. Also, *Reflect & Relate* does not shy away from difficult topics, but rather takes students into the "dark side" of interpersonal communication and relationships to help them cope with the damaging encounters that occur all too frequently. Most importantly, *Reflect & Relate* will teach students *how* to systematically reason through interpersonal communication and relationship problems.

Features

The following features of *Reflect & Relate* are designed to address the new realities of the interpersonal communication classroom.

Reflect & Relate *Offers a New Look at the Discipline*

- *Reflect & Relate* **presents a fresh perspective on interpersonal communication.** Across *Reflect & Relate*, discussions of scholarship from interpersonal communication, psychology, sociology, philosophy, and linguistics are woven together. But, unlike other texts, the focus remains on how these concepts are linked to interpersonal communication and on how communication skills can be improved. For example, in Chapter 3, the perceptual process is discussed not just as a general psychological process but in terms of how each stage of perception influences how we view others' communication, and how perceptions of communication can be improved.

- *Reflect & Relate* **balances new topics of growing interest with classic coverage.** The text integrates coverage of online communication, workplace abuse, interpersonal competence, challenging emotions (such as chronic hostility and grief), and other new topics alongside familiar topics like self, listening, and perception. For example, Chapter 2, "Considering Self," balances traditional coverage of Erving Goffman's notion of "face" with a detailed discussion of how to effectively present your self online.

- *Reflect & Relate* **treats individual and cultural influences as integral parts of the story.** *Reflect & Relate* tackles myths and realities of how race, gender, ethnicity, sexuality, class, religion, and age affect communication, engaging students' interest while unpacking common misconceptions. But it does so without treating any particular group as "other" and without relegating coverage of difference to isolated sections of the text. Instead, differences and similarities are integrated naturally throughout the text and are complemented by **Focus on Culture** boxes, which challenge students to think about how the influence of their own cultures shapes their communication. For instance, in Chapter 11 students read about and discuss how class differences may affect parenting styles.

Reflect & Relate *Helps Students Look Deeply at Themselves — and Develop Skills for a Lifetime*

- **"Self-Reflection" questions foster critical self-reflection and self-awareness.** Self-awareness is essential for effective communication, and carefully placed **Self-Reflection** questions teach students how to examine their own experiences and communication in light of theory and research. As a result, students gain a better understanding of concepts—such as emotional intelligence, conflict style, and relationship ethics—and of themselves, and they learn the habit of ongoing critical self-reflection, which leads to better communication outcomes.

informality is the norm. For example, you might be encouraged by your supervisor to communicate openly and to challenge his or her ideas, regardless of your place in the hierarchy. In other organizations, people are expected to communicate more formally and to more strictly observe authority.

The second influence on an organization's culture is its workplace artifacts—the objects and structures that define the organization (Schein, 1985). Workplace artifacts include everything from the physical layout of your workspace to dress codes and even motivational items such as hallway posters urging you to always perform at your best.

The third influence on organizational culture is workplace values—the beliefs people share about work performance, dedication to the organization, and coworker relationships. For example, both places I worked for in my youth stressed employee excellence and productivity. But the ice cream parlor discouraged friendships between coworkers, whereas the pizza restaurant encouraged such relationships. Other examples include workplace beliefs regarding corporate responsibility to the environment, commitment to stakeholders (customers, employees, business partners, shareholders, and so forth), and worker integrity and ethical behavior.

SELF-REFLECTION

Think about the culture of an organization you belong to. What norms exist regarding communication? What expectations? What values are considered most important for the organization's success? Do you buy into this organizational culture? How does the organizational culture shape your work and your feelings about the organization?

When you join an organization, you usually are socialized into its culture (Miller, 1995). Through formal and informal exchanges between new and established coworkers, you discover how you should communicate as well as what's okay or not okay to talk about. You further sense the organization's culture by observing the artifacts you see around you as well as through stated and unstated messages about the organization's values. During my first day as a dishwasher at the ice cream parlor, for example, my trainer (another dishwasher) told me, "People here don't really hang out together; we're all basically in it for the paycheck." My training at the pizza restaurant was conducted by the manager. He encouraged me to stay after work and enjoy free food and drink with my coworkers—an activity he called "new employee training."

Networks in the Workplace

Just as each of us has social networks of acquaintances, friends, and family members linked through communication, workplaces also have systems of communication linkages, known as **organizational networks** (Miller, 1995). Organizational networks are defined by three characteristics: the nature of

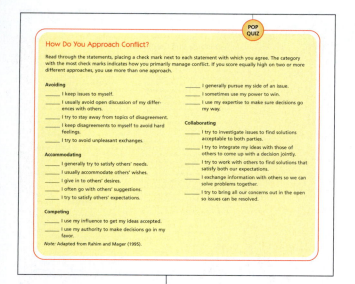

How Do You Approach Conflict?

Read through the statements, placing a check mark next to each statement with which you agree. The category with the most check marks indicates how you primarily manage conflict. If you score equally high on two or more different approaches, you use more than one approach.

Avoiding

_____ I keep issues to myself.
_____ I usually avoid open discussion of my differences with others.
_____ I try to stay away from topics of disagreement.
_____ I keep disagreements to myself to avoid hard feelings.
_____ I try to avoid unpleasant exchanges.

Accommodating

_____ I generally try to satisfy others' needs.
_____ I usually accommodate others' wishes.
_____ I give in to others' desires.
_____ I often go with others' suggestions.
_____ I try to satisfy others' expectations.

Competing

_____ I use my influence to get my ideas accepted.
_____ I use my authority to make decisions go in my favor.

_____ I generally pursue my side of an issue.
_____ I sometimes use my power to win.
_____ I use my expertise to make sure decisions go my way.

Collaborating

_____ I try to investigate issues to find solutions acceptable to both parties.
_____ I try to integrate my ideas with those of others to come up with a decision jointly.
_____ I try to work with others to find solutions that satisfy both our expectations.
_____ I exchange information with others so we can solve problems together.
_____ I try to bring all our concerns out in the open so issues can be resolved.

Note: Adapted from Rahim and Mager (1995).

- **"Pop Quiz" self-tests help students see what they're good at—and where they might need improvement.** Rooted in research, the quizzes help students analyze their strengths and weaknesses so they can focus on how to improve their communication. For example, in Chapter 9, a **Pop Quiz** allows students to assess their communication styles when approaching conflicts.

they tend to be difficult, self-involved, demanding, and ungenerous (Tavris, 1989).

A second common anger management strategy is venting: explosively disclosing all of your angry thoughts to the person or persons who triggered them. Many people view venting as helpful and healthy; it "gets the anger out." The assumption that venting will rid you of anger is rooted in the concept of **catharsis**, which holds that openly expressing your emotions enables you to purge them. But in contrast to popular beliefs about the benefits of venting, research suggests that while venting may provide a temporary sense of pleasure, it actually boosts anger. One field study of engineers and technicians who were fired from their jobs found that the more individuals vented their anger about the company, the angrier they became (Ebbeson, Duncan, & Konecni, 1975).

To effectively manage your anger, it's better to use strategies such as encounter avoidance, encounter structuring, and reappraisal. In cases where something or someone has already triggered anger within you, consider using an alternative approach: the **Jefferson strategy,** named after the third president of the United States. Here's how this strategy works: When a person says or does something that makes you angry, you count slowly to 10 before you speak or act (Tavris, 1989). If you are very angry, count slowly to 100; then speak or act. Thomas Jefferson adopted this simple strategy for reducing his own anger during interpersonal encounters.

Although the Jefferson strategy may seem clichéd, it's effective because it creates a delay between the event that triggered your anger, the accompanying arousal and awareness, and your communication response. The delay between your internal physical and mental reactions and your outward communication allows your arousal to diminish somewhat, including reduction of adrenaline, blood pressure, and heart rate. Therefore, you communi-

140 PART ONE / INTERPERSONAL ESSENTIALS

- **"Skills Practice" exercises strengthen students' repertoires.** Every chapter contains three skills exercises—one devoted to online communication—that give step-by-step instruction in practical skills such as appropriately self-disclosing and interpreting nonverbal codes. **Skills Practice** activities are specifically designed to be easily and practically implemented by students in their lives.

Reflect & Relate *Helps Students Improve Their Relationships*

- **Romantic relationships, friends and family, and workplace relationships are addressed individually.** Tailoring communication strategies to particular relationships is both essential and challenging, so *Reflect & Relate* devotes three full chapters to these key communication contexts, giving students in-depth knowledge along with practical strategies for using communication to improve relationships. In Chapters 10, 11, and 12, research on relationship maintenance is applied to romantic, family, friendship, and

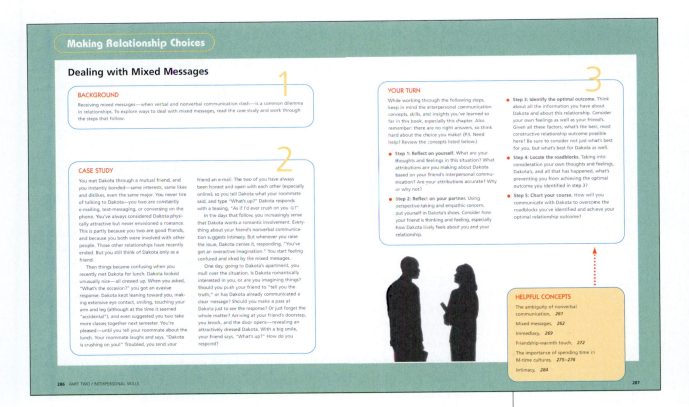

Making Relationship Choices

Dealing with Mixed Messages

1

BACKGROUND

Receiving mixed messages—when verbal and nonverbal communication clash—is a common dilemma in relationships. To explore ways to deal with mixed messages, read the case study and work through the steps that follow.

2

CASE STUDY

You met Dakota through a mutual friend, and you instantly bonded—same interests, same likes and dislikes, even the same major. You never tire of talking to Dakota—you two are constantly e-mailing, text-messaging, or conversing on the phone. You've always considered Dakota physically attractive but never envisioned a romance. This is partly because you two are good friends, and because you both were involved with other people. Those other relationships have recently ended. But you still think of Dakota only as a friend.

Then things became confusing when you recently met Dakota for lunch. Dakota looked unusually nice—all dressed up. When you asked, "What's the occasion?" you got an evasive response. Dakota kept leaning toward you, making extensive eye contact, smiling, touching your arm and leg (although at the time it seemed "accidental"), and even suggested you two take more classes together next semester. You're pleased—until you tell your roommate about the lunch. Your roommate laughs and says, "Dakota is crushing on you!" Troubled, you send your friend an e-mail. The two of you have always been honest and open with each other (especially online), so you tell Dakota what your roommate said, and type "What's up?" Dakota responds with a teasing, "As if I'd ever crush on you ☺!"

In the days that follow, you increasingly sense that Dakota wants a romantic involvement. Everything about your friend's nonverbal communication suggests intimacy. But whenever you raise the issue, Dakota denies it, responding, "You've got an overactive imagination." You start feeling confused and irked by the mixed messages.

One day, going to Dakota's apartment, you mull over the situation. Is Dakota romantically interested in you, or are you imagining things? Should you push your friend to "tell you the truth," or has Dakota already communicated a clear message? Should you make a pass at Dakota just to see the response? Or just forget the whole matter? Arriving at your friend's doorstep, you knock, and the door opens—revealing an attractively dressed Dakota. With a big smile, your friend says, "What's up?" How do you respond?

3

YOUR TURN

While working through the following steps, keep in mind the interpersonal communication concepts, skills, and insights you've learned so far in this book, especially this chapter. Also remember: there are no right answers, so think hard about the choice you make! (P.S. Need help? Review the concepts listed below.)

- **Step 1: Reflect on yourself.** What are your thoughts and feelings in this situation? What attributions are you making about Dakota based on your friend's interpersonal communication? Are your attributions accurate? Why or why not?

- **Step 2: Reflect on your partner.** Using perspective-taking and empathic concern, put yourself in Dakota's shoes. Consider how your friend is thinking and feeling, especially how Dakota likely feels about you and your relationship.

- **Step 3: Identify the optimal outcome.** Think about all the information you have about Dakota and about this relationship. Consider your own feelings as well as your friend's. Given all these factors, what's the best, most constructive relationship outcome possible here? Be sure to consider not just what's best for you, but what's best for Dakota as well.

- **Step 4: Locate the roadblocks.** Taking into consideration your own thoughts and feelings, Dakota's, and all that has happened, what's preventing you from achieving the optimal outcome you identified in step 3?

- **Step 5: Chart your course.** How will you communicate with Dakota to overcome the roadblocks you've identified and achieve your optimal relationship outcome?

HELPFUL CONCEPTS

The ambiguity of nonverbal communication, 261

Mixed messages, 262

Immediacy, 269

Friendship-warmth touch, 272

The importance of spending time in M-time cultures, 275–276

Intimacy, 284

coworker relationships. Students encounter concrete suggestions about how to communicate to foster relationship health and satisfaction. Throughout these chapters, special emphasis is given to relationship maintenance—the key relational concern most students bring to the classroom.

- **"Making Relationship Choices" case studies take application to a new level.** A unique feature, these cases challenge students to draw on all their knowledge when facing difficult relationship issues and to create their own solutions. Instead of just asking students "What would you do?" or offering them solutions, **Making Relationship Choices** teaches students how to systematically reason through problems to generate their own constructive solutions. Students walk step-by-step through realistic scenarios—critically self-reflecting, considering others' perspectives, determining best outcomes, and identifying potential roadblocks—to make informed communication decisions. For instance, in Chapter 8, they project themselves into a situation in which they receive mixed messages from a friend and need to make a choice about how to confront the issue.

Reflect & Relate *Offers a Fresh Look in a Textbook*

- *Reflect & Relate* **offers students a visually stunning design and an unparalleled art program.** Because students today are highly visual learners, *Reflect & Relate* offers a smart, lavish design that will grab their attention and focus them on the subject at hand. More than 350 provocative images complement the written text. For example, in Chapter 2, a photograph showing both Shirley MacLaine and her young daughter wearing makeup and pearls introduces the concept of gender socialization.

- *Reflect & Relate* **offers clear explanations, engaging examples, and a lively voice.** One of my goals was to create a textbook that really is a page-turner—one that holds students' interest with clear and compelling writing. Nearly every major concept is illustrated with examples drawn from pop culture, history, current events, and everyday life—examples that reflect the diversity of students themselves in age, gender, lifestyle, occupations, and culture. In Chapter 2, for instance, I introduce the concept of self through an artist's personal story of his struggle with dyslexia and its effects on his self-esteem. In the same chapter, the concept of "masks" and their relationship to self-presentation is illustrated with references to Rob Halford, lead singer of the heavy metal band Judas Priest, who hid his sexual orientation for years.

- *Reflect & Relate* **offers study aids to help students understand the language of the discipline.** To be able to apply interpersonal communication knowledge in their own lives and relationships, students must be comfortable with the working vocabulary of the discipline. *Reflect &*

The Sources of Self

For most of us, critical self-reflection isn't a new activity. We're already intimately familiar with ourselves. After all, we spend much of our daily lives looking inward, and as a consequence, we feel that we know our selves. But imagine for a moment that you don't. You wake up in your bed at home, and the first thing you notice is people talking in the living room. You recognize their voices as those of your family, but something is terribly wrong. An emptiness is blanketing much of your memory. Although you recognize your surroundings, you have no memory of self. Nothing. How will you find out who you are?

You might first examine your own body. Knowing whether you are male or female would immediately give you a wealth of useful knowledge about your self, such as which clothes you should wear and how you should talk and act. Second, you would likely venture downstairs to talk with family members, gathering as much information from them as you could. You would also watch how they respond to you. Do they seem intimate and caring toward you? Distant and aloof? Unpredictable and uncertain? Last, you would probably turn on the television, surf the web, or even take a walk into town, looking for clues about how people communicate with each other in public, how they dress, and how they behave. From these observations, you might begin to form ideas about where you fit in this culture.

Of course, at the end of the day, you still would have huge holes in your self-knowledge. Biologists and psychologists agree that roughly half of what makes us who we are is inborn, determined by our biological heritage (McCrae et al., 2000; Rothbart, Ahadi, & Evans, 2000). But these same scientists also point out that this biological "hard-wiring" doesn't mean that our self-awareness, self-concept, and self-esteem are 50 percent identical to those of our parents and other ancestors. Instead, regardless of the genetic hand we're dealt, our selves are also shaped by powerful outside forces of gender, family, and culture.

Gender and Self

Arguably the most profound outside force shaping our sense of self is our **gender**—the composite of social, psychological, and cultural attributes that characterize us as male or female (Canary, Emmers-Sommer, & Faulkner, 1997). It may strike you as strange to see gender described as an "outside force." Gender is innate, something you're born with, right? Actually, scholars distinguish gender, which is largely learned, from biological sex, which we're born with. Each of us is born with biological sex organs that distinguish us anatomically as male or female. However, our gender is shaped over time through our interactions with others.

Immediately after birth, we begin a lifelong process of gender socialization, learning from others what it means personally, interpersonally, and culturally to be "male" or "female." Girls are taught feminine behaviors and discover that the most important aspects of the feminine self are sensitivity to one's own and others' emotions, nurturance, and compassion (Lippa, 2002).

"Immediately after birth, we begin a lifelong process of gender socialization."

Relate provides accessible definitions within the text, a comprehensive glossary, checklists, and chapter reviews that focus on giving students a firm knowledge of useful terms and concepts.

Supplements

Book Companion Site at bedfordsmartins.com/reflectrelate
Leah Bryant, *DePaul University*

The student portion of this Web site offers learning tools and study aids such as chapter outlines, chapter quizzes, vocabulary flash cards, and extended learning activities. In addition, the instructor portion of the site includes PowerPoint slides for every chapter, a downloadable version of the instructor's manual, and student quiz tracking.

The Interpersonal Video Glossary at bedfordsmartins.com/reflectrelate
Marion Boyer

The Interpersonal Video Glossary presents short and informative video clips of *Reflect & Relate*'s most important vocabulary terms and concepts, allowing students to visualize and retain what they are learning.

Student Workbook
Jennifer Valencia, *San Diego Miramar Community College*; ISBN-10: 0-312-45910-6, ISBN-13: 978-0-312-45910-9

The comprehensive student workbook provides study outlines built around key terms and concepts to help students develop a strong grasp of the material. In addition, vocabulary activities reinforce terminology, communication and relationship exercises allow students to practice their skills, and practice quizzes help them prepare for examinations.

Course Management Content
Student and instructor resources developed for this textbook are ready for use in online course management systems.

Instructor's Resource Manual
Joseph Ortiz, *Scottsdale Community College*; ISBN-10: 0-312-45187-3, ISBN-13: 978-0-312-0-45187-5

The extensive Instructor's Resource Manual includes teaching notes on managing an interpersonal communication course, organization, and assessment; sample syllabi; advice on addressing ESL and intercultural issues; and tips for using the special features of *Reflect & Relate*. Every chapter includes lecture outlines and class discussion starters, class and group exercises, and assignment suggestions.

Test Bank
Charles J. Korn, *Northern Virginia Community College*; Print: ISBN-10: 0-312-45181-4, ISBN-13: 978-0-312-45181-3; Electronic: ISBN-10: 0-312-45186-5, ISBN-13: 978-0-312-45186-8

Comprising over 100 multiple choice, true/false, short answer, and essay questions for every chapter, the test bank is one of the largest for the introductory interpersonal communication course. This easy-to-use test bank identifies the level of difficulty of each question and connects every question to a learning objective.

Teaching Interpersonal Communication: Resources and Readings

Elizabeth J. Natalle, *University of North Carolina, Greensboro*; ISBN-10: 0-312-45542-9, ISBN-13: 978-0-312-45542-9

The first resource written specifically for the introductory interpersonal communication course, *Teaching Interpersonal Communication* provides instructors with practical advice on course logistics ranging from how to develop a teaching approach to classroom management, constructing a syllabus, administering tests, and integrating theory and skills into a course. The book covers scholarly issues and includes excerpts from five foundational readings in the field and an annotated bibliography of over 75 primary sources.

The Interpersonal Communication e-Newsletter

Kelly Morrison, *Michigan State University*

A teaching and research e-newsletter for instructors of the introductory interpersonal communication course. Sign up at bedfordstmartins.com/reflectrelate.

The Bedford/St. Martin's Video Resource Library

A wide selection of interpersonal communication-related movies is available. Qualified instructors are eligible to select videos from the resource library upon adoption of the textbook.

The Essential Guide to Group Communication

Dan O'Hair, *University of Oklahoma,* and Mary Wiemann, *Santa Barbara City College*; ISBN-10: 0-312-45194-6, ISBN-13: 978-0-312-45194-3

This concise and incisive text explains the role of group communication within organizations and other settings and contains useful guidelines for acting as an effective leader, avoiding groupthink, and achieving optimal results. This resource is available to package with *Reflect & Relate*.

Acknowledgments

I would like to thank everyone at Bedford/St. Martin's who was involved in this project and whose support made it possible, especially President Joan Feinberg, Editorial Director Denise Wydra, Director of Development Erica Appel, and Director of Production Marcia Cohen. Thanks to the editorial team who worked with me throughout the process: Executive Editor Erika Gutierrez, former Publisher Patricia Rossi, Development Editors Hannah Rubenstein and Laurie Johnson, Associate Editor Noel Hohnstine, and Editorial Assistant Barbara Galletly. My most profound thanks go to former Editor Vikram Mukhija: as we often joked, "The only way out is through," and I wouldn't have made it through without his patience, perseverance, unwavering dedication, and creative genius. The book would not have come together without the efforts of Managing Editor Shuli Traub and Senior Project Editor Harold Chester, who oversaw the book's tight schedule; the watchful eyes of Production Manager Pat Ollague and Senior Production Supervisor Joe Ford; and the beautiful design by Anna Palchik and thorough photo research by Sue McDermott. The enthusiasm and support from the marketing team are particularly appreciated: Director of Marketing Karen Melton Soeltz, Executive Marketing Manager Rachel Falk, former Marketing Manager Richard Cadman, Marketing Assistant Zoe Kazmierski, and the entire sales force of Bedford/St. Martin's.

On a more personal level, I want to thank all those who assisted me personally with the book during its development, and those who willingly contributed their extraordinary stories to the text: Helen Torres, Eric Staib, Leigh-Anne Goins, Vivian Derr, and Silvia Amaro. I would like to thank my undergraduate and graduate mentors, Malcolm Parks and Barbara O'Keefe, for instilling within me a fierce love of our discipline and deep respect for the sacred endeavor that is undergraduate teaching. And most of all, I want to thank my colleague, best friend, spouse, and life mate, Kelly Morrison: it was your strength, love, unfailing creative inspiration, and support that enabled me to persevere.

Throughout the development of this textbook, hundreds of interpersonal communication instructors voiced their opinion through surveys, focus groups, and reviews of the manuscript. A special thank you goes to the dedicated members of the editorial board, whose commitment to the project is surpassed only by their help in shaping the book: Kathy Adams, *California State University, Fresno*; Stuart Bonnington, *Austin Peay State University*; Marion Boyer, *Kalamazoo Valley Community College*; Tamala Bulger, *University of North Carolina*; Stephanie Coopman, *San Jose State University*; Susan Drucker, *Hofstra University*; Greg Gardner, *Rollins College*; Kathleen Henning, *Gateway Technical College*; Sarah Kays, *DeVry Institute*; Charles J. Korn, *Northern Virginia Community College*; Karen Krumrey-Fulks, *Lane Community College*; Gary Kuhn, *Chemeketa Community College*; Elizabeth J. Natalle, *University of North Carolina, Greensboro*; Anna Martinez, *Reedley College*; Randall Pugh, *Montana State University*; Marta Walz, *Elgin Community College*; and Cherie White, *Muskingum Area Technical College*.

I would also like to thank everyone else who participated in this process: **Alabama:** Robert Agne, *Auburn University*; Jonathan Amsbary, *University of Alabama*; Bill Huddleston, *University of North Alabama*; James Vickrey, *Troy State University*; Angela Gibson Wible, *Shelton State Community College*. **Arizona:** Anneliese Harper, *Scottsdale Community College*; Douglas Kelley, *Arizona State University, West*; Fred Kester, *Yavapai College, Prescott*; Mark Lewis, *Phoenix College*; Joseph Ortiz, *Scottsdale Community College*. **Arkansas:** Patricia Amason, *University of Arkansas*; Jason Hough, *John Brown University*; Robert Steinmiller, *Henderson State University*. **California:** Katherine Adams, *California State University, Fresno*; Susan Childress, *Santa Rosa Junior College*; Stephanie J. Coopman, *San Jose State University*; Kristin Gatto Correia, *San Francisco State University*; Eve-Anne Doohan, *University of San Francisco*; Jeannette Duarte, *Rio Hondo College*; Anne Duran, *California State University, Bakersfield*; William Eadie, *San Diego State University*; Allison Evans, *California State University, Bakersfield*; G. L. Forward, *Point Loma Nazarene University*; Kimberly Hubbert, *Cerritos College*; Annika Hylmö, *Loyola Marymount University*; Cynthia Johnson, *College of the*

Sequoias; Beverly Kelley, *California Lutheran University*; William Kelly, *University of California, Los Angeles*; Victoria Leonard, *College of the Canyons*; Ben Martin, *Santa Monica College*; Anna Martinez, *Reedley College*; Lawrence Jerome McGill, *Pasadena City College*; William F. Owen, *California State University, Sacramento*; Laurie Pratt, *Fullerton College*; Catherine Puckering, *University of California, Davis*; Jose Rodriguez, *California State University, Long Beach*; Teresa Turner, *Shasta College*; Jennifer Valencia, *San Diego Miramar College*; Richard Wiseman, *California State University, Fullerton.* **Colorado:** Eric Aoki, *Colorado State University*; Diane Blomberg, *Metropolitan State College of Denver*; Cheryl McFarren, *Arapahoe Community College*; Susan Pendell, *Colorado State University*; Dwight Podgurski, *Colorado Christian University.* **Connecticut:** Yanan Ju, *Central Connecticut State University*; Hugh McCarney, *Western Connecticut State University*; William Petkanas, *Western Connecticut State University*; Terri Toles-Patkin, *Eastern Connecticut State University*; C. Arthur VanLear, *University of Connecticut*; Kathryn Wiss, *Western Connecticut State University.* **Florida:** Kenneth Cissna, *University of South Florida*; Ed Coursey, *Palm Beach Community College*; Susan S. Easton, *Rollins College*; Greg Gardner, *Rollins College*; Katherine Nelson, *Barry University*; Maria Roca, *Florida Gulf Coast University*; Ann Scroggie, *Santa Fe Community College.* **Georgia:** Allison Ainsworth, *Gainesville College*; Marybeth Callison, *University of Georgia*; Michael H. Eaves, *Valdosta State University*; Pamela Hayward, *Augusta State University*; Gail Reid, *University of West Georgia*; Jennifer Samp, *University of Georgia.* **Hawaii:** Chiung Chen, *Brigham Young University, Hawaii*; Cailin Kulp O'Riordan, *University of Hawaii, Manoa*; Alan Ragains, *Windward Community College.* **Idaho:** Robyn Bergstrom, *Brigham Young University, Idaho*; Marcy Horne, *Lewis-Clark State College*; Annie McKinlay, *North Idaho College.* **Illinois:** Leah Bryant, *De Paul University*; Tim Cole, *De Paul University*; James Dittus, *Elgin Community College*; Katy Fonner, *Northwestern University*; Daena Goldsmith, *University of Illinois, Urbana-Champaign*; Sarah Strom Kays, *DeVry Institute*; Betty Jane Lawrence, *Bradley University*; Jody Littleton, *Parkland College*; Jay Martinson, *Nazarene University*; Lisa Miczo, *Western Illinois University*; Willona Olison, *Northwestern University*; Michael Purdy, *Governors State University*; Lesa Stern, *Southern Illinois University, Edwardsville*; Marta Walz, *Elgin Community College.* **Indiana:** Austin Babrow, *Purdue University*; Rebecca Bailey, *Valparaiso University*; Alexandra Corning, *University of Notre Dame*; John Greene, *Purdue University*; Krista Hoffmann-Longtin, *Indiana University–Purdue University, Indianapolis*; Irwin Mallin, *Indiana University–Purdue University, Fort Wayne*; Janet Morrison, *Ivy Tech State College*; James H. Tolhuizen, *Indiana University Northwest*; Ralph Webb, *Purdue University.* **Iowa:** Julie Simanski, *Des Moines Area Community College*; Erik Stroner, *Iowa Central Community College*; Charles Veenstra, *Dordt College.* **Kansas:** David Sherlock, *Independence Community College*; Richard Stine, *Johnson County Community College.* **Kentucky:** Chuck Bryant, *University of Kentucky*; Joy Hart, *University of Louisville*; Mona Leonard, *Jefferson Community College*; Tracy Letcher, *University of Kentucky*; Gregory Rickert, *Bluegrass Community and Technical College*; Kandi L.Walker, *University of Louisville.* **Louisiana:** Terry M. Cunconan, *Louisiana Tech University*; Karen Fontenot, *Southeastern Louisiana University*;

Loretta L. Pecchioni, *Louisiana State University*. **Maine:** Julie Zink, *University of Southern Maine*. **Maryland:** Laura Drake, *University of Maryland*; Linda Heil, *Harford Community College*; Audra McMullen, *Towson University*; Susan Ondercin, *Carroll Community College*. **Massachusetts:** Linda Albright, *Westfield State College*; Clea Andreadis, *Middlesex Community College*; Jonathan Bowman, *Boston College*; Elise Dallimore, *Northeastern University*; Joe Klimavich, *Worcester State College*; Michael Milburn, *University of Massachusetts, Boston*; Derrick TePaske, *Framingham State College*; Nancy Willets, *Cape Cod Community College*. **Michigan:** Patricia Amason, *Ferris State University*; Isolde Anderson, *Hope College*; Julie Apker, *Western Michigan University*; Steve Bennett, *Washtenaw Community College*; Marion Boyer, *Kalamazoo Valley Community College*; James Cantrill, *Northern Michigan University*; Robert Loesch, *Ferris State University*; Jennifer Hubbell Ott, *Kalamazoo Valley Community College*; Dennis Patrick, *Eastern Michigan University*; Cami Sanderson-Harris, *Ferris State University*; Sandi Smith, *Michigan State University*; Patricia Sotirin, *Michigan Technical University*. **Minnesota:** Angela Lynn Blais, *University of Minnesota, Duluth*; Christa Brown, *Minnesota State University, Mankato*; Kari Frisch, *Central Lakes College*; Lori Halverson-Wente, *Rochester Community and Technical College*; Ascan Koerner, *University of Minnesota, Twin Cities*; Mariangela Maguire, *Gustavus Adolphus College*; Minda Orina, *University of Minnesota, Twin Cities*; Patricia Palmerton, *Hamline University*; Daniel Paulnock, *Saint Paul College*; Karri Pearson, *Normandale Community College*; R. Jeffrey Ringer, *St. Cloud State University*; Dan West, *Rochester Community and Technical College*. **Missouri:** Leigh Heisel, *University of Missouri, St. Louis*; Lynette Jachowicz, *Maple Woods Community College*; Virgil Norris, *Park University*; Jennifer Summary, *Southeast Missouri State University*. **Montana:** Randall Pugh, *Montana State University, Billings*; Julie Robinson, *Montana State University, Billings*. **Nebraska:** Karla Jensen, *Nebraska Wesleyan University*; Chad M. McBride, *Creighton University*; Lisa Schreiber, *Dana College*. **New Hampshire:** Phyllis Zrzavy, *Franklin Pierce College*. **New Jersey:** Keith Forrest, *Atlantic Cape Community College*; Rebecca Sanford, *Monmouth University*; Madeline Santoro, *Union County College*. **New Mexico:** Candace Maher, *University of New Mexico*; Virginia McDermott, *University of New Mexico*; Kevin Mitchell, *Eastern New Mexico University*; Pamela Stovall, *University of New Mexico, Gallup*. **New York:** Priya Banerjee, *State University of New York, Brockport*; Rex Butt, *Bronx Community College*; Joseph S. Coppolino, *Nassau Community College*; Susan Drucker, *Hofstra University*; Diane Ferrero-Paluzzi, *Iona College*; Douglas Gaerte, *Houghton College*; Andrew Herman, *State University of New York, Geneseo*; Patricia Iacobazzo, *John Jay College*; Anastacia Kurylo, *Manhattan Marymount College*; Michael Lecesse, *State University of New York, New Paltz*; Linda Reese, *College of Staten Island*; Gordon Young, *Kingsborough Community College*. **North Carolina:** Melissa Atkinson, *Surry Community College*; Alessandra Beasley, *Wake Forest University*; Tamala Bulger, *University of North Carolina, Wilmington*; Allison Carr, *Davidson County Community College*; James Manning, *Western Carolina State University*; Nina-Jo Moore, *Appalachian State University*; Elizabeth J. Natalle, *University of North Carolina, Greensboro*; Chris Poulos, *University of North Carolina, Greensboro*; Melinda Sopher, *North Carolina State University*. **Ohio:** Yemi Akande, *John Carroll University*; Carolyn

Anderson, *University of Akron*; Christina S. Beck, *Ohio University*; Kathleen Clark, *University of Akron*; Rozell Duncan, *Kent State University*; David Foster, *University of Findlay*; Stephen Haas, *University of Cincinnati*; William Harpine, *University of Akron*; Kathryn C. Maguire, *Cleveland State University*; Lisa Murray-Johnson, *Ohio State University*; Artemio Ramirez, *Ohio State University*; Deleasa Randall-Griffiths, *Ashland University*; Teresa Sabourin, *University of Cincinnati*; Teresa Thompson, *University of Dayton*; John Warren, *Bowling Green State University*; Cherie White, *Muskingum Area Technical College* (now *Zane State College*). **Oklahoma:** Penny Eubank, *Oklahoma Christian University*; Billy Wolfe Jr., *University of Oklahoma*. **Oregon:** Nick Backus, *Western Oregon University*; Cynthia Golledge, *Portland Community College, Sylvania*; Karen Krumrey-Fulks, *Lane Community College*; Gary Kuhn, *Chemeketa Community College*; Paula Usrey, *Umpqua Community College*. **Pennsylvania:** Mary Badami, *Bloomsburg University of Pennsylvania*; Janet Bodenman, *Bloomsburg University of Pennsylvania*; Denise Danford, *Delaware County Community College*; Joseph Donato, *Harrisburg Area Community College, Lebanon*; Karen Lada, *Delaware County Community College*; David Paterno, *Delaware County Community College*; Elaine Zelley, *La Salle University*. **South Carolina:** Merissa Ferrara, *College of Charleston*; Charmaine Wilson, *University of South Carolina, Aiken*. **Tennessee:** Stuart Bonnington, *Austin Peay State University*; Katherine Hendrix, *University of Memphis*. **Texas:** Shae Adkins, *North Harris College*; Richard Bello, *Sam Houston State University*; Ceilidh Charleson-Jennings, *Collin County Community College*; Karen Daas, *St. Mary's University*; Jill Gibson, *Amarillo College*; Marian Houser, *Texas State University, San Marcos*; Shelly D. Lane, *Collin County Community College*; Laurie Metcalf, *Texas A&M University*; Mark Morman, *Baylor University*; John Nicholson, *Angelo State University*; James Pauff, *Tarleton State University*; Frank G. Pérez, *University of Texas, El Paso*; Lori Peterson, *St. Edward's University*; Narissra Punyanunt-Carter, *Texas Tech University*; Juliann Scholl, *Texas Tech University*; Susan Selk, *El Paso Community College*; Barbara Yancy-Tooks, *El Paso Community College*. **Utah:** Matthew Barton, *Southern Utah University*; Brian Heuett, *Southern Utah University*. **Vermont:** Genevieve Jacobs, *Champlain College*. **Virginia:** Melissa Aleman, *James Madison University*; Jill Jurgens, *Old Dominion University*; Charles J. Korn, *Northern Virginia Community College, Manassas*; Melanie Laliker, *Bridgewater College*; Michaela Meyer, *Christopher Newport University*; Thomas Morra, *Northern Virginia Community College, Annandale*; Nan Peck, *Northern Virginia Community College, Annandale*; Jeffrey Pierson, *Bridgewater College*; James Roux, *Lynchburg College*. **Washington:** Mara Adelman, *Seattle University*; Margaret Kreiner, *Spokane Community College*; Mark Murphy, *Everett Community College*; Roxane Sutherland, *Clark College*. **Washington, D.C.:** Robert Harrison, *Gallaudet University*; Clay Warren, *George Washington University*. **West Virginia:** Robert Bookwalter, *Marshall University*; Matthew Martin, *West Virginia University*. **Wisconsin:** Cheri Campbell, *University of Wisconsin, Waukesha;* Valerie Hennen, *Gateway Technical College*; Craig Hullett, *University of Wisconsin, Madison*; Rebecca Imes, *Carroll College*; Carol Knudson, *Gateway Technical College*; Lindsay Timmerman, *University of Wisconsin, Milwaukee*.

Finally, no textbook is created by one person. Thank you to the interpersonal communication discipline and its students.

Brief Contents

Contents

4 Experiencing and Expressing Emotions   115

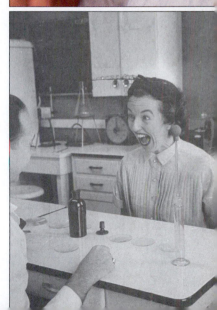

Part Two. INTERPERSONAL SKILLS

7 Communicating Verbally *217*

8 Communicating Nonverbally   *257*

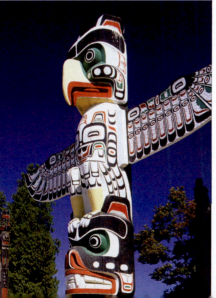

12 Relationships in the Workplace   *417*

From the Reviewers...

"*Reflect & Relate* takes on the tough topics that most authors are hesitant to discuss. If you want your students to take interpersonal communication into the real world, this is the textbook for you!"
—VICTORIA LEONARD, College of the Canyons

"The scholarship is impeccable."
—CRAIG HULLETT, University of Wisconsin, Madison

"*Reflect & Relate* is different from most introductory texts in that it provides practical tools for prompting students to reflect in deep and meaningful ways on how they can put theory and skill to use in their own interpersonal relationships."
—JOSEPH ORTIZ, Scottsdale Community College

"I love *Reflect & Relate's* continued focus on the student, I love the currency of both the concepts and the examples, and I love that this textbook will make a difference in their relationships."
—MARTA WALZ, Elgin College

"At each juncture, readers are given explanations, illustrations, and thought-provoking materials that are stimulating and that they can relate to their lives."
—KAREN KRUMREY-FULKS, Lane Community College

About the Author

Steven McCornack grew up in Seattle, Washington, in the years before Microsoft and grunge music. For as long as he can remember, he has been fascinated with how people create, maintain, and disband close relationships, especially the challenges confronting romantic couples. As an undergraduate at the University of Washington, he pursued this passion by studying with John Stewart and Malcolm Parks, who inspired within Steve the desire to devote his life to interpersonal communication teaching and research.

Steve moved to the Midwest in 1984, pursuing his graduate studies under the tutelage of Barbara O'Keefe at the University of Illinois, where he received his master's and PhD. Hired in 1988 to teach in the Department of Communication at Michigan State University, Steve has remained there ever since and now serves as associate professor, coordinator of the undergraduate program, and faculty adviser to the Undergraduate Communication Association. He has published over 20 articles in leading communication journals and has received several prestigious awards and fellowships related to undergraduate teaching, including the Lilly Endowment Teaching Fellowship, the Amoco Foundation Excellence-in-Teaching Award, and the MSU All-University Teacher/Scholar Award.

To Steve, authoring *Reflect & Relate* represents the culmination of over 20 years of devout interest in how best to share knowledge of interpersonal communication theory and research with undergraduate students. His courses are some of the most popular on campus. Other than his love of teaching, Steve's principal passions are his family (wife Kelly and three red-headed sons, Kyle, Colin, and Conor), his music (he plays drums in a punk band), his yoga practice, and karate training.

"I believe that the most important thing a textbook can teach students is how to make better communicaton decisions so that they can build happier and healthier interpersonal relationships."

Reflect & Relate

An Introduction to Interpersonal Communication

1

Introducing Interpersonal Communication

My office hours were about to end when Helen, a student from my interpersonal communication course the previous semester, arrived. She smiled and said, "Last term you talked in class about the field of interpersonal communication. I want to go into it and do research. How do I do this?"[1] Now it's not every day that a former student boldly declares a desire to become a communication scholar. But my initial skepticism soon disappeared as Helen and I discussed the history behind her visit. As we talked, it became clear that her interest was genuine and her motivation to study interpersonal communication deeply personal.

Helen Torres was born in Puerto Rico but spent her early childhood in Detroit in a neighborhood of Hispanic, Lebanese, and Euro-American families. The summer before Helen entered third grade, her family moved to a suburb that was almost entirely Euro-American; the Torreses were the only Hispanic family in the area.

[1] All information in this narrative is provided by Helen Torres to the author with full permission to publish.

Excited about the change, Helen's mother immediately volunteered to help out with activities at Helen's school, including fund-raising and school parties.

Soon an incident occurred that changed Helen's view of interpersonal communication forever. A parent called Helen's mother and asked her to bake cupcakes for an upcoming school event. Helen's mother, bilingual but a dominant Spanish-speaker, didn't know what "cupcakes" were. Why would anyone in their right mind want a *cup*-size cake? she wondered. Concluding that the caller was confused, Helen's mom baked a beautiful full-size cake and brought it to school. Seeing the cake, some of the kids teased Helen. "I shut them up," Helen explains. "[I said] 'My mom can speak two languages. *Can yours?*'"

But Mrs. Torres was mortified. She stopped volunteering for school functions, afraid of embarrassing her daughters. She also curtailed Helen's and her sister's interactions with schoolmates, worried that she couldn't

defend them if they got into conflicts with fellow students. "It was basically 'Come right home, do your homework, and do your chores,'" recalls Helen.

The stigma associated with the cupcake incident quickly faded from Helen's classmates' memories. But for Helen's mother it fostered a sense of alienation and insurmountable difference between her and the other mothers at Helen's school. And for Helen, it inspired a fierce intellectual curiosity regarding people's perception of difference and the importance of interpersonal communication in shaping relationships. A decade later, when Helen was a college student, this curiosity brought her to my office door.

In the years after our conversation, Helen earned bachelor's and master's degrees in communication. As she put it, "Learning about interpersonal communication provided a different lens for looking at the world than what I previously had. It made me a more alert

and savvy person in interpreting communication, and allowed me to ask better questions and make better decisions. It also gave me the tools to critically analyze myself, others, and situations—I now can step back when I need to and reflect on my own messages, putting myself in others' shoes."

Today, Helen Iris Torres is executive director of Hispanas Organized for Political Equality (HOPE), an influential nonprofit organization committed to achieving political and economic equality for Latinas through leadership, advocacy, and education. But she still recalls the cupcake incident and its impact on her life. "It's a silly story, but it illustrates a profound point: even small communication events can have big consequences. For me, this incident sparked a lifelong quest to better understand communication. And the knowledge I have gained has proven indispensable. In my daily dealings with politicians and other people in positions of power, it always comes down to interpersonal communication."

$\mathbb{W}$e spend our lives communicating. From the moment we're born we interact in meaningful ways with other humans beings—the first hugs we receive from parents or caregivers following birth; the realization months later that we can use spoken words to express thoughts, feelings, and emotions. Eventually, we discover that communication enables us to connect with and understand the unique inner worlds of others. When this happens, communication is transformed from a vehicle for self-expression to a means for building relationships.

Since communication is our central tool for exchanging meaning with others and forging relationships, the study of communication is critically important. For over 4,000 years, scholars have explored the intrigues and challenges of human communication. Across this enormous time span, a wealth of knowledge has been generated regarding the nature of communication and how communication skills can be refined—knowledge that you can learn and apply to your life to build healthier and more satisfying interactions and relationships.

In this chapter, we start our study of interpersonal communication at the beginning—by learning about the field of communication and the nature of interpersonal communication. You'll learn:

- What communication is and how people have studied it—in the past and today

- Different models that describe the process of communication

- The nature of interpersonal communication and the important needs and goals that it helps us to fulfill

- Major issues related to the study of interpersonal communication

- The key elements to studying interpersonal communication

● Whether we are watching a movie or visiting with friends, communication plays a significant role in our everyday experiences.

What Is Communication?

Every day, you communicate with friends, coworkers, family members, and romantic partners. You communicate through e-mail, text messages, phone calls, and face-to-face exchanges. But these aren't the only communication phenomena you experience. You also watch television shows and Webcasts, taking in information and viewing advertisements. You attend public speeches, participate in group projects, go on job interviews, and consume magazine articles, movies, and music.

At the same time communication surrounds us, it intrigues us. We think about communication constantly—everything from thought-provoking course lectures to the meaning of warm smiles displayed by attractive new neighbors. But taking a class on communication is different from personally pondering it. When you're formally educated about communication, you learn knowledge that goes far beyond your intuition, allowing you to broaden and deepen your skills as a communicator. The process of learning about communication begins by answering the most basic question of all: what exactly *is* communication?

Defining Communication

The National Communication Association (NCA), a professional organization representing teachers and scholars of speech and communication in the United States, defines **communication** as the process through which people use messages to generate meanings within and across contexts, cultures, channels, and media (2002). This definition highlights the five features that characterize communication.

First, communication is a process. By "process," we mean that communication unfolds over time through a series of interconnected actions carried out by the participants. For example, your friend dials your cell-phone number, your phone rings, you answer the call, your friend asks if you want to go to a movie, you say yes, and so forth. Although encounters have definite starting and ending points (you say "Hi"; you sign off from an Internet chatroom), everything you say and do now will impact what is said and done in the future, just as your past communicative actions shape what you currently are experiencing.

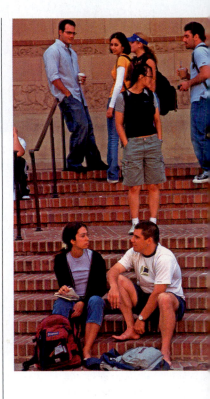

Second, those engaged in communication ("communicators") use messages to convey meaning. At its core, communication is the transportation of information, and a **message** is the "package" of information that is transported during communication. When someone creates a communication message, he or she thinks of information that is relevant to be sent and then forms it into a package ready for transport and delivery. A single communicational unit is a message, and when people exchange a series of messages, the result is called an **interaction** (Watzlawick, Beavin, & Jackson, 1967). For example, you explain that you can't see the movie with your friend because you have too much homework (a message). Then your friend boasts about the movie's action-packed scenes and suspense (another message). Intrigued, you tell your friend you want to see the film after all (yet another message).

Third, communication occurs in a seemingly endless variety of situations, known as **contexts.** We communicate with others at ballgames, while at work, and in household kitchens. And in each context, a host of factors influence how we communicate with one another, such as time constraints on our encounter, the number of other people in the vicinity, and whether the setting is personal or professional. An encounter with a romantic partner necessarily will be different when enacted in a classroom as opposed to in an intimate café, just as a conversation with a friend will be different in the library compared to in your living room.

Fourth, people communicate through various channels. A communication **channel** is the sensory dimension along which communicators transmit information: auditory (sound), visual (sight), tactile (touch), olfactory (scent), or oral (taste). For example, during a visit home, your mother smiles at you and then says, "I'm so proud of you for doing well in school," communicating through both visual and auditory channels. A visually impaired friend "reads" a tactile message you left her, touching the Braille letters with her fingertips. A person you've recently begun dating invites you to his or her house for dinner. When you arrive, your date exudes an alluring scent and presents you with an elegant meal, communicating through the channels of scent and taste that tonight is special.

Fifth, to transmit information, communicators employ a broad range of tools known as communication **media.** We can exchange messages with others using forms of online communication such as e-mail, text messages, or chatrooms. We can communicate in person — "face-to-face" — or interact via videoconferencing or cell phone. And we can communicate through handwriting — exchanging scrawled notes with roommates about who is going to cook dinner or sending a handwritten letter of affection to grandparents.

SELF-REFLECTION

What communication media do you use most often? Why have you begun relying more on these media than on others? Does the type of relationship you have with a person — close or casual, personal or professional — influence what media you use for communicating? If so, how?

Forms of Communication

The rich diversity that exists in communication media, channels, contexts, and messages is reflected in the enormous breadth of the communication field and in the forms of communication studied in colleges and universities. The scholarly discipline of communication embraces everything from critical analyses of historical speeches to the effects of beer commercials on consumer purchasing patterns. And interest in communication is truly interdisciplinary: communication scholars collaborate with colleagues in other academic disciplines as varied as ethnic and women's studies, English, linguistics, philosophy, public health, psychology, and sociology.

Given all of this diversity, how can we distinguish among communication's many different forms? According to the National Communication Association, the field of communication can be divided into four broad domains: speech and rhetorical studies, communication studies, mass communication and media studies, and telecommunication studies.

The domain of speech and rhetorical studies examines how people use words to compel audiences to change or solidify their beliefs. Specific interest areas include political speeches, audience analysis, argumentation (how to structure more compelling arguments), rhetorical criticism (analysis of speeches and written texts), and rhetorical theory (the underlying principles that guide compelling speech).

The communication studies domain comprises research in topics such as interpersonal communication (the focus of this textbook), organizational communication (interactions within organizations), and intercultural communication (communication between and within various cultures). Other topics in this domain are instructional communication (how teachers can be more effective), family communication (patterns that influence family relationships), health and risk communication (health provider-patient interaction; techniques for communicating healthy lifestyles to people), and social influence (communication designed to get others to do what you want).

Scholars and students interested in mass communication and media studies study the history and current state of the media industries (books, newspapers, television, movies, the Internet, etc.), critically analyze the messages transmitted by media institutions (e.g., Google, the FOX News Channel, *The New York Times*), and examine the relationship between the mass media and culture.

The final domain—telecommunication technologies—examines the development, use, regulation, and impact of radio, television, telephony, the Internet, and other such technologies. For example, scholars may study population trends in television viewing, the impact of violent video games

on human behavior, or challenges raised by the use of online communication such as e-mail and online chatrooms.

A Brief History of Communication

The field of communication is undeniably modern, with its attention to topics such as online relationships and the effects of video games. But it has ancient roots. By gaining familiarity with the field's history, you can better appreciate how contemporary communication experts have built on earlier work, as well as the role that *interpersonal* communication plays in the broader field.

Communication in Antiquity.   By taking this class, you are participating in an academic discipline that goes back thousands of years and traverses many different cultures. As such, the field of communication parallels other ancient domains of human intellectual interest, including astronomy, mathe-

---

POP QUIZ

Test Your Knowledge of the Communication Field

Read each of the following phrases. Place a check mark next to the phrases that you believe describe common areas of study in the field of communication.

_____ Ways in which teachers can more effectively interact with and instruct students

_____ The impact of radio, television, media technology, and Web design with streaming audio

_____ Provider-client interaction in health settings, and the diffusion of health information to the public through health campaigns

_____ Interactions between individuals from diverse cultural and ethnic backgrounds

_____ The behaviors of pairs of people and their relationships

_____ The role of verbal and nonverbal behaviors in human interaction

_____ Social interaction processes within organizations, and relations between supervisors and employees

_____ The interaction between performers and audiences in various performance settings

_____ Speakers and speeches, including political campaigns and movements

_____ Groups of three or more individuals who interact around a common purpose and influence each other

Scoring:

All 10 of these areas are commonly studied by communication scholars.

Note: This *Pop Quiz* is adapted from National Communication Association (2003).

matics, and medicine. For example, one of the earliest books ever written—the maxims of the Egyptian sage Ptah Hotep (2200 b.c.e.)—offers suggestions for enhancing interpersonal communication skills (Horne, 1917). In this ancient guidebook, Ptah Hotep encouraged people to be truthful, kind, and tolerant in their communication. He urged actively listening, especially for situations in which people lack experience, because "to not do so is to embrace ignorance." And he emphasized mindfulness in word choice, noting that "good words are more difficult to find than emeralds."

Almost 2,000 years after Ptah Hotep wrote, the communication tradition known as rhetoric arose. Rhetoric comprises the theory and practice of persuading others through speech (Dues & Brown, 2004), and it became a formal discipline of study in ancient Greece and Rome (Kennedy, 1999). In Greece, Socrates and his student Plato were among the first to debate the nature of rhetoric. Socrates thought of rhetoric not as a knowledge-based philosophy but as a skill gained through experience (Kennedy, 1999). Plato viewed rhetoric as the practical complement of dialectic, the form of philosophical reasoning through which one could attain enlightenment. Both viewed rhetorical expertise with caution. They realized that communication skill can be used to attain unethical as well as ethical ends, and they argued strongly against wielding words in manipulative and exploitative ways.

In ancient Rome, statesman and orator Cicero noted three practical objectives of public speaking (Clarke, 1953)—to instruct, to please, and to win over—goals still found in the required speeches of modern public speaking courses. Cicero also outlined the five steps to speech crafting and presentation that we continue to practice: invention (reasoning out truth in order to make your case compelling), arrangement (organizing the information you want to present), style (selecting suitable words to convey the information), memory (having a firm grasp of your subject and words), and delivery (controlling your body and voice when presenting your speech).

Communication in the Early Twentieth Century.

Throughout the lengthy period from ancient Rome to the early twentieth century, the study of communication remained focused on rhetoric. In the 1900s, however, things began to change (see Table 1.1). Stimulated by philosophical interest in the human mind and behavior, scholars across a broad range of disciplines began studying forms of communication other than rhetoric (Knapp, Daly, Albada, & Miller, 2002). During this same era, social psychology (the study of individual behavior when in the presence of others) shifted from explaining human behavior in terms of natural instincts to an emphasis on social

SELF-REFLECTION

Have you ever known someone who was a skilled communicator but used this ability in unethical ways? How did he or she communicate unethically? What does this experience suggest about the responsibility that comes with building your communication skills?

environments and relationships (Delia, 1987). Topics such as interaction, empathy, and interpersonal conflict began to be formally studied, setting the stage for the later study of interpersonal communication (Knapp et al., 2002).

Especially influential in laying the groundwork for modern communication studies was the work of sociologists at the University of Chicago, who refined experimental designs, sampling techniques, and means of statistical analysis for reliably studying people and their communication. In doing so,

Field	Scholar	Contribution
Sociology	Georg Simmel	Introduced the "dyad," or two-person unit, as a focus of study.
Political science	Harold Lasswell	Detailed the four persuasive aims of governmental propaganda: create hatred against the enemy, preserve friendships with allies, procure the cooperation of neutral parties, and demoralize the enemy.
Business	Elton Mayo	Examined effects of coworker interactions on productivity, giving rise to the "human relations" movement and the recognition that supportiveness is crucial for effective workplace communication.
Psychology	Jean Piaget	Analyzed the role that children's ability to perspective-take (see things from their partner's viewpoint) plays in shaping their communication.
Anthropology	Gregory Bateson	Lived among the Iatmul tribe of New Guinea, documenting that although the needs, desires, and feelings of people constantly change, people in satisfying relationships strive to treat each other in a consistent and equal way, despite this flux.

Note: Table 1-1 is based on Lasswell (1927), Simmel (1950), Roethlisberger and Dickson (1939), Piaget (1926), and Bateson (1958).

TABLE 1.1

Selected Historical Milestones in Early-Twentieth-Century Communication Scholarship, 1900–1940

● People have always communicated with each other and were interested in the best way to communicate long before communication became a formal academic discipline.

they helped to establish modern **social science,** the scientific study of the mental, behavioral, and relational actions of human beings.

Communication after World War II.   Although the early twentieth century witnessed an explosion of intellectual interest in communication, not until after World War II did communication became a distinct academic field. This occurred for two reasons (Delia, 1987). First, by the late 1940s and early 1950s, the term "communication" began to be widely used to define a domain of research and teaching, and the emergence and usage of this term symbolically unified the field. Not only did scholars begin to identify their research as "communication" and themselves as "communication scholars," but universities began creating "communication" departments. Some schools housed communication studies researchers alongside rhetoric and speech scholars. The result was "speech communication" departments.

Second, for the first time in history, scholars embraced a standard conception of the communication process. They defined the central question of study to be, "if *who* says *what*, through what *channels* of communication, to *whom*, what will be the *results?*" (Smith, Lasswell, & Casey, 1946). Agreement that communication is a process through which people create messages, send them through channels, and generate outcomes helped to further unify the field.

In the following years, scholarly interest in communication intensified. Anthropologists Ray Birdwhistell (1952) and Edward T. Hall (1959) laid the groundwork for modern study of nonverbal communication through observing and writing about body movement, gestures, postures, and the use of space. In 1967, Paul Watzlawick, Janet Beavin, and Don Jackson published the book *Pragmatics of Human Communication*, which many consider the first modern text outlining principles of interpersonal communication. *Pragmatics* echoed the writings of Ptah Hotep—focusing on how people can communicate more effectively to improve their relationships.

By the early 1970s, dozens of communication and speech communication departments existed, and the first interpersonal communication courses emerged. As the discipline became further unified, it attracted even more interest among scholars and students. From 1970 to 2000, the number of undergraduates majoring in communication in the United States expanded from more than 10,000 annually to 56,000 (NCA, 2002). And in each year of the new millennium thus far, more than 5,000 students have received master's (MA) degrees in communication and over 400 students have received doctorate degrees (PhD) in the field.

Research and Theory in Communication

One of the primary goals of this textbook and the class you're taking is to provide you with trustworthy and useful knowledge regarding communication that will aid you in improving your interpersonal communication skills and relationships. But before information about communication can be taught and learned, scholars must first *have* the information that will be taught and learned. This prompts an obvious question: "How is trustworthy knowledge of communication acquired in the first place?"

The answer is through conducting research and developing theory. When you conduct research, you establish a set of initial questions and then systematically try to answer them, either through careful observation or through creating some type of controlled "test." When you develop theory, you create a set of descriptive statements (propositions) that define your phenomenon of interest and that identify various factors relevant to it, as well as how those factors interrelate (Chaffee & Berger, 1987).

To illustrate how research and theory give rise to trustworthy communication knowledge, let's walk through an example. Imagine that you post a message in one of your favorite online discussion groups, then later find a couple of nasty messages posted in response—messages best described as "flames" (inappropriately aggressive online messages that most people wouldn't communicate face-to-face, as we will discuss in Chapter 5). In the wake of this experience, you're hurt, shocked, and confused. But more than anything else, you want to know *why* this happened, and you want to go beyond merely pondering the event. So you decide to conduct research and develop theory.

Communication scholars typically take one of two approaches when conducting research and developing theory. Qualitative approaches involve the careful observation and description of events in an attempt to identify general patterns and glean principles that govern the events (Znaniecki, 1934). If you opted to study flaming qualitatively, you would follow several steps (Goetz & LeCompte, 1981; Katz, 1983; Robinson, 1951; Znaniecki, 1934). First, you would carefully define what you meant by "flaming," based on observation of various flame messages. You would consider questions such as these: What characteristics of an online message make it a "flame"? How is flaming different from other negative messages? Once you had a clear definition of flaming, you would formulate tentative hypotheses—predictions that describe the relationship between your phenomenon of interest and other related factors. For example, you might hypothesize that flaming is more likely to occur in certain discussion forums than in others or that certain types of messages are especially likely to trigger flames. Then you would test your hypotheses by observing multiple instances of flaming in

online discussion groups. If your observations consistently confirmed your hypotheses, you would conclude that your hypotheses were likely correct. If your observations disconfirmed your hypotheses, you would revise your hypotheses until they matched your observations. After intensive observation and analysis, you would develop a solid understanding of flaming and its causes, one rooted in direct observations of reality (Glaser & Strauss, 1967). You then would create a set of propositions describing the nature of flaming and the factors that influence it—propositions that, taken together, would comprise your theory of flames.

In contrast, quantitative approaches involve the testing of hypotheses within carefully controlled settings, oftentimes in experimental laboratories (Popper, 2004). Whereas qualitative approaches begin with observation and description and then flow toward development of theory, quantitative approaches follow the opposite order. Theory is identified or created, hypotheses are formulated based on theory, and tests of the hypotheses are conducted. To study flaming from a quantitative perspective, you would begin by reading previous research and theory on flaming. You then would select an existing theory or create your own. From this theory, you would choose specific hypotheses to test, and you would design and conduct a controlled test of these hypotheses. For example, you might conduct a study in which people are provided with either anonymous or identifiable accounts and you check to see whether anonymity boosts flaming frequency. If the results from the controlled test support your hypotheses, you would consider your theory plausible. If the results do not match the hypotheses, you would reject the hypotheses and view your theory as suspect.

Although qualitative and quantitative approaches often are characterized as "opposites" or even "rivals," they are equally valid approaches to the study of communication and equally effective for generating valuable and trustworthy knowledge. Qualitative approaches are especially well suited for learning the details, nuances, and richness of real-life communication patterns; and quantitative approaches are excellent for determining the frequency of various communication behaviors, as well as systematically testing the influence of various factors on such behaviors (Pomerantz, 1990).

The Communication Process

The movie *Gallipoli* details the Allied attack on Gallipoli, Turkey in World War I, during which over 26,000 British and Australian soldiers died (Weir, Williamson, & Lovell, 1981). In the climactic scene, a British commanding officer stationed in the rear of the battlefield repeatedly orders Major Barton, leader of the Australian regiment on the front line, to send his troops charging toward entrenched Turkish machine gun positions—despite the fact that every soldier attempting such an attack has been killed. After several disastrous charges, Barton decides to try to thwart the officer's order by getting an Australian general stationed nearby to overrule it. Lacking phone contact with the general, Barton sends Frank—an Olympic-caliber sprinter—to run through the trenches to the general's position and deliver a message: the

SKILLS PRACTICE

This exercise helps you use communication research methods to analyze online communication challenges.

1 Identify a problem you commonly face when communicating with others online—a situation or person you find perplexing or difficult to deal with.

2 Identify all the factors that seem to contribute to the problem.

3 Carefully observe online encounters in which the problem occurs, "testing" whether the factors you've identified are really the causes.

4 Identify ways you can change or control the factors that cause the problem.

5 Test the effectiveness of these solutions by trying them in your future online encounters.

attacks are failing and must be stopped! Frank succeeds, and the general instructs Frank to return with the order: cancel the attacks. As Frank races back with his message, the British officer phones Major Barton and orders him to immediately charge his remaining troops:

"Do I make myself clear!?"

"Yes, sir."

Hanging up, Barton and his soldiers exchange looks: they must do their duty, even if it means certain death. As Frank nears their position with his message of reprieve, Barton leads his troops "over the top," charging the Turkish positions, and they all are killed.

Although most of our daily communication doesn't involve the life and death consequences depicted in *Gallipoli*, it nevertheless is experienced in similar forms. Sometimes, like Barton sending Frank racing through the trenches to the general, we create messages and send them to receivers; the messages flow in a single direction from origin to destination. In other instances, like the phone call between the British officer and Barton, we present messages to recipients and the recipients signal to us that they're receiving and understanding them. Still other times, like Barton and his soldiers sharing doomed glances, communication is mutually created as we and other participants collaboratively construct meanings with no one serving as "sender" or "receiver."

These three different ways of experiencing communication are reflected in three different models of the communication process: the linear model, the interactive model, and the transactional model. These models represent an evolution of thought regarding the nature of communication from a relatively simplistic depiction of communication as a linear process to one that views communication as a complicated process that is mutually crafted. At the same time, these models don't necessarily represent "good" or "bad" ways of thinking about communication. Instead, as we'll see, each of them is useful for thinking about different forms of communication.

FIGURE 1.1

**Linear Model of
Communication**

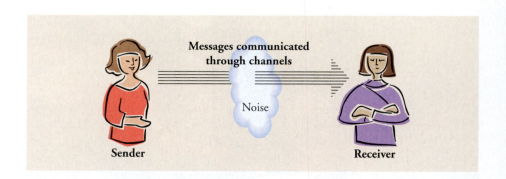

Linear Communication Model

According to the **linear communication model,** communication is an activity in which information flows in one direction, from a starting point to an end point (see Figure 1.1). The linear model contains five components (Lasswell, 1948; Shannon & Weaver, 1949). First, there must be a message, as noted earlier in the chapter. Second, there must be a channel—the sensory dimension or dimensions along which the message is sent. Third, there must be a **sender** (or senders) of the message—the individual (or individuals) who generate the information to be communicated, package it into a message, and choose the channel (or channels) for sending it. Fourth, there exists **noise**—factors in the environment that impede messages from reaching their destination. Noise includes anything that affects our senses and causes our attention to drift from messages: static or the "cutting in and out" that occurs with cell phones, the smell of fresh coffee or pastries nearby, having a stranger sitting behind us who repeatedly bumps or kicks the back of our seat, and so forth. Last, there must be a **receiver** (or receivers)—the people for whom the message is intended and to whom the message is delivered.

Although the linear model is now more than 50 years old, it accurately represents a broad range of communication forms. For example, much of online communication—including text-messaging, e-mail, and spam—fits this model. Certain public speaking contexts may also fit, especially those in which speakers present prepared scripts to large audiences who are expected to sit quietly and listen without responding to or challenging the speaker. But the linear model doesn't work with other communication forms such as face-to-face conversation. For example, when you converse with a friend face-to-face, you may speak in partial sentences and rely on one another to mentally fill in the missing information.

Interactive Communication Model

The **interactive communication model** also views communication as a process involving senders and receivers (see Figure 1.2), but it suggests that this transmission is influenced by two additional factors: feedback and fields of experience (Schramm, 1954). **Feedback** comprises the verbal and nonverbal messages that recipients convey to indicate their reaction to communication. Whether it's eye contact, utterances such as "uh-huh" and "that's right," or head nodding, receivers use feedback to let senders know they've received and understood the message and to indicate their approval or disapproval of

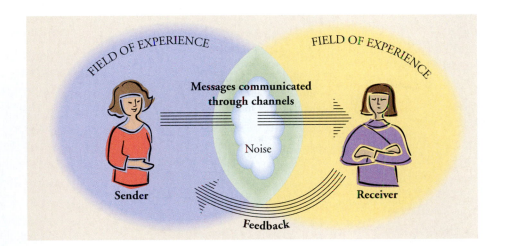

FIGURE 1.2

Interactive Model of Communication

the message's content. **Fields of experience** consist of the beliefs, attitudes, values, and experiences that each participant brings to a communication event. Such fields can powerfully shape how messages are sent and received. For instance, two people with similar beliefs, attitudes, values, and experiences are more likely to understand each other while communicating than are two with nothing in common.

Like the linear model, the interactive model accurately describes a range of communication forms. For example, skillful public speakers interpret audience feedback—"reading" reactions such as fidgeting or interested facial expressions, then modifying their messages as needed to capture the audience's attention and get their message across. Classroom instruction, group presentations, and weekly team meetings among coworkers may also be interactive.

Like the linear model, the interactive model presents communication as largely a linear process in which there is a clearly designated and active "sender" and a passive "receiver." Thus it neglects the active role that receivers often play in constructing the meaning of a communication event. For example, at a family reunion, your uncle starts droning on as usual about his fishing trips. You and your sister glance at each other and immediately understand the meaning of your shared look. If you were to put words to this meaning, you both would be saying, "Oh no, here he goes again!" But neither of you is a sender or receiver in this instance; instead, you *jointly* create communication meaning.

Transactional Communication Model

The most refined and elaborate communication model is the **transactional communication model** (see Figure 1.3). It suggests that communication is not a linear, one-directional process but instead is fundamentally multidirectional—that is, each party involved in a communication event equally influences the communication behavior of the other parties involved (Cappella, 1987; Miller & Steinberg, 1975). From the transactional perspective, there really isn't a "sender" and a "receiver." Instead, the constant exchange of verbal and nonverbal messages and feedback among all parties involved

FIGURE 1.3

Transactional Model of
Communication

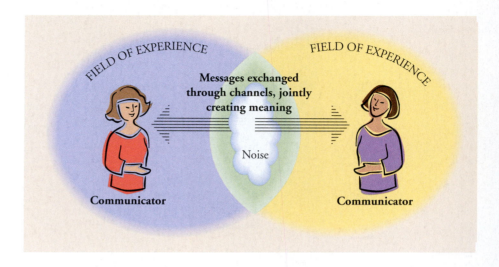

in the encounter makes the participants co-communicators who *collaboratively* create communication meanings (Streek, 1980). The collaborative creation of meaning may be something as simple as a shared look, as in the example above with your uncle. It may be an animated and engrossing conversation between you and a close family member, in which you both seem to know what the other is going to say before it's said. It may even involve two people jointly collaborating to create a single act of communication. Sociologist Jurgen Streek, in discussing the transactional nature of conversation (1980), describes a classroom roll call he once observed. The teacher asked, "Now where is . . .," and before she could complete her query, a student chimed in "Ernesto?" knowing just who the teacher was seeking.

Most interpersonal communication scholars have embraced the transactional model, and with good reason. The majority of encounters that intuitively seem "interpersonal" are transactional—for instance, encounters you have face-to-face or over the phone with your romantic partner, in which the words seem secondary to the intensity of feelings and intentions being conveyed; interactions with family members online via live chat or e-mail messages you send, which include "secret meanings" that only the recipient knows; conversations between close friends, where a few key words or looks instantly convey a wealth of shared information. In these examples and others like them, you and others are collaborating in a transactional fashion to create mutual meanings.

What Is Interpersonal Communication?

When, more than twenty years ago, I first began telling people I was going to major in communication, the common reaction I got was, "Communication? Do you study radio, or TV?" When I told them, "No, actually, I'm interested in *interpersonal communication*," I almost always received a confused stare, followed by the inevitable question, "Oh . . . what's that?"

SELF-REFLECTION

Think about a recent encounter that you consider transactional. How was it different from interactions you've had that were inter-active or linear? Is one type of communication process more "interpersonal" than the others, or are they all equivalent? Why?

"Interpersonal communication is constantly
in motion and changing over time."

Interpersonal communication is a dynamic form of communication between two (or more) people in which the messages exchanged significantly influence their thoughts, emotions, behaviors, and relationships. This definition has four important implications. First, interpersonal communication differs from some other forms of communication—such as organizational memos, spam, and formal lectures or speeches—because it's *dynamic*. Dynamic means that interpersonal communication is constantly in motion and changing over time. Most interpersonal communication is spontaneously created—arising from our thoughts, moods, and emotions of the moment—unlike the carefully planned scripts and messages that dominate advertisements, print and online journalism, and formal public speeches. And because people's thoughts, moods, and emotions are always in flux, their interpersonal communication continually shifts as well. For example, consider a phone conversation you have with a sibling who's in the military and stationed overseas. The first few moments may be awkward and tense as you strive to reconnect with one another. This tension is reflected with long pauses between short sentences. Then suddenly one of you cracks a joke, and the whole exchange suddenly feels warmer. Just a few minutes later, as you realize you have to hang up, the conversation slows, and the mood shifts yet again to sadness and regret, as each of you takes longer and longer turns, trying to delay the inevitable disconnection.

Second, interpersonal communication is typically transactional, though it may occasionally be linear or interactive—depending on the parties involved, the context, and the medium through which you're communicating. Many people think of interpersonal as *only* transactional. Indeed, as noted earlier, the transactional model meets our intuitive sense of interpersonal and most interpersonal communication is transactional. You and a romantic partner share an intimate dinner, jointly reminiscing about past times together and exchanging expressions of affection fluidly back and forth. But some interpersonal communication isn't transactional. For example, you know that your best friend is feeling depressed, so you send her a text message of emotional support in the middle of her workday. You don't expect her to respond, and she doesn't because she's busy with a project. There is no feedback and no interplay between you and your friend. Instead, there is a sender (you), a message (your expression of support), and a receiver (your friend).

Third, interpersonal communication is primarily **dyadic**—that is, involving pairs of people, or dyads. Similar to the predominantly transactional nature of most interpersonal communication, the majority of encounters you consider "interpersonal" likely are dyadic: a conversation with your daughter while driving her to school, talking over lunch with your lover, or e-mails exchanged with your long-distance friend. The dyadic nature of interpersonal communication allows us to distinguish it from **intrapersonal communication**—communication involving only one person, in the form of talking out loud to oneself or having a mental "conversation" inside your head.

Although interpersonal communication is primarily dyadic, defining it as exclusively dyadic would be overly constraining. We most certainly can engage in interpersonal communication with several family members at once while sitting around the dinner table or with groups of friends while enjoying an evening out.

Finally, interpersonal communication changes the participants' thoughts, emotions, behavior, and relationships. The impact on relationships is one of the most profound and unique effects created through interpersonal communication. Through the latter, we forge meaningful bonds with others—easing the distance that naturally arises from differences between people. Philosopher Martin Buber (1965) argued that we can make that distance seem "thinner" through our communication. Specifically, when we embrace the fundamental similarities that connect us with others, strive to see things from others' points of view, and communicate in ways that emphasize honesty and kindness, we feel closer to others. Relationships also deepen when we treat one another as unique individuals and affirm each other's uniqueness through our interpersonal communication (Buber, 1965). We don't have to agree with everything another person says and does, but to communicate effectively with others, we do need to receive them with an open heart. According to Buber, we then perceive our relationship with that person as **I-Thou.**

In contrast, when we focus on our differences, refuse to accept or even acknowledge rival viewpoints as legitimate, and communicate in ways that emphasize our own supposed superiority over others or that disregard their desires, the distance between us "thickens" to the point where it becomes impenetrable (Buber, 1965). As a consequence, we increasingly perceive our relationships with others as **I-It:** we regard other people as "objects which we observe, that are there for our use and exploitation" (1965, p. 24). The more we view others as objects, the greater is the likelihood that we'll communicate with them in disrespectful, manipulative, or exploitative ways. And when we treat others this way, our relationships deteriorate.

Interpersonal communication contrasts sharply with **impersonal communication**—exchanges that have a negligible perceived impact on our thoughts, emotions, behaviors, and relationships. For example, you're watching TV with your lover, and one of you reminds the other that you need to

SKILLS PRACTICE

This exercise helps you shift your communication from I-It to I-Thou.

❶ Think of someone whom you perceive as I-It.

❷ Identify the characteristics that lead you to see this person as fundamentally different from or inferior to you.

❸ Critically analyze these presumed differences. Are they really a cause for concern?

❹ Identify the fundamental similarities that you share with this person.

❺ Develop a plan for communicating with the person in ways that respect differences while also appreciating similarities.

In many of our closest relationships, we often communicate impersonally and interpersonally within the same interaction.

buy groceries for tomorrow night's dinner party. Within most close relationships, at least some communication has this impersonal quality. But we can shift to interpersonal at a moment's notice. A while after the grocery reminder, you snuggle up to your partner and murmur, "I love you." You're rewarded by warm eye contact, a tender smile, and a gentle hug—all signs that your message has had a significant impact on your partner.

Of course, what constitutes "interpersonal" and "significant impact" lies in the hearts and minds of those participating in an encounter. For example, you may not consider an encounter interpersonal unless you feel emotionally moved, learn new knowledge, make different decisions, or—like Martin Buber—forge an I-Thou connection with the other person. Alternatively, you might consider any encounter in which information is conveyed—however minimal—as interpersonal, provided you gained *something* from the exchange. In either view, the measure of whether a communicative exchange—be it online, over the phone, or face-to-face—is truly interpersonal is whether the participants in the encounter view it as such.

Highlighting mental, emotional, behavioral, and relational impact as a defining feature of interpersonal communication emphasizes the important connection that exists between interpersonal communication and its effects or outcomes. *Interpersonal communication actively creates personal, interpersonal, and relationship outcomes.* Through communicating interpersonally with others, you can change your own feelings and thoughts about both yourself and others; alter others' opinions of you; cause heartbreak or happiness; incite hugs or hostility; and create, maintain, or dissolve relationships. This power makes your communication choices critically important.

Goals of Interpersonal Communication

At 19 months of age, Helen Keller fell ill with a severe fever that destroyed her sight and hearing (Dash, 2001). Helen had learned to speak quite early and had a substantial vocabulary (for a toddler), but when she stopped hearing she stopped trying to talk. In the years that followed, she created primitive messages through pulling, shoving, pinching, and shivering, but she had lost the knowledge of how to *interpersonally* communicate.

With no ability to connect with others through communication, she became filled with hatred and an all-encompassing sense of isolation. She called the resulting sense of self "The Phantom." This miserable being routinely flew into screaming tantrums that ceased only when utter exhaustion set in. In one of her early lessons with Annie Sullivan—the woman who eventually taught Helen how to communicate through hand signals—The Phantom became so enraged that she punched Annie in the mouth, knocking out one of her front teeth.

But when Annie finally succeeded in teaching Helen how to communicate through sign language, The Phantom was slain. As Helen explained years later, "It seemed that something of the mystery of communication was revealed to me . . . and suddenly I felt a misty consciousness as of something remembered—a thrill of returning thought." Helen Keller went on to master sign language, Braille, and spoken language and graduated magna cum laude from Radcliffe College.

So far, we've discussed what communication is, how it works, and its interpersonal form. But as the Helen Keller story powerfully illustrates, the issue of *why* we communicate is equally if not more important. Through interpersonal communication, we connect with others—fulfilling a profound human need. We also achieve important personal and professional goals. When these outcomes are denied us, we lapse into isolation and loneliness or, worse yet, have a violent "Phantom" emerge from within, as did Helen Keller.

Interpersonal Communication and Human Needs. Psychologist Abraham Maslow (1943, 1970) suggested a hierarchy of needs that we seek to fulfill in our daily lives (see Figure 1.4). Only when the most basic needs (at the bottom of the hierarchy) are fulfilled do we turn our attention to pursuing higher-level ones, and interpersonal communication helps us fulfill all of these needs. At the foundational level are physical necessities such as air, food, water, sleep, and shelter. When we can't satisfy these needs, we prioritize them over all others. Once they are met, we concern ourselves with security needs—such as job security and protection from violence. Then we seek to address social needs. We try to form satisfying and healthy emotional bonds with friends, family members, and romantic partners. According to Maslow, we particularly strive to be accepted by others and to feel that we belong. People who fail to fulfill these needs are prone to loneliness, anxiety, and depression. Next are ego needs, the desire to have others' respect and admiration. We fulfill these needs by contributing something of value to the world (Maslow, 1970). Finally, we strive to satisfy self-actualization needs. We articulate our unique abilities and use them to give our best in our work, family, and personal life.

● Helen Keller

FIGURE 1.4

Maslow's Hierarchy of Needs

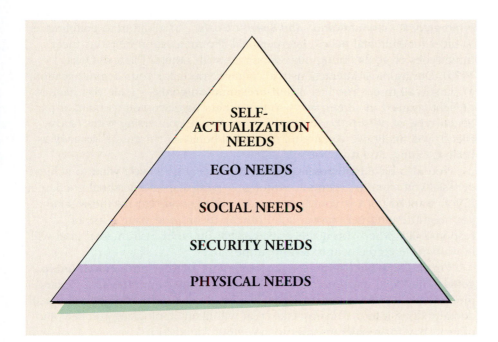

SELF-ACTUALIZATION NEEDS

EGO NEEDS

SOCIAL NEEDS

SECURITY NEEDS

PHYSICAL NEEDS

● Within most interactions, your communication will be tailored toward pursuing all three goals. You'll be concerned with how you appear to people (self-presentation), what you want to get accomplished (instrumental), and how your communication affects your relationships with others in the situation (relationship).

SELF-REFLECTION

Think of a recent encounter you had. What were your self-presentation goals during that encounter? Your instrumental goals? Your relationship goals? How did you use interpersonal communication to fulfill each goal? Was one of these goals more important to you than the others? If so, which one? Why was it most important?

Interpersonal Communication and Specific Goals. In addition to enabling us to meet fundamental needs, interpersonal communication helps us meet three types of goals during our encounters with others (Clark & Delia, 1979). During most interactions with others, you tailor your communication to pursue all three. The first is **self-presentation goals**—goals you have to present yourself in certain ways so that others perceive you as being a particular type of person. For example, when you're conversing with a close friend, you likely use verbal and nonverbal behavior to present yourself as honest, caring, and trustworthy.

You also have **instrumental goals**—practical goals you want to achieve or tasks you want to accomplish through a particular interpersonal encounter. If you want to borrow your best friend's prized sports car for the weekend, you might remind her of your solid driving record and your sense of responsibility when you make your request. But your instrumental goal will be to win her agreement to lend you the car.

Finally, you use interpersonal communication to achieve **relationship goals**—building, maintaining, or terminating bonds with others. For example, if you succeed in borrowing your friend's car for the weekend and accidentally drive it into a nearby lake, you will likely apologize profusely and offer to pay for repairs in order to save your friendship.

Principles of Interpersonal Communication

When one reflects on all that scholars know about interpersonal communication based on decades of research and theory development, five general principles emerge—tenets that both build on and take us deeper into the nature of interpersonal communication than our prior discussion of definition and goals. These principles are affirmed repeatedly throughout this text, and as you read them, consider how they mesh with your own communication experiences and your relationships.

Interpersonal communication conveys both content and relationship information.

During every interpersonal encounter, you and the people with whom you are communicating simultaneously exchange two types of information (Watzlawick et al., 1967). Content information is the actual meaning of the words you exchange. Relationship information consists of signals indicating how each of you views your bond. These signals may indicate whether you consider yourself superior, equal, or inferior to the other person and whether you see the relationship as intimate, acquainted, or estranged.

Whereas you convey content information verbally (through words), you communicate relationship information primarily through nonverbal cues such as vocal tone, pitch, and volume; facial expression and eye contact; hand gestures; height in relation to the listener; and posture. For example, suppose your housemate hasn't been doing his fair share of kitchen cleanup. One evening, after he leaves his dirty dishes in the sink (again!), you walk into the living room where he's curled up on the couch and watching TV. You sit down next to him, smile, and say in a friendly tone of voice, "Do you think you could rinse your dishes off and put them in the dishwasher when you're done with them?" Now, imagine the exact same situation—except that this time you stand between the TV and your housemate, scowl, point your finger at him, and shout, "Do you think you could rinse your dishes off and put them in the dishwasher when you're done with them?!" In both scenarios, the content information is identical—you use exactly the same words. But you communicate very different relationship information. In the first scene, you indicate that you like and respect your housemate. In the second, you communicate anger and dislike.

Relationship information strongly influences how people interpret content information (Watzlawick et al., 1967). In the example above, your housemate will decide how you feel about him and your mutual relationship not so much from your words but from your behavior during the encounter. During most interpersonal encounters, however, people aren't consciously aware of the relationship information being delivered. You don't usually sit there thinking, "Gee, what's this person trying to convey to me about how she sees our relationship?" Relationship information becomes most obvious when it is unexpected or suggests that the sender's view of the relationship is different from the receiver's. Suppose a stranger or new acquaintance says something overly intimate to you, your normally affectionate sister sounds aloof and reserved during a phone conversation, or a coworker starts ordering you around as if he's your manager. When such

---

SKILLS PRACTICE

This exercise is designed to help you convey relationship information.

1 Recall an encounter in which the relationship information you conveyed clashed with the other person's view of your bond (you communicated too much or too little intimacy or a different status from that which the other person perceived you as having).

2 Identify your own feelings about the relationship. Why do you view the relationship in this way?

3 Consider the other person's perspective.

4 Determine how you can communicate in ways that strike a better balance between his or her view of the relationship and yours.

5 Communicate in these ways in your future encounters.

events occur, we often experience annoyance or anxiety. Consequently, it's important to communicate relationship information in ways that are sensitive to and respect others' impressions of the relationship while at the same time staying true to your own relationship feelings.

Because relationship information influences people's interpretation of the content that is presented, it can be considered a specific form of **meta-communication**—communication about communication (Watzlawick et al., 1967). Meta-communication includes any message or interaction that has as its central focus communication—everything from scientific pondering of how communication works to verbal and nonverbal communication between friends clarifying how messages should be interpreted (such as a facial expression or comment suggesting, "Don't take what I just said too seriously"). During interpersonal encounters meta-communication helps us to understand each other's communication, giving us additional guidance regarding how messages should be correctly perceived.

Interpersonal communication can be intentional or unintentional. During interpersonal encounters, people attach meaning to nearly everything you say and do—whether you intend to send a message or not. Scholars Paul Watzlawick, Janet Beavin, and Don Jackson (1967) expressed this as: "One cannot not communicate" (p. 51). As they put it, when you're interacting with others:

> Activity or inactivity, words or silence all have message value: The man at a crowded lunch counter who looks straight ahead, or the airplane passenger who sits with his eyes closed, are both communicating that they do not want to speak to anybody or be spoken to, and their neighbors usually get the message and respond appropriately. This is just as much an interchange of communication as an animated discussion. (p. 49)

SELF-REFLECTION

Consider an instance in which you didn't intend to communicate a message but someone saw your behavior as communication. How did this person interpret your behavior? What were the consequences for your relationship? What did you say and do to correct the individual's misperception?

Consider an illustration from my own teaching experience. One of my greatest pleasures is talking with people who challenge me to think about things in new ways. When I'm chatting with someone and he or she makes a comment that strikes me as really smart, provocative, or interesting, I frequently laugh out loud. This laugh has no intended communication meaning. It's simply a physical expression of pleasure at hearing a cool point, and a gleeful laugh leaps out my mouth. But other people have sometimes interpreted the laugh differently. In particular, when I've been in front of a new class of students who don't know me well and I've laughed after someone made a good point, some students have thought I was making fun of them. Now I explain to every new class, "If I laugh at something you've said, it's not because I think it's stupid, but because I think it's really smart."

Interpersonal communication is irreversible. Every time you communicate interpersonally, you and the other person affect your future communication and the quality of your relationship. Consider something as seemingly simple as answering your cell phone. The ring tone prompts you to look at the incoming number. Your identification of the caller influences how you answer—warm and enthusiastic "Hi!" or detached and terse "Yeah?" depending on how you feel about the caller. Your answer influences how the caller responds. His or her response further affects your next comment. And so on.

This fundamental interconnectedness of action not only defines interpersonal communication but also makes all interpersonal communication irreversible. By sending an e-mail, leaving a phone message, or expressing a thought out loud during a face-to-face encounter, you set in motion the series of outcomes that follow. Simply, once you've said something, you can't take it back. So it's important to think carefully before you communicate. Ask yourself, "Is what I'm about to say going to lead to outcomes I want?" If not, revise your message accordingly.

The fact that all interpersonal communication is irreversible highlights a central theme that runs through this textbook: *the communication choices you make directly determine the personal, interpersonal, and relationship outcomes that follow.* Your decisions about how to communicate, and the messages that result, affect how you think and feel in the future (personal outcomes), how others think and feel (interpersonal outcomes), and how your connections with these individuals will evolve (relationship outcomes). When you communicate thoughtlessly (as we all do on occasion), negative outcomes will ensue, such as interpersonal conflict, painful emotions felt by you or the other person, or mutual dissatisfaction with the relationship. When it comes to interpersonal communication and relationships, there are no "freebies" or "get out of jail free" cards.

At the same time, when you communicate thoughtfully, you activate an equally irreversible—and much more positive—series of outcomes. These outcomes include personal contentment, positive emotions, and mutually satisfying relationships—all essential ingredients for a healthy, happy life.

Interpersonal communication is dynamic. As we've seen, interpersonal communication is dynamic. This means that as we interact with others, our communication and all that influences it—perceptions, thoughts, feelings,

● Whether positive or negative, the communication choices you make directly determine the personal, interpersonal, and relationship outcomes that follow.

and emotions—are constantly in a state of flux. Consider two significant practical implications of this principle. First, no two interactions with the same person will ever be identical. People with whom we once interacted effortlessly and joyfully can seem difficult to talk with during our next encounter. And those we once felt awkward around may become our closest confidants. For example, my wife and I took an almost instant dislike to each other upon our first meeting—a feeling that endured across several encounters that followed. Only after nearly two months and a dozen additional encounters did something "click" between us. Our interactions changed from brief and irksome to long and intimate, and we've now been married almost twenty years.

Second, no two moments within the *same* interaction will ever be identical. The complex combination of perceptions, thoughts, moods, and emotions that fuel our interpersonal communication choices are in a constant state of flux, and as a result, the course of interaction between people is constantly changing as well. For instance, you meet your long-distance partner at the airport, and for the first few minutes after he or she debarks from the plane you both feel incredibly joyous as you bask and revel in being in each other's company once again. But half an hour later, while driving home, you both suddenly find yourselves at a loss for things to talk about. As the minutes pass, the tension increases as you both silently ponder "what happened?"

Interpersonal communication is intertwined with ethics. Our interpersonal communication choices and messages are intertwined with **ethics**—the moral principles that guide our behavior toward others. Ethics involve the translation of our inner moral beliefs into outward action, and given that interpersonal communication is our principal vehicle for conveying our inner world to others, our ethics and our interpersonal communication will naturally be intertwined.

One needn't be ethical in order to interpersonally communicate, although in Chapter 5 I argue that to be interpersonally competent you must

SELF-REFLECTION

Recall an interaction that took a sudden turn for the worse. How did each person's communication contribute to the change in the interaction's quality? What did you say or do to deal with the problem? Could you have communicated differently so the encounter didn't become negative? If so, how?

communicate ethically. You can interpersonally communicate in ethical ways, avoiding the intentional hurting of others and consistently displaying respect, kindness, and compassion. Or you can interpersonally communicate in unethical ways, creating messages designed to exploit or deceive, erode others' self-esteem, express intolerance or hatred, or even intimidate or threaten others' well-being. In either case, the interpersonal communication choices you make—how you opt to interact with and treat others—will be a direct reflection of your personal ethics.

● Understanding the relationship between culture and interpersonal communication will help you communicate more effectively.

Issues in Interpersonal Communication

As we move into the twenty-first century, scholars and students alike share an understanding of what interpersonal communication is and why it's so important in our daily lives and relationships. Armed with this shared clarity regarding the field, scholars have begun to broaden their study of topics related to interpersonal communication. In particular, five issues have begun attracting more attention. As you strive to improve your interpersonal communication skills in an increasingly diverse and technologically advanced world, these five issues will have growing relevance for you, other students of communication, and your teachers. The issues are culture, gender, sexual orientation, online communication, and the dark side of interpersonal relationships.

Culture

We define **culture** as a set of beliefs, attitudes, values, and practices shared by a large group of people (Keesing, 1974). Each of us learns these beliefs, attitudes, values, and practices from parents, teachers, religious leaders, peers, and the mass media (Gudykunst & Kim, 2003). Culture may include your nationality as well as your ethnicity, religion, gender, sexual orientation, and even your age.

Different cultures have very different views of interpersonal communication and the very nature of culture itself. For example, Western cultures (the

United States, the United Kingdom, Europe) conceive of interpersonal communication as a form of behavior that involves exchanging messages and that can be observed and studied objectively (Imahori, 2005). Eastern cultures (India and East Asia) often view interpersonal communication as something that exists "between" people—an "atmosphere" built on how people treat one another—and that can be understood only by considering the specific relationships in which communication occurs, such as parent-child or teacher-student (Imahori, 2005). As our world gets more diverse, scholars and students must consider cultural differences when discussing interpersonal communication theory and research and how communication skills can be improved.

Throughout this text, we examine many differences and similarities related to culture and interpersonal communication, and we assess their

FOCUS ON CULTURE

Interpersonal Communication across Cultures

Formal study of interpersonal communication occurs almost exclusively in the United States; only a handful of scholars in Great Britain, Europe, Australia, and Asia study and teach interpersonal communication (Knapp et al., 2002). As of 2005, only one university outside the United States offered a regular undergraduate course on interpersonal communication—a class titled "Lecture on Personal Relationships" offered by Toyo University, in Tokyo, Japan.[1]

Why isn't Interpersonal communication studied and taught in other cultures? Because it's not recognized as an academic field of interest. Instead, people view interpersonal communication knowledge and skills as a private matter—to be taught by parents to their children—rather than a public matter to be scientifically examined and taught in school. Min Soo, a student at my university, expresses this view:[2]

> Although I'm Korean, I grew up in Bolivia. Schools in Bolivia do not teach interpersonal communication. There's a good reason for that. Interpersonal communication is considered a personal matter, and people tend to go

to their families for that kind of teaching. Bolivian culture, like many other Spanish-speaking countries, values family greatly, and Bolivians believe that the family is the best resource for learning relationship and communication skills. Schools in Bolivia are expected to teach things that cannot be taught by parents—things like math, science, and biology. We understand the importance of interpersonal communication and realize that there's much to learn about it, but most Bolivians would consider that a nonschool subject.

YOUR TURN

- Do you believe that interpersonal communication skills should be taught to children in school or left to parents and caregivers to teach?

- Who taught you the interpersonal communication knowledge and skills you currently possess?

- How has your cultural background influenced your view of who should teach interpersonal communication skills to young people?

[1] M. Ferrara (personal communication, March 1, 2004).
[2] Published with full permission of Min Soo.

practical implications. In each chapter, a *Focus on Culture* feature highlights a particular aspect of culture as it relates to the content being discussed. This feature is designed not simply to inform you about cultural differences but to critically examine the role that this issue plays in your own communication. See the first *Focus on Culture* on page 30 to give yourself a sense of how this feature works.

Gender and Sexual Orientation

Gender consists of social, psychological, and cultural traits generally associated with one sex or the other (Canary, Emmers-Sommer, & Faulkner, 1997). Unlike biological sex, which we're born with, gender is largely learned. Gender influences how people communicate interpersonally, but scholars disagree about how. For example, you may have read in popular magazines or heard on TV that women are more "open" and "expressive" communicators than men and that men "have difficulty communicating their feelings" and "sharing their inner vulnerabilities." But when these beliefs are compared with the research and theory on gender and interpersonal communication, it turns out that men and women often are surprisingly similar in how they communicate. Throughout this book, we will discuss these popular beliefs and look at scholarly research on the impact of gender on interpersonal communication.

Each of us also possesses a **sexual orientation:** an enduring emotional, romantic, sexual, or affectionate attraction to another person that exists along a continuum ranging from exclusive homosexuality to exclusive heterosexuality and that includes various forms of bisexuality (APA Online, n.d.). You may have heard that gays and lesbians communicate in ways different than "straights," or heterosexuals, or build, maintain, and end relationships in distinct ways. But as with common beliefs about gender, research tells us that same-gender and opposite-gender relationships are built up, maintained, and deteriorate in similar ways. We will discuss these assumptions about sexual orientations, as well as what interpersonal communication research tells us about its effects throughout this text.

Online Communication

Radical changes in communication technology in the last few decades have had a profound effect on our ability to interpersonally communicate. Cell phones keep us in almost constant contact with friends, family members, and romantic partners. Our ability to communicate easily and frequently, even when separated by geographic distance, is further enhanced through **online communication:** interaction by means of e-mail, text- or instant-messaging, videoconferences, chatrooms, multiuser discussions listservs and other mailing lists, and Usenet newsgroups (Walther & Parks, 2002).

In this book, we treat such technologies as sophisticated tools for connecting people interpersonally—tools that have become pervasive and naturally integrated into our lives. In every chapter, you'll find frequent mention of these technologies as they relate to various specific topics. Each chapter also provides one *Skills Practice* exercise devoted to helping you strengthen your online interpersonal communication skills.

The Dark Side of Interpersonal Relationships

Interpersonal relationships are central to our life happiness. When our involvements with lovers, family, friends, and coworkers are satisfying, we typically find ourselves happier in general (Myers, 2002). But the fact that relationships can bring us joy obscures the fact that relationships, and the interpersonal communication that occurs within them, often can be destructive. As relational scholars Steve Duck and Julia Wood (1995) note, "the processes of relationship dissolution dog ordinary experience, violence occurs in intimate relationships, and friends and lovers can be mean, petty, vindictive, and cruel to one another" (pp. 1–2).

In studying interpersonal communication, you can learn much by looking beyond constructive encounters to the types of damaging exchanges that occur all too frequently in life. The greatest challenges to your interpersonal communication skills lie not in communicating effectively when it is easy to do so but in practicing skilled interpersonal communication when doing so is difficult. Throughout the text, we will discuss many of these negative aspects that you may experience, as well as recommendations for how to deal with them.

Learning Interpersonal Communication

When Helen Torres (described in the chapter opening) came into my office and declared that she wanted to "go into" the field of interpersonal communication, what she really meant was that she wanted to learn information from the discipline to share with others—assisting them in making better communication decisions that would improve their lives. In a similar fashion, your experience learning about interpersonal communication will be one of mastering knowledge and skills that will enable you to make informed and improved communication choices, resulting in healthier and happier interpersonal relationships.

As you journey through all that lies before you in this book, you won't learn a simple solution to every dilemma that you face, nor will you learn the answer to every question you have. But you will see how to create your own solutions and generate your own answers to interpersonal problems and challenges.

The organization of this text flows directly from our definition of interpersonal communication and the implications of this definition. Your interpersonal communication derives from the communication choices you make, and the communication that flows from those choices creates the personal, interpersonal, and relationship outcomes you experience. To improve your outcomes, therefore, you must learn the knowledge necessary to make better choices, acquire the skills necessary to implement those decisions, and then wrestle with the outcomes of your actions within your interpersonal relationships. This three-part model—essential knowledge about interpersonal communication, the skills that translate this knowledge into constructive action, and the outcomes these skills have for your interpersonal relationships—forms the underlying organizing structure of our book.

● Learning about three factors that influence your communication decisions—your self, your perception of others, and your emotions—is the first step to improving your interpersonal communication.

Interpersonal Essentials

In the three chapters comprising Part One, "Interpersonal Essentials" (Chapters 2–4), you will discover how your awareness of your self, self-esteem, and self-concept all shape your interpersonal communication. You will also explore the process by which you form perceptions of others, as well as learn how to avoid perceptual errors. And you will find strategies for managing difficult emotions—such as anger and grief—that can prevent you from communicating competently and thus can damage your relationships.

Part One also explains the concept of critical self-reflection—a systematic process for analyzing the connections between your thoughts, your communication choices, and the resulting relationship outcomes. Throughout the text, you'll find two features designed to help you master this process. *Self-Reflection* exercises pose questions that encourage you to relate the ideas in the book to your own experiences and relationships. *Pop Quizzes* help you assess your knowledge and identify areas for improvement.

"Would you mind talking to me for a while? I forgot my cell phone."

POP QUIZ

The Dark Side of Interpersonal Relationships

Read the following phrases describing relationship challenges. Place a check mark next to each challenge that you believe you could address by improving your interpersonal communication skills. Then read the instructions that follow to interpret your score.

_____ Feeling plagued by the sense that you're not the kind of person you should be or that others expect you to be

_____ Thinking of and treating others in a negative, stereotypical fashion

_____ Dealing with unwanted anger in ways that avoid chronic hostility and aggression

_____ Managing grief related to the loss of a loved one

_____ Feeling extreme fear and anxiety when interacting with others

_____ Creating messages in ways that avoid triggering defensiveness in others

_____ Managing people who are verbally and physically aggressive toward you

_____ Reducing the likelihood of violence during interpersonal conflicts

_____ Overcoming dysfunctional, intimacy-eroding beliefs about relationships

_____ Managing romantic jealousy in yourself and your partners

_____ Dealing with betrayal in intimate relationships

_____ Responding effectively to abuse from a coworker or supervisor

Scoring

You can better manage all of these relationship challenges by improving your interpersonal communication, as you'll discover throughout this text.

A Misunderstanding between Friends

1

BACKGROUND

Communication misunderstandings can be painful to experience and difficult to overcome. But just as communication occasionally provokes misunderstandings, it also can be used to solve them. Read the case study; then, drawing upon all you know about interpersonal communication thus far, work through the problem-solving model at the end of the exercise — a model designed to help you make more systematic and better relationship decisions in your own life.

2

CASE STUDY

Since freshman year of college, you've been best friends with Pujita. Pujita is smart, funny, and blunt — qualities you admire. You share many interests — music, movies, food. But you also have many differences. Pujita is much less serious than you and is more spontaneous, and you both come from different cultural backgrounds. Over the years, she has been a good friend, and without her help and support, you might not have survived college.

As graduation nears, you find yourself thinking more about your differences. Pujita is graduating with a straight-A average, and already received several promising job offers. You've done well in school, but unlike Pujita, you have not received any job offers despite energetic interviewing.

One night, you and Pujita are hanging out with friends at their apartment, talking about jobs and exchanging interview horror stories. You're having a great time, the most fun you've had in weeks. Suddenly, everything changes. One of your friends asks you how the job search is going, and after you jokingly respond, "I don't know if I'll *ever* get a job," Pujita laughs and says loudly, "I can always throw you my left-overs." Shocked, you ask what she means. She responds, "I'm thinking about taking next year off and just traveling. I can tell the companies that want me to hire you instead." Your friends all chuckle, but you feel hurt and humiliated. Thinking that Pujita's comment is her way of expressing her superiority, you snap, "You know, I don't need your leftovers — I can't believe how full of yourself you are!" and storm out.

That night, you receive an e-mail from Pujita. She says she was just joking and doesn't under-stand why you're so mad. She also demands that you apologize both to her and to your friends for *your* rudeness. As you read her message, a thousand thoughts run through your head. Did she intend to mock you, or was she being playful? Was she trying to pull rank and act superior? Did you overreact because you're feeling sensitive about your lack of job offers? Should you, *can* you, repair the relationship? Pondering these questions, you begin writing a response: "Pujita . . ."

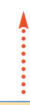

YOUR TURN

Think about the ideas and insights about interpersonal communication you've learned while reading this chapter. Keep them in mind while working through the following five steps. These steps constitute a process that can help you make more effective interpersonal communication choices in important relationships. Remember, there are no right answers to the questions posed here. So think hard about what choice you will make! (P.S. Need help? See the helpful concepts listed below.)

- **Step 1: Reflect on yourself.** What are your thoughts and feelings in this situation? What assumptions are you making about Pujita and her interpersonal communication? Are your assumptions accurate? Why or why not?

- **Step 2: Reflect on your partners.** Put yourself in Pujita's shoes. Consider how she is thinking and feeling. Are her views valid?

- **Step 3: Identify the optimal outcome.** Think about what's happened. Consider your own feelings as well as those of Pujita. Given all these factors, what's the best, most constructive relationship outcome possible here? Be sure to consider not just what's best for *you,* but what's best for Pujita as well.

- **Step 4: Locate the roadblocks.** Taking into consideration your own thoughts and feelings, those of Pujita, and all that has happened in this situation, what's preventing you from achieving the optimal outcome you identified in step 3?

- **Step 5: Chart your course.** What can you say and do to overcome the roadblocks you identified in step 4 and to achieve your optimal relationship outcome?

HELPFUL CONCEPTS

I-Thou and I-It, *21*

Relationship information, *25*

The impossibility of not communicating, *26*

The dynamic nature of interpersonal communication, *27*

The irreversibility of interpersonal communication, *27*

Interpersonal Skills

The five chapters in Part Two, "Interpersonal Skills" (Chapters 5–9), show you how to put your knowledge of interpersonal communication into action. In these chapters, you learn how to strengthen your **interpersonal communication competence** by consistently communicating in appropriate, effective, and ethical ways (Spitzberg & Cupach, 1984). You will also master new **communication skills**—repeatable behaviors that enable you to improve the quality of your interpersonal encounters and relationships (Spitzberg & Cupach, 2002). Although the chapters in Part Two focus on improving interpersonal skills, throughout the entire text, you will find ample opportunity to practice your interpersonal communication skills in real-world applications by completing the *Skills Practice* features contained in each chapter.

Interpersonal Relationships

Interpersonal relationships are the emotional, mental, and physical involvements that you forge with others through communication. In the three chapters that form Part Three, "Interpersonal Relationships" (Chapters 10–12), you will gain familiarity with the unique challenges of communicating with romantic partners, family members and friends, and individuals you encounter in the workplace. These chapters also provide ideas on how to address challenges and maintain positive relationships with key individuals in your life.

Throughout the text, you'll put your interpersonal communication knowledge and skills to the test by completing *Making Relationship Choices*—hands-on exercises challenging you to resolve common relationship predicaments. Try your hand at the *Making Relationship Choices* exercise on pages 34–35 to begin familiarizing yourself with this feature.

● The power of interpersonal communication can bridge the differences and distances that exist between us in life's "big" moments and during everyday encounters.

The Foundation Laid and the Journey Ahead

Interpersonal communication is our primary vehicle for exchanging meaning, emotionally connecting, and building relationships with others. This makes it essential that we base our interpersonal decisions on the best knowledge to which we have access. No one would consider making choices about collegiate majors, future careers, or monetary interests without first gathering the most trustworthy information available. Interpersonal communication should be no different.

This chapter—which introduces the interpersonal communication field, key definitions, and important principles—will start you on your journey into the study of interpersonal communication. And as we travel together through interpersonal essentials, skills, and relationships, the transformative potential of your interpersonal communication will become apparent. Through learning about interpersonal communication, you can improve your interpersonal skills, and this change will directly and positively impact your life and relationships.

POSTSCRIPT

We began this chapter with an inquisitive student and a cake bigger than a cup. When Helen Torres's mother misinterpreted a request from another parent, it set in motion a chain of events that led Helen to study interpersonal communication. Helen's interpersonal communication education provided her with the knowledge and skills necessary to collaborate with

powerful people on behalf of individuals in need.

What motivated *you* to decide to learn more about interpersonal communication? How do you think the knowledge you'll gain in this course will improve your life? Through pursuing *your* communication education by reading this book, you too can gain a different lens for

looking at the world, become more savvy in interpreting interaction, and improve your communication and relationship decision making.

Key Terms

Key Concepts

What Is Communication?

- Scholars have studied **communication** for over 4,000 years. The **message** is the basic unit of communication, and we exchange messages while engaging in **interaction** with others. During communication, **contexts** shape how we create and interpret messages, and messages are conveyed through a variety of **channels** and **media.**

- In antiquity, the study of communication was focused on **rhetoric.** Much of what the ancient Greeks and Romans learned about rhetoric is still taught today in public speaking classes.

- Many communication studies scholars view communication as a **social science.** They conduct **research** and create **theory** to better understand how people interact. Both qualitative approaches and quantitative approaches to research and theory involve the creation and testing of hypotheses, although the manner in which such tests are conducted is quite different.

The Communication Process

- The **linear communication model** describes the basic set of components necessary for communication to occur, including a **sender,** a message, a channel, **noise,** and a **receiver.** The **interactive communication model** builds on the linear model, adding both **feedback** and **fields of experience.** The **transactional communication model** is the most sophisticated and refined model of communication and is widely embraced by scholars as the best model for describing interpersonal communication.

What Is Interpersonal Communication?

- When most people think of **interpersonal communication,** they think of **dyadic** communication. This allows us to distinguish it from **intrapersonal communication.** But we also think of interpersonal communication as **I-Thou** rather than **I-It.** Interpersonal communication allows us to connect with others in ways that are more meaningful and profound than **impersonal communication.**

- We use interpersonal communication for a broad range of purposes, including the pursuit of **self-presentation, instrumental,** and **relationship goals.**

- Whenever we interpersonally communicate with others, we exchange both content and relationship information. Because relationship information influences how others interpret the content of what we have said, it can be considered a form of **meta-communication.**

- Because interpersonal communication is our primary vehicle for expressing ourselves to others, how we choose to communicate will be a direct reflection of our personal **ethics.**

Issues in Interpersonal Communication

- Five issues are becoming increasingly relevant for students and teachers of interpersonal communication: **culture, gender, sexual orientation, online communication,** and the dark side of interpersonal relationships.

Learning Interpersonal Communication

- This text follows a three-part model designed to help you improve your interpersonal communication. First, you will learn essential information about interpersonal communication that will help you to make better choices. Second, you will develop **interpersonal communication competence** and **communication skills.** Third, you will learn how your communication creates outcomes within your **interpersonal relationships** and how your communication can be changed to improve these outcomes.

Key Skills

- What interpersonal communication recommendations did the Egyptian sage Ptah Hotep offer more than 4,000 years ago? Discover the answer on page 10.

- How can you use knowledge of interpersonal communication research methods to solve problems in your own online relationships? Find out by doing the *Skills Practice* on page 14.

- How might you shift your communication from I-It to I-Thou? Complete the *Skills Practice* on page 21 to find out.

- How can you improve the relationship information you communicate to others? Complete the *Skills Practice* on page 25.

- What is the fundamental connection between communication knowledge, communication choices, and relationship outcomes? Review the answer on page 26.

- What are the two practical implications of viewing interpersonal communication as dynamic? Review the answer on page 28.

- What challenges from the dark side of interpersonal relationships can be better managed through building your interpersonal skills? Find the answer by taking the *Pop Quiz* on page 33.

- How would you deal with a challenging relationship dilemma? Complete the *Making Relationship Choices* exercise on page 35 to find out.

2
Considering Self

Artist Eric Staib describes his 2002 painting *labeled* as a self-portrait. "It depicts my feelings about how my peers saw me when I was growing up. The hands pointing, words said under people's breath. You can tell what they're thinking: you're an idiot, you're stupid, you're a joke."[1]

By the time Eric was in third grade, he knew he was different. Whereas his classmates progressed rapidly in reading and writing, Eric couldn't make sense of words on the written page. But it wasn't until fifth grade that Eric finally was given a label for his difference: learning disabled, or "LD." The LD label stained Eric's sense of self, making him feel ashamed. His low self-esteem spread outward, constraining his communication and relationships. "My whole approach was *Don't get noticed!* I'd slouch down in class, hide in my seat. And I would never open up to people. I let nobody in."

[1] All information presented in the introductory segment regarding artist Eric Staib was provided with his permission, from an interview conducted by the author in February of 2005.

41

Frustrated with the seemingly insurmountable challenges of reading and writing, Eric channeled intense energy into art. By eleventh grade, Eric had the reading and writing abilities of a fifth grader, but managed to pass his classes through hard work and artistic ability. He graduated from high school with a D average.

Many of Eric's LD peers turned to substance abuse and dropped out of school, but Eric pursued his education further, taking classes at a local community college. There, something happened that transformed his view of his self, his self-esteem, and the entire course of his life. While taking his first written exam of the semester, Eric knew the answers, but he couldn't write them down. No matter how hard he focused, he couldn't convert the knowledge in his head into written words. Rather than complete the exam, he wrote the story of his disability on the answer sheet, including his struggles with reading and writing and the pain associated with being

labeled LD. He turned in his exam and left. Eric's professor took his exam to the college dean, and the two of them called Eric to the dean's office. They told him, "You need help, and we're going to help you." Their compassion changed Eric's life. Eric's professor arranged for Eric to meet with a learning specialist, who immediately diagnosed him as dyslexic. As Eric explains, "For the first time in my life, I had a label for myself other than 'learning disabled.' To me, the LD label meant I couldn't learn. But dyslexia was different. It could be overcome. The specialist taught me strategies for working with my dyslexia, and gave me my most important tool—my Franklin Spellchecker—to check spellings. But most importantly, I was taught that it was okay to be dyslexic."

Armed with an improving sense of self, Eric went from hiding to asserting himself, "from low self-esteem to being comfortable voicing my opinion, from fear to confidence." That confidence led him to transfer to a Big 10 university, where he graduated with a degree in studio arts, percussion, and horticulture. He subsequently earned a postgraduate degree in K–12 art education, graduating with a straight-A average.

Eric Staib is now an art instructor in the Midwest, and was a 2006 recipient of the Robert Rauschenberg Foundation Power of Art Award, given to the top arts educators in the country each year. He also teaches instructors how to use art to engage learning-disabled students. What means the most to him is the opportunity to pass the legacy of his personal transformation down to others. "When I think about my dyslexia, it's really incredible. What was my greatest personal punishment is now the most profound gift I have to offer to others."

Every word you've ever spoken during an encounter with someone else, every act of goodness or malevolence you've committed in a relationship, has the same root source—your self. When you look inward to your self, you are peering into the wellspring from which all of your interpersonal triumphs and tribulations, large and small, have flowed. At the same time, your self does not simply influence your interpersonal communication and behavior; it is shaped by these as well. Through communicating and relating with others, we learn who we are, what we're worth, and how we should act.

Because your self both affects and is affected by your interpersonal communication, the starting point for improving your communication skills is to understand your self. By deepening your self-understanding, you can begin to clarify your thoughts and feelings about your self; comprehend how these are linked to your interpersonal communication; and develop strategies for enhancing your sense of self, your communication skills, and your interpersonal relationships.

In this chapter, we explore the source of all interpersonal communication: the self. You'll learn:

- The components of self, as well as how critical self-reflection can be used to improve your communication skills and your self-esteem

- The ways in which gender, family, and culture shape your sense of self

- How to present and maintain a positive self when interacting with others

- The challenges of managing selves in relationships, including suggestions for successful self-disclosure

● For years, researchers believed that only humans and apes possess self-awareness, but recent research has documented that dolphins also are self-aware. When marked with a harmless sunscreen cream on their faces, dolphins twist and turn in front of mirrors, carefully examining the marks on themselves.

SELF-REFLECTION

Consider people in your life whom you admire. What is it about them you hold in high regard? Are they better communicators than you? More successful at building relationships? How does socially comparing yourself against admired others affect your feelings about your self?

The Components of Self

At Delphi in ancient Greece, the temple of the sun-god Apollo was adorned with the inscription "Gnothi se auton"—*Know thyself.* According to legend, when one of the seven sages of Greece, Chilon of Sparta, asked Apollo, "What is best for people?" the deity responded with that simple admonition. More than 2,500 years later, these words still ring true, especially in the realm of interpersonal communication and relationships. To understand our interactions with others and the bonds we forge, we must first comprehend ourselves. But what exactly is "thyself" that we need to know?

The **self** is an evolving composite of self-awareness, self-concept, and self-esteem. Although each of us experiences the self as a single entity ("This is who I am"), the self actually comprises three components that develop continually over time, based on a person's life experiences.

Self-Awareness

The first component of self is **self-awareness**—the ability to step outside yourself (so to speak); view yourself as a unique person distinct from your surrounding environment; and reflect on your thoughts, feelings, and behaviors. Scientists have questioned for years whether nonhuman species are self-aware (Parker, Mitchell, & Boccia, 1995). One test they've used is to anesthetize an animal, place a harmless mark on its face, and then present it with a mirror after it awakens. Animals lacking self-awareness ignore the facial mark, perceiving the mirror and their reflection in it as novelties and nothing more. Animals with self-awareness recognize the image in the mirror as themselves, notice the facial mark, and begin touching *their own* faces to investigate. Of the entire animal kingdom, only humans, apes, and dolphins pass this test.

How does self-awareness help create self? According to sociologist George Herbert Mead, we observe our own behaviors during interpersonal encounters, forming impressions of ourselves that lead to an evolving sense of self (Mead, 1934). For example, when you warmly greet a passing coworker or fellow student in the hallway, your awareness of your behavior leads you to think of yourself as a "friendly person." As we're watching and judging our own actions, we also engage in **social comparison,** observing

STONE SOUP © 1996 Jan Eliot. Reprinted with permission of UNIVERSAL PRESS SYNDICATE. All rights reserved.

● When we compare favorably against others, our sense of positive self-awareness is strengthened, but when we compare negatively, the effects can range from poor self-image to serious eating or body-image disorders.

and assigning meaning to others' behavior and then comparing their behavior against ours. Social comparison has a particularly potent effect on self when we compare ourselves against people we admire and wish to emulate. When we compare favorably against respected others, we think well of ourselves ("I'm as hardworking and successful as the best employees in this company"). When we don't compare favorably, we think less of ourselves ("I wish I could be as open and outgoing as my friends").

You can greatly enhance your interpersonal communication skills by practicing a targeted kind of self-awareness known as critical self-reflection. To engage in critical self-reflection, ask yourself the following questions:

- What am I thinking and feeling?
- Why am I thinking and feeling the way I am?
- How am I communicating?
- How are my inner thoughts and feelings affecting my communication behavior?
- How can I improve my thoughts, feelings, and communication behavior?

SKILLS PRACTICE

This exercise reveals the role of critical self-reflection in improving interpersonal communication.

❶ Recall an interaction that left you feeling bad about your self.

❷ Describe what happened.

❸ Answer the five critical self-reflection questions, focusing on what you could have thought, felt, and done differently to improve the situation.

❹ The next time you're in a similar situation, apply your new insights as the situation unfolds. Be patient with yourself! Changing your communication takes enormous time, effort, and practice.

SELF-REFLECTION

Consider your looking-glass self. What kind of labels do your friends use to describe you? Your family? Your coworkers? Do people like or dislike you in general? How do you feel about others' impressions of you? How do these feelings shape your interpersonal communication and relationships?

The ultimate goal of critical self-reflection is embodied in the last question: How can I improve? Improving your interpersonal communication skills is possible only when you accurately understand how your self drives your communication behavior. In the remainder of this chapter, and in the marginal exercises you'll find throughout this book, we help you make links between your inner self and your outer communication behavior.

Self-Concept

The second component of self is your **self-concept,** your overall perception of who you are ("On the whole, I'm a _____ person"). Your self-concept is based on the beliefs, attitudes, and values you have about yourself. Beliefs are convictions that certain things are true—for example, "I'm an excellent student" or "I'm a caring person." Attitudes are evaluative appraisals, such as "I'm happy with my achievements in life" or "I'm unhappy with my appearance." Values represent enduring principles that guide your interpersonal actions—for example, "I think it's wrong to…" Together, the beliefs, attitudes, and values you have about yourself create the overall sense of self that is your self-concept.

Your self-concept is shaped by a host of factors, including gender, family attachments, and culture (Vallacher, Nowak, Froehlich, & Rockloff, 2002). And as we saw in the opening story about Eric Staib, one of the biggest influences on your self-concept is the labels others put on you. Sociologist Charles Horton Cooley described the impact that labeling has on our self-concepts as the **looking-glass self** (Cooley, 1902). According to Cooley, our self-concepts are strongly influenced by our beliefs about how others see and evaluate us ("People think I'm talented, and they like me") and our emotional response to those beliefs ("I feel good/bad about how others see me").

In considering your self-concept and its impact on your interpersonal communication, keep two implications in mind. First, because your self-concept consists of deeply held beliefs, attitudes, and values, it is difficult to change. Once you've decided you're a compassionate person, for example, you'll likely perceive yourself that way for a long time (Fiske & Taylor, 1991). Second, our self-concepts often lead us to make **self-fulfilling prophecies,** predictions about future interactions that lead us to behave in ways that ensure the interaction unfolds as we predicted. Some self-fulfilling prophecies set positive events in motion. For instance, you may see yourself as professionally competent and highly skilled at communicating. This view of self ("I'm a competent professional and skilled communicator") leads you to predict job interview success. During the actual interview, your prophecy of success leads you to communicate in a calm, confident, and impressive fashion, which consequently creates success; the interviewers like and are impressed by you, and their reaction thus confirms your prophecy. Other self-fulfilling prophecies set negative events in motion. I once had a friend who believed he was unattractive and undesirable. Whenever we went out to parties or clubs, his self-concept would lead him to predict interpersonal failure: "What's the point; no one will talk to me anyway." He would then

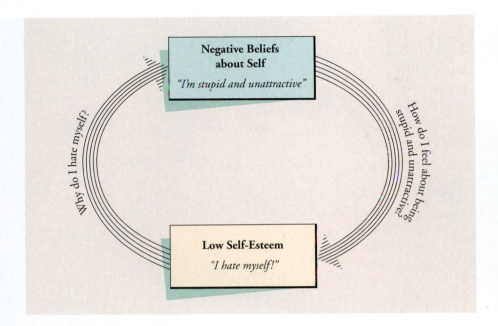

FIGURE 2.1

Low Self-Esteem: A Vicious Cycle

Negative Beliefs about Self

"I'm stupid and unattractive"

Why do I hate myself?

How do I feel about being stupid and unattractive?

Low Self-Esteem

"I hate myself!"

● Our self-concept is influenced by our beliefs about how others perceive us.

SKILLS PRACTICE

This exercise helps you overcome negative self-fulfilling prophecies.

❶ Identify a communication problem that happens repeatedly in your life.

❷ Describe a recent situation when this occurred, including what you thought, said, and did and the results.

❸ Critically self-reflect on the situation, identifying links between your thoughts and feelings and your behavior.

❹ Prevent the prophecy from recurring by blocking any negative links between your thoughts and feelings and your behavior.

spend the entire time sitting at our table, scowling and staring morosely into his drink. Needless to say, no one would approach him or try to talk to him. At the end of the evening, he'd say, "See, I told you no one would want to talk to me!"

Self-Esteem

The third component of self is the overall value that we assign to ourselves, known as our **self-esteem.** Whereas self-awareness prompts us to ask "Who am I?" and self-concept is the answer to that question, self-esteem is the answer to the follow-up question, "Given who I am, what's my evaluation of my worth?" When your overall estimation of self based on all of the characteristics you perceive in yourself (mental, physical, and emotional) is negative, you'll have a meager sense of worth and suffer from low self-esteem. When your evaluation of self is positive, you'll enjoy high self-esteem.

Your self-esteem strongly shapes your interpersonal communication, relationships, and general outlook on life. In simple terms, when you're happy with yourself, this happiness radiates outward. People with high self-esteem report greater life satisfaction, communicate more positively with others, and experience more happiness in their relationships than do people with low self-esteem (Fox, 1997). People with high self-esteem also exhibit greater leadership ability, athleticism, and academic performance (Fox, 1992). By contrast, low self-esteem can spawn a destructive feedback loop, as depicted in Figure 2.1.

● **"Why can't I be the person I want to be?"** This question haunts people who experience a discrepancy between themselves and their ideal self. They may become obsessed with their own failures and sense of worthlessness.

Measuring Up to Your Own Standards. The key to bolstering your self-esteem is understanding its roots. **Self-discrepancy theory** suggests that your self-esteem is determined by how you compare to two mental standards (Higgins, 1987, 1989). The first is your ideal self, the characteristics you want to possess based on your desires. This is the "perfect you"—the embodiment of all the attributes you consider admirable. These characteristics may be mental, physical, emotional, material, and even spiritual. The second standard is your ought self, the person others wish and expect you to be; it stems from expectations of your family, friends, colleagues, and romantic partners as well as cultural norms. According to self-discrepancy theory, you feel happy and content when your perception of your self matches both your ideal and ought selves ("I'm the kind of person I want to be" and "I'm the kind of person others wish me to be") (Katz & Farrow, 2000). However, when you perceive your self to be inferior to both your ideal and ought selves, you experience a discrepancy between your self and these standards and are likely to suffer low self-esteem.

Improving Your Self-Esteem. When asked how people can best address chronic low self-esteem, the Dalai Lama, the spiritual leader of Tibetan Buddhism, responded:

> All human beings have the capacity to be very determined and to direct that strong sense of determination in whatever direction they like. If one maintains an awareness of these potentials and reminds oneself of them repeatedly until it becomes part of one's customary way of perceiving oneself, this can serve to reduce feelings of discouragement, helplessness, and self-contempt. (Cutler & Dalai Lama, 1998)

The Dalai Lama's advice serves as an excellent starting point for boosting your self-esteem and

● **"Why can't I be the person others want me to be?"** This question dogs people who see a discrepancy between themselves and their ought self. They are driven by the inescapable feeling that they're not living up to others' expectations.

experiencing the resulting interpersonal benefits. But your self-esteem can start to improve only when you reduce discrepancies between your self and your ideal and ought selves. How can you do this? Begin by assessing your self-concept. Make a list of the beliefs, attitudes, and values that make up your self-concept. Be sure to include both positive and negative attributes. Then think about your self-esteem. In reviewing the list you've made, do you see yourself positively or negatively?

Next, analyze your ideal self. Who do you wish you were? Be sure to consider the physical, mental, emotional, material, and spiritual aspects of your desired self. Is this ideal attainable, or is it unrealistic? If it is attainable,

FOCUS ON CULTURE

Self-Esteem and the Appearance Culture

Korean American comedian Margaret Cho describes herself as a "trash-talkin' girl comic." In this excerpt from her one-woman show *The Notorious C.H.O.,* she offers her thoughts on self-esteem (Custudio, 2002):

> You know when you look in the mirror and think, "Oh, I'm so fat, I'm so old, I'm so ugly"? That is not your authentic self speaking. That is billions upon billions of dollars of advertising—magazines, movies, billboards—all geared to make you feel bad about yourself so that you'll take your hard-earned money and spend it at the mall. When you don't have self-esteem, you will hesitate before you do anything. You will hesitate to go for the job you really want. You will hesitate to ask for a raise. You will hesitate to defend yourself when you're discriminated against. You will hesitate to vote. You will hesitate to dream. For those of us plagued with low self-esteem, improving [it] is truly an act of revolution!

Cho is right. We live in an "appearance culture," a society that values and reinforces extreme, unrealistic ideals of beauty and body shape (Thompson, Heinberg, Altabe, & Tantleff-Dunn, 1999). In an appearance culture, standards for appearance are defined not by individuals but through digitally enhanced images of bodily perfection produced by the mass media (Field et al., 1999). When we internalize media standards of perfect body and perfect beauty, we end up despising our own bodies and craving unattainable perfection (Jones, Vigfusdottir, & Lee, 2004). Results? Low self-esteem, depression, and, in some cases, self-destructive behaviors such as eating disorders (Harrison, 2001).

YOUR TURN

- Consider your own body. How have images of ideal beauty in magazines and on TV influenced your ideas about what constitutes an attractive body?

- Does your body meet these standards set by our "appearance culture"? If not, could it? What would you have to do to attain the standards?

- How do your feelings about your body affect your self-esteem? How do they affect your interpersonal communication and relationships?

what would you have to change to become this person? If you made these changes, would you be satisfied with yourself, or would your expectations for yourself simply escalate further?

Third, analyze your ought self. Who do others want you to be? Can you ever become the person others expect? What would you have to do to become this person? If you did all of these things, would others be satisfied with you, or would their expectations escalate?

Fourth, revisit and redefine your standards. This step requires intense, concentrated effort over a long period of time. If you find, through our first three steps, that your ideal and ought selves are realistic and attainable, move to the final step—creating an action plan for resolving any self-discrepancies. If you decide that your ideal and ought selves are unrealistic and unattainable, redefine these standards so that each can be attainable through sustained work. Frame your new standards as a list of goals, and post them in your planner, bedroom, or kitchen to remind yourself of these goals. If you find yourself unable to abandon unrealistic and unattainable standards, don't be afraid to consult with a professional therapist or other trusted resource for assistance.

Finally, create an action plan. Map out the specific actions necessary to eventually attain your ideal and ought selves. Since self-esteem can't be changed in a day, a week, or even a month, establish a realistic time line. Then implement this action plan in your daily life, checking your progress as you go.

"Really, only you can tell yourself to giddyup."

POP QUIZ

Test Your Self-Esteem

This quiz can help you gauge your self-esteem. For each statement, mark whether you strongly agree with the statement (SA), agree with it (A), disagree with it (DA), or strongly disagree with it (SD). Give yourself a 3 for each statement marked SA, 2 for A, 1 for DA, and 0 for SD, and total your score.

_____ On the whole, I am satisfied with myself.

_____ I feel that I have a number of good qualities.

_____ I am able to do things as well as most other people.

_____ I feel that I am a person of worth, at least on an equal plane with others.

_____ I have a positive attitude toward myself.

Scoring:

Scores of 7 and below indicate low self-esteem; scores of 8 and above represent high self-esteem.

Note: This *Pop Quiz* is adapted from the self-esteem scale developed by Rosenburg (1965).

The Sources of Self

For most of us, critical self-reflection isn't a new activity. We're already intimately familiar with ourselves. After all, we spend much of our daily lives looking inward, and as a consequence, we feel that we know our selves. But imagine for a moment that you don't. You wake up in your bed at home, and the first thing you notice is people talking in the living room. You recognize their voices as those of your family, but something is terribly wrong. An emptiness is blanketing much of your memory. Although you recognize your surroundings, you have no memory of self. Nothing. How will you find out who you are?

You might first examine your own body. Knowing whether you are male or female would immediately give you a wealth of useful knowledge about your self, such as which clothes you should wear and how you should talk and act. Second, you would likely venture downstairs to talk with family members, gathering as much information from them as you could. You would also watch how they respond to you. Do they seem intimate and caring toward you? Distant and aloof? Unpredictable and uncertain? Last, you would probably turn on the television, surf the web, or even take a walk into town, looking for clues about how people communicate with each other in public, how they dress, and how they behave. From these observations, you might begin to form ideas about where you fit in this culture.

Of course, at the end of the day, you still would have huge holes in your self-knowledge. Biologists and psychologists agree that roughly half of what makes us who we are is inborn, determined by our biological heritage (McCrae et al., 2000; Rothbart, Ahadi, & Evans, 2000). But these same scientists also point out that this biological "hard-wiring" doesn't mean that our self-awareness, self-concept, and self-esteem are 50 percent identical to those of our parents and other ancestors. Instead, regardless of the genetic hand we're dealt, our selves are also shaped by powerful outside forces of gender, family, and culture.

Gender and Self

Arguably the most profound outside force shaping our sense of self is our **gender**—the composite of social, psychological, and cultural attributes that characterize us as male or female (Canary, Emmers-Sommer, & Faulkner, 1997). It may strike you as strange to see gender described as an "outside force." Gender is innate, something you're born with, right? Actually, scholars distinguish gender, which is largely learned, from biological sex, which we're born with. Each of us is born with biological sex organs that distinguish us anatomically as male or female. However, our gender is shaped over time through our interactions with others.

Immediately after birth, we begin a lifelong process of gender socialization, learning from others what it means personally, interpersonally, and culturally to be "male" or "female." Girls are taught feminine behaviors and discover that the most important aspects of the feminine self are sensitivity to one's own and others' emotions, nurturance, and compassion (Lippa, 2002).

"Immediately after birth, we begin a lifelong process of gender socialization."

Dilbert: © Scott Adams/Dist. by United Feature Syndicate, Inc.

SELF-REFLECTION

What lessons about gender did you learn from your family when you were growing up? From your friends? Based on these lessons, what aspects of your self did you bolster—and bury—given what others deemed appropriate for your gender? How did learning about gender affect your interpersonal communication? Your relationships?

Boys are taught masculine behaviors and learn that the most important aspects of the masculine self are assertiveness, competitiveness, and independence from others. As a result of gender socialization, men and women end up forming very different self-concepts (Cross & Madson, 1997). Men are more likely than women to think of themselves as a composite of their individual achievements, abilities, and beliefs—viewing themselves as separate from other people. Women are more likely than men to perceive themselves as connected to others and to assess themselves based on the quality of these interpersonal connections.

Family and Self

When we're born, we have no self-awareness, self-concept, or self-esteem. As we mature, we slowly become aware of ourselves as unique and separate from our environments and begin developing self-concepts. Our caregivers play a crucial role in this process, providing us with ready-made sets of beliefs, attitudes, and values on which we construct our fledgling selves. We also forge emotional bonds with our caregivers, attachments that form the foundation for all our future interpersonal connections (Ainsworth, Blehar, Waters, & Wall, 1978; Bowlby, 1969). Our communication and interactions with caregivers powerfully shape our beliefs regarding the functions, rewards, and dependability of interpersonal relationships (Sarason, Pierce, & Sarason, 1990). These relationship beliefs, as a whole, lead us to adopt one of three attachment styles.

A **secure attachment style** develops when a caregiver is highly affectionate and responsive during a person's infancy and early childhood, providing the child with a sense of security and dependability. The two develop a strong emotional bond. Over time, the child develops the perception that love is dependable, desirable, and predictable.

Others receive only limited attention from their caregivers. At times the caregiver may be responsive, but at other times he or she may be highly unresponsive and perhaps even abusive. These children grow up with an **anxious attachment style,** simultaneously a desire to be loved and an inability to trust love. As a result, they display an intense dependency on others and a desire for commitment from others (Feeney & Noller, 1990).

Finally, some children grow up receiving little care or attention from any caregiver. They develop an **avoidant attachment style,** viewing love as something that only causes pain and unhappiness (Hendrick & Hendrick, 1992). During their adult lives, they avoid intimacy at all costs.

Research suggests that about 60 percent of people are secure, 25 percent avoidant, and 10 percent anxious (Mickelson, Kessler, & Shaver, 1997). And not surprisingly, attachment styles influence our self-concept, self-esteem, and interpersonal relationships. Secure people are more trusting and higher in self-esteem than either anxious or avoidant people (Hazan & Shaver, 1987). They report warmer relationships with their parents and between their parents than do people with the other two styles. Secure people also are more trusting, committed, and satisfied in their romantic involvements (Hendrick & Hendrick, 1992). When faced with relationship crises, they turn to others for comfort and support, whereas avoidant people withdraw from their partners and become hostile, and anxious people grow excessively upset and worried (Simpson, Rholes, & Nelligan, 1992).

Culture and Self

At the 1968 Summer Olympics, U.S. sprinter Tommie Smith won the men's 200-meter gold medal, and teammate John Carlos won the bronze. During the medal ceremony, as the American flag was raised and "The Star-Spangled Banner" played, both runners closed their eyes, lowered their heads, and raised black-gloved fists. Smith's right fist represented black

● Cultural identity is part of a sophisticated definition of self, as Alfred Guillaume, Jr., passionately describes, "I am a 50-year-old American. I am black, Roman Catholic, and Creole.... The segregated South wanted me to believe that I was inferior. The Catholic Church taught me that all of God's people were equal. My French Creole heritage gave me a special bond to Native Americans, to Europeans, and to Africans. This is the composite portrait of who I am. I like who I am and can imagine being no other."

"Culture means different things to different people."

power, and Carlos's left fist represented black unity (Gettings, 2005). The two fists, raised next to each other, created an arch of black unity and power. Smith wore a black scarf around his neck for black pride, and both men wore black socks with no shoes, representing African American poverty. These symbols and gestures, taken together, clearly spoke of the runners' allegiance to black culture and their protest of the poor treatment of African Americans in the United States.

Many Euro-Americans viewed Smith's and Carlos's behavior at the ceremony as a betrayal of "American" culture. Both men were suspended from the U.S. team and thrown out of the Olympic Village, the athletes' home during the games. They and their families began receiving death threats. Over time, however, people of all American ethnicities began to sympathize with their protest. Thirty years later, in 1998, Smith and Carlos were commemorated in an anniversary celebration of their protest.

In addition to gender and family, our culture is a powerful source of self. But what exactly is "culture"? Although we've all heard and used the word before, culture means different things to different people (Martin & Nakayama, 1997). Given the variation in views, we define culture broadly and inclusively. **Culture** is an established, coherent set of beliefs, attitudes, values, and practices shared by a large group of people (Keesing, 1974). If this strikes you as similar to our definition of self-concept, you're right; culture is like a collective sense of self shared by a large group of people.

Thinking of culture in this way has three important implications. First, culture includes many different types of large-group influences. Culture may include your nationality as well as your ethnicity, religion, gender, sexual orientation, and even age. We learn our cultural beliefs, attitudes, and values from parents, teachers, religious leaders, peers, and the mass media (Gudykunst & Kim, 2003). Second, most of us belong to more than one culture simultaneously—possessing the beliefs, attitudes, and values of each. Third, the various cultures to which we belong sometimes clash. When they do, we—like Smith and Carlos on the Olympic podium—often have to choose the culture to which we pledge our primary allegiance.

Numerous distinctions exist between cultures that shape differences in our selves, our communication, and our relationships. As we explore in Chapter 7 on verbal communication, certain cultures stress clarity and direct expression in their verbal messages, whereas others value ambiguity and indirection. Or as we will see in Chapter 9 on conflict and power, some cultures consider it desirable for people to be widely separated in terms of power and social status while others stress equality among all people. A cultural difference that especially shapes our view of self is whether our culture of origin is individualistic or collectivistic. If you were raised in an **individualistic culture,** you likely were taught that individual goals are more important than group or societal goals. People in individualistic cultures are encouraged to focus on themselves and their immediate family (Hofstede, 1998), and individual achievement is praised as the highest good (Waterman, 1984). If you were raised in a **collectivistic culture,** you likely were taught the importance of belonging to groups or "collectives" that look after you in exchange for your loyalty (Hofstede, 2001). In collectivistic

TABLE 2.1

Most Individualistic and Collectivistic Countries (Ranked in Order)

Individualistic Countries	Collectivistic Countries
1. United States	1. Guatemala
2. Australia	2. Ecuador
3. Great Britain	3. Panama
4. Canada	4. Venezuela
5. Netherlands	5. Colombia
6. New Zealand	6. Indonesia
7. Italy	7. Pakistan
8. Belgium	8. Costa Rica
9. Denmark	9. Peru
10. Sweden	10. Taiwan

Note: Information in this table is derived from Hofstede (2001).

cultures, the goals, needs, and views of groups are emphasized over those of individuals, and the highest good is cooperation with others rather than individual achievement.

Presenting Your Self

For more than twenty years, Rob Halford served as the lead singer for heavy metal band Judas Priest. Halford played the role of the "metal god" to the max—riding a Harley-Davidson motorcycle onstage and cladding himself head to toe in black leather. But his public image masked a private secret. During a late '90s interview with MTV, the truth slipped out when Halford prefaced a comment with, "Speaking as a gay man." The disclosure made Halford the first metal singer to come out of the closet. It also ended more than two decades of tension between his public and private selves. Halford now suffers more subtle clashes. When he's not riding his Harley or performing with Judas Priest, he likes to "kick back with a cup of tea, and watch TV, maybe watch *Survivor;* not exactly the rock n' roll stereotype" (Parry, 2002).

Our discussion thus far has focused on our private selves, the self that exists inside each of us and consists of our self-awareness, self-concept, and self-esteem. But in addition to our private selves, each of us also has a public self—the self we present to others, the person we want others to see (Fenigstein, Scheier, & Buss, 1975). We actively create our public selves through our interpersonal communication and behavior.

In many encounters, our private and public selves mirror one another. At other times, they seem disconnected. But regardless of the nature of your private self, it is your public self that your friends, family members, and romantic partners hold dear. Most (if not all) of others' impressions of you are based on their appraisals of your public self. Simply put, people know and judge the "you" who communicates with them—not the "you" you keep inside. Thus, managing your public self is a crucial part of effective interpersonal communication.

Maintaining Your Public Self

Arguably the best-known analysis of public self is the work of sociologist Erving Goffman. Goffman noted that whenever you communicate with others, you present a public self—your **face**—that you want others to see and know (Goffman, 1955). Face doesn't just happen; you actively create and present it through your communication. Your face can be anything you want it to be—"perky and upbeat," "cool and level-headed," or "tough as nails." We create different faces for different moments and relationships in our lives, such as our face as a parent, college student, café regular, or homeless-shelter volunteer.

Sometimes your face is a **mask,** a public self designed to strategically veil your private self (Goffman, 1959). Masks can be dramatic, such as the provocative poses Rob Halford struck with female models in Judas Priest videos, designed to make fans think he's heterosexual. Masks can be subtle—for example, the parent who acts calm in front of an injured child so the youngster doesn't become frightened by the injury. Some masks are designed to inflate one's estimation in the eyes of others. For example, one study found that 90 percent of college students surveyed admitted telling at least one lie in order to impress a person they were romantically interested in (Rowatt, Cunningham, & Druen, 1998). Other masks are crafted to create the opposite impression—one of underestimating us and our abilities (Gibson & Sachau, 2000). For instance, you might act sad and lethargic around a future opponent during a racquetball tournament, letting it slip "how bad" you've been playing all day (even though you've actually won all your games), so your opponent won't adequately prepare, thereby gaining yourself a competitive advantage.

Regardless of the form our face takes—a genuine representation of our private self, or a mask designed to hide this self from others—Goffman argued that we often form a strong emotional attachment to our face because it represents the person we most want others to see when they communicate with and relate to us.

Sometimes after we've created a certain face, information is revealed that contradicts it, causing us to lose face (Goffman, 1955). Losing face provokes feelings of shame, humiliation, and sadness—in a word, **embarrassment.** For example, in October 2004, teen singer Ashlee Simpson performed live on NBC's *Saturday Night Live*. Or did she? Simpson and her band performed her first song, "Pieces of Me," without a hitch. Later, when they began playing their second song, the music for "Pieces of Me" began playing over the loudspeakers, complete with Simpson's vocal track. The faux pas revealed to viewers that Simpson and her band had lip-synched their first song. Embarrassed, Simpson ran off the stage. At the end of the show, she came back onstage with host Jude Law and tried to alleviate her embarrassment by blaming her band for the gaffe, telling audience members, "My band started playing the wrong song, and I didn't know what to do."

As the Ashlee Simpson example illustrates, losing face can cause intense embarrassment, but this is not the only cost. When others see us lose face, they may begin to question whether the public self with which they're familiar is a genuine reflection of our private self. For example, suppose your workplace face is "dedicated, hardworking employee." Everything you say and do at the office bolsters this image. You ask your boss if there's extra work to be done, help fellow coworkers, show up early, stay late, and so forth. But if you tell your manager that you need your afternoon schedule cleared to work on an urgent report and then she sees you playing the video game *World of Warcraft,* she'll undoubtedly view your actions as inconsistent with your communication. Your face as the "hardworking employee" will be called into question, as will your credibility.

Because losing face can damage others' impressions of you, maintaining face during interpersonal interactions is extremely important. How can you effectively maintain face?[2] Use words and actions consistent with the face you're trying to craft. From one moment to the next and from one behavior to the next, your interpersonal communication and behaviors must complement your face, rather than clash with it as in the example above. Also, make sure your communication and behaviors mesh with the knowledge that others already have about you. If you say or do things that contradict what others know is true about you, they'll see your face as false. For example, if your neighbor knows you don't like him because a friend of yours told him so, he's likely to be skeptical the next time you adopt the face of "friendly, caring neighbor" by warmly greeting him and telling him how glad you are to see him.

Finally, for your face to be maintained, your communication and behavior must be reinforced by objects and events in the surrounding environment—things over which you have only limited control. You can communicate in a consistent fashion and have everyone believe you, but if a contradictory event occurs, you will lose face. For example, imagine that your romantic partner is overseas for the summer, and you agree you'll "talk" by exchanging messages in an Internet chatroom. Your first scheduled chat is this Friday at 5 p.m. But when 5 p.m. Friday rolls around, your server is down, preventing you from Internet access. By the time the server is finally up again, your partner has already signed off, leaving perplexed e-mails regarding your "neglect."

Of course, all of us fall from grace on occasion, whether it's getting caught computer-gaming when we should be working, failing to be available when we've promised, or lip-synching when we should be singing. But remember, most people want you to be able to maintain face, because your face is the positive, public "you" with whom they're most familiar. So when something happens that causes you to lose face, promptly acknowledge

---

[2]All of the information that follows regarding how to successfully maintain face is adapted from Goffman (1955).

that the event happened, admit responsibility for any of your actions that contributed to the event, apologize for your actions and for disappointing others, and move to maintain your face again. Apologies are fairly successful at reducing people's negative impressions and the anger that may have been triggered—especially when such apologies avoid excuses that contradict what people know really happened (Cody & McLaughlin, 1990; Ohbuchi & Sato, 1994). People who consistently deny their inconsistencies or who blame others for their lapses (like Ashlee Simpson) are judged much more harshly.

Presenting Your Self Online

Every evening, rain or shine, school night or weekend, the same query resounds in my household: "Dad, can I go online?" My preteen son and his male and female friends regularly congregate online at 8 p.m. to exchange instant messages, meet in chatrooms, and explore new Web sites and games. When I asked him why they didn't just call each other, he said, "Because it's easier to talk and tell people stuff online." And when I asked why they instant message, chat, e-mail, and text all at the same time, he said, "Because it's fun!"

My son's nightly gatherings with his friends illustrate how for many people, online communication has become simply another way to interpersonally interact—one that in some instances is more convenient and interactive than interacting face-to-face or on the telephone. Whereas the online world was initially considered "virtual" and separate from the "real world," this distinction no longer has much relevance to those who have access to and a degree of comfort with online forms of communication. Instead, we shift easily between different media, often in the same time frame, choosing whichever medium strikes us as convenient or best suited to the communication task at hand.

For all of this, online communication provides us with unique benefits and challenges for self-presentation. When you talk with others face-to-face, people judge your public self not just on the content of your communication but also on your visual appearance—age, gender, clothing, and so forth. Each of these cues provides others with information about who you are, independent from anything you might say. Similarly, when you're conversing on the phone, you and the other person listen for vocal cues—tone, pitch, volume—to judge one another. But when people communicate online, they have no such clues to public self, unless they choose to provide them by posting photos, audio files, or video streams. This can be liberating, especially for those with physical disabilities that in face-to-face contacts lead others to judge them negatively (Fox, 2000).

With the freedom that online communication affords us in how we craft our selves comes an associated cost. Unless you have met someone in person, you will have great difficulty determining whether an online mask is authentic. Through misleading screen names, false profiles, or dishonest verbal communication, people communicating online can assume identities that would be impossible to maintain in offline encounters (Rintel & Pittam, 1997). Without some prior knowledge of them, you can't verify or invalidate their online selves; you can only take their selves at face value, presuming that they really are who they say they are.

SKILLS PRACTICE

This exercise helps you restore your face online after losing it.

1 Choose an online relationship you value.

2 List the characteristics comprising your face in this relationship.

3 Monitor your online communication. How well do your messages match the face you've described?

4 When something happens that causes you to lose face, immediately send an online message to acknowledge what happened; if necessary, admit responsibility for what happened and apologize.

5 Analyze the outcomes; did your message help restore your face?

For example, many people "gender-swap" online, portraying themselves as female when they're male, or vice versa. Photographs do little to validate gender; gender-swappers frequently bolster their online masks with fake photos (Turkle, 1995). For this reason, online communication scholars suggest that you should never presume the gender of someone you interact with online if you haven't met the person face-to-face, even if you're offered photos (Savicki, Kelley, & Oesterreich, 1999). Another type of mask commonly adopted online is that of the "expert." In Internet chatrooms, men are somewhat more likely than women to represent themselves as having expertise in particular topics, and they are more eager to answer questions and supply information, regardless of their actual knowledge level (Soukup, 1999). In contrast, women are more likely to produce supportive messages, express appreciation and gratitude, and make others feel welcome to a group.

How do we present our selves online? Through nearly every formatting choice we make—from the font we choose and the e-mail signatures we create, to the wallpapers and photos that adorn our home pages. For example, an artist friend of mine uses a cursive-style font for all of her e-mails *("Just checking in to see how you're doing")*. This simple shift in visual style creates an immediate impression of "artistry" to all who receive her messages, an impression that she feels accurately presents her self. Not surprisingly, given the potency of visual information in shaping our impressions (something we talk more about in Chapter 3 on perception), photos play a critical role in presenting our online selves. For example, many professional women recognize that they are more likely than their male peers to be judged on appearance, and as a result, they post more "serious" photos of themselves, avoiding ones that are silly or humorous (Miller & Arnold, 2001).

One of the most important means through which we create our selves online is also one of the simplest: our choice of a screen name (Barnes, 2001). Online communicators often use screen names to form first impressions of one another. For example, if you're in a chatroom and you meet "Skatepunk," you'll likely have a vastly different impression of him or her than you will upon meeting "Treehugger" or "Holyman." A screen name's power to create first impressions suggests the importance of choosing an appropriate screen name rather than one that strikes your whimsy at that particular moment. When choosing a screen name, select one that you feel best represents the online self you wish to display—the positive "you" you want others to see in all your online interactions.

The Relational Self

One of the reasons we carefully craft the presentation of our selves is to create interpersonal relationships. We present our selves to acquaintances, coworkers, friends, family members, and romantic partners, and through our interpersonal communication, relationships are fostered, maintained, and sometimes ended. Within each of these relationships, the intimacy we experience is defined largely by how much of our selves we and our partners reveal to each other.

Managing the self in interpersonal relationships isn't easy. Exposing our selves to others can make us feel vulnerable, provoking tension between how much to reveal versus how much to veil. And in even the closest of relationships certain aspects of self remain hidden, from our partners as well as ourselves.

Opening Your Self to Others

In the 2001 movie *Shrek*, the ogre Shrek forges a friendship with a likable but occasionally irksome donkey (Adamson & Jenson, 2001). As their acquaintanceship deepens to friendship, Shrek tries to explain the nature of his inner self to his companion:

SHREK: For your information, there's a lot more to ogres than people think!
DONKEY: Example … ?
SHREK: Example … Ok … Um … Ogres … are like onions.
DONKEY: They stink?
SHREK: Yes … NO!
DONKEY: Or they make you cry?
SHREK: No!
DONKEY: Oh … You leave 'em out in the sun and they get all brown and start sprouting little white hairs!
SHREK: No! Layers! Onions have layers—OGRES have layers! Onions have layers! You get it!? We both have layers!
DONKEY: Ooohhhh … you both have layers … oh. You know, not everybody likes onions…CAKE! Everybody loves cakes! Cakes have layers!

FIGURE 2.2

The Layers of Self

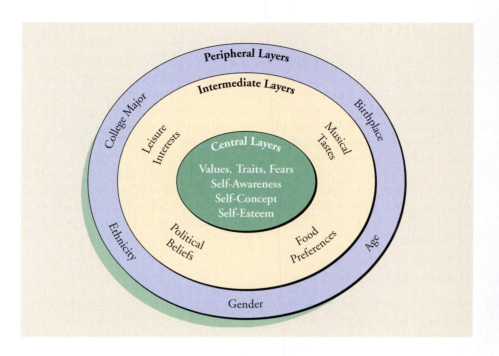

Shrek was not the first to use the onion as a metaphor for self. In fact, the idea that revealing the self to others involves peeling back or penetrating layers was first suggested by psychologists Irwin Altman and Dalmas Taylor in their **social penetration theory** (Altman & Taylor, 1973). Like Shrek, Altman and Taylor envisioned the self as an "onion-skin structure," consisting of sets of layers.[3]

At the outermost, peripheral layers of your self are demographic characteristics such as birthplace, age, gender, and ethnicity (see Figure 2.2). Discussion of these characteristics dominates first conversations with new acquaintances: What's your name? What's your major? Where are you from? In the intermediate layers reside your attitudes and opinions about music, politics, food, entertainment, and other such matters. Deep within the "onion" are the central layers of your self—core characteristics such as self-awareness, self-concept, self-esteem, personal values, fears, and distinctive personality traits. We'll discuss these in more detail in Chapter 3.

The notion of layers of self helps explain the development of interpersonal relationships, as well as the ways in which we distinguish between casual and close involvements. As relationships progress from casual to intimate, partners communicate increasingly personal information to each other. This allows them to mutually penetrate one another's peripheral, then intermediate, and finally central selves. Relationship development, therefore, is like the hypothetical movement of a pin into an onion: it proceeds layer by layer, without skipping layers.

---

[3]Although Altman and Taylor use *personality* to describe the self, they define personality in terms of self-concept and self-esteem, and use the terms *personality* and *self* interchangeably throughout their text (for example, see 1973, pp. 17–19).

The penetration into selves that occurs during relationship development involves both breadth and depth. Breadth is the number of different aspects of self each partner reveals at each layer—the insertion of more and more pins into the onion, so to speak. Depth involves how deeply into one another's self the partners have penetrated: have you revealed only your peripheral self, or have you given the other person access into your intermediate or central selves as well?

Although social penetration occurs in all relationships, the rate at which it occurs is not consistent. For example, some people let others in quickly, or they never grant them access to certain elements of themselves no matter how long they know a person. The speed with which people grant one another access to the broader and deeper aspects of their selves depends on a variety of factors. But in all relationships, intimacy and access to previously hidden areas of the self are fundamentally intertwined: the deeper and broader we penetrate into each other's selves, the more intimate we feel; the more intimate we feel, the more we allow each other access to broad and deep aspects of our selves.

Your Hidden and Revealed Self

The image of self and relationship development offered by social penetration theory suggests a relatively straightforward evolution of intimacy, with partners gradually penetrating broadly and deeply into each other's selves over time. But in thinking about our selves and our relationships with others, two important questions arise. First, are we really aware of all aspects of ourselves? Second, are we willing to grant others access to all aspects of ourselves?

We can explore possible answers to these questions by looking at the model of the relational self called the Johari Window, named after the psychologists who developed it, Joe Luft and Harry Ingham (Luft, 1970). The

● The ability to share ourselves with someone else feels like a rare experience, but when the opportunity arises, information flows more freely and greater relational intimacy develops.

FIGURE 2.3

The Johari Window

Quadrant I	Quadrant II
Public Area	*Blind Area*
Aspects of your self that you and others are aware of. Includes everything you openly disclose—from music and food preferences to religious beliefs and moral values.	Facets of your self that are readily apparent to others through your interpersonal communication but that you're not aware of. Includes strengths that you may not see in yourself or character flaws that don't mesh with your self-concept.
Quadrant III	**Quadrant IV**
Hidden Area	*Unknown Area*
Parts of your self that you're aware of but that you hide from most others. These include destructive thoughts, impulses, and fantasies, and disturbing life experiences that don't fit comfortably with your public self or your own self-concept.	Aspects of your self that you and others aren't aware of, such as unconscious motives and impulses that strongly influence your interpersonal communication and relationships. While you can't gain access to your unknown area through critical self-reflection, you can indirectly infer aspects of your unknown area by observing consistent patterns in your own behavior.

Johari Window (see Figure 2.3) suggests that some "quadrants" of our selves are open to self-reflection and sharing with other people, while others remain hidden—to both ourselves and others.

During the early stages of an interpersonal relationship and especially during first encounters, our public area of self is much smaller than our hidden area. As relationships progress, partners gain access to broader and deeper information about their selves; consequently, the public area expands and the hidden area diminishes. The Johari Window thus provides us with a useful alternative metaphor to social penetration. As relationships develop, we don't just let people "penetrate inward" to our central selves; we let them "peer into" more parts of our selves by revealing information that we previously hid from them.

Importantly, as our interpersonal relationships develop and we increasingly share previously hidden information with our partners, our unknown and blind quadrants remain fairly stable. By their very nature, our unknown areas remain unknown throughout much of our lives. And for most of us, the blind area remains imperceptible. That's because our blind area is defined by our deepest-rooted beliefs about ourselves—those beliefs that make up our self-concept. Consequently, when others challenge us to open our eyes to our blind areas, we resist.

To improve our interpersonal communication, we must be able to see into our blind area and then change the aspects within it that lead to ineffective communication and relationship challenges. But this isn't easy. After all, how can you correct misperceptions about yourself that you don't even know exist or flaws that you consider your greatest strengths? Delving into your blind area means challenging fundamental beliefs about yourself—subjecting your self-concept to hard scrutiny. Your goal is to overturn your most treasured personal misconceptions. Most people accomplish this only over a long period of time and with the assistance of trustworthy and willing relationship partners.

Relational Tensions

You're out to dinner with your romantic partner when he or she asks you, "How are you feeling about our relationship?" After thinking about it, you realize you're not sure. On the one hand, you haven't felt attracted to your partner for some time. But you also know that external stresses—your job, your classes, financial pressures—have been distracting you. You're uncertain whether your lukewarm feelings are stemming from stress or indicate that you're falling out of love. Do you share this information openly, copping to your uncertainty about your feelings ("I really have no idea about how I'm feeling toward you right now")? Or do you soft-pedal your response ("I've been too tired to think about how our relationship is going")?

As scholar Leslie Baxter describes, interpersonal relationships are "a dynamic knot of contradictions, a ceaseless interplay between contrary or opposing tendencies" (Baxter & Montgomery, 1996). These tendencies manifest themselves in the form of competing impulses—tensions—between our selves and our feelings toward others known as **relational dialectics** (Baxter, 1988, 1990; Rawlins, 1992). Relational dialectics take three common forms.

Openness versus Protection.
The first relational dialectic is illustrated in the example above, openness versus protection. Think back to social penetration and the Johari Window models of relationship development. As your relationships become more intimate, you and your partners naturally penetrate from one another's peripheral to intermediate to central selves, gaining broader and deeper information about each other. Your public quadrant grows and your hidden area shrinks. Though a natural occurrence in developing relationships, this increasing openness provokes an obvious tension. While we want to be open with our partners, we also want to keep certain aspects of our selves—such as our most private thoughts and feelings—protected.

This struggle between openness and protecting our privacy influences our decisions about how honest to be in our interpersonal communication. **Honesty** is defined as the revealing of all information that is relevant to share in a situation (McCornack, 1997). In many encounters, we have information that's relevant and important to share, but we know that revealing that information could damage our face, our partner's face, and our relationship. In such situations, most of us resolve this dialectic by responding in a way that protects the relationship. For example, in one study, participants recorded an important conversation with a relational partner and then evaluated the honesty of their own statements. The researchers found that only 38.5 percent of statements people presented to their partners were completely honest (Turner, Edgley, & Olmstead, 1975). The remaining 61.5 percent of statements "spun" the information in some way—concealing problems, exaggerating feelings, conveying false information, and so forth. When asked why they chose to sacrifice openness for protection, participants argued that openness in close relationships doesn't mean unbridled honesty. Rather, it means "fidelity to the maintenance of our relationship"—that is, disclosing to your partner only information that maintains relational happiness.

The decision to reconcile the openness-versus-protection dialectic by "saying what's good for the relationship" needn't be a choice you make on your own. Instead, as researcher Sandra Petronio notes, we can define the boundaries of honesty collaboratively with our relational partners, negotiating rules for exchanging personal information (Petronio, 1991, 2000). Working with our partners to clarify what needs to be shared—and what doesn't—is the surest way to prevent conflicts regarding honesty while still preserving the sense of privacy that we all value and to which we're all entitled. For example, during our engagement, my wife Kelly and I lived long-distance. When Kelly would go out with her friends, they inevitably would meet and hang out with a group of attractive men. Afterward, her natural instinct was to be completely honest and regale me with the details of how much fun they had and how impressive or attractive the men happened to be. But such revelations made me jealous and provoked repeated fights. So we negotiated an honesty rule: whenever she went out with her friends, she would tell me that she went out and whether she had a good time. But no details! I trusted her completely but had learned that if I heard the specifics, I would get jealous. Negotiating this rule prevented many long-distance conflicts from erupting.

Autonomy versus Connection.   The second dialectic common to relationships is autonomy versus connection. We're driven to communicate with others and forge relationships out of a desire for connectedness, and the central element of our bonds with friends, family, and romantic partners is our sense of emotional attachment (Bowlby, 1969). At the same time, when we feel too connected to others—when they've penetrated so deeply into our selves that we begin to lose our sense of individual identity—we crave autonomy.

Novelty versus Predictability.   The final dialectic is the clash between our need for stability and our need for excitement and change—known as novelty versus predictability. We all like the security that comes with knowing how our partners will behave, how we'll behave, and how our relationships will unfold. The more we know about our partners' central selves, the more predictable and explainable their behavior becomes to us and the more we trust them to behave in the ways we expect (Berger & Bradac, 1982). However, predictability often spawns boredom. As we get to know our partners, the novelty and excitement of the relationship wears off, and things seem increasingly monotonous. Reconciling the desire for predictability with the need for novelty is one of the most profound emotional challenges facing relational partners, particularly those in romantic relationships.

Disclosing Your Self to Others

Early in his 1976 campaign for the U.S. presidency, Jimmy Carter granted an interview with *Playboy* magazine. At the time, Carter was enjoying a 30-point lead in national polls over rival Gerald Ford. During Carter's interview, the reporter asked what his opinion on adultery was and whether he had ever committed it. Carter responded (Jimmy Carter The *Playboy* Interview, 1976):

> I'm just human and I'm tempted. Christ said anyone who looks on a woman with lust has in his heart already committed adultery. I've looked on a lot of women with lust. I've committed adultery in my heart many times. This is something that God recognizes, and God forgives me for it.

Following this disclosure, Carter's lead in the polls evaporated. People disapproved of his granting an interview to *Playboy* in the first place, but his plummeting poll numbers stemmed mainly from his adultery disclosure. People perceived Carter's comments as too personal and too revealing. As Altman and Taylor might suggest, Carter had allowed people to penetrate his central self. And people were uncomfortable with what they saw. By the eve of the election, Carter and Ford were locked in a virtual dead heat, with Carter eventually winning only by a slim margin. To this day, political scientists consider Carter's candor one of the greatest gaffes in presidential campaign history, and contemporary candidates are counseled to steadfastly avoid such disclosures.

We all can think of situations where we've revealed personal information to others and instances in which the information we revealed wasn't well received. Revealing private information about your self to others is known as **self-disclosure** (Wheeless, 1978). Self-disclosure plays a critical role in interpersonal communication and relationship development. You can't boost intimacy in relationships without openly sharing your private thoughts, feelings, and beliefs. At the same time, as the Carter example illustrates, disclosing information that's perceived as *too* personal can create strongly negative impressions. Research suggests that one of the most damaging events that can happen in interpersonal relationships is a partner's sharing information that the other person finds inappropriate and perplexing (Planalp & Honeycutt, 1985).

Differences in Disclosure. Researchers have conducted literally thousands of self-disclosure studies over the last forty years (Tardy & Dindia, 1997). These studies suggest five important facts regarding how people self-disclose. By honing your awareness of these facts, you can improve your self-disclosure skills with an eye toward strengthening your relationships.

First, in any culture, people vary widely in the degree to which they self-disclose. Some people are naturally transparent; others are more opaque

"ALWAYS WITH THE 'V'... WOULD IT KILL US TO TRY A 'W'? EVEN AN 'I' WOULD BE COOL."

BREVITY: © Guy & Rodd/Dist. by United Feature Syndicate, Inc.

SELF-REFLECTION

Consider Carter's response to *Playboy*'s question. Was it inappropriately revealing? If you were in Carter's shoes, how would you have responded? What aspects of self are appropriate to share publicly? If a close friend had asked you the same questions, would you have answered differently?

● Willingness to disclose information about ourselves varies as we go through life. For example, disclosure rates tend to be extremely low during adolescence, when self-concepts and self-image are taking shape. While teens' caregivers should be open to discussing adolescent concerns, forcing teens to reveal their central selves during this time can foster resentment and anger.

(Jourard, 1964). Trying to force someone who has a different idea of self-disclosure than yours to open up or be more discreet not only is presumptuous but can damage the relationship (Luft, 1970).

Second, people across cultures differ in their self-disclosure. For instance, people of Asian descent tend to disclose less than do people of European ancestry. Japanese disclose substantially less than Americans in both friendships and romantic relationships, and they view self-disclosure as a less important aspect of intimacy development than do Americans

(Barnlund, 1975). Researchers found similar tendencies among people of Chinese heritage. In general, Euro-Americans tend to disclose more frequently than just about any other cultural group, including Asians, Hispanics, and African Americans (Klopf, 2001).

Third, people disclose more quickly, broadly, and deeply when interacting online than face-to-face. One reason for this is that during online encounters, people are more aware of themselves and less aware of the people to whom they are talking, so the consequences of such disclosure seem less salient (Joinson, 2001). Of course, the ease of online divulgence sometimes results in "post-cyber-disclosure panic"—that awful moment at which you wonder who else might be reading the innermost thoughts and secrets you just unveiled in an e-mail message to a friend (Barnes, 2001).

Fourth, self-disclosure appears to promote mental health and relieve stress (Tardy, 2000). Especially when the information is troubling, keeping it inside can escalate your stress levels substantially, resulting in immune system breakdown, ulcers, and high blood pressure (Pennebaker, 1997). Keeping troubling information trapped inside can also lead it to dominate your thoughts because you must constantly monitor what you say to avoid disclosing the secret (Kelly & McKillop, 1996). Of course, the flip side of disclosing troubling secrets to others is that people might react negatively and you might be more vulnerable.

Finally, women disclose more than do men, and both genders are more willing to disclose to female than to male recipients (Dindia & Allen, 1992). Teenage boys *and* girls are more likely to disclose to mothers and best female friends than to fathers and best male friends—suggesting that

POP QUIZ

Test Your Self-Disclosure

Think about the person you currently consider closest to you, such as your best friend, a close family member, or your romantic partner. For each phrase below, rate your self-disclosure between 0 and 4, 0 indicating no self-disclosure to your partner and 4 denoting full self-disclosure. Add your ratings to arrive at your total score.

1. My personal habits
2. Things I've done that I feel guilty about
3. Things I wouldn't do in public
4. My deepest feelings
5. What I like and dislike about myself

6. What is important to me in life
7. What makes me the person I am
8. My worst fear
9. Things I've done that I'm proud of
10. My close relationships with other people

Scoring:

0–15 = low disclosure; 16–25 = moderate disclosure; 26–40 = high disclosure.
Repeat this exercise for other people in your life, such as same-sex friends, coworkers, and casual acquaintances. Examine your pattern of scores. Do you tend to be high, moderate, or low in disclosure? Does your willingness to disclose depend on the relationship? What do your scores generally tell you about how you self-disclose?

Note: The material provided in this *Pop Quiz* is adapted from Miller, Berg, and Archer (1983, p. 1236).

Ethics and Self-Disclosure

1

BACKGROUND

Self-disclosure is the primary vehicle people use to communicate their private selves to others in interpersonal relationships. Yet choosing when and how to self-disclose or ask for self-disclosure can be tricky, particularly when ethical considerations are involved. Read the following case study, and work through the five steps that follow to learn how you can ethically self-disclose.

2

CASE STUDY

You've worked for Acme Industries for more than a year, and it's the best job you've ever had. You make good money, have excellent benefits, and share great relationships with your supervisor and coworkers, to whom you feel very loyal.

A few months ago, a friend of yours, Jonathan, joined Acme. You've known Jonathan since grade school, and his parents and yours are good friends. Jonathan's public self is impressive; he's funny, charming, and intelligent. He always manages to cheer you up no matter what's happening in your life. But you've always wondered whether his public self is really just a mask. Jonathan doesn't let people in to his central self; he keeps everyone, including you, at a distance. Whenever conversations get too personal, he cracks a joke. And over the past many years, no matter what the situation—a group project, dinner out with colleagues, or weekend trips with friends—things always seem to miraculously work out so that Jonathan contributes the least effort and benefits the most. You can't help but wonder whether he's a nice guy with incredible luck or someone who constantly manipulates situations to his advantage.

As part of its scholarship program, Acme offers to cover the costs of Jonathan's earning his BA at a local college, in exchange for his agreeing to work for the organization for three years after completing his degree. Jonathan enthusiastically accepts. That night, the two of you celebrate. When you tell him how excited you are that you'll be working together for years into the future, Jonathan laughs. "We'll see," he says. You suddenly have the uncomfortable feeling that he's planning to renege on his end of the deal once he gets his degree. You decide to press him: "You're not planning on bailing on the company after they've paid for your college, are you?" Jonathan hesitates for a moment, then suddenly smiles and shifts into joke mode, "Do you have a *wiretap* on you or something? Are you a *company spy?*"

You realize you can't press Jonathan further without disclosing your long-term suspicions about his hidden self or forcing him to disclose something he obviously doesn't want to discuss. At the same time, your loyalty to Acme compels you to discover the truth about his motives.

YOUR TURN

Think about the interpersonal communication skills and insights you gained while reading this chapter. Work through the following five steps, which will give you practice making thoughtful interpersonal communication choices in your relationships. Remember, there is no one right answer, so think hard about what choice you will make!

● **Step 1: Reflect on yourself.** What are your thoughts and feelings about Jonathan? Is your impression of him and his motives accurate, or could you be mistaken? Do you feel more loyal to Jonathan or to Acme? What role should loyalty play in shaping your relationship choice?

● **Step 2: Reflect on your partner.** Put yourself in Jonathan's shoes. What is he is thinking and feeling about you? What is his perspective on Acme's tuition offer? Is his viewpoint legitimate?

● **Step 3: Identify the optimal outcome.** What's the most constructive relationship outcome for you and Jonathan? Can you maintain your relationship with Jonathan and your loyalty to Acme? Consider what's best not only for you but for all those involved as well.

● **Step 4: Locate the roadblocks.** Taking into consideration your own thoughts and feelings, those of Jonathan, and all that has happened in this situation, what is keeping you from achieving the optimal outcome you defined in step 3?

● **Step 5: Chart your course.** What might you say to Jonathan to overcome the roadblocks and achieve your optimal relationship outcome?

HELPFUL CONCEPTS

Face and masks, *59*

Maintaining face, *60*

Openness, protection, and honesty, *67–68*

Recommendations for effective self-disclosure, *74*

adolescents may perceive females as more empathic and understanding than males (Garcia & Geisler, 1988).

Effectively Disclosing Your Self. Based on all we know about self-disclosure, how can you improve your self-disclosure skills? Consider these recommendations:

- **Follow the advice of Apollo: know your self.** Before disclosing, make sure that the aspects of your self you reveal to others are aspects that you want to reveal and that you feel certain about. This is particularly important when disclosing intimate feelings, such as romantic interest. When you disclose feelings about others directly to them, you affect their lives and relationship decisions. Consequently, you're ethically obligated to be certain about the truth of your own feelings before sharing them with others.

- **Know your audience.** Whether it's a magazine interview or an intimate conversation with a friend, think carefully about how others will perceive your disclosure and how it will impact their thoughts and feelings about you. If you're unsure of the appropriateness of a disclosure, don't disclose. This holds equally true for online and face-to-face encounters. Instead of disclosing, talk more generally about the issue or topic first, gauging the person's level of comfort with the conversation before revealing deeper information.

- **Don't force others to self-disclose.** We often presume it's good for people to "open up" and share their secrets, particularly those that are troubling them. Although it's perfectly appropriate to let someone know you're available to listen, it's unethical and destructive to force or cajole others into sharing information against their will. People have reasons for not wanting to tell you things—just as you have reasons for protecting your own privacy.

- **Don't presume gender preferences.** Although it's true that women disclose more than men, don't fall into the trap of thinking that because someone is a woman, she will disclose freely. Conversely, don't presume because you're talking with a woman it's appropriate for you to freely disclose.

- **Be sensitive to cultural differences.** When interacting with people from different backgrounds, disclose gradually. And as with gender, don't presume disclosure patterns based on ethnicity. Just because someone is of European descent doesn't mean he or she will want to openly share intimate thoughts and feelings, and just because someone is Asian doesn't mean he or she will be comparatively reluctant to disclose.

- **Go slowly.** Share intermediate and central aspects of your self gradually and only after thorough discussion of peripheral information. Moving too quickly to discussion of your deepest fears, self-esteem concerns, and personal values not only increases your sense of vulnerability, but it may make others uncomfortable enough to avoid you.

Improving Your Self

One of the greatest gifts we possess is our capacity for self-awareness. Through self-awareness, we can ponder the kind of person we are, what we're worth, where we come from, and how we can improve. We can craft face and strive to maintain it. We can openly disclose some aspects of our selves and protect other aspects. And all the while, we can stand apart from our selves, critically reflecting on our interpersonal communication and relationship decisions: Was I right or was I wrong?

At the same time, we're often hampered by the beliefs, attitudes, and values we hold about our selves. Our self-concepts can trap us in destructive self-fulfilling prophecies. Whether imposed by gender, culture, or family, the standards we embrace suggesting who we should be are often unattainable. When we inevitably fall short of these standards, we condemn our selves, destroying our own self-esteem.

But our selves are not static. We constantly evolve, so we always have the opportunity to improve our selves and enhance our interpersonal communication and relationships. Through dedicated and focused effort, you can learn to avoid destructive self-fulfilling prophecies and resolve discrepancies between your self-concept and standards that damage your self-esteem. You can also maintain your face and disclose your self effectively to others. The starting point for improving your self is the same as it ever was: the advice mythically offered to Chilon by Apollo. Know thyself.

POSTSCRIPT

Look again at the painting *labeled.* Note that this work of art isn't simply a portrait of the pain and isolation felt by one artist suffering from dyslexia. It embraces all of us. We've all had fingers pointed and names hurled at us.

What metaphorical fingers point at you? Are some of those fingers your own? What names go with them? How do these shape the ways in which you communicate with others and make choices in your relationships?

This chapter began with a self-portrait of suffering—an artist stigmatized in youth by labels. But we can all draw inspiration from Eric Staib's story. Each of us possesses the uniquely

human capacity to turn our personal punishments into profound gifts, just as Eric did.

Chapter Review

Key Terms

Key Concepts

The Components of Self

- The root source of all interpersonal communication is the **self;** thus understanding the self and its connection to communication is critical for improving interpersonal skills. The ability to reflect on our selves distinguishes us from most other mammals, which lack **self-awareness.**

- During interpersonal encounters, we make sense of our selves and our communication in part by comparing our behaviors with those of others. **Social comparison** has a particularly pronounced impact on our sense of self when the people to whom we're comparing ourselves are those whom we admire.

- When most of us think of our selves, what comes to mind is our **self-concept.** Our self-concept is defined at least in part through our **looking-glass self.** Our self-concept can sometimes trap us in **self-fulfilling prophecies,** although we can overcome these by analyzing our underlying beliefs about self.

- It is a daunting challenge to have positive **self-esteem** while living in an appearance culture dominated by images of bodily and facial perfection. Many of us have unnatural and unrealistic appearance standards. **Self-discrepancy theory** explains the link between these standards and our feelings about ourselves, as well as ways in which we can overcome low self-esteem.

The Sources of Self

- Our self-concept and self-esteem come from many sources, one of which is **gender.** At the same time that our families teach us gender lessons, they also create emotional bonds with us that form the foundation for various attachment styles, including the **secure attachment style,** the **anxious attachment style,** and the **avoidant attachment style.** These attachment styles influence our adult interpersonal relationships.

- Many of us identify with more than one **culture.** As a consequence, we're occasionally thrust into situations in which we must choose a primary cultural allegiance. Depending on whether we're raised in a primarily **individualistic culture** or **collectivistic culture,** we learn values and beliefs about effective interpersonal communication that may put us at odds with those raised in different cultures.

Presenting Your Self

- The **face** we present to others is the self others perceive and evaluate. Sometimes our face reflects our inner selves, and sometimes we adopt **masks.** When we fall from grace into wrong face, **embarrassment** results.

The Relational Self

- According to **social penetration theory,** we develop relationships by gradually delving deeper and more broadly into different layers of self, a process complicated by **relational dialectics.** A common dilemma is balancing the need for **honesty** with the need for sensitivity toward our partners.

- Relationships can't take root without effective **self-disclosure** from both partners.

Key Skills

- Want to refine your critical self-reflection ability? Learn how by reviewing the steps of critical self-reflection on page 45 and completing the *Skills Practice* on page 46.

- Interested in overcoming self-fulfilling prophecies that plague your communication? Do the *Skills Practice* on page 47.

- Ever feel as if you're not the person you wish you could be or the person others want you to be? Find out why on pages 47–48.

- How can you improve your self-esteem and consequently your communication and relationships? Learn how by reviewing the information on pages 49–51 and taking the *Pop Quiz* on page 51.

- How can you effectively maintain face during interpersonal encounters? Follow the recommendations on pages 59–61.

- What can you do to save your face when it's been threatened? Review the skills described on page 60; then do the *Skills Practice* on page 61 to learn how to restore face in online relationships.

- Why is the choice of screen name so important? Find the answer on page 62.

- How can you improve your self-disclosure skills? Review pages 69–75 to refresh your memory, take the *Pop Quiz* on page 71, and then put your skills to the test by working through the *Making Relationship Choices* exercise on pages 72–73.

3

Perceiving Others

Marian Keech was fascinated by the occult. And like many people sharing this interest, she lived an ordinary life — that is, until one morning in 1954 when she woke with a tingling in her arm. As Keech describes in the book *When Prophecy Fails,* "Without knowing why, I picked up a pencil and began writing. I looked at the hand-writing, but it was not my own. I realized that somebody was using my hand."[1] Keech believed she was receiving messages from "Sananda," an entity communicating on behalf of aliens from the planet Clarion. Sananda began sending her daily messages, and in the weeks that followed, several commu-nity residents began consulting Keech regarding Sananda's communiqués, forming a tight-knit group of believers.

In late July, Sananda's mes-sages took a sinister turn. He warned that on December 21,

---

[1] All quotes and related information are adapted from Festinger, Riecken, and Schachter (1956).

"Earthlings shall awaken to great destruction." A tidal wave would swallow the United States, and England would sink to the bottom of the Atlantic. Most of Keech's disciples perceived this prophecy as infallible. Their perceptions led them to sever all interpersonal ties except those with other group members, quit their jobs, and sell their possessions. Sananda promised that before the wave struck, a spaceship would spirit them away to safety.

In mid-December, a man identifying himself as "Sananda in earthly guise" began calling the group. He discussed the forthcoming apocalypse and plans for escape. One evening, this man and four of his friends arrived at Marian's house. They talked for several hours with Marian and her followers, then left. Following this encounter, perceptions sharply diverged depending on the degree to which group members believed in Keech's prophetic powers. Dr. Thomas Armstrong, Marian's most devout disciple,

declared, "They were spacemen all right." But less devout members perceived the visitors and their communication differently. Their impression was one of college kids pulling a prank. Follower Kurt Freund shared his skepticism, stating, "I must say I saw nothing. They just looked like college kids to me. It looked as though they just came here for a lark." Freund's difference in perception, and his decision to disclose it, cost him dearly—group members denounced and shunned him. The next morning, Freund left the house and the group behind, never to return.

Of course, no cataclysm occurred on December 21. Keech's followers were devastated. They had forfeited relationships, belongings, and jobs, all because of their belief in a false prophecy. In the weeks that followed, most of them abandoned their faith in Keech and moved on with their lives. As their perceptions changed,

many lamented the impact their previous perceptions had had on their personal and interpersonal decisions. Follower Kitty O'Donnell said it best: "I don't believe in it any more, and I just regret that I made such an ass of myself, giving away my money and stuff."

It's easy to stereotype Marian Keech and her disciples as "nuts." But she was not mentally ill, nor were her devotees: prior to the failed prophecy, they underwent extensive psychiatric testing at the behest of local media and passed with flying colors. Instead, Keech and her followers were fundamentally similar to you and me, at least in the way they formed their perceptions of the people around them. Though their beliefs were different, they used the same perceptual process we all use. And their perceptions, like yours and mine, not only actively shaped their interpersonal communication and relationship choices but created profound and life-altering consequences as a result.

Perception is our window to the world. All that we experience while interacting with others is filtered through perception. And although information seems to enter into our conscious minds clean and pure, our perception is not an untainted reflection of the reality that surrounds us, an objective "lens." Instead, our perception of what people mean and who they are is a product of our own mental creation. When we perceive, we actively create the meanings we assign to people, their communication, and our relationships, and we look to our perception—not reality itself—to guide our interpersonal communication and relationship decisions.

For this reason, it's essential that we understand precisely how perception works. By honing our awareness of the perception process and how to create more flexible and accurate impressions, we can improve the quality of our interpersonal communication and forge better relationships.

In this chapter, we explore how you can improve your perception to become a more effective interpersonal communicator. You'll learn:

- How the perception process unfolds and which perceptual errors you need to watch for

- The influence that culture, gender, and personality have in shaping your perception of others and your interpersonal communication

- How you form impressions of others, and the benefits and limitations of the methods you use

- Strategies for improving your perceptual accuracy

Perception as a Process

Our lives are filled with interpersonal interactions and relationships. Each day we communicate in ways designed to meet new people, reaffirm acquaintanceships, maintain long-standing involvements, and solve problems at school or work. We make sense of these encounters and plot our own communication paths within them by selecting, organizing, and interpreting information from our senses, a process known as **perception.** Perception begins when we select information to focus our attention on. We then organize information into an understandable pattern inside our minds and interpret its meaning. Each activity influences the other: our mental organization of information shapes how we interpret it, and our interpretation of information influences how we mentally organize it. In the section that follows, we take a closer look at each phase of the perception process. (See Figure 3.1.)

Selecting Information

It's finals week, and you're in your room studying for a difficult exam you'll take in the morning. Exhausted, you decide to take a break and listen to some music. You don your headphones, press the "play" button, and close your eyes. Suddenly you hear a noise. Startled, you open your eyes and remove your headphones, to find that your housemate has just slammed open your bedroom door. "I've been yelling at you for the last five minutes," she snaps. "What's going on?!"

The first step of perception, **selection,** involves focusing attention on certain sights, sounds, tastes, touches, or smells in our environment. One estimate suggests that, even though our senses take in 11 million bits of information per second, we select only about 40 bits to pay attention to (Wilson, 2002). The reason for such a narrow sampling is that our brains can process only so much data at a time.

Consider the housemate example. Once you hear her enter, you likely would select her communication as the focus of your attention. The moment you do this, the process of perception begins: you watch and listen, trying to organize what she is saying into a coherent mental image and to make sense of its meaning. You might even select a more narrow aspect of her verbal or nonverbal communication as your attention focus: her loud and angry voice perhaps, or a certain phrase that she uses. While you're doing this, literally millions of other stimuli are also bombarding your senses, information that remains outside of your conscious awareness. There's your

FIGURE 3.1

The Process of Perception

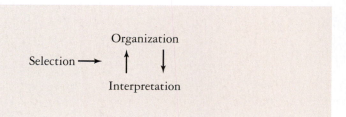

housemate's outfit and her unkempt hair. There are also unnoticed environmental stimuli: the smell of dinner from your apartment kitchen, the blue light from your cell phone, and so forth.

The degree to which particular people or aspects of their communication attract our attention is known as **salience** (Fiske & Taylor, 1991). When something—a person's comment, facial expression, action—is salient, it seems especially noticeable and significant to us. We view aspects of interpersonal communication as salient—and therefore select them as the focus for our attention—under three conditions (Fiske & Taylor, 1991). First, communication is more salient if the communicator behaves in a visually and audibly stimulating fashion. A loudly yelling and energetically gesturing housemate is more salient than a housemate standing motionless and quietly informing us that a phone call is waiting. Second, communication becomes salient if our goals or expectations lead us to view it as important. Our housemate's softly spoken phone announcement will command our immediate attention if we are anticipating a call. Last, communication that deviates from our expectations is salient. An unexpected verbal attack will always be more salient than an expected polite remark.

Organizing the Information You've Selected

Once you've selected something as the focus of your attention, you take the information you have selected and structure it into a coherent pattern inside your mind, a phase of the perception process known as **organization** (Fiske & Taylor, 1991). For example, imagine that a female relative is telling you about a recent visit to your hometown. As she shares her story with you, you select certain bits of her narrative to focus your attention on based on salience, such as a mutual friend she saw during her visit or a favorite old hangout she saw. You then organize your own representation of her story inside your head.

During organization, you engage in **punctuation,** structuring the information you've selected into a chronological sequence that matches how you experienced the order of events (Watzlawick, Beavin, & Jackson, 1967). You determine which words and actions occurred first, second, and so on and which comments or behaviors caused subsequent actions to occur. To illustrate punctuation, think about how you might punctuate the sequence of events in our housemate example. You hear a noise, open your eyes, see your housemate in your room, and then hear her yelling at you. But two people involved in the same interpersonal encounter may punctuate it in very different ways. Here's how your housemate might punctuate the same situation:

"I was in my room studying for finals, but my cell phone kept ringing. I got so irritated that I turned my phone off and put an away message on my instant-messenger. But then the apartment phone rang. I yelled for my housemate to get it, but the phone kept ringing. I ran out to the kitchen, grabbed the phone, and found out it was my housemate's parents calling. I shouted outside his door, 'Your folks are on the phone!' and went back to my room. But then I realized that he hadn't come out to the kitchen. I blew up, charged into his room, and found him there with his headphones on, listening to music. I said, 'I've been yelling at you for the last five minutes! What's going on?' "

If you and another person organize and punctuate information from an encounter differently, the two of you may well feel frustrated with one another. Disagreements about punctuation, and especially disputes about who "started" unpleasant encounters, are a common source of interpersonal conflict (Watzlawick et al., 1967). For example, your housemate may contend that "you started it" because she told you to get the phone but you ignored her. You may believe that "she started it" because she barged into your room without knocking.

Such examples suggest that we can avoid perceptual misunderstandings that lead to conflict by working to understand how our organization and punctuation of information differs from that of other people. For instance, if you asked your housemate why she was yelling at you and learned that she thought you were ignoring her request to get the phone, you might suddenly realize that she wasn't interrupting your study break just to be annoying. And if she asked why you didn't get the phone and learned that you simply didn't hear her, her frustration might dissipate as well. One helpful way to forestall such conflicts is to practice asking others to share their views of encounters in which you both participated. You might say, "Here's what I saw, but that's just my perspective. What do *you* think happened?"

Interpreting the Information

As we organize information we have selected into a coherent mental model, we also engage in **interpretation,** assigning meaning to information we've selected. We call to mind familiar information that's relevant to the current interpersonal encounter, and we use that information to make sense of what we're hearing and seeing. We also create explanations for why things are happening as they are.

Using Familiar Information.   We make sense of others' communication in part by comparing what we currently perceive with knowledge that we already possess. For example, I proposed to my wife by surprising her after class. I had decorated her apartment with several dozen roses and carnations, was dressed in my best (and only!) suit, and was spinning "our song" on her turntable—The Spinners' "Could It Be I'm Falling in Love." When she opened the door, and I asked her to marry me, she immediately interpreted my communication correctly. But how, given that she never had been proposed to before? Because she knew from friends, family members, movies, and television shows what a marriage proposal looked and sounded like. Drawing on this familiar information, she correctly figured out what I was up to and (thank goodness!) accepted my proposal.

The knowledge we draw on when interpreting interpersonal communication resides in **schemata,** mental structures containing information defining concepts' characteristics as well as those characteristics' interrelationships (Macrae & Bodenhausen, 2001). Each of us develops schemata for individual people, groups of people, places, events, objects, and relationships. (Schemata play a key role in forming Gestalt impressions and stereotypes, as we'll discuss later in this chapter.)

SELF-REFLECTION

Recall a conflict in which you and a friend disagreed about "who started it." How did you punctuate the encounter? How did your partner punctuate it? If you both punctuated differently, how did those differences contribute to the conflict? If you could revisit the situation, what might you say or do differently to resolve the dispute?

Because we use familiar information to make sense of current interactions, our interpretations reflect what we presume to be true. For example, suppose you're interviewing for a job with a manager who has been at the company for 18 years. In this case, you'll likely interpret everything she says in light of your knowledge about "employees with long-term company connections." This knowledge includes your assumption that "company veterans generally know insider information." So, when your interviewer talks in glowing terms about the company's future, you'll probably interpret her comments as credible. Now imagine that you're interviewing with someone who has been with the company only a few weeks. Although he may present the exact same message to you about the company's future, your interpretation of his comments likely will prove quite different. Based solely on your perception of him as "new employee," and on the information you have in your schemata related to "new employees," you may interpret his message as naïve speculation rather than the "expert commentary" offered by the company veteran—even if his statements are accurate.

> ● Schemata are mental structures that help us understand a concept's characteristics, and we use them to interpret communication. Together, a bunch of roses, a nice suit, and a diamond ring are schemata that suggest a marriage proposal.

Creating Explanations.   In addition to drawing on our schemata to interpret information from interpersonal encounters, we create explanations for others' comments or behaviors, known as **attributions.** Attributions are our answers to the "why" questions we ask multiple times every day. "Why didn't my romantic partner return my instant message?" "Why did my best friend just yell at me?"

Consider an example shared with me by a friend of mine. She had finished teaching for the semester and was visiting her mother who lived out-of-state. A student of hers, whom we'll call "Janet," had failed her course. During the time my friend was out of town, Janet e-mailed to ask if there was anything she could do to change her grade. However, my friend was offline for the week and missed Janet's e-mail. Checking her messages upon her return, she discovered Janet's original e-mail, along with a second, follow-up message:

> Maybe my situation isn't a priority to you, and that's fine, but a response e-mail would've been appreciated! Even if all you had to say was "there's nothing I can do." I came to you seeking help, not a hand-out! –Janet.[2]

Put yourself in Janet's shoes for a moment. What attributions did Janet obviously make about my friend's failure to respond? How did these

---

[2] Example e-mail contributed to author by professional colleague, with all identifying information removed so as to protect the identity of the student in question.

attributions shape Janet's communication in her second e-mail? Now consider this situation from my friend's perspective. If you were in her shoes, what attributions would you make about Janet and how would they shape how you interpreted her e-mail?

Attributions take two forms, internal and external (see Table 3.1). Internal attributions presume that a person's communication or behavior stems from internal causes, such as character or personality. For example, "My professor didn't respond to my e-mail because she doesn't care about students," or "Janet sent this message because she's rude." External attributions hold that a person's communication is caused by factors unrelated to personal qualities: "My professor didn't respond to my e-mail because she hasn't checked her messages yet," or "Janet sent this message because I didn't respond to her first message."

Like schemata, the attributions we make powerfully influence how we interpret and respond to others' communication. For example, if you think Janet's e-mail was caused by her having a terrible day, you'll likely interpret her message as an understandable venting of frustration. If you think her message was caused by her personal rudeness, you'll probably interpret the e-mail as inappropriate and offensive.

Given the dozens of people with whom we communicate each day, it's not surprising that we occasionally form invalid attributions. One common mistake is the **fundamental attribution error,** the tendency to attribute others' behaviors to internal causes (the kind of person they are) rather than the social or environmental forces affecting them (Heider, 1958). The fundamental attribution error is so named because it is the most prevalent of all perceptual biases and each of us falls prey to it (Langdridge & Butt, 2004). Why does this error occur? Because when we communicate with others, they dominate our perception. They—not the surrounding factors that may be causing their behavior—are most salient for us. Consequently, when we make judgments about why someone is acting or communicating in a certain way, we overestimate the influence of the person and underestimate the significance of his or her immediate environment (Heider, 1958; Langdridge & Butt, 2004).

The fundamental attribution error is particularly common during online communication such as e-mailing or instant-messaging (Shedletsky & Aitken,

TABLE 3.1
Internal versus External Attributions

Communication Event	Internal Attribution	External Attribution
Your romantic partner doesn't reply after you spontaneously send a romantic e-mail.	"My partner is being unromantic."	"My partner is probably too busy to respond."
Your unfriendly coworker greets you warmly.	"My coworker is friendlier than I thought."	"Something unusual must have happened to make my coworker act so friendly."
Your friend ridicules your taste in music.	"My friend has an unpredictable mean streak."	"My friend must be having a really bad day."

2004). Because we aren't privy to the rich array of environmental factors that may be shaping our communication partners' messages—all we perceive is words on a screen—we're more likely than ever to interpret others' communication as stemming solely from internal causes (Wallace, 1999). As a consequence, when an e-mail or instant message is even slightly negative in tone, we're very likely to blame that negativity on bad character or personality flaws. Such was the case when my professor friend presumed that Janet was a "rude person" based on her e-mail.

A related error is the **actor-observer effect,** the tendency of people to make external attributions regarding their own behaviors (Fiske & Taylor, 1991). Because our mental focus during interpersonal encounters is on factors external to us—and especially the person with whom we're interacting—we tend to credit these factors as causing our own communication. This is particularly prevalent during unpleasant interactions. Our own impolite remarks during family conflicts are viewed as "reactions to their hurtful communication" rather than "messages caused by our own insensitivity." Our terseness toward coworkers is seen as "a natural response to incessant work interruptions" rather than "communication resulting from our own prickly personality."

However, we don't always make external attributions regarding our own behaviors. In cases where our actions result in noteworthy success, either personal or professional, we typically take credit for the success by making an internal attribution, a tendency known as the **self-serving bias** (Fiske & Taylor, 1991). Suppose, for example, you've successfully persuaded a friend to lend you her car for the weekend—something you've never pulled off before. In this case, you will probably attribute this success to your charm and persuasive skill rather than luck or your friend's generosity. The self-serving bias is driven by ego-protection: by crediting ourselves for our life successes, we each can feel happier about who we are and the skills we possess.

Clearly, attributions play a powerful role in interpreting the meaning of communication. For this reason, it's important to consider the attributions you make while you're interacting with others. Check your attributions frequently, watching for the fundamental attribution error, the actor-observer effect, and the self-serving bias. If you think someone has spoken to you in a rude or otherwise offensive way, ask yourself if it's possible that outside forces—including your own communication behavior—could have caused the problem. Also keep in mind that communication (like other forms of human behavior) rarely stems from *only* external *or* internal causes. It's caused by a combination of both, which is why making only one type of attribution typically constitutes an "error" in itself (Langdridge & Butt, 2004).

Finally, when you can, check the accuracy of your attributions by asking people for the reasons behind their behavior. And when you've made attribution errors that lead you to criticize or lose your patience with someone else, apologize and explain your mistake to the person. After Janet learned that my friend hadn't responded because she had been out-of-state—as opposed to intentionally blowing her off—Janet apologized for her error. She also explained why her message was so terse: she thought my friend was intentionally ignoring her. Upon receiving Janet's apology, my friend apologized also. She realized that she, too, had succumbed to the

SKILLS PRACTICE

This exercise helps you make better online attributions.

1 Recall an unpleasant e-mail exchange.

2 Identify your attribution about why the other person sent the message.

3 Consider how your attribution influenced your messages.

4 List other possible causes for the person's messages.

5 Envision how your messages would have been different if you made one of these other attributions.

6 Before responding to the next e-mail you perceive negatively, evaluate your attributions and make plausible ones that will lead to more effective messages.

● When we are uncertain about other people's behavior, we can learn more about them by observing them, by asking their friends about them, or even by interacting with them directly. The information we gain by engaging in passive, active, or interactive strategies helps us make decisions about our future communication with them.

fundamental attribution error: she had presumed that Janet was rude, when in fact Janet's frustration over not getting a response was what caused her to communicate as she did.

Experiencing Uncertainty

When intercultural communication scholar Patricia Covarrubias was a young girl, she and her family immigrated to the United States from Mexico (Covarrubias, 2000). On her first day of school in her adoptive country, Patricia's third-grade teacher, Mrs. Williams, led her to the front of the classroom to introduce her to her new classmates. As Patricia stood excitedly before them, she waited for Mrs. Williams to introduce her as "Patricia Covarrubias," or perhaps "Patricia." Of course, when Patricia was growing up in Mexico, her friends and family members rarely used either of these names. Instead, they called her *la chiquita* (the little one) or *mi Rosita de Jerico* (my rose of Jericho). But in the more formal setting of the classroom, Patricia expected her teacher to introduce her using her first and last name. Instead, Mrs. Williams, her hand gently resting on Patricia's shoulder, turned to the class and said, "Class, this is *Pat.*"

Patricia was dumbfounded. In her entire life, she had never been "Pat," nor could she understand why someone would call her "Pat." As she explains, "In one unexpected moment, all that I was and had been was abridged into three-letter, bottom-line efficiency" (Covarrubias, 2000, pp. 10–11). And although Mrs. Williams was simply trying to be friendly—using an abbreviation most Euro-Americans would consider "informal"—Patricia was mortified. The encounter bolstered her feeling that she was an outsider in an uncertain environment.

In most interpersonal interactions, the perception process unfolds in a rapid, straightforward manner. But sometimes we find ourselves in situations where people communicate in perplexing ways. In such contexts, we experience uncertainty, the anxious feeling that comes when we can't predict or explain someone else's communication.

Uncertainty is common during first encounters with new acquaintances, when we don't know much about the people with whom we're communicating. According to **Uncertainty Reduction Theory,** our primary compulsion during initial interactions is reducing uncertainty about our conversational partners, by gathering enough information about them that their communication is rendered predictable and explainable (Berger & Calabrese, 1975). When we're able to reduce uncertainty, we're inclined to perceive people as attractive and likable, talk further, and consider forming relationships with them (Berger, 1987; Burgoon & Hoobler, 2002; Kellermann & Reynolds, 1990). When we can't predict or explain people's communication or behavior, our uncertainty escalates, we're inclined to not communicate further, to form negative impressions, and to avoid developing relationships.

Uncertainty can be reduced in several ways, each of which has advantages and disadvantages (Berger & Bradac, 1982). Sometimes we use passive strategies, gathering information about others by watching them without their knowledge. If you opt for this type of strategy, you don't approach and talk with another person; you simply watch the individual to see how he or she acts when communicating with others. Observing how others talk with their coworkers, close friends, family members, or strangers can provide you with information that helps you predict how they'll behave when they interact with you, allowing you to reduce uncertainty before you even talk with them. Examples of passive strategies include observing someone hanging out with friends at a party, watching a person having lunch with his or her coworkers, and watching a person interact with family members at a football tailgate party.

We can also reduce uncertainty through active strategies. Similar to passive strategies, active strategies don't involve directly interacting with the person we're sizing up. The most common active strategy is third-person questioning, asking other people questions about the person we're interested in. You might find someone who knows the person you're assessing and then get him or her to disclose as much information as possible about that individual. Or you might ask a mutual friend to tell you what he knows about a classmate you're romantically interested in. Active strategies pose risks, though. The person you're querying may tell the target person you've been asking questions. That could embarrass you—and make the target individual angry, especially if he or she perceives what you've been doing as personally invasive. In addition, the third-party information you acquire may not be trustworthy. The person you're asking for information may unknowingly have false information or may intentionally mislead you.

Finally, you can use interactive strategies to reduce uncertainty. Interactive strategies involve direct interaction between you and the person you're interested in. Two interactive strategies are common, the first of which is asking questions. This is the most direct and effective means of gathering the information you need to ease uncertainty. You might ask where the person is originally from, what he or she does for a living, and what interests he or she shares with you. The second active strategy is disclosing personal information about yourself. This enables you to test the other person's reactions to you. For instance, upon meeting someone new at a party, you might chat a bit about your classes or mention that you play drums in a punk band, then gauge whether the person seems intrigued or bored. That information can help you decide whether you want to continue the conversation or get together with your new acquaintance again in the future.

Influences on Perception

A sense of immediacy and directness pervades the perceptual process. Someone says something to us, and with lightning speed we focus our attention, organize information, and interpret its meaning. This leads to a reduction, an increase, or no change in our uncertainty. But although this process seems straightforward, powerful forces outside of our conscious awareness shape our perception during every encounter, whether we're communicating with colleagues, friends, family members, or lovers. Three of the most powerful influences on perception are culture, gender, and personality.

SELF-REFLECTION

In what types of interpersonal encounters do you use passive strategies to reduce your uncertainty? Active strategies? Interactive? Judging from your experiences, which of the three types of strategies is most effective? Why? In your view, are passive and active strategies ethical? Why or why not?

Perception and Culture

The culture in which you grew up influences your perception of others during interpersonal communication in at least two ways. Recall from Chapter 2
that *culture* is an established, coherent set of beliefs, attitudes, values, and
practices shared by a large group of people. Whenever you interact with
others, you interpret their communication in part by drawing on information
from your schemata. But your schemata are filled with the beliefs, attitudes,
values, and practices you learned in your own culture (Gudykunst & Kim,
2003). Consequently, people raised in different cultures have different
knowledge in their schemata, so they interpret one another's communication
in very different ways. Skilled interpersonal communicators recognize this
fact. When necessary and appropriate, they check the accuracy of their
interpretation by asking questions such as "I'm sorry, could you clarify what
you just said for me?"

Second, culture affects whether you perceive others as similar to or different from yourself. When you grow up valuing certain cultural beliefs, attitudes, and values as your own, you naturally come to perceive those who
share these with you as fundamentally similar to yourself—people you
consider **ingroupers** (Allport, 1954). You may consider individuals from
many different groups as your ingroupers as long as they share a substantial
point of commonality, such as religious beliefs, ethnicity, socioeconomic
class, hometown, or taste in movies. In contrast, you may perceive people
who aren't fundamentally similar to yourself as **outgroupers.**

Perceiving others as ingroupers or outgroupers has important implications. For example, we're more likely to form positive impressions of people
we perceive as ingroupers (Triandis, 1995). One study of 30 different ethnic

groups in East Africa found that members of each group perceived ingroupers' communication as substantially more trustworthy, friendly, and honest than outgroupers' communication (Brewer & Campbell, 1976). And in cases where people communicate in rude or inappropriate ways, you're substantially more inclined to form negative, internal attributions if you perceive them as outgroupers (Brewer, 1999). So, for example, if a city bus driver chides you for not having the exact change but he's wearing a T-shirt emblazoned with a message advocating your beliefs and values, you're likely to make an external attribution: "He's just having a bad day." The same communication coming from someone who is proudly displaying chestwide messages attacking your beliefs likely will provoke a negative, internal attribution: "What a jerk! He's just like all those other people who believe that stuff!"

While categorizing people as ingroupers or outgroupers, it's easy to make mistakes. For example, even if people dress differently than you do, they may hold beliefs, attitudes, and values similar to your own. If you assume they're outgroupers based on surface-level differences, you may communicate with them in ways that prevent the two of you from getting to know one another better. You may never discover that you share other important qualities, losing an opportunity to make a friend, gain a new colleague, or forge a romantic bond.

Perception and Gender

Pick any group of your male and female friends and get them talking about the differences in men's and women's perception. Chances are you'll hear a number of arguments fired back and forth, most of them claiming that men and women perceive differently and therefore interpret their interpersonal communication experiences differently. Your friends may insist that "Men are cool and logical in their perception of others" while "Women see everything through a lens of sentiment and emotion."

However, the relationship between gender and perception is more complex than common beliefs. For example, through magnetic resonance imaging and positron emission tomography, we have learned that the structure of the brain's cerebral cortex differs in men and women (Frederikse, Lu, Aylward, Barta, & Pearlson, 1999). Researchers maintain that this difference enables men to perceive time and speed more accurately than women and to mentally rotate three-dimensional figures more easily. The difference in cerebral cortex structure allows women to understand and manipulate spatial relationships between objects more skillfully than men do and to more accurately identify others' emotions. Women also have a greater ability to process information related to language simultaneously in both of the brain's frontal lobes, resulting in higher scores on tests of language comprehension and vocabulary (Schlaepfer et al., 1995).

But whether differences in brain structure and corresponding perceptual abilities translate into substantial gender differences in interpersonal communication remains a matter of debate. Linguist Deborah Tannen argues that gender socialization amplifies innate differences between men and women to the point where they perceive and produce communication in vastly

SELF-REFLECTION

Consider people you view as ingroupers and those you consider outgroupers. How does your communication with each type differ? Have you ever perceived someone initially as an outgrouper, only to decide later that he or she is an ingrouper? If so, what does this suggest about the limitations of categorizing people in this way?

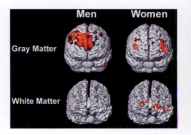

different ways (Tannen, 1990). For example, Tannen suggests that when problems arise, men focus on solutions, and women offer emotional support. Consequently, women perceive men's solutions as unsympathetic, and men perceive women's need for emotional support as unreasonable. In contrast, researchers from communication and psychology argue that men and women are actually more similar than different in how they interpersonally communicate (Aries, 1996; Hall, Carter, & Horgan, 2000; Hyde & Linn, 1988,

FOCUS ON CULTURE

Perceiving Race

Race is a way we classify people based on common ancestry or descent and is almost entirely judged by physical features (Lustig & Koester, 2006). Once we perceive race, other perceptual judgments follow, most notably the assignment of people to ingrouper versus outgrouper status (Brewer, 1999). People we perceive as being the "same race" we see as being ingroupers. Their communication is perceived more positively than the communication of people of "other races," and we're more likely to make positive attributions about their behavior.

Not surprisingly, the perception of racial categories is more salient for people who suffer racial discrimination than for those who don't. Consider the experience of Canadian professor Tara Goldstein. She asked students in her teacher education class to sort themselves into "same race" groups for a discussion exercise (2001). Four black women immediately grouped together; several East Asian students did the same. But the white students were perplexed. One shouted, "All Italians—over here!" while another inquired, "Any other students of Celtic ancestry?" One white female approached Dr. Goldstein and said, "I'm not white, I'm Jewish." Following the exercise, the white students commented that they had never been sorted by their whiteness and didn't perceive themselves or each other as white.

Whiteness has been questioned only recently. Whiteness often can mean "natural" or "normal" to individuals who are white, but for scholars interested in whiteness and for people of color, it means privilege. In her book *White Privilege,* Peggy McIntosh lists 26 privileges that she largely takes for granted and that result from her skin color (1999). For example, as a white person, McIntosh is able to swear, dress in second-hand clothes, or not answer e-mail without having members of her race or other races attribute these behaviors to bad morals, poverty, or computer illiteracy. This perception of verbal and nonverbal communication may seem mundane, but as McIntosh says, it is part of white privilege, "an invisible package of unearned assets which I can count on cashing in each day, but about which I was meant to remain oblivious" (p. 79).

YOUR TURN

- Consider race in your own life. What race do you identify with?

- How does your race affect your perception of ingrouper versus outgrouper communication? How does your race affect other people's perception of your communication?

- Is race an ethical way to perceive how others communicate or choose relationship partners? Do you think some races have more or less privilege in their interpersonal communication? If so, why?

Wilkins & Andersen, 1991). Researchers Dan Canary, Tara Emmers-Sommer, and Sandra Faulkner reviewed data from over 1,000 gender studies and found that if you consider all of the factors that influence our communication and compare their impact, only about 1 percent of people's communication behavior is caused by gender (1997). They concluded that when it comes to interpersonal communication, "men and women respond in a similar manner 99% of the time" (p. 9).

If men and women aren't that different in their interpersonal communication, why do people think they are? Because people are socialized to believe that men and women communicate differently. Within Western culture, a long tradition exists of emphasizing fundamental communication differences between men and women. People believe that women talk more about their feelings than men, talk about "less important" issues than men (women "gossip" whereas men "discuss"), and generally talk more than men (Spender, 1990). Because of these strong beliefs in gender differences, we perceive differences in male or female communication even where few or none exist.

Consider the case of perceived gender differences in language usage. For more than a hundred years now, people in Britain and the United States have believed that men and women speak differently, with women using "indirect" and "flowery" language, and men speaking in "direct, clear, and concise" ways (Jesperson, 1922; Spender, 1990). But in one of the best-known studies of this phenomenon, researchers found that this was more a

---

POP QUIZ

Is It a Man or a Woman?

Drawing on all that you know about men, women, and their communication, identify the genders of the people who made these speeches. Then check your answers. What does your score tell you about your perception of gender and language?

❑ 1. "Perhaps a new spirit is rising among us. If it is, let us trace its movements and pray that our own inner being may be sensitive to its guidance, for we are deeply in need of a new way beyond the darkness that seems so close around us."

❑ 2. "I am happy to be here at this time before this audience because I must speak of that issue that comes first of all in the hearts and minds of all of us—that issue which most urgently challenges and summons the wisdom and the

courage of our whole people. This issue is peace."

❑ 3. "Let tyrants fear; I have come amongst you at this time to live or die amongst you all; to lay down, for my God, and for my kingdom, and for my people, my honor and my blood."

❑ 4. "There is so much suffering, so much hatred, so much misery, and we with our sacrifice are beginning at home. Love begins at home, and it is not how much we do, but how much love we put in the action that we do."

Answers:

1. *A Time to Break Silence,* Martin Luther King Jr., 1963

2. *The Chance for Peace,* Dwight D. Eisenhower, 1953

3. *The Spanish Armada,* Queen Elizabeth I, 1588

4. *Nobel Lecture,* Mother Teresa, 1979

matter of perception than real difference (Mulac, Incontro, & James, 1985). In the study, two groups of participants were given the same speech. One group was told that a man had authored and presented the speech; the other was told that a woman had written and given it. Participants who thought the speech was a woman's perceived it as having more "artistic quality." Those who believed it was a man's saw the speech as having more "dynamism." Participants also described the "man's" language as strong, active, and aggressive and the "woman's" language as pleasing, sweet, and beautiful, despite the fact that the speeches were identical.

The widespread predisposition to perceive gender differences in our interpersonal communication creates at least two costs. First, when problems arise in cross-sex relationships, we may presume that they are unbridgeable, given the perceived communication gulf that separates the sexes. Instead of directly discussing our concerns, we may instead avoid the issue or even end the relationship, thinking, "What's the point of talking about it—men and women never see things the same way!" (Metts & Cupach, 1990). Second, the perceived gender differences in communication do not place men and women on equal footing. Instead, they depict women's communication as inferior. Women communicate with skill equal to that of men, yet they are routinely perceived as lacking comparable authority, effectiveness, and persuasiveness, especially in professional settings (Spender, 1990).

Given our tendency to presume broad gender differences in communication, can we still improve the accuracy of our perception? Yes—if we challenge the assumptions we make about gender and if we remind ourselves that male and female approaches to communication are more similar than different. The next time you find yourself thinking "Oh, she said that because she's a woman," or "He sees things that way because he is man," question your perception. Are the people you are observing really communicating differently because of their gender, or are you simply perceiving them as different based on *your* beliefs about their gender?

Personality

In S. E. Hinton's classic tale of teen relationships, *The Outsiders,* Ponyboy is the youngest of three brothers growing up amid poverty and violence in the 1960s (Hinton, 1967). Orphaned by his parents' fatal car crash, Ponyboy lives with his two brothers, Sodapop and Darry, whose personalities are complete opposites. Soda's warmth, outgoing nature, and utter lack of responsibility contrast sharply with Darry's cool reserve, meticulousness, and maturity. Hanging out with friends Two-Bit and Johnny one night, Ponyboy unveils bitter feelings toward Darry when a girl he has met, Cherry, asks Ponyboy to describe him:

> Cherry turned to me. "Tell me about your oldest brother. You don't talk much about him. Is he wild and reckless like Soda? Dreamy, like you?" My face got hot as I bit my lip. Darry . . . what was Darry like?
> "He's . . ." I started to say he was a good ol' guy but I couldn't. I burst out bitterly: "He's not like Sodapop at all and he sure ain't like me. He's hard as rock and about as human. He's got eyes exactly like frozen ice.

SELF-REFLECTION

Recall an encounter in which you perceived gender differences in communication. What differences did you perceive? How did your perception shape your communication? Reconsidering the encounter, do you now believe there was an actual communication difference? If so, what factors other than gender might have caused it?

He thinks I'm a pain in the neck. He likes Soda—everybody likes Soda—but he can't stand me. I bet he wishes he could stick me in a home somewhere, and he'd do it too, if Soda'd let him." Two-Bit and Johnny were staring at me now. "No . . ." Two-Bit said, dumbfounded. "No, Ponyboy, that ain't right . . . you got it wrong . . ." (p. 39)

The Outsiders paints a vivid portrait of how personality shapes our perception of others, our interpersonal communication, and our relationships. Although you may not be able to relate to the story's setting—gang warfare in 1960s Oklahoma—you probably *can* relate to the characters. We all can think of warm, outgoing, irresponsible people in our lives, just as we can call to mind those who are cool, reserved, and meticulous. And when we think of these people and their personalities, visceral reactions are commonly evoked. We resent, like, loathe, or even love people based on our perception of their personalities and how their personalities mesh with our own.

Personality is an individual's characteristic way of thinking, feeling, and acting, based on the traits that he or she possesses (McCrae & Costa, 2001). Traits are enduring motives and impulses. Contemporary psychologists argue that although thousands of different personalities exist, they each comprise only five primary traits, referred to as the "Big Five" (John, 1990; Loehlin, McCrae, Costa, & John, 1998; McCrae & Costa, 1996, 1997, 2001). The Big Five are extraversion, agreeableness, conscientiousness, neuroticism, and openness (see Table 3.2). The degree to which a person possesses each of the Big Five traits determines his or her personality. The Big Five are quite stable during adulthood and appear to describe personalities across cultures (McCrae, 2001). You can discover where you score on the Big Five by taking the test at www.sulloway.org.

Prioritizing Our Own Traits When Perceiving Others.   Our perception of others is strongly guided by the personality traits we see in ourselves and how we evaluate these traits. If you're an extravert, for example, another person's extraversion becomes highly salient to you when you're communicating with him or her. Likewise, if you pride yourself on being friendly, other people's friendliness becomes your perceptual focus.

But it's not just a matter of focusing on certain traits to the exclusion of others. We evaluate people positively or negatively in accordance with how we feel about our own traits. We typically like in others the same traits we like in ourselves, and we dislike in others the traits that we dislike in ourselves. For example, in *The Outsiders,* Ponyboy criticized Darry's conscientiousness in part because he saw himself as a very responsible person but he longed to be reckless and wild like Sodapop. And Ponyboy's quietness led him to loathe this trait in Darry, just as his friendliness caused him to admire Sodapop's warmth.

To avoid this preoccupation with our own traits, carefully observe how you focus your attention on other people's traits and how your evaluation of these traits in others is a reflection of your own feelings about yourself. Strive to perceive people broadly, taking into consideration all of their traits and not just the positive or negative ones that you share. Then evaluate

TABLE 3.2

The Big Five Personality
Traits

Extraversion	The degree to which a person is interested in interacting regularly with others and actively seeks out interpersonal encounters. People high in extraversion are outgoing and sociable; those low in extraversion are quiet and reserved.
Agreeableness	The degree to which a person is trusting, friendly, and cooperative. People low in agreeableness are aggressive, suspicious, and uncooperative. Also known as *friendliness.*
Conscientiousness	The degree to which a person is organized and persistent in pursuing goals. People high in conscientiousness are methodical, well organized, and dutiful; those low in conscientiousness are less careful, less focused, and more easily distracted. Also known as *dependability.*
Neuroticism	The degree to which a person experiences negative thoughts about oneself. People high in neuroticism are prone to insecurity and emotional distress; people low in neuroticism are relaxed, less emotional, and less prone to distress. Also known as *emotional stability.*
Openness	The degree to which a person is willing to consider new ideas and take an interest in culture. People high in openness are more imaginative, creative, and interested in seeking out new experiences than those low in openness.

SELF-REFLECTION

What personality traits of
yours do you like? When
you see these traits in others, how does that impact
your communication toward
them? How do you perceive
people who possess traits
you don't like in yourself?
How do these perceptions
affect your relationships
with others?

them and communicate toward them independently of your own positive and negative evaluations of yourself.

Generalizing from the Traits We Know. Another effect that personality has on perception is the presumption that because a person is high or low on a certain trait, he or she must be high or low on other traits. For example, say that I introduce you to a friend of mine, Shoshanna. Within the first minute of interaction you perceive her as highly friendly. Based on your perception of her high friendliness, you'll likely also presume that she is highly extraverted, simply because high friendliness and high extraversion intuitively seem to "go together." If people you've known in the past who were highly friendly and extraverted also were highly open, you may go further, perceiving Shoshanna as highly open as well.

Your perception of Shoshanna was created using **implicit personality theories,** the information we have about different types of personalities and the ways in which traits cluster together (Bruner & Taguiri, 1954). When we meet people for the first time, implicit personality theories are particularly useful. They allow us to perceive just a little about a person's personality and then presume a great deal more, making us feel that we know the person and helping to reduce uncertainty. At the same time, making

"We evaluate people based on how we feel about ourselves. We like in others the traits we like in ourselves, and we dislike in others the traits we dislike in ourselves."

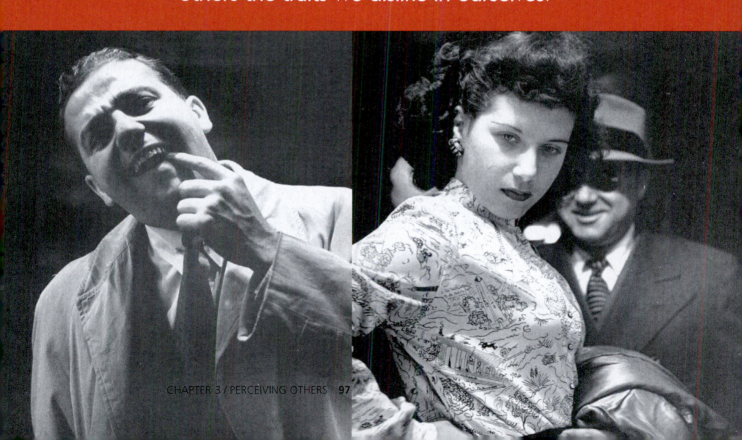

SELF-REFLECTION

Recall an encounter where you mistakenly presumed someone had certain traits and you communicated toward them based on this presumption. How did the person react? What did you say to repair your error? How did you feel afterward?

presumptions about people's personalities is risky. Presuming that someone is high or low on one trait because he or she is high or low on others can lead you to communicate in inappropriate and ineffective ways. For example, if you presume that Shoshanna is high on openness, you might also presume she has certain political or cultural beliefs, leading you to say things to her that cut directly against her actual values: "Don't you just hate people who try to cut federal arts funding?" "No, actually I think that government should have no role in the arts!"

Forming Impressions of Others

When we use the perception process to size up other people, we form **interpersonal impressions**—mental pictures of who people are and how we feel about them. All aspects of the perception process shape our interpersonal impressions: the information we select as the focus of our attention, the way we organize this information, the interpretations we make based on knowledge in our schemata and our attributions, and even our uncertainty.

Given the complexity of the process, it's not surprising that impressions vary widely, both in the speed with which we form them and in the shape they take. Some impressions come quickly into focus. We meet a person and take an immediate dislike to him. Or we quickly decide that someone's a "fun person" after chatting with her briefly. Other impressions form slowly, over a series of encounters. Some impressions are intensely positive, others neutral, and still others negative. But regardless of their form, interpersonal impressions exert a profound impact on our interpersonal communication and relationship choices. To illustrate this impact, imagine yourself in the following situation.

It's summer, and you're at a local lake, hanging out with friends. As you lie on the beach, enjoying the sun, the man pictured in the photo on the next page approaches you. He introduces himself as "Ted" and tells you that he's waiting for some friends who were supposed to help him load his sailboat onto his car. He's easy to talk to, friendly, and he has a nice smile. His left arm is in a sling, and he holds the arm tightly against his body. He casually mentions that he injured it playing racquetball and asks if you've ever played. ("You should try it—it's fun!" he says.) But his arm is hurting, and his friends are missing, so he asks if you would help him with his boat. You say, "Sure." You walk with him to the parking lot, and during your walk Ted admires the gorgeous day and all the people at the park.

You get to Ted's car, but you don't see a boat. When you ask him where his boat is, he says, "It's at my folks' house, just up the hill. Do you mind going with me? It'll just take a couple of minutes." You tell him you can't go with him because your friends will wonder where you are. "That's OK," Ted says cheerily, "I should have told you it wasn't in the parking lot. Thanks for bothering anyways." As the two of you walk back to the beach, Ted repeats his apology and expresses gratitude for your willingness to help him. He's polite and strikes you as very sincere.

Think about your encounter with Ted, and all that you've perceived. What's your impression of him? What traits besides the ones you've observed would you expect him to have? What do you predict would have happened if you had gone with him to his folks' house to help load the boat? Would you want to play racquetball with him? Would he make a good friend? Does he interest you as a possible romantic partner?

The scenario you've read actually happened to someone in 1974. The above description is drawn from the police testimony of Janice Graham, who was approached by Ted on the afternoon of Sunday, July 14, at Lake Sammamish Park, near Seattle, Washington (Michaud & Aynesworth, 1989). Graham's decision not to accompany Ted saved her life. Two other women—Janice Ott and Denise Naslund—were not so fortunate. Each of them did go with Ted that afternoon, and he raped and murdered them, discarding their bodies in a forest near the park. Friendly, handsome, and polite Ted was none other than Ted Bundy, one of the most notorious serial killers in U.S. history.

Thankfully, most of the interpersonal impressions we form don't have life or death consequences. But all impressions do exert a powerful impact on how we communicate with others and whether we pursue relationships with them. For this reason, it's important to understand the advantages and disadvantages of each kind of interpersonal impression as well as how we can flexibly adapt our impressions to create more accurate and reliable preconceptions of others.

Constructing Gestalts

One way we form impressions of others is to construct a **Gestalt,** a general and global impression of a person that's either positive or negative. We discern a few traits and drawing upon information in our mental schemata, we arrive at a judgment based on these traits. The result is an impression of the person as a whole rather than as the sum of individual parts (Asch, 1946). For example, suppose you strike up a conversation with the person sitting next to you at a lunch restaurant. The person is funny, friendly, and attractive—characteristics associated with positive information in your schemata. You immediately construct an overall positive impression ("I like this person!") rather than spending additional time weighing the significance of his or her separate traits.

The primary advantages of Gestalts are that they are formed rapidly and require relatively little mental or communicative effort. This makes them useful for encounters in which we must render quick judgments about others with only limited information—an interview at a job fair in which you have only few minutes to size up the interviewer or an encounter in which you suspect a stranger may be about to rob you. Gestalts also are useful for interactions involving casual relationships (contacts with acquaintances or service providers) and contexts in which we are meeting and talking with a large number of people in a small time (business conferences or parties). During such exchanges, it isn't reasonable or even possible to carefully scrutinize every piece of information we perceive about others. Instead, we quickly form broad impressions and then mentally walk away from them. But this also means that Gestalts have significant shortcomings.

The Positivity Bias.   In 1913, author E. H. Porter published a novel titled *Pollyanna,* about a young child who was happy nearly all of the time. Even when faced with horrible tragedies, Pollyanna saw the positive side of things. Research on human perception suggests that some Pollyanna exists inside each of us (Matlin & Stang, 1978). Examples of Pollyanna effects include the facts that people perceive pleasant events as more likely to happen than unpleasant ones, most people deem their lives "happy" and describe themselves as "optimists," and when asked to rate themselves in terms of physical attractiveness and intellect, most people view themselves as "better than average" (Matlin & Stang, 1978; Silvera, Krull, & Sassler, 2002; Van Rooijen, 1973).

Pollyanna effects come into play when we form Gestalts. When Gestalts are formed, they are more likely to be positive than negative, an effect known as the **positivity bias.** Let's say you're at an office party at a company where you just started working. During the party, you meet six new coworkers for the first time and talk with each of them for a few minutes. You form a Gestalt for each. Owing to the positivity bias, most or all of your Gestalts are likely to be positive. Although the positivity bias is helpful in initiating relationships, it can also lead us to make bad interpersonal decisions, such as when we pursue relationships with people who turn out to be unethical or even abusive.

All Information Is Not Created Equal.   When we create Gestalts, we don't treat all information that we learn about people as equally important. We place extra emphasis on the first information we take in about the person, a tendency known as the **primacy effect.** The primacy effect is one reason people consider first impressions so consequential. In truth, it isn't first impressions that are so important; all impressions, whether formed quickly or slowly, are important in shaping our communication and relationship decisions. Rather, it's the first information we learn about people that plays a critical role in shaping our impressions (Asch, 1946). For example, suppose you meet someone new at a party, and the first thing you notice is that he seems nervous. You form a negative Gestalt, deciding that he's "a loser." Even though you may learn later that he is actually very social, the initial characteristic of "nervous" remains prominent in your mind.

We also place emphasis on the negative information we learn about others, a pattern known as the **negativity effect.** Across cultures, people perceive negative information as more informative about someone's "true" character than positive information (Kellermann, 1989). Though you may be wondering whether the negativity effect contradicts Pollyanna effects, it actually derives from them. People tend to believe that positive events, information, and personal characteristics are more commonplace than negative events, information, and characteristics. So when we learn something negative about another person, we see it as unusual. Consequently, we judge that information as more truly representative of a person's character than positive information (Kellermann, 1989).

Sometimes primacy and negativity effects lead us to accurate perceptions of people. One of the women who rejected Ted Bundy's request for assistance at Lake Sammamish Park reported that she had seen him "stalking" other women before he approached her. This initial information led her to form a negative Gestalt before he even talked with her—an impression that saved her life. But just as often, primacy and negativity effects lead us away from accurate perception. Accurate perception is rooted in carefully and critically assessing everything we learn about people, then flexibly adapting our impressions to match this data. When we base impressions only on the first information we receive or weight negative information more heavily than positive, we perceive only a small part of people, aspects that may or may not be representative of who they are and how they normally communicate.

Halos and Horns.   Once we form a Gestalt, it influences how we interpret the other person's subsequent communication and the attributions we make regarding the individual. For example, think about someone for whom you've formed a strongly positive Gestalt. Now imagine that this person discloses a dark secret: he or she lied to a lover, cheated on taxes, or stole supplies from the office. Because of your positive Gestalt, you will likely dismiss the significance of this behavior, telling yourself instead that the person "had no choice" or "wasn't acting normally." This tendency to positively interpret nearly anything someone says or does because we have a positive Gestalt of them is known as the **halo effect** (see Table 3.3).

The counterpart of the halo effect is the **horn effect,** the tendency to negatively interpret the communication and behavior of people for whom we have negative Gestalts (see Table 3.4). Call to mind someone you can't stand. Imagine that this person discloses the same secret as the individual described above. Although the information in both cases is the same, you will likely chalk up this individual's unethical behavior to bad character or lack of values.

Calculating Algebraic Impressions

A second way we form interpersonal impressions stands in stark contrast to Gestalts. Rather than quickly forming a general impression of someone based on a few observed traits, we develop what are called **algebraic impressions** by carefully evaluating each new thing we learn about a person (Anderson, 1981). Although this term may sound like jargon, it's actually an apt description. Algebraic impressions involve comparing and assessing the positive and negative things we learn about a person in order to calculate an overall impression, then modifying this impression as we learn new information. It's similar to solving an algebra equation, whereby we add and subtract different values from each other to compute a final result.

Consider how you might form an algebraic impression of Ted Bundy from our earlier example. At the outset, his warmth, humor, and ability to chat easily with you strike you as "friendly" and "extraverted." These traits, when added together, lead you to calculate a positive impression: friendly + extraverted = positive impression. But when you accompany Bundy to the

SELF-REFLECTION

Think of someone for whom you have a negative Gestalt. How did primacy and negativity effects shape your impression? Now call to mind personal flaws or embarrassing events from your past. If someone learned of this information and formed a negative Gestalt of you, would his or her impression be accurate?

TABLE 3.3	Impression	Behavior	Attribution
The Halo Effect	Person we like :-)	Positive behavior	Internal
	Person we like :-)	Negative behavior	External

Note: Information in this table is adapted from Guerin (1999).

TABLE 3.4	Impression	Behavior	Attribution
The Horn Effect	Person we dislike :-(	Positive behavior	External
	Person we dislike :-(	Negative behavior	Internal

Note: Information in this table is adapted from Guerin (1999).

parking lot to help with his sailboat and realize the boat isn't there, you perceive this information as strange and possibly deceptive. This new information—Ted may be a liar and have ulterior motives—immediately causes you to revise your computation: friendly + extraverted + potential liar + ulterior motives = negative impression.

When we form algebraic impressions, we don't place an equal value on every piece of information in the equation. Instead, we weight some pieces of information more heavily than others, depending on the information's importance and its positivity or negativity. For example, your perception of potential romantic partners' physical attractiveness, intelligence, and personal values will likely carry more weight when calculating your impression than their favorite color or breakfast cereal—unless you view colors and cereals as important.

As this discussion illustrates, algebraic impressions are more flexible and accurate than Gestalts. For encounters in which we have the time and energy to ponder someone's traits and how they add up, algebraic impressions offer us the opportunity to form refined impressions of people. We can also flexibly change them every time we receive new information about people. But since algebraic impressions require a fair amount of mental effort, they aren't as efficient as Gestalts. In unexpected encounters or casual conversations, such mental calculations are unnecessary and may even work to our disadvantage, especially if we need to render rapid judgments and act on them.

Using Stereotypes

A final way we form impressions is to perceptually categorize people into a social group and then evaluate them based on information we have in our mental schemata related to this group (Bodenhausen, Macrae, & Sherman, 1999). This is known as **stereotyping,** a term first coined by journalist Walter Lippmann to describe overly simplistic interpersonal impressions (1922). When we stereotype others, we often replace the subtle complexities that make people unique with blanket assumptions about their character and worth based solely on their social group affiliation.

SKILLS PRACTICE

This exercise strengthens your ability to use algebraic impressions.

1 When you next make a new acquaintance, spend time observing everything you can about the person.

2 Afterward, make a list of the traits you perceived.

3 Scrutinize your list, considering each trait's importance and its positivity or negativity, and then form an algebraic impression of the person.

4 Do the same thing after subsequent interactions.

5 Pay close attention to how any new information changes your impression.

We stereotype because doing so streamlines the perception process. Once we've categorized a person as a member of a particular group, we can apply all of the information we have about that group to form a quick impression (Bodenhausen et al., 1999). For example, suppose a friend introduces you to Conor, an Irish transfer student. Once you perceive Conor as "Irish," beliefs that you might hold about Irish people could come to mind: they love to tell exaggerated stories (the blarney), have bad tempers, like to drink, and are passionate about soccer. Mind you, none of these assumptions may be accurate about Irish people or relevant to Conor. But if this is what you believe about the Irish, you'll keep it in mind during your conversation with Conor and look for ways to confirm your beliefs. So when he tells you about "seeing a great match" last weekend, you might assume he's talking about soccer rather than tennis or chess. If he discloses that he went to a party last night, you might picture him with a pint of Guinness in his hand rather than a root beer.

As this example suggests, stereotyping frequently leads us to form flawed impressions of others. One study of workplace perception found that male supervisors who stereotyped women as "the weaker sex" perceived female employees' work performance as deficient and gave women low job evaluations—regardless of the women's actual job performance (Cleveland, Stockdale, & Murphy, 2000). A separate study examining college students' perceptions of professors found a similar biasing effect for ethnic stereotypes. Euro-American students who stereotyped Hispanics as "laidback" and "relaxed" perceived Hispanic professors who set high expectations for classroom performance as "colder" and "more unprofessional" than Euro-American professors who set identical standards (Smith & Anderson, 2005).

However, stereotyping doesn't automatically lead to negative outcomes. Communication scholars Valerie Manusov and Radha Hegde (1993) found that during encounters between American and Indian students, the Americans who held positive or negative stereotypes about Indians were more inquisitive and actively engaged during the interaction than those who lacked stereotypes. As this study suggests, stereotyping can create an opportunity for communication, but the quality of the communication will depend on the nature of the stereotype.

Stereotyping is almost impossible to avoid. Researchers have documented that categorizing people in terms of their social group affiliation is the most common way we form impressions, more common than either Gestalts or algebraic impressions (Bodenhausen et al., 1999). Why? Social group categories such as race and gender are among the first things we notice about others upon meeting them. As a consequence, we often perceive people in terms of their social group membership before any other impression is even possible (Devine, 1989). And the Internet provides no escape from this tendency. Without the nonverbal cues and additional information that can distinguish a person as a unique individual, people communicating online are even more likely than those communicating face-to-face to form stereotypical impressions when meeting others for the first time (Lea & Spears, 1992; Spears, Postmes, Lea, & Watt, 2001; Wallace, 1999).

People rarely question the accuracy of their stereotyping. Most of us presume that our beliefs about groups are valid. As a consequence, we have

a high degree of confidence in the legitimacy of our stereotypical impressions, despite the fact that such impressions are frequently flawed (Brewer, 1993). We also continue to believe in stereotypes even when members of a stereotyped group repeatedly behave in ways that contradict the stereotype. In fact, contradictory behavior may actually *strengthen* stereotypes. For example, if you think of Buddhists as quiet and contemplative and meet a talkative and funny Buddhist, you may dismiss his or her behavior as atypical and not worthy of your attention (Seta & Seta, 1993). You'll then actively seek examples of behavior that confirm the stereotype to compensate for the uncertainty that the unexpected behavior aroused (Seta & Seta, 1993). As a result, the stereotype is reinforced.

To lay the groundwork for more flexible and accurate interpersonal impressions, you can overcome stereotypes by critically assessing your beliefs about various groups, especially those you dislike. Is the information in your mental schemata related to these groups accurate or flawed? Then educate yourself about these groups. Pick several groups you feel positively or negatively about. Read a variety of materials about these groups' histories, beliefs, attitudes, values, and behaviors. Look for similarities and differences between people affiliated with these groups and yourself.

Finally, when interacting with members of these groups, keep in mind that just because someone belongs to a certain group doesn't necessarily mean that all of the defining characteristics of that group apply to that person. And since each of us simultaneously belongs to multiple social groups, don't form a narrow and biased impression of someone by slotting him or her into just one group.

Improving Your Perception of Others

Malcolm X is most remembered for his fiery rhetoric denouncing white racism and his rejection of nonviolent protest as a means for dealing with oppression. Less well known is the marked change in his perception and communication that occurred following his April 1964 visit to Saudi Arabia. Malcolm traveled to Mecca for a traditional Muslim Hajj, or pilgrimage, and during his visit underwent a dramatic shift, one he later detailed in a letter home,[3]

> You may be shocked by these words coming from me. But on this pilgrimage, what I have seen and experienced has forced me to rearrange my thought-patterns and toss aside some of my previous conclusions. This was not too difficult. I have always been a man who tries to face facts, and to accept the reality of life as new experience and new knowledge unfolds. I have always kept an open mind, which is necessary to the flexibility that must go hand in hand with every form of intelligent search for truth. During the past eleven days, I have eaten from the same plate, drunk from the same glass, and slept on the same rug—while praying to the same God—with fellow Muslims, whose eyes were the bluest of blue, whose hair was the blondest of blonde, and whose skin was the whitest of white. And in the words and deeds of the white Muslims, I felt the same sincerity I felt among the black Muslims of Nigeria, Sudan and Ghana.

Malcolm's transformation suggests important lessons for everyone interested in improving his or her own perception and communication. Malcolm was able to appreciate the perspectives and feel a strong emotional kinship toward others he previously had dismissed and disparaged based on skin color. He also freely called into question his own judgments, critically assessing prior perceptions and correcting those found to deviate from "the reality of life."

Forty years later, Malcolm X's words of anger and alienation still sound a clarion call for people of all colors to challenge racism and oppression. But his ability to empathize with those he once despised and to question his own perceptual accuracy point us in the direction toward improved perception and interpersonal communication.

Offering Empathy

Empathy counts among the most valuable tools for communicating more effectively with others (Campbell & Babrow, 2004). The word "empathy"

---
[3] Adapted from personal letter of Malcolm X (1964).

SKILLS PRACTICE

This exercise helps you challenge your stereotypes.

❶ Pick a group you've stereotyped.

❷ List characteristics you associate with this group.

❸ Read about this group's history, culture, and traditions.

❹ Identify an acquaintance who is affiliated with this group.

❺ Communicate regularly (but not intrusively) with this person, finding out as much as you can about him or her as an individual.

❻ Revise your initial group description, based on everything you've learned.

● Malcolm X's perception changed after 1964 as shown in these quotes: *(above left)* "Concerning nonviolence, it is criminal to teach a man not to defend himself when he is the constant victim of brutal attacks." *(above right)* "I believe in recognizing every human being as a human being, neither white, black, brown, nor red—when you are dealing with humanity as one family, it's just one human being marrying another human being, or one human being living around or with another human being."

comes from the Greek word *empatheia,* meaning "feeling into." When we experience **empathy,** we "feel into" others' thoughts and emotions, making an attempt to identify with them (Kuhn, 2001).

Although many people think of empathy as a single concept, it actually consists of two separate facets (Davis, 1994). The first is *perspective-taking*—the ability to see things from someone else's vantage point without necessarily experiencing that person's emotions (Duan & Hill, 1996). The second is *empathic concern* (Stiff, Dillard, Somera, Kim, & Sleight, 1988). Empathic concern encompasses the emotional side of considering another's perspective. When you experience empathic concern, you become aware of how the other person is feeling and perhaps even experience some of his or her emotions yourself. You also feel a sense of concern and compassion regarding the other person's emotional state.

Together, perspective-taking and empathic concern create empathy. But experiencing empathy isn't sufficient in itself to improve your interpersonal communication and relationships. You must also *convey* your empathy to others. To effectively communicate the perspective-taking part of empathy, let others know that you're genuinely interested in hearing their viewpoints ("I'd love to get your impression," "What's your take on what's happening?") and tell them that you think their views are important and understandable ("Your perspective on this is really insightful," "Seeing it from your side makes a lot of sense"). To communicate empathic concern, disclose to others that you're concerned about them and their feelings ("I hope you're doing OK," "I'm really concerned about how you're feeling"). Share with them your own emotions regarding their situation ("I feel terrible that you're going through this," "I'm so happy for you!").

Importantly, avoid using "I know" messages ("*I know* just how you feel," "*I know* just what you're going through"). Even if you make such comments with kind intentions, others will likely view you as presumptuous and perhaps even patronizing, particularly if they suspect that you don't or can't feel as they do. For example, when people suffer a great loss—such as the death of a loved one—many don't believe that anyone else could feel the depth of anguish they're experiencing. Saying "I know how you feel" isn't helpful under these conditions.

Checking Your Perception

The second part of improving your perception is embracing willingness, as Malcolm X put it, to "rearrange your thought-patterns" and "toss aside previous conclusions" when they prove to be wrong. This is accomplished through **perception-checking,** a five-step process in which you apply all that you've learned in this chapter to your own perception of others.

1. *Check your punctuation.* People punctuate encounters in different ways, often disagreeing on "who/what started it" or "who/what ended it." This kind of disagreement crops up especially during interpersonal conflicts. When you experience a conflict, be aware of your own punctuation and keep in mind that other people may see things differently. Practice asking others to share their punctuation with you.

2. *Check your knowledge.* Your perception of others is only as accurate as the information you have in your schemata. Never presume that you know the "truth" about what others "really" mean or what they're "really" like. When in doubt, ask others to explain their meaning to you.

3. *Check your attributions.* Avoid the common temptation to attribute others' communication and behavior exclusively to internal causes such

POP QUIZ

Test Your Empathy

Read these statements, marking the ones with which you agree. Total up your check marks and interpret your score below.

Perspective-Taking

_____ Before I criticize a person, I try to imagine how I would view the situation in his or her place.

_____ I believe there are two sides to every question, and I try to look at both sides.

_____ I find it easy to see things from another person's point of view.

_____ I try to look at everybody's side of a disagreement before I make a decision.

_____ When I am upset with someone, I usually try to put myself in his or her "shoes" for a while.

Empathic Concern

_____ When I see a person being taken advantage of, I feel protective toward him or her.

_____ I often have tender, concerned feelings for people who seem less fortunate than I.

_____ I would describe myself as a pretty soft-hearted person.

_____ Other people's misfortunes disturb me a great deal.

_____ I am often touched by the things that I see happen to people around me.

Scoring:

For each section, a score of 0–1 indicates that you have low empathy; 2–3 indicates moderate empathy; and 4–5 indicates high empathy.

Note: This *Pop Quiz* is adapted from Stiff et al. (1988).

Reconciling Intimacy and Uncertainty

1

BACKGROUND

One relationship challenge we face is discovering information about people close to us that increases our uncertainty and changes our impression of them. To understand how you might effectively manage such a relationship challenge, read the case study and work through the five steps that follow.

2

CASE STUDY

Early in the semester, your professor pairs you with Alex for a class project. Although Alex is attractive, you don't really like Alex because the two of you seem very different. But as you get to know Alex better, it turns out both of you like the same music, video games, movies, and food. Although Alex isn't publicly warm or outgoing, in private Alex is kind, honest, and generous. As you spend more time together, you begin to feel attracted to Alex. In time, the two of you become a couple.

Despite your escalating intimacy, Alex's family is a closed topic. One evening at Alex's apartment, you press for more: "I'm always talking about my family, but you never talk about yours," you say. "That's because my family is *my* business," Alex snaps. Stung, you ask, "But can't you at least tell me *something*? I mean, what about your folks. . . ." Alex interrupts you, saying, "My *folks*? You don't have a clue what you're talking about." Hurt, you murmur, "You don't have to be rude." Alex responds, "Congratulations, you've discovered the real me." Angry, you storm out.

The walk home helps you cool off, and you begin reflecting on your relationship. While you have deep feelings for Alex, tonight's incident jacked your uncertainty sky high. You feel unable to predict or explain Alex's next move. You find yourself wondering whether Alex is emotionally unstable and what other undesirable aspects of Alex's personality might emerge.

Arriving home, you call Alex's childhood friend Chris, who approves of the relationship. You tell Chris what happened. Chris says, "Alex will be upset I told you this, but the reason Alex never talks about family is because of fear of what you might think if you knew. Alex doesn't really have a family—Alex was bounced around various foster homes for years, dad left when Alex was a kid and Mom has been in and out of rehab. But you should know that despite all this, Alex is a good person and really loves you."

Afterwards, a million questions race through your mind. Was Alex's outburst triggered by your pressing the issue? Or does it indicate emotional instability? Has your impression of Alex changed in negative, irreparable ways? Is it ethical to hide your knowledge of Alex's childhood, or should you tell Alex what you know? Do you try to patch things up and continue your relationship, or do you use this evening's conflict as a convenient excuse to bail?

YOUR TURN

Think about the interpersonal communication concepts, skills, and insights you have learned while reading this book, especially this chapter. Try to keep all of this in mind while working through the following five steps, which will help you become aware of how you can make better interpersonal communication choices in your relationships. Remember, there are no right answers, so think hard about what choice you will make! (P.S. Need help? See the helpful concepts listed below.)

● **Step 1: Reflect on yourself.** What are your thoughts and feelings in this situation? What attributions are you making about Alex and the interpersonal communication you experienced? Are your attributions accurate? Why or why not?

● **Step 2: Reflect on your partner.** Using perspective-taking and empathic concern, put yourself in Alex's shoes. Consider how your lover is thinking and feeling. How did Alex likely perceive the encounter tonight?

How did this perception shape the exchange you two had? How does Alex likely feel about you and your relationship?

● **Step 3: Identify the optimal outcome.** Think about all the information you have about Alex and about this relationship. Consider your own feelings as well as Alex's. Given all these factors, what's the best, most constructive relationship outcome possible here? Be sure to consider not just what's best for *you*, but what's best for Alex as well.

● **Step 4: Locate the roadblocks.** Taking into consideration your own thoughts and feelings, your partner's, and all that has happened in this situation, what's preventing you from achieving the optimal outcome you identified in step 3?

● **Step 5: Chart your course.** What can you say and do to overcome the roadblocks you've identified and achieve your optimal relationship outcome?

HELPFUL CONCEPTS

as character or personality. Question the legitimacy of any internal attributions you make. Remember that all behavior—including interpersonal communication—stems from a complex combination of internal and external forces.

4. *Check perceptual influences.* Reflect on how culture, gender, and personality are shaping your perception of others. Are you perceiving others as ingroupers or outgroupers? If so, on what basis? How is this perception affecting your communication? Your relationships?

5. *Check your impressions.* Reflect on your impressions as you're forming them. If you find yourself making Gestalts, realize that your Gestalts may bias your perception of subsequent information you learn about a person. Resist stereotyping but also realize that it's difficult to avoid, given the natural human tendency to categorize people into groups upon first meeting. Strive to create flexible impressions, thoughtfully weighing new information you learn about a person and reshaping your overall impression based on new data.

Perception-checking is an intense mental exercise. Mastering it takes time and effort, but the ability to critically check your own perception goes, as Malcolm X wrote, "hand in hand with every form of intelligent search for truth," whether the truth is personal, interpersonal, or universal. When you routinely perception-check, errors are corrected and perception becomes more accurate, balanced, and objective. As a result, you will make fewer communication blunders, and you will be able to tailor your communication to people as they really are, making your messages more sensitive and effective. The ultimate result will also be perceptual: *others* seeing *you* as a skilled and responsive communicator.

Practicing Responsible Perception

We experience our interpersonal reality—the people who surround us, the communicative contacts that join us with them, and the relationships that result—through the lens of perception. But perception is a product of our own creation, metaphorical clay we can shape in whatever ways we want. At each stage of the perception process, decision points exist, choices that empower us to mold our perception in constructive or destructive ways. What do I select as the focus of my attention? What attributions do I make? Do I form initial impressions and cling to them in the face of contradictory evidence? Or do I strive to flexibly adapt my impressions of others as I learn new information about them? The choices we make at each of these decision points feed directly into how we communicate with and relate to others. When we negatively stereotype people, for example, or presume that their behavior derives exclusively from their personality, we immediately destine ourselves to ineffective communication. If someone looks or talks this way, he obviously is an outgrouper, so why empathize with him? If someone is communicating in this way because of who she is, there's nothing *I* can do to change that, so why try?

An essential part of improving our interpersonal communication and relationship decision making is practicing responsible perception. This means routinely perception-checking, correcting errors we make. It means striving to form flexible impressions of people that shift and adapt as we get to know them better. It means striving to see those who populate our interpersonal world through eyes of empathy, honoring their perspectives, emotionally reaching out to them, and communicating this perspective-taking and empathic concern in open, appropriate ways. Practicing responsible perception means not just mastering the knowledge of perception presented in these pages, but translating this intellectual mastery into active practice within interpersonal encounters. We all use perception as the basis for our communication and relationship decision making. But when we practice responsible perception, the natural result is more effective communication and wiser relationship decisions.

POSTSCRIPT

We began this chapter with a tale of failed prophecy. Marian Keech and her core followers believed deeply that Earth was going to be destroyed and that aliens from the planet Clarion were going to rescue them. Their beliefs led them to perceive others and their interpersonal communication in ways that can conservatively be described as unusual.

We often perceive people like Keech as "crazy" or "delusional." How could any sane person perceive prank-pulling college students as extraterrestrials? But to stereotype her in this fashion is to miss the Marian Keech that

exists in all of us. We all like to believe that we're in touch with the real truth about reality and that our perceptions, communication, and relationship decisions are inspired by wisdom that transcends our mundane lives.

What metaphorical "aliens" do you perceive inside the people you meet? How often do you perceive "extraterrestrial brilliance" in others who are merely playing games with you?

The tragedy of Marian Keech and her followers provides us with a powerful parable regarding perception. If we

don't take active responsibility for the perceptions we create, they can lead us to make dramatic and sometimes damaging interpersonal and life decisions. And although we never will be right about all people, all communication, and all of our relationships, we can strive to be right much of the time and in doing so build relationships and lives that avoid interpersonal apocalypses.

Chapter Review

Key Terms

Key Concepts

Perception as a Process

- We make sense of our interpersonal world through **perception,** a process during which we engage in **selection, organization,** and **interpretion** of information received from our senses. This process begins when we focus our attention on certain things, a decision guided by **salience.**

- When we mentally organize information related to interpersonal encounters, we order this information into a chronological sequence that reflects how we experienced the event. When people disagree on **punctuation,** conflicts can arise.

- We interpret the meaning of communication in part by drawing on known information stored in our mental **schemata.** We also make **attributions** regarding why people said and did certain things. Sometimes we fall prey to the **fundamental attribution error,** the **actor-observer effect,** and the **self-serving bias,** all of which draw us away from interpreting communication accurately.

- According to **Uncertainty Reduction Theory,** we commonly experience uncertainty during first encounters with new acquaintances. A number of strategies are available for reducing uncertainty, each of which has advantages and disadvantages.

Influences on Perception

- Culture plays a major role in shaping our perception of communication. When we perceive people as **ingroupers,** we typically view them and their communication more positively than if we perceive them as **outgroupers.**

- Although few gender differences actually exist in how people communicate, people perceive the communication of men and women in very different ways.

- **Personality** influences our perception of the traits we possess and how we perceive the traits of others. **Implicit personality theories** help guide our perceptions of others' personalities. Sometimes they lead us to presume in others traits that they actually don't possess, resulting in ineffective and inappropriate communication.

Forming Impressions of Others

- When we perceive others, we form **interpersonal impressions.** Sometimes we create general **Gestalts,** which quite often are positive, thanks to the **positivity bias.**

- People consider "first impressions" critical because of the **primacy effect.** But the **negativity effect** also plays an important role in shaping how we perceive information that we learn about others.

- When we form strong positive or negative Gestalts, this sometimes leads to a **halo effect** or a **horn effect.** Both of these cause us to perceive subsequent information we learn about people in distorted ways.

- The most accurate and refined impressions of others are **algebraic impressions.** When we carefully calculate our impressions based on each individual trait, we're more likely to see people as they really are and be able to adapt our communication accordingly.

- The most common form of interpersonal impression is **stereotyping** because the first thing we perceive about people is often their social group membership.

Improving Your Perception of Others

- You can improve your perception and communication by feeling and expressing **empathy.** When you can take the perspective of others and experience empathic concern toward them, your communication naturally becomes more sensitive and adaptive.

- Responsible perception is rooted in **perception-checking,** routinely questioning your own perceptions and correcting errors that may lead to ineffective communication.

Key Skills

- Ever experience disputes regarding "who started it"? See pages 82–84 to find out why, as well as how such conflicts can be avoided.

- Want to improve your attribution accuracy, both online and face-to-face? Read the tips on page 87, and check out the *Skills Practice* on page 87.

- How can you reduce uncertainty during first encounters? Learn the different strategies and their advantages and disadvantages on pages 88–89.

- Can you tell the difference between male and female communicators? Test your gender perception in the *Pop Quiz* on page 93.

- Curious about personality and how it shapes perception? Take the online personality test suggested on page 95, and read about the effects of personality on perception on pages 95–98.

- Why do people think first impressions are so important? Review the importance of first and negative information in shaping impressions on pages 100–101, as well as the risks associated with placing too much emphasis on this information.

- Want to form more accurate, balanced, and flexible impressions of others? Learn how by reading pages 101–102 and completing the *Skills Practice* on page 102.

- Interested in overcoming stereotypes? Read the suggestions on pages 104–105, and do the *Skills Practice* on page 105.

- Not sure how to effectively express empathy toward others? See the suggestions on pages 105–106 for how to communicate perspective-taking and empathic concern, including the one phrase you always want to avoid.

- Are you an empathic person? Take the *Pop Quiz* on page 107 to discover your level of perspective-taking and empathic concern.

- Want to master a straightforward process for checking your perceptual accuracy? Consult the steps of perception-checking on pages 107 and 110.

- What relationship decision do you make when you discover uncertainty-increasing information about a loved one that changes your impression? Work through *Making Relationship Choices* on pages 108–109 to find out.

4

Experiencing and Expressing Emotions

Two teenage sisters, growing up in eighteenth-century England. One with "regular features and a remarkably pretty figure," the other "more striking . . . her face so lovely that in the common cant of praise she was called a beautiful girl."[1] Two sisters, doomed to live parallel lives of emotional heartbreak. Two sisters, similar in many ways except one: their firm beliefs regarding how best to manage life's deepest joys, passions, and sorrows.

Published in 1811 (and reenacted in the 1995 movie) Jane Austen's novel *Sense and Sensibility* tells the story of the Dashwood family, focusing on the romantic entanglements and resulting emotions of the sisters Elinor and Marianne. United in family and close friendship, the sisters are divided in their views on expressing emotion. Marianne believes that emotions should be openly vented; Elinor maintains they should be silenced (Ballaster, 1995).

---

[1] All quotes that follow are adapted from Austen, J. (1811/1995).

115

Throughout the story, Elinor and Marianne clash over how emotion should be communicated in relationships. Elinor falls in love with Edward, an unassuming English gentleman. Knowing her family's tendency to exaggeration, Elinor tempers her words carefully when sharing her feelings about Edward: "I do not attempt to deny that I think very highly of him— that I greatly esteem, that I like him." Marianne is outraged by such tepid expression of romantic passion. "Esteem him! Like him! Cold-hearted Elinor! Use those words again and I will leave the room this moment."

When Marianne falls for Willoughby, a dashingly handsome and equally ardent connoisseur of life's passions, her expressions of love contrast sharply with Elinor's cool reserve. Marianne's uninhibited communication prompts Elinor to chide her, provoking Marianne to lash back: "I see what you mean. I have been open and sincere where I ought to have been reserved, spiritless, dull, and deceitful."

In Marianne and Elinor, Austen gave human form to rival notions of emotion management in nineteenth-century British society. Marianne embodied "sensibility": She experienced unmediated emotional reactions and communicated them uninhibitedly (Ballaster, 1995). In extreme form, sensibility is characterized by selfish wallowing in emotion to the exclusion of concern for others. The opposite of sensibility is "sense," personified by Elinor. People who use this approach to emotion management perceive the surrounding world in a dispassionate fashion and suppress their emotions for the betterment of others (Ballaster, 1995).

In her novel, Austen pits Elinor's sense against Marianne's sensibility, demonstrating how these rival approaches lead the sisters to respond to similar events in contrasting ways. For example, when Marianne discovers that Willoughby is engaged, she

explodes into hysterics and sinks into a deep depression. When Elinor finds out that Edward is betrothed, she suppresses her reaction so as not to worry her sisters and mother. Importantly, neither response yields particularly positive outcomes. Elinor suffers months of unspoken torment because of her sense, and Marianne falls gravely ill owing to her sensibility.

Two hundred years ago, Jane Austen used rival approaches to managing emotional experience and expression as narrative tools to divide fictional characters. Today, sense and sensibility continue to divide many of us from constructive relationship outcomes that would be attainable by managing our emotions differently. But we needn't emulate Elinor and Marianne. Instead, we can learn to skillfully manage our emotions in ways that avoid extremes of sense *and* sensibility, improve our communication, and create satisfying interpersonal relationships.

Emotion is the most powerful of human experiences. We bring children into the world, pledge ourselves to others until death does us part, or commit grievous acts of violence, all as a consequence of emotions. Our emotions fill our lives with meaning (Berscheid & Peplau, 2002); to experience emotion is to feel "alive," and to lack emotion is to view life itself as colorless and meaningless (Frijda, 2005).

Because emotion is so powerful, we feel compelled to express this experience to others through communication. When we do, emotion makes a transition from the purely personal to the intensely interpersonal. We have long discussions with loved ones about our feelings toward them and others. In concert with friends, family members, and romantic partners, we poke and prod our emotional states, questioning their authenticity, meaning, and appropriateness. We also make decisions about how best to manage our experience and expression of emotion—decisions that strongly shape our lives. When we skillfully manage emotional experience and expression, our relationship satisfaction and overall life happiness increases. When we ineffectively manage our emotions, our relationships suffer, and these lapses are reflected in relationships and lives torn by anger and sadness.

In this chapter, we examine how to effectively communicate that most personal and interpersonal of human experiences—emotion. You'll learn:

- The important differences between emotions, feelings, and moods, as well as the best approaches to managing negative moods

- Ways in which gender, personality, and culture influence emotion

- Different approaches to managing your experience and expression of emotion, as well as the best strategy for skillfully managing undesirable emotions

- How to deal effectively with passion, anger, and grief, three of the most challenging emotions you'll face in your close interpersonal relationships

The Nature of Emotion

In the movie *Bend It like Beckham*, Jesminder Bahmra is a British girl of Indian descent and a passionate and gifted soccer player (Chadha, 2002). Her parents disapprove strongly of her soccer interest because Indian girls aren't "supposed" to be "footballers" and because of her father's bitter past experience with discrimination when he played sports. After Jess discloses to her parents that she has earned a full-ride soccer scholarship to a U.S. university, she braces herself for a negative response from them. Instead, she is surprised, and then overjoyed, to hear her father express his vehement approval:

> "When those bloody English cricket players threw me out of their club like a dog, I never complained. On the contrary, I vowed that I would never play again. Who suffered? Me. But I don't want Jessy to suffer. I don't want her to make the same mistakes that her father made of accepting life, accepting situations. I want her to *fight*. And I want her to *win*. Because I've seen her play—she's brilliant. I don't think anybody has the right of stopping her."

When we recall emotions we've felt, we typically remember "hot" emotions—physically and mentally intense experiences such as Jesminder's reaction when her father surprises her with loving support. We think of our own joys, angers, sadness, and surprises—experiences during which our palms sweated, our mouths felt dry, and our hearts pounded (Berscheid & Regan, 2005). When we strive to translate these emotions into words, we often use vivid physical metaphors. Sadness is "pain" or "heaviness"; grief, "a living hell." Fear is a sense of "threat lurking everywhere," and love is "an intense longing to be close to someone" (Frijda, 2005).

Defining Emotion

Scholarly definitions of emotion reflect the powerful nature of emotional experience and expression with which we're all familiar. **Emotion** is an intense reaction to an event that involves interpreting the meaning of the event, becoming physiologically aroused, labeling the experience as emotional, attempting to manage our reaction, and communicating this reaction in the form of emotional displays and disclosures (Cacioppo, Klein, Berntson, & Hatfield, 1993; Gross, Richards, & John, 2006). This definition highlights the five key features of emotion. First, emotion is reactive, triggered by our perception of outside events (Cacioppo et al., 1993). The news that a friend's cancer is in remission and that she will make a full recovery leads you to experience joy. You discover an e-mail from your romantic partner's ex-boyfriend in your partner's inbox, and you read with surprise and anger. Your favorite roommate announces that she's switching to a different school, triggering sadness. When an emotion-inducing event occurs, we engage in the same perceptual process as we do with other types of interpersonal events—selecting, organizing, and interpreting information related to that event. As we interpret the event's meaning, we decide whether the incident is positive, neutral, negative, or somewhere in between. Events that are appraised as strongly positive or strongly negative are likely to trigger corresponding emotions (Smith & Kirby, 2004), as are events that we perceive as "unusual" or "unexpected" (Berscheid, 2002).

A second feature of emotion is that it involves physiological arousal, in the form of increased heart rate, blood pressure, and adrenaline release. Many researchers consider arousal the defining feature of emotion, a belief mirrored in most people's descriptions of emotion as "intense" and "hot" (Berscheid, 2002).

Third, to experience emotion, you must become aware of your interpretation and arousal as "an emotion"—that is, you must consciously label them as such (Berscheid, 2002). For example, imagine that you and a good friend have struck a bargain not to discuss with anyone else an event that embarrassed you. One evening at a party, you hear your friend regaling those around him with the tale of your humiliation. Within seconds, you interpret his behavior as negative—a betrayal of your trust. Your face grows hot, and your breathing quickens. But not until several more seconds have passed do you become consciously aware of these physical sensations. This awareness, combined with your assessment of the situation, causes you to label your experience as the emotion "anger."

Fourth, how we each experience and express our emotions is constrained by historical, cultural, relational, and situational norms governing what is and isn't appropriate (Metts & Planalp, 2002). As a consequence, once we become aware that we're experiencing an emotion, we try to

SELF-REFLECTION

Recall a recent event in a close interpersonal relationship that caused you to feel an intense emotion. Then consider all of the physical and mental sensations you experienced. If you had to put your emotional experience into words, what words would you use?

TABLE 4.1

Common Emoticons

:-o	Surprise
:-D	Joyous
:-(	Sad
:-)	Happy
8-O	Astonished
>:-(	Annoyed
>:-<	Angry

manage that experience and express that emotion in ways we consider acceptable. We may allow our emotion to dominate our thoughts and communication, try to channel it in constructive ways, or suppress our emotion completely. Emotion management results largely from the recognition that the totally unrestrained experience and expression of emotion will lead to negative consequences.

And last, when emotion occurs, the choices you make regarding emotion management are reflected outward in your verbal and nonverbal displays, in the form of word choices, exclamations or expletives, facial expressions, body posture, and gestures. Other than arousal, many scholars of emotion consider the central defining feature of emotions to be communication displays that are distinct to only one emotion (Mauss, Levenson, McCarter, Wilhelm, & Gross, 2005).

The communicative nature of emotion is so fundamental that online communicators have developed emoticons, symbols that represent emotional expressions in a text-only fashion in e-mail or during instant-messaging. Emoticons enable people to convey happiness, sadness, anger, and other emotions in a text-only environment (see Table 4.1).

Another way in which emotion is communicative is that we talk about our emotional experiences with our relationship partners, a form of communication known as **emotion-sharing.** Much of interpersonal communication consists of emotion-sharing—disclosing emotions, talking about them, and pondering them. Studies on emotion-sharing suggest that people share between 75 and 95 percent of their emotional experiences with at least one other person, usually a spouse, parent, or friend (Frijda, 2005). The people with whom we share our emotions generally enjoy being confided in. Often, they share the incident with others, weaving a socially intimate network of emotion-sharing.

Sometimes emotion-sharing leads to **emotional contagion,** when the experience of the same emotion rapidly spreads from one person to others. Emotional contagion can be positive, such as when the joy you experience over an unexpected job promotion spreads to your family members as you tell them about it. At other times, emotional contagion can be negative, such as when fear moves quickly from person to person in a large crowd. Such was the case in the 1903 stampede in Chicago's Iroquois Theater, one of the deadliest disasters in American history. A small fire broke out, and although it was quickly extinguished, people's fear regarding the fire spread quickly through the crowd, causing a panicked stampede that killed more than 500 people (Brown, 1965).

Types of Emotion

Take a moment and look at the emotion communicated by the people in the photos on the next two pages. How can you discern the emotion expressed in each picture? One way to distinguish between different types of emotions is to examine consistent patterns of facial expressions, hand gestures, and body postures that characterize specific emotions. By considering these patterns, scholars have identified six emotions they consider **primary emotions**—emotions that involve unique and consistent behavioral displays across cultures (Ekman, 1972). The six primary emotions are surprise, joy, disgust, anger, fear, and sadness. Most of them—disgust, anger, fear, and sadness—also involve distinct patterns of internal physiological arousal as well (Ekman, 1999).

Some situations, like an unexpected gift from a romantic partner or the death of a close relative, provoke especially intense primary emotions. In such cases, we often use different words to describe the emotion, even though what we're experiencing is simply a more intense version of the same primary emotion (Plutchik, 1980). For instance, a gift we receive from a romantic partner may cause intense joy that we think of as "ecstasy," just as the passing of a close relative likely will trigger intense sadness that we label as "grief" (see Table 4.2).

Primary Emotion	High-Intensity Counterpart
Joy	Ecstasy
Surprise	Amazement
Anger	Rage
Disgust	Loathing
Sadness	Grief
Fear	Terror

With whom do you share your emotional experiences? Why do you share your emotions with others? Does such sharing always have a positive impact on your relationships, or does it cause problems at times? Have you ever shared an emotion with someone, only to have the person tell others about it when you wished they hadn't? What does this tell you about the ethics governing emotion-sharing?

TABLE 4.2

Intense Primary Emotions

According to studies performed by psychologist Paul Ekman (1972), people around the world associate the same facial expressions with particular feelings. Part of improving your interpersonal communication is to recognize others' emotions. Can you identify the ones displayed in each of these photographs? (From left to right, the emotions shown are joy, surprise, anger, disgust, fear, and sadness.)

In other situations, an event may trigger two or more primary emotions simultaneously, resulting in an experience known as **blended emotions** (Plutchik, 1993). For example, imagine that you're at a party enjoying the evening with your romantic partner. After a brief bathroom break, you return to find that your partner has disappeared. Then, wandering through the party, you suddenly spy your partner standing in a dark corner of the living room, laughing and smiling with a very attractive person. What emotion do you experience at that moment? Many people in this situation would experience jealousy, a blended emotion because it combines the primary emotions anger, fear, and sadness (Guerrero & Andersen, 1998)—in this case, *anger* at your partner's behavior, *fear* that your relationship may be threatened, and *sadness* at the thought of potentially losing your partner to a rival. Other examples of blended emotions include contempt (anger and disgust), remorse (disgust and sadness), and awe (surprise and fear) (Plutchik, 1993).

Blended emotions can even involve feeling emotions that conflict with each other. For example, after teaching my oldest son Kyle a karate move designed to knock down an opponent, I saw him use the technique against my middle son, Colin. I simultaneously experienced two conflicting emotions: joy at seeing Kyle perfectly render a skill I had taught him and anger that he would recklessly use a self-defense move against his younger brother.

The six primary emotions distinguished by scholars closely approximate Americans' intuitive impressions of emotion types. When asked to identify primary emotions, Americans list six—surprise, joy, love, anger, fear, and sadness (Shaver, Wu, & Schwartz, 1992). At the same time, the American idea of six primary emotions—three positive and three negative—isn't necessarily shared across cultures. In traditional Chinese culture, shame and sad love, an emotion concerning attachment to former lovers, are primary emotions. Traditional Hindu philosophy suggests nine primary emotions: sexual passion, amusement, sorrow, anger, fear, perseverance, disgust, wonder, and serenity (Shweder, 1993).

Feelings and Moods

We often talk about emotions, feelings, and moods as if they are the same thing. But they're not. **Feelings** are short-term emotional reactions to events that generate only limited arousal; they typically do not trigger attempts to manage their experience or expression (Berscheid, 2002). We experience dozens, if not hundreds, of feelings daily—most of them lasting only a few

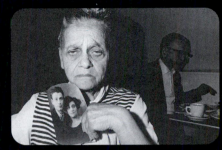

seconds or minutes. An attractive stranger casts you an approving smile, causing you to feel momentarily flattered. A parent calls you unexpectedly when you're trying to work, making you feel briefly annoyed. You find a lost photo of a former romantic partner, triggering a fleeting sense of sentimentality. Feelings are like "small emotions." Common feelings include gratitude, concern, pleasure, tension, hope, bewilderment, relief, and resentment.

Whereas emotions occur occasionally in response to substantial events and feelings arise frequently in response to everyday incidents, moods are different. **Moods** are low-intensity states—such as boredom, contentment, grouchiness, or serenity—that are not caused by particular events and typically last longer than feelings or emotions (Parkinson, Totterdell, Briner, & Reynolds, 1996). Positive or negative, moods are the slow-flowing emotional currents in our everyday lives. We can think of our frequent, fleeting feelings and occasional intense emotions as riding on top of these currents, as displayed in Figure 4.1.

Moods powerfully influence our perception and interpersonal communication. People who describe their moods as "good" are more likely to form positive impressions of others than those who report being in "bad" moods (Forgas & Bower, 1987). People in good moods also are more likely than those in bad moods to perceive new acquaintances as sociable, honest, giving, and creative (Fiedler, Pampe, & Scherf, 1986).

FIGURE 4.1

The Flow of Emotions, Feelings, and Moods

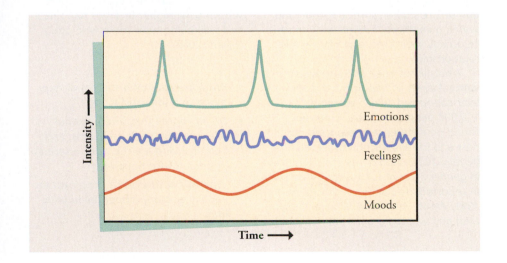

Our moods also influence how we talk with partners in close relationships (Cunningham, 1988). People in positive moods are significantly more likely to openly disclose relationship thoughts and concerns to close friends, family members, and romantic partners. People in negative moods typically prefer to sit and think, to be left alone, and to avoid social and leisure activities (Cunningham, 1988).

FOCUS ON CULTURE

Happiness across Cultures

A Chinese proverb warns, "We are never happy for a thousand days, a flower never blooms for a hundred" (Myers, 2002, p. 47). Although most of us understand that our positive emotions may be more passing than permanent, we tend to presume that greater joy lies on the other side of various cultural fences. If only we made more money, lived in a better place, or even were a different age or gender, *then* we truly would be happy. But the science of human happiness has torn down these fences, suggesting instead that happiness is interpersonally based.

Consider class, the most common cultural fence believed to divide the happy from the unhappy. Studies suggest that wealth actually has little effect on happiness. Across countries and cultures, happiness is unaffected by the gain of additional money once people have basic human rights, safe and secure shelter, sufficient food and water, meaningful activity with which to occupy their time, and worthwhile relationships.

What about age? The largest cross-cultural study of happiness and age ever conducted, which examined 170,000 people in sixteen countries, found no difference in reported happiness and life satisfaction based on age (Myers, 2002). And gender? Differences in gender account for less than 1 percent in reported life happiness (Michalos, 1991; Wood, Rhodes, & Whelan, 1989). Men and women around the globe all report roughly similar levels of happiness. Even population density drops as a predictor of joy: people in rural areas, towns, suburbs, and big cities report similar levels of happiness (Crider, Willits, & Kanagy, 1991).

When asked, "What is necessary for your happiness?" people overwhelmingly cite satisfying close relationships with family, friends, and romantic partners at the top of their lists (Berscheid & Peplau, 2002). Faith also matters. Studies over the last 20 years in both Europe and the United States repeatedly have documented that people who are religious are more likely to report being happy and satisfied with life than those who are nonreligious (Myers, 2002). Finally, living a healthy life breeds joy. The positive effect of exercise on mood extends to broader life satisfaction: people who routinely exercise report substantially higher levels of happiness and well-being than those who don't (Myers, 2002).

YOUR CULTURE

- What are your own sources of happiness and life satisfaction?

- Do you agree that interpersonal relationships, spiritual beliefs, and healthy living are the most essential ingredients for happiness?

- What other sources of happiness are equally or more influential in your life?

Your mood's profound effect on your perception and interpersonal communication suggests that it's important to learn how to shake yourself out of a bad mood (Thayer, Newman, & McClain, 1994). Unfortunately, some of the most commonly practiced strategies for improving bad moods—drinking alcohol or caffeinated beverages, taking recreational drugs, and eating—are also the least effective and may actually worsen your mood (Thayer et al., 1994). More effective strategies for improving bad moods are ones that involve active expenditures of energy, especially strategies that combine relaxation, stress management, mental focus and energy, and exercise. The most effective strategy of all appears to be rigorous physical exercise (Thayer et al., 1994). Sexual activity does not seem to consistently elevate mood.

Forces Shaping Emotion

What I remember most about that Tuesday morning, besides its absolute normalcy, was the beauty of the day. It was gorgeous outside, with a deep, ocean-blue sky and a bite in the air that seemed to say, "Autumn is coming!" Driving my boys to school before heading to the university, I was listening to my favorite station when the DJ joked about how "some idiot has apparently managed to fly his plane into the Twin Towers." Within minutes, however, the truth of that day filled the television and radio airwaves. As rage and grief surged within me, I felt an almost primal compulsion to communicate with my closest intimates. I rushed home to talk with my wife, phoned my friends in New York to make sure they were OK, and called my parents and my brother.

Arriving in the lecture hall an hour later, I found a classroom full of students equally eager to share their emotions. But although we all felt intense negative emotions, the specific nature of our experiences and expressions cut along lines carved by culture, gender, and personality. Visiting students from other countries displayed widely varying reactions. Some remained sad

● It can be tempting to improve bad moods by drinking alcohol or caffeinated beverages, taking recreational drugs, or eating. However, studies show that one of the best ways to feel better is through physical exercise.

SKILLS PRACTICE

This exercise helps you manage negative moods.

❶ Recall a bad mood you experienced and how it influenced your perception and communication.

❷ Identify strategies you used to change your mood. How effective were they?

❸ The next time you're in a bad mood, use one or a combination of the mood-improving strategies suggested in this chapter.

❹ Compare the results of both sets of strategies. Which strategies have the most positive impact on your perception of others and your interpersonal communication?

and silent; others offered quiet condolences or openly vented their anger. Whereas most of the women in my class expressed grief over the loss of life, the men felt blindingly angry. Personality also seemed to make a difference. For example, my less agreeable students vocalized their anger and insisted that the attacks confirmed "the innate evil of human nature."

After September 11, 2001, people around the globe were united by emotional pain. British, German, French, Italian, and Russian heads of state and citizens expressed their unity with Americans. But the faces and voices I saw and heard in my classroom on the morning of 9/11 were both united and divided. We were united in a newly forged bond of anger and sadness over the loss of so many innocent lives, but divided along lines of culture, gender, and personality in how we each experienced this bitter bond.

Culture

In all cultures, children are taught guidelines for where, when, and how to manage and communicate emotions (Saarni, 1993). When people in a given culture agree about which forms of emotion management and communication are socially desirable and appropriate, these norms are called **display rules.** Display rules powerfully shape how we each communicate our emotional experiences to others. For example, on the morning of 9/11, when individuals from disparate cultures experienced the same negative emotions, the manner in which they communicated these emotions differed widely depending on the students' cultural display rules. Some openly wept or angrily shouted; others silently mourned.

Because of differences in socialization, traditions, and ideals, display rules show considerable variation across cultures (Soto, Levenson, & Ebling, 2005). Consider the two fastest-growing ethnic groups in the United States—Mexican Americans and Chinese Americans (Buriel & De Ment, 1997). In traditional Chinese culture, emotional control and moderation are emphasized above all else; intense emotions are considered dangerous and are even thought to cause illness (Wu & Tseng, 1985). This belief shapes communication in close relationships as well; Chinese American couples discussing their relationships display fewer periods of openly expressed positive emotion toward one another than do Euro-American couples (Tsai & Levenson, 1997). In contrast, traditional Mexican culture encourages Mexican Americans

BIG TOP © 2003 Harrell. Dist. By UNIVERSAL PRESS SYNDICATE. Reprinted with permission. All rights reserved.

● In response to tragedy, women experience and express sadness and fear more than men. Men more frequently respond to tragic events with anger.

to openly express emotion, even more so than in Euro-American culture (Soto et al., 2005). For people of Mexican descent, the experience, open expression, and deep discussion of emotions and feelings provide some of life's greatest rewards and satisfactions.

When families from other cultures emigrate to a multicultural society like the one in the United States, the move often provokes tension over which set of display rules should be honored. People more closely oriented to their cultures of origin continue to communicate their emotions in traditional ways; others—usually first-generation American-born children—move away from traditional forms of expression, creating communication differences based on their degree of "Americanization" (Soto et al., 2005). For example, Chinese Americans who adhere strongly to traditional Chinese culture openly display fewer negative emotions than those who are Americanized (Soto et al., 2005). Similarly, Mexican Americans with strong ties to traditional Mexican culture express intense negative emotion more openly than "Americanized" Mexican Americans.

Skilled interpersonal communicators adjust their expression of emotion according to the cultural background of the people with whom they're interacting. Keep in mind that the exact same emotional expression—for example, an open and vivid venting of intense joy—might be considered an enormous breach of social etiquette in some cultures but a healthy and normal behavior in others.

Gender

Across cultures, women who are surveyed report experiencing more sadness, fear, shame, and guilt than men, whereas men report feeling more anger and other hostile emotions (Fischer, Rodriguez Mosquera, van Vianen, & Manstead, 2004). In the United States, gender differences in emotion derive in part from differences in how men and women orient to interpersonal relationships (Brody & Hall, 2000). Women are more likely than men to express emotions that support relationships and suppress emotions that assert their own interests over another's (Zahn-Waxler, 2001). As a consequence, women may feel sadness more often than men because sadness, unlike anger, isn't directed outward at another person; thus it doesn't threaten relationships. Sadness communicates personal vulnerability and signals the need for comforting from others. It therefore reflects a willingness to submit oneself to the care of another. By contrast, anger conveys a motivation to achieve one's own goals or to take satisfaction in one's success over another's (Chaplin, Cole, & Zahn-Waxler, 2005).

Though men and women may experience emotions with different frequency and express these emotions differently, when they experience the same emotions, there is no gender difference in the intensity of the emotion experienced (Fischer et al., 2004). Whether it's anger, sadness, joy, or disgust, men *and* women experience these emotions with equal intensity.

Personality

Like culture and gender, personality exerts a pronounced impact on our emotions. Recall the Big Five personality traits described in Chapter 3—extraversion, agreeableness, conscientiousness, neuroticism, and openness. Of these five, three strongly influence our inward experience and outward communication of emotion (Pervin, 1993). The first is extraversion, the degree to which one is outgoing and sociable versus quiet and reserved. High-extraversion people experience positive emotions more frequently than low-extraversion people. The greater occurrence of positive emotions appears to be due to enhanced sensitivity to positive events. Put simply, high-extraversion people "look for happiness" in their everyday lives, focusing their attention more on positive events than on negative (Larsen & Ketelaar, 1991). High-extraversion people also rate themselves as better able to cope with stress and more skilled at managing their emotional communication than do low-extraversion people (Lopes, Salovey, Cote, & Beers, 2005).

The tendency to think negative thoughts about oneself, known as neuroticism, also affects emotional experience and expression. In a fashion inverse to that of high-extraversion people, high-neurotic people focus their attention primarily on negative events (Larsen & Ketelaar, 1991). Consequently, they report more frequent negative emotions than do low-neurotic people and rate themselves as less happy overall. They also describe themselves as less skilled at emotional communication, and they test lower on scientific measures of emotion management than do low-neurotic people (Lopes et al., 2005).

Another personality trait that influences emotion is agreeableness. People high in agreeableness—those who are trusting, friendly, and cooperative—report being happier in general, better able to manage stress, and more skilled at managing their emotional communication than low-agreeable people. High-agreeable people also score substantially higher on measures of emotion management and are rated by their peers as having superior emotion management skills (Lopes et al., 2005).

SELF-REFLECTION

What emotions do you consider more appropriate to experience than others given your gender? Do you experience these emotions more frequently than other emotions that seem more appropriate for the other gender? What gender-based display rules do you follow when communicating your emotions?

Clearly, your degree of extraversion, neuroticism, and agreeableness influences how often you experience positive and negative emotions and how effectively you manage and communicate these emotions to others. At the same time, keep in mind that personality is merely one of many pieces that contribute to the overall complex puzzle that is emotion. Part of becoming a skilled emotional communicator is learning how your personality traits shade your emotional experience and expression, and treating personality-based emotion differences in others with sensitivity and understanding.

Managing Your Emotional Experience and Expression

On May 23, 2005, actor Tom Cruise appeared on the *Oprah* show. In disclosing his love for Katie Holmes to Oprah Winfrey and her audience, Cruise got so emotionally worked up that he repeatedly dropped onto one knee and punched the air, shouted, and eventually leapt onto Winfrey's sofa and jumped up and down. Cruise's emotional communication was so poorly managed that it set off widespread speculation regarding his emotional stability, possible drug usage, and the question of whether the whole episode was a staged publicity stunt. By August 2005, Cruise's mismanaged emotional communication had spawned a new phrase in the English language—"jumped the couch"—meaning the defining moment when someone completely loses control of his or her behavior and emotions.

Although emotions deeply enrich our relationships and lives, failure to effectively manage our experience and expression of emotion can lead us to behave in ways that can only be described as dysfunctional (Gross et al., 2006). Best friends scream unthinkable things at each other that cause irreparable relationship damage, family members refuse to discuss tensions or resentments for months or even years, and world-famous movie stars leap onto talk-show sofas, all because of ineffectively managed emotions.

Effectively managing your emotions is part of **emotional intelligence:** the broader ability to interpret your own and others' emotions accurately and use this information to manage emotions, communicate them constructively, and solve relationship problems (Gross & John, 2002; Lopes et al., 2005; Salovey, Mayer, & Caruso, 2002). Although you may already have heard or read about "emotional IQ" on television or in magazines, very little media information regarding emotional intelligence is based on scientific study (Salovey et al., 2002). Moreover, most popular tests of emotional intelligence measure little more than existing personality traits such as extraversion and friendliness (Davies, Stankov, & Roberts, 1998). In fact, emotional intelligence can't be accurately measured using pencil-and-paper-type self-report tests at all (Salovey et al., 2002). Instead, you can determine your emotional intelligence only by closely examining your ability to perceive emotions, use emotions to facilitate thinking, understand emotions, and manage your own experience and expression of emotion (Mayer & Salovey, 1997).

Of the skills comprising emotional intelligence, emotion management is the most important for effective interpersonal communication because it is the one that directly influences emotional experience and expression (Lopes et al., 2005). **Emotion management** involves attempts to influence which emotions you have, when you have them, and your experience and expression of them (Gross et al., 2006). As you saw at the beginning of this chapter, emotions naturally trigger attempts to manage them. Consequently, the practical issue is not whether you will manage your emotions but how you can most effectively manage your emotions in ways that improve your interpersonal communication and relationships. Although people use dozens of different strategies to manage their emotions (Gross, 1998), we can distinguish among these strategies based on when they are employed during the emotional experience (Gross et al., 2006).

"You might want to save some of this rage for your woodpecking."

©The New Yorker Collection 2003
Bruce Eric Kaplan from
cartoonbank.com. All Rights Reserved.

Managing Your Emotions After They Occur

One strategy for managing emotions is to try to modify or control them after we become aware of them (Gross et al., 2006). An event triggers arousal, interpretation, and awareness of an emotion. We then consciously try to modify our internal experience and outward communication of that emotion.

The two most common ways people manage emotions after they have been triggered are suppression and venting, strategies that mirror the "sense" and "sensibility" approaches described at the beginning of the chapter. The modern label for Elinor's strategy of sense is **suppression:** inhibiting thoughts, arousal, and outward behavioral displays of emotion (Richards, Butler, &

POP QUIZ

Test Your Chronic Hostility

Place a check mark next to the statements with which you agree. Count up all your check marks, and then use the key below to interpret your score.

_____ Most people are sexually immoral.

_____ Human nature is innately sinful.

_____ I am often annoyed by the behaviors of people around me.

_____ I don't try to cover up my poor opinions of others when they do things that are wrong.

_____ People are basically inconsiderate and selfish.

_____ I've had to sometimes be rough with people who were rude or annoying.

_____ Friends and family members often do things that bother me.

_____ I've often met people who were supposed to be "experts" who were no smarter or better than me.

_____ People often try to take advantage of me.

_____ It's human nature to be self-centered and rude.

Scoring

A score of 0–4 means low hostility. If you've scored in this range, you likely experience anger on an occasional basis, triggered in the normal way by events that you perceive negatively. A score of 5–7 means moderate hostility. If you fall into this range, anger may be an issue of concern in your interpersonal relationships. A score of 8–10 means high hostility. You likely experience anger frequently, and your interpersonal relationships are probably strongly and detrimentally affected by your anger.

Note: Information in this *Pop Quiz* is adapted from the MMPI Hostility subscale (Hathaway & McKinley, 1942).

SELF-REFLECTION

Consider your own use of suppression and venting to manage your emotions. What leads you to choose one or the other strategy? Do you believe that there should be limits to how often you vent or how long you suppress? If so, why? What ethical considerations arise related to each strategy?

Gross, 2003). For example, one participant in an emotion management study describes suppressing his communication of happiness and surprise after scoring well on a college paper in which he had invested little effort (Gross et al., 2006):

> "I didn't work very hard on this paper so I was surprised. My room-mate actually did some work and didn't get a good grade, so he was very down about it. I was very happy inside, but at the same time, I didn't want to show up my roommate because he's my friend. Instead of acting happy and surprised, I kind of put on my academic sad face and said, 'Oh, I didn't do well either.'" (p. 11)

The desire to suppress stems from the recognition that feeling, thinking, and openly communicating certain emotions would be relationally, socially, or culturally inappropriate. Although people sometimes suppress positive emotion, suppression occurs most commonly with negative emotions, especially anger and sadness (Gross et al., 2006). This is because many people recognize that most displays of pleasant emotions elicit favorable responses from others, whereas the expression of negative emotions often drives other people away (Argyle & Lu, 1990; Furr & Funder, 1998).

The inverse of suppression is to manage emotions as Marianne did in *Sense and Sensibility*. This strategy is known as **venting:** allowing emotions to dominate our thoughts and explosively expressing them (Fuendeling, 1998; Kostiuk & Fouts, 2002). Sometimes people vent positive emotion, as Tom Cruise did on *Oprah,* for example. At other times, we vent negative emotions, such as when you "blow up" at a spouse or other family member who has been repeatedly pestering you.

Preventing Emotions

An alternative to managing emotions after they occur is to prevent unwanted emotions from happening in the first place. There are four commonplace strategies for preventing emotions (Gross et al., 2006), the first of which is encounter avoidance. As the label implies, **encounter avoidance** involves staying away from people, places, or activities that you know will provoke emotions that you don't want to experience. For example, suppose that seeing a former romantic partner always provokes intense and unpleasant emotions within you. To use encounter avoidance, you might find out your ex's work or class schedule and then adjust your own schedule so that you systematically avoid running into him or her.

A second preventive strategy is **encounter structuring:** intentionally avoiding specific topics that you know will provoke unwanted emotion during encounters with others. For example, I love my in-laws (honestly!), but my political attitudes are the opposite of theirs. Early in our acquaintance-ship, my father-in-law and I would both get angry whenever we discussed politics. After a few such battles, we agreed to avoid this topic. We have thus structured our encounters so that politics never arises.

A third preventive strategy is **attention focus:** intentionally devoting your attention only to aspects of an event or encounter that you know will not provoke an undesired emotion. Imagine that you're at a family get-together. As your dad is showing everyone DVD footage from your family's recent vacation, two of your cousins sitting in the back of the room are quietly making fun of your father's new haircut. To use attention focus in this situation, you might actively keep watching and listening to your dad so that your cousins' rudeness doesn't set you off.

A fourth way people preventively manage emotion is **deactivation:** systematically desensitizing yourself to emotional experience (Fuendeling, 1998). Some people, especially after experiencing a traumatic emotional event, decide that they no longer want to feel anything. The result is an overall deadening of emotion. Though the desire to use this strategy is understandable, deactivation can trigger deep depression.

Reappraising Your Emotions

Imagine that you receive an affectionate e-mail from a former romantic partner with whom you're in occasional friendly contact. You feel ethically obligated to share this message with your current partner because you've both agreed to be open and honest in your relationship. But you also know that when you show the message to your beloved, he or she will respond by popping off nasty remarks about your ex—the kind of insults that typically anger you. Knowing your own responses to your partner's likely behavior and the destructive communication that will likely ensue, how can you best manage the difficult but unavoidable emotions that will arise when you share the e-mail with your partner?

The most fruitful strategy for engaging difficult and unavoidable emotions is **reappraisal:** actively changing how you think about the meaning of emotion-eliciting situations so that their emotional impact is changed (Gross et al., 2006; Jackson, Malmstadt, Larson, & Davidson, 2000). To use reappraisal in the scenario described above, you might think vividly about your partner's positive aspects, the benefits of your relationship with him or her, and your future together. You could concentrate on your partner's love for you, your love for your partner, the emotional support your partner has offered in the time you've been together, and all the great things you'll be doing together in the coming weeks and months (Richards et al., 2003). As a result of this reappraisal, you'll be more likely to communicate positively in response to your partner—"I know you don't like my ex, and I can totally understand why; I would feel the same if I was in your shoes"—rather than negatively, "Why do you always feel the need to snipe at my ex!?"

Reappraisal is effective because you employ it before a full-blown emotional reaction can commence. This strategy also requires little mental energy and effort compared to trying to suppress or control your emotions after they've occurred. In addition, reappraisal produces interpersonal communication that is appropriately focused on partners and is perceived by partners as emotionally engaged and responsive (Gross et al., 2006). Across studies, people who are most effective at managing their emotional communication report reappraisal as their primary strategy. Reappraisal has been found to decrease emotion and emotion-expressive behavior in situations that elicit negative emotions as well as enhance interpersonal communication effectiveness (John & Gross, 2004).

Although reappraisal is the most effective emotion management strategy, the most widely practiced strategy for managing unavoidable and unwanted emotions is suppression, a strategy with only marginal effectiveness. The effectiveness of suppression is limited because you are trying to modify intense arousal you already are experiencing, the thoughts you already are thinking, and the body's natural inclination to display this arousal and these thoughts in the form of expressions. Research on people who habitually use suppression to manage their emotions suggests that they have lower levels of well-being and substantially lower evaluations of positive relationships with others than people who routinely use reappraisal (Lopes et al., 2005).

Reappraisal demands that you take active responsibility for how you think about interpersonal events. When you reappraise, you literally change your own thoughts about an event before they lead you to experience an undesired emotion. You accomplish this through two steps. First, before or during an encounter that you suspect will trigger an undesired emotion, call to mind the positive aspects of the encounter. Flood your mind with good thoughts. If you truly can't think of any positive things about the other person, your relationship, or the encounter, focus on seeing yourself as the kind of person who can constructively communicate even during unpleasant encounters with people you ardently dislike.

Second, as you hold in mind all the good aspects of the current situation, look ahead to the future. Consider in detail the possible short- and long-term consequences of the current encounter. Think about how you might communicate positively in the here-and-now to shape those consequences in constructive ways.

Although our discussion of reappraisal has focused on the management of negative emotions, you can use reappraisal to effectively manage problematic positive emotions as well. Imagine that you're at work, and you've spent much of your mental downtime this morning pondering a new romantic relationship. You realize that although you're uncertain of your partner's feelings, you know that you are falling in love. A moment later, your partner unexpectedly drops by, saying that he or she "just wanted to see how you were doing." Your adrenaline surges, your heart leaps into your throat, and you feel intense joy bordering on ecstasy. But you also realize that you must manage your emotional communication, lest you "jump the couch" and overwhelm your partner with your intensity, as well as cause a disruption at work.

How might you use reappraisal in this case? You would focus your thoughts on your partner and his or her perspective, recalling that you don't yet know whether the person feels the same way you do. You would also mentally remind yourself why your partner has stopped by (just a casual visit), acknowledge the setting (your workplace, not the appropriate locale for intimate disclosures), and assess your relationship (just beginning). Finally, you would consider the potential consequences of this encounter— such as frightening your partner away. With your emotions managed thanks to your reappraisal, you might say something like, "Wow, it's really great to see you—I was just thinking about you," as opposed to what might have come out of your mouth had you not reappraised: "I can't believe you stopped by—I've been thinking about you nonstop all morning and just realized that I'm totally and completely in love with you!"

Challenging Relationship Emotions

In *Tonto and the Lone Ranger Fistfight in Heaven,* Native American author Sherman Alexie poignantly describes the challenges confronting individuals trying to manage emotions in close interpersonal relationships (1993). In one scene from his book, subsequently depicted in the film *Smoke Signals,* the young boy Victor witnesses his uncles' anger escalate into senseless violence:

> Although it was winter, a hurricane dropped from the sky and fell so hard on the Spokane Indian Reservation that it knocked Victor from his bed. His mother and father were upstairs, hosting the tribal New Year's Eve party, when two Indians began raging. The music was so loud that Victor could barely hear the voices as they escalated their argument. "What is going on?" Victor's father yelled, his voice coming quickly and with force. "Adolph and Arnold are fighting again," Victor's mother said. Adolph and Arnold were her brothers, Victor's uncles. They always fought. Had been fighting since the very beginning. "Well tell them to get out of my house," Victor's father yelled. Victor heard this and ran to his window. He could see his uncles outside, slugging each other with such force that they had to be in love. Strangers would never want to hurt each other that badly. During other hurricanes broadcast on the news, Victor had seen crazy people tie themselves to trees on the beach. Those people wanted to feel the force of the hurricane firsthand, wanted it to be like an amusement ride, but the thin ropes were broken and the people were broken. Sometimes the trees themselves were pulled from the ground and both the trees and the people tied to the trees were carried away. Houses were flattened, their contents thrown in every direction. Memories not destroyed, but forever changed and damaged. Which is worse? Victor wanted to know if memories of his personal hurricanes would be better if he could change them. Or if he just forgot about all of it. Victor had once seen a photograph of a car that a hurricane had picked up and carried for five miles before it fell on a house. Victor remembered everything exactly that way. (pp. 1–3)

Most of us would agree that our emotions are more intense within close relationships than casual ones (Berscheid & Ammazzalorso, 2001). Relationship intimacy enhances the intensity of our emotions because, in close relationships, we forge numerous important connections with our partners. These connections take the form of joint daily activities, common goals, and important, shared life plans. When unexpected events occur that trigger emotions—conflicts, job promotions, accidents—they affect a much broader and personally significant range of activities, goals, and plans within close relationships than within casual attachments (Berscheid, 2002). In simple terms, the higher the intimacy, the higher the personal investment, and consequently the higher the intensity of the emotions springing from life's interruptions.

But with higher intimacy, personal investment, and emotional intensity comes greater personal challenge. Emotional experiences in close relationships are more challenging because the stakes associated with managing them are higher. Skillfully managed, intense emotions fill our relationships with meaning and foster closeness. Improperly managed, these same emotions can lead us to make destructive relationship decisions—choices that leave permanent relationship wreckage akin to the interpersonal hurricane devastation described by Sherman Alexie.

When we ponder the emotions that prove most difficult for us to deal with in our close relationships, several come to mind. For example, romantic jealousy—which we discuss in Chapter 10—is often considered toxic to the health of relationships (Berscheid, 2002) and must be managed effectively for relationships to survive (Guerrero & Andersen, 1998; Salovey & Rodin, 1988). Likewise, fear—of emotional investment, vulnerability, or long-term commitment—can prevent us from forming intimate connections with others (Feeney & Noller, 1990; Mickelson, Kessler, & Shaver, 1997). But of all the emotional experiences we share in our relationships, three—passion, anger, and grief—emerge as especially challenging because they occur frequently, are perceived as uniquely important, and profoundly shape our communication and relationship decision making (Berscheid, 2002).

Passion

Few emotions garner as much media attention and popular concern as passion. Thousands of Web sites, infomercials, books, and magazine articles focus on how to create, maintain, or recapture passion. Feeling passion toward romantic partners seems almost obligatory in American culture, and we often decide to discard relationships when passion fades (Berscheid & Regan, 2005). At the same time, most of us recognize that passion is fleeting and distressingly fragile (Berscheid, 2002).

Passion is a blended emotion, a combination of the surprise and joy coupled with a number of positive feelings such as excitement, amazement, and sexual attraction. People who elicit our passion are those who communicate in ways that deviate from what we expect (triggering surprise and amazement), whom we interpret positively (generating joy and excitement), and whom we perceive as physically pleasing (leading to sexual attraction).

Because passion stems in large part from surprise, the longer and better you know someone, the less passion you will experience toward that person on a daily basis (Berscheid, 2002; Hatfield, Traupman, & Sprecher, 1984; Sprecher & Regan, 1998). In the early stages of romantic involvements, our partners communicate in ways that are novel and positive. The first time our lovers invite us on a date, kiss us, or disclose their love all are surprising events and intensely passionate. But as partners become increasingly familiar with each other, their communication and behavior do too. Things that once were perceived as unique become predictable. Partners who have known each other intimately for years may be familiar with almost all of the com-

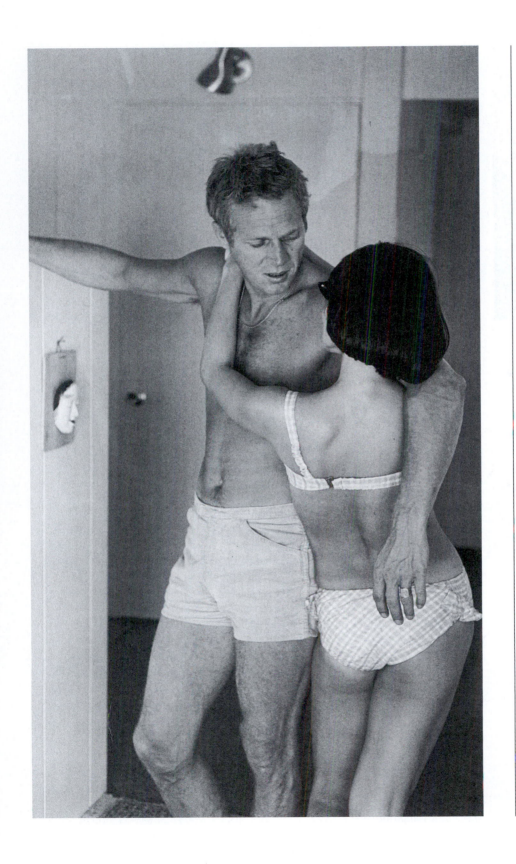

munication behaviors in each other's repertoires (Berscheid, 2002). Consequently, the capacity to surprise partners in dramatic, positive, and unanticipated ways is diminished (Hatfield et al., 1984).

Because passion derives from what we perceive as surprising, you can't engineer a passionate evening by carefully negotiating a dinner or romantic rendezvous. Such surprises could cause you or your partner to experience passion if the event is truly unexpected, but jointly planning and then acting out a romantic candlelight dinner together or spending a weekend in seclusion cannot recapture passion for both you and your partner. When it comes to passion, the best you can hope for in long-term romantic relationships is a warm afterglow (Berscheid, 2002; Reik, 1972). However, this is not to say that you can't maintain a happy *and* a long-term romance; maintaining this kind of relationship requires strategies that we discuss in Chapter 10.

Anger

Anger is our most intense and potentially destructive emotion. It's also common; the average person is mildly to moderately angry anywhere from several times a day to several times a week (Berkowitz & Harmon-Jones, 2004). Anger causes perceptual errors that enhance the likelihood we will respond in a verbally and physically violent fashion toward others (Lemerise & Dodge, 1993). Both men and women report the desire to punch, smash, kick, bite, or do similar actions that will "hurt" others when they are angry (Carlson & Hatfield, 1992).

Anger is a negative primary emotion that occurs when you are blocked or interrupted from attaining an important goal by what you see as the improper action of an external agent—the person who cuts in front of you in line, the doorjamb against which you stub your toe, the rainstorm that disrupts an important ballgame (Berkowitz & Harmon-Jones, 2004). Anger is almost always triggered by someone or something external to us (Scherer, 2001).

SELF-REFLECTION

How has your experience of passion changed over time in your romantic relationships? Have these changes influenced other relationship emotions and feelings? How did you communicate these changes to your partners? Is passion a necessary component of romance, or is it possible to have a romantic relationship without frequent passion?

Anger is driven largely by the perception that the interruption was improper or unfair. Studies manipulating the perceived fairness of outcomes have shown that interruptive events viewed as unfair are much more likely to generate anger than interruptions perceived as fair or just (Weiss, Suckow, & Cropanzano, 1999). So, for example, when your roommate who is always offering to lend you money refuses to give you a much-needed loan, you're more likely to feel angry if you think he or she can afford to give you the loan but is simply choosing not to (you decide that your roommate's behavior is "unjust" given his or her past offers and your current financial standing). By contrast, if you think your roommate is willing but unable to help you (he or she wants to lend you money but has none to give), you'll be less likely to feel anger toward him or her.

The most frequently used strategy for managing anger is suppression. You "bottle it up" inside you rather than let it out. To use this strategy, you might pretend that you're not really feeling angry, blocking your angry thoughts and attempting to control communication of your anger.

Occasional suppression can be constructive, such as when open communication of anger would be unprofessional, or when anger has been triggered by mistaken perceptions or attributions. But *always* suppressing anger can cause physical and mental problems: you put yourself in a near-constant state of arousal and negative thinking known as **chronic hostility.** People suffering from chronic hostility spend most of their waking hours simmering in a thinly veiled state of suppressed rage. Their thoughts and perceptions are dominated by the negative. Chronically hostile people are more likely than others to believe that human nature is innately evil and that most people are immoral, selfish, exploitive, and manipulative. Ironically, because chronically hostile people believe the worst about others, they tend to be difficult, self-involved, demanding, and ungenerous (Tavris, 1989).

A second common anger management strategy is venting: explosively disclosing all of your angry thoughts to the person or persons who triggered them. Many people view venting as helpful and healthy; it "gets the anger out." The assumption that venting will rid you of anger is rooted in the concept of **catharsis,** which holds that openly expressing your emotions enables you to purge them. But in contrast to popular beliefs about the benefits of venting, research suggests that while venting may provide a temporary sense of pleasure, it actually boosts anger. One field study of engineers and technicians who were fired from their jobs found that the more individuals vented their anger about the company, the angrier they became (Ebbeson, Duncan, & Konecni, 1975).

To effectively manage your anger, it's better to use strategies such as encounter avoidance, encounter structuring, and reappraisal. In cases where something or someone has already triggered anger within you, consider using an alternative approach: the **Jefferson strategy,** named after the third president of the United States. Here's how this strategy works: When a person says or does something that makes you angry, you count slowly to 10 before you speak or act (Tavris, 1989). If you are very angry, count slowly to 100; then speak or act. Thomas Jefferson adopted this simple strategy for reducing his own anger during interpersonal encounters.

Although the Jefferson strategy may seem clichéd, it's effective because it creates a delay between the event that triggered your anger, the accompanying arousal and awareness, and your communication response. The delay between your internal physical and mental reactions and your outward communication allows your arousal to diminish somewhat, including reduction of adrenaline, blood pressure, and heart rate. Therefore, you communi-

cate in a less extreme (and possibly less inappropriate) way than if you had not "counted to 10." A delay also gives you time for critical self-reflection, perception-checking, and empathy. These three skills can help you identify errors in your assessment of the event or person and plan an effective response. The Jefferson strategy is especially easy to use when you're communicating by e-mail or instant-messaging, two media that naturally allow for a delay between receiving a message and responding.

Grief

> In the steamer is the trout
> seasoned with slivers of ginger,
> two sprigs of green onion, and sesame oil.
> We shall eat it with rice for lunch,
> brothers, sister, my mother who will
> taste the sweetest meat of the head,
> holding it between her fingers
> deftly, the way my father did
> weeks ago. Then he lay down
> to sleep like a snow-covered road
> winding through pines older than him,
> without any travelers, and lonely for no one.
>   —"Eating Together" by Li-Young Lee

The intense sadness that follows a substantial loss, known as **grief,** is something each of us will experience. We cannot maintain long-term, intimate involvements with other mortal beings without at some point losing a loved one to death, divorce, separation, illness, or some other event. Managing grief is enormously and uniquely taxing. Unlike other negative emotions such as anger, which typically is triggered by a one-time, short-lived event,

TABLE 4.3

Some Online Support Groups

www.griefnet.org	An Internet community of persons dealing with grief, death, and major loss, with almost 60 e-mail support groups
www.compassionatefriends.org	A Web site dedicated to helping families toward the positive resolution of grief following the death of a child
www.webhealing.com	An interactive Web site with online grief discussion
www.caringbridge.org	Free personalized Web sites for those wishing to stay in touch with family and friends by sharing photos, journals, and other information
www.petloss.com	A Web site for people grieving the loss of their pets

grief stays with us for a long time—triggered repeatedly by experiences linked with the loss.

Managing Your Grief.   No magic pill can erase the suffering associated with a grievous loss. It seems ludicrous to think of applying strategies such as reappraisal, encounter structuring, or the Jefferson strategy to such pain. Can you systematically change your thoughts about a friend, family member, or romantic partner you have lost so that the pain goes away? Avoid all mention of your loved one so you feel better? Count to 10 or 100 and find the pain gone? No. Grief is a unique emotional experience, and none of the emotion management strategies discussed in this chapter so far can help you.

Instead, you must use emotion-sharing: talking about your grief with others who are experiencing or have experienced similar pain, or people who are skilled at providing you with much-needed emotional support and comfort. Participating in a support group for people who have lost someone to violent death, HIV/AIDS, cancer, Alzheimer's disease, and so forth can encourage you to share your emotions. When you share you grief, you feel powerfully connected with others—and this sense of connection can be a source of comfort. You also gain affirmation that the grief process you're experiencing is normal. For example, a fellow support-group participant who also lost his mother to cancer might tell you that he, too, finds Mother's Day a particularly painful time or that he, too, finds himself weeping suddenly at inopportune times. Finally, other participants in a support group can help you remember that grief does get gradually more bearable over time.

For those of us without ready access to face-to-face support groups, online support offers a viable alternative (see Table 4.3). Communicating through your computer enables you to emotion-share while at home and overcome the problem of transportation to and from a meeting site (Weinberg, Schmale, Uken, & Wessel, 1995). If you miss a "meeting," you still have direct access to written records of that meeting. Online support groups also provide a certain degree of anonymity for people who feel shy

TABLE 4.4

Examples of Supportive
Communication

Intention	Supportive Communication	Unsupportive Communication
To express sympathy	"I am so very sorry for your loss."	"Believe it or not, you will get over this sooner than you think."
To give support	"Remember that I love you and that you're in my thoughts and prayers."	"You're not helping matters at all by acting like this."
To encourage emotional expression	"Let me know if you need someone just to listen."	"You shouldn't feel so bad."

Note: Information in Table 4.4 is adapted from Burleson and MacGeorge (2002).

or uncomfortable within traditional group settings (Weinberg et al., 1995). You can interact in a way that preserves some degree of privacy. This is an important advantage, as many people find it easier to "discuss" sensitive topics online than face-to-face, where they'd run the risk of embarrassment (Furger, 1996).

Note, however, that individuals participating in online support groups also describe a number of disadvantages of such groups. These include inability to make physical contact with others, lack of nonverbal cues, flaming and off-topic remarks, greater likelihood of deception, and slower responses to messages (Wright, 2000).

Helping Others Manage Their Grief. The challenges you face in helping others manage their grief are compounded by the tendency many have to adopt suppression as the strategy of choice for managing sadness. The decision to use suppression derives from the widespread belief that it's important to maintain a stoic bearing, a "stiff upper lip," during personal tragedies (Beach, 2002). However, a person who uses suppression to manage grief can end up experiencing stress-related disorders such as chronic anxiety or depression. Also, the decision to suppress can lead even normally open and communicative people to stop talking about their feelings. This places you in the awkward position of trying to help them manage emotions that they themselves are unwilling to admit they are experiencing.

The best way you can help others manage their grief is to engage in **supportive communication**—sharing messages that express emotional support and that offer personal assistance (Burleson & MacGeorge, 2002). Effective support messages convey explicit emotional support, sincere expressions of sympathy and condolence, concern for the other person, or encouragement to express emotions (see Table 4.4). Ineffective support messages tell a person how he or she should feel or indicate that the individual is somehow incompetent or blameworthy. Unfortunately, many messages thought to be "supportive" are actually perceived by grieving recipients as unhelpful. In such cases, the supposedly supportive communi-

SELF-REFLECTION

Think about an encounter in which you tried to communicate supportively with a person who was grieving but your efforts only made matters worse. What was it about your communication that was ineffective? Now consider instances in which you successfully comforted a grieving person. How was your communication different?

Making Relationship Choices

Managing Anger and Providing Support

BACKGROUND

1

Managing your anger and providing supportive communication are two skills that can clash when you're trying to support someone who is making you angry. Read the case study, and work through the five steps that follow to learn how you might effectively deal with this situation.

2

CASE STUDY

You're the oldest sibling in a close family in which everyone freely expresses their emotions and often talks about daily events. Of all your siblings, you seem to share an especially close bond with John, the youngest. When John accepts a job offer out of state, you're sad to see him go, but you're excited for his future and take comfort in the daily emails you exchange.

Shortly after John moves away, your grandmother has a heart attack. Doctors initially think she will make a full recovery, so you e-mail John and tell him not to worry. However, her condition suddenly worsens, and she passes away. Everyone is grief-stricken, but John is devastated. He is the only one in your immediate family who didn't see her before she died. John was very close to her because she took care of him during much of his childhood when your mom went back to school.

When John arrives for the funeral, he seems sullen and bitter. But so much is going on that you don't get a chance to talk with him at length. Before you know it, he has left. Following the funeral, John rebuffs your attempts to communicate with him. He doesn't return your e-mails or phone messages, only sending an instant message saying "leave me alone." You become

increasingly worried about how he is dealing with his grief. You leave John a phone message and send an e-mail telling him that you're coming to visit. Despite receiving no response, you opt to go anyway.

Arriving after several hours of grueling travel, you are shocked to find John unwelcoming. Scowling, he says, "What are you *doing* here? I thought I told you to leave me alone." You start getting angry. After all, you spent a good portion of your savings to get here, and you made the trip out of love and concern for John. As you try to manage your anger by using the Jefferson strategy, John attacks: "Oh, I get it. This is the big 'ease your conscience' trip. You figure that if you comfort me, I'll feel better about you lying to me about Grandma's condition. Well, it's not going to work. I didn't get to see her before she died and it's your fault, so why don't you take your self-serving concern and go home!" He slams the door in your face.

You're left standing on the porch, furious. Do you make the several-hour trip home, heeding John's request even though you know he said it out of anger? Or do you pursue your original plan of trying to help John deal with his grief?

YOUR TURN

While working through the following steps, keep in mind the interpersonal communication concepts, skills, and insights you've learned so far in this book, especially this chapter. Also remember: there are no right answers, so think hard about the choice you make! (P.S. Need help? Review the concepts listed below.)

● **Step 1: Reflect on yourself.** What are your thoughts and feelings in this situation? Are your impressions accurate, or could you be mistaken in some way?

● **Step 2: Reflect on your partner.** Put yourself in John's shoes. What is he thinking and feeling? Is his perspective legitimate?

● **Step 3: Identify the optimal outcome.** When you think about this situation, as well as your feelings, John's feelings, and your relationship with him, what's the best, most constructive relationship outcome possible? Be sure to consider not just what's best for *you*, but what's best for all those who are involved.

● **Step 4: Locate the roadblocks.** Taking into consideration your own thoughts and feelings, those of John, and all that has happened in this situation, what obstacles are keeping you from achieving the optimal outcome?

● **Step 5: Chart your course.** What can you say and do to overcome the roadblocks you've identified and achieve your optimal relationship outcome?

HELPFUL CONCEPTS

Gender and emotion, *128*

Emotion management strategies, *131–135*

Intimacy and emotion, *136*

Anger, *138*

Grief, *141*

Supportive communication, *143*

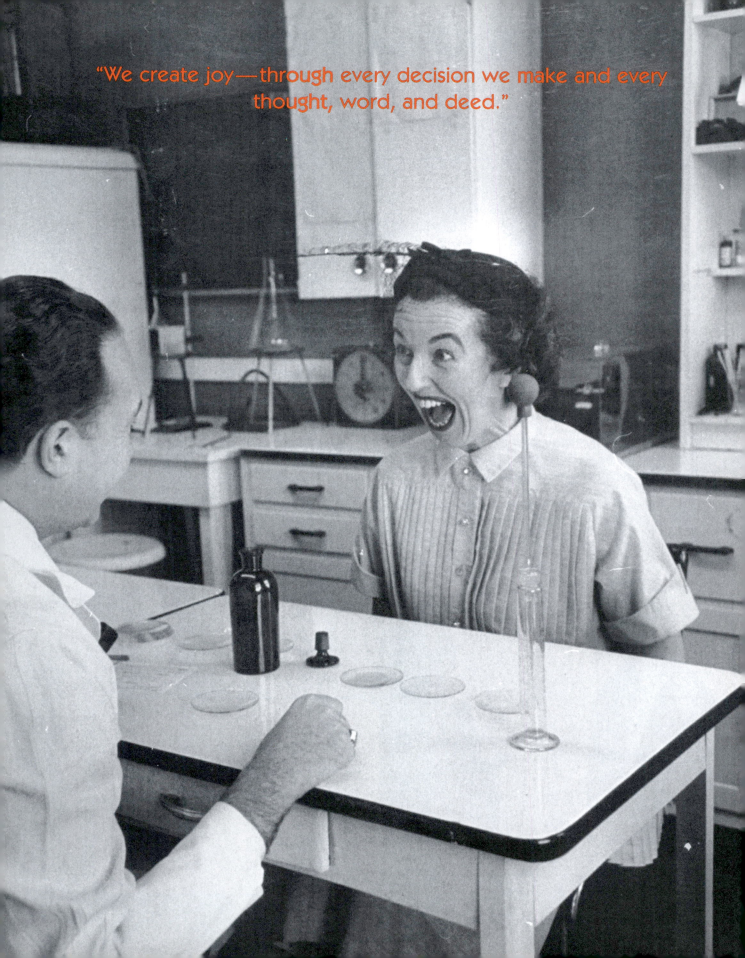

"We create joy—through every decision we make and every thought, word, and deed."

cation may do more harm than good and may damage the relationship between the two individuals (Burleson & MacGeorge, 2002).

Living a Happy Emotional Life

We all live lives rich in relationships and punctuated with emotion. Lovers arrive, bringing gifts of passion and tenderness, and then exit, marking their passage with anger and sadness. Children flash into being, evoking previously unimaginable exhilaration and exhaustion. Friends and family members tread parallel paths, sharing our emotions, and then pass on, leaving grief and memories in their wake.

Across all of our relationship experiences, what balances out our anger and grief is our joy. All human beings share the capacity to relish intense joy and the desire to maintain such happiness in an impermanent and ever-changing world. Also universal is the fact that our personal joy is determined by the quality of our interpersonal connections. When our relationships with family, friends, coworkers, and romantic partners are happy, we are happy, and when they're not, we're not.

Yet joy doesn't drop magically from the sky into our hearts and minds and stay there. *We* create joy—through every decision we make and every thought, word, and deed. When we manage our emotional experiences and communication poorly, the interpersonal sorrows we wreak on others reflect back on us in the form of personal unhappiness. When we steadfastly and skillfully manage our emotions, the positive relationship outcomes we create multiply, and with them, our happiness and the joy of those who surround us.

POSTSCRIPT

In Jane Austen's *Sense and Sensibility*, extreme ways to manage emotion are juxtaposed in the person of two fictional sisters, both of whom suffer because of the way they handle their experience and expression of emotion. Unlike Austen's heroines, however, we have options for emotion management that transcend simple dichotomies. Through our own choice, we can move beyond sense or sensibility into skillfulness. We can manage our emotions after they erupt, prevent unwanted emotions from occurring in the first place, or reshape our thoughts to modulate intense emotions.

How do *you* manage your emotions? Do you retain a cool reserve, or do you love without moderation? What communication choices do you make because of your emotions? How do these choices shape your relationships?

Emotion is indeed the most powerful of human experiences, one that colors our lives with pleasure, pain, and purpose. By learning to effectively manage how we experience emotions and communicate them to others, we can live skillful emotional lives that truly reflect "strength of understanding."

Chapter Review

Key Terms

Key Concepts

The Nature of Emotion

- **Emotion** is the most powerful of human experiences and typically involves thoughts, intense arousal, and communication. Emotions are such significant life events that we feel compelled to engage in **emotion-sharing** with our relationship partners. Sometimes communicating about our emotions leads to **emotional contagion.**

- Six **primary emotions** appear to exist, based on consistent patterns of nonverbal behavior: surprise, joy, disgust, anger, fear, and sadness. Sometimes we experience more than one of these primary emotions simultaneously; the result is **blended emotions.**

- Emotions are relatively rare compared to **feelings,** which occur numerous times daily, and typically arise and decay with little conscious awareness. **Moods** endure much longer than either feelings or emotions and have pronounced effects on our perception and communication. Many of the most widely practiced techniques for improving bad moods are ineffective.

Forces Shaping Emotion

- Culture, gender, and personality all play powerful roles in shaping our experience and expression of emotion. As just one example, we each learn cultural **display rules** growing up that influence what we believe to be socially acceptable and desirable emotional communication.

Managing Your Emotional Experience and Expression

- Effective **emotion management** is a critical part of **emotional intelligence.** Two of the most common ways people manage their emotions after they have occurred are **suppression** and **venting.** Strategies people use for preventing emotions before they occur include **encounter avoidance, encounter structuring, attention focus,** and **deactivation.**

- Of all the strategies available to people for managing emotions, by far the most effective is **reappraisal.** Reappraisal can be used to effectively manage both positive and negative emotions, and it results in dramatically improved emotional communication.

Challenging Relationship Emotions

- Although an entire industry exists offering advice for how to permanently maintain **passion** in romantic relationships, most people experience intense passion in the early stages of their involvements and then a steady decline the longer the relationship endures.
- **Anger** is extremely difficult to manage, given its intensity. People who routinely manage anger through suppression sometimes develop **chronic hostility.** Others mistakenly think that openly venting anger will purge them of it because of their belief in **catharsis.**
- When anger has already been triggered, an additional approach for managing it is the **Jefferson strategy.** Providing a time delay between the onset of anger and your communicative response can be especially effective during online communication.
- **Grief** is intensely demanding. Managing one's own grief is best accomplished through emotion-sharing, whereas providing **supportive communication** is the best approach for aiding others in overcoming their grief.

Key Skills

- Want to improve a bad mood and enhance the effectiveness of your perception and communication as a result? Check out the strategies for improving bad moods on page 125; then complete the *Skills Practice* on page 125.
- Interested in preventing unwanted emotions before they occur? Find out how on pages 132–133.
- Why is reappraisal the most effective strategy for managing emotion? Learn the answer on pages 133–134. Then complete the *Skills Practice* on page 134 to bolster your reappraisal skills.
- Do you use suppression to deal with unwanted anger? You may be putting yourself at risk for chronic hostility. Test your chronic hostility by taking the *Pop Quiz* on page 131.
- Curious about your emotional intelligence? Take the *Pop Quiz* on page 139.
- Interested in an alternative approach for managing anger? Try the Jefferson strategy described on page 140. Then complete the *Skills Practice* on page 140 to learn how it can be used during online communication.
- How can you best manage your own grief? Find out on pages 142–143.
- Want to improve your skill at comforting others when they are suffering grief? Learn how on page 143. Then check out the differences between effective and ineffective support in Table 4.4 on page 143.
- Could you communicate in a supportive fashion toward someone who is making you angry? Find out by completing the *Making Relationship Choices* exercise on pages 144–145.

5

Developing Interpersonal Competence

Cesar Chavez never earned more than $6,000 a year.[1] When he died on April 23, 1993, Chavez left no savings, yet he had transformed the lives of thousands. Through his interpersonal communication competence, Chavez persuaded powerful people to act on behalf of the poorest laborers in America.

During the Great Depression, Chavez's family suffered financial ruin. Leaving their hereditary homestead in Arizona, the Chavezes traveled across the Southwest as migrant workers. Conditions were intolerable. Regularly doused with pesticides by crop-dusting airplanes, workers had to use short-handled hoes that forced them to bend over for hours, which inflicted spinal injuries.

Although young Cesar's home life was poor in material terms, it was interpersonally rich. Cesar's mother, Juana, taught

[1] All information regarding Cesar Chavez is excerpted from the California Department of Education (n.d.), and postings to the Los Angeles County Public Library Cesar Chavez Honorary Web site (Susana, 2004).

151

him to communicate toward others with kindness, regardless of their background or beliefs.

In the late 1940s, Chavez read works by Gandhi, St. Francis, and St. Paul, as well as books on the labor movement. These writings bolstered his belief in the importance of interpersonal communication, in unions as a means for achieving social justice, and in nonviolence. Chavez rallied migrant workers to form a union. From the outset, laborers were inspired by Chavez's word-craft. When he boldly told Euro-American politicians, "It is ironic that those who till the soil, cultivate and harvest the fruits, vegetables, and other foods that fill your tables with abundance have nothing left for themselves," workers knew they had a leader who could communicate in ways that would achieve social justice on their behalf.

In 1962, Chavez founded the National Farm Workers Association, which later became the United Farm Workers (UFW), one of the most powerful unions in the country. Chavez organized strikes and marches protesting work conditions. Although landowners attacked him and his fellow workers with shotguns and dogs, he steadfastly maintained his ethic of nonviolence. His patience and perseverance paid off in the form of legislation ensuring fieldworkers better working conditions and higher wages. In 1975, the U.S. Supreme Court outlawed use of the short-handled hoe.

Although Chavez's successes were public and political, they derived from his interpersonal competence. One UFW volunteer recalled a chance encounter she had with Chavez in Washington, D.C. After delivering a speech, Chavez was ushered away by his bodyguards. When he saw workers who had been volunteering at UFW tables all day, he veered toward them, even as his guards tried to force him toward his car. Chavez shook the workers' hands, saying, "I noticed how you stayed here all day and worked so hard. It is because of you there is a movement. I may be the one who does the speaking, but it is you who make the movement what it is!" The volunteer marveled that Chavez—who by then had attracted worldwide renown— "took the time to learn about each of us; our names, backgrounds, who we were and what we did. I will never forget his humility and kindness."

Before and after his death, Cesar Chavez received many honors, including the Aguila Azteca—the highest civilian award in Mexico—and the U.S. Presidential Medal of Freedom. But his legacy is not just of an American dedicated to justice, nonviolence, and help for the needy. It's proof of the power of interpersonal competence, which can enable any of us to translate the most honorable of personal intentions into interpersonal actions that change the world. Expressed in the simple elegance of Chavez's personal motto, *Sí se puede*— "It can be done."

Interpersonal communication is the means through which we create, maintain, and dissolve human relationships (Burleson, Metts, & Kirch, 2000). But while communication is the "fulcrum upon which the levers of social life are maneuvered," to quote communication scholars Brian Spitzberg and William Cupach (2002, p. 564), it is the competence of our communication that determines the quality of our relationships and life outcomes. Competent communicators report more relational satisfaction (including happier marriages), better psychological and physical health, and higher levels of educational and professional achievement (Spitzberg & Cupach, 2002).

Although people who communicate competently report positive outcomes as a result, they don't all communicate in the same ways. No one recipe for competence exists. To strengthen your interpersonal competence, you must incorporate certain global principles of positive conduct into your everyday life, while also adapting your communication to specific situations and others' needs. And although communicating competently will help you achieve more of your interpersonal goals, it doesn't guarantee that all of your interpersonal problems will be solved.

In this chapter, we focus on general principles for developing interpersonal communication competence. You will learn:

- The three components of interpersonal communication competence and why all three are essential

- Ways to craft competent messages

- Skills for overcoming competence challenges and for coping with incompetent communicators

- Principles for developing your intercultural competence

- Tips for communicating competently online

What Is Interpersonal Communication Competence?

In *The Two Towers*, the second volume in J. R. R. Tolkien's Lord of the Rings trilogy, the army of the wizard Saruman is destroyed and his castle devastated. His conquerors, moving through the wreckage, are astonished to see Saruman appear high above them, in his tower:

> Suddenly another voice spoke, low and melodious, its very sound an enchantment. Those who listened unwarily to that voice could seldom report the words that they heard. Mostly they remembered only that it was a delight to hear the voice speaking, and all that it said seemed wise and reasonable. When others spoke they seemed harsh and uncouth by contrast. For some the spell lasted only while the voice spoke to them. For many the sound of the voice alone was enough to hold them enthralled; but for those whom it conquered the spell endured when they were far away, and ever they heard that soft voice whispering and urging them. But none were unmoved; none rejected its pleas and its commands without effort of mind and will. (Tolkien, 1973, p. 234)

Perhaps you've met people who, like Saruman, leave us spellbound with their words—people who are so skilled in their communication that others seem "harsh and uncouth by contrast." Maybe you have a friend who always sends you just the right e-mail message when you're having a bad day. Or perhaps your boss possesses an uncanny power to explain difficult projects in ways that make them seem doable. Maybe a sibling has won widespread respect for integrity and honesty.

But the truth is there's nothing magical about such abilities. **Interpersonal communication competence** means consistently communicating in ways that meet three criteria: appropriateness (your communication follows accepted norms), effectiveness (your communication enables you to achieve your goals), and ethics (your communication treats people fairly) (Spitzberg & Cupach, 1984; Wiemann, 1977). Each of these three characteristics is essential. Although we sometimes equate competence exclusively with politeness or ability to achieve goals, it is only through the fusion of appropriateness, effectiveness, and ethics that true competence is achieved.

Acquiring knowledge of what it means to communicate competently is the first step in developing interpersonal communication competence (Spitzberg, 1997). As we learn information about what it means to interpersonally communicate in a competent fashion, we transcend the merely intuitive, developing a level of comprehension and knowledge far beyond what we could have achieved through common sense alone. The second step is learning how to translate this communication knowledge into **communication skills**, repeatable goal-directed behaviors, behavioral patterns, and behavioral sequences that you routinely practice in your interpersonal encounters and relationships (Spitzberg & Cupach, 2002). Both steps require something that is often overlooked. To become a competent communicator, you must be motivated to improve your communication. If you do not believe your communication needs improvement, or if you believe that competence is unimportant or no more than common sense, competence

SELF-REFLECTION

How would you define interpersonal communication competence? Is it appropriate, effective, and ethical or some other set of qualities and actions? Is competence just common sense?

will be difficult, if not impossible, to refine. But if you are strongly motivated to improve interpersonal communication, you can master the knowledge and skills necessary to develop competence.

Appropriateness

In the *Seinfeld* episode "The Pitch," Jerry and George are waiting in the NBC corporate office when "Crazy Joe Davola," an acquaintance of Jerry's, approaches them, and the following encounter transpires (David & Cherones, 1992).

JOE: Hello Jerry.

JERRY (EXTENDING HIS HAND): Hey Joe! How you doing?

JOE: You're under no obligation to shake my hand.

JERRY: Oh, no, just a custom. . . . You look good!

JOE: Why shouldn't I look good?

JERRY: Oh, no reason. You're into karate, right?

JOE: You want to hit me?

JERRY: What are you doing here?

JOE: I dropped a script off.

JERRY: Ahh, good for you. Well. . . .

JOE: You don't have to say anything.

SELF-REFLECTION

Think of an interpersonal encounter in which different people expected very different things from you in your communication. How did you choose which expectations to honor? What were the consequences of your decision? How could you have communicated in a way perceived as appropriate by the other participants in the encounter?

● A German submarine captain during World War I, Martin Niemöller (1892–1984) was a Lutheran pastor who denounced Adolf Hitler as "anti-Christian" and a "false prophet." Sacrificing appropriateness to state the truth, Niemöller wrote the following celebrated poem in 1945, while imprisoned in the Dachau concentration camp.

First they came for the communists, and I did not speak out—
Because I was not a communist;
Then they came for the socialists, and I did not speak out—
Because I was not a socialist;
Then they came for the trade unionists, and I did not speak out—
Because I was not a trade unionist;
Then they came for the Jews, and I did not speak out—
Because I was not a Jew;
Then they came for me—
And there was no one left to speak out.

The first characteristic of competent interpersonal communication is **appropriateness**—the degree to which your communication matches situational, relational, and cultural expectations regarding how people should communicate. In any interpersonal encounter, norms exist regarding what people "should" and "shouldn't" say, and how they "should" and "shouldn't" act. Part of developing communication competence is refining your sensitivity to these norms and adapting your communication accordingly. People who fail to adapt their communication to situational norms are perceived by others as incompetent communicators, like Joe in the *Seinfeld* example.

People who are highly sensitive to appropriateness and adapt their communication accordingly are called **high self-monitors** (Snyder, 1974). As the name implies, such individuals closely monitor their own communication to ensure they're acting in accordance with situational expectations (Giles & Street, 1994). Not surprisingly, because their communication is influenced by an overarching concern for appropriateness, high self-monitors prefer situations in which clear expectations exist regarding how they're supposed to communicate. And they may feel uncertain when such expectations are not clearly defined (Miller, Cody, & McLaughlin, 1994).

In contrast, **low self-monitors** are not sensitive to appropriateness. Instead, they believe that people should communicate the same way regardless of the situation. They don't assess their own communication or the situation, and they prefer encounters in which they can "act like themselves" rather than having to abide by norms (Snyder, 1974). As a consequence, they are more likely than high self-monitors to communicate in ways that others perceive as inappropriate.

Communicating appropriately is a key part of competence. Yet *overemphasizing* appropriateness can backfire. If you focus exclusively on appropriateness and always adapt your communication to what others want, you may end up forfeiting your freedom of communicative choice to peer pressure and being perceived negatively (Burgoon, 1995). For example, think of a person who always gives in to what others want and never advocates for his or her own goals. Is this individual a competent communicator? How about the friend who always tells people only what they want to hear rather than conveying the truth? Or the colleague who never raises a dissenting voice, even when it's critically important to do so, out of fear that others will consider opposition inappropriate? As these examples suggest, exclusive attention to appropriateness can hurt both the communicator and those around him or her.

Effectiveness

The second characteristic of competent interpersonal communication is **effectiveness**, the ability to use communication to accomplish interpersonal goals (Parks, 1994). Recall the three kinds of interpersonal goals discussed in Chapter 1. Self-presentational goals represent your desire for others to perceive you as a certain kind of person. Instrumental goals are the practical things you want to achieve in a particular situation. And relational goals represent the connections you want to cultivate with your communication partners. Effective communication enables you to accomplish all three types of interpersonal goals.

Yet there's rarely a single communicative path for achieving all of these goals. Indeed, sometimes you must make trade-offs among the three types of goals. For example, a critical part of maintaining satisfying close relationships is the willingness to occasionally sacrifice instrumental goals in order to achieve important relational goals. Suppose you badly want to see a movie tonight, but your romantic partner needs your emotional support to handle a serious family problem. Would you say, "I'm sorry you're feeling bad—I'll call you after I get home from the movie" (emphasizing your instrumental goals)? Or would you say, "I can see the movie some other time—tonight I'll hang out with you" (emphasizing your relational goals)? The latter approach, which facilitates relationship health and happiness, is obviously more competent.

Ethics

You meet "Chaz" in an Internet chatroom. He introduces himself as a full-time staff member for a national charity. Over the weeks that follow, Chaz befriends several people in the chatroom. Through his articulate and persuasive e-mails and postings, he manages to get you and the rest of his virtual friends to donate money to his charity. Then you discover that he and his charity are fraudulent. In the aftermath, you certainly would have to credit Chaz for both appropriateness and effectiveness. His online communication always adhered to Web site norms; in fact he was charming and polite. He also successfully used his interpersonal communication to accomplish his

SELF-REFLECTION

Consider how you balance the three types of interpersonal goals in your communication. In what situations do you prioritize one type of goal over another? Which of the three types do you tend to emphasize most often? Why?

POP QUIZ

Test Your Self-Monitoring

Place a check mark next to the statements you agree with. Then count the total number of statements you checked to see if you're a high or low self-monitor.

_____ I find it easy to imitate others' behavior.

_____ When I'm uncertain how to act during an interpersonal encounter, I look to others' behaviors for cues.

_____ I would probably make a good actor.

_____ In different situations and with different people, I often act like very different persons.

_____ Even if I'm not enjoying myself, I often behave as if I'm having a good time.

_____ I find it easy to change my behavior to suit different people and situations.

_____ I sometimes appear to others to be experiencing deeper emotions than I really am.

_____ I'm pretty good at making other people like me.

_____ I'm not always the person I appear to be.

Scoring:

0–4 indicates you're probably a low self-monitor; 5–9 suggests you're a high self-monitor.

Note: This *Pop Quiz* is adapted from the self-monitoring scale provided by Snyder (1974).

self-presentation, instrumental, and relational goals. Yet you also would be correct to view him as an incompetent communicator, given the unethical way in which he applied his communication skills.

The final defining characteristic of competent interpersonal communication is that communication decisions are driven by a set of standards regarding moral behavior, known as **ethics** (Spitzberg & Cupach, 2002). But what standards underlie competence? Scholars interested in ethics and interpersonal communication suggest that, at a minimum, we are obligated to avoid intentionally hurting others through our communication. By this standard, communication that's intended to erode a person's self-esteem, that expresses intolerance or hatred, that intimidates or threatens others' physical well-being, or that expresses violence is unethical and therefore incompetent (Parks, 1994). Such communication damages others' well-being, our interpersonal relationships, and the broader society in which we live (National Communication Association, 1999).

But to practice ethical communication, we must go beyond simply not doing harm. Competent communication is also founded on treating others with respect (Cupach & Canary, 1997). During every interpersonal encounter, we need to strive to treat others as valuable and worthy and to communicate with them honestly, kindly, and positively (Englehardt, 2001).

Crafting Competent Messages

A plaque posted on the wall of the karate dojo where I train reads, "Patience when it is easy is not patience; only in situations where waiting is intolerable can true patience be achieved." In an analogous fashion, all of us are capable of competence in contexts that demand little of us—situations where it's easy to behave appropriately, effectively, and ethically. True competence is developed when we consistently communicate competently across *all* situations that we face—contexts that are uncertain, complex, and unpleasant as well as those that are simple, comfortable, and pleasant. Consider the following situation (O'Keefe, 1988).

You've been assigned to a group project in one of your classes. Your final grade will depend to a great extent on how well the group project turns out. You were assigned to your group by the professor, who also designated you as the group leader. Your duties include telling the professor what grade you think each individual in the group deserves, based on his or her individual contributions to the project.

As the project gets under way, one group member, Ron, begins presenting some problems. Ron seldom makes it to group meetings on time and he skipped one meeting without calling anyone in advance to let the group know. At the next meeting, Ron arrived late. He apologized for missing the previous meeting, and mentioned something about "family problems." Ron then volunteered to do all the background research on one important aspect of the project, saying he had a special interest in that topic.

The group project is due next week. The group planned to put together the final draft of the report presentation at a meeting scheduled for tomorrow afternoon. Ron calls you up today and says he doesn't have his library research done and can't get it finished before the meeting. He says he needs more time. *What would you say to Ron?*

This situation is difficult precisely because it forces you to consider complex and competing goals. You probably feel frustration with Ron that you're tempted to vent in inappropriate and unethical ways: "You just don't care about this project, do you, Ron?" Yet it's also possible that Ron failed to complete his work for legitimate reasons—he may actually have serious family problems. Your overarching objective is to motivate Ron to get his work done. Figuring out how to communicate with him in an appropriate, effective, and ethical fashion is a vivid test of your competence.

Three Kinds of Messages

Communication scholar Barbara O'Keefe devoted more than a decade to studying people's responses to communication situations such as the one involving Ron (O'Keefe, 1988; O'Keefe & Lambert, 1995). She found that

● The ways people express respect vary across culture and time. This statue with bent knees illustrates the way Baule people showed respect in Ivory Coast in the nineteenth century.

when asked what they would say to Ron, people consistently created one of three types of messages.

- "Ron, you jerk! I can't believe you don't have the work done! This is why I hate group projects—no one ever gets the work done that they're supposed to. Things like this always happen to me."

- "Ron, you said you'd get the work done on time, so you have to stick to your promise. I know you've been having problems, but everyone

FOCUS ON CULTURE

Competence and Age

The aging of the American population is a demographic change that highlights the importance of communicating competently with seniors. For example, although only 12.4 percent of Americans are currently over the age of 65, by the year 2100 this percentage will almost double to 23 percent (Gist & Hetzel, 2004).

Unfortunately, when communicating with seniors, many young and middle-aged people shift to "elderspeak"—a form of language characterized by a slower-than-usual rate, a sing-song voice, elevated pitch and volume, frivolous terms ("cutie-pie," "sweety"), and simplified vocabulary and grammar (Williams, Kemper, & Hummert, 2003). Elderspeak is sometimes referred to as "secondary baby talk" because it mirrors the way adults speak to very young children (Kemper & Harden, 1999).

More than 20 percent of nursing home staff communication with seniors consists of elderspeak (O'Connor & Rigby, 1996). In other settings, young and middle-aged communicators use elderspeak when talking with seniors. The longer any particular cross-age encounter endures, the more likely the younger participant is to resort to elderspeak (Kemper, Ferrell, Harden, Finter-Urczyk, & Billington, 1998).

Why do people use elderspeak? In part, they may presume that seniors are incompetent communicators. Some research does suggest that elderspeak can be effective with seniors who are quite elderly or hearing-impaired, but seniors consistently report perceiving elderspeak as patronizing and insulting, and they almost never use it with each other—the most telling indicator of its perceived incompetence. When used consistently over a period of time, elderspeak can trigger decreased self-esteem, depression, withdrawal, and dependence (Kemper & Harden, 1999; Ng, 1998). So how can you communicate competently with seniors? The same way you communicate with any other person—respectfully and with genuine appreciation for their worth.

YOUR TURN

- Think of an encounter in which someone modified his or her communication with you because of your age. How did this communication affect you?

- Now consider how you modify your communication when talking with others who are substantially older or younger than you. Is modifying your communication in this way a sign of competence or incompetence? Why?

● The Tupperware party became popular in the 1950s as a marketing strategy and as a social event. It was a complex and highly uncertain communication environment in which saleswomen tried to sell plastic containers while socializing. A high degree of interpersonal competence was required if the saleswoman were to be successful.

has problems, and our first priority is completing this project. As group leader, it's my responsibility to make sure you have it done. Have the work done by the group meeting tomorrow, or I'll have to fail you from the group."

• "Ron, thanks for letting me know. How much more time do you need? What's going on with your family that's keeping you from getting this work done? Is there anything I can do to help? How about this: I'm planning on going to the library tomorrow morning anyway, so why don't I swing by your place around ten, and pick you up? That way we can both get our work done. What do you think?"

As you can see, in the first message, the speaker sacrifices communication competence by ignoring appropriateness, effectiveness, and ethics altogether. This individual expresses random and negative thoughts and feelings toward Ron. In the second message, the speaker focuses solely on effectiveness, demanding that Ron accomplish his goals and making threats, such as "have the work done . . . or I'll have to. . . ." In the third message, the speaker successfully blends appropriateness, effectiveness, and ethics by negotiating agreements with Ron to complete his required work. O'Keefe labeled these differences in message design "expressive," "conventional," and "rhetorical" (McCornack, 2004).

SELF-REFLECTION

What are the pros and cons of each message to Ron? Which one would you describe as the most competent? What message would you use to communicate with Ron? Why?

Expressive messages have one and only one purpose: to convey what you think and feel so that others know what you think and feel. Although these messages are perfectly acceptable within casual and friendly encounters of the "how's it going" variety, in more difficult and perplexing situations such as the Ron encounter these messages prove problematic. People who use expressive messages divulge thoughts and feelings even if doing so is inappropriate, ineffective, or unethical. For example, "What are you talking about, Ron? You don't have it done? You must be crazy! Man, I should have known better than to trust a loser like you."

Conventional messages emphasize the achievement of instrumental goals in a situation; thus, they focus narrowly on effectiveness. People who craft this type of message attempt to achieve their goals by citing social roles and obligations and wielding power over the other person. For example, "Ron, everyone is expecting me, as group leader, to make sure that this project gets done. You promised to have the work done for tomorrow, so you're obligated to have it done. Everyone is expecting you to have it done. Make sure that you turn it in on time!"

Rhetorical messages signal an attempt to answer the question "How can I best talk about this situation so that the problems we're facing are solved?" Individuals who use rhetorical messages recognize that something can be a "big deal" or "no big deal," depending on how the people involved communicate about it. Rhetorical messages successfully blend all three ingredients of competent communication—appropriateness, effectiveness, and ethics. For example, "Hey Ron, thanks for calling and letting me know. No big deal—we have until next week to wrap the project anyway. How's your family doing? Is there anything I can do to help? I know what it's like to have personal problems that interfere with school work—I went through that myself last semester. We do need to get rolling on this stuff, though. I'm planning on heading to the library tonight. Can I pick you up so we can work on the project together? What do you think?"

Using Rhetorical Messages

Rhetorical messages feature four characteristics that make them uniquely competent. These messages address a situation's problems in neutral and nonjudgmental ways ("No big deal—we have until next week to wrap up the project"). They also openly express empathy in the form of both perspective-taking and empathic concern ("I know what it's like to have personal problems"). In addition, such messages offer specific, workable solutions to the practical problems at hand and suggestions for how these solutions can best be implemented, making them exceptionally effective in accomplishing interpersonal goals ("I'm planning on going to the library tonight. Can I pick you up so we can work on the project together?"). Last, rhetorical messages open doors to negotiation. Rather than trying to wield power over the other person, speakers who use rhetorical messages convey equality in status and strive to negotiate mutual consensus ("What do you think?").

"People who craft rhetorical messages treat others as unique human beings whose feelings, attitudes, and goals deserve acceptance and respect."

Viewed from both humanistic and scientific perspectives, rhetorical messages are more competent than conventional and expressive messages. People who craft this type of message treat others as unique human beings whose feelings, attitudes, and goals deserve acceptance and respect—an approach to communication that facilitates interpersonal relationships (Buber, 1970). These qualities contrast sharply with those of conventional messages, which emphasize others' social roles (Ron is a "group member" rather than a person). They also trump expressive messages, which dehumanize recipients and treat them as objects. And scientific research over the last two decades documents that across people and situations rhetorical messages are perceived as more competent than both conventional and expressive messages (McCornack, 2004). People view those who consistently use rhetorical messages as more effective leaders and more likable individuals (O'Keefe & McCornack, 1987).

How can you craft rhetorical messages? Practice incorporating the four characteristics described above. The next time you find yourself in a difficult situation, talk about it in a neutral and nonjudgmental way. You don't have to be dishonest in your description of what's going on, but keep in mind that how you describe an event goes a long way toward shaping others' perceptions of that event. Also, strive to experience and express empathy toward the other person through perspective-taking and empathic concern—no matter how difficult this may be. When others know that you can appreciate their feelings and perspectives, they'll be more willing to accommodate your goals. And rather than simply telling people what you want them to do, offer ideas for removing obstacles to accomplishing those objectives. Finally, as you present these suggestions, frame them as possibilities rather than dictates. The goal of rhetorical messages is always to create mutual consensus with others rather than wielding power over others or trying to threaten or coerce them.

Preventing Interpersonal Incompetence

Tyrus "Ty" Cobb was arguably the greatest baseball player of all time.[2] Across the 24 seasons he played, he compiled a .367 batting average, the highest in the history of the game. And he was the first player inducted into the Baseball Hall of Fame. But Cobb was also notorious for his interpersonal communication incompetence. Cobb viewed communication as a means for aggressively manipulating people in self-serving ways.

For example, in 1911, Cobb, playing for the Detroit Tigers, was vying with Cleveland's Shoeless Joe Jackson for the batting title. As the two teams entered a six-game series, Jackson had a 9-point lead over Cobb. Jackson

---

[2] All information that follows regarding Ty Cobb is excerpted from Ty Cobb (n.d.).

● "The base paths belonged to me. The rules gave me the right. I always went into a bag full of speed, feet first. I had sharp spikes on my shoes. If the baseman stood where he had no business to be and got hurt, that was his own fault." –Ty Cobb

was one of the few players in the league who got along with Cobb, and the two had been friends on and off the field for years. But Cobb badly wanted the title, so he decided to play a communication "head game" with Jackson. Every time Jackson greeted him, Cobb ignored the greeting and snapped rude and hostile remarks in response. Jackson became so worried that he had done something to jeopardize their friendship that he became distracted and his batting deteriorated. To complete his ploy, Cobb gave Jackson a warm farewell as the series wrapped up, further bewildering him. Cobb won the batting title. Later, he boasted about how he had successfully manipulated Jackson and exploited their friendship to his advantage.

However, Cobb's notoriously incompetent interpersonal communication was not without costs. He died on July 17, 1961, a sad and lonely man, twice divorced and nearly friendless. From all of baseball—a sport he had dominated for more than 20 years—only three former players attended his funeral.

Interpersonal communication incompetence can take a wide range of forms—from extreme manipulation of others to refusal to accept constructive criticism to profound discomfort with meeting strangers. But regardless of the form, we each must combat incompetence in ourselves as well as cope with others' incompetence in productive ways. In the following sections, you'll discover strategies for dealing with three particularly common forms of communication incompetence.

Communication Apprehension

You move into a rental house that is shared with four other people. In the days that follow, you learn that each of your new housemates has a different fear regarding communication. Meta seems to dread interaction of any kind. She rarely leaves her room and never hangs out with the rest of the housemates. Despite your best efforts at getting her to "open up," she appears anxious and uncomfortable whenever you try to initiate a conversation. Jonathan is the house goof. He's always cracking jokes and playing pranks. Yet one day he reveals that he's terrified of talking in front of groups, and he doesn't know how he's going to survive his public-speaking class this semester. Confident and friendly, Shekinah serves as the house manager, organizing the finances, setting schedules, and doing repairs when needed. One evening, as you're giving her a lift home from work, you're pulled over for speeding. After the officer gives you a ticket, you notice that Shekinah seems agitated, almost panicked. When you ask her what's wrong, she says that two weeks ago she and her brother were pulled over and roughed up by the same officer, simply because they were African Americans driving through a white neighborhood at night. Your fourth housemate, Sarah, seems very down-to-earth. But one afternoon, she appears distressed. She tells you that she's dreading going home this weekend because she and her mother had a fight and she knows she has to resolve the situation.

Each of these housemates is suffering from **communication apprehension**—fear or anxiety associated with real or anticipated communication with another person or persons (Daly, McCroskey, Ayres, Hopf, & Ayres, 2004). Four types of communication apprehension exist, as displayed by the four housemates (McCroskey & Richmond, 1987, 1991). Trait communication apprehension, represented by Meta, is an enduring tendency to experience fear and anxiety with all communication (spoken, written, face-to-face, online) and regardless of the situation (home, office, classroom). Context communication apprehension, illustrated by Jonathan, is fear and anxiety in response to communication in a particular type of situation, including public speaking, first meetings, job interviews, and oral exams. Receiver communication apprehension, experienced by Shekinah, is fear and anxiety consistently experienced during communication with a particular type of person or group. Temporary communication apprehension, shown by Sarah, is a spontaneous, short-term experience of fear and anxiety regarding communication with a particular person or group. Fundamentally different from the other three types, temporary communication apprehension is triggered by an interpersonal event that causes a person to become briefly apprehensive about communicating.

Communication apprehension can create severe problems for sufferers. People with high degrees of apprehension experience intense discomfort while interacting with others and therefore have difficulty forging productive relationships. Such individuals also commonly experience physical symptoms including nervous stomach, dry mouth, sweating, increased blood pressure and heart rate, mental disorganization, and shakiness (McCroskey & Richmond, 1987).

Overcoming Communication Apprehension. Most of us experience context, receiver, or temporary communication apprehension at some points in our lives. And we can overcome each of these through hard work and perseverance. But trait communication apprehension, the rarest of the four types, is a serious and disabling problem that requires professional treatment with a licensed therapist who specializes in this area.

The key to overcoming context, receiver, and temporary communication apprehension is to develop competent **communication plans**—mental maps that describe exactly how communication encounters will unfold—*prior* to interacting in the situation or with the person or types of people who cause your communication apprehension. Competent communication plans comprise two elements. The first is **plan actions**, the "moves" you think you'll perform in an encounter that causes you anxiety. In creating a competent communication plan, you need to map out in advance the topics you will talk about, the messages you will say in relation to these topics, and the physical behaviors in which you will engage.

The second part of a competent communication plan is **plan contingencies**, the messages you think your communication partner or partners will say during the encounter and how you will respond. To develop plan contingencies, think about the topics your partner will likely talk about, the messages your partner will likely present, your partner's reaction to your communication, and your response to your partner's messages and behaviors.

When you create and then implement a communication plan during an encounter that causes you apprehension, the experience is akin to playing chess. While you're communicating, envision your next two, three, or four possible moves—your plan actions. Try to anticipate how the other person will respond to those moves and how you will respond in turn. The goal of this process is to interact with enough confidence and certainty to reduce the anxiety and fear you normally feel during such encounters.

Shyness and Loneliness. Many people who experience communication apprehension also report suffering from shyness and loneliness. **Shyness** is the tendency to be timid and reserved, and to talk less when in the presence of others (Daly & McCroskey, 1984). It's the third most common psychological problem reported in the United States. Shyness affects 40 to 50 percent of Americans; 15 to 20 percent suffer from chronic shyness (Carducci & Zimbardo, 1995). Shy people often commit speech errors, fail to contribute to conversations, appear tense, produce disorganized and incoherent messages, and avoid eye contact with conversational partners (Buss, 1984; Daly & Stafford, 1984).

Loneliness is defined as feelings of social isolation and lack of companionship (Russell, Peplau, & Cutrona, 1980). Loneliness also is associated with communication shortcomings. People suffering from chronic loneliness are perceived by others as poor communicators (Berger & Bell, 1988). They express difficulty in talking with new acquaintances, have trouble making friends, and find it hard to share their feelings with others (Chelune, Sultan, & Williams, 1980).

Both shyness and loneliness hamper people's ability to create competent communication plans. Communication researchers Charles Berger and

---

SKILLS PRACTICE

This exercise helps you create competent communication plans.

1 Think of a situation or person with whom you consistently suffer communication apprehension.

2 Envision yourself interacting in this situation or with this person.

3 List detailed plan actions: topics you will discuss, messages you will present, and actions you will take. Keep in mind appropriateness, effectiveness, and ethics.

4 List detailed plan contingencies: events that might happen during the encounter, things the other person will likely say and do, and your responses.

5 Implement your plan the next time you communicate in that situation or with that person.

● Shyness and loneliness affect a person's verbal and nonverbal communication, creating a vicious cycle from which it is difficult to extricate oneself.

Robert Bell (1988) found that when asked to generate communication plans for various situations, people scoring high on shyness and loneliness generated the least competent plans. In fact, shyness, loneliness, and the inability to create competent communication plans are intertwined. Shy people report not knowing what to say or do during interpersonal encounters. Because they lack communication plans and don't know how to create them, they avoid interaction with others, and they suffer from high levels of loneliness as a result.

Defensiveness

Your mother criticizes you repeatedly about the clothes you wear, prompting you to lash back, "What makes you think I care about your opinion?!" At work, you suggest an alternative approach to a coworker, but she snaps, "We've *always* done it this way." You broach the topic of relationship concerns with your romantic partner, but he or she shuts you down, telling you to "Just drop it!"

A second type of interpersonal incompetence is **defensive communication,** incompetent messages delivered in response to suggestions, criticism, or perceived slights. People who communicate defensively rudely dismiss the validity of what another person has just said. They also refuse to make internal attributions about their own behavior, especially when they are at fault. Instead, they focus their responses away from themselves and on the other person.

Four types of defensive communication are common (Alexander, 1973; Waldron, Turner, Alexander, & Barton, 1993). Through **dogmatic messages,** a person dismisses suggestions for improvement or constructive criticism, refuses to consider other views, and continues to believe that his or her behaviors are acceptable. With **superiority messages,** the speaker suggests that he or she possesses special knowledge, ability, or status far beyond that of the other individual. In using **indifference messages,** a person implies that the suggestion or criticism being offered is irrelevant, uninteresting, or unimportant. Through **control messages,** a person seeks to squelch criticism by controlling the other individual or the encounter.

Defensiveness is undeniably incompetent, because it violates norms for appropriate behavior, rarely succeeds in effectively achieving interpersonal goals, and treats others with disrespect (Waldron et al., 1993). People who communicate in a chronically defensive fashion suffer a host of negative consequences, including high rates of conflict and lower satisfaction in their

● Chronic loneliness may be in part genetic. Studies of twins have found that if one twin suffers from chronic loneliness, the other twin likely does as well. This pattern does not occur for adopted siblings.

Dogmatic message	"Why would I change? I've always done it like this!"
Superiority message	"I have more experience and have been doing this longer than you."
Indifference message	"*This* is supposed to interest me?"
Control message	"You need to remember who you're talking to" or "Let's talk about something else, shall we?"

TABLE 5.1

Examples of Defensive Communication

SELF-REFLECTION

Recall a situation in which you were offered a suggestion, advice, or criticism and you reacted defensively. What caused your reaction? What attributions did you make about the other person's communication? What were the interpersonal outcomes of your defensive communication? How could you have prevented a defensive response?

personal and professional relationships (Infante, Myers, & Burkel, 1994). Yet even highly competent communicators behave defensively on occasion. Defensiveness is an almost instinctive reaction to behavior that makes us angry—communication we perceive as inappropriate, unfair, or unduly harsh. Consequently, the key to overcoming it is to control its triggering factors. For example, if a certain person or situation invariably provokes defensiveness in you, practice preventive anger management strategies such as encounter avoidance or encounter restructuring (discussed in Chapter 4). If you can't avoid the person or situation, use techniques such as reappraisal and the Jefferson Strategy (also in Chapter 4). Given that defensiveness frequently stems from attributional errors—thinking the other person is "absolutely wrong" and you're "absolutely right"—perception-checking (Chapter 3) also can help you reduce your defensiveness.

To prevent others from communicating defensively with you, use rhetorical rather than conventional or expressive messages when communicating suggestions, advice, or criticism. At the same time, realize that communicating rhetorically is not a panacea for curing chronic defensiveness in another person. Some people are so deeply entrenched in their defensiveness that any communication you offer, no matter how competent, will still trigger a defensive response. In such situations, the best you can do is strive to maintain ethical communication by treating the person with respect. You might also consider removing yourself from the encounter before it can escalate into intense conflict.

Verbal Aggression

The most notable aspect of Ty Cobb's interpersonal incompetence was his **verbal aggression**, the tendency to attack others' self-concepts rather than their positions on topics of conversation (Infante & Wigley, 1986). Verbally aggressive people denigrate others' character, abilities, or physical appearance rather than constructively discussing different points of view. They may also use profanity against them. Verbal aggression can be expressed not only through speech but also through behaviors, such as physically mocking another's appearance, displaying rude gestures, or assaulting others (Sabourin, Infante, & Rudd, 1993). For example, Ty Cobb once verbally abused a groundskeeper who was tending a training field, and when the groundskeeper's wife tried to intervene, Cobb grabbed her by the throat and choked her, leading to his arrest on charges of assault.

Why are some people verbally aggressive? At times, such aggression stems from a temporary mental state. Most of us have found ourselves in situations at one time or another where various factors—stress, exhaustion, frustration or anger, relationship difficulties—converge. As a result, we "lose our heads" and spontaneously "go off" on another person. Some people who are verbally aggressive suffer from chronic hostility. Others frequently aggress because it helps them achieve short-term interpersonal goals (Infante & Wigley, 1986). For example, people who want to cut in front of you in line, win an argument with you, or steal your parking spot before you can slide your car into it may believe that they stand a better chance of achieving these objectives if they use insults, profanity, and threats. And their experiences may bolster this belief. After all, many people give in to those who are verbally aggressive, which encourages the aggressor to use the same technique again.

If you find yourself consistently communicating in a verbally aggressive fashion, identify and address the root causes behind your aggression. Has external stress (job pressure, a troubled relationship, a family conflict) triggered your aggression? Do you suffer from chronic hostility? If you find that anger management strategies don't help you reduce your aggression, seek professional assistance.

Communicating with others who are verbally aggressive is also a daunting challenge. Dominic Infante, a leading aggression researcher, offers three tips. First, avoid communication behaviors such as teasing, baiting, or insulting that may trigger verbal aggression in others. Second, if you know someone who is chronically verbally aggressive, avoid or minimize contact with that person. For better or worse, the most competent, practical solution for dealing with such individuals is to not interact with them at all. Third, if you can't avoid interacting with a verbally aggressive person, remain polite and respectful during your encounters with him or her. Allow the individual to speak without interruption. Stay calm, and express empathy (when possible). Avoid retaliating with personal attacks of your own; they will only further escalate the aggression. And finally, end interactions when someone becomes aggressive, explaining gently but firmly, "I'm sorry, but I don't feel comfortable continuing this conversation."

Improving Your Intercultural Competence

In the summer of 2002, graduate student Min Liu flew from her home in Shanghai, China, to the United States to begin work on her communication PhD.[3] Ten days after her arrival she was teaching American undergraduates in a university classroom, despite the fact that she felt unprepared. "Had I known the problems I was to get myself into," she commented later, "I wouldn't have come." From the start, Ms. Liu's students criticized her as being "difficult to understand" and "not speaking English well enough to teach," despite the fact that she spoke fluent English and had passed a battery of language proficiency exams.

This scenario has become increasingly common. More than 30 percent of university graduate teaching assistants are foreign-born, and complaints regarding their communication competence in university classrooms have skyrocketed in recent years (Gravois, 2005). But although students put the blame for incompetence squarely on their instructors' shoulders, education and speech communication professor Donald Rubin says the blame has been misplaced. Rubin argues that much of the difficulty American students experience when communicating with foreign-born instructors stems from

---

[3] Information regarding Min Liu is adapted from Gravois (2005).

● Competence is a useful guide in new contexts where we have little to tell us what to do. But what might be effective, appropriate, and ethical for us might not be to someone else, so it is important to remain flexible and accepting.

students' tendency to presume that "nonnative instructors will be poor instructors and unintelligible speakers" (Gravois, 2005). This presumption leads students to experience comprehension difficulties that do not correlate with the actual quality of instructors' communication. To document this, Rubin conducted a series of studies. American students listened to an audiotape lecture, and either they were told the speaker was "John Smith from Portland" and were shown a photo of a Euro-American instructor or they were told the speaker was "Li Wenshu of Beijing" and were shown a photo of a Chinese instructor. When students were asked afterward to fill in missing words from a printed transcript of the lecture, students who had listened to "Li Wenshu" made 20 percent more errors than students who had listened to "John Smith," despite the fact that the audiotape was identical. From this outcome, Rubin concluded, "All the pronunciation improvement in the world [by foreign instructors] will not by itself halt the problem of students' dropping classes or complaining about their instructors' language" (Gravois, 2005).

Clearly, given the ever-increasing cultural diversity of the American population, we all must work harder to develop **intercultural competence**, the ability to communicate appropriately, effectively, and ethically with people from diverse backgrounds. But strengthening intercultural competence is no small feat because definitions of competent communication vary across cultures. Take appropriateness. Most Americans link smiling with happiness and view smiling as appropriate in positive social contexts. Many Japanese, however, smile not only to express happiness and affection but also to mask embarrassment and unpleasantness. Japanese smile at funeral guests, and badly defeated Japanese athletes or students who receive poor grades veil their shame by smiling (Chen & Starosta, 1998). Such differences easily can lead to communication misunderstandings. For example, an American interacting with a Japanese acquaintance might say something inappropriate or

offensive and then misinterpret the acquaintance's resulting smile of embarrassment as enjoyment or supportiveness for what has been said and continue their offensive conduct as a result.

Consider effectiveness and ethics (Martin, Flores, & Nakayama, 1998). In collectivistic cultures, people expect one another to put self-presentation and relational goals above instrumental goals, if necessary, to maintain harmony during interpersonal encounters. For example, suppose you're a participant in a group project and the other members agree to pursue the project in a particular way. If you lived in a collectivistic culture, you would be expected to support the group's decision even if you favored an alternative approach. Withholding your dissenting opinion would equal effective communication.

In individualistic cultures, however, the inverse is true. People who strongly voice their opinions and emphasize instrumental goals during encounters are typically judged as competent communicators. If you openly challenged the group's decision by suggesting an alternative approach and your approach ended up netting everyone a high grade, you would be praised for your "out-of-the-box" thinking. And if you withheld your opinion and the others discovered this fact, they might well decide that you acted unethically.

You can strengthen your intercultural competence by applying two broad principles: world-mindedness and attributional complexity (Bush, Rose, Gilbert, & Ingram, 2001; Shah, King, & Patel, 2004).

Are You World-Minded?

When you possess **world-mindedness**, you demonstrate acceptance and respect toward other cultures' beliefs, values, and customs (Hammer, Bennett, & Wiseman, 2003). You can practice world-mindedness in three

● Intercultural competence is so important that the United States Air Force now provides intercultural competence training to its overseas service members. In a course taught at the Special Operations School, students learn about communication traditions in Latin America, Africa, and Asia.

● Margaret Mead was the most famous female anthropologist of the twentieth century. She visited American Samoa, New Guinea, and Bali to learn more about the societies that thrived there, befriending the people while studying their customs and rituals.

ways. First, accept others' expression of their culture as a natural element in their interpersonal communication, in the same way that your interpersonal communication is a reflection of your cultural background (Chen & Starosta, 1998). Second, avoid the temptation to evaluate others' viewpoints as "better" or "worse" than your own cultural beliefs, attitudes, and values. Third, consistently treat people from different cultures with respect. This can be especially challenging when differences between you in race, nationality, religion, or sexual orientation seem unbridgeable or when the other person's cultural ways conflict with your own beliefs, attitudes, and values. But in the same way that communicating ethically means more than just "do no harm," practicing world-mindedness means more than just coldly "tolerating" cultural differences you find perplexing or problematic. Treating people with respect means communicating in a consistently kind and courteous fashion, and endeavoring to preserve others' personal dignity by respecting their rights to possess viewpoints that differ from yours.

World-mindedness is the opposite of **ethnocentrism**, the belief that one's own cultural beliefs, attitudes, values, and practices are superior to those of others. Highly ethnocentric people view their own culture as the center of everything and the standard against which all other cultures should be judged (Neulip & McCroskey, 1997; Sumner, 1906). Ethnocentric people tend to presume that their own communication is competent while that of people from other cultures is incompetent.

Remember: Check Your Perceptions and Practice Empathy

Another way to improve your intercultural competence is to acknowledge **attributional complexity**, the fact that other people's behaviors have multiple and complicated causes. To develop awareness of attributional complexity, observe others' behavior and analyze the forces influencing it. Also, take the initiative to learn more about other cultures, so you can better understand why others communicate as they do.

In addition, routinely check your perceptions of others (a practice discussed in Chapter 3) to avoid attributional errors, and regularly demonstrate empathy. In situations where the cultural gaps between you and others seem impossibly wide, try to see things from others' perspectives. Consider the motivations underlying their interpersonal communication and relationship choices. Examine how people from diverse backgrounds make deci-

---

POP QUIZ

Test Your Intercultural Competence

Place a check mark next to each statement you agree with. Then total your check marks to determine your intercultural competence score.

World-Mindedness:

_____ It would be better to be a citizen of the world than of any particular nation.

_____ Lifestyles in other cultures are just as valid as those in my culture.

_____ Our responsibility to people of other cultures ought to be as great as our responsibility to people of our own culture.

_____ I respect the values and customs of other cultures.

_____ Our schools should teach the history of other cultures as well as that of our own culture.

Attributional Complexity:

_____ I enjoy analyzing the reasons for behavior of people from other cultures.

_____ I'm interested in how my own thinking works when I make judgments about people from other cultures.

_____ To understand the personality or behavior of someone from another culture, I have found it important to know how that person's attitudes, beliefs, and character traits fit together.

_____ I think a lot about how culture influences other people's thoughts, attitudes, and behaviors.

_____ I enjoy learning about other cultures through reading, watching foreign films, and surfing the Internet.

Scoring:

0–4 represents low intercultural competence; 5–10 represents high intercultural competence.

Note: Items in this *Pop Quiz* were developed from adaptation of Neulip and McCroskey (1997) and Shah, King, and Patel (2004).

sions, and compare their approaches to how you make your own choices. And finally, ask others to explain the reasons underlying their behavior, and then accept and validate their explanations ("That makes sense to me") rather than challenging them ("You've got to be kidding!"). Avoid making statements indicating that you presume you understand others' motivations—such as, "I know that people like you act this way because you think that . . ." or "I'm sure, given your background, you thought that. . . ."

Improving Your Competence Online

Early in Helen Fielding's novel *Bridget Jones's Diary*, Bridget receives an unexpected—and shocking—e-mail message from her philandering boss (Fielding, 2001):

> *Message Pending* suddenly flashed up on top of screen. Delighted by, well, anything—as always am if is not work—I nearly jumped out of my skin when I saw *Cleave* at the bottom of the message. I instantly thought he had been able to tap into the computer and see that I was not getting on with my work. But then I read the message:
>
> *Message Jones:* You appear to have forgotten your skirt. As I think is made perfectly clear in your contract of employment, staff are expected to be fully dressed at all times. (p. 20)

Online communication—whether e-mail, instant messaging, or some other form—provides enormous benefits. It enables us to meet and form friendships and romances with people we wouldn't encounter otherwise, and it helps us maintain established relationships (Howard, Rainie, & Jones, 2001). It bolsters our sense of community. Whereas people used to gather around the proverbial water cooler to chat, now they can use discussion groups, listservs, and blogs as social gathering places (Shedletsky & Aitken, 2004). And when communicating online, we're judged by the quality of what we say rather than how we look. As researcher Mac Parks notes, this has a liberating effect: people can form relationships based on who they are rather than how they physically appear (1996).

But as Cleave's inappropriate e-mail to Bridget demonstrates, online communication also poses unique challenges for those interested in developing interpersonal competence. When we communicate face-to-face, we draw upon nonverbal cues such as facial expression, vocal tone, and the surrounding environment to help us understand one another. When interacting online, we don't have access to such cues, and this constraint makes miscommunication more likely (Shedletsky & Aitken, 2004). Jokes can be easily misinterpreted as insults, and sarcastic messages perceived as literal. In addition, because online communication involves the exchange of written text without accompanying nonverbal cues (emoticons notwithstanding), the words take on more importance and intensity than those exchanged during face-to-face interactions (Shedletsky & Aitken, 2004). The result is that inap-

SELF-REFLECTION

Compare the experiences you've had with online communication and face-to-face encounters. How are norms for appropriateness different online than face-to-face? Which interpersonal goals do you find easier to achieve online? When interacting online, what ethical challenges do you face that don't arise when you're communicating in person?

propriate messages—such as Cleave's e-mail to Bridget—can seem especially shocking and incompetent.

The benefits and pervasiveness of online communication are undeniable. But given its specific challenges, how can you ensure that you communicate competently in this medium? Throughout this text, we discuss strategies and skills such as the use of emoticons and the significance of usernames. In this chapter, however, we look at the broad principles of competent online communication.

Adapting to Online Norms

How might you develop your interpersonal competence online? Begin by understanding and adapting to the norms for appropriateness that govern online communication. In general, rules determining what is said and how it is said are much looser online than face-to-face. Indeed, an overall norm of **online disinhibition** exists, whereby people more openly and directly share personal information during online interactions (Suler, 2004). Online disinhibition stems from several factors, including a feeling that online communication is more anonymous, the lack of immediate feedback, and the perception that online communication occurs in a space separate from our day-to-day reality.

Consider the impact that online disinhibition has on first encounters. Because the only source of information during such interactions is the text that is exchanged, people expect each other to quickly disclose detailed and personal information (Walther & Parks, 2002). Online conversational partners meeting for the first time ask more direct, personal questions of each other and share more personal information than do face-to-face partners (Tidwell & Walther, 2002). And online communication partners who ask personal questions and give personal answers during first meetings rate one another highly in terms of competence. In contrast, individuals who ask personal questions or who share intimate information during initial face-to-face encounters are often judged as incompetent.

However, online disinhibition also gives rise to **flaming:** inappropriately aggressive messages that people typically wouldn't communicate face-to-face. Flaming is a predictable product of online disinhibition because people are more willing to discuss and react to controversial ideas online than they are face-to-face. Moreover, the lack of softening nonverbal cues worsens the impact of flaming; insulting words traded online are more readily perceived as personal attacks than the same words exchanged face-to-face (Shedletsky & Aitken, 2004). For these reasons, flaming constitutes incompetent communication.

Some people intentionally post flaming messages in discussion groups just to get attention or disrupt the interaction, a practice known as **trolling** (Barnes, 2003). Although it may seem harmless or even amusing, trolling can spawn serious consequences. One British computer user hacked into an American high school student's account to flame a discussion group. The student was blamed for the incident; she lost her e-mail account and was expelled from her high school for abusing the computer system (Barnes, 2003).

Making Relationship Choices

When a Friend Fails You

1

BACKGROUND

A particularly daunting challenge to practicing interpersonal competence is trying to balance appropriateness, effectiveness, and ethics when a friend or romantic partner disappoints you deeply. To consider how you might effectively deal with such a situation, read the case study and work through the five steps that follow.

2

CASE STUDY

Tara is a close friend of several years. You count on her for emotional support and share many interests. A few months ago, Tara started a demanding degree program, and now it seems you never get to talk or spend time with her. You only communicate via e-mail, and Tara's messages sound distant and preoccupied. You care about Tara a great deal and still consider her a close friend, but you have begun to feel that you're putting more effort into this relationship than she is.

Recently, Tara has made dates to go to the movies, hang out, or attend a party with you. But in each case, she has e-mailed you at the last minute to cancel. Tara's messages have been kind and apologetic, and she has always explained that the intense demands of school are preventing her from socializing much. Though you understand that Tara's school work is demanding, you're beginning to feel frustrated by her repeated cancellations.

After two weeks of no communication, Tara e-mails you and apologizes for her unavailability and explains that she had been working on an important project. Now the project is done, and she wants to spend some time with you and get caught up. Tara invites you to lunch on Wednesday and offers to treat, "to make up for the last couple of months." Delighted, you immediately accept Tara's invitation.

On Wednesday morning, you check your e-mail. You see a message from Tara, with the subject line: "PLEASE READ IMMEDIATELY!" To your immense annoyance, you read, "I hate to do this, because I was really looking forward to seeing you, but I'm going to have to cancel our lunch today. I'm running behind on my project, and I've got to get it done now. Please e-mail me to let me know you got this message in time. Thanks!"

Preparing to respond, you find yourself struggling with competing emotions. You're hurt and angry, and your gut impulse is to flame Tara. But you also want to get together with her and rebuild your friendship. At the same time, her actions make you wonder if she values the relationship. With all of these thoughts and emotions, you begin writing a response: "Tara. . . . "

Note: This *Making Relationship Choices* exercise is adapted from the "friend lunch" situation originally developed by O'Keefe and Lambert (1989).

3

YOUR TURN

While working through the following steps, keep in mind the interpersonal communication concepts, skills, and insights you've learned so far in this book, especially in this chapter. Also remember: there are no right answers, so think hard about the choice you make! (P.S. Need help? Review the concepts listed below.)

- **Step 1: Reflect on yourself.** What are your thoughts and feelings in this situation? What attributions are you making about Tara and her interpersonal communication? Are your attributions accurate? Why or why not?

- **Step 2: Reflect on your partner.** Using perspective-taking and empathic concern, put yourself in Tara's shoes. Consider how your friend is thinking and feeling. How did Tara likely perceive your planned lunch together? How is her graduate work affecting your friendship? How does Tara likely feel about you and your relationship?

- **Step 3: Identify the optimal outcome.** Think about all the information you have about Tara and about this relationship. Consider your own feelings as well as hers. Given all these factors, what's the best, most constructive relationship outcome possible here? Be sure to consider not just what's best for *you* but what's best for Tara as well.

- **Step 4: Locate the roadblocks.** Taking into consideration your own thoughts and feelings, Tara's, and all that has happened, what's preventing you from achieving the optimal outcome you identified in step 3?

- **Step 5: Chart your course.** How will you respond to Tara to overcome the roadblocks you've identified and achieve your optimal relationship outcome?

HELPFUL CONCEPTS

Ethics and respect, *158–159*

Crafting rhetorical messages, *164*

Formatting online messages, *176*

Communicating online versus face-to-face, *180–181*

As this example illustrates, trolling is intrinsically incompetent since it unethically manipulates and provokes people through blatant inappropriateness.

If you're new to an online environment (game, chatroom, discussion group) and uncertain about what kind of information is appropriate to disclose, one way to get a firm sense of norms is to lurk. Through **lurking,** you observe others communicate in an online environment, but you don't participate. Although lurking was once considered inappropriate and even unethical (hence the pejorative name), it is common practice. In most online groups, only about 10 percent of the members actively contribute to conversations; most participants lurk (Barnes, 2001). The majority of discussion groups now recommend lurking as a means for new members to learn how established members interact, a practice that helps new members competently communicate once they join the conversation (Barnes, 2003).

Some online communication norms govern how to format your message content, and it's vital to follow these. For example, use acronyms correctly and sparingly. Also limit your use of capitalized letters, excessive punctuation, and doubles (repeating letters multiple times, such as "YYOOUURR KKIIDDIINNGG!!"). In a text-only environment, content requires little additional amplification or emphasis. Avoid critiquing others' spelling and grammar. Many people use online communication because of its speed and efficiency and aren't concerned about precision. And finally, in discussion groups particularly, restrict your comments to the topic at hand.

Online or Face-to-Face?

Being competent online also means knowing when to communicate online instead of face-to-face. For many interpersonal goals, communicating online is more effective. Text-messaging a friend to invite her to coffee makes more sense than dropping by her workplace and interrupting her work, and it's probably quicker and less disruptive than calling her on your cell phone. Quick and simple requests and casual invitations like this are easily done online. E-mail also can help you communicate effectively and ethically when dealing with problematic people or certain types of conflicts. That's because you can take time to think and carefully draft and revise responses before sending them—something that isn't possible during face-to-face interactions.

But online communication is not the best medium for giving in-depth, lengthy, and detailed explanations of professional or personal dilemmas or for conveying weighty relationship decisions. Despite the ubiquity of online

DOONESBURY © 1996 G. B. Trudeau. Reprinted with permission of UNIVERSAL PRESS SYNDICATE. All rights reserved.

communication, many people still expect important news to be shared in person. Most individuals would think it incompetent for a spouse to reveal a long-awaited pregnancy or announce his or her desire for a divorce through e-mail. Likewise, you would probably be surprised if your best friend came out of the closet or disclosed a cancer relapse through instant-messaging.

Taking Control of Competence

All of our interpersonal desires, dreams, and goals converge and are born into existence at the point of contact with other human beings, when we create encounters through communication. Our interpersonal communication forges the relationships that in turn fuel our life outcomes. But it is not our interpersonal communication per se that determines the *quality* of our outcomes; it is the competence of our interpersonal communication. People who communicate competently enjoy a wealth of benefits, from greater relationship satisfaction and professional success to more contentment with their lives overall. Those who fail to communicate competently—owing to obstacles such as apprehension or a desire to wield power over and manipulate others—miss out on these valuable benefits.

Thankfully, each of us can develop our interpersonal competence by taking active control of our communication choices and striving to master and refine key communication skills. By strengthening the abilities necessary to communicate appropriately, effectively, and ethically face-to-face, across cultures, and online, you improve the quality of your own life and the lives of others. Although personal and professional relationships will always present challenges, developing interpersonal competence is your best means for facing those challenges confidently and adroitly.

POSTSCRIPT

We began this chapter with an American hero. Cesar Chavez was a humble and compassionate defender of truth who built a human rights movement on the foundation of his own exceptional ability to communicate appropriately, effectively, and ethically in public and private settings.

How have you used your communication competence to improve your life and the lives of those around you? What metaphorical battles or protests have you waged on behalf of others, armed only with your interpersonal effectiveness?

Like you and me, Chavez faced innumerable challenges in deciding how to communicate with and relate to others. His greatness lay in his consistent

desire to communicate in ways that brought hope and light to tens of thousands of underprivileged human beings.

Chapter Review

Key Terms

interpersonal communication competence, *154*

communication skills, *154*

appropriateness, *156*

high self-monitors, *156*

low self-monitors, *156*

effectiveness, *156*

ethics, *158*

expressive messages, *162*

conventional messages, *162*

rhetorical messages, *162*

communication apprehension, *166*

communication plans, *167*

plan actions, *167*

plan contingencies, *167*

shyness, *167*

loneliness, *167*

defensive communication, *169*

dogmatic messages, *169*

superiority messages, *169*

indifference messages, *169*

control messages, *169*

verbal aggression, *170*

intercultural competence, *172*

world-mindedness, *173*

ethnocentrism, *174*

attributional complexity, *175*

online disinhibition, *177*

flaming, *177*

trolling, *177*

lurking, *180*

Key Concepts

What Is Interpersonal Communication Competence?

- Although we sometimes view exceptional communicators as having "special powers," **interpersonal communication competence** is simply the ability to communicate with others in ways that are appropriate, effective, and ethical. To strengthen your interpersonal competence, you must understand the defining characteristics of communication competence, translate this understanding into action in the form of **communication skills**, and consistently strive for excellence in your communication.

- Competent interpersonal communicators are sensitive to norms of **appropriateness**. People can be distinguished as **high** and **low self-monitors**, depending on the degree to which they are aware of and adaptive to situational norms. To be truly competent, you must strike a balance among appropriateness, effectiveness, and attention to ethics in your communication. Too much concern for appropriateness can render your communication ineffective.

- We often consider people who demonstrate **effectiveness** in achieving their interpersonal goals as being interpersonally competent. But people can be exceptionally effective communicators and still be unethical or inappropriate. In such cases, their communication is incompetent.

- The final component of competence is **ethics**. Although a minimum standard for ethical communication is "do no harm to others," many people feel that true competence can be achieved only through consistent demonstration of respect toward others.

Crafting Competent Messages

- It is easy to be competent in situations that aren't demanding. You demonstrate true competence when you can communicate appropriately, effectively, and ethically across all situations. Although some people use **expressive messages** and others use **conventional messages** for dealing with challenging situations, **rhetorical messages** are the most competent.

Preventing Interpersonal Incompetence

- One way to better understand competent communication is to examine different types of incompetence—communication that is inappropriate, ineffective, or unethical. One form of incompetence is **communication apprehension**. The best strategy for remedying communication apprehension is to generate **communication plans** for encounters that cause apprehension, paying careful attention to your **plan actions** and **plan contingencies**.

- A second type of interpersonal incompetence is **defensive communication**, which typically takes one of four forms: **dogmatic messages**, **superiority messages**, **indifference messages**, or **control messages**. Creating rhetorical messages is the best approach for dealing with others' defensive communication. However, this approach may generate only limited success when you're dealing with chronically defensive individuals.

- A close cousin of defensive communication is **verbal aggression**, a form of communication that is best prevented in oneself through anger management. When others display verbal aggression, it's best to remain polite and respectful or to remove yourself from the encounter.

Improving Your Intercultural Competence

- **Intercultural competence** is challenging because people from different cultures possess different views of what it means to communicate appropriately, effectively, and ethically. To be a competent intercultural communicator, you must embrace **world-mindedness** and **attributional complexity**, and avoid **ethnocentrism**.

Improving Your Competence Online

- Because online communication doesn't allow for nonverbal indicators of mood, tone, and nuance of meaning, interacting competently online can be difficult. To communicate competently online, you need to be sensitive to the effect of **online disinhibition** on norms regarding appropriateness of disclosure. Avoid **flaming** and **trolling**, and use **lurking** only to familiarize yourself with the norms for appropriate communication in a specific online environment.

Key Skills

- How sensitive and adaptive are you to situational appropriateness norms? Discover the answer by taking the *Pop Quiz* on page 157. Be sure to consider the importance of balancing appropriateness with other concerns, discussed on page 157.

- Curious about how to incorporate ethics into your interpersonal communication? Review the National Communication Association's "Credo for Ethical Communication" on page 158.

- How can you competently communicate with seniors? Find out in *Focus on Culture* on page 160.

- Interested in creating competent messages? Read pages 159–162 to find out how; then complete the *Skills Practice* on page 164 to try your hand at designing and using rhetorical messages.

- Do you suffer from communication apprehension? If so, revisit the discussion of communication plans on page 167; then complete the *Skills Practice* on page 167.

- Interested in overcoming your own defensiveness or in dealing more competently with people who communicate defensively? Review the recommendations on pages 169–170.

- What's the best way to communicate with verbally aggressive people? Learn the answer on page 171.

- How can you master intercultural competence? Review the two principles that underlie intercultural competence on pages 173–176. Then take the *Pop Quiz* on page 175 to see how world-minded you are and gauge your awareness of attributional complexity.

- Have you had difficulty communicating competently online? Discover suggestions for improvement on pages 177, 180–181. Then complete the *Skills Practice* on page 180 to put these principles into action.

- What would you do if a close friend repeatedly disappointed you? Put your interpersonal competence to the test by working through the *Making Relationship Choices* exercise on pages 178–179.

6

Listening Actively

Fred McFeely Rogers began each day by swimming laps in a local pool.[1] A nonsmoking, nondrinking vegetarian, he was happily married for close to 50 years, and helped raise two sons. He also was the most awarded person in television history: two Peabody awards, numerous Emmys, two Lifetime Achievement Awards, the Presidential Medal of Freedom, and a star on the Hollywood Walk of Fame. But Rogers saw himself primarily as a minister who believed in the power of listening. From his perspective, the greatest communicative gift people could give was attentive silence that encouraged others to openly express their deepest emotions.

Although he eventually would receive honorary degrees from more than 40 different institutions—including Yale, Carnegie Mellon, and Boston University—Rogers's first degree was in music composition from Rollins College in Florida.

---

[1] All information regarding Fred Rogers were obtained from Millman (1999), Stimson (1998), and Mister Rogers (n.d.).

Rogers planned on entering the seminary after graduation but was sidetracked by the chance to help establish the first public television station, WQED in Pittsburgh. As he later explained, "I got into television because I hated it so, and I thought there's some way of using this fabulous instrument to nurture those who would watch and listen" (Stimson, 1998). While working at the station, Rogers attended classes at Pittsburgh Theological Seminary. Ordained in 1963, he decided to minister to children and their families by creating *Mister Rogers' Neighborhood*, a TV program emphasizing affirmation, acceptance, and, most of all, listening. In Rogers's words, "being a good listener is a vital part of ministry, especially ministry with children. . . . I cultivated my own listening skills in part by integrating silence into my life as a part of my daily spiritual discipline." By providing children with an adult who would listen to their concerns, Rogers's show helped youngsters express their emotions in healthy ways. During the Gulf War, for example, Rogers dedicated a series of episodes to parents and children with close relatives fighting in Desert Storm. He encouraged parents to discuss life and death openly with their children rather than lying to them or avoiding their questions.

Rogers's renowned listening ability matched a talent for speaking powerfully in ways that made *others* listen. In the late 1960s, a congressional committee headed by notoriously gruff Senator John Pastore was considering halving public broadcasting's funding. Rogers testified before the committee, describing the importance of providing children with a compassionate adult listener on television. After hearing Rogers's testimony, Pastore remarked, "I'm supposed to be a pretty tough guy, but this is the first time I've had goose bumps in the last two days." The committee then voted to approve full funding for public broadcasting.

Mister Rogers' Neighborhood became the longest-running show in television history. During a 33-year span, Rogers welcomed guests as diverse as the Harlem Boys Choir, chef Julia Child, and cellist Yo-Yo Ma. The show became so well known that it remains a cultural cliché—many people still remember the opening song, the gentle lilt of Rogers's voice, and his famous cardigan sweaters. Rogers was lampooned by everyone from comedian Eddie Murphy to the writers of the animated series *Family Guy*. But through it all, he remained committed to the central message of his subtle, nondenominational television ministry: listen to others and offer them love, respect, and kindness. Even after his death in 2003, the words he shared at the end of each episode still linger: "I'll be back when the day is new, and I'll have more ideas for you. And you'll have things you'll want to talk about. I will too."

We often take listening for granted. It's a natural but otherwise unremarkable part of our interpersonal communication. Compared with the knowledge, motivation, and skill that competent speaking requires, listening seems to just happen. And listening sometimes feels more like an inconvenience than a pleasure; after a hard day, you collapse onto your sofa to watch television, when your best friend instant-messages you and wants an immediate response.

But viewing listening as secondary to speaking—or worse yet, an irksome obligation—misses two truths about listening, communication, and interpersonal relationships. First, listening is our most primal and primary communication skill. As children, we develop the ability to listen long before we learn how to speak, read, or write; listening is our first communicative link with other human beings (Wolvin & Coakley, 1996). And as adults, we spend more time listening than we do in any other type of communication activity (Wolvin & Coakley, 1996). A U.S. Department of Labor study found that the average American worker spends 55 percent of his or her workplace communication listening (U.S. Department of Labor, 1991). Second, we each have the potential to develop our listening into something far more profound than passive action. When we listen actively, we transcend our own thoughts, ideas, and beliefs, and we begin to directly experience the words and worlds of other people. Through focusing our attention, tailoring our listening to the situation, and letting others know we understand them, we move beyond the personal and create the *interpersonal*. The result is improved relationships and people perceiving us as more sensitive and skilled communicators (Chesebro, 1999).

In this chapter, you'll learn how to build your active listening skills. You'll gain familiarity with:

- The five stages of the listening process and strategies for improving your listening skills

- The many purposes listening serves

- The advantages and disadvantages of different listening styles

- Ways to avoid common forms of ineffective listening

Listening: A Five-Step Process

Listening is commonly thought of as a single activity, ability, or skill. But listening actually comprises a series of separate yet linked actions that together form a process. Specifically, **listening** involves receiving, attending to, understanding, responding to, and recalling sounds and visual images during interpersonal encounters (Wolvin & Coakley, 1996). When you're listening to someone else, you draw on both auditory and visual cues. In addition to spoken messages, behaviors such as head nodding, smiling, gestures, and eye contact affect how you listen to others and interpret their communication. The process of listening also unfolds over time, rather than instantaneously, through the five steps discussed here.

Receiving

You're walking to class when you unexpectedly run into a good friend. You stop to chat with her. As she talks, you listen to her words as well as observe her behavior. But how does this process happen in terms of your senses? As you observe your friend, light reflects off her skin, clothes, and hair and travels through the lens of your eye to your retina, which contains optic nerves. These nerves become stimulated, sending information to your brain, which translates the information into visual images such as your friend smiling or shaking her head, an effect we call **seeing** (see Figure 6.1). At the same time, sound waves generated by her voice enter your inner ear, causing your eardrum to vibrate. These vibrations travel along acoustic nerves to your brain, which interprets them as your friend's words and voice tone, an effect known as **hearing** (see Figure 6.2).

Together, seeing and hearing constitute **receiving,** the first step in the listening process. Receiving is critical to listening—you can't listen if you don't see or hear the other person. Unfortunately, our ability to receive is often hampered by noise pollution, sound in the surrounding environment that obscures or distracts our attention from auditory input. Sources of noise pollution include crowds, road and air traffic, construction equipment, and music.

FIGURE 6.1

How the Eye Sees

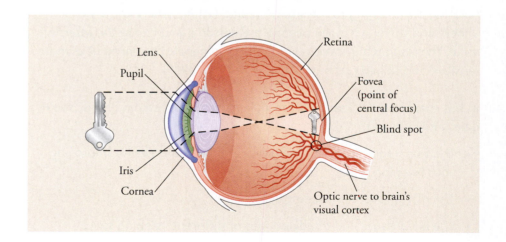

Although noise pollution often is inescapable, especially in large cities, some people intentionally expose themselves to intense levels of noise pollution. This can result in hearing impairment, the restricted ability to receive sound input across the humanly audible frequency range. For example, research suggests that more than 40 percent of college students have measurable hearing impairment due to loud music in bars, home stereos and headphones, and rock concerts, but only 8 percent believe that it is a "big problem" compared with other health issues (Chung, Des Roches, Meunier, & Eavey, 2005). One study of rock and jazz musicians found that 75 percent suffered substantial hearing loss from exposure to chronic noise pollution (Kaharit, Zachau, Eklof, Sandsjo, & Moller, 2003).

You can enhance your ability to receive—and improve your listening as a result—by becoming aware of noise pollution and adjusting your interactions accordingly. Practice monitoring the noise level in your environment during your interpersonal encounters, and notice how it impedes your listening. When possible, avoid interactions in loud and noisy environments, or physically move to quieter locations when you wish to exchange important information with others. And if you enjoy exposure to high levels of noise pollution such as loud music or live concerts, always use ear protection to ensure your auditory safety. As a lifelong musician, I myself never practice, play a gig, or attend a concert without earplugs.

● Repeated exposure to intense levels of noise pollution can result in hearing impairment. Guitarist Pete Townsend of The Who, after years of exposure to his own noise pollution, can no longer hear spoken words during normal conversations.

FIGURE 6.2

How the Ear Hears

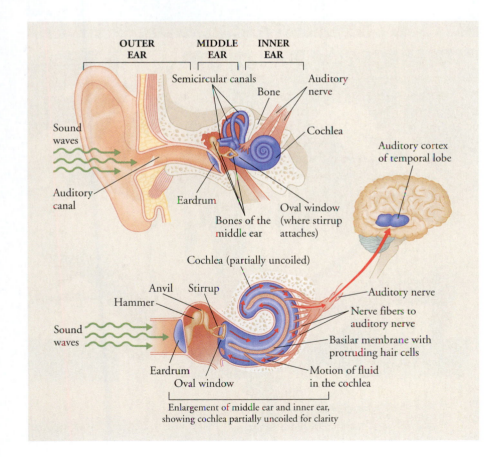

OUTER EAR   MIDDLE EAR   INNER EAR

Semicircular canals   Bone   Auditory nerve

Sound waves

Cochlea

Auditory canal

Eardrum

Bones of the middle ear   Oval window (where stirrup attaches)

Auditory cortex of temporal lobe

Cochlea (partially uncoiled)

Anvil   Stirrup

Hammer

Sound waves

Auditory nerve

Nerve fibers to auditory nerve

Basilar membrane with protruding hair cells

Eardrum

Oval window

Motion of fluid in the cochlea

Enlargement of middle ear and inner ear, showing cochlea partially uncoiled for clarity

● The Heidi incident, in which NBC executives opted to preempt a football play-off game to broadcast the movie *Heidi,* is considered by ESPN to be one of the five most shocking moments in NFL history.

Attending

With only 65 seconds left in the Nov. 17, 1968 Jets-Raiders game and the Jets up 32–29, NBC abruptly preempted the game and switched to the movie *Heidi*, its previously scheduled program. Stunned football fans, including my father-in-law, watched in disbelief as Raiders and Jets suddenly morphed into a young shepherdess dancing on a flowered mountainside. While Heidi capered on-screen, the Raiders rallied for two touchdowns in the last minute, winning the game 43–32. Thousands of angry callers flooded the NBC phone lines, overloading the network's switchboard and causing it to break down.

Attending, the second step in the listening process, involves devoting attention to the information you've received. If you don't attend to information, you can't go on to interpret and understand it, or respond to it in ways that constructively contribute to the encounter (Kahneman, 1973). The extent to which you attend to received information is determined largely by its salience. As discussed in Chapter 3, we view information as salient and therefore select it as the focus for our attention when it's visually or audibly stimulating, unexpected, or personally important (Fiske & Taylor, 1991). In the Heidi incident, the Jets-Raiders game was important to football fans because the teams were fierce rivals and each team wanted to win as a way to improve their chance of going to that season's playoffs.

We have only limited control over salience; whether people communicate in stimulating, unexpected, or important ways is largely determined by them, not us. However, we do control our overall attention level. To boost your attention, follow these steps (Marzano & Arredondo, 1996; Marzano, Arredondo, & Brandt, 1987). First, develop awareness of your attention level. Throughout the day and especially during interpersonal interactions, monitor how your attention naturally waxes and wanes. Notice how various internal and external factors, such as fatigue, stress, or hunger, influence your attention. Second, take note of encounters in which you *should* listen carefully, given their important short- and long-term consequences, but that nevertheless seem to trigger low levels of attention on your part. These might include interactions with parents, teachers, spouses, friends, or work managers or situations such as the classroom, work meetings, or family get-togethers. Third, consider the optimal level of attention required for adequate listening during these encounters. Fourth, compare the level of attention you observed in yourself versus the level of attention that is required, identifying the "attention gap" that needs to be bridged in order for you to improve your attention.

Finally, and most important, raise your level of attention to the point necessary to take in the auditory and visual information you're receiving. You can do this in several ways. Before and during an encounter, boost the salience of the exchange by reminding yourself of how it will impact your life and relationships. Take active control of the factors that may diminish your attention. When possible, avoid important encounters when you are overly stressed, hungry, ill, fatigued, or under the influence of alcohol, for such factors substantially impair attention (Haider, 1972). If you have higher energy levels in the morning or early in the week, try to schedule attention-demanding activities and encounters such as classes, work meetings, and

1 Identify an important person to whom you find it difficult to listen.

2 List factors—fatigue, time pressure—that impede your attention when you're interacting with this person.

3 Before your next encounter with the individual, address factors you can control.

4 During the encounter, increase the person's salience by reminding yourself of his or her importance to you.

5 As the encounter unfolds, practice mental bracketing to stay focused on your partner's communication.

job interviews during those times. Finally, when you find your attention wandering, practice **mental bracketing,** systematically putting aside thoughts that aren't relevant to the interaction at hand. When irrelevant thoughts arise, let them pass through your conscious awareness and drift away without allowing them to occupy your attention fully.

Understanding

In the movie *Memento,* actor Guy Pearce plays Leonard Shelby, an insurance investigator searching for the man responsible for his wife's murder (Todd, Todd, & Nolan, 2000). During the attack that caused his wife's death, Leonard suffered a brain injury. He remembers everything about his life before the attack, but he cannot form new memories. As soon as something fades from his short-term memory, he forgets it permanently. As a consequence, he faces grave difficulties in understanding the meaning of others' communication. In every new encounter, he struggles to answer even the most basic questions, such as "Who is this person?" and "What is she talking about?" In an attempt to compensate, he writes his experiences down on notes, takes photos of people and captions them before he forgets, and even tattoos important information on his body.

Leonard's story illustrates the essential role that memory plays in shaping the third stage of listening. **Understanding** involves interpreting the meaning of another person's communication by comparing newly received information against our past knowledge (Macrae & Bodenhausen, 2001). Whenever you receive and attend to new information, you place it in your **short-term memory,** the part of your mind that temporarily houses the

information while you seek to understand its meaning. While the new information sits in your short-term memory, you call up relevant knowledge from your **long-term memory,** the part of your mind devoted to permanent information storage. You then compare relevant prior knowledge from your long-term memory with the new information in your short-term memory to create understanding.

Responding

You're spending the afternoon at your apartment discussing your wedding plans with two friends, John and Sarah. You want them to help you with ideas for your rehearsal dinner, ceremony, and reception. As you talk, John looks directly at you, smiles, nods his head, and leans forward. He also asks questions and makes comments periodically during the discussion. Sarah, in contrast, seems completely uninterested. She alternates between looking at the people strolling by your living-room window and checking her cell phone for messages. She also sits with her body half-turned away from you and leans back in her chair. You become frustrated because it's obvious that John is listening closely and Sarah isn't listening at all.

What leads you to conclude that John is listening and Sarah isn't? It's the way your friends are **responding**—communicating their attention and understanding to you. When you actively listen, you do more than simply attend and understand. You also convey your attention and understanding to others by clearly and constructively responding. Active listening can be communicated by using positive feedback and by paraphrasing and clarifying.

Positive Feedback.   Critical to active listening is using verbal and nonverbal behaviors known as **feedback** to communicate attention and understanding *while* others are talking. Scholars distinguish between two kinds of feedback, positive and negative (Wolvin & Coakley, 1996). When you use positive feedback, like John in our earlier example, you look directly at the person speaking, smile, position your body so that you're facing him or her, and lean forward. You also may offer **back-channel cues,** verbal and nonverbal behaviors such as nodding and making comments—such as "Uh-huh," "Yes," and "That makes sense"—that signal you've paid attention to and understood specific comments (Duncan & Fiske, 1977). All of these behaviors combine to show speakers that you're actively listening. In contrast, people who use negative feedback, like Sarah in our example, send a very different message to speakers: "I'm not interested in paying attention to you or understanding what you're saying." Behaviors that convey negative feedback include avoiding eye contact, turning your body away, looking bored or distracted, and not using back-channel cues.

The type of feedback we provide while we're listening has a dramatic effect on speakers (Wolvin & Coakley, 1996). Receiving positive feedback from listeners can enhance a speaker's confidence and generate positive emotions. Negative feedback can cause speakers to hesitate, make speech errors, or stop altogether to see what's wrong and why we're not listening.

"Uh-huh. Uh-huh. And for precisely how long were you a hunter-gatherer at I.B.M?"

SELF-REFLECTION

Recall an encounter in which you were saying something important but the other person responded with negative feedback. How did the feedback affect your communication with the listener? Your relationship? Is negative feedback ever appropriate? If so, under which circumstances?

To effectively display positive feedback during interpersonal encounters, follow four simple rules (Barker, 1971; Daly, 1975). First, make your feedback obvious. As communication scholar John Daly notes, no matter how actively you listen, unless others perceive your feedback, they won't view you as actively listening. Second, make your feedback appropriate. Different situations, speakers, and messages require more or less intensity of positive feedback. Third, make your feedback clear by avoiding behaviors that might be mistaken as negative feedback. For example, something as simple as innocently stealing a glance at your watch to see what time it is might be mistaken as negative feedback indicating that you're bored or wish the person would stop speaking. Finally, make your feedback *immediate*. Feedback should always be provided quickly in response to what the speaker has just said.

Paraphrasing and Clarifying.   Active listeners also communicate attention and understanding through saying things *after* their conversational partners have finished their turns—things that make it clear they were listening. One way to do this is by **paraphrasing,** summarizing others' comments after they have finished ("My read on your message is that . . . " or "You seem to be saying that . . ."). This practice can help you check the accuracy of your understanding during both face-to-face and online encounters. Paraphrasing should be used judiciously, however. Some conversational partners may find paraphrasing annoying if you use it a lot or they view it as contrived. Paraphrasing also can lead to conversational lapses, silences of three seconds or longer that participants perceive as awkward (McLaughlin & Cody, 1982).

● In many Protestant churches, it is perfectly acceptable for audience members to express their feedback loudly during the minister's sermon by shouting "Amen!" or "Hallelujah!" The same type of positive feedback would be radically inappropriate in a traditional Catholic church.

Paraphrasing can cause lapses because when you paraphrase, you do nothing to usefully advance the conversational topic forward in new and interesting ways (Heritage & Watson, 1979). Instead, you simply rehash what already has been said. In so doing, the only relevant response your conversational partner can then provide is a simple acknowledgment, such as "Yep" or "Uh-huh." For example, a romantic partner shares with you concerns about your relationship, to which you respond, "You seem to be saying that. . . ." What can he or she then say in response to your paraphrase? "Yep" or "Nope," and in either case, a lapse is likely to ensue immediately after, unless one of you has a new topic ready to introduce to advance the conversation. This is an important practical concern for anyone interested in being perceived as interpersonally competent because the more lapses that occur, the more likely your conversational partner is to perceive you as incompetent (McLaughlin & Cody, 1982). To avoid this perception, always couple your paraphrasing with additional comments or questions that usefully build on the previous topic or take the conversation in new directions.

Of course, on some occasions, we simply don't understand what others have said. In such instances, it's perfectly appropriate to respond by seeking clarification rather than paraphrasing, saying, "I'm sorry, but could you explain that again? I want to make sure I understood you correctly." This technique not only helps you clarify the meaning of what you're hearing; it also enables you to communicate your desire to understand the other person.

● The bizarreness effect occurs because something unusual triggers heightened levels of our attention and requires us to work harder to make sense of it.

Recalling

The fifth stage of listening is **recalling,** remembering information after you've received, attended to, understood, and responded to it. As researchers L. Todd Thomas and Timothy Levine note, recalling is a crucial part of the listening process because we judge the effectiveness of listening based on our ability to accurately recall information after we've listened to it (1994). Think about it: when a romantic partner asks, "Were you listening to me?" how do you demonstrate that you really were actively listening? By recalling everything that was said and reciting it back to your partner. Indeed, practically every scientific measure of listening uses recall accuracy as evidence of listening effectiveness (Thomas & Levine, 1994).

Your recall is only as accurate as your perception, however. If you misunderstand information when you first receive and attend to it, your subsequent recall of this information and any communication or relationship decisions you make based on it will be flawed. For instance, the *Saturday Night Live* character Emily Litella, immortalized by the late comedienne Gilda Radner, was famous for her lengthy tirades based on misunderstood information. In a series of skits, she debated "the fuss" over issues ranging from "sax and violins on television" to "pouring money into canker research." In each case, after her error was pointed out to her by others, she would offer her now-famous concession, "Oh, that's very different . . . *never mind!*"

Recall accuracy also varies depending on the situation. When people have no task other than simple memorization, recall accuracy is high. For example, laboratory studies examining facial recall have found that when people are asked to memorize others' faces, they can subsequently recall which faces they've seen with close to 100 percent accuracy (Freides, 1974). But when people are engaged in activities more complicated than rote memorization, recall accuracy plummets. That's because in such cases, we're receiving a lot of information, which increases the likelihood of perceptual

SELF-REFLECTION

When you're listening to others, what information do you find easiest to recall? What information do you tend to forget? When you're participating in an encounter that's important but that you know will be difficult to recall accurately later, what do you do to boost your recall?

and recall errors. Research on the recall accuracy of criminal eyewitnesses, for instance, has found that people frequently err in their recall of crimes, something most jurors and even the eyewitnesses themselves don't realize (Loftus, 1979; Wells, Lindsay, & Tousignant, 1980). And our recall of interpersonal and relational encounters is not exempt from error. Especially for negative and unpleasant interactions, such as conflicts, we tend to recall our own behavior as positive and constructive and the behavior of others as comparatively negative, regardless of what actually happened (Sillars, 1980).

How can you enhance your recall ability? One way is to use **mnemonics,** devices that aid memory. For example, when I was an undergraduate at the University of Washington, I delivered pizzas. Many of my deliveries went to the Wallingford neighborhood, a residential area west of campus. Wallingford was different from other neighborhoods because the streets had names instead of numbers: Eastern, Sunnyside, Corliss, Bagley, Meridian, Burke Wallingford, Densmore, Woodlawn, and Ashworth. No matter how many times my supervisor told me, "No, Woodlawn is *between* Densmore and Ashworth!" I couldn't recall the street order when I was out on a run. So I created a mnemonic. I took the first syllable of each street name, in order from east to west, and created a simple phrase, "Eas-Sun Cor-Bag Mer-Bur Wal-Den Wood-Ash." The phrase was so distinct that it stuck in my mind, and from then on I had no problem locating the streets. The mnemonic was so powerful that even now, more than 20 years later, I can recall it, even though I now live thousands of miles from Seattle and the pizza restaurant for which I delivered no longer exists.

My experience creating a pizza-delivery mnemonic supports one of the most common findings in mnemonic research, the **bizarreness effect,** which causes us to remember unusual information more readily than commonplace information (Worthen, Garcia-Rivas, Green, & Vidos, 2000). The bizarreness effect occurs because unusual information and events trigger heightened levels of our attention and require us to work harder to make sense of them; thus we remember the information and its associated interaction better. The bizarreness effect can be used to enhance your recall of information by creating links between information you are listening to and unusual images or information that you can link with what you're trying to remember. You can create unique phrases or acronyms based on the information you're trying to remember, and use these as memory prompts. For example, the phrase "Cor-Bag" for me was so strange sounding that it was the most memorable part of my mnemonic, and I could remember the entire mnemonic by calling to mind "Cor-Bag."

Several other practices can also help you boost your recall ability. Because listening is rooted in both visual and auditory information and memory is enhanced by using all five senses, try bolstering your memory of an interpersonal communication encounter by linking information you've listened to with pleasant or even silly visuals, scents, or sounds. For example, to create visual images of an interpersonal encounter, you could write detailed notes or draw diagrams documenting the contents of a conversation. You could also link a new acquaintance's name with a unique physical feature characterizing him or her. And you could pay close attention to a presenter's PowerPoint slides during a lecture.

SKILLS PRACTICE

This exercise helps you to boost your recall of information exchanged during online encounters.

❶ Identify online encounters where it's important to recall the information.

❷ During your next encounter, focus your attention on the information in the messages as well as any visual images or emotions you associate with this information.

❸ Immediately after the encounter, print the messages and write down detailed notes regarding the information you consider most important.

❹ Create mnemonics for this information.

❺ Bolster your memory by reciting these mnemonics.

If a friend is making important relationship disclosures, remembering intense emotional reactions can also help you recall the details of the interaction later. Reducing complex information to simple sayings or symbols makes recall easier as well. And finally, when you develop mnemonics or notes, review them repeatedly, including reciting them out loud, because repetition helps aid memory.

FOCUS ON CULTURE

When Nobody Will Listen

On March 6, 1988, the board of trustees at the nation's oldest university for the deaf, Gallaudet University, announced that Elizabeth A. Zinser was selected as the university's president. Zinser was a hearing person with little knowledge of the deaf community. The decision shocked Gallaudet faculty, staff, and students, who had hoped the board (most of whom were hearing) would for the first time hire a deaf president.

A large crowd of student protesters gathered. Board chair Jane Spilman, a hearing person, refused to listen to the students' concerns and defended the board's decision, saying, "Deaf people are not able to function in a hearing world." The protest escalated, and the demonstrators made four demands: Zinser must resign and be replaced by a deaf president, Spilman must resign from the board, deaf representation on the board must be at least 51 percent, and there must be no reprisals toward any of the protesters.

The board refused to listen and the students responded by refusing to meet with Zinser and blocking campus gates (Mercer, 1998). Zinser realized her candidacy was doomed by administrators' and students' refusal to listen to each other. As she notes, "We had found no reasonable means to establish contact or communication on campus. So I resigned." The board then met the remaining demands.

Ten years later, former protesters, board members, and Zinser returned to Gallaudet to remember and honor the protest. Zinser was asked, if she could go back in time, knowing what she now knows, would she change her decision to resign? She responded, "Gallaudet looms large in my life, in the deeper awareness that I gained for what people who have been oppressed feel. I've had fantasies of getting through those gates, talking with all the students and listening to their concerns. But had I found a way to actually sit down and talk to them, in fairly short order I would have concluded the same thing" (Mercer, 1998).

YOUR TURN

- Have you experienced an encounter in which you and another person refused to listen to each other because of perceived differences?

- How did the situation affect your ability to receive, understand, respond to, and recall information during and after the encounter?

- What happened to your relationship with that person? What could you have done differently to facilitate better mutual listening?

Note: All information was obtained from "A watershed moment: Deaf President Now" (n.d.), "Deaf President Now" (n.d.), and Mercer (1998).

Why Listen? Five Purposes

A talent contest in which audience members vote for their favorite performer, *American Idol* features three professional judges who listen to contestants and offer their own evaluations. The judges are Simon Cowell (a BMG record executive), Paula Abdul (a Grammy- and Emmy-award-winning singer), and Randy Jackson (a Grammy-winning record producer and former vice president at Columbia Records).[2] Although each judge is charged with the task of listening, they appear to approach this task with very different purposes in mind. Cowell listens as a means to evaluate performers and make blunt and pointed criticisms. Jackson focuses his listening on enjoying the experience, often giving standing ovations to contestants who have "touched" him, as if he was an audience member rather than a judge. Abdul listens in an almost therapeutic fashion, readily offering praise and comfort and suspending judgment for the sake of support.

The differences among the *American Idol* judges illustrate that how we choose to listen is often shaped by **listening functions,** our purposes for listening. Interpersonal encounters are characterized by five common functions.

Listening to Comprehend

Think for a minute about your interpersonal communication class — the course for which this text was assigned. When you're sitting in class listening to your communication professor, why do you listen? The answer is so obvious it's silly: you listen so that you can comprehend the information he or she is presenting to you. When you listen for this purpose, you work to accurately interpret and store the information you receive, so you can correctly recall it later. Additional examples of this type of listening might include listening to a coworker explain how to use a software application at work and listening to a prospective landlord explain your contractual obligations if you sign a lease on an apartment.

Listening to Support

You're making lunch in your apartment one afternoon, when your best friend calls you on your cell phone. You answer only to hear him sobbing uncontrollably. He tells you that his girlfriend just broke up with him because she discovered his dalliance with someone else. He says he needs someone to talk to.

Providing comfort to a conversational partner is another common purpose for listening. To provide support through listening, you must suspend judgment — taking in what someone else says without evaluating it, and openly expressing empathy. Listening to support is embodied in Paula Abdul's approach to judging on *American Idol*. Other examples include

---

[2] All information regarding *American Idol* is from "American Idol" (n.d.).

comforting a relative after the death of a spouse or responding with a kind e-mail to a coworker who sends you a message complaining that her boss just criticized her at a team meeting.

Listening to Analyze

With supportive listening, you suspend judgment and convey empathy. But when you listen to analyze, you carefully evaluate the message you're receiving, and you judge it. For instance, Simon Cowell evaluates the quality of the performances he listens to on *American Idol*. As another example, you might analyze your father's neutral comments about his recent medical checkup, listening for signs of worry so you can determine whether he's hiding serious health problems.

Listening to Appreciate

The fourth function of listening is to appreciate what is being listened to. When you listen to appreciate, your goal is simply to enjoy the sounds and sights you're experiencing and then to respond by expressing your appreciation. Listening to appreciate is the primary function for which Randy Jackson uses listening on *American Idol*. Other common examples include listening to your child excitedly share the story of his Little League home run or listening while a close friend tells a funny story.

Listening to Discern

Musicians in symphonies and bands must listen carefully when tuning their instruments before a performance. Amid the background noise of the audience and other musicians' tuning, each player carefully isolates the sound of his or her instrument, distinguishing the pitch, tone, and timbre of the strings. Auto mechanics use listening for a similar purpose. After a tune-up, they listen for smoothness while revving the car engine. In close relationships, we often listen carefully to the vocal tone of our intimate partners to assess mood and stress level. For example, if you're concerned about your romantic partner being angry with you, you might listen carefully to the sound of his or her voice rather than to the words, to gauge your partner's state of temper. Each of these activities illustrates the final function of listening: discerning. When you listen, you discern—you focus on distinguishing specific sounds from each other.

Adapting Your Listening Purpose

The five functions that listening commonly serves are not mutually exclusive. You might change your purpose for listening even within the same encounter. You're listening with appreciation to your local symphony when suddenly you realize one of the musicians is out of tune. You might shift to discerning listening (trying to isolate that particular instrument from the others) and ultimately to listening to analyze (trying to assess whether you are in fact correct about its being out of tune). If the musician happens to be a friend of yours, you might even switch to supportive listening following the concert, as she openly laments her disastrous performance!

An essential part of active listening is skillfully and flexibly adapting your listening purposes to the changing demands of interpersonal encounters. To strengthen your ability to adapt your listening purpose, heighten your awareness of the various possible listening functions during your interpersonal encounters. Routinely ask yourself, "What is my primary purpose for listening at this moment, in this situation? Do I want to comprehend, analyze, support, appreciate, or discern?" Then adjust your listening accordingly. As you do this, keep in mind that for some situations, certain approaches to listening may be inappropriate or even unethical, like listening to analyze when a relational partner is seeking emotional support.

SELF-REFLECTION

Recall a situation in which you did not listen for the right purpose. For instance, perhaps a friend needed you to listen supportively, but you instead listened to analyze. What led you to make this error? What consequences ensued from your misread? What can you do in the future to avoid such listening mishaps?

Understanding Listening Styles

When Fred Rogers first began hosting his children's show, he intentionally adopted a nonthreatening listening style that put children at ease and helped them feel safe. His listening style reflected his religious practice of contemplative silence, which emphasizes responding empathically to others.

POP QUIZ

Identify the Right Listening Function

List one or more listening functions that would be appropriate in each of the following situations. Then use the key to award yourself one point for each correct answer. Total your score. Bonus: For additional points, reread the situations, and identify listening functions that might be ineffective and perhaps even unethical.

Situation 1: A friend sends you an e-mail saying that she won't be able to attend your birthday party because she's just been diagnosed with strep throat.

Situation 2: Your professor provides a description of an upcoming assignment.

Situation 3: Your romantic partner, who is very insecure about his or her singing ability, sings a song to you at a local karaoke bar.

Situation 4: A classmate challenges your position on a topic during an in-class discussion.

Situation 5: A coworker inquires as to whether his voice "still sounds funny" after he received Novocain during a dental checkup.

Key

Situation 1: comprehend, support. Situation 2: comprehend. Situation 3: support, appreciate, discern. Situation 4: comprehend, support, analyze. Situation 5: support, analyze, discern. Bonus: Situation 1: analyze. Situation 2: analyze. Situation 3: analyze.

Scoring

6 or above correct: You have a strong ability to adapt your listening purpose. 5 or below correct: You have difficulty adapting your listening purpose.

Note: Items in this *Pop Quiz* are adapted from Watson, Barker, and Weaver (1995).

While Rogers's trademark listening style has earned ridicule from some quarters of our popular culture, it proved extremely effective in the context of his show and with his chosen audience.

What does it mean to have a "listening style"? Your **listening style** is your habitual pattern of listening behaviors, which reflects your attitudes, beliefs, and predispositions regarding the listening process (Watson, Barker, & Weaver, 1995). One of the most important truths about active listening is that different situations require different listening styles. For example, an empathic and supportive listening style such as Fred Rogers's is highly effective for trying to provide guidance to a young child or solace to a heartsick friend. But the same style would be inappropriate and perhaps an impediment during a meeting with an important business client in which an enormous amount of information must be covered in a brief period of time.

Unfortunately, most of us don't adapt our listening styles. Instead, we use only one or two styles in all our interpersonal interactions (Chesebro, 1999). One study found that 36.1 percent of people reported exclusively using a single listening style across all of their interpersonal encounters; an additional 24.8 percent reported that they never use more than two different styles (Watson et al., 1995). We also resist attempts to switch from our dominant styles, even when those styles are ill-suited to the situation at hand. The result is people potentially perceiving us as insensitive, inflexible, and even incompetent communicators.

Four Listening Styles

During his daily briefings with aides, President George W. Bush prefers listening to concise, focused, and clear messages that allow him to quickly render decisions and pursue courses of action (Brookhiser, 2003). He displays little tolerance for listening to communicators he perceives as vague or disorganized. He also demands absolute punctuality to maintain a strict work schedule, requiring aides to present information within allotted time frames. His immediate predecessor, President Bill Clinton, displayed sharply contrastive listening styles. Clinton was renowned for openly expressing empathy when listening, most notably in April 1992 when he told AIDS activist Bob Rafsky, "I feel your pain"—a line that soon became the butt of many jokes. Clinton also demanded that aides provide him with exhaustive detail regarding issues, so much information that meetings would often go hours over schedule.

The contrastive listening styles of Presidents George W. Bush and Bill Clinton illustrate the four different primary listening styles that exist. **Action-oriented listeners** want brief, to-the-point, and accurate messages from others—information they can then use to make decisions or initiate courses of action. Like President Bush, action-oriented listeners can grow impatient when communicating with people they perceive as disorganized, long-winded, or imprecise in their talk. For example, when faced with an upset spouse, an action-oriented listener would be more concerned about receiving information related to the cause of the problem so a solution could be generated than in listening to elaborate details of their spouse's feelings.

Time-oriented listeners prefer brief and concise encounters. They tend to let others know in advance exactly how much time they have available for each conversation. Also, like President Bush, time-oriented listeners want to stick to their allotted schedules.

In contrast, **people-oriented listeners** view listening as an opportunity to establish commonalities between themselves and others. When asked to identify the most important part of effective listening, people-oriented listeners cite concern for other people's emotions. Like President Clinton or Fred Rogers, they strive to demonstrate empathy to others when listening by using positive feedback and offering supportive responses.

Content-oriented listeners prefer to be intellectually challenged by the messages they receive during interpersonal encounters. Also, like President Clinton, they enjoy receiving complex and provocative information. Content-oriented listeners often take time to carefully evaluate facts and details before forming an opinion about information they've heard.

Being an active listener requires that you learn to strategically deploy each of the four different listening styles with different people and types

POP QUIZ

Discover Your Listening Styles

Place a check mark next to each of the items you agree with. Then determine how many listening styles you use by seeing which categories have three or more checked statements. Don't be surprised if you have more than one listening style!

People-Oriented Listeners:

_____ I focus my attention on others' feelings when listening to them.

_____ When listening to others, I quickly notice whether they are pleased or disappointed.

_____ I become emotionally involved when listening to others' problems.

_____ I nod my head and use good eye contact to show interest in what others are saying when I listen.

Content-Oriented Listeners:

_____ I enjoy listening to technical information.

_____ I prefer to listen to facts and evidence so I can personally evaluate them.

_____ I like the challenge of listening to complex information.

_____ I enjoy asking probing questions to gather additional information.

Action-Oriented Listeners:

_____ I become frustrated when others don't present their ideas in an orderly, efficient way.

_____ When listening to others, I focus on inconsistencies or errors in what they're saying.

_____ I often jump ahead and finish others' thoughts in my own mind while listening.

_____ I get impatient with people who ramble on during conversations.

Time-Oriented Listeners:

_____ When hurried, I let others know that I have only a limited amount of time to listen.

_____ I often begin discussions by telling others how long I can meet with them.

_____ I interrupt others when I feel pressure to move on to another task.

_____ I look at my watch or at a clock when I have limited time to listen to others.

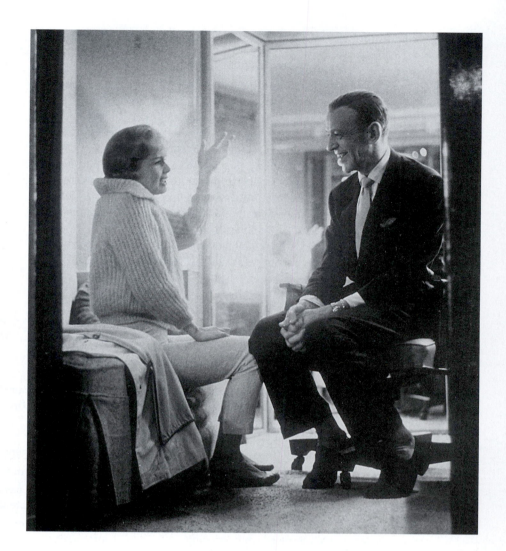

● Debbie Reynolds and Fred Astaire caught in a private moment.

of interpersonal encounters. For example, in situations where your primary listening purpose is to provide emotional support—friends, family members, or romantic partners obviously want to discuss feelings or turn to you for comfort—the ability to rapidly shift to a people-oriented listening style is essential. Studies document that use of a people-oriented listening style substantially boosts others' perceptions of your interpersonal sensitivity (Chesebro, 1999). In such encounters, use of a content-, time-, or action-oriented style would likely be perceived as incompetent. By contrast, in contexts where the dominant function of listening is to comprehend—business or educational settings in which large amounts of complex information are being presented—switching to a content-oriented listening style is required. Similarly, when it's obvious that a conversational partner is interested primarily in abiding by a preset schedule or moving quickly to a decision and the situation requires quick assimilation of information, you must adapt your listening to a more time- or action-oriented style.

Gender Differences in Listening Styles

Women and men consistently differ in their preferences for and practices of the various listening styles (Watson et al., 1995). Women are more likely than men to use people-oriented and content-oriented listening styles, and men are more likely to use time-oriented and action-oriented styles. Among individuals who employ more than one primary listening style, men tend to use time-oriented and action-oriented listening as their combination, and women typically use people-oriented and content-oriented listening. These findings have led researchers to conclude that men (in general) tend to have a task-oriented and hurried approach to listening whereas women perceive listening as an intellectual, emotional, and ultimately relational activity.

Keeping these differences in mind during interpersonal encounters is an important part of active listening. When interacting with men, observe the listening styles they display and adapt your style to match theirs. Don't be surprised if time- or action-oriented styles emerge as the most desired. When conversing with women, follow the same pattern, carefully watching their listening styles and adjusting your style accordingly. Be prepared to quickly shift to more people- or content-oriented styles if needed. And whether you're listening to men or women, always temper any adjustment you make to your listening with the knowledge that just because a person is female or male doesn't necessarily mean that she or he always will listen—or expect you to listen—in certain ways.

Culture and Listening Styles

Culture powerfully shapes the use and perception of listening styles. What's considered effective listening by one culture is often perceived as ineffective by others, something you should always keep in mind when communicating with people from other cultures. For example, in individualistic cultures such as the United States and particularly in the American workplace, time-oriented and action-oriented listening styles dominate. People often approach conversations with an emphasis on time limits ("I have only ten minutes to talk"). Many people also feel and express frustration if others don't communicate their ideas efficiently ("Just say it!").

The value that Americans put on time and efficiency—something we'll discuss more in Chapter 8—frequently places them at odds with people from other cultures. In collectivistic cultures, people- and content-oriented listening is emphasized. In many East Asian countries, for example, Confucian teachings admonish followers to pay close attention when listening, display sensitivity to others' feelings, and be prepared to assimilate complex information—hallmarks of people- and content-oriented listening styles (Chen & Chung, 1997). And studies have found that international students view Americans as less willing and patient listeners than individuals who come from Africa, Asia, South America, and southern Europe, regions that emphasize people-oriented listening (Wolvin, 1987).

SELF-REFLECTION

Do your preferred listening styles reflect research findings about men's and women's style preferences? How have your listening styles affected your interpersonal communication with people of the same and opposite gender? Do you adjust your speaking style to suit your communication partners' listening preferences? If so, how?

SKILLS PRACTICE

This exercise helps you communicate with people from other cultures.

① Identify your listening style in your next interaction with someone from a different culture.

② Use a people-oriented listening style. While the person is speaking, provide positive feedback.

③ Let the person know you've been paying attention by paraphrasing or seeking clarification.

④ Express interest in the speaker's feelings, opinions, and concerns and emphasize points of commonality.

⑤ Gauge reactions to your responses, assessing the effectiveness of this style.

Preventing Ineffective Listening

The material we've covered to this point offers many suggestions for how to improve your active listening skills. To listen actively, you must control factors that impede your attention and boost your attention focus on important aspects of encounters. You must communicate your understanding to others in effective and timely ways and provide obvious, appropriate, clear, and quick feedback. You must devote energy and effort toward improving recall.

And perhaps most important, active listening requires you to develop heightened awareness of the primary listening functions in various situations and to shift your listening style at a moment's notice.

Of course, none of us is a perfect active listener. We make errors during the listening process, fail to listen for the right purpose during an interpersonal encounter, or neglect to use the appropriate listening style. In previous sections of this chapter, we discussed ways to avoid such errors. But being an effective active listener also means systematically avoiding five notoriously incompetent—and all-too-common—types of listening.

Selective Listening

A colleague stops by your office to chat and shares exciting news: a coworker to whom you're romantically attracted is similarly interested in you. As your thoughts become riveted upon this revelation, the remainder of what he says fades from your awareness, including important information he shares with you about an upcoming project deadline.

Perhaps the greatest challenge to active listening is overcoming **selective listening,** taking in only bits and pieces of information (those that are immediately salient) during an interpersonal encounter and dismissing the rest. When we selectively listen, we rob ourselves of the opportunity to learn information from others that may impact important personal or professional outcomes, such as a missed project deadline.

Selective listening is difficult to avoid because it is the natural result of fluctuating attention and salience. To overcome selective listening, you shouldn't strive to "learn how to listen to everything" all at once. Instead, seek to slowly and steadily broaden the range of information you can actively attend to during your encounters with others. The best way to do this is by improving your overall level of attention, through practicing the techniques for enhancing attention discussed earlier in this chapter. Through these means, you boost your chances of noticing information that has important short- and long-term consequences for your personal and professional relationships.

Eavesdropping

In *Wuthering Heights*, Emily Brontë's classic tale of romance and vengeance, a major turning point occurs when Heathcliff eavesdrops on a conversation between his lover Catherine and Nelly, the story's narrator. Catherine's comments cause Heathcliff to abandon her, setting in motion a tragic series of events that lead to Catherine's death (Brontë, 1995):

> "It would degrade me to marry Heathcliff, now; so he shall never know how I love him; and that, not because he's handsome Nelly, but because he's more myself than I am. Whatever our souls are made of, his and mine are the same." Ere this speech ended I became sensible of Heathcliff's presence. Having noticed a slight movement, I turned my head, and saw him rise from the bench, and steal out, noiselessly. He had listened till he heard Catherine say it would degrade her to marry him, and then he staid to hear no farther. (p. 80)

SELF-REFLECTION

What do you find to be the greatest challenges to active listening in your own life? How do these challenges affect your interpersonal communication? How do they affect your relationships? What steps might you take to surmount these challenges?

We often assume that our conversations occur in isolation and that the people standing, sitting, or walking around the participants can't hear the exchange. But they can. As sociologist Erving Goffman noted, the presence of other individuals within the auditory and visual range of a conversation should be considered the rule and not the exception (Goffman, 1979). This is the case even with phone conversations and e-mail. Most cell-phone conversations occur with others in the immediate proximity, and e-mail is no more secure than a postcard.

When people intentionally and systematically set up situations so they can listen to private conversations, they are **eavesdropping** (Goffman, 1979). People eavesdrop for a host of reasons: desire to find out if someone is sharing personally, professionally, or legally incriminating information; suspicion that others are talking behind their backs, or even simple curiosity. Eavesdropping is both inappropriate and unethical because it robs others of their right to privacy and it disrespects their decision to not share certain information with you. Perhaps not surprisingly, the social norms governing this behavior are powerful. If people believe that you eavesdropped on a conversation, they typically will be upset and angry, and they may threaten reprisals. In the United States, a nation that has long emphasized the value of privacy, every state has established laws outlining the consequences for eavesdropping. Depending on the state, personal eavesdropping—particularly recording a conversation without the consent of the participants—is either a misdemeanor or a felony and thus can be punishable by fines and prison time.

Eavesdropping can be personally damaging as well. People occasionally say spiteful or hurtful things that they don't really mean, simply to impress others, fit in, or draw attention to themselves. As the *Wuthering Heights* example illustrates, if you happen to eavesdrop on such conversations, the result can be personally and relationally devastating. The lesson is clear: don't eavesdrop, no matter how tempting it might be.

Pseudo-Listening

You stayed up late the night before to finish a report, and when you finally got to bed, one of your kids got sick and kept you up the rest of the night. Now it's the afternoon and you're sitting in a warm and cozy coffeehouse, listening to your friend tell you a story she's already shared with you several times previously. Try as you might, you find yourself fading. But you don't want to embarrass yourself or your friend, so you do your best to act the part of an active listener—maintaining good eye contact, nodding your head, and contributing appropriate responses when needed.

You're engaging in **pseudo-listening,** behaving as if you're paying attention though you're really not. Pseudo-listening is obviously an ineffective way to listen because it prevents us from attending to or understanding information coming from the other person. Thus we can't recall the encounter later. Pseudo-listening is also somewhat unethical because it's deceptive. To be sure, occasional instances of pseudo-listening to veil fatigue or protect a friend's feelings (such as in our example) are understandable. But if you continually engage in pseudo-listening during your encounters with others, eventually they will realize what's going on and conclude that you're dishonest or disrespectful. Consequently, pseudo-listening should be avoided.

Aggressive Listening

People who engage in **aggressive listening** (also called ambushing) attend to what others say solely to find an opportunity to attack their conversational partners. For example, your friend may routinely ask for your opinions regarding fashion and music, but she then disparages your tastes whenever you share them with her. Or your romantic partner may encourage you to share your feelings, but then mock your feelings when you do share them.

As may be obvious, aggressive listening often goes hand in hand with both verbal aggression and chronic hostility, and consequently, the personal, interpersonal and relational costs are similar. People who consistently use listening to aggressively ambush others typically think less favorably about themselves (Infante & Wigley, 1986), experience lower marital satisfaction (Payne & Sabourin, 1990), and may experience more physical violence in their relationships (Infante, Chandler, & Rudd, 1989).

Some people engage in aggressive listening online. People known as **provocateurs** post messages designed solely to annoy others. They wait for people to post responses, and then they attack the responses. If the attacks of a provocateur are sophisticated enough, naïve group members may side with him or her against participants who seek to oust the instigator from the group. The result can be a flame war that prompts the site manager to shut down the discussion group—the ultimate "victory" for a provocateur.

SELF-REFLECTION

When do you pseudo-listen to others? How do people react when you are pseudo-listening? How do you feel and respond when you sense that someone has been pseudo-listening during an encounter with you? Are there situations in which pseudo-listening is acceptable? If so, when?

● The good cop/bad cop scenario is something we have all seen on television and in movies. The "bad cop" succeeds only if the "good cop" listens well enough to draw information out of the intimidated person both are interrogating. The bad cop's aggressive listening style is unlikely to work on its own.

Making Relationship Choices

Listening When You Don't Want To

1

BACKGROUND

Some of the most difficult listening situations you will face are those in which you feel obligated to listen to information that you find offensive or unethical. To learn how you might competently handle such a situation, read the case study and work through the five steps that follow.

2

CASE STUDY

You've been in a serious relationship with Taylor for several months. The two of you are well matched in beliefs, interests, values, and personalities. You love one another and are considering marriage. Taylor recently met your family, and everyone got along well. Your family is close, emotionally supportive, and ethnically diverse. Several of your siblings married people from different ethnic backgrounds, and many of your nieces and nephews have dual heritages. Now it's your turn to meet Taylor's family. Taylor warns you in advance, however, that "they're a bit old-fashioned" when it comes to diversity. You interpret this to mean that they might be somewhat prejudiced, but don't expect it to be much of a problem.

Arriving at Taylor's home, you receive a warm and hearty welcome. The family turns out to be very outgoing, open, and friendly. You like them immediately, and Taylor seems relieved that you're all getting along so well. As the evening progresses, however, the conversation around the dinner table takes a disturbing turn. Taylor's brother launches into a string of racist jokes that happen to target the same ethnic groups as your siblings' spouses. Then others at the table begin sharing stories that disparage other races.

For much of this conversation, you try to show that you're listening, but you feel sick inside. Finally, you can't take it anymore and politely excuse yourself to use the bathroom. Lingering in the hallway, you ponder your next move, when Taylor walks up and says, "I am *so* sorry. I know how offended and hurt you must be. Trust me, I feel the same way. But my brothers are teasing me about what's taking you so long, and my mom just served dessert. I know she'll be really hurt if you don't come back and join us."

As you stand there, competing impulses run through your mind. Do you protect your relationship with Taylor and maintain your positive image with the family by tolerating the racist storytelling? Do you pseudo-listen, merely playing the part of the active listener? Do you jeopardize your relationship with Taylor's family by expressing your discomfort with the conversation? Or do you support your family by refusing to listen any further and leaving?

YOUR TURN

While working through the following steps, keep in mind the interpersonal communication concepts, skills, and insights you've learned so far, especially in this chapter. Also remember: there are no right answers, so think hard about the choice you make! (P.S. Need help? Review the concepts listed below.)

- **Step 1: Reflect on yourself.** What are your thoughts and feelings in this situation? What attributions are you making about Taylor and Taylor's family? Are your attributions accurate? Why or why not?

- **Step 2: Reflect on your partner.** Using perspective-taking and empathic concern, put yourself in Taylor's shoes. How is Taylor likely perceiving the dinner situation? How does Taylor feel about you and your relationship? Also consider Taylor's family. What are their thoughts, feelings, and perceptions of the dinner? Of you and your relationship with Taylor?

- **Step 3: Identify the optimal outcome.** Think about all the information you have about Taylor and about this relationship. Consider your own feelings as well as those of everyone else involved in the situation. Given all these factors, what's the best, most constructive relationship outcome possible here? Be sure to consider not just what's best for *you*, but what's best for Taylor and your two families as well.

- **Step 4: Locate the roadblocks.** Taking into consideration everyone's thoughts and feelings and what has happened, what's preventing you from achieving the optimal outcome you identified in step 3?

- **Step 5: Chart your course.** What will you say to Taylor and Taylor's family to overcome the roadblocks you've identified and achieve your optimal relationship outcome?

HELPFUL CONCEPTS

Positive and negative feedback, *193*

Listening to analyze, *200*

People-oriented listening, *203*

Pseudo-listening, *208*

● The ability to listen begins to develop well before we are born and serves us throughout our lives.

If you find yourself habitually listening in an aggressive fashion, combat this type of ineffective listening by discovering and dealing with the root causes of your aggression. Oftentimes, external pressures such as job stress, relationship challenges, or family problems can play a role, so be careful to consider all possible causes and solutions for your behavior. Don't hesitate to seek professional assistance if you feel that it would be helpful. If you're in a personal or professional relationship with someone who uses aggressive listening against you, deal with that person by following the recommendations for addressing verbal aggression outlined in Chapter 5. Limit your interactions when possible, be polite and respectful, and use a people-oriented listening style. Avoid retaliating by using aggressive listening yourself because it will only escalate the aggression.

Narcissistic Listening

In Greek mythology, the beautiful nymph Echo falls in love with Narcissus immediately upon seeing him (Bulfinch, 1985). But when she approaches and moves to throw her arms around him, he recoils, telling her that he would rather die than be with her. Heartbroken, Echo flees to the mountains and plans for her revenge. She casts a spell on Narcissus, making him fall in love with his own reflected image in a pool. Upon seeing the enchanted image, Narcissus can't tear himself away. He abandons all thought of food and rest and gazes, entranced, at himself—until he finally dies of starvation.

Like its namesake in Greek mythology, **narcissistic listening** is self-absorbed listening: the perpetrator ignores what others have to say and redirects the conversation to him- or herself and his or her own interests. People who engage in narcissistic listening provide positive feedback as long as they are the center of conversational attention, but the moment the topic switches to something other than them, they give negative feedback. In some cases, the negative feedback may be extreme—narcissistic listeners may pout, whine, or even throw tantrums when the conversation switches away from them and onto the other person (Bushman & Baumeister, 1998). Because of its radical incompetence, you always should avoid narcissistic listening by allowing the conversation to focus on topics other than you and your own interests and offering positive feedback when such topics are discussed.

The Gift of Active Listening

When we are newborns struggling to make sense of a world filled with mysterious noises, we quickly learn to listen. Long before we recognize written words as having meaning, and long before we can produce our own words, we come to understand the words of others. Our lives as interpersonal communicators begin at that point.

It is ironic, then, that this first communicative gift shared by human beings—the gift of listening—poses so many challenges for us when we reach adulthood. We struggle with listening in part because it is exceptionally demanding. Like interpersonal communication competence, active listening requires dedication to mastering knowledge, hard work in practicing skills, and the motivation to continually improve.

Yet when we surmount the challenges of active listening by focusing our attention, training our memories, adapting our listening styles, and avoiding ineffective listening, an amazing thing happens. The activity that we originally mistook as passive begins to crackle with the energy of opportunity. For when we actively listen, the words and worlds of others wash over us, providing us with rich and unanticipated opportunities to move beyond the constraints of our own thoughts and beliefs and to forge interpersonal connections with others.

POSTSCRIPT

We began this chapter with the story of a man who dedicated his life to active listening. Fred Rogers brought his ministerial values of compassion and kindness to the small screen, and through television he touched the lives of millions of children. In addition to establishing the longest-running show in history, he created a safe space in which children felt simultaneously entertained, educated, and affirmed by an adult who genuinely listened to them.

How do you use listening in *your* life? What values underlie your listening? Do you create metaphorical "neighborhoods" through your listening—places in which people feel welcomed and valued? Or, as Eddie Murphy once quipped, do you create places where whenever you "move in, everyone else moves away"?

The PBS soundstage Fred Rogers once strolled through lies abandoned now, just as his famous cardigan hangs empty in a Smithsonian display case.

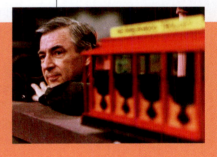

He'll never again "be back when the day is new." Yet the values he espoused will endure as long as people actively, compassionately, and respectfully listen to one another.

Chapter Review

Key Terms

Key Concepts

Listening: A Five-Step Process

- Although we often think of **listening** as a single activity, it's actually a multistep process. The first stage of listening is **receiving**, which involves **seeing** or **hearing** the communication of others.

- Critical to active listening is **attending** to information in an alert and energized fashion. To hone attention skills during interpersonal encounters, you should control factors that impede attention (such as fatigue, stress, and consumption of drugs or alcohol) and practice **mental bracketing.**

- **Understanding** the meaning of others' communication requires us to compare information in our **short-term memory** and **long-term memory,** using prior knowledge to evaluate the meaning of new information.

- Active listening requires **responding** to the communication of others in clear and constructive ways. Indications of effective responding include positive **feedback** and the use of **back-channel cues. Paraphrasing** can also help you convey understanding, but if you use it extensively during face-to-face encounters, your partners may find it annoying, and you run the risk of conversational lapses.

- Listening effectiveness is often measured in terms of our **recalling** ability, something you can improve through the use of **mnemonics.** In creating effective mnemonics, reduce complex information to simpler forms, employ visual images (as well as information from other senses), and use the **bizarreness effect.**

Why Listen? Five Purposes

- Even during a single interpersonal encounter, you will likely have multiple purposes for listening known as **listening functions.** Active listeners recognize the importance of quickly switching from function to function as circumstances dictate.

Understanding Listening Styles

● Although different situations require different approaches to listening, most people have one or two dominant **listening styles** that they use across situations. The four most common listening styles are **people-, action-, content-,** and **time-oriented** listening. Both gender and culture impact perceptions of which styles are most effective, as well as preferences for using particular styles.

Preventing Ineffective Listening

● To listen effectively, you must learn to recognize and avoid incompetent forms of listening. One of the greatest challenges to active listening is **selective listening,** which is a natural result of fluctuating attention. If you use **pseudo-listening** deliberately to deceive others, you're behaving unethically.

● **Eavesdropping** is an especially destructive form of listening and can have serious consequences, such as legal action against you.

● Some people use **aggressive listening** to attack others. People who do so during online encounters are known as **provocateurs.**

● People who engage in **narcissistic listening** constantly seek to turn the focus of the conversation back to themselves and may pout or whine if the talk strays from their interests.

Key Skills

● What can you do to deal with noise pollution and its negative effects on your ability to accurately receive information? Look at page 189 for the answer.

● Interested in improving your attention in ways that enhance your listening? Review the suggestions on pages 191–192; then complete the *Skills Practice* on page 192.

● What two things can you do to effectively communicate your attention and understanding to others when responding? Find out on pages 193–195.

● How can you enhance your positive feedback skills to improve your interpersonal communication? Follow the four rules detailed on page 194.

● Want to improve your recall ability? Apply the practical tips for improving recall skills offered on page 197; then complete the *Skills Practice* on page 197 to boost your recall related to important online encounters.

● Interested in effectively adapting your listening purpose during interpersonal encounters? Review the discussion on pages 199–201; then take the *Pop Quiz* on page 201 to test your skill.

● Curious about your dominant listening style? Complete the *Pop Quiz* on page 203 to find out. Then review the discussion of listening styles on pages 201–205 to discover how listening styles influence your interpersonal effectiveness.

● What are the best listening styles to use when you're engaged in cross-gender or cross-cultural encounters? Find the answers on pages 204–205.

● Want to more effectively deploy different listening styles with people who belong to cultures different from yours? Complete the *Skills Practice* on page 205 to discover how.

● Interested in putting your active listening skills to the test? Complete the *Making Relationship Choices* exercise on pages 210–211.

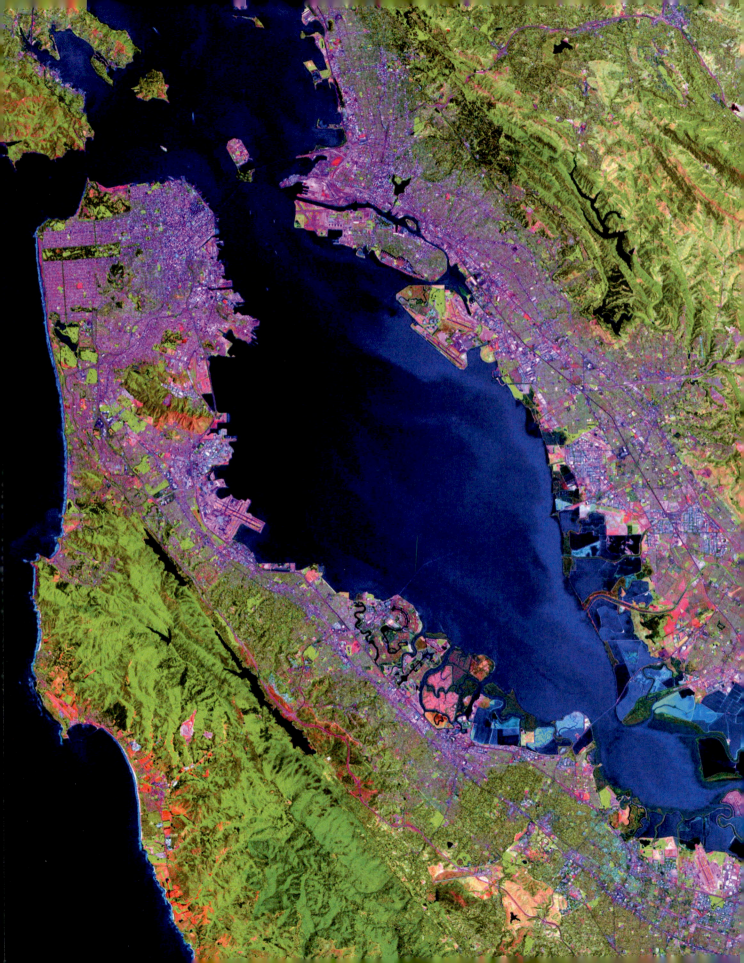

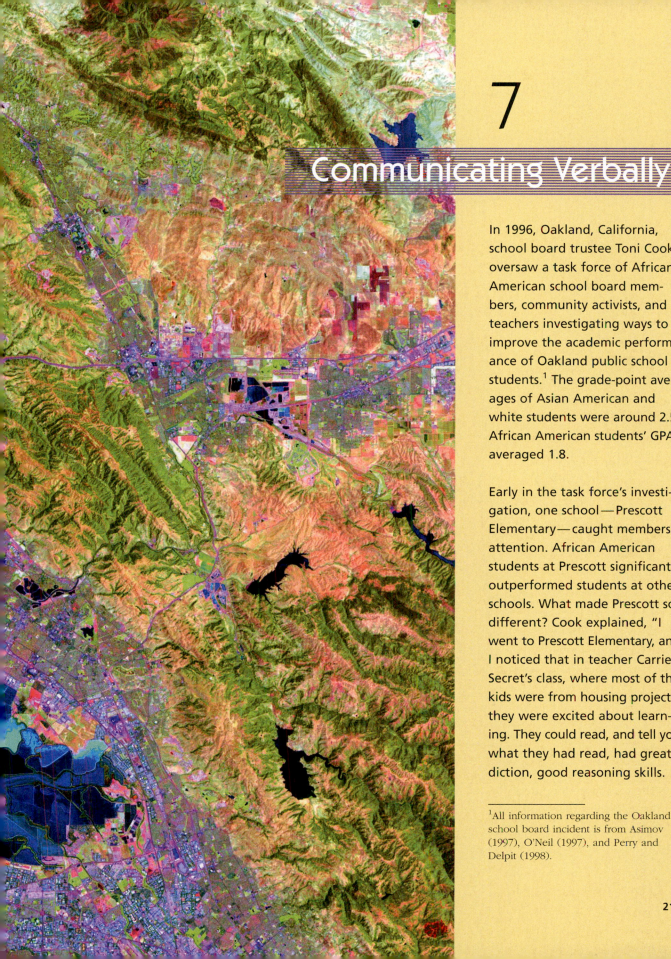

7

Communicating Verbally

In 1996, Oakland, California, school board trustee Toni Cook oversaw a task force of African American school board members, community activists, and teachers investigating ways to improve the academic performance of Oakland public school students.[1] The grade-point averages of Asian American and white students were around 2.5; African American students' GPAs averaged 1.8.

Early in the task force's investigation, one school—Prescott Elementary—caught members' attention. African American students at Prescott significantly outperformed students at other schools. What made Prescott so different? Cook explained, "I went to Prescott Elementary, and I noticed that in teacher Carrie Secret's class, where most of the kids were from housing projects, they were excited about learning. They could read, and tell you what they had read, had great diction, good reasoning skills.

---

[1]All information regarding the Oakland school board incident is from Asimov (1997), O'Neil (1997), and Perry and Delpit (1998).

So I asked Carrie, 'What are you doing differently?' She said, 'The Standard English Proficiency program'" (Asimov, 1997).

The Standard English Proficiency program (SEP) was based on two premises. First, many African American children grow up knowing Black English rather than Standard English. Black English is a distinct language derived from Standard English and African language forms. According to Wayne O'Neil, professor of linguistics at MIT, "Enslaved Africans forced to learn English simply mapped English words onto the grammar structures of their native languages, resulting in Black English" (1997). Second, if students were familiar only with Black English, they should be taught to translate from Black English to Standard English. Noting the SEP's success in helping students learn Standard English and the higher grades that resulted, Toni Cook and the task force members drafted a resolution requiring all Oakland public schools to participate in SEP.

On December 18, the Oakland school board passed the task force's resolution. In informative, honest, and clear language, the resolution declared "that the Superintendent shall immediately implement the best possible academic program for imparting instruction to African American students . . . to facilitate their acquisition and mastery of English language skills." The resolution also officially recognized "the existence, and the cultural and historical bases" of Black English and described it as "the primary language of African-American students."

A firestorm of controversy ensued. Despite the meticulous wording of the document and the clear language used by board members, national media outlets ran stories describing the district as "abandoning Standard English," and political pundits from Rush Limbaugh to George F. Will denounced Toni Cook and the other board members as "lunatics" (Perry & Delpit,

1998). Shocked, the board repeatedly emphasized the resolution's purpose—facilitating students' mastery of Standard English—but it made no difference. One week after passage of the resolution, U.S. education secretary Richard Riley declared that federal funds would not be available to any school district supporting the SEP.

To protect Oakland's funding, the board rescinded the resolution. But the controversy gave members pause for thought. Could they have worded things differently—in their written text or their spoken comments—to inspire a more positive reaction? Should they have used verbal communication that was *less* informative, honest, and clear to veil their recognition of Black English as a language, avoid the controversy, and achieve their goal of implementing the SEP? A month later, trustee Toni Cook bitterly noted, "While Rome is burning, we're trying to figure out whether the song we're singing is politically correct."

In a life filled with firsts—first kiss, first job, first car—it's a first we don't even remember. But it's celebrated by the people around us, who recognize in that fleeting moment the dawning of a life filled with language. Our first word drops from our mouths as the simplest of monosyllables: "cup," "dog," "ball." But once the sound has left our lips, the path has been irrevocably forged. By the end of infancy, we will have a vocabulary of several hundred words, and we will be able to put together brief sentences (Cole & Cole, 1989). By age 6, we will be learning more than 15 new words a day, and our vocabularies will have grown to anywhere between 8,000 and 14,000 words.

As we master native or newer tongues, we discover the power of verbal communication. Through exchanging words with others online, over the phone, and face-to-face, we share ideas, influence others, and make relationship choices. And we learn the responsibility that we have to use language cooperatively. Language itself isn't good or bad; it's merely a tool that allows us to interact with others, but we use it to serve both constructive and destructive ends. Used constructively, verbal communication opens doorways to shared understanding, intimacy, and enduring relationships. Used destructively, verbal communication can mislead others and damage our relationships.

In this chapter, we examine the nature and role of verbal communication in our lives. You'll learn:

- The defining characteristics of language

- The important functions that verbal communication serves in our interpersonal encounters and relationships

- Principles you can apply to use verbal communication more cooperatively

- Sources of miscommunication and ways to avoid them

Characteristics of Verbal Communication

In her essay "Mother Tongue," author Amy Tan describes her use of language in relationships and interactions with others (Tan, 2003):

> I spend a great deal of my time thinking about the power of language—
> the way it can evoke an emotion, a visual image, a complex idea, or a
> simple truth. Recently, I was made keenly aware of the different
> English's I use. I was giving a talk to a large group of people about my
> writing, my life, and my book, *The Joy Luck Club*. The talk was going
> along well enough, until I remembered one major difference that made
> the whole talk sound wrong. My mother was in the room. And it was
> perhaps the first time she had heard me using the kind of English I
> have never used with her. I was saying things like, "The intersection of
> memory upon imagination" and "There is an aspect of my fiction that
> relates to thus-and-thus"—speech filled with carefully wrought gram-
> matical phrases, burdened, it suddenly seemed to me, with past perfect
> tenses, conditional phrases, all the forms of standard English I did not
> use at home. Just last week, I was walking down the street with my
> mother, and I again found myself conscious of the English I was using.
> We were talking about the price of new and used furniture and I heard

FIGURE 7.1

Language Activity in the Brain

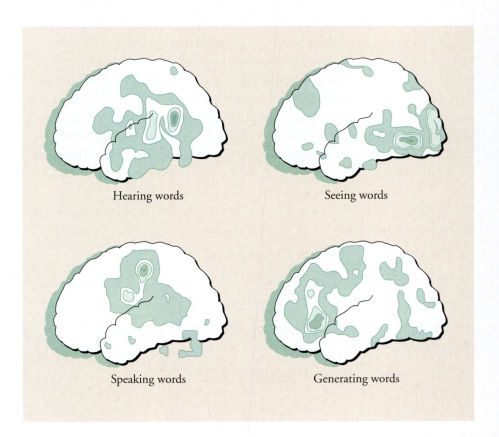

Hearing words

Seeing words

Speaking words

Generating words

myself saying, "Not waste money that way." My husband was with us as well, and he didn't notice any switch. And then I realized why. It's because over the twenty years we've been together I've often used that same kind of English with him, and sometimes he even uses it with me. It has become our language of intimacy, a different sort of English that relates to family talk, the language I grew up with. (pp. 60–61)

When we think of what it means to communicate, what leaps to mind is the exchange of spoken language with others during interaction, known as **verbal communication.** Across any given day, we use words to communicate with coworkers, friends, family members, and romantic partners. Our verbal communication bridges multiple media; we exchange language through e-mail, on the phone, and face-to-face. During each of these encounters, we tailor our language in creative ways, depending on whom we're speaking with. We shift grammar, word choices, and sometimes even the entire language itself—for example, firing off a Spanish text-message to one friend and an English message to another. As Amy Tan notes, our ability to communicate with words gives us the power to transmit simple truths or ideas, create visual images, and evoke emotions. And as you saw in the story of the Oakland school board's resolution, our ability to verbally communicate can intentionally or unintentionally result in misunderstanding and conflict.

Because verbal communication is defined by our use of language while interacting with others, the first step toward improving our verbal communication is to deepen our understanding of the nature of language. Scholars suggest that language has five fundamental characteristics (Ellis, 1999). (See Figure 7.1.)

"We use words as symbols to represent

objects,   actions,   people,   places,   and ideas."

Language Is Symbolic

Look around the room you're sitting in right now. As you do, you'll see a wealth of images: your textbook in front of you, the surface on which it rests, and perhaps people like your roommate or romantic partner. You might experience thoughts and emotions related to what you're seeing—memories of your roommate asking to borrow your laptop or feelings of love toward your partner. Now imagine communicating all of this to others. To do so, you need words to represent these things: "roommate," "lover," "borrow," "laptop," "love," and so forth. Whenever we use items to represent other things, they are considered **symbols.** In verbal communication, words are the primary symbols that we use to represent people, objects, events, and ideas (Foss, Foss, & Trapp, 1991).

All languages are basically giant collections of symbols in the form of words that allow us to communicate with each other. When we agree with others on the meanings of words by mutually recognizing what the words represent, we communicate easily. Your friend probably knows exactly what you mean by the word *roommate,* so when you use it, misunderstanding is unlikely. But some words have several possible meanings, making confusion possible. For instance, in English, the word *table* might mean a piece of furniture, an element in a textbook, or a verb referring to the need to end talk ("Let's table this discussion until our next meeting"). For words that have multiple meanings, we rely on the surrounding context to help clarify meaning. If we're in a classroom and the professor says, "Turn to Table 3 on page 47," you likely won't search the room for furniture. And if your mother says, "Please don't put your feet on the table," you probably won't take this to mean a prohibitive statement against placing your feet on your open textbook.

Language Is Governed by Rules

When we use language to verbally communicate, we follow rules. Rules govern the meaning of words, the way we arrange words into phrases and sentences, and the order in which we exchange words with others during conversations. **Constitutive rules** define word meaning: they tell us which words represent which objects (Searle, 1965). For example, a constitutive rule in the English language is: "The word *dog* refers to a domestic canine." Whenever you learn the vocabulary of a language—words and their corresponding meanings—you're learning the constitutive rules for that language.

Most people master the constitutive rules for their native tongues during early childhood. Many go on to learn a second language as well. For individuals learning a second language, whether English or some other language, the task of mastering constitutive rules becomes even more complicated. You not only must learn a new set of words but also replace familiar words with your new vocabulary—for instance, "The English word for domestic canine is *dog,* not *perro.*"

Regulative rules govern how we use language when we verbally communicate. They're the traffic laws controlling language use—the do's and don'ts. Regulative rules guide everything from spelling ("*i* before *e* except after *c*") to sentence structure ("The article 'the' or 'a' must come *before* the noun 'dog'") to conversation ("If someone asks you a question, you should answer").

To communicate skillfully, you must understand and follow the constitutive and regulative rules governing the language you're using. If you don't know which words represent which meanings (constitutive rules), you can't send clear messages to others or understand messages delivered by others. Likewise, without knowing how to form a grammatically correct sentence and when to say particular things (regulative rules), you can't communicate clearly with others or accurately interpret their messages to you.

Language Is Flexible

Although all languages have constitutive and regulative rules, people often bend those rules. For example, Amy Tan's family created their own special version of English to communicate with each other. Many people, especially those in close relationships, generate **personal idioms**—words and phrases that have unique meanings within their relationship (Bell, Buerkel-Rothfuss, & Gore, 1987). One study of personal idioms used by romantic partners found that the average couple had created more than a half dozen idioms. The most common idioms identified in the study were nicknames (referring to one's partner as "Pookers" or "Putsy"), teasing insults (calling partner "Hogmo" or "Fat Piggy" because of bad table manners), and sexual invitations (saying "I want some ice cream" to convey desire).

SELF-REFLECTION

What personal idioms do you have for your friends, family, and romantic partners? Who do you have the most idioms with? The least? What does this say about the relationship between idioms and intimacy?

POP QUIZ

Test Your Knowledge of American Dialects

Each of the following phrases is common to a specific U.S. dialect. See if you know what each one means and where it is from.

❏ 1. "Are you packing a card?"

❏ 2. "Check out the second growth."

❏ 3. "Mind if I use your commode?"

❏ 4. "Hey, that guy just budged!"

❏ 5. "Is there a bubbler nearby?"

❏ 6. "You're blocking my dooryard."

❏ 7. "He's just a leafer."

❏ 8. "Let's sit in the parlor."

❏ 9. "It's in the locker."

Answers:

(1) Union membership, Pacific Northwest. (2) Timber that has grown back on a previously harvested area, Pacific Northwest. (3) Bathroom, Deep South. (4) Cut in line, eastern Wisconsin and Minnesota. (5) Drinking fountain, eastern Wisconsin. (6) Driveway, Maine and northern New England. (7) Tourist traveling to see the seasonal foliage, northern New England. (8) Living room, Delaware Valley. (9) Closet, New Orleans.

Note: Information in this *Pop Quiz* was obtained from "Regional vocabularies of American English" (n.d.).

● L. L. Zamenhof invented Esperanto, a constructed language, in the late nineteenth century. It was intended to be a universal language, one that would permit easy intercultural and international communication. Although Esperanto did not originate with a nationality and remains unaligned with a place or society, it was created in a cultural context that valued the goal of universal communication.

When large groups of people share creative variations on language rules, those variations are called **dialects** (Gleason, 1989). A dialect may include unique phrases, words, and pronunciations (what we call "accents"). Dialects can be shared by people living in a certain region (Midwestern, Southern, or Northeastern United States), people with a common socioeconomic status (upper-middle-class suburban, working class), or people of similar ethnic or religious ancestry (Yiddish English, Irish English, Amish English) (Chen & Starosta, 1998). And if you're like most people, you prefer your own dialect. Communication scholar Jesse Delia conducted a study that asked people to form impressions of others based solely on voice recordings of dialects (1972). Listeners formed positive impressions of persons who used dialects similar to their own. Listeners also used negative stereotypes in judging people with dissimilar dialects. For instance, study participants who lived in regions other than New England and the South assumed that people using New England dialects came from "urban areas" and people using Southern dialects were "uneducated"—even if the speakers did not in fact have these characteristics.

Clearly, dialects powerfully influence our perceptions of others. If you remain unaware of this influence, you may unwittingly communicate with others in ways that damage your relationships or prevent you from forging what could have been positive connections. For example, if you assume that someone is "uneducated" because he or she speaks with a Southern U.S. dialect, you may decline to have anything to do with the person—and miss out on an opportunity to make a new friend or build a mutually beneficial relationship with a new colleague. To avoid such scenarios, resist making negative or stereotypical judgments about others who speak with dialects different from your own. Remember: Just because someone uses words, phrases, or an accent that indicates a certain regional or ethnic affiliation, that person doesn't necessarily possess attributes you might associate with people from that region or group.

Language Is Cultural

When I was in high school, I tried to learn German. I mastered the constitutive rules—German nouns, verbs, adjectives, and their meanings. I familiarized myself with the regulative rules—how to shape sentences and what to say when. But still something was missing: a deeper understanding of the richer cultural meanings beyond the words (Streek, 2002). This became clear when I befriended a German exchange student, Geli. When she spoke to me, I could understand the literal meanings of her words but often missed implied meanings, ironies, cultural "in jokes," and hints. As she put it, "Du sprichst Deutsch wie ein Lehrbuch und nicht wie eine Person" (You speak German like a textbook and not like a person).

It's obvious that different cultures have different languages. But beyond this simple observation lies a more profound truth: languages and cultures are fused in fundamental ways. Language is the set of symbols that members of a culture create to communicate their thoughts, beliefs, attitudes, and values with one another. Once created, a language is used to bolster a sense of cultural identity and connectedness (Whorf, 1952). Thus, languages both reflect the cultures that created them and enable people to perpetuate those cultures while also sustaining a sense of collective identity—for example, "We are Japanese" or "We are Kenyans."

Moreover, people use language differently depending on the extent to which they assume that others share their cultural beliefs, attitudes, and values. For example, people living in what scholars term **low-context cultures** tend *not* to presume that listeners share their beliefs, attitudes, and values; they tailor their verbal communication to be informative, clear, and direct as a result (Hall & Hall, 1987). They openly express their own viewpoints and attempt to persuade others to accept them (Hall, 1976, 1997a). Within such cultures, which include Germany, Scandinavia, and the United States, people strive to make important information obvious in the words themselves ("Here are my thoughts on this situation . . .") rather than convey information through less direct means such as implying or hinting.

In **high-context cultures,** such as China, Korea, and Japan, people presume that listeners share extensive knowledge in common with them. As a result, they don't feel a need to provide a lot of explicit information to gain listeners' understanding. People can hint, imply, or suggest meanings and feel confident that they will be understood. Consequently, communicators in high-context cultures rely more on indirect and ambiguous language and even silence to convey important meanings, and often "talk around" points rather than addressing them directly.

As with dialects, people often view their own language and culture as superior to others. Such individuals may believe that their language is more sophisticated or that it enables them to communicate more complex thoughts or ideas than other languages can. Some people even believe that their language, owing to its supposed innate superiority, should be widely adopted. For example, the lobbying group English First contends that English has a "natural supremacy" over all other languages. Their principal goals are to see English recognized as the official language of the United States and to discontinue government funding for bilingual and multilingual educational programs.

Despite strong beliefs that some languages are superior to others, research indicates that no one language is more effective than others in enabling its speakers to communicate verbally. Nevertheless, people do have strong expectations regarding the appropriateness of language use in specific situations. In fact, this was a driving force behind the Oakland school board's decision to support the SEP program. As Oakland school board trustee Toni Cook maintained, "Standard English is necessary to go to a four-year college, to being accepted in an apprenticeship program, to understanding the world of technology, to communicating" (Asimov, 1997).

Language Evolves

When University of Colorado assistant athletic director Dave Plati first began distinguishing the area inside an opponents' 20-yard line as a unique place on the football field, he had no idea he was setting in motion a linguistic

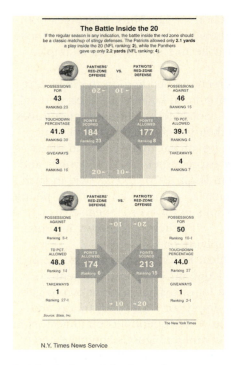

The Battle Inside the 20

● A football team's "red zone."   ● A natural disaster's "red zone."

evolution that would lead to a near-universal phrase. As Plati describes, "In 1980, I started charting game statistics inside the opponents' 20 for both CU and the Denver Broncos, and described it as 'scoring percentage inside the 20,' or 'inside the 20' for short."[2] Other offensive coordinators and coaches followed suit. Soon, NFL coach Joe Gibbs dubbed the newly defined region "The Red Zone," based on where his team (the Washington Redskins) needed to get to optimize their scoring chances (Attner, 1982). But the phrase didn't enter public parlance until 1989, when a *Sports Illustrated* article described inside the 20 as "The Red Zone" (King, 1989). Sports announcers and fans alike adopted the catchy phrase, and in the years that followed it became not just football lingo but a metaphor for dangerous and volatile areas. On November 27, 2005, when the South Pacific volcano Mount Manaro erupted, threatening the lives of thousands of island residents, vulcanologists described the area needing evacuation as "The Red Zone" (Lilley, 2005).

Many people view language as immutable. But in fact, language constantly changes. A particular language's constitutive rules—which define the meanings of words—may shift. As time passes, people add new words and phrases to their language and discard old ones. Sometimes people create new phrases, such as "the red zone," that eventually see wide use. Other

---

[2]Information regarding evolution of "The Red Zone" was obtained through personal interview with Dave Plati conducted by the author in December 2005.

times, speakers of a language borrow words and phrases from other languages and incorporate them into their own.

Consider these examples of how English-speakers have borrowed from other languages: If you tell friends that you want to *take* a *whirl* around the United States, you're using Norse (Viking) words, and if your trip takes you to *Wisconsin, Oregon,* and *Wyoming,* you're visiting places with Native American names.[3] If you stop at a café and request a cup of Chai *tea* along the way, you're speaking Amoy (eastern China), but if you ask the waiter to spike your coffee with *alcohol,* you're using Arabic. If, at the end of trip, you express an eagerness to return to your *job,* you're employing Breton (western France), but if you call in sick and tell your *manager* that you have *influenza,* you're speaking Italian.

A language's regulative rules also change. When you learned to speak and write English, for example, you probably were taught that *they* is inappropriate as a singular pronoun. But before the 1850s, people commonly used *they* as the singular pronoun for individuals whose gender was unknown—for example, "the owner went out to the stables, where they fed the horses" (Spender, 1990). In 1850, male grammarians petitioned the British Parliament to pass a law declaring that all gender-indeterminate references be labeled *he* instead of *they* (Spender, 1990). Since that time, teachers of English worldwide have taught their students that *they* used as a singular pronoun is "not proper."

Functions of Verbal Communication

Throughout human history, many cultures have been *nonliterate;* they developed spoken languages but not written ones. Beliefs, values, and traditions in such cultures are handed down generation to generation through oral communication rather than written records. For example, the Celts, ancient forebears of the modern Irish, Scottish, and Welsh, were nonliterate, and their cultural history was preserved through the writings of their Roman conquerors (MacCulloch, 1911). Many Native American cultures have been preserved solely through storytelling. As Tatanga Mani, a Stoney Indian living in the early 1900s, argued, "People depend too much on man-made printed pages—I turn to the Great Spirit's book which is the whole of his creation" (MacEwan, 1969). But throughout all of recorded human history, no known culture has lacked *spoken* language.

The universality of spoken language raise an interesting question: What purpose does verbal communication serve? The answer isn't one but many. The use of language during verbal communication serves six important functions, all of which strongly influence our interpersonal communication and relationships.

---

[3]Information regarding the origins of these words was obtained from "The English language: Words borrowed from other languages" (n.d.).

● Oral storytelling is an ancient art, one that creates and passes histories and mythologies down from generation to generation. Through blogs and podcasts, this tradition continues to take on new forms.

Sharing Meaning

In the movie *High Fidelity*, actor John Cusack plays Rob Gordon, a self-absorbed record-store owner whose romantic partner Laura recently left him for his upstairs neighbor Ian (Bevan et al., 2000). When Laura stops by Rob's apartment, Rob asks her if sex is better with Ian than it was with him. "I don't know," Laura tells him, "we haven't made love . . . not *yet*." In the scenes that follow, Rob ponders the meaning of Laura's "not yet." He asks his employee Barry (Jack Black) for his opinion on the word *yet,* using a hypothetical question:

ROB: What would it mean to you—"I haven't seen Evil Dead 2 *yet*"?

BARRY: Well, to me it would mean you're a liar; you've seen it twice!

ROB: No, listen to me, would you get the impression that I really *wanted* to see it?

BARRY: Well, you couldn't have been desperate to see it; otherwise you'd have already gone!

ROB: Right! I'm *not* going to see that movie . . .

BARRY: But the word "yet" . . . yeah . . . you know what . . . I get the impression that you *wanted* to see it . . . otherwise you'd have said you didn't want to go!

Verbal communication enables us to share meanings with others during interpersonal encounters. When you use language to verbally communicate, you share two kinds of meanings. The first is the literal meaning of your words, as agreed on by members of your culture, known as **denotative meaning.** Denotative meanings are what you find in dictionaries—for example, the word *yet* means "up to the time specified; thus far" (*Webster's New World College Dictionary,* 1997). So, when Laura says "not yet," to Rob in *High Fidelity*, part of the meaning she is sharing with Rob is "not up to the time specified."

But when we verbally communicate, we also exchange **connotative meaning:** additional understandings of a word's meaning based on the situation and the knowledge we and our communication partners share. Connotative meaning is implied, suggested, or hinted at by the words you choose while communicating with others. For example, Rob stews over Laura's use of "not yet" because he interprets her words as meaning that she wants to have sex with Ian.

"We always see the world through
the lens of our language."

SELF-REFLECTION

Recall an encounter in which someone communicated connotative meanings—that is, hinted or implied information beyond the literal meaning of the words. How did you figure out what the person really meant? Did your relationship with her or him help or hinder you in making sense of the message?

Scholar Edward T. Hall suggests that relationship intimacy plays a major role in shaping how we use and interpret connotative meanings while communicating with others (1997a). People who know each other extremely well can convey connotative meanings to one another that others don't pick up on. They also can exploit their intimacy to send each other confusing and perplexing connotations, such as when Laura uses "not yet."

Shaping Thought

In addition to enabling us to share meaning during interpersonal encounters, verbal communication also shapes our thoughts and perceptions of reality. Feminist scholar Dale Spender describes the relationship between words and our inner world in this way (1990):

> To speak metaphorically, the brain is blind and deaf; it has no direct contact with light or sound. The brain has to interpret: it only deals in symbols and never knows the real thing. And the program for encoding and decoding is set up by the language which we possess. What we *see* in the world around us depends in large part on our language. (pp. 139–140)

Consider an encounter I had at a family gathering. My 6-year-old niece told me that a female neighbor of hers had helped several children escape a

"Yet different people from different cultures use different languages."

house fire. When I commended the neighbor's heroism, my niece corrected me. "Girls can't be heroes," she scolded. "Only boys can be heroes!" In talking with her further, I discovered she knew of no word representing "brave woman." Her only exposure to "heroine" was through her mother's romantic novels. Not knowing a word for "female bravery," she considered the concept unfathomable: "The neighbor lady wasn't a hero, she just saved the kids."

The idea that language shapes how we think about things was first suggested by researcher Edward Sapir, who conducted an intensive study of Native American languages. Sapir argued that because language is our primary means of sharing meaning with others, it powerfully affects how we perceive others and our relationships with them (Gumperz & Levinson, 1996). Almost fifty years later, Benjamin Lee Whorf expanded on Sapir's ideas in what has become known as the Sapir-Whorf Hypothesis. Whorf argued that we cannot conceive of that for which we lack a vocabulary—that language quite literally defines the boundaries of our thinking. This view is known as **linguistic determinism.** As contemporary scholars note, linguistic determinism suggests that our ability to think is "at the mercy" of language (Gumperz & Levinson, 1996). We are mentally "constrained" by language to only think certain thoughts, and not one of us is free to interpret the world in neutral ways, because we always see the world through the lens of our languages.

Both Sapir and Whorf also recognized the dramatic impact that culture has on language. Because language determines our thoughts and different people from different cultures use different languages, Sapir and Whorf agreed that people from different cultures would perceive and think about the world in very different ways, an effect known as **linguistic relativity.**

FOCUS ON CULTURE

Names and Prejudice

Individuals in culturally oppressed groups face a unique challenge in naming themselves. The names they embrace often are used against them as insults. Here, four college friends discuss their thoughts about names used to describe sexual orientation.

DAVE: "Gay" is not an inclusive word, because it's the lesbian, bi, transgender, queer, *and* gay community. "Queer" can be offensive depending on who's saying it and how they mean it. I use "queer" to describe myself, but it's different if I say it, versus someone coming up and saying to me "You're a %$#@ queer, aren't you!?"

KYEORDA: When people say "gay," they think white male, and that's not me. I use "queer" because it includes a lot of different people. I started referring to myself as queer because I don't like the word "bisexual." When you say you're bisexual, people assume things, like that person is in a phase and they're really a lesbian or when I walk in the room I'm going to be attracted to half males and half females, and it's just not like that. "Queer" is more ambiguous and I like that.

BRANDON: I like the word "queer" but I don't use it to identify myself. I use it when I speak about the community in a broad context because "LBGT" [lesbian-bisexual-gay-transgendered]

doesn't encompass everyone. When you think about "gay" you think male; that eliminates other genders. "Queer" is questionable, depending on who you are. Older LBGT members don't like it; there are too many difficult memories. You see the younger generation reclaiming it and making "queer" something we can believe in.

SARAH: "Gay" is *not* an inclusive word. So far as "queer," I don't think it's a bad word to use, and it's convenient as opposed to the acronyms, but I don't use it myself. Also, I think there are some people outside the community who view "queer" as different or oddball and that's not an image we want to project.

BRANDON: I think breaking that image is something important though. I'm normal, and I'm queer!

YOUR TURN

- Think about groups you belong to—religious, social, ethnic, etc. What are some positive and negative names attached to these groups?

- What impact do these names have on you and your relationships with other group members?

- Can the negative names applied to your group be challenged? How?

Note: All information in this *Focus on Culture* was obtained during voluntary focus group sessions conducted in 2005 by MSU master's student Leigh-Anne Goins on behalf of the author. Participants granted permission to publish these materials.

As Sapir himself once noted (1929), "Even comparatively simple acts of perception are very much more at the mercy of words than we might suppose . . . We see and hear and experience largely as we do because the language of our community predisposes certain choices of interpretation" (p. 210).

Naming

In the early 1990s, the Attorney General's Office for the State of Michigan declared that the enormous tree displayed every winter in front of the state capitol should be called a "Holiday Tree," not a "Christmas tree" (Andrews, 2005). It based its decision on a court ruling that barred the state from spending money on "religious observances." The renaming of the tree triggered a bitter controversy. Conservatives denounced liberals for attacking their religious traditions and for being politically correct. Liberals accused conservatives of excluding members of other faiths. On December 13, 2005, after more than 15 years of annual acrimony, the Michigan state legislature passed a senate resolution declaring, "From this day forward, the tree and its graceful branches that adorn the Capitol lawn will be known as the Michigan Christmas Tree." As State Senator Alan Cropsey, the bill's sponsor, said, "It's a *Christmas tree*, not a 'holiday tree.' Everyone knows it" (Andrews, 2005).

Another important function of verbal communication is **naming**—that is, creating linguistic symbols for objects. The process of naming is one of humankind's most profound and unique abilities (Spender, 1984). When we name people, places, objects, and ideas, we create symbols that represent them. We then use these symbols during our interactions with others to communicate meaning about these things. Because of the powerful impact language exerts on our thoughts, the decisions we make about what to name things ultimately determine not just the meanings we exchange but also our perceptions of the people, places, and objects we communicate about.

The issue of naming is especially potent for people who face cultural prejudice, given that others outside the group often label them with derogatory names. Consider the case of gays and lesbians. For many years, gays and lesbians were referred to as "homosexual." But, as scholar Julia Wood notes, many people shortened "homosexual" to "homo" and used the new term as an insult, along with "fairy," "dyke," and "faggot" (1998). In response, lesbian and gay activists in the 1960s renamed themselves "gay." This move also triggered disputes, however. Antigay activists protested the use of a term that traditionally meant "joyous and lively." Some lesbian activists argued that "gay" meant only men and was therefore exclusionary to women. Many straight people began using "gay" as an insult in the same manner as earlier epithets. In response, some gays and lesbians in the 1990s began searching for yet another name to identify themselves by. They chose to embrace and redefine the old slur of "queer." But as Wood notes, in the new millennium, no clear consensus exists on the best name to be used (1998).

SELF REFLECTION

Think about the vocabulary you inherited from your culture for thinking and talking about intimate relationships. What terms exist for describing serious romantic involvements? Casual relationships that are more physical than emotional? Relationships that are purely platonic? How do these terms shape your thinking about these relationships in your life?

SELF-REFLECTION

What names of people, places, objects, or ideas in your life have you questioned? What about these names made you uncomfortable or upset? Do you know who named the object and why they had the ability to do so? What would be an alternative name? How would that new name change your or others' perception?

Performing Actions

Alice Walker's Pulitzer Prize–winning novel *The Color Purple* reaches an emotional climax when the principal character Celie, following years of abuse by Albert, stands up to him (Walker, 1992):

> I curse you, I say.
> What that mean? He say.
> I say, Until you do right by me, everything you touch will crumble.
> He laugh. Who you think you is? He say. You can't curse nobody. Look at you. You black, you pore, you ugly, you a woman, you nothing at all.
> Until you do right by me, I say, everything you even dream about will fail.
> Whoever heard of such a thing, say Mr. _____. I probably didn't whup your ass enough.
> Every lick you hit me you will suffer twice, I say. Then I say, You better stop talking because all I'm telling you ain't coming just from me. Look like when I open my mouth the air rush in and shape words. (p. 204)

Verbal communication enables us to take action. We make requests, issue invitations, deliver commands, or even curse—as Celie did to Albert. We also try to influence others' behaviors. We want our listeners to grant our requests, accept our invitations, obey our commands, or suffer from our curses. The actions that we perform with language are **speech acts** (Searle, 1969). (See Table 7.1 for types of speech acts.)

During interpersonal encounters, the structure of our back-and-forth exchange is based on the speech acts we perform (Jacobs, 1994; Levinson, 1985). Think about it: when your professor asks you a question, how do you know what to do next? You recognize that the words she has spoken constitute a "question," and you realize that an "answer" is expected as the relevant response. Similarly, when your best friend text-messages you and inquires, "Can I borrow your car tonight?" you immediately recognize his message as a "request." You also understand that two speech acts are possible as relevant responses: "granting" his request ("no problem") or "rejecting" it ("I don't think so").

TABLE 7.1

Types of Speech Acts

Act	Function	Example
Representative	Commits the speaker to the truth of what has been said	"It sure is a beautiful day." "That's definitely what we should do."
Directive	Attempts to get listeners to do things	"Get over here this minute!" "What chapter are we supposed to read for tomorrow?"
Commissive	Commits speakers to future action	"I will always love you, no matter what happens." "If you don't eat your vegetables, I will ground you!"
Expressive	Conveys a psychological or emotional state that the speaker is experiencing	"Thank you so much for the wonderful gift!" "I am so sorry I hurt your feelings."
Declarative	Produces dramatic, observable effects	"From this point onward, you are no longer an employee of this organization." "Until you do right by me, everything you touch will crumble!"

Note: Information in this table is adapted from Searle (1976).

Crafting Conversations

Language meanings, thoughts, names, and acts don't happen in the abstract, they occur within conversations. Conversation is the most common type of language activity. Although each of us intuitively knows what a conversation is, scientists distinguish conversations from other forms of talk based on three characteristics (Nofsinger, 1999). First, conversations are interactive. At least two people must participate in a talk exchange for it to count as a conversation. Participants must take turns exchanging messages, and the exchange must occur in real time (immediately back and forth). This means that talk in real-time Internet chatrooms and instant-messaging can be considered a conversation, but traditional e-mail, in which there is a time delay between messages being sent, cannot.

Second, conversations are locally managed. Local management means the people having the conversation choose who gets to speak, what they get to talk about, when, and for how long. This makes conversation different from other talk exchanges such as debate, in which the order and length of turns are decided before the event begins, and drama, in which people speak words that have been written down in advance.

Third, conversation is universal. Conversation forms the foundation for most forms of interpersonal communication and for social organization generally. Our relationships and our places in society are created and maintained through conversations.

9 Chickweed Lane © Brooke McEldowney/Dist. By UFS, Inc.

Managing Relationships

Verbal communication's most profound purpose in our lives is to help us forge, maintain, and end relationships. Our personal and professional relationships are largely defined through the verbal information we exchange online, over the phone, and face-to-face (Duck, 1994). For example, how often you communicate with your romantic partner and his or her friends and family, regardless of what you and they talk about, powerfully predicts your feelings toward your partner and your relationship's survival. People who communicate frequently with their partners and their partners' friends and family experience less uncertainty in their relationships and are less likely to break up than those who communicate less often (Parks & Adelman, 1983).

Of course, the content of language exchanged in relationships also matters. Couples who share more compliments, assurances of their commitment, and emotionally supportive comments and who behave in a generally upbeat manner in their verbal communication are more likely to survive than those who don't (Stafford, Dainton, & Haas, 2000). One study found that when spouses were asked to talk about something they would like to change in themselves, supportive comments from their spouses predicted marital satisfaction for two years following the conversations (Pasch, Bradbury, & Davila, 1997). And spouses who provide positive and supportive comments during conflicts in the early months of marriage report substantially higher levels of marital satisfaction and face a dramatically lower likelihood of divorce (Gottman, 1994; Gottman, Coan, Carrere, & Swanson, 1998).

Cooperative Verbal Communication

Eager to connect with your teenage son, you ask him about his day when he arrives home from school. But you get only a grunted, "Fine," in return, as he quickly disappears to his room to play computer games. You invite your romantic partner over for dinner, excited to demonstrate a new recipe. But when you query your partner's opinion of the dish, the response is, "It's interesting." You text-message your best friend, asking for her feedback on an in-class presentation you gave today. She responds, "You talked way too fast!"

Although these examples seem widely disparate, they share an underlying commonality: people failing to verbally communicate in a fully cooperative fashion. To understand how these messages are comparatively uncooperative, consider their cooperative counterparts. Your son tells you, "It was all right—I didn't do as well on my trig test as I wanted, but I got an A on my history report." Your partner says, "It's good, but I think it'd be even better with a little more salt." Your friend text-messages you, saying, "It went well, but I thought it could have been presented a little slower."

When you use **cooperative verbal communication,** you produce messages that others can easily and fully understand, that take active ownership for what you're saying, and that make others feel included rather than excluded. Underlying these goals is the **Cooperative Principle,** philosopher Paul Grice's argument that meaningful interactions rest on our ability to tailor our verbal communication in certain ways so that others can understand us. To be cooperative verbal communicators, we must make our conversational contributions as informative, honest, relevant, and clear as is required, given the purposes and directions of the encounters in which we're involved (Grice, 1989).

Being aware of situational demands is a critical aspect of applying the Cooperative Principle. For example, although cooperative verbal communication requires that we avoid verbosity, some contexts encourage overly informative speech, such as mentoring an inexperienced coworker or teaching a child how to make pancakes. Similarly, while we're ethically bound to share important information with others, this doesn't mean we *always* should. When a romantic partner discloses a confidential secret to us and a friend subsequently asks us to reveal it, it would be unethical to share this information without the permission of our partner.

Be Informative

According to Grice, being informative during interpersonal encounters means two things (1989). First, you should present all of the information that is relevant and appropriate to share, given the demands of the situation. When a coworker passes you in the hallway and greets you with a quick "How's it going?" the situation requires that you provide little information in return—"Great! How are you?" The same question asked by a concerned friend during a personal crisis creates very different demands; your friend likely wants a detailed accounting of your thoughts and feelings.

The responsibility to be informative overlaps with the responsibility to be ethical. To be a cooperative verbal communicator, you must share information with others that has important personal and relational implications for them. If you discover that your friend's spouse is having an affair, you're ethically obligated to disclose this information when your friend asks you about it. Being informative, however, doesn't mean disclosing information that isn't appropriate or important in a particular situation. A detailed description of your personal woes ("I haven't been sleeping well lately, and my cat is sick . . .") in response to your colleague's quick "How's it going?" query likely would be perceived as inappropriate and even strange.

Be Honest

Honesty is the single most important characteristic of cooperative verbal communication because other people count on the fact that the information you share with them is truthful (Grice, 1989). Honesty means not sharing information that you're uncertain about and not disclosing information that you know is false. When you are dishonest in your verbal communication, you violate standards for ethical behavior and you lead others to believe false things (Jacobs, Dawson, & Brashers, 1996). For example, if you assure your romantic partner that your feelings haven't changed when in fact they have, you not only provide your partner with false hope about your future together, but also lay the groundwork for your partner making continued investments into a relationship that you know is already doomed.

SELF-REFLECTION

Recall an encounter where you possessed important information but knew that disclosing it would be personally or relationally problematic. What did you do? How did your decision impact your relationship? Was your choice ethical? Based on your experience, is it always cooperative to disclose important information?

FIGURE 7.2

Conversational Pattern

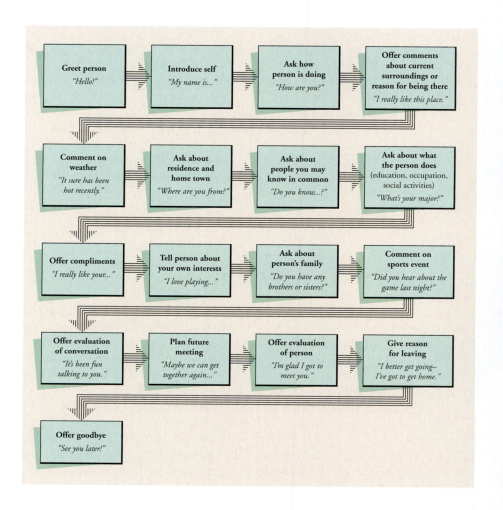

Be Relevant

Relevance means making your conversational contributions responsive to what others have said. When people ask you questions, you provide answers. When they make requests, you grant or reject their requests. When certain topics arise in the conversation, you tie your contributions to that topic. And across the course of conversations, you stick with topics that are relevant and avoid those that aren't. Dodging questions or abruptly changing topics would be uncooperative, and in some instances, it may be perceived as an attempt at deception—especially if you change topics to avoid discussing something you want to keep hidden (McCornack, 1992).

Being relevant often means adhering to conversational scripts—rigidly structured patterns of talk—especially in first encounters where you are trying to reduce other people's uncertainty. For example, the topics that college students discuss when they first meet follows a set script, as illustrated in Figure 7.2 (Kellermann, 1991). Communication researcher Kathy Kellermann conducted several studies looking at the first conversations of college students and found that 95 percent of the topic changes followed the same pattern regardless of gender, age, race, or geographic region. This suggests that a critical aspect of relevance is not only making responsive conversational contributions but grasping and following relevant conversational scripts.

Does the fact that we frequently use scripts to guide our conversations mean this type of communication is inauthentic? If we expect more from an exchange than a prepackaged response, scripted communication may strike us as such. However, communication scripts allow us to relevantly *and* efficiently exchange greetings, respond to simple questions and answers, trade pleasantries, and get to know people in a preliminary fashion, without putting much active thought into our communication. This saves us from mental exertion and allows us to focus our energy on more involved or important interpersonal encounters.

Be Clear

Using clear language means presenting information in a straightforward fashion rather than framing it in obscure or ambiguous terms. For example, telling a partner that you like a recipe but that it needs more salt is easier to understand than veiling your meaning by vaguely saying, "It's interesting." Importantly, using clear language doesn't mean being brutally frank or dumping offensive and hurtful information on others. As we've discussed in earlier chapters, skilled interpersonal communicators always consider others' feelings when designing their messages. When information is important and relevant to disclose, choose your words carefully to be both respectful *and* clear, so that others won't misconstrue your intended meaning.

Use "I" Language

It's the biggest intramural basketball game of the year, and your team is down by a point with 5 seconds left when your teammate is fouled. Stepping to the line for two free throws and a chance to win the game, she misses both, and your team loses. As you leave the court, you angrily snap at her, "You really let us down!"

SKILLS PRACTICE

This exercise helps you create a cooperative first encounter with a new acquaintance.

1 Review the sequence of topics presented in Figure 7.2.

2 Create a communication plan in your head by talking through these topics in the order in which they are presented and by thinking of specific things to say.

3 Initiate an encounter with a fellow college student who is a new acquaintance.

4 Follow the communication plan you have created.

5 As the encounter unfolds, allow for flexibility in the pattern of topics if your conversational partner goes slightly out of order or introduces a different topic.

"You" Language	"I" Language
You make me so angry!	I'm feeling so angry!
You totally messed things up.	I feel like things are totally messed up.
You need to do a better job.	I think this job needs to be done better.
You really hurt my feelings.	I'm feeling really hurt.
You never pay any attention to me.	I feel like I never get any attention.

TABLE 7.2

"You" Language versus "I" Language

The second key to cooperative verbal communication is taking ownership of the things you say to others, especially in situations where you're expressing negative feelings or criticism. You can do this by avoiding **"you" language,** phrases that place the focus of attention and blame on other people, such as "*You* let us down" and "*You* blew it." Instead, rearrange your statements so that you use **"I" language,** phrases that emphasize ownership of your feelings, opinions, and beliefs (see Table 7.2). The difference between "I" and "you" may strike you as minor, but it actually has powerful effects: "I" language is less likely to trigger defensiveness on the part of your listeners than is "you" language (Kubany, Richard, Bauer, & Muraoka, 1992). "I" language creates a clearer impression on the part of listeners that you're responsible for what you are saying and that what you are doing is expressing your own perceptions rather than accusations and unquestionable truths.

Using "We" Language

It's Thursday night, and you're standing in line waiting to get into a club. In front of you are two couples, and you can't help but overhear their conversations. As you listen, you notice an interesting difference in their verbal communication. One couple expresses everything in terms of "I" and "you"—"What do you want to do later tonight?" "I don't know, but I'm hungry, so I'll probably get something to eat. Do you want to come?" The other couple consistently uses "we"—"What should we do later?" "Why don't we get something to eat?"

What effect does this simple difference in pronoun usage—"we" rather than "I" or "you"—have on your impressions of the two couples? If you're like most people, you would perceive the couple using "we" as being closer than the couple using "I" and "you." And like most people, you would be right! "We" is a common way people signal their closeness (Dreyer, Dreyer, & Davis, 1987), and couples who use "we" language tend to be more satisfied with their relationships than those who routinely rely on "I" and "you" messages (Honeycutt, 1999).

An important part of cooperative verbal communication is using **"we" language**—wordings that emphasize inclusion—to express your connection to others. In a sense, "we" language is the inverse of "I" language. We use "I" language when we want to show others that our feelings, thoughts, and opinions are separate from them and that we take sole responsibility for our feelings, thoughts, and opinions. But "we" language is used to bolster feelings of connection and similarity with not only romantic partners but also with anyone to whom you want to signal a collaborative and cooperative relationship. When I went through my training to become a certified Yoga instructor, part of the instruction was to replace the use of "you" with "we" and "let's" during in-class verbal cueing of moves. Rather than saying, "You should lunge forward with your left leg" or "I want you to step forward left," we were taught to say, "*Let's* step forward with *our* left legs." After I implemented "we" language in my Yoga classes, my students repeatedly commented on how they liked the "more personal" and "inclusive" nature of my verbal cueing.

● Tête-à-tête chairs were developed to support a culture of frequent face-to-face verbal communication. The design of the chairs was intended to facilitate conversation.

Gender and Cooperative Verbal Communication

Powerful stereotypes exist regarding what men and women value in verbal communication. These stereotypes suggest that men appreciate informative, honest, relevant, and clear language more than women do. In Western cultures, many people believe that men communicate in a clear and straightforward fashion, whereas women are more indirect and wordy (Tannen, 1990). These stereotypes are reinforced powerfully through television, in programs in which female characters often use more polite language than men ("I'm *sorry* to bother you . . ."), more uncertain phrases ("I *suppose* . . ."), and more flowery adjectives ("that's *silly*," "oh, how *beautiful*") and male characters fill their language with action verbs ("let's *get a move on!*") (Mulac, Bradac, & Mann, 1985).

How do men's and women's actual verbal communication compare with the stereotypes? Research suggests that when it comes to language, men and women are more similar than different. For example, data from 165 studies involving nearly a million and a half subjects found that women do not use more vague and wordy verbal communication than men (Canary & Hause, 1993; Dindia & Allen, 1992; Hyde & Linn, 1988). The primary determinant of whether people's language is clear and concise or vague and wordy is not gender but whether the encounter is competitive or collaborative (Fisher, 1983). Both women and men use clear and concise language in competitive interpersonal encounters, such as when arguing with a family member or debating a project proposal in a work meeting, and they use comparatively vaguer and wordier language during collaborative encounters, such as eating lunch with a friend or relaxing in the evening with a spouse.

Women are not more likely than men to want their verbal communication to focus on personal feelings. A review of 205 studies involving 23,702 women and men found very small differences between the genders in personal disclosure (Dindia & Allen, 1992). Women do disclose more than men during same-gender encounters but not more than men within cross-gender encounters. This finding led the researchers who conducted the review to conclude, "It is time to stop perpetuating the myth that there are large sex differences in men's and women's self-disclosure" (Dindia & Allen, 1992).

Finally, one of the most common beliefs related to broader considerations of communication cooperativeness is that men interrupt more than women do. This is false. A series of studies by communication researcher Kathryn Dindia found no gender differences in interruption patterns (1987). Instead, both men and women interrupt cross-gender partners more than they interrupt same-gender partners.

Culture and Cooperative Verbal Communication

Unlike gender, culture exerts a significant impact on verbal communication. As we noted at the beginning of this chapter, language is cultural, and each culture has its own idea of what constitutes cooperative verbal communication. So how can you tailor your use of language when communicating with people from other cultures? For starters, you can study a particular culture's guidelines for verbal expression before communicating with members of

● Male and female television characters speak in ways that reinforce stereotypes about women, men, and verbal communication. Sex differences in television dialogue lead viewers to perceive female characters as "beautiful, nice, sweet" and male characters as "strong, aggressive, loud."

that culture and then adapt your own use of language according to those guidelines (Chen & Starosta, 1998).

But also consider **communication accommodation theory,** which holds that people are especially motivated to adapt their language when they seek social approval, when they wish to establish relationships with others, and when they view others' language usage as appropriate (Giles, Coupland, & Coupland, 1991). In contrast, people tend to accentuate differences between their language and others' when they wish to convey emotional distance and disassociate themselves from others. Suppose you've just met someone from a different culture who speaks the same language as you but speaks more slowly than you, takes longer to reply, and uses vaguer language than you do. Communication accommodation theory suggests that if you like that person and want to be impressive, you'll adapt your language use to match his or hers over the course of your encounter—slowing your speech rate, taking longer turns, and using ambiguous wording. If you don't wish to impress, you'll do the opposite—accentuating your verbal communication differences by talking rapidly, taking short turns, and striving for a high degree of clarity.

Research on verbal communication accommodation suggests that when you moderately adjust your language use to match that of others from different cultures, you will be perceived as having high communication skill (Coupland, Giles, & Wiemann, 1991; Giles et al., 1991). The key to such adjustments is adapting to others' speech rate, clarity of language, and desired balance of turn-taking (Bianconi, 2002). This means attuning yourself early in the conversation to how long the other person takes with his or her turns, how rapidly the individual speaks, how direct he or she is, and how much the person appears to want to talk compared to you. You then fine-tune your verbal communication accordingly: matching the person's speech rate, employing appropriately direct or more ambiguous language, using turn lengths you believe will please the person, and monitoring the other's feedback while you are speaking to see whether he or she wants you to continue or stop.

However, *never* try to match the other person's dialect or word choices. He or she will likely perceive your behavior as inappropriate and insulting. For example, in the 1980s, many American businesspeople adjusted their voice tone and word choices in an attempt to "sound Japanese" while conversing with Japanese partners. Japanese businesspeople consistently found such imitations offensive and patronizing (Boylan, 2001), just as any of us would if we heard someone else trying to imitate our dialect or voice.

Barriers to Cooperative Verbal Communication

In the spy-movie spoof *Austin Powers: The Spy Who Shagged Me*, Mike Myers plays several roles, including the arch-villain Dr. Evil (Lyons et al., 1999). In one scene, Dr. Evil, who has time-traveled back to 1969, tries to blackmail the president of the United States, while Evil's son Scott watches. Unfortunately for Dr. Evil, the president can't understand his allusions to the (future) movie *Jerry McGuire:*

DR. EVIL: Mr. President, after I destroy Washington, D.C., I will destroy another major city every hour on the hour unless of course you pay me . . . *ONE HUNDRED BILLION DOLLARS!*

PRESIDENT (LAUGHING UPROARIOUSLY): Dr. Evil, this is 1969. That amount of money doesn't even *exist!* That's like saying I want a bajillion bajillion dollars!

DR. EVIL: Come on, Mr. President, *show me the money!*

PRESIDENT: Show you *what* money?

DR. EVIL: *Show me the money! Show me the money!*

PRESIDENT: What?

DR. EVIL: *You had me at hello . . . tear . . .* nothing, no?

SCOTT (WHISPERING TO DR. EVIL): Pssst! It's 1969—*Jerry McGuire* won't even come out for another thirty years. Nobody knows what you're talking about!

Despite our best intent, our verbal communication doesn't always generate the positive results we expect—even if it is cooperatively expressed. Sometimes we speak in ways that are easy to understand, take ownership for what we say, and are appropriately inclusive, but misunderstandings or problems still ensue. At other times, *we* may communicate cooperatively, but others with whom we're interacting—like Dr. Evil—communicate in ways we can't comprehend. Communicating online only complicates the situation. Although only 12.7 percent of respondents in a study of online

communication agreed that e-mail is likely to result in miscommunication of message content, 27.2 percent of respondents agreed that e-mail is likely to result in miscommunication of intent and 53.6 percent agreed that it is relatively easy to misinterpret an e-mail message (Rainey, 2000).

In this section, we explore two common barriers to cooperative verbal communication: mispresentation and misunderstanding.

Mispresentation

Have you ever listened to someone who was striving to make sense but who was so uninformative, wordy, vague, or imprecise that you just couldn't understand what he or she was trying to say? In such cases of unintentional **mispresentation,** or ineffective presentation of language, a communicator doesn't mean to miscommunicate. The speaker simply doesn't realize that his or her verbal communication is deficient. This includes instances in which a person honestly doesn't believe that certain information is relevant, unwittingly presents false facts, or believes wrongly that he or she is being clear.

In most cultures, instances of unintentional mispresentation are considered innocent errors (Goffman, 1955). To avoid unintentional mispresentation, consistently practice the principles for cooperative verbal communication discussed previously. In addition, hone your awareness of others' responses to your messages. By doing so, you can learn to identify when others think you've mispresented and correct your errors as they become apparent.

Sometimes mispresentation is intentional, however. Consider the White House press conference that President Bill Clinton held on January 26, 1998, in response to a scandal involving his behavior with intern Monica Lewinsky. His fist clenched, Clinton angrily insisted, "I did not have sexual relations with that woman, Miss Lewinsky. I never told anybody to lie, not a single time, never. These allegations are false and I need to get back to work for the American people." Several months later, on July 17, Clinton admitted the affair in a televised speech to the grand jury investigating the matter, making it clear that he had lied in his former statement.

When people deliberately use uninformative, untruthful, irrelevant, or vague language for the specific purpose of misleading others, they're engaging in intentional mispresentation, more commonly called **deception.** Clinton, for example, sought to deceive people by baldly presenting false information. He *had* engaged in sexual relations with Lewinsky, and he *had* told people who were aware of the relationship to lie. Still, people more often deceive by leaving important information out of messages; indeed, concealment is the most frequent form of intentional mispresentation (McCornack, 1997).

Deception is also commonplace during online encounters. People communicating in chatrooms and via e-mail and text-messaging distort and hide whatever information they want, providing little opportunity for the recipients of their messages to check accuracy. Some people provide false information about their backgrounds, professions, appearances, and gender online for amusement, to form alternative relationships unavailable to them offline, or to take advantage of others through online scams (Rainey, 2000).

Of course, even someone who intentionally mispresents information may not be doing so out of malicious intent. As noted earlier, many cultures view ambiguous and indirect language as hallmarks of cooperative verbal communication. In addition, sometimes people intentionally mispresent information out of kindness and desire to maintain the relationship, such as when you tell a close friend that her awful new hairstyle looks great because you know she'll be agonizingly self-conscious if she knew how bad it really looked (McCornack, 1997; Metts & Chronis, 1986).

Misunderstanding

Miscommunication is just as likely to occur when hearers misunderstand language used cooperatively as it is when speakers unintentionally or intentionally use language uncooperatively. **Misunderstanding** occurs when one person misperceives another's thoughts, feelings, or beliefs as expressed in

POP QUIZ

Test Your Deception Acceptance

People vary widely in the degree to which they think deception is an acceptable and appropriate form of verbal communication. To test your deception acceptance, check each statement that you agree with. Then total your score and compare it to the scoring key.

❏ 1. You should never tell anyone the real reason you did something unless it is useful to do so.

❏ 2. It is okay to lie in order to achieve your goals.

❏ 3. What people don't know can't hurt them.

❏ 4. The best way to handle people is to tell them what they want to hear.

❏ 5. It is often better to lie than to hurt someone's feelings.

❏ 6. There is nothing wrong with lying as long as you don't get caught.

❏ 7. In some situations lying can be the most ethical thing to do.

❏ 8. Honesty isn't always the best policy.

❏ 9. There are many instances in which lying is justified.

❏10. Lying can sometimes solve problems more effectively than telling the truth.

Scoring:

0–3: Low deception acceptance. You believe that deception is unacceptable no matter the circumstance, and you likely react extremely negatively when you find out people have lied to you. 4–6: Moderate deception acceptance. You believe that deception is acceptable under certain circumstances, and you probably are more accepting when others lie to you. 7–10: High deception acceptance. You believe that deception is an acceptable form of behavior, and you likely use it regularly to deal with difficult communication and relationship situations.

Note: This *Pop Quiz* is adapted from the lie acceptability scale developed by Levine, McCornack, and Baldwin Avery (1992).

the other individual's verbal communication. As with mispresentation, misunderstanding can be unintentional or intentional.

Unintentional misunderstanding occurs when people mean to understand someone else, but walk away from encounters with a faulty perception of that person's thoughts, feelings, or beliefs. Unintentional misunderstandings have three origins. The first—and perhaps most common—is failure to actively listen. Recall, for example, our discussion of action-oriented listeners in Chapter 6. Action-oriented listeners often become impatient with others while listening and frequently jump ahead and finish other people's (presumed) points (Watson, Barker, & Weaver, 1995). This listening style can lead them to misunderstand others' messages. To overcome this source of misunderstanding, practice the active listening skills described in Chapter 6.

Another cause of unintentional misunderstanding, strangely enough, is relationship intimacy. As we'll see in Chapter 10, when we're involved in romantic relationships, we often presume that our partners share our opinions. This assumption can lead us to unintentionally misunderstand our part-

● We all encounter chronically hostile people at some point. When people are chronically hostile, it is hard to determine how our behavior will affect theirs and how we should communicate with them.

ners' actual attitudes and beliefs ("But I thought you loved Usher as much as I do!") (Sillars, Folwell, Hill, Maki, Hurst, & Casano, 1994; Sillars, Pike, Jones, & Murphy, 1984).

Finally, unintentional misunderstanding can arise when people innocently misinterpret others' messages. This occurs often when people are communicating online because they lack nonverbal cues to clarify one another's meaning. The tendency to misunderstand online verbal communication is so prevalent that online scholars suggest the following practices: If a particular message absolutely must be error-free, don't use e-mail or text-messaging to communicate it. Avoid using e-mail and text-messaging when the content of your message is controversial. Whenever possible, conduct high-stakes encounters, such as important attempts at persuasion, face-to-face. Finally, never use e-mail for sensitive actions such as professional reprimands or dismissals (Rainey, 2000).

Misunderstanding can also happen intentionally. Sometimes, no matter what you say, a person who is biased against you will look for excuses to twist your words and make negative judgments about you. Individuals

SELF-REFLECTION

Recall an online encounter in which you thought you understood someone's e-mail or text message, then later found out you were wrong. How did you discover that your impression was mistaken? What led to the misunderstanding? What could you have done differently to avoid the misunderstanding?

Making Relationship Choices

Honesty in Verbal Communication

1

BACKGROUND

Cooperative verbal communicators constantly strive to use language that is appropriately informative, honest, relevant, and clear. But sometimes information that is relevant to share with others can be damaging. In such situations, deception becomes a tempting alternative. To find out how you would cope with such a situation, read this case study and work through the five steps that follow.

2

CASE STUDY

You've been dating Kieran for two years, and the relationship is the most serious you've experienced. Your best friend and lover, Kieran is smart, funny, kind, and honest. Your families and circles of friends support the relationship, and at various points over the last year, the two of you have discussed possibly living together or getting married.

Recently, however, your feelings for Kieran have changed. You both are graduating and you're uncomfortable making a permanent commitment at this point. In fact, you've found yourself craving freedom—to do what you want when you want without having to account for your time and to go out with other people. Kieran, however, is moving in the opposite direction and lately has been pushing for a firmer commitment. Although you haven't discussed your changing feelings with Kieran, the tension between your competing relationship goals is obvious. The two of you have been fighting a lot and Kieran has been acting uncharacteristically jealous and possessive.

Cael, a friend from class, has made the situation even more complicated. Cael has qualities you feel Kieran lacks—including light-heartedness and a relaxed attitude about relationships. A few nights ago, you ran into Cael at a party. You hung out, one thing led to another, and the two of you ended up spending the night together. The next morning, you felt intensely guilty, but the experience also made you realize that you aren't ready to commit to one person yet.

Soon after, you're at Kieran's house studying. Kieran is uptight and grouchy, responding to you with one-word answers. The tension mounts, and suddenly Kieran says, "You've seemed really distant lately. It's like there's this big wall between us, and I'm tired of it. Is something wrong?"

Immediately, a million thoughts race through your head. You love Kieran, and you want to protect the relationship. You also respect and admire Kieran as a friend, and don't want to be hurtful. But you feel that Kieran should know about your feelings and your recent dalliance with Cael. And you want freedom to pursue other relationships, including one with Cael. What do you say to Kieran?

YOUR TURN

While working through the following steps, keep in mind the interpersonal communication concepts, skills, and insights you've learned so far in this book, especially in this chapter. Also remember: there are no right answers, so think hard about the choice you make! (P.S. Need help? Review the concepts listed below.)

● **Step 1: Reflect on yourself.** What are your thoughts and feelings in this situation? What attributions are you making about Kieran? Are your attributions accurate? Why or why not?

● **Step 2: Reflect on your partner.** Using perspective-taking and empathic concern, put yourself in Kieran's shoes. Consider how your partner is thinking and feeling. How does Kieran likely perceive you and your behavior? How does Kieran feel about you and your relationship?

● **Step 3: Identify the optimal outcome.** Think about all the information you have about Kieran and about this relationship. Consider your own feelings as well as your partner's. Given all these factors, what's the best, most constructive relationship outcome possible here? Be sure to consider not just what's best for *you*, but what's best for Kieran as well.

● **Step 4: Locate the roadblocks.** Taking into consideration your own thoughts and feelings, Kieran's, and recent events in this situation, what's preventing you from achieving the optimal outcome you identified in step 3?

● **Step 5: Chart your course.** What will you say to Kieran to overcome the roadblocks you've identified and achieve your optimal relationship outcome?

suffering from chronic hostility (discussed in Chapter 4) also commonly engage in intentional misunderstanding. Because chronically hostile people believe that others are exploitive, manipulative, and immoral, they interpret others' language in ways that provoke conflict. Another example of intentional misunderstanding occurs within intimate relationships. Sometimes when individuals repeatedly misbehave (lying, cheating, complaining), their romantic partners intentionally misunderstand them to preserve relationship harmony—"overlooking their flaws," as people say (McCornack, 1997).

Unfortunately, little can be done to combat intentional misunderstanding. You can communicate in a perfectly cooperative fashion, but if someone possesses unalterable beliefs that lead him or her to misunderstand your meanings, you have no power to change this. The best recommendation for dealing with such encounters is to practice the principles of cooperative verbal communication; treat the person with kindness, respect, and empathy; and extricate yourself from the encounter as quickly as possible.

The Power of Verbal Communication

One can't help but marvel at the power of verbal communication. Words are our symbolic vehicle for creating and exchanging meanings, performing actions, and forging relationships. We use language to name all that surrounds us; and in turn, the names we have created shape how we think and feel about these things.

But for most of us, the power of language is experienced as intensely personal. Call to mind the most important relationship events in your life. When you do, you'll likely find they were not merely accompanied by verbal communication but were defined and created through it. Perhaps it was the first time you said "I love you" to a partner or posed the heart-stopping query "Will you marry me?" Maybe it was a doctor declaring, "It's a boy!" "It's a girl!" "It's twins!" Or perhaps the relational events that float upward into memory are sadder in nature, the words bitter remnants you wish you could forget: "I don't love you anymore." "I never want to see you again." "I'm sorry, but the prognosis is grim."

With great power comes great responsibility, as the saying goes, and our power to shape and use verbal communication is no different. The words we exchange profoundly affect not only our interpersonal communication and relationships but also others'. And the responsibility we bear because of this power is to communicate cooperatively.

POSTSCRIPT

We began this chapter with a nationally publicized example of the misunderstanding that can arise from verbal communication. Toni Cook and the members of the Oakland school board wanted nothing other than to improve the education of African American students in their district by enhancing their Standard English skills. They communicated their resolution to the public using the most informative, honest, and clear communication possible . . . and disaster resulted.

What important "resolutions" have you communicated to others that ended up being misunderstood? What have you done when your verbal communication—no matter how cooperative—was turned upside down by people determined to twist your words and see you in a critical light?

The Oakland School District story doesn't mean that cooperative verbal communication is fruitless. Instead, it serves as a powerful reminder of the limits of language. Just because you choose your words wisely doesn't mean that others will understand your meaning or respond in the way you intended. People will always hear what they want to hear and believe what they want to believe. In the end, cooperative verbal communication means doing everything in *your* power to ensure positive outcomes from your interactions with others.

Chapter Review

Key Terms

Key Concepts

Characteristics of Verbal Communication

- We use **verbal communication** when interacting with coworkers, friends, family members, and romantic partners. In doing so, we employ words as **symbols** to represent people, objects, and ideas.

- Verbal communication is governed by both **constitutive rules** and **regulative rules.** These rules define meanings and clarify appropriate spelling, grammar, and even conversational structure.

- Partners in close relationships often develop **personal idioms** for each other that convey intimacy and uniqueness. Large groups develop common **dialects** that include distinct pronunciations and word choices. People are inclined to judge others with dissimilar dialects more negatively than they judge those with similar dialects.

- Culture has an enormous impact on language perception and usage. People within **low-context cultures** tend not to presume commonly shared knowledge with others, and consequently use direct, informative language. Because individuals in **high-context cultures** assume a high degree of shared knowledge in others, they tend to rely more on implied meanings and indirect expression.

Functions of Verbal Communication

- When we speak, we convey both **denotative meaning** and **connotative meaning** to others. People in intimate relationships often communicate to each other connotative meanings that others are incapable of interpreting.

- Proponents of **linguistic determinism** suggest that our capacity for thought is defined by the limits of our language. Because language is defined by culture, people from different cultures perceive and experience different realities, due to **linguistic relativity.**

- Although language shapes our thoughts, we control language through the power of **naming.** Groups who face prejudice often seek out names that are more positive in order to offset the social stigma they face in daily life.

- Words don't merely express meanings; they also perform actions. Whenever we interact with others, we use language to perform **speech acts,** and our conversations are in large part structured in accordance with the types of speech acts we perform.

Cooperative Verbal Communication

- Using **cooperative verbal communication** requires that you abide by the **Cooperative Principle.** You also should avoid expressing negative evaluations and opinions through **"you" language;** instead, replace it with **"I" language. "We" language** is a good means for fostering the sense of inclusiveness characteristic of cooperative communication.

- Although men and women perceive cooperative communication in largely similar ways, substantial cultural differences exist. A good approach for communicating cooperatively across cultures is to follow the guidelines of **communication accommodation theory,** adapting your language use in appropriate ways to match those of your conversational partners.

Barriers to Cooperative Verbal Communication

- Even the most ardent of cooperative verbal communicators occasionally fall prey to unintentional **mispresentation.** But when misrepresentation is performed intentionally, we consider it **deception.**

- Sometimes we communicate in a perfectly cooperative fashion, but **misunderstanding** still results. This can stem from people not listening to us, hearing only what they want to hear, or intentionally distorting our words because they are biased against us.

Key Skills

- How do dialects shape your perception, and how might you best communicate verbally with people who use different dialects? Review the answers on page 224; then complete the *Pop Quiz* on page 223 to test your knowledge of American dialects.

- What responsibilities do cooperative communicators face related to the language that they choose? Find out on pages 238–239.

- How much information should you share with others to be a cooperative verbal communicator? The answer is on page 239.

- What topics should you discuss when communicating with a fellow college student for the first time? Review Figure 7.2 on page 240 to refresh your memory; then do the *Skills Practice* on page 241.

- How can you better take ownership over your negative opinions and evaluations of others? Find out on page 242.

- What can you do to express inclusion and closeness through your language? Discover the answer on page 242.

- What is the key to cooperative verbal communication across cultures, and the one thing you never want to do in a cross-cultural encounter? Find out on pages 243–244; then do the *Skills Practice* on page 244.

- How can you avoid unintentional mispresentation online and face-to-face? Follow the recommendations on page 246; then do the *Skills Practice* on page 246.

- Are you inclined to intentionally mispresent information? Discover your level of deception acceptance by taking the *Pop Quiz* on page 247.

- What can you do to prevent misunderstandings during online encounters? Discover the answer on pages 246–247.

- Interested in finding out how to be appropriately honest in intimate relationships? Complete the *Making Relationship Choices* exercise on pages 250–251.

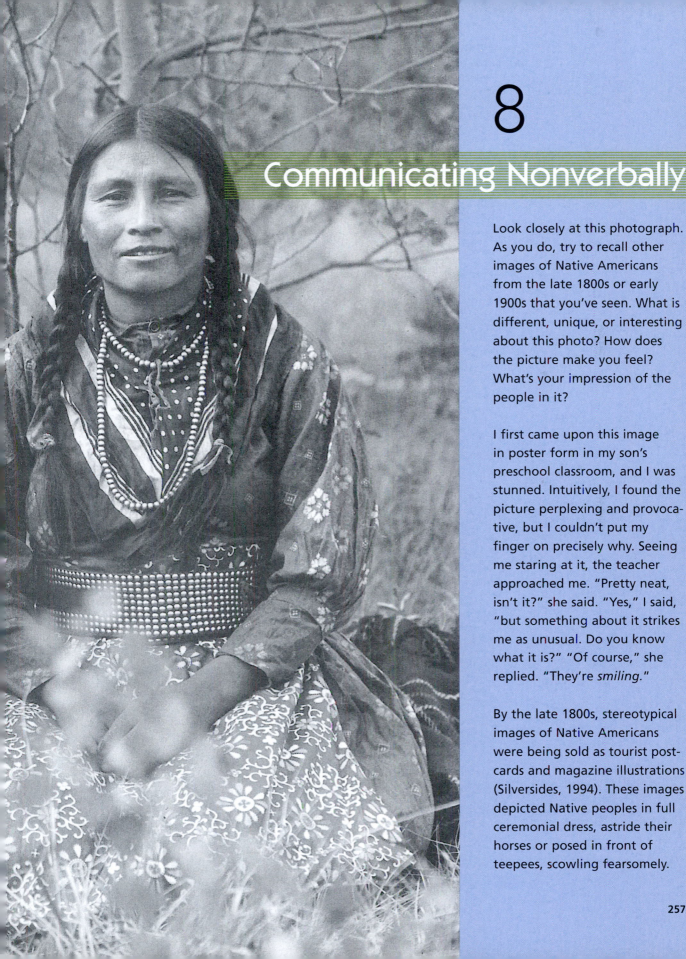

8

Communicating Nonverbally

Look closely at this photograph. As you do, try to recall other images of Native Americans from the late 1800s or early 1900s that you've seen. What is different, unique, or interesting about this photo? How does the picture make you feel? What's your impression of the people in it?

I first came upon this image in poster form in my son's preschool classroom, and I was stunned. Intuitively, I found the picture perplexing and provocative, but I couldn't put my finger on precisely why. Seeing me staring at it, the teacher approached me. "Pretty neat, isn't it?" she said. "Yes," I said, "but something about it strikes me as unusual. Do you know what it is?" "Of course," she replied. "They're *smiling*."

By the late 1800s, stereotypical images of Native Americans were being sold as tourist postcards and magazine illustrations (Silversides, 1994). These images depicted Native peoples in full ceremonial dress, astride their horses or posed in front of teepees, scowling fearsomely.

As Cambridge University professor Maria Tippett (1994) notes, "The image one gets throughout this seventy year period is of a blank-faced, stiff, and unengaged people" (p. 2). When I surveyed more than 5,000 photos from this era, I found not a single image portraying Native Americans with smiles—except for this family photo.[1]

In contrast, this rare portrait, taken by amateur photographer Mary Schaffer (1861–1939), shows people who, rather than staring blankly into the camera, "communicate with the eyes behind it" (Tippett, 1994). The image has an intriguing history. Schaffer, with her friend Mollie Adams and two guides, were exploring the headwaters of the Saskatchewan and

Athabasca rivers in Canada, where they met a band of Stoney Indians who befriended them. Among them were Samson Beaver, his wife Leah, and their young daughter Frances, who invited Mary to dinner. After the meal, Mary asked them if she could take their picture, and they agreed.

The Beaver family photo provides a literal and metaphorical snapshot of an interpersonal encounter: the postures, faces, dress, and use of space during a family meeting with a new friend late one sunny afternoon. You can almost feel the fellowship that must have infused the conversation, communicated through Samson's smile, his forward lean, and his direct gaze—all cues conveying

intimacy and closeness. If you feel an immediate connection and empathy with Samson, you're not alone. This is a typical human reaction to the sight of a smiling person. A scowling face has quite the opposite effect.

The Beaver family photo reminds us of the universal and transcendent nature of human nonverbal expression and of its powerful role in shaping our impressions of others. A hundred years ago, a family joined new friends to share a meal and something of themselves with each other. Although they're all long since dead, the image of their encounter serves as an enduring reminder of the power of human nonverbal expression to shape our interpersonal communication and relationships.

---

[1] Author review of 5,000 photos in the Curtis Archives; http://curtis.library.northwestern.edu/toc.cgi

Chapter 7 noted the impact of language on our interpersonal communication and relationships. But the potency of verbal communication pales in comparison to that of nonverbal communication. Researchers have found that most of the meaning we exchange during interpersonal encounters comes from our nonverbal expressions (Birdwhistell, 1955). And if forced to choose which to believe—verbal or nonverbal messages—we select the nonverbal (Burgoon & Hoobler, 2002).

Learning to manage your nonverbal communication responsibly poses a great challenge because skillful nonverbal expression involves mastery of different aspects of behavior. When you communicate nonverbally, you manipulate your bodily movements, your voice, and the way you touch others. You also decide how to occupy space, craft your appearance, and use time. And you do all of this simultaneously. To do so *skillfully* requires knowledge of the various means of nonverbal communication, the ability to shape and adapt nonverbal expression, and the motivation to do so. But it's worth it. Nonverbal skill is associated with higher levels of self-esteem and life satisfaction, perceptions of attractiveness and popularity by others, greater interpersonal influence in situations requiring persuasive ability, and higher satisfaction rates in interpersonal relationships (Burgoon & Hoobler, 2002; Carton, Kessler, & Pape, 1999; Hodgins & Belch, 2000).

In this chapter, we discuss communication without words and offer guidelines for strengthening your nonverbal communication skills. You'll learn:

- How nonverbal communication differs from verbal, and how gender and culture affect our nonverbal communication

- The eight codes of nonverbal communication, and how you can more effectively use these codes when interacting with others

- What purposes nonverbal communication serves in our everyday lives

- How to responsibly manage your nonverbal communication

● What comes to mind when you think about nonverbal communication? Is it as subtle as the look in your partner's eyes when you've said something funny? Is it as dramatic as an image from a movie that sticks in your memory?

Principles of Nonverbal Communication

Most of us share an intuitive sense of what nonverbal communication is: it's "body language"—gestures, facial expressions, and posture. But challenges arise when we try to pin down a precise definition (Burgoon & Hoobler, 2002). Some scholars argue that *all* nonverbal behavior should be considered communication; that during interpersonal encounters with others, "you cannot not communicate" (Watzlawick, Beavin, & Jackson, 1967). If your manager at work perceives your poorly stifled yawn of fatigue as a sign of boredom and lack of interest, communication has occurred, even though you didn't intend it to. Others suggest that only those behaviors through which we intend to convey meaning count as nonverbal communication (Ekman & Friesen, 1969). From this perspective, the yawn seen by your boss wouldn't constitute nonverbal communication, but a yawn used intentionally to tease a friend about a story she's told one too many times *would* count as communication.

In this book, we define **nonverbal communication** as the intentional or unintentional transmission of meaning through an individual's nonspoken physical and behavioral cues (Patterson, 1983, 1995). This definition embraces both intentional and unintentional nonverbal behaviors as communication. Sometimes we do things like yawn, sigh, or grimace and mean nothing by them; but others interpret them as acts of communication, and their perceptions lead them to respond in ways that affect us, our interpersonal communication, and our relationships. A boss who catches you yawning may express concern that you're "not paying attention," even though you're closely attending to your work. At other times, we intentionally craft nonverbal behaviors to communicate information to others. We add frowning emoticons :-(to e-mails to show family members we're sad, or we look at coworkers to signal we're ready for meetings.

As you might have gathered, nonverbal communication differs markedly from verbal communication, a fact reflected in the very label we use to describe it: *non*verbal. Below, we take a closer look at the key distinctions between nonverbal and verbal forms of expression.

Nonverbal Communication Uses Multiple Channels

In contrast with verbal communication, which we transmit through a single auditory channel (the human voice), our nonverbal messages are expressed through multiple channels—including auditory, visual, and tactile. When you talk with a good friend, for example, you simultaneously listen to your friend's tone of voice (auditory); watch your friend's facial expressions, use of eye contact, and hand gestures (visual); and perhaps even touch and receive touch from your friend (tactile). What's more, you do this while also listening to and making sense of your friend's verbal communication.

Nonverbal Communication Is More Ambiguous

Nonverbal meanings are more flexible and ambiguous than verbal meanings. A smile can express comfort or contempt, just as a shared glance can convey intimacy or warning—depending on the situation. The ambiguity of nonverbal messages can pose difficulties for interpersonal communication and relationships. For instance, suppose a friend you suspect of harboring romantic feelings for you gives you an extra-long hug. Is he or she just being friendly or signaling romantic interest? Some people exploit the ambiguity of nonverbal messages, intentionally communicating in ways designed to create confusion. Consider a manager who believes he can get more work out of his employees by keeping them guessing about his mood. "If they're not sure of my mood," the boss tells himself, "they may worry that I'm not pleased with their performance and work harder just to be on the safe side." This boss may suddenly put his hand on the back of your neck and give it a firm grip while you're working on an important and difficult project. You don't know if the touch is meant to communicate intimidation or emotional support—so, just to play it safe, you step up your efforts on the project.

Nonverbal Communication Has Fewer Rules

Nonverbal communication is more ambiguous than verbal communication because it is governed by fewer rules. As you saw in Chapter 7, you learn literally thousands of constitutive and regulative rules regarding grammar, spelling, pronunciation, and meaning as you master your first and any additional languages. But consider how rarely you've been instructed in the use of nonverbal communication. To be sure, nonverbal rules do exist, such as "Raise your hand if you want to be called on." However, most of these rules are informal norms—for instance, "It's not polite to stare at people," and "You shouldn't stand too close to another person in an elevator, if there are only two of you riding."

Nonverbal Communication Has More Meaning

When we interact with others, we often deduce more meaning from people's nonverbal communication than from their verbal, and we convey more meaning to them from our nonverbal than from our verbal. Suppose you meet someone new at a party and find yourself intrigued. To assess the person's attractiveness, you probably gather a lot more information from his or her facial expressions, eye contact, posture, gestures, vocal tone, clothing, and other nonverbal signals than you do from the person's words. This is because during first encounters, nonverbal communication has a greater impact on our overall impressions of attractiveness than does verbal communication (Raines, Hechtman, & Rosenthal, 1990; Zuckerman, Miyake, & Hodgins, 1991). Some scholars argue that as much as 93 percent of the meaning exchanged during interpersonal encounters comes from nonverbal sources (Mehrabian & Wiener, 1967), while others suggest that from 60 to 65 percent of meaning is communicated nonverbally (Birdwhistell, 1955).

Our reliance on nonverbal communication escalates even higher when people display **mixed messages,** verbal and nonverbal behaviors that convey contradictory meanings (Burgoon & Hoobler, 2002). A friend says she "isn't sad," but her slumped shoulders and frowning mouth suggest otherwise; your child insists he's "not scared" by a theme park ride, but his wide eyes and death grip on your arm show he is. In such cases, we almost always trust the nonverbal messages over the verbal ones. In contrast, when verbal and nonverbal messages align ("Yes, I'm sad" coupled with slumped shoulders and frown, or "Yes, I'm scared!" accompanying wide eyes and death grip), the amount of attention we pay to verbal communication rises (Burgoon & Hoobler, 2002).

Nonverbal and Verbal Combine to Create Communication

Despite the differences between verbal and nonverbal forms of expression and the weight we give nonverbal communication when sending and receiving information, they both are essential. When we interact with others, our verbal and nonverbal behaviors combine to create meaning (Jones & LeBaron, 2002). And in everyday encounters, verbal and nonverbal communication are not experienced or expressed separately but are used jointly to create interpersonal communication (Birdwhistell, 1970). Keep this in mind: your skill as a nonverbal communicator goes hand in hand with your skill as a verbal communicator, so you need *both* to communicate effectively.

Nonverbal Communication Is Influenced by Gender

When Irish singer Sinéad O'Connor's first album, *The Lion and the Cobra,* was released in 1987, the American cover depicted the shorn singer demurely gazing downward (O'Connor, 1987). But the version released to the rest of the globe showed a vastly different image: a screaming face that far more accurately represented the anger in O'Connor's songs. Why the difference? U.S. record distributors feared that Americans would react negatively to such a hostile facial expression displayed by a woman.

As with other forms of communication, people possess stereotypes about how the different genders use nonverbal communication and what men and women consider appropriate nonverbal expression. Men presumably display strong and forceful nonverbal expressions—such as dramatic gestures and expansive use of space—to convey dominance, and such behavior is seen as acceptable for males. Women, in contrast, are "supposed" to use supportive, nurturing, and submissive nonverbal communication—for example, the lowered gaze shown on O'Connor's American album cover. Common wisdom also holds that women are more skilled at nonverbal communication than men. Women reputedly can better read others' emotions

SELF-REFLECTION

When you receive mixed messages from someone else, which do you put more faith in, the verbal or the nonverbal communication? Why? Have you ever deliberately sent mixed messages to someone else during an interpersonal encounter? Was it ethical to do so?

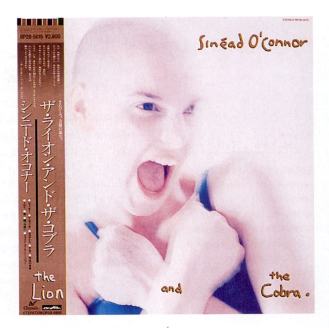

from nonverbal expression, can accurately display their own emotions, and can more easily distinguish between friendly nonverbal messages and sexual interest (Baldwin-Avery, McCornack, & Pickett, 1992).

Research on nonverbal communication affirms some of these beliefs. For example, psychologist Judith Hall has examined data from hundreds of gender studies, assessing patterns of similarity and difference in nonverbal communication (Hall, 1984, 1998; Hall, Carter, & Horgan, 2000). Her findings suggest four consistent patterns. First, women are better than men at both sending and receiving nonverbal messages. In 71 percent of the gender studies Hall examined, women were better than men at nonverbally communicating in ways receivers could correctly interpret, and in 84 percent of the studies women were more accurate than men in their interpretations of others' nonverbal expressions.

Second, women show greater facial expressiveness than men, and they smile more. The difference in smiling stems in part from cultural expectations that women should exhibit only positive and pleasant nonverbal expressions (Spender, 1990). Many feminists argue that the smiling difference also derives from men's greater dominance. Numerous studies have shown that people associate nonsmiling faces with dominance and smiling faces with submissiveness (Deutsch, 1990).

Third, women gaze more at others during interpersonal interactions. This is especially apparent within same-gender conversations, where mutual gaze occurs much more often between females than between males.

Finally, men are more territorial than women. Men maintain more physical space between themselves and others during encounters. Women tolerate more intrusion into their personal space, give way to others more frequently if space is scarce, and try to take up less space than do men. Women also adopt closer conversational distances during same-gender encounters than do men, prefer side-by-side seating more than men, and perceive crowded situations more favorably.

You can use your knowledge of these differences to improve your nonverbal skills. When interacting with men, be aware that they may prefer greater conversational distance and a less direct gaze than women, and take pains to convey nonverbal messages as clearly as possible. During encounters with women, don't be surprised if they adopt a closer conversational distance, and be sensitive to their likely preference for a more direct gaze and more frequent eye contact. Failing to recognize these differences may result in frustration or misunderstandings. For example, a friend of mine celebrated her first anniversary with her husband by returning to the spot where their wedding had occurred: underneath a large tree overlooking beautiful fields. She expected that they would sit down facing each other, open up their picnic basket, and gaze lovingly into each other's eyes while eating and reviewing their first year of married life. Instead, he sat next to her and gazed off into the distance for a good part of the time. She felt that he was ignoring her and got angry. He later explained to her that he felt very intimate sitting next to her and looking out over the fields surrounding their wedding spot. She told me later that if she had known ahead of time that men often prefer less direct gaze, she might have interpreted the incident differently and experienced not only far less pain but possibly a greater feeling of intimacy by knowing that *he* felt intimate.

Nonverbal Communication Is Influenced by Culture

You're at a dinner party, and an Iranian student named Amid introduces himself. Amid approaches you very closely—standing so close that his face is only about 12 inches from yours. You think, "Close talker," and back up, but he closes the distance again. The two of you end up repeating this little "distance dance" throughout your conversation—him closing the distance, you expanding it again, and both of you feeling uncertain and uncomfortable.

This "hypothetical" example happened to me when I was in college. And although Amid and I went on to become close friends, our initial conversation was awkward because of our competing views regarding the appropriate amount of distance that should exist during first encounters. As I learned later, Amid perceived my moves to establish greater distance as communicating "aloofness" and "desire to not interact," whereas I viewed his desire for close distance as intrusive and unsettling.

As my encounter with Amid illustrates, nonverbal communication and culture are inextricably linked, in ways we will discuss throughout this chapter. You can wrinkle your brow, use a hand gesture, or speak loudly to make a point, but if people in the culture surrounding you don't understand your behavior, you haven't communicated your message. Consider cultural differences in the meaning of eye contact, for example (Chen & Starosta, 1998). In the United States, it's considered impolite or even offensive for men to gaze openly at women, but in Italy, people view it as perfectly appropriate. Middle Easterners view gazing as a sign of respect during conversation, but Cambodians see direct eye contact as insulting and an

SELF-REFLECTION

Do the women you know perceive and display nonverbal messages more accurately than men? Do they smile more and hold their gaze longer? Are men more territorial than women in their use of space during interpersonal communication?

invasion of privacy. Euro-Americans use more eye contact when they're listening than when they're talking, but for African Americans, the opposite often is true.

The tight link between culture and nonverbal communication makes cross-cultural communication difficult to master. Sure, the nonverbal symbols used in different cultures are easy enough to learn. But familiarity with the full tapestry of cues—use of personal space, attitudes toward time, perception of touch, appropriateness of gaze, facial expressions—takes much longer. Most people need many years of immersion in a culture before they fully understand the meanings of that culture's nonverbal communication (Chen & Starosta, 1998).

Nonverbal Communication Codes

One reason nonverbal communication contains such rich information is that during interpersonal encounters, we use many different aspects of our behavior, appearance, and surrounding environment simultaneously to communicate meaning. You can greatly strengthen your nonverbal communication skills by understanding **nonverbal communication codes,** the different means used for transmitting information nonverbally (Burgoon & Hoobler, 2002). Scholars distinguish eight different nonverbal communication codes, summarized in Table 8.1.

Communicating through Body Movements

It is arguably one of the most chilling moments in cinematic history. In the Oscar award-winning film *The Silence of the Lambs* (Demme, Tally, & Bozman, 1991), FBI agent Clarice Starling approaches the top-security underground jail cell of infamous mass-murderer Dr. Hannibal Lecter. As Starling gains her first glimpse of Lecter, she finds him standing erectly, staring intensely. His arms held rigidly by his side, he wears an expectant expression on his face. Neither says a word. Yet Lecter's posture, facial

Kinesics: visible body movements, including facial expressions, eye contact, gestures, and body postures

Vocalics: vocal characteristics such as loudness, pitch, speech rate, and tone

Haptics: duration, placement, and strength of touch

Proxemics: use of physical distance

Chronemics: organization and use of time

Physical appearance: appearance of hair, clothing, body type, and other physical features

Artifacts: personal possessions displayed to others

Environment: structure of physical surroundings

TABLE 8.1

The Eight Codes of Nonverbal Communication

"A person's character is written on the face."

expression, and eyes create an intense sense of menace.

Lecter's behaviors exemplify the power of **kinesics** (from the Greek *kinesis,* meaning "movement")—visible body movements. Kinesics is the richest nonverbal code in terms of its power to communicate meaning, and it includes most of the behaviors we associate with nonverbal communication: facial expression, eye contact, gestures, and body postures.

Facial Expression. A person's character is clearly written on the face. As this traditional Chinese saying suggests, the face plays a pivotal role in shaping our perception of others. In fact, some scholars argue that facial cues rank first among all forms of communication in their influence on our interpersonal impressions (Knapp & Hall, 2002). We use facial expression to communicate an endless stream of emotions, and we make judgments about what others are feeling by assessing their facial expressions. Our use of emoticons (such as ☺ and ☹) to communicate attitudes and emotions online

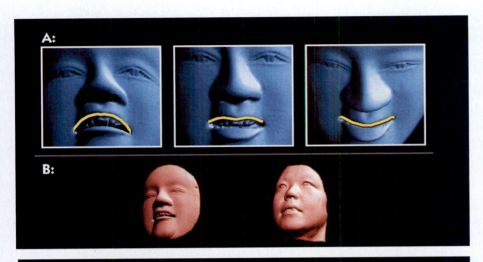

FIGURE 8.1

Traditional Japanese Noh Masks

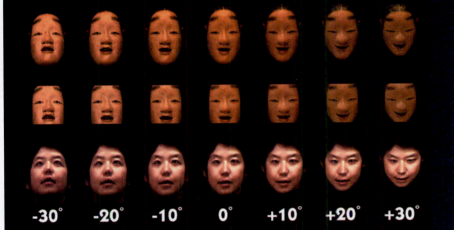

-30°   -20°   -10°   0°   +10°   +20°   +30°

FIGURE 8.2

Full Sequence of Seven Noh Mask Photos

testifies to our reliance on this type of kinesics, and the primacy of the face even influences our labeling of interpersonal encounters ("face-to-face") and Web sites devoted to social networking (www.facebook.com).

As with all kinesics, we perceive facial expression visually. Consequently, our visual perspective—where we are in relation to the person we're observing—affects our perception. Consider the three traditional Japanese Noh masks, displayed in Figure 8.1. What do they communicate to you? The three images are actually the same mask, viewed from different angles. Don't believe it? Look at the seven photos in Figure 8.2, displaying the same mask slowly being tilted forward and backward. This shift in facial expressions is known as the "Noh mask effect," which communication researchers in Japan and London tested in a series of studies by asking viewers to judge the mask's changing expression based on its tilt (Lyons et al., 2000).

The Noh mask effect suggests several practical tips to keep in mind about facial expressions. For one thing, it's not the entirety of the face but its specific features—angle of the eyebrows, curve of the mouth, width of the eyes—that communicate the other person's expressions. Thus a quick assessment of all these features can help you arrive at the most accurate

"Within a few days of birth, infants can communicate with caregivers through eye contact."

interpretation of what you're seeing. Moreover, it's wise to take care while judging facial expressions; depending on your viewing angle, you may be misreading them! For instance, if your roommate is glancing down at some paperwork on his desk while you're talking with him, his face may appear more pensive or moody than he actually feels.

Eye Contact.   Margaret Atwood's novel *The Handmaid's Tale* (1985) tells of a futuristic culture in which young women are forced to be "Handmaids," living only to produce offspring. Handmaids must avoid all eye contact, particularly with other Handmaids, because sharing a gaze might convey conspiracy. In one scene, the story's narrator—Offred—accidentally catches the gaze of her shopping companion Ofglen:[2]

> Ofglen and I stand outside, looking through the shatterproof windows. Now I shift my gaze. What I see is not the machines, but Ofglen, reflected in the glass of the window. She's looking straight at me. We can see into each other's eyes. This is the first time I've seen Ofglen's eyes, directly, steadily, not aslant. She holds my stare in the glass, level, unwavering. Now it's hard to look away. There's a shock in this seeing; it's like seeing somebody naked, for the first time. There is risk, suddenly, in the air between us, where there was none before. This meeting of eyes holds danger.

Eye contact serves a multiplicity of purposes during interpersonal communication. We use our eyes to express emotions, signal when it's someone else's turn to talk, and show others that we're listening to them.

SELF-REFLECTION

Recall a recent encounter in which you exchanged looks with someone but not words. What messages did each of you communicate through the exchange of eye contact? Was the encounter positive or negative? What aspects of the eye contact made the encounter pleasant or unpleasant?

_____

[2] Atwood, M. (1985). *The Handmaid's Tale*. New York: Fawcett Crest, pp. 216–217.

We can also demonstrate our interest in a conversation by increasing our eye contact or signal relationship intimacy by locking eyes with a close friend or romantic partner.

Eye contact also can convey hostility. One of the most aggressive forms of nonverbal expression is prolonged staring—fixed and unwavering eye contact of several seconds' duration (typically accompanied by a hostile facial expression). Although women seldom stare, men use this behavior to threaten others, invite aggression ("staring someone down" to provoke a fight), and assert their status (Burgoon, Buller, & Woodall, 1996).

Gestures.   Imagine that you're driving to an appointment and someone is riding right on your bumper. Scowling at the offender in your rearview mirror, you're tempted to raise your middle finger and show it to the other driver, but you restrain yourself. The raised finger is an example of a gesture, a hand motion used to communicate messages (Streek, 1993). "Flipping" someone "the bird" falls into a category of gestures known as **emblems,** which represent specific verbal meanings (Ekman, 1976). With emblems, the gesture and its verbal meaning are interchangeable. You can say the words or use the gesture, and you'll send the same message.

Unlike emblems, **illustrators** accent or illustrate verbal messages. You tell your spouse about a rough road you recently biked, and as you describe the road you bounce your hand up and down to illustrate the bumpy ride. Your father points to a new house being built in your old neighborhood while relating details about the project.

Regulators control the exchange of conversational turns during interpersonal encounters (Rosenfeld, 1987). Listeners use regulators to tell speakers to keep talking, repeat something, hurry up, or let another person talk (Ekman & Friesen, 1969). Speakers use them to tell listeners to pay attention or to wait longer for their turn. Common examples include pointing a finger while trying to interrupt and holding a palm straight up to keep a person from interrupting. During online communication, abbreviations such as *BRB* ("be right back") and *JAS* ("just a second") serve as textual substitutes for gestural regulators.

Adaptors are touching gestures that serve a psychological or physical purpose (Ekman & Friesen, 1969). For example, you smooth your hair to make a better impression while meeting a potential new romantic partner, or you adjust your child's coat to make sure she stays warm on a cold day.

Posture.   The fourth kinesic is your bodily posture, which includes straightness of back (erect or slouched), body lean (forward, backward, or vertical), straightness of shoulders (firm and broad or slumped), and head position (tilted or straight up). Your posture communicates two primary messages to others: immediacy and power (Kudoh & Matsumoto, 1985; Mehrabian, 1972). **Immediacy** is the degree to which you find someone interesting and attractive. Want to nonverbally communicate that you like someone? Lean forward, keep your back straight and your arms open, and hold your head up and facing toward the person when talking. Want to convey dislike? Lean back, close your arms, and look away.

Power is the ability to influence or control other people or events (discussed in detail in Chapter 9). Imagine attending two job interviews in the same afternoon. The first interviewer sits bolt upright, with a tense, rigid

● Our postures are determined by conditions and tools. Within Western cultures, where many people work in offices, the greatest influence on body posture is the chair. In agrarian and pastoral societies, where people spend most of their lives working outside, body postures are shaped accordingly. Within Asia and Africa, for example, a common posture is the deep squat.

This exercise helps you use kinesics to communicate immediacy during interpersonal encounters.

❶ Initiate an encounter with someone you're interested in and whom you want to impress as an attentive and involved communicator (such as a new friend or a potential romantic partner).

❷ While talking, keep your facial expression pleasant. Don't be afraid to smile!

❸ Make eye contact, especially while listening, but avoid prolonged staring.

❹ Directly face the person, keep your back straight, lean gently forward, and keep your arms open and relaxed (rather than crossing them across your chest).

❺ Use illustrators to enhance important descriptions, and regulators to control your exchange of turns.

body posture. The second interviewer leans back in his chair, with his feet up on his desk and his hands behind his head. Which interviewer has more power? Most Americans would say the second. In the United States, high-status communicators typically use relaxed postures (Burgoon et al., 1996), but in Japan, the opposite is true. Japanese display power through erect posture and feet planted firmly on the floor.

Communicating through Voice

In the third season of the NBC show *Friends* (Crane & Kauffman, 1998), Chandler introduced his new girlfriend Janice (played by actor Maggie Wheeler) to his roommate, Joey. Although Janice is physically attractive, intelligent, and friendly, Joey takes an instant dislike to her because he finds her voice grating and her laugh annoying.

Joey's reaction to Janice reveals the impact of **vocalics**—vocal characteristics we use to communicate nonverbal messages—on our interpersonal communication and relationships. Indeed, vocalics rival kinesics in their communicative power (Burgoon et al., 1996) because our voices communicate our social, ethnic, and individual identities to others. Consider a study that recorded people from diverse backgrounds answering a series of "small talk" questions such as "How are you?" (Harms, 1961). People who listened to these recordings afterward were able to accurately judge participants' ethnicity, gender, and social class, often within only 10 to 15 seconds, based solely on their voices. And as the *Friends* episode with Janice spoofed, vocalics strongly shape our perception of others when we first meet them. If we perceive a person's voice as calm and smooth (not nasal or shrill), we are more likely to view him or her as attractive, form a positive impression, and judge the person as extraverted, open, and conscientious (Zuckerman, Hodgins, & Miyake, 1990).

When we interact with others, we typically experience their voices as a totality—they "talk in certain ways" or "have a particular kind of voice." But people's voices are actually complex combinations of four characteristics: loudness, pitch, speech rate, and tone.

Loudness. Consider the following sentence: *Will John leave the room* (Searle, 1965). Say the sentence aloud, each time emphasizing a different word. Notice that emphasizing one word over another can alter the meaning from statement to question to command, depending on which word is emphasized.

Loudness affects meaning so powerfully that people mimic it online by USING CAPITAL LETTERS TO EMPHASIZE CERTAIN POINTS. Indeed, people who extensively cap are punished for being "too loud." For example, a member of a music Web site I routinely visit accidentally left his "cap lock" key on while posting during a visit to a chatroom, and all of his messages were capped. Several other members immediately pounced, scolding him, "Stop shouting!"

Pitch. You're introduced to two new coworkers, Rashad and Paul. Both are tall and muscular. Rashad has a deep, low-pitched voice; Paul, an unusually

● A breathy, soft voice helped establish Marilyn Monroe as an international sex symbol.

high-pitched one. How do their voices shape your impressions of them? If you're like most people, you'll conclude that Rashad is strong and competent, while Paul is weak (Spender, 1990). Not coincidentally, people believe that women have higher-pitched voices than men and that women's voices are more "shrill" and "whining" (Spender, 1990). But although women across cultures do use higher pitch than men, most men are capable of using a higher pitch than they normally do but *choose* to intentionally limit their range to lower pitch levels in order to convey strength (Brend, 1975).

Speech Rate.   Talking at a moderate and steady rate is often considered a critical technique for effective speaking. Public-speaking educators urge students to "slow down," and people in conversations often reduce their speech rate if they believe that their listeners don't understand them. But MIT computer science researcher Jean Krause found that speech rate is not the primary determinant of intelligibility (Krause, 2001). Instead, it's pronunciation and articulation of words. People who speak quickly but clearly enunciate are just as effective communicators as those who speak moderately or slowly.

Tone.   The fourth, and most complex, vocalic characteristic is vocal tone, which is a combination of resonance and breathiness. You can control your vocal tone by allowing your voice to resonate deep in your chest and throat—achieving a deep rich tone that conveys an authoritative quality while giving a formal talk, for example. By contrast, letting your voice resonate through your sinus cavity creates a more whiny and nasal tone—often unpleasant to others. Your use of breath also affects tone. If you expel a great deal of air

SELF-REFLECTION

Has someone ever judged you from your voice? If so, how did this experience make you feel? Now think about your reactions to others' voices. Is there anyone you know whose voice you find funny, strange, or irritating? What is it about this person's voice that fosters your negative impression? Is it ethical to judge someone solely from his or her voice? Why or why not?

when speaking (think Marilyn Monroe), you convey sexiness. If you constrict the airflow when speaking, you create a "thin" and "hard" tone that may communicate nervousness or anxiety.

English-speakers use vocal tone to emphasize and alter the meanings of verbal messages. Regardless of the words you use, your tone can make your statements serious, silly, or even sarcastic, and you can shift tone extremely rapidly to convey different emphases. For example, when talking with your friends, you can suddenly switch from your normal tone to a much more deeply chest-resonant tone to mimic a pompous politician, then nearly instantly constrict your airflow and make your voice sound like "SpongeBob SquarePants." In online communication, we use italics to convey tone change ("I can't *believe* you did that").

Communicating through Touch

The ancient Greeks called touch *haptein*, and the nonverbal communication code of touch is known more formally as **haptics.** Touch likely is the first sense we develop in the womb, and receiving touch is a critical part of infant development (Knapp & Hall, 2002). Infants deprived of affectionate touch walk and talk later than others and suffer impaired emotional development in adulthood (Montagu, 1971).

Even the most casual touch conveys volumes during interpersonal encounters. For example, researchers at Purdue University conducted an experiment in which male and female library clerks handed back users' library cards by either placing their hand directly over the other's palm—touching each user—or simply handing the cards back without any contact (Fisher, Rytting, & Heslin, 1976). Upon exiting the library, students were asked to rate their feelings toward the library clerk and the library in general. Students who were touched evaluated the clerk and the library significantly more favorably than those who weren't.

Touch can vary based on its duration, part of the body being touched, and strength of contact, and these varieties influence how we interpret the physical contact (Floyd, 1999). Scholars distinguish between five types of touch (Heslin, 1974). We use **functional-professional touch** to accomplish some type of task. Three examples are touch between physicians and patients, between teachers and students, and between coaches and athletes. **Social-polite touch** derives from social norms and expectations. The most common form of social-polite touch is the handshake, which has been practiced as a form of greeting in one form or another for over 2,000 years (Heslin, 1974). Other examples include light hugging between friends or relatives, and the light cheek kiss. We rely on **friendship-warmth touch**— for example, gently grasping a friend's arm and giving it a squeeze—to express liking for another person. **Love-intimacy touch**—cupping a romantic partner's face tenderly in your hands, giving him or her a big, lingering hug—lets you convey deep emotional feelings. **Sexual-arousal touch,** as the name implies, is intended to physically stimulate another person.

People differ in the degree to which they feel comfortable giving and receiving touch; some people are more touch avoidant than others (Andersen, 1999). Consequently, consider adapting your use of touch to others' preferences, employing more or less touch depending on your conversational partner's behavior responses to your touching. If you are talking with a "touchy" person, who repeatedly touches your arm gently while talking (a form of social-polite touch), you can probably presume that such a mild form of touch would be acceptable to reciprocate. But if a person offers you no touch at all, not even a greeting handshake, you would be wise to inhibit your touching.

Cultural upbringing has a strong impact on how people use and perceive touching. For example, many Hispanics use friendship-warmth touch more frequently than do Europeans and Euro-Americans. Researchers in one study monitored casual conversations occurring in outdoor cafés in two different locales: San Juan, Puerto Rico, and London, England. They then averaged the number of touches between conversational partners.[3] The Puerto Ricans touched each other an average of 180 times per hour. The British average? Zero.

Communicating through Personal Space

The fourth nonverbal communication code, **proxemics** (from the Latin *proximus*, meaning "*near*"), is communication through the use of physical distance. Edward T. Hall, one of the first scholars to study proxemics, identified four communication distances: intimate, personal, social, and public (Hall, 1966). **Intimate space** ranges from 0 to 18 inches. Sharing intimate space with someone counts among the defining nonverbal features of close relationships (see Figure 8.3). **Personal space** ranges between 18 inches and 4 feet and is the distance we occupy during encounters with friends. For most Americans, personal space is about your "wingspan"—that is, the distance from fingertip to fingertip when you extend your arms. **Social space** ranges from about 4 to 12 feet. Many people use it when communicating in the workplace or with acquaintances and strangers. In **public space**, the distance between persons ranges upward from 12 feet, including great distances; this span occurs most often during formal occasions such as public speeches or college lectures.

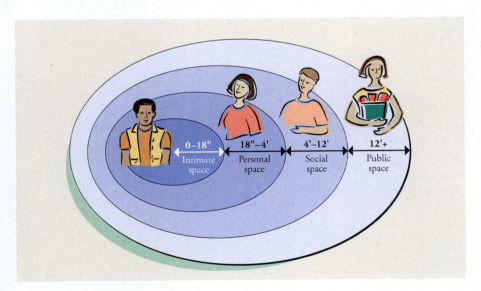

FIGURE 8.3

Physical Distance in Communication

0–18"
Intimate space

18"–4'
Personal space

4'–12'
Social space

12'+
Public space

[3] www.epa.gov (2003). Cross-cultural communication primer.

● In this 1957 series of photographs, future President Lyndon B. Johnson, then Senate majority leader, uses nonverbal communication to intimidate a colleague. Johnson's use of proxemics was known—and feared—as the "Johnson Treatment."

As noted earlier in our chapter, cultures differ substantially in their use of personal space (Chen & Starosta, 1998). North Americans feel most comfortable an arm's-length distance apart while conversing. Latin Americans tend to keep a closer distance, and Japanese and Chinese tend to keep a longer distance. North Americans may feel that people from North Africa and the northern and western Middle East intrude on their personal space, just as people from those cultures may judge North Americans' desire for larger distance as off-putting.

In addition to the distance we each claim for ourselves during interpersonal encounters, we also have certain physical areas or spaces in our lives that we consider our turf. **Territoriality** is the tendency to claim physical spaces as our own and to define certain locations as areas we don't want others to invade without permission (Chen & Starosta, 1998). Human beings react negatively to others who invade their perceived territory, and we respond positively to those who respect it (King, 2001). Imagine coming home to your apartment after school. Walking into your bedroom, you find your housemate sitting at your desk, listening to music on your computer. How would you respond? If you're like most people, you would feel angry and upset. Even though your housemate is not violating your personal space (distance from your body), he or she is inappropriately encroaching on physical space that you consider your territory.

What can you do to become more sensitive to differences in the use of personal space? Keep in mind that North Americans' notions of personal space tend to be larger than those in most other cultures, especially people from Latin America or the Middle East. When interacting with people from other cultures, adjust your use of space in accordance with your conversational partner's preferences. Realize, also, that if you're from a culture that values large personal space, others will feel most comfortable interacting at a closer distance than you're used to. If you insist on maintaining a large personal space bubble around yourself when interacting with people from other cultures, they may think you're aloof or distant or that you don't want to talk with them.

Communicating through Time

It's the middle of a busy workday. Looming over you is a 3 p.m. deadline for a report and a 3:30 appointment with the dentist. Suddenly your father calls. He wants to talk to you about plans for an upcoming surprise party for your mother. Should you disrupt your work schedule and talk or tell your father that another time would be more convenient?

Dilemmas such as this revolve around **chronemics,** the way you use time to communicate during interpersonal encounters. Edward Hall, who pioneered work on proxemics, also wrote extensively on chronemics (from the Greek word *khronos,* meaning "time"). Hall distinguished between two time orientations: *M-time* and *P-time* (Hall, 1981, 1983, 1997b).

People who have an **M-time** (or monochronic) orientation value careful scheduling and time management. They view time as a precious resource: it can be saved, spent, wasted, lost, or made up, and it can even run out. So, if you have an M-time view, you likely would perceive your father's call as an interruption and time taken during the workday to discuss a party as "misspent." Many people living in cultures where M-time is emphasized (such as the United States) think M-time is the only reasonable way of organizing life. As Hall notes, time for M-time people "is so thoroughly woven into the fabric of our existence that we hardly are aware of the degree to which it determines and coordinates everything we do, including our relationships with others—social and business life, even one's sex life, is commonly schedule-dominated" (1997b, pp. 278–279).

If you're an M-time person, "spending time" with someone, or "making time" in your schedule to share activities with him or her, sends the message

FOCUS ON CULTURE

Touch and Distance

Cultures vary in their norms regarding appropriate touch and distance, some with lots of touching and close distance during interpersonal encounters and others with less (Hall, 1966). Often, these differences correlate with latitude and climate. People living in cooler climes tend to be low contact and people living in warmer areas tend to be high contact (Andersen, 1997). The effect of climate on nonverbal touch and distance is even present in countries that have both colder and hotter regions. Below, Cindy, a former student, describes her experience juggling norms for touch and distance.*

"I'm a Mexican American from El Paso, Texas, which is predominantly Latino. There, most everyone hugs hello and goodbye. And I'm not talking about a short slap on the back—I mean a nice encompassing *abrazo* (hug). While I can't say that strangers greet each other this way, I do recall times where I've done it. Growing up, it just seemed like touching is natural, and I never knew how much I expected it, maybe even relied on it, until I moved.

"I came to Michigan as a grad student. My transition here was relatively smooth, but it was odd to me the first time I hung out with friends and didn't hug them hello and goodbye. A couple

of times on instinct I did greet them this way, and I'll never forget the strange tension that was created. Some people readily hugged me back, but most were uneasy. Quickly I learned that touching was unacceptable.

"Now I find that I hold back from engaging people in this manner. I feel like I'm hiding a part of myself, and it is frustrating. Nonetheless, this is the way things are done here, and I've had to adjust. Fortunately, I now have a few friends who recognize my need to express myself in this way and have opened themselves up to it. I'm grateful for that, and through these people a piece of me and my identity is saved."

YOUR TURN

- What has your culture taught you about the use of touch and distance? Are you a high- or low-contact person?

- When communicating with people from other cultures, how do you adapt your use of touch and distance?

- Have you ever had to alter your touching and distance to adapt to others' preferences? How did this change make you feel?

* Cindy's narrative was provided voluntarily to the author with full permission for publication.

that you consider that person and your relationship important (Hall, 1983). You may view time as a gift you give to others to show love or caring, or a tool with which you can punish ("I no longer have time for you"). Men and women differ in their perception of time's importance in intimate relationships. Activities that "take time away" from a relationship by removing one partner from the other's presence (such as personal hobbies) are more likely to be seen as a threat to the relationship and to provoke jealousy by women than by men (Hansen, 1985).

In contrast to M-time, people who have a **P-time** (or polychronic) orientation don't view time as a resource to be spent, saved, or guarded. And they rarely think of time as "wasted." If you're a P-time person, you might view your father's phone call as a welcome reprieve from the stress of work and an opportunity for an enjoyable and lengthy conversation.

POP QUIZ

Are You an M-Time or a P-Time Person?

Read the questions below and choose the answer that reflects your view of time. If you don't agree with either of the answers, choose the one that most closely approximates your view. When you're done, review your answers and see what they suggest about your personal time orientation; are you an M-time person or a P-time person?

❏ 1. Do you have a personal planner or Blackberry in which you carefully keep track of your daily schedule and appointments?

(a) _____ "Of course! How could I survive without one?"

(b) _____ "What exactly do I need to plan? What's a Blackberry?"

❏ 2. Do you often check the time during the day to see if you're "on schedule"?

(a) _____ "All the time. I also make sure that my watch is synchronized with my cell phone, and I program my cell to issue alarm reminders for key appointments."

(b) _____ "Never. I don't even own a watch."

❏ 3. Do you get stressed out about not having enough time to do the things you're supposed to?

(a) _____ "Not having enough time to do what I'm supposed to do is the number-one source of stress in my life."

(b) _____ "What exactly are 'the things we're supposed to do,' other than share life with those we love and be happy?"

❏ 4. Your best friend calls you at work, says that she has been dumped by her romantic partner, and badly needs to talk with you. You:

(a) _____ "Check my Blackberry/planner, to see if there's an opening in my schedule at some point later in the day."

(b) _____ "Arrange to leave work to go comfort my friend."

❏ 5. You have to renew your driver's license because it expires tomorrow. You use your lunch hour to do so, but there are only two people working the counter at the registry of motor vehicles, and the line is long. You:

(a) _____ "Check my watch and feel my stress increase as the hour passes and I'm still not at the head of the line. Finally, I cut to the front, and ask 'Is there any way I can go next? I've been waiting for an hour!'"

(b) _____ "Take the opportunity to chat with other people who are waiting, making new acquaintances."

Note: Information in this Pop Quiz was gathered by the author from undergraduate volunteers.

● The Slow Food Movement began in Italy in response to the changing pace of eating in modern society. Followers of this movement emphasize relaxed and pleasurable meals, a practice that draws on the literally close relationships of many families in southern Europe.

Differences in time orientation can create problems when people from different cultures make appointments with each other (Hall, 1983). For example, those with an M-time orientation, such as many Americans, often become impatient if P-time people show up late for a meeting. In cultures with a heavy P-time emphasis, such as those in Arabian, African, Caribbean, and Latin American countries, arriving 30 minutes or more after a meeting's scheduled start is considered "on time," and changing important plans at the last minute is viewed as acceptable.

How can you become more sensitive to other people's time frames and, as a result, improve your nonverbal communication? Learn about the time orientation of a destination or country before traveling there. Also, respect others' time orientation. If you're an M-time person interacting with a P-time individual, don't abruptly end the encounter because you feel you have to stick to your schedule. Your communication partner will likely view you as rude. If you're a P-time person interacting with an M-time partner, realize that he or she likely views the interaction as time-bounded. This individual may view a lengthy, leisurely conversation or late arrival to an appointment as inconsiderate. In addition, avoid criticizing or complaining about behaviors that stem from others' alternative time orientations. Instead, accept the unavoidable fact that others may have views of time markedly different from yours, and be willing to adapt your own use of time when interacting with them.

Communicating through Physical Appearance

The ABC show *Extreme Makeovers* first aired on April 23, 2003, and became an instant ratings hit (Schultz, 2003). The show featured a team of plastic surgeons, eye surgeons, cosmetic dentists, and hair and makeup artists who reconfigured a volunteer's physical appearance, including changing his or her weight (through liposuction), body shape (through surgical implants), hair, facial structure, eye color and shape, and teeth. The network described the experience thusly: "These men and women are given a truly Cinderella-like experience: a real life fairy tale in which their wishes come true, not just to change their looks, but their lives and destinies."[4]

As shows like *Extreme Makeovers* demonstrate, **physical appearance**— visible attributes such as hair, clothing, body type, and other physical features—profoundly influences interpersonal communication and relationships. In simple terms, how you look conveys as much about you as what you say. And beauty counts. Across cultures, people credit individuals they find physically attractive with higher levels of intelligence, persuasiveness, poise, sociability, warmth, power, and employment success than they credit to unattractive individuals (Hatfield & Sprecher, 1986).

What physical appearance characteristics does it take to be judged attractive? Standards of beauty are highly variable, both across cultures and across time periods. But one factor that's related to attractiveness across cultures is facial symmetry—the degree to which each side of your face precisely matches the other. Look in the mirror at your own

---

[4] Excerpted from ABC Extreme Makeover Web site (n.d.).

face. Are your eyes the same shape? Are your ears at the exact same height? People with symmetrical faces are judged as more attractive than people with asymmetrical faces (Grammer & Thornhill, 1994), although absolute perfect facial symmetry may be seen as artificial and unattractive (Kowner, 1996).

Gender differences in perceptions of the importance of beauty also exist. Men have long placed more emphasis on the physical attractiveness of romantic partners than do women (Hatfield & Sprecher, 1986). For example, a study conducted in 1939 asked male and female college students if they would marry a person who ranked low in such qualities as money, looks, personality, morals, education, and intelligence (Baber, 1939). Men placed particular emphasis on beauty as a requirement for a life mate, whereas women rated the other qualities (financial standing, morals, and so forth) as equally important.

Your clothing also has a profound impact on others' perceptions of you. More than 40 years of research suggests that clothing strongly influences people's judgments of profession, level of education, socioeconomic status, and even personality and personal values (Burgoon et al., 1996; Fortenberry, Maclean, Morris, & O'Connell, 1978; Rosencranz, 1965). The effect that clothing has on perception makes it essential that you consider the appropriateness of your dress, the context for which you are dressing, and the image of self you wish to nonverbally communicate. When I worked for a Seattle trucking company, I was expected to wear clothes that could withstand rough treatment. On my first day, I "dressed to impress" and was teased by coworkers and management for dressing as if I was an executive at a large corporation. But expectations like this can change in other situations. During job interviews, for example, dress as nicely as you can. Being even moderately formally dressed is one of the strongest predictors of whether an interviewer will perceive you as socially skilled and highly motivated (Gifford, Ng, & Wilkinson, 1985).

Communicating through Objects

Take a moment to examine the objects that you're wearing and that surround you: jewelry, watch, cell phone, notebook, computer, and so forth. These **artifacts**—the things we possess that influence how we see ourselves and that we use to express our identity to others—constitute another code of nonverbal communication. As with to our use of posture and of personal space, we use artifacts to communicate power and status. For example, by displaying expensive watches, cars, or living spaces, people "tell" others that they're wealthy and influential (Burgoon et al., 1996).

Communicating through the Environment

A final way in which we communicate nonverbally is through our **environment,** the physical features of our surroundings. As the illustration of the New York Yankees locker room shows, our environment envelops us, shapes our communication, and implies certain things about us, often without our realizing it.

SELF-REFLECTION

Which objects do you believe best communicate who you are? What do these objects say about you? Over the next few hours, study the objects that other people surround themselves with. What do those objects convey about their gender, ethnicity, and social class?

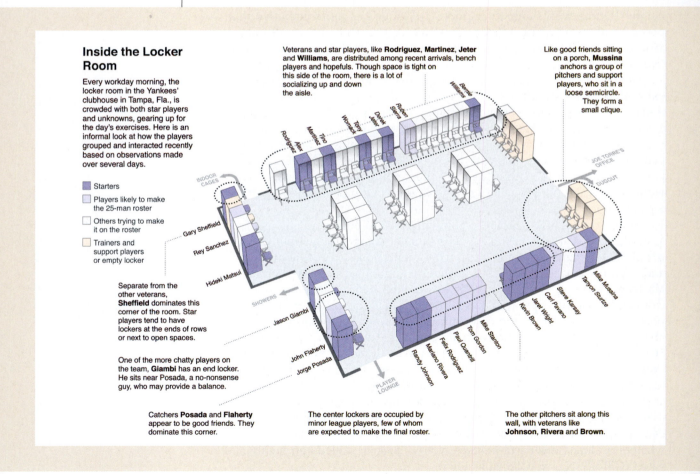

Inside the Locker Room

Every workday morning, the locker room in the Yankees' clubhouse in Tampa, Fla., is crowded with both star players and unknowns, gearing up for the day's exercises. Here is an informal look at how the players grouped and interacted recently based on observations made over several days.

- ■ Starters
- ▨ Players likely to make the 25-man roster
- □ Others trying to make it on the roster
- ▨ Trainers and support players or empty locker

Separate from the other veterans, **Sheffield** dominates this corner of the room. Star players tend to have lockers at the ends of rows or next to open spaces.

One of the more chatty players on the team, **Giambi** has an end locker. He sits near Posada, a no-nonsense guy, who may provide a balance.

Catchers **Posada** and **Flaherty** appear to be good friends. They dominate this corner.

Veterans and star players, like **Rodriguez**, **Martinez**, **Jeter** and **Williams**, are distributed among recent arrivals, bench players and hopefuls. Though space is tight on this side of the room, there is a lot of socializing up and down the aisle.

The center lockers are occupied by minor league players, few of whom are expected to make the final roster.

Like good friends sitting on a porch, **Mussina** anchors a group of pitchers and support players, who sit in a loose semicircle. They form a small clique.

The other pitchers sit along this wall, with veterans like **Johnson**, **Rivera** and **Brown**.

Gary Sheffield · Rey Sanchez · Hideki Matsui · Jason Giambi · John Flaherty · Jorge Posada · Randy Johnson · Mariano Rivera · Felix Rodriguez · Paul Quantrill · Tom Gordon · Mike Stanton · Kevin Brown · Jarel Wright · Carl Pavano · Steve Karsay · Tanyon Sturtze · Mike Mussina

Alex Rodriguez · Tino Martinez · Tony Womack · Derek Jeter · Ruben Sierra · Bernie Williams

INDOOR CAGES · SHOWERS · PLAYER LOUNGE · JOE TORRES OFFICE · DUGOUT

Two types of environmental factors play a role in shaping interpersonal communication (Hall, 1981): fixed features and semifixed features. *Fixed features* are stable and unchanging environmental elements such as walls, ceilings, floors, and doors. Fixed features define the size of a particular environment, and size has an enormous emotional and communicative impact on people. For example, the size of structures communicates power, with bigger often being better. In corporations, it's often assumed that larger offices equal greater power for their occupants, and historically, the square footage of homes has communicated the occupant's degree of wealth.

Semi-fixed features are impermanent and usually easy to change; they include furniture, lighting, and color. We associate bright lighting with environments that are very active and soft lighting with environments that are calmer and more intimate. Color also exerts a powerful effect on our mood states and communication: we experience blues and greens as relaxing, yellows and oranges as arousing and energizing, reds and blacks as sensuous, and grays and browns as depressing (Burgoon et al., 1996).

Functions of Nonverbal Communication

On July 10, 1999, the U.S. women's soccer team faced China in the World Cup finals, in front of 90,185 fans (and more than 40 million television viewers)—the largest crowd ever to witness a women's sporting event. Tied at 0–0, the game went to a penalty shoot-out, in which each team takes a series of five kicks on the goal to break a tie score. U.S. goalkeeper Brianna Scurry provided the opportunity for victory by stopping the shot of China's top scorer, Liu Ying. When Scurry's teammate Brandi Chastain blasted her kick past goalkeeper Gao Hong, the United States won the game and the world championship. Chastain's fist pumping and elated expression, and the ecstatic hugs exchanged between the players, powerfully communicated the team's joy, exultation, and championship status. But more than anything else, their nonverbal communication revealed the team's sense of camaraderie—the intensely close relationships they shared as friends and teammates. As this example illustrates, nonverbal communication can serve many different purposes—from communicating meanings and expressing emotions to presenting ourselves to others, managing interactions, and defining relationships (Argyle, 1969).

Conveying Meanings

Just as we use words to signify unique meanings, we often use nonverbal communication to directly convey meanings. Your boss flips you a thumbs-up gesture following a presentation, and you know she means "Good job!" A friend makes a two-finger "V" at a campus rally, and you recognize it as an emblem for peace. Members of the U.S. women's soccer team do a "victory lap" around the Rose Bowl following their win, holding up their index fingers to indicate that "We're number one!"

At other times we use nonverbal communication more indirectly, as a means for accenting or augmenting verbal communication meanings (Malandro

SELF-REFLECTION

Look around the room you're in right now. How does this room make you feel? What mood or feeling is created by the size of the space, furniture, lighting, and color? What does the room say to others about who you are? What kind of interpersonal communication would be most appropriate for this space—personal or professional? Why?

& Barker, 1983). We do this in five ways, the first of which is by reiterating. Nonverbal communication is used to reiterate or repeat verbal messages, as when you say "Up!" and then point upward. Second, we contradict our verbal messages with our nonverbal communication. For example, a friend may ask if you're angry, but you respond by scowling and angrily shouting "No, I'm not angry!" Third, we use nonverbal communication to enhance the meaning of verbal messages, such as when you tell an intimate "I love you" while smiling and offering a gentle touch to emphasize the point. Fourth, we sometimes use nonverbal communication to replace verbal expressions—such as when you shake your head instead of saying "no." And finally, we use nonverbal communication to spotlight certain parts of verbal messages, such as when you increase the loudness of just one word: "STOP hitting your brother with the toy sword!"

Expressing Emotion

We communicate emotion nonverbally through **affect displays**—intentional or unintentional nonverbal behaviors that display actual or feigned emotions (Burgoon et al., 1996). Affect displays are presented primarily through the face and voice. Intentional use of the face to communicate emotion begins during late infancy, when babies learn to facially communicate anger and happiness to get what they want (Burgoon et al., 1996). Unintentional affect displays begin even earlier. Infants in the first few weeks of life instinctively and reflexively display facial expressions of distress, disgust, and interest. And as adults, we communicate hundreds, if not thousands, of real and faked emotional states with our faces.

People also use vocalics to convey emotions. Consider how you communicate love through your voice. What changes do you make in pitch, tone, volume, and speech rate? How does your "love" voice differ from your "anger" voice? Most people express emotions such as grief and love through lowered vocal pitch, and hostile emotions such as anger and contempt through loudness (Costanzo, Markel, & Costanzo, 1969). Pitch conveys emotion so powerfully that the source of the sound (human voice or other) is irrelevant, and words aren't necessary. Researcher Klaus Scherer mimicked voice patterns on a music synthesizer and had listeners judge the emotion conveyed (1974). Participants strongly associated high pitch with emotions such as anger, fear, and surprise, and they linked low pitch with pleasantness, boredom, and sadness.

Presenting Self

Think about your interactions with your manager at work. How do you let him or her know—without words—that you're a dedicated and hardworking employee? Chances are, you employ almost all the nonverbal codes discussed above, simultaneously. You convey attentiveness through focused eye contact and pleasant facial expression, and you communicate seriousness through moderate speech rate and pitch. You likely avoid crowding your boss and touching him or her. You strive to show up at meetings on time if you sense that your manager is M-time oriented. You also dress appropriately for the office and try to obey workplace norms regarding how you decorate your work space.

Now imagine that your manager confides to you a recent diagnosis of terminal illness. How would you use nonverbal communication to convey a different self—one who's compassionate, supportive, and concerned? You'd likely adopt a facial expression conveying sadness and concern. You'd slow your speech rate and lower the pitch of your voice to convey empathy. You'd decrease your interpersonal distance to communicate support. And you might touch your boss lightly on the elbow or gently clasp his or her shoulder to signify caring.

As these examples suggest, nonverbal communication can help us present different aspects of our self to others. We use all nonverbal communication codes to create our identities during interpersonal encounters. And an important part of being an effective nonverbal communicator is recognizing the need to shift our nonverbal communication quickly to present ourselves in different ways when the situation demands—for example, dedicated employee one moment, concerned fellow human being another.

Managing Interactions

Nonverbal communication also helps us to manage interpersonal interactions. For example, during conversations, we use regulators, eye contact, touch, smiling, head nods, and posture shifts to signal who gets to speak and for how long (Patterson, 1988). While chatting with a friend, you probably look at him or her anywhere from 30 to 50 percent of your talk time. Then, when you're approaching the end of your conversational turn, you invite your friend to talk by decreasing your pitch and loudness, stopping any gestures, and focusing your gaze on the other person. As your friend begins speaking, you now look at your partner almost 100 percent of his or her talk time, nodding your head to show you're listening (Goodwin, 1981).

During conversations, we also read our partners' nonverbal communication to check their level of interest in what we're saying—watching for signals like eye contact, smiles, and head nods. Yet we're usually unaware that we're doing this until people behave in unexpected ways. For example, if a partner *fails* to react to something we've said that we consider provocative or funny, we may shoot them a glance or frown to express our displeasure nonverbally.

Nonverbal communication also helps us regulate others' attention and behavior. For example, a sudden glance and stern facial expression from a parent or babysitter can stop a child from reaching for the forbidden cookie jar. In my sons' school, the principal gains students' attention by clapping loudly three times—Clap! Clap! Clap!—a pattern that students then repeat back to him, falling silent afterward to listen for an important announcement.

Defining Relationships

You're sitting at a local diner, eating lunch and people-watching. Two couples are sitting in nearby booths. One couple sits very close to one another.

SKILLS PRACTICE

This exercise helps you non-verbally present yourself in an effective fashion in the workplace.

❶ Display a pleasant facial expression, make good eye contact, lean forward, and exhibit upright posture.

❷ Use a moderately resonant and breathy vocal tone, medium pitch and volume, and moderate speech rate.

❸ Adapt your use of proxemics to others' needs for personal space, and respect their territory.

❹ Adjust your haptics to match others' preferences.

❺ Keep appointments or allow flexibility regarding punctuality.

❻ Ensure that your physical appearance and artifacts are appropriate, asking your coworkers' and manager's opinions if you're uncertain.

They cuddle, touch, and occasionally kiss. When they're not touching, they're smiling and gazing at each other. The couple sitting at the next booth over is behaving very differently. The man sits up tall and straight, his arms extended on both sides of the table. He glares at his partner, interrupts her, and doesn't look at her when she's talking. Her eyes are downcast, her hands are folded in her lap, and she speaks softly. What does the nonverbal communication of each of these couples tell you about the degree of intimacy in their relationship? The partners' relative dominance? A final function of nonverbal communication is to define the nature of our interpersonal relationships. In particular, we use our nonverbal communication to create intimacy and define dominance or submissiveness in our relationships (Burgoon & Hoobler, 2002).

Intimacy.   One crucial function nonverbal communication serves is to create **intimacy,** a feeling of emotional bonding or union between ourselves and others (Register & Henley, 1992; Rubin, 1973). For example, in her novel *Written on the Body,* acclaimed British author Jeanette Winterson offers a vivid and poignant description of how the nonverbal code of touch defines intimacy:

> Articulacy of fingers, the language of the deaf. Who taught you to write on my back? Who taught you to use your hands as branding irons? You have scored your name into my shoulders, referenced me with your mark. The pads of your fingers have become printing blocks, you tap a message on to my skin, tap meaning into my body. Your Morse code interferes with my heart beat. I had a steady heart before I met you, I relied upon it, it had seen active service and grown strong. Now you alter its pace with your rhythm, you play upon me, drumming me taut. (1993, p. 89)

But intimacy isn't defined solely through touch. Physical closeness, shared gaze, soft voices, postural openness, sharing of personal objects, and, of course, spending time together—each of these nonverbal behaviors highlights and enhances intimacy. Consider just a few specifics. Smiling and gazing are associated with intimacy (Floyd & Burgoon, 1999), something vividly illustrated in the Beaver family photo in our chapter opening. Individuals share more personal space with intimates and liked others than with strangers and use proximity to convey affection (Floyd & Morman, 1999). Studies that have instructed people to communicate liking to others have found that the primary way people do so is through increasing gaze, smiling, and leaning forward (Palmer & Simmons, 1995). Conversely, one can communicate lack of intimacy and greater formality through distance, lack of eye contact, decreased vocal expressiveness, precise articulation, and postural tension (Burgoon & Hoobler, 2002).

In general, more intimate relationships—particularly romantic bonds— show higher levels of nonverbal involvement across all of the codes (more eye contact, more touch, more smiling, closer distance, and so forth). For romantic couples, level of nonverbal involvement is a direct indicator of the relationship's health (Patterson, 1988). Think back to the highly engaged couple in the café booth. Although you don't know who they are, what they're saying, or what culture they're from, you could reasonably conclude that they have a healthy relationship, based solely on their nonverbal behavior.

Dominance and Submissiveness. Recall the physically distant couple in the other diner booth. Rather than conveying intimacy, their nonverbal communication displays dominance and submissiveness. **Dominance** refers to the interpersonal behaviors we use to exert power and influence over others (Burgoon & Dunbar, 2000). Larger-than-normal use of space; access to other people's space, time, and possessions; one-sided use of touch (giving more, receiving less); indirect body orientation; direct gaze and staring; frowning and scowling; and silence—all of these codes signal the dominance of the person who employs them (Burgoon & Hoobler, 2002; Carney, Hall, & Smith LeBeau, 2005). And gender has little effect—these behaviors are perceived as dominant when displayed by both men and women (Carney et al., 2005).

In contrast, **submissiveness** is the willingness to allow others to exert power over us. We communicate submissiveness to others nonverbally by engaging in behaviors that are opposite to those that express dominance, such as taking up less space; letting others control our time, space, and possessions; smiling more; and permitting others to interrupt us.

POP QUIZ

Test Your Nonverbal Dominance Knowledge

Knowing which behaviors people perceive as dominant is an important part of being a skilled nonverbal communicator (Carney et al., 2005). Review the following list of behaviors, identify and rank the top five nonverbal cues that you think communicate dominance, and check your answers.

_____ (a) Using a loud voice while you talk

_____ (b) Exhibiting confident and self-assured facial expressions

_____ (c) Initiating the shaking of an interaction partner's hand

_____ (d) Having your arms crossed or folded on your chest during an encounter

_____ (e) Displaying unresponsive facial expressions toward your conversational partner

_____ (f) Using broad, large, and expansive hand gestures while you talk

_____ (g) Showing facial disgust

_____ (h) Paying attention to your conversational partner

_____ (i) Manipulating objects during the conversation (such as playing with your pencil or fiddling with a piece of paper)

_____ (j) Engaging in "invasive" behaviors with your conversational partner, such as standing too close, touching, and pointing

Scoring

The most to least dominating nonverbal cues are: b, c, f, j, and g.

Note: Items in this Pop Quiz are derived from Table 1 of Carney, Hall, and Smith LeBeau (2005).

Making Relationship Choices

Dealing with Mixed Messages

BACKGROUND

Receiving mixed messages—when verbal and nonverbal communication clash—is a common dilemma in relationships. To explore ways to deal with mixed messages, read the case study and work through the steps that follow.

CASE STUDY

You met Dakota through a mutual friend, and you instantly bonded—same interests, same likes and dislikes, even the same major. You never tire of talking to Dakota—you two are constantly e-mailing, text-messaging, or conversing on the phone. You've always considered Dakota physically attractive but never envisioned a romance. This is partly because you two are good friends, and because you both were involved with other people. Those other relationships have recently ended. But you still think of Dakota only as a friend.

Then things became confusing when you recently met Dakota for lunch. Dakota looked unusually nice—all dressed up. When you asked, "What's the occasion?" you got an evasive response. Dakota kept leaning toward you, making extensive eye contact, smiling, touching your arm and leg (although at the time it seemed "accidental"), and even suggested you two take more classes together next semester. You're pleased—until you tell your roommate about the lunch. Your roommate laughs and says, "Dakota is crushing on you!" Troubled, you send your friend an e-mail. The two of you have always been honest and open with each other (especially online), so you tell Dakota what your roommate said, and type "What's up?" Dakota responds with a teasing, "As if I'd ever crush on you ☺!"

In the days that follow, you increasingly sense that Dakota wants a romantic involvement. Everything about your friend's nonverbal communication suggests intimacy. But whenever you raise the issue, Dakota denies it, responding, "You've got an overactive imagination." You start feeling confused and irked by the mixed messages.

One day, going to Dakota's apartment, you mull over the situation. Is Dakota romantically interested in you, or are you imagining things? Should you push your friend to "tell you the truth," or has Dakota already communicated a clear message? Should you make a pass at Dakota just to see the response? Or just forget the whole matter? Arriving at your friend's doorstep, you knock, and the door opens—revealing an attractively dressed Dakota. With a big smile, your friend says, "What's up?" How do you respond?

3

YOUR TURN

While working through the following steps, keep in mind the interpersonal communication concepts, skills, and insights you've learned so far in this book, especially this chapter. Also remember: there are no right answers, so think hard about the choice you make! (P.S. Need help? Review the concepts listed below.)

- **Step 1: Reflect on yourself.** What are your thoughts and feelings in this situation? What attributions are you making about Dakota based on your friend's interpersonal communication? Are your attributions accurate? Why or why not?

- **Step 2: Reflect on your partner.** Using perspective-taking and empathic concern, put yourself in Dakota's shoes. Consider how your friend is thinking and feeling, especially how Dakota likely feels about you and your relationship.

- **Step 3: Identify the optimal outcome.** Think about all the information you have about Dakota and about this relationship. Consider your own feelings as well as your friend's. Given all these factors, what's the best, most constructive relationship outcome possible here? Be sure to consider not just what's best for *you*, but what's best for Dakota as well.

- **Step 4: Locate the roadblocks.** Taking into consideration your own thoughts and feelings, Dakota's, and all that has happened, what's preventing you from achieving the optimal outcome you identified in step 3?

- **Step 5: Chart your course.** How will you communicate with Dakota to overcome the roadblocks you've identified and achieve your optimal relationship outcome?

● For romantic couples, the level of nonverbal involvement is a direct indicator of the relationship's health.

Responsibly Managing Your Nonverbal Communication

As you interact with others, you use various nonverbal communication codes naturally and simultaneously. Similarly, you take in and interpret others' nonverbal communication instinctively. Look again at the Beaver family photo at the beginning of the chapter. While viewing this image, you probably don't think, "What's Samson's mouth doing?" or "Gee, Frances's arm is touching Samson's shoulder." When it comes to nonverbal communication, although all the parts are important, it's the overall package that delivers the message.

Given the nature of nonverbal communication, it's important to highlight general guidelines for how you can responsibly manage your nonverbal communication. In this chapter we've offered very specific advice for improving your use of particular nonverbal codes. But we conclude with four principles for responsible nonverbal conduct.

First, when interacting with others, remember that your nonverbal communication often speaks louder than your verbal communication. This means that people view your nonverbal communication as at least as important as what you say, if not more so. So, although you should endeavor to build your interpersonal communication competence (Chapter 5), active listening skills (Chapter 6), and use of effective language (Chapter 7), bear in mind that people will often assign the greatest weight to what you do nonverbally.

Second, nonverbal communication effectiveness is inextricably tied to culture. In our discussion you've repeatedly seen the vast cultural differences that exist in body movements (kinesics), space (proxemics), touch (haptics), and time (chronemics), to mention just four. Part of responsibly managing your nonverbal communication is knowing the cultural display rules for appropriate nonverbal expression prior to interpersonally interacting within a culture and then adapting your nonverbal communication to match those rules. In addition, responsible managers of nonverbal communication are respectful of cultural differences. When someone from another culture uses more or less touch than you, has a different orientation toward time, or adjusts personal distance in ways at odds with your own practice, your first duty and obligation is to be tolerant and accepting of this difference rather than dismissive or disparaging and to adapt your own nonverbal communication in ways sensitive to the validity of this difference.

Third, be sensitive to the demands of interpersonal situations. For example, if an interaction seems to call for more formal or more casual behavior, adapt your nonverbal communication accordingly. Remind yourself, if necessary, that being interviewed for a job, sharing a relaxed evening with your roommate, and deepening the level of intimacy in a love relationship all call for different nonverbal messages. And recall that you can craft those messages through careful use of the many different codes available to you.

Finally, remember that verbal communication and nonverbal communication flow with one another. Your experience of nonverbal communication from others and your nonverbal expression to others is fundamentally fused with the words you and they choose to use. As a consequence, you cannot become a skilled interpersonal communicator by focusing time, effort, and energy only on verbal or only on nonverbal. Instead, you must devote yourself to both because it is only when both are joined as a union of skills that more competent interpersonal ability is achieved.

POSTSCRIPT

Reflect on the postures, dress, use of space, eye contact, and facial expressions depicted in the Beaver family photo. Then think about how nonverbal communication shapes your life. What judgments do you make about others, based on their scowls and smiles? Their postures? Their appearance and voice? Do you draw accurate conclusions about certain groups of people based on their nonverbal communication? And how do others see you? As you communicate with others throughout a typical day, what do your facial expressions, posture, dress, use of space, and eye contact convey?

We began this chapter with a family of smiles. The smile— one of the simplest, most commonplace expressions. Yet like so many nonverbal expressions, the smile has the power to fundamentally shift interpersonal perceptions. In the case of the Beaver family, seeing the smiles that talking with a friend evoked 100 years ago helps erase more than a century of Native American stereotypes. But the power of the Beaver family smiles goes beyond simply remedying a historical distortion. It highlights the power that even the simplest nonverbal communication of yours has in shaping and shifting others' perceptions of you.

289

Key Terms

Key Concepts

Principles of Nonverbal Communication

- Scholars continue to debate whether **nonverbal communication** includes all unspoken behavioral displays or only those we use intentionally to convey meaning. This chapter takes an inclusive approach to defining nonverbal communication.

- Nonverbal communication generally carries more meaning than verbal, especially when we send or receive **mixed messages.**

- Both gender and culture shape people's perceptions and use of nonverbal communication.

Nonverbal Communication Codes

- Although eight different **nonverbal communication codes** exist, the behaviors that most people associate with nonverbal communication, such as facial expressions, gestures, and body posture, are **kinesics.** Four different forms of gestures are commonly used during our interpersonal encounters: **emblems, illustrators, regulators, and adaptors.**

- Something as seemingly simple as body posture—how we lean, position our shoulders, and hold our heads—can communicate substantial information regarding **immediacy** and power to others.

- Although we often think of the voice as one thing, many different specific features (such as loudness, pitch, speech rate, and tone) contribute to the complex nonverbal code of **vocalics.**

- People vary their duration, placement, and strength of touch (known as **haptics**) to communicate a broad range of meanings, including **functional-professional touch, social-polite touch, friendship-warmth touch, love-intimacy touch,** and **sexual-arousal touch.** People's impressions of these various forms of touch are strongly influenced by culture.

- Culture also influences **proxemics,** or use of space and interpersonal distance during encounters with others. Forms of distance include **intimate, personal, social,** and **public space.** All human beings experience **territoriality** and resent perceived invasions of personal domains.

- We send powerful messages about intimacy and caring through **chronemics,** or our use of time. People differ in their perceptions of the significance of time. Some have an **M-time** orientation, others a **P-time** view.

- Like it or not, our **physical appearance** strongly molds others' impressions of us. Many people favor those they perceive as attractive over those they perceive as unattractive.

- We use personal **artifacts** to portray who we are to others and to communicate information regarding our worth, status, and power.

- Features of our physical **environment**—such as size, furnishings, and materials used in our home or office—also send distinct messages about status and mood.

Functions of Nonverbal Communication

- Our nonverbal communication serves many purposes in our interpersonal encounters and relationships. One of the most common is **affect displays,** which function to show others how we are feeling.

- We can harness all of the nonverbal communication codes to send powerful messages of **intimacy, dominance,** and **submissiveness** to others.

Key Skills

- How might you use your knowledge of gender differences to improve your nonverbal communication skills? Review the practical tips on page 264.

- What does the Noh mask effect suggest about how best to use and interpret facial expressions? Find the answer on pages 267–268.

- Want to nonverbally communicate that you like someone? Follow the suggestions on page 269 for how to effectively convey immediacy; then do the *Skills Practice* on page 270.

- How can you effectively adapt vocalics to online communication? Find out by completing the *Skills Practice* on page 272.

- What should you do to effectively use touch during interpersonal encounters? Find out on page 272.

- What can you do to enhance your use of personal space during encounters with people from other cultures? Review the suggestions on page 273.

- Do you understand the differences between M-time and P-time orientations? Take the *Pop Quiz* on page 277, and review the rules for increasing sensitivity to others with different time orientations on page 278.

- Why is it important to dress appropriately for the situations and encounters you're going to face? Find out on page 279.

- Want to improve your nonverbal communication in the workplace? See the tips for effective nonverbal self-presentation in the workplace on pages 282–283; then do the *Skills Practice* on page 283.

- Do you know which nonverbal cues are most likely to be perceived by others as communicating dominance? Test your dominance knowledge by taking the *Pop Quiz* on page 285.

- What are mixed messages, and how can you most effectively deal with them if you receive them from others? Review *Making Relationship Choices* on pages 286–287 to find out.

- What general guidelines can help you responsibly manage your nonverbal communication? Refresh your memory by consulting pages 288–289.

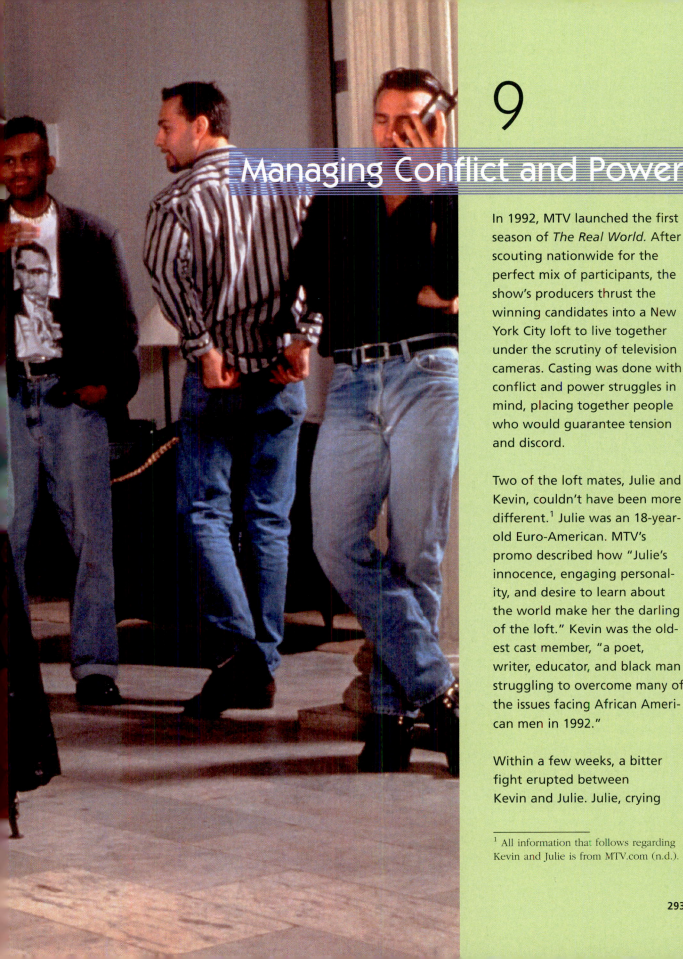

9

Managing Conflict and Power

In 1992, MTV launched the first season of *The Real World.* After scouting nationwide for the perfect mix of participants, the show's producers thrust the winning candidates into a New York City loft to live together under the scrutiny of television cameras. Casting was done with conflict and power struggles in mind, placing together people who would guarantee tension and discord.

Two of the loft mates, Julie and Kevin, couldn't have been more different.[1] Julie was an 18-year-old Euro-American. MTV's promo described how "Julie's innocence, engaging personality, and desire to learn about the world make her the darling of the loft." Kevin was the oldest cast member, "a poet, writer, educator, and black man struggling to overcome many of the issues facing African American men in 1992."

Within a few weeks, a bitter fight erupted between Kevin and Julie. Julie, crying

---

[1] All information that follows regarding Kevin and Julie is from MTV.com (n.d.).

hysterically, explains to two other loft mates that she and Kevin had a fight about a phone call and that Kevin threw a candleholder at her. She is afraid of Kevin, thinks he is crazy, and never wants to be alone with him again. Kevin denies brandishing the candle-holder and insists that the fight wasn't his fault. Julie was rude to him first, he contends. At a later party, the conflict breaks out again with Julie shouting at Kevin, "What are you going to do, hit me?!"

The conflict between Kevin and Julie sparked intense viewer interest, as it cut across lines of gender, power, and ethnicity. Who was to blame—Kevin or Julie? After the show aired, communication researchers Mark Orbe and Kiesha Warren (2000) had groups of Euro-American and African Ameri-can men and women watch the episode and articulate their perceptions.

Although the research partici-pants all viewed the same episode, each group perceived

a different conflict. Euro-American women saw Kevin as the aggressor who used his physical strength to wield power over Julie. "Race was irrelevant," said these women. "Not so," maintained the African American women in the study, who felt the conflict was all about race. Although Julie and Kevin were equally aggressive, the fight escalated because Julie played the "powerless victim." As one of the African American women said, "I think the 'big black guy' perception did play a part, and he wasn't even physically big, so the stereotype was there" (Orbe & Warren, 2000, p. 54).

The African American male participants agreed that race was an issue, but said the dif-ferences between Kevin's and Julie's ages and backgrounds played the largest role in the conflict. In contrast to all other groups, Euro-American men thought it had nothing to do with power or race. They believed that the problem

between Kevin and Julie was a personality clash.

The four groups in Orbe and Warren's study viewed the same dispute, but each made distinctly different judgments about the protagonists' inter-personal communication, the role of power in shaping their interactions, and the meaning of the conflict itself. Although this early episode of *The Real World* has now receded into popular culture memory, the study's findings reveal the fun-damentally subjective nature of conflict. For participants and witnesses alike, the nature of Julie's and Kevin's battle lay very much in the eyes of the beholders. Yet, for all the vari-ation in viewpoints, one point of perceptual agreement was shared across people: had Kevin and Julie both communi-cated more effectively with one another, they might have constructively managed their disagreements and therefore prevented things from spiral-ing out of control.

In the entertainment industry, conflict and power struggles sell. From Hollywood to Bollywood, producers of movies, TV programs, and music videos exploit the allure of confrontation, contriving situations in which people are guaranteed to clash. Why do so many people feel compelled to watch others fight? Perhaps doing so enables us to experience the intensity of conflict without suffering the interpersonal costs. But when we get embroiled in actual discord, the consequences become all too painfully real. Consider the words people most commonly associate with interpersonal conflict: "destruction," "anger," "anxiety," "heartache," "hopelessness" (Wilmot & Hocker, 2001).

Yet real-life conflicts and struggles over power have a constructive side as well. For one thing, they give us opportunities to change and improve our relationships. Through conflict, we clarify our own and others' perspectives and goals and learn how to adapt our communication to work more productively together (Donohue & Kolt, 1992). The capacity of conflict and power struggles to both damage and improve relationships makes effectively managing them an essential interpersonal skill.

In this chapter, we explore the nature of interpersonal conflict and power and examine how best to manage both. You'll learn:

- The nature of conflict and the conflict-related challenges facing people in close relationships

- The role power plays in conflict

- Different approaches for dealing with interpersonal conflict

- Resolutions and long-term outcomes of conflict

- The impact of gender and culture on interpersonal communication during conflicts

Conflict and Interpersonal Communication

Almost any issue can spark conflict. People clash over sex, money, property, work, love, politics, religion, relatives, children, time, personal habits, jealousies—and these are just a few of the many possible examples! Studies asking married couples about their conflicts found 100 different categories of causes specified (Gottman, 1979). For people who are dating, common conflict triggers include the amount of energy devoted to relationship maintenance, criticism about partner's appearance or lack of fitness, and the frequency and type of sexual activity (Surra & Longstreth, 1990).

Given all the things people fight about, it's not surprising that conflicts assume many different forms, as displayed in Table 9.1. It's also no shock that conflict is a daily constant. On average, people report seven conflicts a week, mostly among relatives, friends, and lovers with whom they've argued before (Benoit & Benoit, 1990).

What Is Conflict?

Though it can take many different forms, **conflict** is a transactional process between people who perceive incompatible goals, scarce resources, or interference in achieving their objectives (Wilmot & Hocker, 2001). This definition highlights several key features of conflict. First, conflict unfolds over time, and its course is determined by the communication choices we make. Although people often describe conflict as a series of unrelated events ("I sent her this carefully worded e-mail, and for no reason, she flamed me!"),

TABLE 9.1

Types of Conflict

Type	Description	Example
Blow-up	Erupts suddenly and involves heated emotional exchanges	"I've had it! Get out of my face or you'll be sorry."
Civil	Calmly and rationally discussed by participants	"Let's talk this through. We can figure it out."
Déjà vu	Follows a predictable and repeated pattern	"Oh no, here we go again."
Indirect	Not discussed or explicitly recognized by participants	"The tension is so thick you can cut it with a knife."
Mock	Playful in intent	"We're just joking."
Sarcastic sniping	Marked by exchanges of hostile sarcasm	"How can you afford that? Did you win the lottery?"
Silent treatment	Characterized by one partner's silence across two or more encounters	"He's freezing me out."

Note: Table 9.1 is adapted from Baxter, Wilmot, Simmons, and Swartz (1993).

conflict is transactional; everything we say and do during a conflict influences everything our partner says and does, and vice versa. Moreover, most conflicts proceed through several stages, each involving decisions and actions that affect the conflict's direction and its consequences for the individuals and relationships involved.

Second, as illustrated by the Orbe and Warren (2000) study discussed earlier, conflict is strongly shaped by perception. Our interpretations of what's happening influence how we define a conflict—for instance, viewing a dispute as "a power struggle" versus "a personality clash." These perceptions also affect whom we blame for a disagreement as well as which communication choices we make as the situation progresses.

Third, as the definition suggests, conflicts are rooted in our perceptions regarding goals and resources (Cahn, 1992; Canary, Cupach, & Messman, 1995; Roloff & Soule, 2002). Some conflicts revolve around incompatible goals, ranging from everyday leisure activity disputes ("I want to go out dancing! Why do you want to stay home?") to serious arguments regarding personal values ("I want our children to be raised Jewish, not Christian"). Because most people pursue a wide range of goals at any one time (Ohbuchi & Tedeschi, 1997), interpersonal conflict is inevitable. Other disputes break out when people compete over resources—whether it's a coveted position in a long checkout line or a cherished family heirloom that grown children clamor for after a grandparent has passed on. Still other conflicts erupt when we believe that someone else is preventing us from achieving our goals—intentionally or not. A friend calls repeatedly while you're studying, and you snap at him. Your manager demands that you work over a holiday weekend, and you refuse.

Conflict in Relationships

Most conflicts occur between people who know each other and are involved in close relationships, such as romantic partners, friends, family members, and coworkers (Benoit & Benoit, 1990). Conflicts happen comparatively rarely between complete strangers, and most violent conflicts happen in the home between family members and romantic partners (Berscheid, 2002).

Unlike people who don't know each other well, people in close relationships experience prolonged contact and frequent interaction, which can set the stage for disagreements over goals and resources. And relationship partners often develop consistent patterns of communication for dealing with conflict that either promote or undermine their happiness. As just one example, happily married couples are more likely than unhappily married couples to avoid personal attacks during conflicts and instead focus their discussion on the differences at hand (Peterson, 2002). Such patterns are self-perpetuating: happy couples remain motivated to behave in ways guaranteed to keep them happy, and because they believe they can solve their problems, they are more likely to cooperatively resolve conflict (Caughlin & Vangelisti, 2000).

Managing conflicts in close relationships presents unique challenges. Consider the extensive personal information that you and your romantic partners or friends have disclosed to each other over the time you've been

conflict

opportunity

danger

● The Chinese character for *conflict* is made up of two different symbols, for *danger* and for *opportunity*, that express the dualistic nature of conflict. All conflict encounters contain the potential for dangerous outcomes as well as the opportunity for positive change.

SELF-REFLECTION

Think about a recent conflict you've experienced. What triggered it? Did you and the other person realize you had incompatible goals? Were you competing over a valued resource? Was one of you preventing the other from achieving an important objective?

together. Although this information bonds you together, it also provides a tempting arsenal to use when conflict erupts. For example, in a tactic known as **kitchen-sinking** (from the expression, "throwing everything but the kitchen sink at them"), combatants throw accusations at each other that have little to do with the disagreement at hand—"Oh yeah? What about the time when you completely forgot our anniversary?"

The emotional investment we make in our close relationships further adds to the complexity of conflict. We feel connected to and interdependent with our intimate partners, so when disputes erupt and threaten that sense of connection, emotion naturally results (Berscheid, 2002). Your conflicts with loved ones are guaranteed to be intense and draining emotional experiences.

Last, conflicts aren't discrete and isolated events, independent from the future of your relationship with your intimate partners. Instead, they're events that powerfully affect your future interpersonal encounters with them as well as your relationship satisfaction. For example, if you and a sibling attack each other through a caustic e-mail exchange, this conflict will shape not only how you feel about your relationship in the coming weeks and months but also how the two of you communicate when you once again are face-to-face. As conflict researcher Donald Peterson (2002) notes, "Every conflict and every resolution, as well as every failure at resolution, becomes a part of your overall relationship history."

Power and Conflict

In the opening scene of a dance piece by Les Ballets Africains, the European Colonial Governor visits a local village on market day, where he meets and becomes smitten with one of the dancers, Sona. When he reaches to kiss

"Power is central to conflict."

her hand, Sona refuses him and runs to her fiancé Balake for help. During the confrontation that follows, the Governor slaps Balake in the face and then orders his guards to haul Balake to prison. Later, the Governor orders the death of Balake and sends a messenger to the village to announce his death. But Sona defies the Governor's desire for her by leaving the village, swallowing poison, and joining her lover Balake in death.

As this tale of confrontation suggests, conflict often has close ties with **power,** the ability to influence or control other people and events (Donohue & Kolt, 1992). Because people in conflict believe that others are challenging, competing with, or opposing them, they often feel compelled to wield whatever means of influence they have to overcome the opposition and achieve their goals. And in situations where one person in the conflict has more power than the other—like the Governor over Sona and Balake—they tend to get what they want, unless others defy them in extreme ways like Sona's decision to die rather than become the Governor's concubine.

Power's Defining Characteristics

You might think of power as something that only people in official positions of authority possess, such as politicians or police officers. But we all have some degree of power, and it influences our interpersonal communication and relationships every day, including the conflicts we experience. Consider the defining characteristics of power outlined below (Wilmot & Hocker, 2001).

Power Is Always Present. Whether you're talking with your manager, instant-messaging your best friend, or spending time with your children, power is present in all your interpersonal encounters and relationships. Power may be balanced (friend to friend) or imbalanced (manager to employee, parent to young child, dominant spouse to submissive spouse). When power is balanced, **symmetrical relationships** result. When power is unbalanced, **complementary relationships** are the outcome. We're usually not aware of power until a conflict erupts in which the relationship's power balance is tested: a friend with whom you have a symmetrical relationship starts bullying you, or an employee with whom you have a complementary relationship questions a decision you've made.

People differ in their beliefs about the appropriate power balance that should exist in relationships. In traditional Mexican culture, for instance, the value of *respeto* emphasizes complementary power balance between those who are younger and those in positions of power, especially elders within one's family (Delgado-Gaitan, 1993). As part of *respeto,* children are expected to defer to elders' authority and to avoid openly disagreeing with elders. In contrast, many European Americans believe that once children reach the age of adulthood, power in family relationships should be balanced—children and their elders orienting to one another in a symmetrical fashion as friends (Kagawa & McCornack, 2004).

Many people also view successful intimate relationships as achievable only through a complementary power balance. For instance, in June 1998, the Southern Baptist Convention in the United States issued the 18th article of the Baptist Faith and Message, declaring that "a wife is to submit graciously to the servant leadership of her husband, even as the Church willingly submits to the headship of Christ" (Cline, 2006). Both women and men supported this article, and Baptist delegates overwhelmingly rejected an amendment by more liberal members that would have had husbands and wives "submit to each another."

Power Can Be Used Ethically or Unethically. Power itself isn't good or bad—it's the way people wield it that matters. Many happy marriages, family relationships, and long-term friendships are complementary. One person controls more resources and has more decision-making influence than the other. Yet the person in charge uses his or her power only to benefit both people and the relationship. In other relationships, the powerful partner wields his or her power unethically or recklessly. For

example, a boss threatens to fire her employee unless he sleeps with her, or an abusive husband tells his unhappy wife that she'll never see their kids again if she leaves him.

Power Is Granted.   Power doesn't reside within people. Instead, it is granted by individuals or groups who allow another person or group to exert influence and control over them. Power is thus a social construct and exists only between individuals and groups. For example, a friend of mine invited his parents to stay with him and his wife for the weekend. His parents had planned on leaving Monday, but come Monday morning, they announced that they were having so much fun that they had decided to stay through the end of the week. My friend accepted their decision even though he could have insisted that they leave at the originally agreed-upon time. In doing so, he granted his parents the power to decide their departure date without his input or consent. As he explained to me later, "They're my *parents.*"

Power Influences Most Conflicts.   If you strip away the particulars of what's said and done during most conflicts, you'll find power struggles underneath. Who has more influence? Who controls the resources, decisions, and feelings involved? During most conflicts, people struggle to see whose goals will prevail, and they wield whatever power they have to pursue their own goals. But power struggles rarely lead to mutually beneficial solutions. As we'll see, the more constructive approach is to set aside your power and instead work collaboratively to resolve the conflict at hand.

Power Currencies

Given that power is not innate but something that some people grant to others, how do you get people to give you power? In order to acquire power, you must possess or control some form of **power currency,** a resource that other people value (Wilmot & Hocker, 2001). Possessing or controlling a valued resource gives you influence over individuals who value that resource. Likewise, if individuals have resources you view as valuable, you will in turn grant power to them.

  Five power currencies are common in interpersonal relationships. **Resource currency** includes material things such as money, property, and food. If you possess material things that someone else needs or wants, you have resource power over them. Parents have nearly total resource power over young children because they control all the money, food, shelter, clothing, and other items their children need and want. Managers have

● Power expresses itself in the form of different power currencies. As shown here, these include resource currency, expertise currency, social network currency, personal currency, and intimacy currency.

high levels of resource power over employees, as they control employees' continued employment and salaries.

Expertise currency comprises special skills or knowledge. The more highly specialized and unique the skill or knowledge you have, the more expertise power you possess. A Stuttgart-trained Porsche mechanic commands a substantially higher wage and choicer selection of clients than a minimally trained Quick Lube oil-change attendant.

A person who is linked with a network of friends, family, and acquaintances with substantial influence has **social network currency.** Others may value his or her ability to introduce them to people who can land them jobs, "talk them up" to potential romantic partners, or get them invitations to exclusive parties or vacations.

Personal characteristics—physical beauty, intelligence, charm, communication skill, and sense of humor—that people prize as desirable in a particular culture constitute **personal currency.** Even if you lack resource, expertise, and social network power, you can still achieve a certain degree of influence and stature through being beautiful, funny, or smart.

Finally, you acquire **intimacy currency** when you share with someone else a close bond that no one else shares. If you have a unique intimate bond with someone—lover, friend, or family member—you possess intimacy power over him or her, as my friend's parents did in the example above.

Power and Culture

Views of power differ substantially across cultures. Power derives from the perception of power currencies, so people are granted power not only according to which power currencies they possess but also by the degree to which power currencies are valued in a given culture. In Asian and Latino cultures, very high value is placed on resource currency; consequently, people without wealth, property, or other such material resources are likely to grant those who possess them power (Gudykunst & Kim, 2003). In contrast, in northern European countries and the United States, people with wealth may be admired or even envied, but they are not granted unusual power.

SELF-REFLECTION

What power currencies do you possess? What ethical responsibilities do you have in using these currencies? For example, is it ethical to pit your personal currency against someone else's social network currency to get a job? What about leveraging your resource currency to get your children to obey you?

TABLE 9.2

Power-Distance across Countries

High Power-Distance Countries	Moderate Power-Distance Countries	Low Power-Distance Countries
Malaysia	Spain	Norway
Panama	Pakistan	Sweden
Guatemala	Italy	Ireland
Philippines	South Africa	New Zealand
Mexico	Hungary	Denmark
Venezuela	Jamaica	Israel
China	United States	Austria

Source: Hofstede (2001).

Cultures also differ widely in the degree to which people view the unequal distribution of power as acceptable, known as **power-distance** (Hofstede, 1991, 2001). In high power-distance cultures, it's considered normal and even desirable for people of different social and professional status to be widely separated in terms of their power. Within such cultures, people give privileged treatment and extreme respect to those in high-status positions (Ting-Toomey, 1999). People of lesser status are expected to behave humbly, especially when they're around people of higher status, and high-status people are expected to act superior. In low power-distance cultures, people in high-status positions strive to minimize the differences between themselves and lower-status persons, often interacting with lower-status persons in an informal and equal fashion (see Table 9.2).

Power-distance influences how people choose to deal with conflict. In low power-distance cultures, people who possess few if any power currencies still may choose to engage in conflict with high-power people. Employees may question management decisions, or people may attend a town meeting and argue with the mayor. These behaviors are much less likely in high power-distance cultures (Bochner & Hesketh, 1994). For example, several years ago, a teacher friend of mine moved from an American university to an Asian university. In the United States, students perceived only moderate power-distance between themselves and him. As a consequence, they routinely challenged his opinions in class, and

POP QUIZ

Are You a High or a Low Power-Distance Person?

Read each statement. Place a check mark next to the statements with which you agree. Then follow the instructions for interpreting your score.

_____ Obedience and respect for authority are the most important values children should learn.

_____ What young people need most is strict discipline, rugged determination, and the willingness to sacrifice for family and country.

_____ Every person should have complete faith in some supernatural power whose decisions he or she obeys without question.

_____ Young people sometimes get rebellious ideas, but as they grow up they ought to get over these ideas and settle down.

_____ There are few things worse than a person who doesn't feel gratitude and respect for his or her parents.

_____ What this country needs most is a few courageous, tireless, and devoted leaders in whom the people can put their faith.

_____ In times of doubt, people should trust our country's leaders to do what's right.

Interpreting your score

If your total score is 5–7, you're likely a high authoritarian; a score of 3–4 suggests you're a moderate authoritarian; 0–2 indicates you're a low authoritarian.

Note: Information in this Pop Quiz is adapted from Ray (1972).

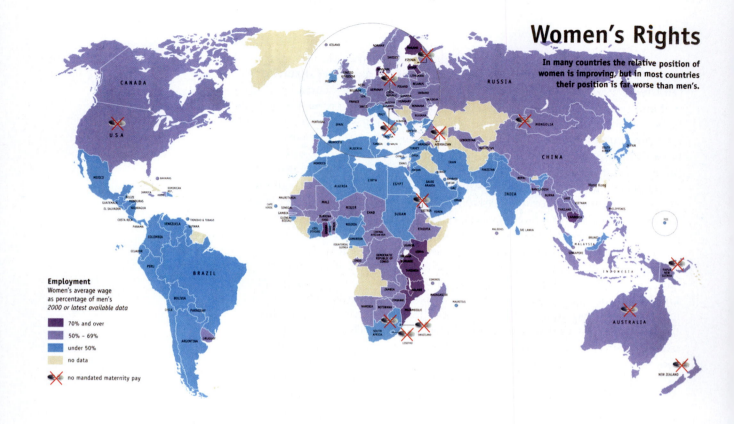

Women's Rights

In many countries the relative position of women is improving, but in most countries their position is far worse than men's.

Employment
Women's average wage as percentage of men's
2000 or latest available data

- 70% and over
- 50% – 69%
- under 50%
- no data
- ✖ no mandated maternity pay

being an argumentative sort, my friend enjoyed this type of conflict. Overseas, his teaching experience proved very different. People throughout the community treated him with extreme deference. Students avoided challenging his opinion in class—even when he wanted them to—because they perceived the power-distance as too great.

People in high power-distance cultures also tend to be highly authoritarian. Regardless of whether they themselves occupy powerful positions, they believe that authority figures should be believed and obeyed (Adorno, Frenkel-Brunswik, Levinson, & Sanford, 1950). If you're a high authoritarian, you likely trust people such as parents, police officers, teachers, managers, ministers, and political leaders. Consequently, you're less likely to challenge these individuals in cases of conflict and more likely to simply accommodate their wishes. If you're a low authoritarian, you're much more likely to challenge authority figures and engage in conflict with people who have more power than you.

Power and Gender

To say that power and gender are intertwined is an understatement. Throughout history and across cultures, *the* defining distinction between the genders has been men's power over women. Through patriarchy, which means "the rule of fathers," men have used cultural practices to maintain their societal, political, and economic power (Mies, 1991). Men have built and sustained patriarchy by denying women access to power currencies. In

Greater Percentage Than the United States	Equal Percentage to the United States
Cuba	Congo
Peru	Uruguay
Rwanda	Slovenia
Turkmenistan	Singapore
Uganda	Tajikistan
Source: IANWGE (2002).	

TABLE 9.3

Women's Political Representation Compared to the United States

many countries around the world, women lack access to education, receive lower wages than men do, have lower-quality health care, and have scant political representation (United Nations, 2002). Consequently, women globally have lower resource, expertise, and social network power.[2] In Central American and central African countries, for example, fewer than 50 percent of girls attend secondary schools. Only 34 percent of countries around the world have achieved gender equality in youth literacy rates. And just 45 percent of the world's nations have female employment rates equal to those of men. Most damaging to female power, women across cultures are largely excluded from positions of political authority. A mere 14 percent of all political representatives worldwide are women. And within the United States—which prides itself on its purported gender equality—only 12 percent of elected representatives are women. Thirty-eight developing countries have a substantially higher percentage of female political leaders than this (see Table 9.3).

How does lack of power affect women's interpersonal communication? As gender scholar Cheris Kramarae (1981) notes, women with little or no power "are not as free or as able as men are to say what they wish, when and where they wish. . . . Their talk is often not considered of much value by men" (p. 1). By contrast, what men say and do is counted as important, and women's voices are muted. In interpersonal relationships, this power difference manifests itself in men's tendency to expect women to listen attentively to everything they say while men select the topics they wish to attend to when women are speaking (Fishman, 1977). While men may feel satisfied that their voices are being heard in their relationships, women often feel as though their viewpoints are being ignored or minimized, both at home and in the workplace (Spender, 1990).

Approaching Conflict

You're standing in a long checkout line at a local bookstore, when suddenly a woman casually slips into the line ahead of you (Forni, 2002). What do you do? Ignore the situation and wait in line behind her? Leave the line in

---

[2] All information that follows is excerpted from United Nations (2002).

frustration? Ask her politely to go to the end of the line? Or perhaps challenge her, demanding that she leave and threatening to call the store manager over if she doesn't?

In any such situation—when someone is challenging your goals or competing for desired resources—your most important decision is how to deal with the conflict (Sillars & Wilmot, 1994). Your choice about what you'll say and do will shape everything that follows—whether the situation will go unresolved, escalate, or reach resolution. Your communication choice will also influence whether your relationship with the other person (if one exists) will be damaged or grow stronger. People generally manage conflict in one of four ways: avoiding, accommodating, competing, or collaborating. Before reading about each approach, take the Pop Quiz on the facing page to find out how you approach conflict.

Avoiding Conflict

In her standup routine, comedienne Ellen DeGeneres spoofs people's passive reactions to rude behavior. Sitting in the theater and watching a movie, someone behind you keeps kicking your seat either intentionally or unwittingly. How do most people respond? By fidgeting in their chairs, occasionally turning halfway around, sighing loudly, or making little under-the-breath remarks about "discourtesy." All these reactions suggest that they notice the person's rude behavior but won't directly communicate about it or challenge it.

This demonstrates the **avoidance** approach to conflict, in which you ignore or communicate ambiguously about the situation. Avoidance is the most frequently used approach to managing conflict (Sillars, 1980). One common form of avoidance is **skirting,** in which a person avoids a serious source of conflict by joking about it or changing the topic. Say you feel that your romantic partner doesn't compliment you enough. When you broach the subject, he or she laughs and starts singing the chorus to the 1970s hit "Cold as Ice" to change the subject. Another form of avoidance is **sniping**—communicating in a negative fashion and then abandoning the encounter by physically leaving the scene or refusing to interact further. You're trying to work through a conflict with your long-distance partner by instant-messaging when she or he writes something nasty and signs off before you have a chance to reply.

Many people opt for avoidance because it seems safe, but it actually poses substantial risks. Avoiding conflicts that center on important issues can create ambivalence in relationships or even spawn hostility (Roloff & Soule, 2002). This is due to **cumulative annoyance** in which our repressed annoyance grows as the mental list of grievances we have against our partner accumulates (Peterson, 2002). Eventually, cumulative annoyance overwhelms our capacity to suppress it further, and the result is a sudden explosion of anger, frequently accompanied by kitchen-sink messages. For example, you find yourself constantly reminding your teenage son about his homework, chores, personal hygiene, and room cleanliness. This bothers you immensely because you feel these matters are his responsibility, but you swallow your anger because you don't want to make a fuss and don't want to be seen by him as "nagging." One evening, after reminding him twice to hang up his expensive new leather jacket, you walk into his bedroom to find the coat crumpled in a ball on the floor. You go on a tirade, listing all of the things he has done to upset you in the past month.

A second risk posed by avoidance is **pseudo-conflict,** the perception that a conflict exists when in fact it doesn't. For example, you think a new acquaintance dislikes you because he always cuts your encounters short, so you begin avoiding him. But he does like you—it's just he's been really busy recently—so you lose a possible friendship. Or you mistakenly perceive an incompatibility in goals with your romantic partner, thinking he or she is about to break up with you. So you decide to preemptively end your relationship even though your partner actually has no desire to leave you.

POP QUIZ

How Do You Approach Conflict?

Read through the statements, placing a check mark next to each statement with which you agree. The category with the most check marks indicates how you primarily manage conflict. If you score equally high on two or more different approaches, you use more than one approach.

Avoiding

_____ I keep issues to myself.

_____ I usually avoid open discussion of my differences with others.

_____ I try to stay away from topics of disagreement.

_____ I keep disagreements to myself to avoid hard feelings.

_____ I try to avoid unpleasant exchanges.

Accommodating

_____ I generally try to satisfy others' needs.

_____ I usually accommodate others' wishes.

_____ I give in to others' desires.

_____ I often go with others' suggestions.

_____ I try to satisfy others' expectations.

Competing

_____ I use my influence to get my ideas accepted.

_____ I use my authority to make decisions go in my favor.

_____ I generally pursue my side of an issue.

_____ I sometimes use my power to win.

_____ I use my expertise to make sure decisions go my way.

Collaborating

_____ I try to investigate issues to find solutions acceptable to both parties.

_____ I try to integrate my ideas with those of others to come up with a decision jointly.

_____ I try to work with others to find solutions that satisfy both our expectations.

_____ I exchange information with others so we can solve problems together.

_____ I try to bring all our concerns out in the open so issues can be resolved.

Note: Adapted from Rahim and Mager (1995).

Accommodating Conflict

Through **accommodation,** one person abandons his or her own goals and acquiesces to the desires of the other person. For example, your supervisor at work asks you to stay an extra hour tonight because a coworker is showing up late. Although you had plans for the evening, you cancel them and act as if it's not a problem.

If you're like most people, you probably accommodate people who have more power than you. Why? If you don't, they might use their power to control or even punish you until they get what they want. This suggests an important lesson regarding the relationship between power and conflict: if you possess few or no power currencies, people who are more powerful probably won't accommodate your goals during conflicts.

FOCUS ON CULTURE

Accommodation and Radical Pacifism

You're walking down the street, and a man approaches you and demands your wallet. You immediately give it and then ask him whether he also wants your coat. Or suppose you badly want an open position at work. When you find out that a coworker also wants it, you inform your supervisor that you no longer want the job and encourage her to give it to your colleague instead.

As the biblical verse "When a man takes your coat, offer him your shirt as well" (Luke 6:29) suggests, one way to deal with conflict is an extreme form of accommodation known as *radical pacifism.* Although it is often associated with antiwar movements (Bennett, 2003), *radical pacifism* embodies a broader philosophy about the nature of interpersonal connections between human beings and how conflict is best resolved. Those practicing radical pacifism believe in a moral obligation to behave in selfless and self-sacrificial ways that quickly end conflicts and that assist others. During interpersonal conflict, this means discovering what someone else wants and needs, then aiding that person in attaining these goals, even if it means sacrificing your own.

The practice of radical pacifism cuts across countries, ethnicities, and social classes; it is primarily rooted in the religious cultures. For example, in the Buddhist text *Punnovada Sutta* (Bodhi & Nanamoli translation, 1995), the Buddha asks his disciple Punna what he would do if someone attacked him with a knife. "I would think they were truly kind, for not taking my life." "What if they kill you?" asks the Buddha. "I would be happy, because many disciples, disgusted by the body, sought to have their lives ended with a knife, but I was fortunate enough to have it happen without even seeking it!" Amish Church elders embracing radical pacifism share a similar view: "Even if the result of our pacifism is death at the hands of an attacker during a violent conflict, so be it; death is not threatening to us as Christians. Hopefully the attacker will have at least had a glimpse of the love of Christ in our nonviolent response" (Pennsylvania Dutch Country Welcome Center, n.d.).

YOUR TURN

- What are your beliefs regarding the practice of radical pacifism?

- Do you have an ethical obligation to accommodate others when their interests clash with yours? At what point, if any, does this obligation end?

- How would your interpersonal communication be affected if you practiced radical pacifism?

Another factor that influences people's decision to accommodate is love. Especially in romantic relationships, we tend to prioritize our partners' needs before our own (Hendrick & Hendrick, 1992). For example, your romantic partner is accepted into a summer study-abroad program in Europe. Although you had planned on spending the summer together, you encourage him or her to accept the offer, even though the thought of separation pains you bitterly. Many romantic relationship scholars consider the willingness to forsake our own goals to make our romantic partners happy a defining feature of love (Rubin, 1973).

Competitively Managing Conflict

Think back to Kevin and Julie's conflict on *The Real World*. Each of them aggressively challenged the other and expressed little concern for the other's perspective or goals. The approach they took to managing their conflict was **competition.** When you use that approach, you confront others and pursue your own goals to the exclusion of theirs. The two defining characteristics of competitive approaches are open and clear discussion of the goal clash that exists and pursuit of one's own goals without regard for others' (Sillars, 1980).

Competitive approaches may be more common online than face-to-face. The inability to see online partners and to witness their nonverbal reactions to messages makes people less aware of the consequences of their communication choices (Joinson, 2001). As a result, people are more likely to prioritize their own goals, minimize partner's goals, and use hostile personal attacks in pursuit of their goals online than face-to-face (Shedletsky & Aitken, 2004).

As with accommodation, power plays a strong role in the use of competitive approaches to conflict. People who have substantial power currencies are more inclined to use competition than those with less power (Peterson, 2002). Because they have more power to begin with, they feel they can wield it over others to serve their own ends. However, people with

less power may opt for competitive approaches on occasion, particularly when they feel they've been abused, exploited, or bullied for a long period of time.

At a minimum, competitive approaches can trigger defensive communication (described in Chapter 5)—partners refusing to consider your goals or dismissing them as unimportant, acting superior to you, or attempting to squelch your disagreement by wielding power over you (Waldron, Turner, Alexander, & Barton, 1993). But the primary risk of choosing a competitive approach is **escalation,** a dramatic rise in emotional intensity and increasingly negative and aggressive communication. And if you and your partner are unwilling to back down from a dispute, escalation is guaranteed. Even initially trivial conflicts can quickly explode into intense exchanges.

When conflicts escalate, people often begin communicating in ways they normally would shun. During close relationship conflict, for example, escalation can lead partners to say things that permanently damage their bond (McCornack & Husband, 1986). **Sudden-death statements** occur when people get so angry and frustrated that they declare the end of the relationship, even though breaking up wasn't a possibility before the conflict. When my wife Kelly and I had been married for two years, we had a major argument while visiting her parents. A small dispute over family differences quickly escalated into a full-blown conflict. After flinging a number of kitchen-sink messages at each other, we both shouted, "Why are we even together!? We're so different!" Fortunately, this sudden-death statement caused us to immediately calm down. But many couples who blurt out such things during escalation follow through on them.

Perhaps most destructive, conflict escalation can cause people to reveal **dirty secrets,** messages that are honest in content but have been kept hidden to protect a partner's feelings. Dirty secrets can include acts of infidelity ("Remember when you thought I was cheating on you? Well, you were right; I did cheat, and it was great!"). They can also include intense criticism of a partner's appearance ("You know how I said I always liked your nose? Well, I don't!"), and even a lack of feelings ("I haven't been in love with you for years; I've just stayed with you for the kids' sake!"). Dirty secrets are designed to hurt, and because the content is true, they can irreparably damage the recipient and the relationship.

SELF-REFLECTION

Recall a conflict in which you and the other person used competitive approaches, the conflict escalated, and you exchanged negative messages such as defensive communication, sudden-death statements, or dirty secrets. What impact did these messages have on the conflict? How did they affect your relationship?

Needless to say, the intensely negative messages that often mark conflict escalation have destructive effects on relationships. Couples who exchange more critical, contemptuous, and defensive messages during the first seven years of marriage are substantially more likely to end up divorcing than are couples who refrain from such negative forms of communication (Gottman & Levenson, 2000).

Collaboratively Managing Conflict

Imagine that it's a few weeks before Thanksgiving, and you and your new romantic partner are making holiday plans. Each of you has always shared the day with family. But now that you're a couple, you face the obvious dilemma of which family to spend the holiday with. You both want to share the day together, but neither of you wants to miss your traditional family

"You're much more likely to talk directly and constructively with a partner when you think he or she is cooperative."

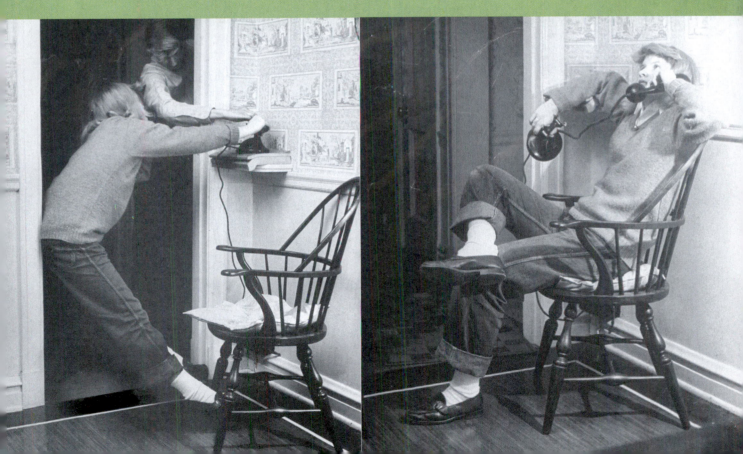

TABLE 9.4

Competitive versus Collaborative Conflict Approaches

	Competitive Approach	Collaborative Approach
Roommate hasn't been doing his or her share of housework.	"I'm sick and tired of you never doing anything around here to help out! From now on, you are doing all the chores!"	"We've both been really busy, but I'm concerned that things are not getting done. Let's make a list of all the chores and figure out how to fairly divide it up."
Coworker is draining large blocks of your work time by socializing with you.	"It's obvious to me from how you're always goofing around that you don't care about your job or whether you get fired. But I need this job, so stop bugging me all the time and let me get my work done!"	"I enjoy spending time with you, but I'm finding I don't have enough time left to get everything done. Let's figure out how we can better balance hanging out and getting our work done."
Romantic partner wants you to abandon a beloved pastime because it seems too dangerous.	"I've been racing dirt bikes long before I met you, and there's no way I'm giving them up. If you really loved me, you'd accept that instead of pestering me to quit!"	"Sorry my racing worries you; I know the reason you're concerned is because you care about me. Let's talk about what we can both do so I don't worry you so much."

gathering. Do you simply ignore the issue, avoiding the conflict until it's too late? Does one of you accommodate the other, and agree to forsake his or her family's get-together? Do you compete with each other, each person trying to dominate the ultimate decision? Or do you search for a solution that will make both of you happy?

The most constructive approach for managing conflict is **collaboration,** treating conflict as a mutual problem-solving challenge rather than something that must avoided, accommodated, or competed over. Collaboration tends to increase relationship satisfaction (Sillars, 1980) and to enhance trust and relational commitment (Canary & Cupach, 1988; Canary & Spitzberg, 1989).

To use a collaborative approach, openly discuss the incompatibility of goals or the competition for resources that has fueled your conflict (see Table 9.4). Give equal attention to both persons' needs and desires. For example, to collaboratively manage the conflict over Thanksgiving, you would honestly discuss the matter with your partner, expressing empathic concern and perspective-taking ("I know this is hard for each of us, and I completely understand how important our family traditions are"). Also, use rhetorical messages (discussed in Chapter 5), keeping the conversation focused on solutions and taking a flexible, respectful stance toward your partner ("Let's try to figure out a plan together so we can both end up happy"). Perhaps most valuable, be courteous, respectful, and positive toward your partner, and avoid personal attacks.

Communication scholars William Wilmot and Joyce Hocker offer four additional suggestions for collaboratively managing conflict (2001). First, attack problems not people. When talking about the conflict, separate the problem that's the source of the conflict from the people who are involved. For example, in the Thanksgiving scenario, you would stress that it's the practice of spending the holidays with your families that is the source of the conflict and not the personality, values, or attitudes of your partner. Avoid personalizing the conflict through statements such as "You don't care about my family!" or "You're always out for yourself!" Second, focus on common interests and long-term goals ("I know we both want to maintain close ties to our families as well as spend important holidays together"). Arguing over positions ("I want this" "Well, I want that!") endangers relationships because the conflict quickly becomes a destructive contest of wills. Third, create options before arriving at decisions. Identify different possible routes for resolving the conflict, and then combine the best parts of them to come up with a solution. For instance, solutions to the Thanksgiving dilemma might include spending the holiday with one family this year and with the other family next year, or eating turkey with one family and having dessert and coffee with the other family. Don't get bogged down searching for the one "perfect" solution—it may not exist. Finally, critically evaluate your solution. Ask: is it equally fair for both of us?

Barriers to Constructive Conflict

Imagine two conflicts. The first is with John, one of your housemates. You and John seem to disagree about everything from food and music to politics and religion. You perceive John as uncooperative, and he always seems to being doing things intentionally designed to provoke you. Recently, some of your food has been disappearing from the house refrigerator, and you suspect that John has taken it. The second conflict is with a coworker, Jane. Unlike John, Jane strikes you as a cooperative person who rarely is to blame for the few problems that have arisen between you. What's more, when you disagree, it seems that such conflicts are generally the result of temporary causes (such as bad moods or work stress) rather than differences like the ones between you and John. In your latest conflict with Jane, you got upset when she seized an opportunity to work overtime. You blame yourself, though, because when Jane said she was interested in earning extra pay, you didn't mention that you also wanted the overtime.

Now think about how you might approach your conflicts with Jane and John. How does your view of Jane as cooperative, comparatively blameless, and agreeable shape how you will approach your conflict with her? Given your opinion of John as uncooperative, blameworthy, and fundamentally different from you, is working things out with him worth the time and effort?

SKILLS PRACTICE

This exercise helps you effectively work through conflict online.

❶ Watch for an online message that triggers conflict.

❷ Before responding, question your presumption that the person you're clashing with is uncooperative.

❸ Avoid exclusively blaming the other person; instead, consider how you may have contributed to the conflict.

❹ Critically assess whether the conflict is due to ongoing differences or to temporary factors such as stress, fatigue, misunderstanding, or bad moods.

❺ Once you've checked your attributions, create a reply that focuses on the problem not the person, emphasizes points of commonality, and offers several possible solutions to the dispute.

Based on everything you have read in this chapter so far, adopting a collaborative approach with both Jane and John is the most constructive way to manage your conflicts with them. Unfortunately, adopting this approach is not that simple. Sometimes, substantial barriers—in the form of inaccurate perceptions and attributions—prevent us from using collaboration. When we get into conflicts with others, we don't judge ourselves, others, and the communication that occurs objectively. Instead, we perceive these things in ways that make us look right and others look wrong (Sillars, Roberts, Leonard, & Dun, 2000). For example, one study found that husbands and wives blamed their spouses for their own negative remarks made during conflicts, claiming that their destructive communication behavior was triggered by their partner's inappropriate actions (Schutz, 1999). Spouses also consistently attributed their communication to good intentions and described their partner's communication as irrational and inconsistent. When asked who was to blame for the conflict, each spouse blamed the other.

As the example of your conflicts with John and Jane suggests, these perceptual tendencies are not limited to conflicts in marriages. During any disagreement, we *all* make errors in perception and attributions that lead us away from using a collaborative approach. For example, we often perceive our antagonists as uncooperative and ourselves as cooperative (Sillars et al., 2000), a comparison that discourages collaboration. And instead of acknowledging our own role in a dispute, which encourages a collaborative approach, we often blame our partners (Schutz, 1999). Finally, we tend to attribute conflicts to long-term differences that can't be overcome, which also discourages collaboration ("There's nothing I can do about the fact that we don't get along, so why talk about it!?") (Sillars, 1980).

As you can see, errors in perception and attribution play a significant role in blocking the use of collaboration to manage conflict. Consequently, to improve your conflict-management skills, practice assessing your perceptions and attributions during disputes. Although you might not achieve complete objectivity or neutrality in your judgments, try testing yourself by going through this mental checklist:

- Is my partner really being uncooperative, or am I making a faulty attribution?

- Is my partner really solely to blame, or have I also done something to cause the conflict?

- Is the conflict really due to ongoing differences between us, or is it due to temporary factors such as stress or fatigue?

Conflict and Violence

The most physically and emotionally destructive response to conflict is physical violence, a strategy to which people may resort if they cannot think of a better way or they believe no other options are available (Klein, 1998). In the National Violence against Women Survey (Tjaden & Thoennes, 1999),

52 percent of women and 66 percent of men reported that at some time in their lives they had been physically assaulted during conflicts. And both men and women *use* violence as a strategy for dealing with conflicts. Approximately 12 percent of women and 11 percent of men surveyed report having committed a violent act during conflict with their spouse in the preceding year (Barnett, Miller-Perrin, & Perrin, 1997). Moreover, in an analysis of data from 82 violence studies, researcher John Archer found no substantial difference between men and women in their propensity toward violence as a conflict strategy (2000). At the same time, although women perpetrate as much violence during conflicts as do men, they are substantially more likely to be injured or killed, owing to their lesser physical size and strength (Archer, 2000; O'Leary & Vivian, 1990). And physical violence doesn't restrict itself to heterosexual relationships; nearly 50 percent of lesbian and 30 to 40 percent of gay respondents have been victims of violence during interpersonal conflicts at some time in their lives (Peplau & Spalding, 2000).

If you find yourself in a relationship in which your partner behaves violently toward you, seek help from family members, friends, and law enforcement officials if necessary. Realize that your best option might be to end the relationship and avoid all contact with the person.

If you find that you are inclined to violence in relationships, revisit the anger management techniques described in Chapter 4 as well as the suggestions for constructively handling conflict described previously. Most aggression during conflicts stems from people's perception that they have no other options. Although situations may exist where there truly are no other options—for example, self-defense during a violent assault or robbery—within most encounters more constructive alternatives are available. If you are unable to control your impulses toward violence, seek professional counseling.

Conflict Resolutions and Outcomes

Think about the most recent serious conflict you experienced, and consider the way it ended. Did one of you "win" and the other "lose"? Were you both left dissatisfied, or were you each pleased with the resolution? More important, were you able to resolve the underlying goal dispute, competition for resources, or goal disruption that triggered the disagreement in the first place, or did you merely create a short-term fix that won't last?

Given their emotional intensity and the fact that they typically occur in relationships, conflicts conclude more gradually than many people would like. You may arrive at a short-term resolution leading you and the other person to consider the conflict over. But afterward, you'll experience long-term outcomes as you spend time remembering, pondering, and regretting the incident. During this latter phase, you'll mull over whether you truly resolved the causes of the conflict and how the interpersonal communication you and the other person exchanged during the dispute has affected your relationship.

Short-Term Conflict Resolutions

Short-term conflict resolutions typically take one of five forms (Peterson, 2002). Some conflicts end through **separation**, the sudden withdrawal of one person from the encounter. This resolution is characteristic of approaching conflict through avoidance, but not all separations are preceded by negative communication. For example, you may be talking about a disagreement with your mother when she suddenly hangs up on you. Or you're discussing a concern with your roommate when he unexpectedly gets up, walks into his bedroom, and shuts the door behind him. Separation may end the immediate encounter, but it does nothing to solve the underlying incompatibility of goals or competition for resources that triggered the dispute in the first place.

On the other hand, separation isn't always negative. In some cases, short-term separation may help bring about long-term resolution. For example, if you and your partner have both used competitive approaches, your conflict may have escalated so much that any further contact may result in irreparable relationship damage. In such cases, temporary separation may help you both to cool off, regroup, and consider how to collaborate. You can then come back and work together to better resolve the situation.

Domination occurs when one person gets his or her way by influencing the other to engage in accommodation and abandon goals. Conflicts that end with domination often are called "win-lose" solutions. The strongest predictor of domination is the power balance in the relationship. In cases where one person has substantial power over the other, he or she will likely use domination to prevail.

In some cases, domination may be acceptable. For example, when one person doesn't feel strongly about achieving his or her goals, being dominated by the other may have few costs. However, domination is destructive when it becomes a chronic pattern and an individual consistently sacrifices his or her goals to keep the peace. Over time, the consistent abandonment of goals can spawn resentment and hostility. And while the accommodating "losers" are silently suffering, the dominating "victors" may think everything is fine because they are used to achieving their goals.

Through **compromise,** both parties change their goals to make them compatible. Often, both people abandon part of their original desires, and neither feels completely happy about it. Compromise typically results from people using a collaborative approach and is most effective in situations where both people have relatively equal power and the clashing goals aren't particularly important. In cases where the two parties consider their goals important, however, compromise is likely to foster mutual resentment and regret (Peterson, 2002). Say that you and your spouse want to spend this weekend away. You planned for months to share the weekend, but your spouse now wants to attend a two-day workshop that same weekend. A compromise would involve you cutting the trip short by a night, and your spouse missing a day of his or her workshop, leaving both of you with substantially less than you originally desired.

Through **integrative agreements,** the two sides preserve and attain their goals by developing a creative solution to their problem. Creating a "win-win" solution in which both people benefit from the outcome is the goal of collaborative conflict approaches. In order to achieve integrative agreements, the parties must remain committed to their individual goals but be flexible in how they achieve them (Pruitt & Carnevale, 1993). An integrative agreement for the example given above would involve rescheduling the weekend so that you and your spouse could enjoy both the vacation and the workshop.

In cases of especially intense conflict, **structural improvements** may result if the people involved are able to control their negative emotions and still collaboratively manage the conflict. In this type of resolution, the parties change the basic rules or understandings that govern their relationship in order to forestall further instances of conflict. Suppose your romantic partner is much wealthier than you. Your partner enjoys paying for all of your leisure activities and buying you expensive gifts, but you can't reciprocate. Although his or her generosity is well intended, it begins to create conflict; each new gesture of generosity further highlights the fundamental difference between your respective economic situations. After a particularly bitter battle about money, you and partner might sit down and collaboratively hash out a budget that lays down guidelines for fair and balanced spending in your relationship.

In cases of structural improvement, the conflict itself becomes a vehicle for reshaping the relationship in positive ways—rebalancing power or redefining expectations about who plays what roles in the relationship. The intensity of the conflict makes it clear that there are broader issues at play, and the partners work together to address those issues by making substantial changes.

SKILLS PRACTICE

This exercise helps you to create better conflict resolutions.

❶ When a conflict arises in a close relationship, manage your negative emotions.

❷ Before communicating with your partner, call to mind the long-term relational consequences of your various communication choices.

❸ Employ a collaborative approach, and avoid kitchen-sinking.

❹ As you negotiate solutions, keep your original goals in mind but remain flexible about how they can be attained.

❺ Revisit relationship rules or agreements that might have triggered the conflict, and consider redefining them in ways that prevent future disputes.

Long-Term Conflict Outcomes

After the comparatively short-term phase of conflict resolution, you begin to ponder the long-term outcomes. In particular, you consider whether the conflict was truly resolved, and you assess the dispute's impact on your relationship. Research examining long-term conflict outcomes and relationship satisfaction has found that certain approaches for dealing with conflict—in particular, avoidant and collaborative approaches—strongly predict the effect that conflicts have on relationship quality.

As noted earlier, the most commonly used conflict approach is avoidance. People overwhelmingly deal with conflicts by avoiding them, suppressing them, or communicating about them indirectly. Because avoidance doesn't address the goal clash, competition for resources, or goal disruption that sparked the conflict, tensions will likely continue resurfacing. As a consequence, people who use avoidance have lower relationship satisfaction and endure longer and more frequent conflicts than people who don't avoid (Sillars, 1980). Consequently, try not to use avoidance unless you're certain the issue is unimportant. And this is a judgment call; sometimes an issue that seems unimportant at the time ends up eating away at you over the long run. So when in doubt, communicate directly with your partner about the issue.

People who use collaborative approaches experience much better long-term outcomes. They tend to resolve their conflicts, they report higher satisfaction in their relationships, and they experience shorter and fewer disputes. The lesson from this is to strive to deal with conflict by directly and openly discussing it in a way that emphasizes mutual interests and protects your partner's self-esteem.

If collaborating yields positive long-term outcomes and avoiding yields negative ones, what about accommodating and competing? This is difficult to predict. Sometimes, you'll compete and get what you want; the conflict will be resolved, and you'll be satisfied with the outcome. Or you'll compete, the conflict will escalate wildly out of control, and you'll end up incredibly unsatisfied. Or you'll accommodate, the conflict will be resolved, and you'll be satisfied. Other times, you'll accommodate, and the other person will exploit you further, causing you deep dissatisfaction. This makes both accommodation and competition risky; you can't count on either as a constructive way to manage conflict for the long term.

Unsolvable Conflicts

In the climactic scene of Margaret Mitchell's Civil War classic *Gone with the Wind,* the principal character Scarlett O'Hara declares her love for Rhett Butler, only to find that he no longer feels the same about her (Mitchell, 1936).

> "Stop," she said suddenly. She knew she could no longer endure with any fortitude the sound of his voice when there was no love in it. He paused and looked at her quizzically. "Well, you get my meaning, don't you?" he questioned, rising to his feet. "No," she cried, "All I know is that you do not love me and you are going away! Oh, my darling, if

"Some conflicts are impossible to solve."

you go, what shall I do?" For a moment he hesitated as if debating whether a kind lie were kinder in the long run than the truth. Then he shrugged. "Scarlett, I was never one to patiently pick up broken fragments and glue them together and tell myself that the mended whole was as good as new. What is broken is broken—and I'd rather remember it as it was at its best than mend it and see the broken places as long as I lived. I wish I could care what you do or where you go, but I can't." He drew a short breath, and said lightly but softly: "My dear, I don't give a damn." (p. 732)

As this famous fictional scene illustrates, some conflicts are simply unsolvable. If one person loves another but the feeling isn't reciprocated, no amount of collaborating will fix things. Part of effectively managing conflict is accepting that some conflicts are impossible to resolve. How can you recognize such disputes? Clues include the following: you and the other person aren't willing to change your negative opinions of one another, your goals are irreconcilable and strongly held, and one or the other partner is uncooperative, chronically defensive, or even violent. In these cases, the only options are to avoid the conflict, hope that your attitudes or goals will change over time, or abandon the relationship, as Rhett Butler did.

SELF-REFLECTION

Think of an unsolvable conflict you've had. Why was it unsolvable? How did you communicate after realizing it was unsolvable? How did the dispute affect your relationship? Looking back on the situation, could you have done anything different to prevent the conflict from becoming unsolvable? If so, what?

Gender and Culture's Influence on Conflict

In the movie *Napoleon Dynamite,* high school student Pedro comes into conflict with popular cheerleader Summer Wheatley when he decides to compete for the same valued resource she is pursuing—the school presidency (Hess, Hess, Coon, Wyatt, & Covel, 2004). Their clash escalates when Pedro creates a piñata that looks like Summer. Although he perceives it as a friendly jibe, school officials see it as a personal attack. The stunt earns Pedro a firm reprimand from the principal. Later, a bewildered Pedro commiserates with his friend Deb, noting that he had no idea that a piñata could be perceived so negatively: "I don't understand. He says you're not allowed to smash piñatas that look like real people, but we do it in Mexico all the time." As this incident reveals, our perceptions of a conflict and the moves we make during a dispute are fundamentally intertwined with our gender and culture.

Conflict and Gender

Traditional gender socialization creates challenges for men and women as they seek to constructively resolve conflicts. Women are encouraged to avoid and suppress conflict and to sacrifice their own goals to accommodate others when conflict is inevitable (Wood, 1998). Consequently, many women have little experience in constructively pursuing their goals during a dispute. Men, in contrast, learn to adopt competitive or even violent approaches to interpersonal clashes, as such approaches suggest strength and manliness (Wood, 1998). At the same time, they're taught not to harm women. Thus, during a contentious exchange with a woman, men face a dilemma: compete or avoid? Many men handle the dilemma by downplaying conflicts or simply leaving the scene instead of seeking constructive resolution.

In close relationships, these traditional gender roles can trigger a **demand-withdraw pattern,** in which a woman pursues conflict by demanding that her goals be met and a man responds by withdrawing from the encounter. Some scholars suggest that demand-withdraw patterns stem from unequal power in relationships (Klinetob & Smith, 1996). Because women often lack power in their involvements with men, they may feel less satisfied (Jacobson, 1990). Given this dissatisfaction, women may be more likely to want changes in their relationships, a desire that eventually expresses itself as a demand. In contrast, men, given their comparative power, desire few relational changes. Because confronting conflict might make things worse for them, they tend to withdraw from their female partners' demands for change.

Other scholars have argued that, rather than power and desire for change, the tendency for women to demand and men to withdraw stems from women's greater interest in dealing with relationship issues and men's discomfort discussing these concerns (Caughlin & Vangelisti, 1999). Regardless of the cause, however, demand-withdraw patterns characterize unhappy relationships and are associated with marital discord and divorce (Caughlin & Vangelisti, 1999). Consequently, if you find yourself in a close

SELF-REFLECTION

What differences do you believe exist in how men and women deal with conflict? How do your beliefs about these differences shape your own approach to conflict with men and women? Is it ethical to manage conflict in different ways depending on the other person's gender?

relationship in which the demand-withdraw pattern has emerged, discuss this situation with your partner. Using a collaborative approach, critically examine the forces that trigger the pattern, and work to generate solutions that will enable you to avoid the pattern in the future.

Given that gender can sometimes interfere with constructive conflict management, reconsider how you approach conflict with men and women. When experiencing conflicts with women, you should encourage the open expression of goals to allow for a collaborative solution. Above all, avoid assuming that no conflict exists just because the other person hasn't voiced any concerns. When managing conflicts with men, be aware of the male emphasis on competitive approaches. Stress collaboration, and as you communicate, steadfastly avoid forms of communication such as personal criticism, insults, or threats that may unnecessarily escalate the conflict.

Conflict and Culture

The strongest cultural factor that influences your choice of a specific conflict approach is whether you belong to an individualistic or collectivistic culture (Ting-Toomey 1997). People raised in collectivistic cultures often view direct messages regarding conflict as personal attacks (Nishiyama, 1971) and consequently are more likely to manage conflict through avoidance or accommodation. People raised in individualistic cultures feel comfortable agreeing to disagree and don't necessarily see such clashes as personal affronts (Ting-Toomey, 1985) and hence are more likely to compete or collaborate.

Given these differences, how might you manage conflict effectively across cultures? If you're an individualist embroiled in a dispute with someone from a collectivistic culture, consider the following practices, suggested by communication scholars William Gudykunst and Young Yun Kim (2003):

- Recognize that collectivists may prefer to have a third person mediate the conflict (Kozan & Ergin, 1998). Mediators allow those in conflict to manage their disagreement without direct confrontation. And the lack of confrontation helps maintain harmony in the relationship—which is particularly important to collectivists.

- Help the other person save face. Avoid humiliating or embarrassing a collectivist, especially in public.

- Closely observe the other person's nonverbal communication and implied verbal messages. Collectivists often express opinions more

● TV shows perpetuate the conflict stereotype of wives constantly demanding change from their husbands, and husbands responding by avoiding and withdrawing. As is so often the case, the truth about husbands, wives, and demand-withdraw patterns is more complicated than the stereotype.

Making Relationship Choices

Dealing with Family Conflict

1

BACKGROUND

Conflict poses complex challenges for your interpersonal communication and relationships. But when you throw in parental expectations, power differences between generations, and the emotional connections within families, effectively managing conflict becomes even more difficult. To see how you would deal with family conflict, read the case study and work through the five steps that follow.

2

CASE STUDY

Your parents are first-generation Americans and take great pride in the fact that they arrived with next to nothing but managed through hard work to provide for you and your younger brother Amul. Your folks built a thriving business in your neighborhood, and during much of your youth, Amul and you helped out.

You love your family dearly, but you've dreamed of relocating once you complete your degree and starting your own life. The time you've spent working for your parents convinced you that you don't want to follow in their footsteps. Your parents support your decision to go to college and are paying your tuition. But you haven't told them about your desire to move or your professional goals. You figure you have plenty of time to discuss it after you graduate. Luckily, your brother seems to love the family business and has made no mention of going to college. Everyone in the family appears to presume that Amul will inherit the business.

Your family gathers for a weekend meal. All week, your mother has been hinting that big

news is coming. From e-mails that Amul sent, you suspect that he proposed to Priti, his girl-friend. You're excited, and at dinner, your parents announce the engagement. But what follows staggers you. Your father says, "After their honeymoon, Amul will begin an apprenticeship with Priti's father." Your brother shoots you a look as if to say, "Sorry, but I couldn't pass up such a great deal."

Later, your mother asks if you're happy for Amul. "Yes," you say, "but I'm confused—I always thought Amul would take over the business when you retired." "Oh no," says your mother, laughing, "He's just been filling in while you're at college. *You* are going to run it, of course. Why else would we have paid all that money for your tuition?" Your head begins to spin. All of your goals and dreams for your future are in jeopardy—put there by the very people who made them possible in the first place. Your father then walks in and says, "So, has your mother been talking to you about our little plan? What do you think?"

YOUR TURN

While working through the following steps, keep in mind the concepts, skills, and insights you've learned so far in this book, especially in this chapter. Also remember: there are no right answers, so think hard about the choice you make! (P.S. Need help? Review the concepts listed below.)

- **Step 1: Reflect on yourself.** What are your thoughts and feelings in this situation? What attributions are you making about your parents? Are your attributions accurate? Why or why not?

- **Step 2: Reflect on your parents.** Using perspective-taking and empathic concern, put yourself in your parents' shoes. Consider how they are thinking and feeling. How do they likely perceive you and your goals?

- **Step 3: Identify the optimal outcome.** Think about all the information you have about your family (your parents and Amul), and your relationship with them. Consider your own feelings as well as theirs. Given all these factors, what's the best, most constructive outcome possible here? Be sure to consider not just what's best for *you*, but what's best for your family as well.

- **Step 4: Locate the roadblocks.** Taking into consideration your own thoughts and feelings, those of your parents and Amul, and recent events in this situation, what's preventing you from achieving the optimal outcome you identified in step 3?

- **Step 5: Chart your course.** What will you say to your parents to overcome the roadblocks you've identified and achieve your optimal outcome?

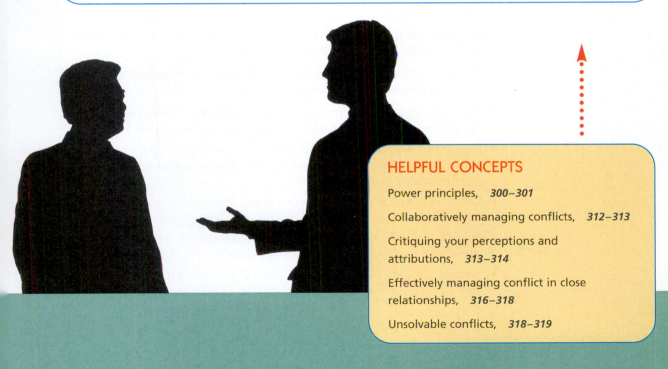

HELPFUL CONCEPTS

Power principles, *300–301*

Collaboratively managing conflicts, *312–313*

Critiquing your perceptions and attributions, *313–314*

Effectively managing conflict in close relationships, *316–318*

Unsolvable conflicts, *318–319*

through nonverbal means such as facial expression and eye contact than through direct verbal expression.

- Use indirect verbal messages more than you usually do. For example, sprinkle your comments with "maybe" and "possibly," and avoid blunt responses such as "no."

- Let go of the situation if the other person does not recognize that the conflict exists or does not want to deal with it.

If you're a collectivist in contention with someone from an individualistic culture, the following guidelines may help:

- Recognize that individualists often separate conflicts from people. Just because you're in conflict doesn't mean that the situation is personal.

- Focus your attention on the issues involved in the conflict, not on the personalities. Many individualists see the clash between goals as the most important thing to resolve.

- Use an assertive style and be more direct than you usually are. For example, use "I" messages and directly state your opinions and feelings.

- Provide verbal feedback more than you typically do. Individualists attend more to spoken messages than you do.

- Manage conflicts when they arise, even if you'd much rather avoid them.

The Challenge of Managing Conflict and Power

Whether it's big or small, when a dispute arises, you may feel that no one else has ever had the same thoughts and emotions. The anger, fear of escalation, pain of hurtful things that should have been left unsaid, and uncertainty associated with not knowing the long-term relationship outcomes combine to make the experience intense and draining.

But conflicts and struggles over power needn't be destructive. Though they carry risk, they also provide the opportunity to engineer positive change in the way you communicate with others and manage your relationships. Through conflict, you can resolve problems that, left untouched, would have eroded your relationship or deprived you of greater happiness in the future. The key distinguishing feature between conflict and power struggles that destroy and those that create opportunities for improvement is how you interpersonally communicate.

In this chapter, you've learned about a broad range of communication skills that can help you manage conflict and power more effectively. Whether it's using collaborative approaches, critiquing your perceptions and attributions, or being sensitive to gender and cultural differences, you now know the skills necessary for successfully managing the disagreements, disputes, and contests that will erupt in your life. The challenge facing you now is to take these skills and put them into practice.

POSTSCRIPT

We began this chapter with an interpersonal dispute packaged as a product for televised mass consumption. Kevin and Julie were cast on MTV's *The Real World* in part because producers suspected their differences in attitude and background would lead to conflicts and power struggles between them. Indeed, their relationship soon became mired in turmoil, and rather than managing it collaboratively, they blamed each other and communicated in ways that guaranteed a lack of resolution and destructive relationship outcomes.

Who in your "real world" is perfectly cast to provoke conflict and power struggles? How often do you blame them for your disputes and disagreements? Does your perception of them as uncooperative and blameworthy drive you to compete with them, or do you strive to collaborate with them in constructively managing your conflicts?

When Kevin and Julie waged their private war, it was publicly splashed across TV screens. Most conflicts you experience won't be so dramatic, and they certainly won't be shared vicariously by millions of coparticipants watching from living rooms and experimental labs. But

like the infamous clash of Kevin and Julie, the resolutions and outcomes of your conflicts and power struggles will rest on your willingness and ability to manage conflict and power.

Key Terms

conflict, *296*

kitchen-sinking, *298*

power, *299*

symmetrical relationships, *300*

complementary relationships, *300*

power currency, *301*

resource currency, *301*

expertise currency, *302*

social network currency, *302*

personal currency, *302*

intimacy currency, *302*

power-distance, *303*

avoidance, *306*

skirting, *306*

sniping, *306*

cumulative annoyance, *306*

pseudo-conflict, *307*

accommodation, *308*

competition, *309*

escalation, *310*

sudden-death statements, *310*

dirty secrets, *310*

collaboration, *312*

separation, *316*

domination, *316*

compromise, *317*

integrative agreements, *317*

structural improvements, *317*

demand-withdraw pattern, *320*

Key Concepts

Conflict and Interpersonal Communication

- **Conflict** arises whenever people's goals clash or they compete for valued resources. Because everyone is pursuing important goals at any point in time, conflict is an inevitable part of everyday life.

- Conflict in close relationships poses unique challenges. Avoid **kitchen-sinking,** which uses the negative information you know about someone against that person when you're angry.

Power and Conflict

- Conflict and **power** go hand in hand because whenever people perceive their goals as clashing, they often wield whatever influence they have in order to achieve their goals.

- Power is present in all interpersonal encounters and relationships. Friendships and romantic involvements are typically expected to be **symmetrical relationships,** whereas parent-child, manager-employee, and teacher-student are **complementary relationships.**

- Power isn't innate. It's something granted to you by others, depending on the **power currency** you possess. Types of power currency include **resource, expertise, social network, personal,** and **intimacy.**

- People from different cultures have very different beliefs about what constitutes appropriate **power-distance.** High power-distance cultures emphasize disparities between people of different social standing. Low power-distance cultures typically encourage power equality across all people, regardless of their social standing.

- Across cultures and time, men have consolidated power over women by strategically depriving women of access to power currencies.

Approaching Conflict

- The most commonly used approach to managing conflict is **avoidance.** Although avoidance often seems easier than other approaches, it can lead to damaging behaviors, including **skirting, sniping, cumulative annoyance,** and the inability to overcome **pseudo-conflict.**

- **Accommodation,** another approach to managing conflict, often is motivated by the desire to please the people we love or to acquiesce to those who have power over us.

- As an approach to managing conflict, **competition** involves the aggressive pursuit of one's own goals at the expense of others'. Competition is more likely to occur during online conflicts than in face-to-face disputes.

- Competition creates severe risk of **escalation,** when people communicate in ways they never would use under other circumstances. In particular, disputants may make **sudden-death statements** and hurl **dirty secrets** at one another.

- The most constructive approach to conflict is **collaboration.** This is your best bet for reinforcing trust and commitment in your relationships, and building relational satisfaction.

- When people believe that no other option exists, they will commit violence. Both men and women resort to violence, which severely damages individuals and their relationships.

Conflict Resolutions and Outcomes

- In the short term, conflicts resolve through **separation, domination, compromise, integrative agreements,** or **structural improvements.** Then, partners involved in the conflict ponder whether they've resolved the underlying goal clash that triggered the conflict, and consider the long-term impact on their relationship.

Gender and Culture's Influence on Conflict

- Although men are socialized to approach conflict competitively, they also are encouraged to avoid behaving aggressively toward women. As a result, in many close cross-gender relationships, a **demand-withdraw pattern** emerges: women actively voice their concerns, and men withdraw from the encounter.

- Whether a culture is individualistic or collectivistic determines how people manage conflict: individualistic cultures are inclined to approach conflicts more competitively and directly than collectivistic cultures.

Key Skills

- Why does power make managing conflict constructively difficult? Find out on page 299.

- Are you inclined to competitively challenge authority during a conflict? Find the answer by taking the *Pop Quiz* on page 303.

- Do you manage conflicts through avoidance? If so, you may want to revisit the risks associated with this approach, described on pages 306–307.

- What is your approach for managing conflict? Find out by taking the *Pop Quiz* on page 307.

- Do you use a competitive approach to deal with conflict? Review the consequences associated with competitiveness on pages 309–310 to see why this might not be the wisest choice.

- Want to improve your ability to use collaboration to constructively manage conflicts? Review the suggestions on pages 312–313; then do the *Skills Practice* on page 313.

- Want to avoid common perceptual and attributional errors when handling conflicts? Follow the recommendations on page 314; then do the *Skills Practice* on page 314 to learn how to implement these suggestions during online disputes.

- How might you reduce the likelihood of violence during intense disagreements? Follow the guidelines on page 315.

- When can avoidance be better than collaboration? Find the answer on page 316.

- Want the best possible outcome for your conflicts? Check out the long-term effects of the various conflict approaches on page 318.

- How might you use your knowledge of gender differences to improve your conflict skills? Revisit the suggestions on pages 320–321.

- What can people do to constructively manage conflict with individuals from other cultures? See the recommendations on pages 321 and 324.

- How would you approach a seemingly unresolvable family conflict? Find out by completing the *Making Relationship Choices* exercise on pages 322–323.

10

Relationships with Romantic Partners

Two households, both alike in dignity
In fair Verona, where we lay
*   our scene*
From ancient grudge break to
*   new mutiny,*
Where civil blood makes civil
*   hands unclean.*
From forth the fatal loins of
*   these two foes*
A pair of star-cross'd lovers take
*   their life;*
Whose misadventured piteous
*   overthrows*
Do with their death bury their
*   parents' strife.*
*   —ROMEO AND JULIET,*
*   PROLOGUE, 1–8.*

Consider the enduring appeal of Shakespeare's greatest romance. Penned in 1595, *The Tragedy of Romeo and Juliet* has inspired artistic works as diverse as an 1870 Tchaikovsky orchestral piece, a 1935 ballet by Sergei Prokofiev, a 1957 Jerome Robbins musical (*West Side Story*), the 1979 Bugs Bunny cartoon *Rabbit Romeo*, and even a song on Dire Straits's 1980 album *Making Movies*. Film directors have committed *The Tragedy of Romeo and Juliet* to celluloid no fewer than eight times, most recently in a version by Baz Luhrmann

starring Leonardo DiCaprio and Claire Danes.

I was 10 years old when I first saw Italian director Franco Zeffirelli's 1968 movie, and the film forever altered my view of love. The speed with which Romeo and Juliet's passion overtook them, the futility of their scheme to escape the enmity of their families, and the fatal mistakes that led to their deaths burned dramatic and enduring romantic images into my mind. Although my parents were deeply in love, no one in my family ever talked about romantic love—what it is, where it comes from, how it's maintained, and what happens when it dies. Instead, romantic love formed an unquestioned backdrop for our lives. Zeffirelli's *Romeo and*

Juliet explained love for me through intense and poignant visual images. What is it about Shakespeare's story of romance and despair that resonates with so many people throughout the ages? The saga taps into a number of beliefs many of us share about the nature of romantic love—that it strikes quickly; that communication between lovers flows easily and naturally; that love is dramatic, bigger than life, and at the same time tragic and painful. The very title "*The Tragedy. . .*" infuses love with a sense of disaster and intrigue that's irresistible to anyone of romantic heart. But perhaps the most important belief conveyed by the story is that love must be intensely passionate to qualify as "real." If Romeo and Juliet were so impassioned that they were willing to die for their love, we should be, too. But of course theater isn't reality. Although *The Tragedy*

of Romeo and Juliet forced me to reflect for the first time on the nature of love, it also led me away from the truth. Love lived is rarely the same as love imagined. Real-life romance is much grittier—and ultimately more satisfying—than stylized, theatrical portrayals. As I stumbled through my first fledgling romances, I quickly learned that I knew very little about how to build and maintain real love, much less how to use communication to sustain my relationships through the inevitable problems and challenges. Eventually I came to realize that the quiet romance my parents shared—a nondramatic bond rooted in the joint sharing of everyday triumphs and tragedies—was true love and *Romeo and Juliet* merely fiction.

Romantic love is the most universal yet intimately personal of human experiences. People from all cultures and periods of history have experienced falling in love (Jankowiak & Fischer, 1992). Romantic love has shaped poetry, art, philosophy, religion, film, and literature for millennia. Still, for most of us, our concerns about love center not on art and literature but instead on how we can build and sustain our romantic relationships.

As you can probably attest, when you're immersed in a real-life romance you quickly learn that despite idealized images, maintaining such relationships requires communication skill and effort. "Interpersonal skills are the means through which all human relationships are initiated, negotiated, maintained, and transformed," note communication scholars Brian Spitzberg and William Cupach (2002, p. 564), and romantic relationships are no exception. To successfully build and maintain a romantic relationship requires an understanding of love and a practiced grasp of the communication tactics needed to maintain and protect it. And when you look at romantic couples who've flourished for long periods of time, rather than being a testimony to the "magic of destiny," their success is a monument to the energy they've invested into making their love thrive.

In this chapter, the first of three on relationships (see Chapter 11 on relationships with family and friends and Chapter 12 on relationships in the workplace), you'll learn:

- The defining characteristics of romantic love and relationships

- What drives you to feel attracted to some people and not others

- How communication changes as your love relationships come together ... and fall apart

- How to communicate in ways that keep your love alive

- How to deal effectively with challenges to romantic relationships

Defining Romantic Relationships

Romantic love may not be essential to life, but it may be essential to joy. Life without love would be for many people like a black-and-white movie—full of events and activities but without the color that gives vibrancy and provides a sense of celebration. Beyond the theories, beyond the research, romantic love is one of life's compensations for drudgery, illness, and, perhaps in some small way, for mortality.[1]

— LOVE RESEARCHERS CLYDE AND SUSAN HENDRICK

We often think of romantic relationships as exciting and filled with promise—a joyful fusion of closeness, communication, and sexual connection. When researchers Pamela Regan, Elizabeth Kocan, and Teresa Whitlock (1998) asked several hundred people to list the things they associated most with "being in love," the most frequent responses were trust, honesty, happiness, bondedness, companionship, communication, caring, intimacy, sharing laughter, and sexual desire. But apart from such associations, what exactly *is* romantic love? How does it differ from liking? And how does interpersonal communication shape love relationships? The answers to these questions can help you build more satisfying romantic partnerships, as well as negotiate the dissolution of bonds that are no longer working.

Liking and Loving

Most scholars agree that liking and loving are separate emotional states, with different causes and outcomes (Berscheid & Regan, 2005). **Liking** is a feeling of affection and respect that we typically have for our friends (Rubin,

SELF-REFLECTION

Consider the characteristics of romantic love cited by the participants in the Regan, Kocan, and Whitlock study. Do you agree with this list? If not, what additional items would you include that weren't mentioned? What characteristics were listed that you think should not be included?

TABLE 10.1

The Intersection of Liking and Loving

Feeling	Description
No liking or loving	No feelings of warmth, admiration, concern for the other's well-being, sense of union, or desire to be with the other.
Liking but not loving	Warmth, admiration, concern for the other's well-being, sense of union, fondness, but no intense desire to be with the other. Characteristic of most friendships and many family relationships, especially those with extended relatives or in-laws.
Loving but not liking	Sense of union, intense desire to be with the other, concern for the other's well-being, but no warmth or admiration. Characteristic of romantic involvements following some form of relational betrayal, such as infidelity or deception.
Liking and loving	Warmth, admiration, concern for the other's well-being, sense of union, fondness, and intense desire to be with the other—the ideal combination for long-term success in romantic relationships.

---

[1] The quote is excerpted from Hendrick and Hendrick (1992, p. 117).

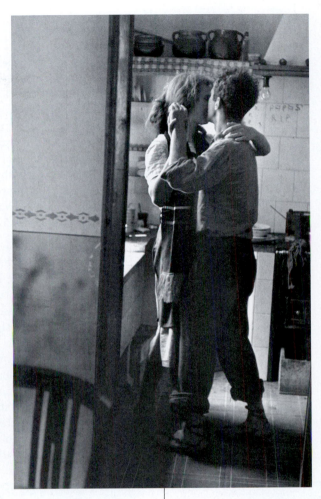

● People who love each other do not just feel differently than people who only like each other. Their verbal and nonverbal communication with each other is different, too. Even if we cannot hear these two couples, their nonverbal behaviors distinguish them from one another.

1973). *Affection* is a sense of warmth and fondness toward another person, while *respect* is admiration for another person apart from how he or she treats you and communicates with you. **Loving,** in contrast, is a vastly deeper and more intense emotional commitment and consists of three components: intimacy, caring, and attachment (Rubin, 1973). *Intimacy* is a feeling of closeness and "union" between you and your partner (Mashek & Aron, 2004). *Caring* is the concern you have for your partner's welfare and the desire to keep him or her happy. *Attachment* is a longing to be in your partner's presence as much as possible.

The Colors of Love

Though most people recognize that loving differs from liking, many also believe that only one "true" type of romantic love exists: **passionate love,** a state of intense emotional and physical longing for union with another (Hendrick & Hendrick, 1992). For example, in Laura Esquivel's novel *Como agua para chocolate* ("Like Water for Chocolate"), two lovers, Tita and

Pedro, experience passionate love that due to circumstance cannot be consummated (Esquivel, 1992):

> Pedro couldn't resist the smells from the kitchen and was heading toward them. But he stopped stock still in the doorway transfixed by the sight of Tita. Tita looked up without stopping her grinding and her eyes met Pedro's. At once their passionate glances fused so perfectly that whoever saw them would have seen but a single look, a single rhythmic and sensual motion, a single trembling breath, a single desire. After that look that saw through clothes, nothing would ever be the same. Tita knew through her own flesh how fire transformed the elements, how a lump of corn flour is changed into a tortilla, how a soul that hasn't been warmed by the fire of love is lifeless, like a useless ball of corn flour. (p. 67)

Studies of passionate love such as that illustrated in *Como agua para chocolate* suggest five important facts regarding its experience and expression. First, passionate love is driven (in part) by idealization of partners. People in the throes of passionate love often view their loved ones and relationships in an excessively idealistic light—and this tendency is associated with relationship satisfaction (Fletcher & Simpson, 2000). For instance, many partners in passionate love relationships talk about how "perfect" they are for each other and how their relationship is the "best ever."

Second, no gender or age differences exist in people's experience of passionate love. Men and women report experiencing this type of love with equal frequency and intensity, and studies using a "Juvenile Love Scale" (which excludes references to sexual feelings) have found that children as young as age 4 report passionate love toward others (Hatfield & Rapson, 1987). The latter finding is important to consider when talking with children

about their romantic feelings. Although they lack the emotional maturity to fully understand the consequences of their relationship decisions, their feelings toward romantic interests are every bit as intense and turbulent as our adult emotions. So if your 6- or 7-year-old child or sibling reveals a crush on a schoolmate, treat the disclosure with respect and empathy, rather than teasing him or her.

Third, people from all cultures feel passionate love. Studies comparing members of individualistic versus collectivistic cultures have found no differences in the amount of passionate love experienced (Hatfield & Rapson, 1987). And although certain ethnicities, especially Latinos, often are stereotyped as more "passionate," studies comparing Latino and non-Latino experiences of romantic love suggest no differences in intensity (Cerpas, 2002).

Fourth, for adults, passionate love is integrally linked with sexuality and sexual desire (Berscheid & Regan, 2005). In one study, undergraduates were asked whether they thought there was a difference between "being in love" and "loving" another person (Ridge & Berscheid, 1989). Eighty-seven percent of respondents said that there was a difference and that sexual attraction was the critical distinguishing feature of being in love.

Finally, passionate love is *negatively* related to relationship duration. Like it or not, the longer you're with a romantic partner, the less intense your passionate love will feel (Berscheid, 2002; Sprecher & Regan, 1998). Although the "fire" of passionate love captures our imagination and dominates media depictions of romance, not all people view romantic love as intense passion. **Companionate love** is an intense form of liking defined by emotional investment and deeply intertwined lives (Berscheid & Walster, 1978). Many long-term romantic relationships evolve into companionate love. As Susan and Clyde Hendrick explain, "Sexual attraction, intense communication, and emotional turbulence early in a relationship give way to quiet intimacy, predictability, and shared attitudes, values, and life experiences later in the relationship" (1992, p. 48).

Between the poles of passionate and companionate lies a range of other types of romantic love. Canadian sociologist John Alan Lee was among the first scholars to suggest that people differ widely in their beliefs about what constitutes true love (1973). Using a color wheel as an analogy, Lee posited six different **colors of love** and gave each color a traditional Greek name: *storge, agape, mania, pragma, ludus,* and *eros* (see Figure 10.1). As Lee noted, just as there is no "right" color, there also is no "right" love. Different types of love appeal to different people, and no one type of love is good or bad (Lee, 1973).

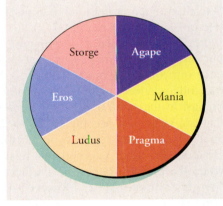

FIGURE 10.1

The Colors of Love

Despite similarities between men and women in their experiences of passionate love, substantial gender differences exist related to one of Lee's "love colors"—pragma, or "practical love." Across numerous studies, women score higher than men on pragma (Hendrick & Hendrick, 1988, 1992), refuting the common stereotype that women are "starry-eyed" and "sentimental" about romantic love (Hill, Rubin, & Peplau, 1976). What's more, although men are often stereotyped as being "cool" and "logical" about love (Hill et al., 1976), they apparently are anything but. Men (more than women) perceive their romantic partners as "perfect" and believe that "love at first sight is possible," that "true love can overcome any obstacles," and that "there's only one true love for each person" (Sprecher & Metts, 1989).

Key Elements of Romantic Relationships

We know that loving differs from liking and that people experience different types of love. But what exactly does it mean to have a romantic *relationship*? A **romantic relationship** is a chosen interpersonal involvement forged through communication in which both participants perceive the bond as romantic. This definition highlights four key elements of romantic relationships.

Perception.   A romantic relationship exists whenever the two partners perceive that it does. And as perceptions change, so too does the relationship. For example, a couple may consider their relationship "casual," marked by only small stirrings of love, but still define it as "romantic" (rather than friendly). And a long-term, committed couple may feel more companionate than passionate but still consider themselves "in love." If two partners' perceptions of their relationship differ—for example, one person feels romantic and the other does not—they do not have a romantic relationship (Miller & Steinberg, 1975).

Choice.   We enter into romantic relationships through choice, selecting not only whom we initiate involvements with but also whether and how we maintain these bonds. Thus, contrary to widespread belief, love doesn't "strike us out of the blue" or "sweep us away" (Hendrick & Hendrick, 1992). Choice plays a role even in arranged marriages: the spouses' families and social networks select an appropriate partner, and in many cases the betrothed retain at least some control over whether the choice is acceptable (Hendrick & Hendrick, 1992).

Relational dialectics—competing impulses between our feelings about our selves and others that we first explored in Chapter 2—powerfully influence our romantic choices (Baxter & Montgomery, 1996). We elect to form romantic relationships largely out of a desire to "connect" with other human beings. At the same time, if we come to feel so connected to our partners that our individual identity seems to dissolve, we may choose to "pull back." Similarly, our need for both predictability and spontaneity molds our choices. Like other interpersonal relationships, romances are more successful when the partners behave in predictable ways and thus reduce uncertainty (Berger & Bradac, 1982). However, too much predictability can cause boredom, prompting us to change the relationship or even terminate it. Last, we struggle to balance openness and self-protection in our romances. Most of us want to share our innermost thoughts and feelings with our partners. But such openness can also give us that uncomfortable sense that we've lost our privacy and must share *everything* with our lovers.

Diversity.   Romantic relationships exhibit remarkable diversity in the ages and genders of the partners, as well as their ethnic and religious backgrounds and sexual orientation. Consider gay and lesbian couples, for example. Most such romantic relationships are as "traditional" as cross-gender relationships in terms of the importance that the partners place on their relationship, the amount of time and energy they devote to maintaining their

SELF-REFLECTION

Have you ever ended or backed off from a relationship because you felt too connected to the other person? Because things had become too predictable and you felt bored? What degree of openness do you prefer in your love relationships? Do you feel comfortable sharing everything with romantic partners, or do you think some things should remain private?

relationship, and the openness of their communication (Fitzpatrick, Jandt, Myrick, & Edgar, 1994). As relationship scholar Sharon Brehm describes, gay and lesbian couples "fall in love in the same way, feel the same passions, experience the same doubts, and feel the same commitments as straights" (Brehm, Miller, Perlman, & Campbell, 2002, p. 27).

Communication.   Romantic involvements, like all interpersonal relationships, are forged through interpersonal communication. By interacting with others online, over the phone, and face-to-face, we build a variety of relationships—some of which blossom into romantic love. And once love is born, we use interpersonal communication to foster and maintain it. Thus the strength of your interpersonal communication skills determines the health and quality of your romances.

Romantic Attraction

The first meeting between John Adams and Abigail Smith went poorly.[2] John had been dragged to the Smith homestead by his friend Richard Cranch, who was courting Abigail's older sister, Mary. Cranch had hoped to kindle a romance between John and Abigail, which would provide an excuse for him to visit Mary more frequently. But the two didn't click. The tall and slender Abigail—15 years old and with striking features—was shy and reserved around strangers. John was 27, short and pudgy, with a round, plain face. Following their initial encounter, John thought Abigail had a fine "wit," but he also wrote in his journal that she was "silly" and her reserved nature caused her to be "not frank or candid." She thought him "pompous."

But in the months that followed, as Cranch courted Mary—often with John in tow—the paths of John and Abigail continued to cross. And as they spent more time together, they realized they shared similar interests, beliefs, and values. Adams marveled that he had met his intellectual equal, if not superior, in Abigail, and he was smitten by her physical attractiveness. Abigail considered John her best friend, and even in her elder years "remembered the thrill of the first time he held her hand" (Akers, 1980). By the time of Cranch's marriage to Mary, in November 1762, the romantic attraction between John and Abigail had blossomed. They wed on October 25, 1764, and remained married for the next 54 years, until death parted them. During this time, John would become U.S. president, and the two would raise several children, including John Quincy Adams, who would ascend to the presidency as well. Throughout it all, John and Abigail considered themselves best friends as well as lovers and spouses. Their friendship was rooted in intellectual kinship and companionship. And

---

[2] All information regarding John and Abigail Adams is from Akers (1980); Butterfield, Friedlander, and Kline (1975); Levin (1987); and McCullough (2001).

they maintained their romantic love through open communication when they were together and intimate letters when circumstances kept them apart.

Every day, you meet and interact with new people while walking across campus, standing in line at the local coffee shop, or working. Like John Adams, perhaps you've been dragged along by friends to meet siblings of their romantic interests. Despite these encounters, few of these individuals make a lasting impression on you, and even fewer strike a chord of romantic attraction. What draws you to those special few and shies you away from the forgotten remainder?

Resources: What Can They Offer?

One spark that kindles romantic attraction is the resources another person offers, such as physical attractiveness, intelligence, humor, money, and sexual interplay. But what leads you to desire some people's resources and not others?

Social exchange theory proposes that you'll feel drawn to those you see as offering substantial benefits (things you like and want) with few associated costs (things demanded of you in return). In judging the benefits and costs others bring, you use two standards: a comparison level and a comparison level for alternatives (Kelley & Thibaut, 1978). Your comparison level is your personal belief regarding the benefits and costs you think you deserve in a love relationship. In other words, what kind of romantic partner do you merit? Your comparison level for alternatives is your perception of the benefits and costs currently available to you from alternative romantic relationships. Simply put: Can you get the same benefits from others, with fewer costs? Or does this person offer unique value?

Consider how these standards influence your evaluation of potential romantic partners. Imagine, for example, that as you're warming up for a workout at your health club, you strike up a conversation with someone new. As you talk, you begin sizing the person up, evaluating him or her in terms of your comparison level. How does this individual's looks, attitude, and intelligence compare with what you think you deserve in a romantic partner? If the person matches up well against your comparison level, you'll be attracted ("I could see dating this person!"). If the person doesn't compare favorably, you won't find him or her attractive.

Now think about your comparison level for alternatives. As you're comparing the person against what you think you deserve, you're also comparing him or her against other current and potential romantic partners in your life. You're weighing how comfortable you feel talking with these different individuals, how attractive they are, and other such matters. How does this individual compare to these alternatives? If you perceive him or her as superior to current alternatives, you'll likely feel an attraction ("Wow, this person is really special!"). If not, you probably won't consider pursuing a relationship.

Feeling attracted doesn't guarantee that a love relationship will develop, however. Once you've experienced an initial spark, the balance of benefits

SELF-REFLECTION

Consider the potential gains and drawbacks of getting involved romantically with a new person you've recently met. What benefits might you gain from a love relationship with this person? What might the relationship cost you in personal demands and responsibilities? How does the balance of benefits and costs you associate with this person compare with the balance that other potential partners may bring?

and costs exchanged by you and the other person, known as **equity,** determines whether your attraction will continue and whether a relationship will take root (Canary & Stafford, 1992, 1994; Stafford, 2003). Romantic partners are happiest when the balance of giving and getting in their relationship is equal for both, and they're least happy when inequity exists (Hatfield, Traupmann, Sprecher, Utne, & Hay, 1985).

What is inequity? People in relationships have a strong sense of proportional justice: the balance between benefits gained from the relationship versus contributions made to the relationship (Hatfield, 1983). Inequity occurs when the benefits or contributions provided by one person are greater than those provided by the other. People who get more rewards from their relationships for fewer costs than their partners are overbenefited; people who get fewer rewards from their relationships for more costs than their partners are underbenefited. Overbenefited individuals experience negative emotions such as guilt, while underbenefited partners experience emotions such as sadness and anger (Sprecher, 1986, 2001).

Equity strongly determines the short- and long-term success of romantic relationships. One study found that only 23 percent of equitable romances broke up during a several-month period, whereas 54 percent of inequitable romantic relationships broke up (Sprecher, 2001).

Proximity

The simple fact of physical proximity—being in one another's presence frequently—exerts far more impact on romantic attraction than many people think. In general, you'll feel more attracted to those with whom you have frequent contact and less attracted to those with whom you interact rarely. This is known as the **mere exposure effect:** the more you're exposed to others (regularly seeing them and/or interacting with them), the more likely you are to perceive them as attractive (Bornstein, 1989). For example, although John Adams and Abigail Smith initially disliked each other, they came to view one another as attractive the more time they spent together.

Proximity's pronounced effect on attraction is one reason that "mixed-race" romantic relationships are much rarer than same-race pairings in the United States. Despite this nation's enormous ethnic diversity, most Americans cluster into ethnically homogeneous groups, communities, and neighborhoods. This clustering reduces the likelihood that they will meet, regularly interact with, and eventually become attracted to individuals outside their own cultural group (Gaines, Chalfin, Kim, & Taing, 1998). Those who do form interethnic romances typically have living arrangements, work

● You're more likely to be attracted to people you're around a lot, but the effect of proximity on attraction depends on your experience with the people. At least one study has found that people feel most negatively toward those whom they find bothersome and those whom they live nearest to.

situations, or educational interests that place them in close proximity with diverse others, fostering attraction (Gaines et al., 1998).

Beauty or the Beast: The Power of Physical Attractiveness

It's no secret that many people feel attracted to those they perceive as physically appealing, a phenomenon known as the **beautiful-is-good effect.** We view beautiful people as competent communicators, intelligent, and well adjusted (Eagly, Ashmore, Makhijani, & Longo, 1991), although some studies suggest that we also see them as more conceited and sexually promiscuous (Dermer & Thiel, 1975). But although most of us find physical beauty attractive, we tend not to form long-term romantic relationships with people we judge as substantially different from ourselves in physical attractiveness. This is known as **matching** (Feingold, 1988). Research documents that people don't want to be paired with those they think are substantially "below" or "above" themselves in looks (White, 1980).

Similarity: Do Birds of a Feather Flock Together?

No doubt you've heard the contradictory clichés regarding similarity and attraction: "Opposites attract" versus "Birds of a feather flock together." Which is correct? The scientific evidence suggests that we are attracted to those we perceive as similar to ourselves (Brehm et al., 2002). This is known as the **birds-of-a-feather effect.** One explanation for this is that people whom we perceive as similar to us are less likely to provoke uncertainty. In first encounters, they seem easier to predict and explain than people we perceive as dissimilar (Berger & Calabrese, 1975).

The effect of similarity goes far beyond initial attraction. Although "soul mate" may be an esoteric label, studies repeatedly have shown that highly similar couples are more likely than dissimilar couples to stay together in the long run. Criteria for similarity include physical attributes, attitudes toward women's rights, religion and religiosity (how intensely you believe in your particular faith), number of children desired, age, beauty, educational aspirations, and even SAT scores (Hill et al., 1976).

● Although people lust after gorgeous others, most of us end up in long-term relationships with those we perceive to be our equals in physical attractiveness.

● Approximately 50 percent of students surveyed think interracial dating is acceptable, but this masks substantial race and gender differences. While 81 percent of Euro-American and 75 percent of African American men express willingness to date outside their ethnicity, the majority of Euro-American and African American women report negative attitudes toward interracial dating.

Although the birds-of-a-feather effect is generally true, bear in mind several important qualifications. For one thing, perceived similarity is not the same as actual similarity. Just because you *think* someone is similar to you doesn't mean that he or she actually is. For example, we tend to overestimate our own physical attractiveness, and this commonly leads us to perceive ourselves as being similar to physically attractive persons and dissimilar to unattractive persons (Marks, Miller, & Maruyama, 1981). Moreover, in order for similarity to breed attraction, the characteristic you share in common has to be one you like about yourself. If the point of commonality is something you dislike about yourself, you won't be attracted to that quality in others.

In addition, similarity means more than physical attractiveness; it means sharing parallel personalities, values, and personal likes and dislikes (Neimeyer & Mitchell, 1988). Fundamentally different personalities or widely disparate values erode attraction in the long run. At the same time, differences in mere tastes and preferences have no long-term negative impact on relationship health, as long as you and your partner are similar in other, more important ways. For example, I like heavier music (Tool, Motorhead, Pantera), and my wife hates it. But we have very similar personalities and values, so our attraction and our relationship endure.

Because differences in tastes and preferences don't predict relationship success, you shouldn't dismiss potential romantic partners because of their minor likes and dislikes. Whether you think, "Wow, I have so much in common with this person—he or she is amazing," or "This person is so different—just look at the kind of food/music/movies/fashion he or she likes," try to discover if you have similarities in personality and values before you make any definitive decisions.

Finally, you can share fundamental similarities with someone else, but if you're missing the most important ingredient that translates similarity into attraction, it won't matter. What's this ingredient? Interpersonal communication. Think back to John Adams and Abigail Smith. They shared similarities in intellect, beliefs, attitudes, and values. But they had no idea these similarities existed until they *talked* about them with one another. The effects of similarity on attraction presume that partners communicate about these similarities, and when people share information with each other about their similarities, they are more likely to find attraction triggered (Sunnafrank, 1991).

FIGURE 10.2

"Coming Together"

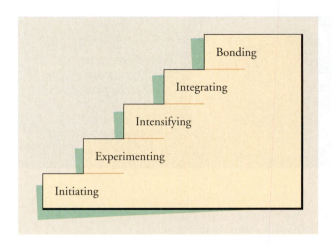

Relationship Development and Deterioration

Romantic relationships come together and apart in as many different ways and at as many different speeds as there are partners who fall for each other (Surra & Hughes, 1997). Some develop and deteriorate like wildfire: love quickly flaming and then fading, perhaps even in a single blowup that leaves the lovers and those around them emotionally torn and bewildered. Other relationships are more like a controlled burn: the partners cautiously watch and deepen their involvement, then slowly extinguish it if the fuel that fired their love is exhausted.

But all romantic relationships undergo stages marked by distinctive patterns in the partners' communication, thoughts, and feelings. We know these transitions intuitively, referring to them as "taking things to the next level," "kicking it up a notch," "taking a step back, or "taking a break." Communication scholar Mark Knapp distinguished ten relational stages—five of coming together and five of coming apart—with each stage characterized by unique communication patterns.[3]

Coming Together

Each of our romantic relationships develops in its own way, at its own pace, depending on the intensity of attraction present and the nature of the love shared between us and our partners (passionate or companionate, storgic or manic, and so forth). Mark Knapp's stages of coming together illustrate one possible flow of relationship development but not necessarily the exact map your romances will always follow (see Figure 10.2). Thus, in reviewing these stages, consider how they mesh with your own experiences of romantic development, and then use this knowledge to gain insights into how you can better negotiate your way through future relationship transitions.

---

[3] The content that follows regarding coming together and coming apart is excerpted and adapted from Knapp and Vangelisti (2000).

Initiating.   During the **initiating** stage, you size up a new person you've just met or noticed. You draw on all available visual information (physical attractiveness, body type, age, ethnicity, gender, clothing, and posture) to assess possible similarities and thereby determine whether you find him or her attractive. You also ponder and present a greeting you deem appropriate. Your primary concern at this stage is to portray yourself in a positive light.

The Internet provides a unique and fertile ground for initiating (Rabby & Walther, 2003). As the label "www" reminds us, the Web is quite literally worldwide. Thus it enables us to initiate relationships with a diverse range of people whom we never would meet otherwise. And unlike face-to-face meetings, where we rely heavily on visual cues to assess others' attractiveness, online communication—whether in chatrooms, on dating Web sites, or elsewhere—enables us to initiate and develop relationships based solely on our communication skills. As scholars Michael Rabby and Joseph Walther note, "one's currency online is the quality of one's information and the wit with which one presents it" (2003, p. 145).

Experimenting.   Once you've initiated an encounter with someone else, you enter the **experimenting** stage to relationship development, during which the two of you exchange demographic information (names, majors, where you grew up). As you share these details, you continue looking for points of commonality on which you can base further interaction. Communication

---

POP QUIZ

Most and Least Effective Opening Lines

You're about to approach someone you think is attractive. What are the first words that come out of your mouth? Psychologists Chris Kleinke, Frederick Meeker, and Richard Staneski polled more than 1,000 university students and employees to find out which opening lines they tended to use and which they liked the most and least. See if you can pick out the three most and least effective lines for men and women.

Opening lines used by men:

❑ 1. Is that really your hair?

❑ 2. Hi.

❑ 3. You remind me of a woman I used to date.

❑ 4. Hi, my name is _____.

❑ 5. Isn't it cold? Let's make some body heat.

❑ 6. That's a really pretty _____ (sweater, dress, etc.) you have on.

Opening lines used by women:

❑ 1. Since we're both sitting alone, would you care to join me?

❑ 2. It's been a long time since I've had a boyfriend.

❑ 3. Hi.

❑ 4. I'm easy, are you?

❑ 5. I don't have anyone to introduce me, but I'd like to meet you.

❑ 6. Didn't we meet in a previous life?

Answers:

Most effective lines for men: 2, 4, 6; least effective: 1, 3, 5.
Most effective lines for women: 1, 3, 5; least effective: 2, 4, 6.

Note: Information in this *Pop Quiz* is from Kleinke, Meeker, and Staneski (1986).

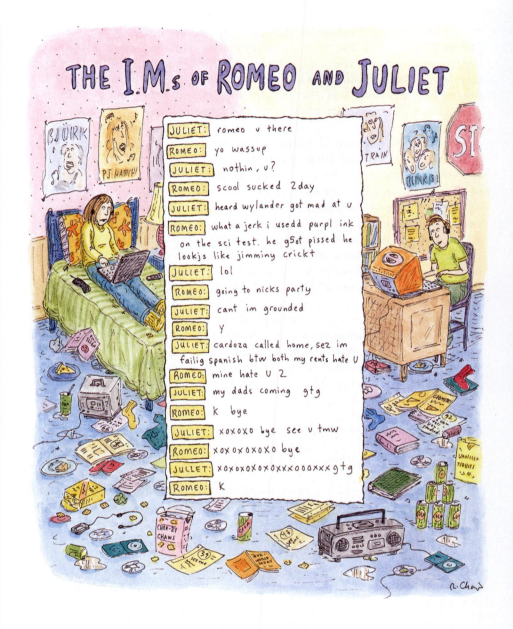

during experimenting is dominated by **small talk,** facts that you and the other person consider relatively unimportant but that enable you to introduce yourselves in a safe and controlled fashion. Although commonly dismissed as trivial, small talk serves several important functions in relational development. For one thing, it lays the groundwork for deeper conversation. As you engage in small talk, you and the other person discern which topics you might safely explore in more depth. Small talk also serves as a kind of relationship audition. You use it to decide whether to have a future relationship with the other person.

At the experimenting stage, relationships are generally pleasant and casual. Still, it should be noted that most involvements never progress beyond this stage. For better or worse, we go through life experimenting with many people but achieving deeper connections with very few. This is true for online experimenting as well as face-to-face. For instance, relational scholar Malcolm Parks found that among people who met each other and formed relationships online through general discussion groups (sites *not* devoted to matchmaking), only 10 percent of these relationships evolved beyond experimenting into a deeper romantic involvement (Parks & Floyd, 1996; Parks & Roberts, 1998).

Intensifying. Occasionally, you'll progress beyond the experimenting stage and find yourself experiencing strong feelings of attraction toward another person because of perceived rewards, proximity, physical attractiveness, similarity, or a combination of these factors. When this happens, your verbal and nonverbal communication becomes increasingly intimate, and your relationship deepens. During the **intensifying** stage of relationship development, the depth of personal disclosure increases. You and your partner begin to reveal previously withheld information, such as secrets about your past or important life dreams and goals. You may begin to use informal forms of address or terms of endearment ("honey" versus "Joe") and employ "we" instead of "you and I." One particularly strong sign that your relationship is intensifying is the direct expression of commitment ("I think I'm falling for you"). Nonverbally, your personal space boundaries become permeable. You can move into my personal space and I can move into yours, without evoking discomfort and perhaps even generating pleasure. At this stage, you may also begin sharing physical expressions of affection, such as hand-holding, cuddling, or sexual activity.

Integrating. During the **integrating** stage of relationship development, your and your partner's personalities seem to become one. You find it increasingly difficult to separate your identities. Physically, this integration is reinforced through sexual activity and the exchange of belongings (items of clothing, books, CDs, music or photographic downloads, and so forth). In terms of communication, you may begin to finish each other's sentences and rely more on nonverbal expression to communicate thoughts and feelings. For instance, if you're window-shopping together, you can share your impressions of an outfit on display through a quick exchange of glances rather than discussing it.

When you've integrated with a romantic partner, you cultivate attitudes, activities, and interests that clearly join you together as a couple—"*our* favorite movie," "*our* song," and "*our* favorite restaurant." Friends, colleagues, and family members begin to treat you as a couple. For example, this can occur when they always invite the two of you to parties or dinners. Not surprisingly, many people begin to struggle with the dialectical tension of connectedness versus autonomy, as was discussed previously. As a student of mine once told his partner when describing this stage, "I'm not me any more, I'm *us*."

Type	Quality of Bond	Balance of Power	Level of Interdependence	Communication and Conflict
Traditional	Bond is viewed as a "union of souls" and marriage is "'til death does us part."	Partners believe that power should be imbalanced, such as when one partner is the "decision maker" and the other is the "helpmate."	Partners are highly interdependent and spend the majority of their leisure time together.	Partners are open and expressive. They aren't assertive about individual goals but will confront issues that could damage the marriage.
Independent	Bond is viewed as a pact between autonomous individuals.	Partners presume an equal power balance; some reverse gender roles, such as when women are "breadwinners" and men are "stay-at-home dads."	Partners spend a great deal of time together, but they also value solitary leisure activities.	Partners are open and expressive, but they're willing to displease each other to pursue individual goals.
Separate	Bond is weak. Many "separate" marriages begin as "traditional" ones, but the partners fall out of love with each other.	Like "traditional" partners, "separate" partners believe that one partner should be the decision maker.	Partners share little leisure time together.	Partners are constrained in their communication; they steadfastly avoid and suppress conflict.
Mixed	Bond is viewed differently by each partner. Approximately 40% of all marriages are "mixed."	Varies according to partners' perception of the marriage bond.	Varies according to partners' perception of the marriage bond.	Varies according to partners' perception of the marriage bond.

Note: Information in this table is derived from Vangelisti (2002) and Fitzpatrick (1988).

TABLE 10.2

Four Different Marriages

Bonding. The ultimate stage of coming together is **bonding,** a public ritual that announces to the world that you and your partner have made a commitment to one another. Bonding is something you'll share with very few people—perhaps only one—during your lifetime. Couples bond primarily to seek public validation of their private commitment to each other. The most obvious example of bonding is marriage, though marriage can take many forms. Table 10.2 shows four different types of marriage bonds.

Bonding institutionalizes your relationship. Before this stage, the ground rules for your relationship and your communication within it remain a private matter, to be negotiated between you and your partner. In the bonding stage, you import into your relationship a set of laws and customs determined by governmental and often religious authorities. Although these laws and customs help to solidify your relationship, they can also make your relationship feel more rigid and structured.

Coming Apart

Most romantic relationships that come together end up coming apart as well. One study of college dating found that across a typical three-month period, 30 percent of the couples surveyed broke up (Parks & Adelman, 1983). Similar trends occur in the married adult population. For example,

FOCUS ON CULTURE

Arranged and Assisted Marriages

Although the experience of romantic love is universal, the forces shaping how couples come to bond vary widely across cultures. In many Middle Eastern and Asian countries, marriages are arranged by parents or local religious figures. Within the United States, individuals from cultures in which marriages traditionally are arranged often blend American and their own cultural practices. For example, first-generation Indian Americans have shifted away from arranged marriages to what can be described as "assisted marriages." In assisted marriages, parents "screen potential nominees" for caste, lineage, and a host of other factors, but they allow the partners to make the final decision regarding suitability (Bellafante, 2005). This model helps preserve traditional Indian class, religious, and regional identities, while at the same time providing potential spouses greater freedom of choice than they might have outside the United States.

Although arranged or assisted marriage may strike you as radically different from "American tradition," the practice in the United States of basing marriage on romantic love is actually comparatively new (Hendrick & Hendrick, 1992). Couples like John and Abigail Adams notwithstanding, most American marriages historically were *not* "love matches," and as recently as 1967, 76 percent of women and 35 percent of men said they'd marry someone who had all of the qualities they wanted in a spouse, even if they weren't in love with that person (Kephart, 1967).

YOUR TURN

- Think about your own cultural and family traditions and how they've shaped your views on romantic love and marriage. Were you raised to believe that people should marry for love—or for other reasons? Did your parents or caregivers marry primarily for love? How about your grandparents?

- Ask yourself the same question asked of men and women in 1967: Would *you* spend your life bonded with someone you didn't love, if he or she was a good partner for you in every other way? Why or why not?

the divorce rate since the early 1980s has been fairly stable: approximately 40 percent of American couples who marry end up divorcing (Hurley, 2005; Kreider, 2005).[4]

In some relationships, breaking up is the right thing to do: the partners have grown apart, they've lost interest in one another, or perhaps one person has been abusive to the other and caused irreparable damage. In other relationships, coming apart has unfortunate consequences. Perhaps the partners could have resolved their differences but didn't make the effort. Thus they needlessly suffer the pain of breaking up. Friends and family members who felt attached to the couple also experience pain. If the couple has children, the youngsters pay a high price as well—for example, in the form of separation from one parent.

Like coming together, coming apart unfolds over stages marked by changes in thoughts, feelings, and communication (see Figure 10.3). But different from coming together, the stages of coming apart often entail emo-

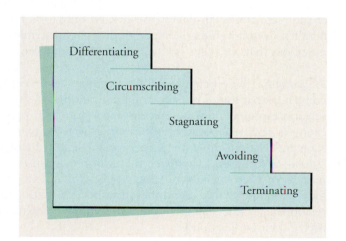

FIGURE 10.3

"Coming Apart"

---

[4] For years, news media, politicians, and even academics have quoted the American divorce rate as "50 percent." This is false. The 50 percent calculation was based on census data comparing the number of marriages per year versus the number of divorces. However, this is obviously flawed, as the people marrying each year are not the same people getting divorced (Hurley, 2005). Accurate estimates of the American divorce rate suggest that since the 1980s, the percentage has remained relatively stable: around 40 percent of marriages end in divorce.

tional turmoil, making them difficult to negotiate skillfully. Learning how to communicate supportively and empathically while a romantic relationship is coming apart is a challenging but important part of being a skilled interpersonal communicator. By applying the right communication practices during this process, you minimize the emotional pain and damage that breaking up can cause. You also preserve your own and the other person's dignity as much as possible.

Differentiating.   In all romantic relationships, the partners share differences as well as similarities. But during the first stage of coming apart, **differentiating,** the beliefs, attitudes, and values that distinguish you from your partner come to dominate your thoughts and communication ("I can't *believe* you think that!" and "We are *so* different!").

Most healthy romances experience occasional periods of differentiating. These moments are unpleasant because your time with your partner is tainted by clashes and bickering over differences in viewpoints, tastes, or goals. But you can move your relationship through this difficulty—and thus halt the coming-apart process—by openly, directly, and collaboratively discussing your points of difference and working together to resolve them. To help overcome differentiating, when it occurs, you should review the constructive conflict skills discussed in Chapter 9—especially the relational conflict pitfalls—as well as refresh your memory on how to craft competent messages (discussed in Chapter 5).

Circumscribing.   If one or both of you respond to problematic differences by ignoring them and spending less time talking, you enter the **circumscribing** stage. You actively begin to restrict the quantity and quality of information you exchange with your partner. Instead of sharing information, you seek to create "safe zones" in which you discuss only topics that won't provoke conflict. Common remarks made during circumscribing include, "Don't ask me about that" or "Let's not talk about that anymore."

Stagnating.   When circumscribing becomes so severe that almost no safe conversational topics remain, communication slows to a standstill, and your relationship enters the **stagnating** stage. You both presume that communicating is pointless because it will only lead to further problems. People in stagnant relationships often experience a sense of resignation; they feel "stuck" or "trapped." However, they can remain in the relationship for months or even years. Why? Some believe that it's better to leave things as they are rather than expend the effort necessary to break up or rebuild the relationship. Others simply don't know how to repair the damage and revive their earlier bond.

Avoiding.   During the **avoiding** stage, one or both of you decide that you no longer can be around each other, and you begin distancing yourself physically. Some people communicate avoidance directly to their partner ("I don't want to see you anymore"). Others do so indirectly—for example, by staying away from the partner's haunts, screening cell-phone calls, deleting e-mail messages without responding, and so forth.

● Gender stereotypes dominate our thinking about men and women in romantic relationships, but research discredits many of these damaging stereotypes. For example, although women in Western cultures are depicted as sentimental and men as rational, women actually are more likely than men to base their romantic relationship decisions on practical considerations.

SELF-REFLECTION

Have most of your romantic relationships ended by avoiding? Or have you sought the closure provided by terminating? In what situations is one approach to ending relationships better than the other? Is one more ethical than the other? Why or why not?

Terminating. In ending a relationship, some people feel the need to come together for a final encounter in order to create closure. During this **terminating** stage, the two of you might discuss the past, present, and future of the relationship. Couples often exchange summary statements about the past—comments reflecting "how our relationship was" that are either accusations ("No one has ever treated me so badly!") or laments ("I'll never be able to find someone as perfect as you"). Verbal and nonverbal behaviors indicating the lack of intimacy are readily apparent—including crossed arms, physical distance between the two individuals, and reluctance to make eye contact. The partners may also discuss the future status of their relationship. Some couples may agree to end all contact from this point forward. Others may choose to maintain some level of physical intimacy even though the emotional side of the relationship is now officially over. Still others may express interest in "being friends."

Many people find the terminating stage of coming apart especially painful or awkward. It's hard to tell someone else that you no longer want to be involved, and it can be equally painful to hear it. How can you best negotiate your way through this dreaded moment? Draw on the interpersonal communication skills you've learned from previous chapters. Infuse your communication with empathy—offering empathic concern and perspective-taking (Chapter 3). Realize that romantic breakups are a kind of death and that it's normal to experience grief. Consequently, offer supportive communication (Chapter 4) to help your partner work through his or her grief ("I'm sorry things had to end this way"; "I know this is going to be painful for both of us"). Practice the recommendations for competent messages in Chapter 5. And make your communication as informative, honest, relevant, and clear as needed, abiding by the requirements for cooperative communication outlined in Chapter 7. Terminating conversations are never pleasant or easy. But the communication tools you've learned throughout this text can help you minimize the pain and damage, enabling you and your former partner to move on to other relationships.

Maintaining Romantic Relationships

In the movie *The Eternal Sunshine of the Spotless Mind*, Joel (Jim Carrey) and Clementine (Kate Winslett) are lovers struggling to maintain a bittersweet romance (Bregman, Golin, Gondry, & Kaufman, 2004). Clementine, an outgoing, self-described "high-maintenance girl," is the opposite of quiet, bookish Joel, who communicates more with his private journal than with her. Following a fight, Clementine impetuously visits a clinic that specializes in memory erasure and has Joel expunged from her mind. Despondent, Joel follows suit. But the two meet again and find themselves attracted. Eventually discovering the truth—that they aren't strangers at all but long-time lovers—they face a momentous decision. Do they invest the time and energy necessary to maintain their romance a second time, knowing that they failed so terribly before that they chose to obliterate their memories? Or do they end it before their history of relational disaster can repeat itself? They discuss their dilemma:

CLEMENTINE: I'm not a concept, Joel, I'm just a messed-up girl who's looking for my own peace of mind. I'm not perfect.

JOEL: I can't see anything that I don't like about you.

CLEMENTINE: But you will!

JOEL: I can't.

CLEMENTINE: But you *will!* You know, you *will* think of things, and I'll get bored with you and feel trapped because that's what happens with me!

JOEL: OK.

CLEMENTINE: OK?

JOEL: OK.

Romantic relationships aren't always about happiness and celebration. No matter how much you love your partner, you will still experience unpleasant moments such as feeling annoyed by something the other person does, bored by the routines you've established, or trapped by the expectation that the two of you must spend all of your time together. Though such emotions are normal in all close relationships, many people find them disturbing and wonder whether negative feelings indicate the need to end the relationship. But Clementine's and Joel's choice in the conclusion of *Eternal Sunshine*—to accept the inevitable negatives as natural and move forward regardless—offers a message of hope. Wiping our mental slates clean and leaving our partners behind is not the only solution to romantic relationship challenges. Instead, we can choose to harness our interpersonal communication skills and invest the effort necessary to maintain our love.

To this point we've talked a good deal about the nature of love, and we've traced the stages through which many romances progress as they come together and dissolve. Now let's shift focus to a more practical concern: If you have a satisfying, healthy romantic relationship that you want to sustain, how can you use interpersonal communication to maintain your bond on a day-to-day basis? Simply put, how can you keep your love alive?

Maintenance Strategies

Many people believe that love just happens—that once it strikes, it endures. But a foundational principle of romantic love is that maintenance is necessary to keep relationships from deteriorating (Stafford, 2003). **Relational maintenance** refers to romantic partners' efforts to keep their relationships in a desired state or condition (Dindia & Canary, 1993). Across several studies, communication researchers Laura Stafford and Dan Canary have observed a range of strategies that satisfied couples routinely use to maintain their romances (Canary & Stafford, 1992; Stafford, 2003; Stafford & Canary, 1991; Stafford, Dainton, & Haas, 2000). These strategies are used by partners in a diverse range of relationships, including African American, Euro-American, and Korean heterosexual romantic partners, as well as gay and lesbian couples (Diggs & Stafford, 1998; Haas & Stafford, 1998; Yum & Canary, 2003).

Positivity.   Positivity is the most frequently reported relationship maintenance tactic used by satisfied romantic couples (Dainton & Stafford, 1993). Positivity includes communicating with your partner in a cheerful and optimistic fashion, doing unsolicited favors for him or her, and giving your partner gifts.

You use positivity when:[5]

- You try to make each interaction with your partner enjoyable
- You try to build your partner up by giving him or her compliments
- You try to be romantic, fun, and interesting with your partner

You undermine positivity when:

- You constantly look for and complain about problems in your relationship without offering solutions
- You openly criticize, ridicule, and insult your partner
- You demand that your partner do you favors and give you gifts (without offering anything in return), and you pout and sulk when your partner doesn't do so

Openness.   The second most commonly reported maintenance tactic is openness. Through openness, you create a climate of security and trust within your relationship. Openness in a romance doesn't just happen; it emerges when each person behaves in ways that are predictable, trustworthy, and ethical. Over time, consistency in behavior fosters mutual respect and the perception that feelings and concerns can be discussed honestly without fear of repercussion.

You use openness when:

- You take time to talk periodically with your partner about your relationship
- You encourage your partner to disclose his or her thoughts and feelings, and offer empathy in return
- You regularly share (in a constructive fashion) your relationship feelings, wants, and needs with your partner

---

[5] All bulleted items that follow are adapted from the maintenance scale of Stafford and Canary (1991).

● Constant, daily maintenance is needed to keep romantic relationships alive and healthy.

You undermine openness when:

- You avoid or refuse to have "relationship talks" with your partner
- You react defensively when your partner shares his or her feelings, attacking and disparaging your partner's perspective
- You routinely keep things hidden from your partner or betray your partner by sharing confidential information about him or her with others

Assurances.   Although it may seem obvious, one tactic that satisfied, committed couples use to maintain their romances is to regularly reaffirm their commitment to each other. Assurances are messages that emphasize the relationship's depth of intimacy, stress mutual commitment, and describe the couple's future as certain. Assurances may be expressed directly, such as telling your partner, "I love you with all my heart," or "I will never leave you." Or you may communicate assurances more indirectly, by emphasizing

the value you place on your time together—for example, sending your partner an e-mail or text message that says, "I can't wait to see you again," or "I'm really looking forward to tonight" (Rabby, 1997).

You use assurances when:

- You regularly tell your partner how committed you are to your relationship
- You let your partner know that you believe your relationship has a strong future
- You do and say things to demonstrate your love for your partner

You undermine assurances when:

- You flirt with others and talk about how attractive they are in front of your partner
- You tell your partner not to count on anything long-term
- You systematically avoid pledging love or fidelity to your partner

Sharing Activities.   A critical part of maintaining love is sharing enjoyable activities. Happy, committed couples often develop unique routines: Wednesday mornings become your "coffee date," Saturday evenings become your "private time," and so forth. They also make an effort to involve each other in their personal hobbies and outside interests.

You share activities when:

- You make an effort to block out time in your schedule each week for your partner
- You take an interest in your partner's hobbies and interests
- You invite your partner to participate in your leisure activities

You undermine shared activities when:

- You structure your schedule so that little time is left for your partner
- You make it clear to your partner that you're not interested in his or her hobbies
- You intentionally exclude your partner from participating in things you like to do

Sharing Tasks.   Another strategy for maintaining your romantic relationship is to jointly share the "grunt work" of practical, day-to-day tasks and demands. Sharing tasks involves taking mutual responsibility for chores and negotiating an equitable division of labor within the relationship. Although this may sound like something that only married or cohabiting couples face, sharing tasks is relevant for all long-term couples and includes responsibilities such as transportation to work or campus, running errands, and making reservations for travel, dinner, or movies.

You share tasks when:

- You try to pitch in equally on everyday responsibilities

- You ask your partner how you can help out
- You make an effort to handle tasks before your partner asks you to do them

You undermine task sharing when:

- You strategically avoid having to do your share of the work
- You never ask your partner how you can help out
- You expect your partner to run errands and do chores for you, without reciprocating

Social Networks.   Romances are more likely to survive if important members of the couples' social networks approve of the relationship (Felmlee, 2001). For example, communication scholars Malcolm Parks and Mara Adelman measured how much support romantically involved individuals received from their partners' friends and family, what percentage of their partners' network they had met, and how often they communicated with these people (Parks & Adelman, 1983). Using these factors, along with perceived similarity to partner and frequency of communication with partner, Parks and Adelman were able to predict with 88 percent accuracy which couples would survive. The strongest determinants of whether couples stayed together? Social network support and regular communication with partner.

Fostering healthy relationships with surrounding friends and family appears especially crucial for those involved in interethnic relationships (Baptiste, 1990) and for gay and lesbian couples. Approximately 67 percent of interethnic marriages end in divorce, compared with an overall divorce rate of 40 percent, the largest reasons being lack of network support and cultural disapproval (Gaines & Agnew, 2003). Gay and lesbian couples report having supportive environments such as churches or clubs and being treated as "the same" as straight couples by their network members as being especially important for their relationship stability and satisfaction (Haas & Stafford, 1998).

You foster supportive social networks when you:

- Tell your partner how much you like his or her friends and family
- Invite your partner's friends or family members to share activities with the two of you
- Willingly sacrifice your own needs and desires for the sake of your partner's friends and family—for example, supporting your partner's desire to spend several weeks with his or her ill parent

You undermine social networks when you:

- Make critical and disparaging remarks regarding your partner's friends and family to him or her
- Intentionally avoid encounters with your partner's friends and family
- Demand that your partner choose between spending time with you and spending it with friends and family

Confronting Relationship Crises

As we've seen, forging a long-term romantic commitment with another human being means confronting the minor difficulties that inevitably arise between people who are intimately involved with one another. But love relationships also experience crises that, left unaddressed or handled ineptly, can damage a relationship beyond repair. How can you respond most constructively to crises as they arise? Couples use numerous different strategies, which vary in their effectiveness.

Strategies differ along two broad dimensions: the degree to which they are active or passive, and the degree to which they are constructive or destructive (Rusbult, 1987). Couples who approach relationship crises in an active fashion aggressively confront problems at the first sign of trouble. Others take a passive approach, believing that problems that are left alone will resolve themselves eventually. And some couples approach problems constructively, viewing relationship crises as opportunities for positive collaboration. Others take a more destructive approach, seeing problems as symptoms of a doomed future and using them as an excuse to end the relationship.

Voice Strategy. Through use of the **voice strategy,** an active, constructive approach, a couple talks directly about a problem they're experiencing without attacking, blaming, or accusing one another of wrongdoing. To use this strategy, let your partner know how you're feeling about a problem that has arisen, and ask for his or her perspective: "I was really hurt when you canceled our anniversary dinner again because of work. What was going through your mind when that happened?" Once you've shared perspectives, name the problem and decide how you can best deal with the root cause: "We've let work pressures bleed into our personal life too much. We need to establish firmer boundaries between work and our life together." If the source of the problem is your or your partner's behavior, consider whether and how these problematic behaviors can be changed: "Could you try planning your workload more carefully in the weeks leading up to important dates, such as our anniversary? And I'll do my part by being willing to shift our dinner plans to the next night if you simply can't reschedule your work."

The voice strategy helps you negotiate constructive, workable solutions to serious relationship problems. Couples using this strategy may and often do solicit help from third parties, including close friends and family members and in some cases trained therapists.

Loyalty Strategy. In contrast to the active nature of the voice strategy, couples who use the **loyalty strategy** take a more "passive constructive"

TABLE 10.3

Approaches to Relationship Crises

	Passive Approach	Active Approach
Constructive Approach	Loyalty	Voice
Destructive Approach	Neglect	Exit

approach to crises. If you rely on loyalty for dealing with your relationship crises, you avoid directly confronting a problem. If your partner raises a concern, you do your best to suppress and avoid discussion of it. Instead, you wait for things to get better, believing that problems eventually work out for the best.

Exit Strategy.   Instead of aggressively and constructively confronting problems when they arise, some couples respond to relationship crises with an **exit strategy,** an "active destructive" approach. As the name implies, exiting means dealing with relationship problems by thinking about leaving the relationship, threatening to leave, or actually leaving.

Neglect Strategy.   Some couples approach problems using a **neglect strategy,** a destructive approach, albeit a passive one. If you use neglect, you withdraw from your relationship, cut back on the time you spend with your partner, and avoid discussing your relationship problems. You may also treat your partner badly and complain about the relationship without offering solutions.

Not surprisingly, research looking at these tactics documents that the more active and constructive the approach you take for dealing with your relationship problems, the happier your relationship will be and thus the more likely you will be to successfully maintain your relationship (Rusbult, 1987). In particular, use of the voice strategy substantially boosts couples' relationship satisfaction. The loyalty strategy, in contrast, is only weakly related to satisfaction and thus success at maintaining ongoing relationships. The tactics of both exit and neglect have strong negative effects on relationship happiness: couples who use either strategy report substantially lower happiness and less likelihood of survival (Metts & Cupach, 1990).

Deciding Whether to Maintain

Of course, not all romantic involvements are worth the effort to maintain. In some cases, it may be healthier to purge yourself of the involvement rather than communicate in ways designed to foster its survival. The decision whether to maintain or dissolve a struggling romance is one of the most bitter and challenging interpersonal decisions we face.

As one way to work through this decision, familiarize yourself with the characteristics distinguishing couples whose relationships survive from those whose involvements don't last. Then compare your own relationship against these criteria. If your bond has those same characteristics, it may be worth investing effort to maintain it.

Four factors—each of which we've discussed earlier in this chapter—appear to be most important in predicting survival of a romantic relationship. First, is the degree to which the partners consider themselves "in love." Couples are more likely to stay together if they think of themselves as in love, are considering marriage or a lifelong commitment, rate their relationship as high in closeness, and date each other exclusively (Hill et al., 1976). Second is equity. Romantic relationships are happiest and most stable when the balance of giving and getting is equal for both partners (Hatfield et al.,

SELF-REFLECTION

Think about your most recent romantic crisis. Which approach—voice, loyalty, exit, or neglect—best captures how you dealt with the situation? What happened as a result of your strategy? Now imagine that a similar crisis happens again in the future. Could you use the voice strategy to deal with it? If so, how would you apply that strategy? What would you say to your partner?

1985). Third, similarity. Highly similar couples are more likely to stay together than couples who are dissimilar (Hill et al., 1976). And fourth, network support. A romance is more likely to endure when the couple's social networks approve of the relationship (Felmlee, 2001; Parks & Adelman, 1983).

How well does your relationship meet these four criteria? Ask yourself the following questions:

1. Are you still in love with your partner? Do you see yourself always being with him or her, and do you still want to date him or her exclusively?
2. Is your relationship equitable?
3. Do you and your partner share values and personality traits?
4. Do your family and friends support your relationship? Do they and your partner communicate well, share time and activities together, and generally approve of each other?

If you answer "yes" to these questions, your relationship may warrant investment in maintenance. But remember: *deciding whether to maintain a struggling relationship or to let it go is a choice only you can make.* Friends, family members, pop-culture relationship experts, and even textbooks can't tell you when to keep or when to leave a romantic involvement. That being said, romantic relationships are in many ways practical endeavors. Your decision to maintain or end a struggling romance should be based on a long-term forecast of your relationship. Stacking your relationship up against those four questions can give you insight into whether your relationship has a solid foundation on which to invest further maintenance effort, and it can help guide you in making a wise relationship choice.

The Dark Side of Romantic Relationships

Think back to *Romeo and Juliet*, with which this chapter opened. Part of the enduring appeal of Shakespeare's tragedy is that it reminds us of the joyful, ennobling nature of love. Even in the midst of bitter enmity, love can arise, joining people together who previously were enemies. Of course, love also can turn tragic, and when it does it has the capacity to spawn the deepest despair. In this section, we explore three potent challenges to love—dysfunctional relationship beliefs, jealousy, and betrayal—and present communication strategies for addressing them.

Dysfunctional Relationship Beliefs

Many of us harbor harmful illusions, or **dysfunctional relationship beliefs,** about what constitutes the "perfect" romantic relationship. These beliefs lead us to communicate with our partners in destructive ways and to make disastrous decisions. Five dysfunctional relationship beliefs exert a particularly poisonous effect on romantic unions (Metts & Cupach, 1990). The first of these is the conviction that "all disagreement is destructive." Many people

"That's the fourth time this week you've worked late because 'the game went into double overtime.' Well, I'm not falling for it, Charles. ...Who's the tramp?"

believe that their thoughts, attitudes, and goals for their relationship must align perfectly with those of their partner for the relationship to survive. But in both casual and committed romantic relationships, it's commonplace for partners to disagree. The challenge for those of us interested in maintaining our romances is to constructively resolve such disagreements—as we discussed in Chapter 9 on conflict—rather than believing that such disagreements will never arise.

Second, many people believe that "mind-reading is mandatory" for relational health—that "If you *really* loved me, you'd know my every thought, desire, and emotion," no matter how nuanced or subtle they may be. People who hold this belief view any empathic failure by their partners as proof of a lack of closeness rather than the natural limits of human perception. Messages that display this belief include "I shouldn't have to tell you—you should just *know* what I'm thinking," and "if you really loved me, you'd understand how I feel."

Third, romantic partners often hold fast to the notion that their partners "can't change" their behaviors, particularly those perceived as negative. At base is the belief that people are incapable of improving over time. People who believe that partners can't change think, "You can't teach an old dog new tricks," and "A person who hurts you once will hurt you again."

Fourth, we often think that every sexual encounter with a romantic partner should be "perfect." For most people, the experience of romantic love is tied to sexuality. However, the belief that sex always should be perfect reflects an extreme and unrealistic expectation about the ever-changing nature of sexual expression. People who possess this belief view sexual problems (including the occasional less-than-fabulous encounter) as indicative of waning love and dwindling passion.

Finally, people often believe that "men and women are monumentally different" in their perceptions, emotions, and communication. People possessing this belief view the differences between men and women as outweighing the similarities, and they see communication between genders as intrinsically challenging and difficult. Examples of this belief include "You can never really understand someone of the other gender" and "Men and women are *so* different, they never can really relate to each other."

These beliefs are difficult to overcome, in part because our popular culture sells them as truths. Web sites, movies, music videos, books, and magazines continually trumpet the importance of having "perfect sex" every time. They push the idea that men and women are so different that they're from different planets and that straightforward communication is impossible. But these beliefs damage communication within romantic relationships and threaten intimate bonds. Thus it's vital to understand and eradicate them if you want to cultivate healthy, satisfying partnerships.

For example, consider how two beliefs—"disagreement is destructive" and "partners can't change"—affect communication strategies in relationship crises (Metts & Cupach, 1990). Say that you've been casually dating someone for the last few weeks. It's not especially serious—at least not yet—but you do enjoy the person's company and the activities you share together. Then you discover that your partner doesn't share one of your core values—for example, he or she doesn't believe in God, but you do. If you're

convinced that "disagreement is destructive" and that "partners can't change," you'll likely deal with this dilemma by simply terminating the relationship (exit strategy). If you had talked directly and respectfully with your partner about the issue (voice strategy), you may have discovered that the two of you in fact could resolve the issue and develop a deeper, more satisfying bond.

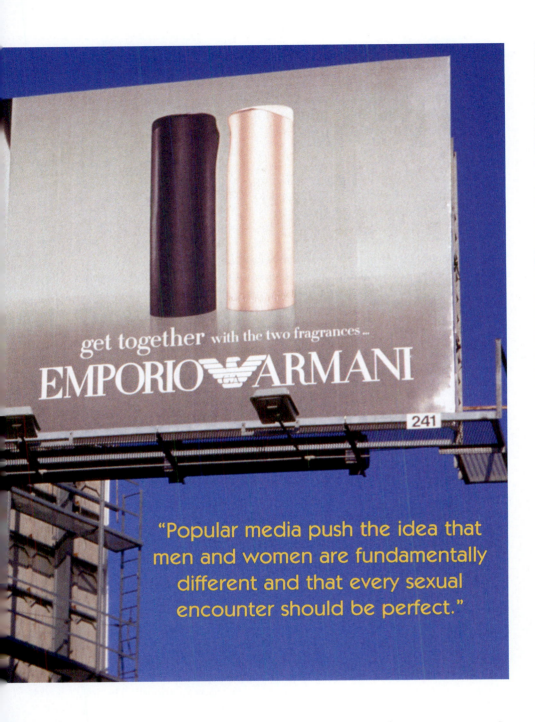

"Popular media push the idea that men and women are fundamentally different and that every sexual encounter should be perfect."

The starting point for overcoming these beliefs and preventing them from contaminating your communication is to recognize that they are false. Disagreements *will* arise in both casual and committed romantic relationships, partners *can't* read each other's minds, people *can* change their behaviors, sex *won't* always be perfect, and men and women are more *similar* than different. Then, perception-check (see Chapter 3) by critically examining how the degree to which you accept these beliefs shapes your thoughts and communication, especially during relationship crises. Embrace voice (talking directly and respectfully with your partner) as a strategy for dealing with relational problems, and resist the temptation to neglect or exit romantic relationships simply because of these beliefs.

Jealousy

A second problem that plagues many romantic relationships is **jealousy**—a protective reaction to a perceived threat to a valued relationship (Hansen, 1985). Most scholars agree that jealousy isn't a singular emotion per se but rather a combination of negative emotions—primarily hurt, anger, and fear (Guerrero & Andersen, 1998).

Jealousy can strike in several forms (Pfeiffer & Wong, 1989). When we experience *cognitive* jealousy, we become paranoid and suspicious about our partner's behavior. In particular, we suspect that he or she is being unfaithful. These suspicions are not necessarily rooted in reality: cognitive jealousy can stem from imagined as well as actual threats. *Behavioral* jealousy is jealousy in action. Rather than merely worrying, we actively try to determine whether our jealous thoughts have a basis in fact. For example, we question mutual friends, verify a partner's whereabouts, or even search our partner's belongings. Last is *emotional* jealousy, an emotional response to certain people that occurs independently of any conscious appraisal of threat. For instance, you may experience an uncontrollable surge of resentment and worry when you see your partner's ex, even though you know that the ex poses no threat to your relationship.

Although the experience of jealousy in romantic relationships is perfectly normal, it's also decidedly unpleasant. Imagine yourself in a jealousy-provoking situation. You're at a party with partner, and you go to the bathroom. Upon returning, you can't find your partner anywhere. Suddenly you see him or her standing in a dark corner of the living room, huddled closely with an attractive person, laughing and smiling. How can you best deal with the jealousy that you're bound to feel?

Romantic partners use several jealousy-reducing strategies, which vary in effectiveness (Salovey & Rodin, 1988). One is *self-reliance:* allowing yourself to feel jealous but not letting whatever sparked your jealousy interrupt what you already were doing. You continue your current activities and give yourself time to cool off. To use self-reliance in the party situation, you would recognize your jealousy as a normal reaction, rejoin your partner, and say, "There you are! I was looking around for you and couldn't find you, and was starting to get worried. Please introduce me to your friend!" The idea with self-reliance is to accept jealousy as a normal reaction and not let it derail you.

Another commonly used strategy is *self-bolstering*—combating jealous thoughts and feelings with positive affirmations about yourself. If you used this strategy in the party scenario, you might stand across the room, evaluate the other person who's talking with your partner, and tell yourself how much more attractive or interesting you are than your apparent romantic rival.

Finally, many people use *selective ignoring*—discounting or devaluing the event that ignited your jealousy in the first place. You pretend that what has made you jealous isn't really that important. At the party, for example, you would pretend that you hadn't seen your partner with someone else or tell yourself that it's not a big deal.

None of these tactics alleviates jealousy completely, but research on their effectiveness suggests that self-reliance works best (Salovey & Rodin, 1988). Self-bolstering and selective ignoring do little to reduce jealousy and may actually generate frustration and additional negative emotion. Think about it: when you're feeling jealous, can you really pretend it's no big deal? Your reaction suggests otherwise. And can you really think positive thoughts about yourself when jealousy has a hold on you? Not if you're feeling angry, hurt, and scared. The best approach you can take is to accept the experience as normal, continue with what you were doing, and allow the intensity of the experience to fade. Avoid communicating with your partner until you're able to do so in a cooperative and constructive fashion.

Betrayal

Although dysfunctional beliefs and jealousy plague many romantic relationships, the negative outcomes they create pale in comparison to the damage wrought by intimate **betrayal**—hurtful actions inflicted by one partner on another (Couch, Jones, & Moore, 1999). Common acts of intimate betrayal include sexual infidelity (engaging in sexual activity with someone else), emotional infidelity (developing a strong romantic attachment to someone else), deception (intentional mispresentation, such as lying), and disloyalty (hurting your partner to benefit yourself). But any behavior that violates norms of loyalty and trustworthiness can be considered betrayal. One study

POP QUIZ

How Often Do You Betray Romantic Partners?

Read each statement and rate how often you have done the activity: 1 (never), 2 (once), 3 (a few times), 4 (several times), 5 (many times). Get your score by adding up your answers.

_____ Snubbing a romantic partner when you are with a group you want to impress.

_____ Gossiping about a romantic partner behind his or her back.

_____ Making a promise to a romantic partner with no intention of keeping it.

_____ Telling others information given to you in confidence by a romantic partner.

_____ Lying to a romantic partner.

_____ Failing to stand up for a romantic partner when he or she is being criticized or belittled by others.

Scoring:

6–14: You're a very low betrayer. 15–23: You're a moderate betrayer. 24–30: You're a high betrayer.

Note: Information in this *Pop Quiz* adapted for romantic relationships is from Jones and Burdette (1994).

looking at uncertainty-increasing events in close relationships found that "betrayals of confidence" were the second most commonly reported event (Planalp & Honeycutt, 1985). These included acts such as a boyfriend's telling the mother of his girlfriend that they had sex, a woman's telling her friends about her problematic sex life with her partner, and a man's disclosing his partner's family secrets to people outside of the family.

In any intimate relationship, partners inevitably behave in ways that defy expectations and cause disappointment. However, betrayal is different. Betrayal is *intentional*. The driving force behind the pain of betrayal is the overwhelming sense of **relational devaluation**—the realization that our partners do not love and respect us as much as we thought they did (Leary, 2001). This sense of devaluation, which is affected most by sexual infidelity and deception, is difficult to overcome and often leads partners to abandon their relationships.

Sexual Infidelity.   Easily the most intimate and destructive form of romantic betrayal is sexual infidelity. A partner who cheats on you within a sexually committed relationship has broken a fundamental sacrament—the spoken or unspoken pledge to "cleave only unto one another." Not surprisingly, many people react to infidelity with a strong urge to leave their partner. One study found that more than 20 percent of American women and men would consider divorce if a spouse passionately kissed someone else, more than 30 percent would consider divorce if their spouse had a romantic date with another person, and more than 60 percent would consider divorce if their spouse had a serious (sexual) affair (Shackelford & Buss, 1997). Whether or not a sexual dalliance is planned matters little; cheaters' original intentions have no impact on subsequent feelings of blame by their partners (Mongeau, Hale, & Alles, 1994).

Although men and women view infidelity as treasonous, their perceptions diverge when they're asked to compare sexual with emotional cheating. Infidelity researcher David Buss presented study respondents with the following dilemma (Buss, Larsen, Westen, & Semmelroth, 1992). Imagine you discover that your partner has become interested in someone else. What would distress you more: your partner's forming a deep emotional attachment to that person, or your partner's enjoying passionate sex with that person? Sixty percent of men said that sex would upset them more, but 83 percent of women said they'd find the emotional attachment more distressing. The same pattern of results was found in samples of men and women from Sweden, the Netherlands, Germany, Korea, and Japan (Buss et al., 1999; Buunk, Angleitner, Oubaid, & Buss, 1996; Wiederman & Kendall, 1999).

Deception.   The only form of betrayal that comes close to rivaling infidelity in the damage it does to relationships is deception. As defined in Chapter 7, deception is intentional misrepresentation: misleading your partner by intentionally withholding information, presenting false information, or making your message unnecessarily irrelevant or ambiguous (McCornack, 1997).

Despite media images depicting romantic partners catching each other in lies, most people discover lies indirectly through hearing about them

"Most people discover lies indirectly through hearing about them from a third party or stumbling across damning evidence..."

Making Relationship Choices

Dealing with Infidelity

1

BACKGROUND

Sexual infidelity is the most damaging form of betrayal. When a romantic partner cheats, the act forces you to choose between two painful options: repairing a relationship that will never be the same or ending it. To consider how you might deal with such a dilemma, read the case study and work through the five steps that follow.

2

CASE STUDY

You've been with Kelin for five years, and they've been the happiest of your life. The two of you are very much in love, and you plan on spending your lives together. You've talked about marriage, and you currently live together in a neighborhood where you both share many friends. Kelin treats you well, exceeding both your comparison level and your comparison level for alternatives. The two of you enjoy many common interests. Kelin works hard to stay fit and attractive for you and strives to maintain equity in your relationship. It's not a "perfect" romance; you've had the same ups and downs like all long-term couples. But you've managed to work through the rough times, in part because you both regularly exchange assurances and you constructively and actively face problems head-on when they arise.

Kelin is professionally successful and is invited to speak at a conference. Following several nights apart, you meet Kelin at the airport, but you can tell immediately that something's wrong. Your partner seems emotionally withdrawn and down. You suspect that the speech wasn't well received, but Kelin insists it went

fine. You decide to let it go, but the rest of your day is tainted by your partner's foul mood. Back at the house, Kelin retreats into the home office. You begin to get angry because you were stuck at home for several days handling chores while Kelin was off having a good time, thousands of miles away. You decide to confront your partner.

Approaching the home office, you're shocked to hear Kelin weeping. You gently knock, open the door, and ask what's wrong. Kelin says softly, "I've destroyed everything." Feeling your stomach drop and fearing the worst, you ask for an explanation. Kelin tells you that the presentation went great and that afterward several colleagues went out as a group to celebrate. Following many rounds of drinks, one of the other conference participants invited Kelin up to a hotel room—where the two had sex. Your partner insists that this was a "one-time" event. After all, the other person lives several states away, and they're unlikely to ever meet again. Kelin begs for your forgiveness, pleads with you not to leave, and pledges love and future loyalty. You believe that your partner is sincerely remorseful, but you're deeply injured by this betrayal.

YOUR TURN

While working through the following steps, keep in mind the interpersonal communication concepts, skills, and insights you've learned so far in this book, especially this chapter. Also remember: there are no right answers, so think hard about the choice you make! (P.S. Need help? Review the concepts listed below.)

● **Step 1: Reflect on yourself.** What are your thoughts and feelings in this situation? What attributions are you making about Kelin? Are your attributions accurate? Why or why not?

● **Step 2: Reflect on your partner.** Using perspective-taking and empathic concern, put yourself in Kelin's shoes. Consider how your romantic partner is thinking and feeling. How does Kelin likely perceive this situation? How does Kelin feel about you and your relationship?

● **Step 3: Identify the optimal outcome.** Think about all the information you have about Kelin and about this relationship. Consider your own feelings as well as your partner's. Given all these factors, what's the best, most constructive relationship outcome possible here? Be sure to consider not just what's best for *you*, but what's best for Kelin as well.

● **Step 4: Locate the roadblocks.** Taking into consideration your own thoughts and feelings, Kelin's, and the situation, what's preventing you from achieving the optimal outcome you identified in step 3?

● **Step 5: Chart your course.** What will you say to Kelin to overcome the roadblocks you've identified and achieve your optimal relationship outcome?

from a third party or stumbling across damning evidence, such as an ex's phone number on a partner's cell phone (Park, Levine, McCornack, Morrison, & Ferrara, 2002). When partners discover a lie, the experience typically is emotionally intense and negative. One study looking at the emotional and relational aftermath of lies found that 16 percent of people who recalled having discovered a lie reported breaking up their romantic relationship because of the lie (McCornack & Levine, 1990). The strongest determinant of the decision to break up was what was lied about. If people felt the lie was "important" (for example, lying about relationship feelings), they were more likely to end their involvement (McCornack & Levine, 1990).

Dealing with Betrayal.   The truth about romantic betrayal is that no simple solution or skill set exists that will remedy the pain, disillusionment, and relationship damage that accompany betrayal. All the scientific evidence we have suggests that the seriousness of the betrayal is the strongest predictor of what happens afterward. If a betrayal permanently stains your perception of your partner, the relationship will probably not survive. If you believe you can eventually overcome the pain of the betrayal, then your relationship has a chance.

When you are dealing with romantic betrayal, the choices available to you are the same as in other relationship crises: voice, loyalty, neglect, or exit strategies. You can actively confront the betrayal, seeking to understand the conditions that led to it and jointly working with your partner to change those causes (voice strategy). You can quietly stand by your partner, choosing to forgive and forget and trusting that, in time, your love will heal the pain you feel (loyalty strategy). You can stand by your partner but simmer with pain, venting your anger on your partner by constantly reminding the person of his or her transgression or withholding sex or other rewards (neglect strategy). Or you can simply end the relationship, believing that the emotional costs associated with the betrayal are too substantial to surmount (exit strategy).

Regardless of which approach you take, the plain, perhaps harsh, truth is that your relationship will never be the same, and it will never be "better" in terms of trust, intimacy, and satisfaction than it was prior to the betrayal. You can use the voice strategy and possibly rebuild a strong and enduring relationship. But your relationship will always be scarred by the betrayal, and although the wound may heal, the emotional scar tissue will be an enduring reminder of your suffering.

The Hard Work of Successful Love

Romantic relationships are most satisfying and stand a greater chance of enduring when you and your partner view your bond without illusions and embellishments, warts and all. When you do this, when you look love square in the face, what you find may surprise you. Love is hard work. Long-term romantic relationships endure not because the partners exchange upgraded rings every five years. They thrive because partners choose to communicate in ways that maintain their relationship. They last because partners have learned to voice their concerns and to work together to solve the crises they inevitably face. They survive because partners have learned that sex isn't always perfect, that they won't always agree, and that they can't always read each other's minds. These connections prevail because partners have learned that being positive and open; sharing talk, time, and tasks; and providing assurances feeds their love as fertilizer feeds plants and that betraying love—even once—can permanently poison it.

Though passionate sex and the novelty of discovering one another are certainly exciting, it's the everyday communication and effort that you and your partner invest that will most enable you to build a satisfying, intimate bond—and sustain it if that's what you choose to do. Enduring couples succeed at love by working at it day in and day out—helping each other with dishes, cheering each other with kind words while changing the kids' diapers, nursing each other through illness, and even holding each other close as one of them lets go of life.

POSTSCRIPT

This chapter began with the greatest romantic tragedy ever written and its impact on a 10-year-old boy growing up in Seattle, Washington. Franco Zeffirelli's movie version of *Romeo and Juliet* forever changed my perception of romance. In a single evening, it grounded the beliefs about the nature of love that I would carry into adulthood—and that I would revise once I gained personal experience with love.

But what about you? What does love mean to you? Who or what shaped *your* beliefs about romantic love? Was it family? Friends? Your faith? Think about how your beliefs have affected your communica-

tion with romantic partners and the quality of your intimate relationships. What smart and not-so-smart relationship decisions have you made, based on your beliefs? Have your romantic experiences to date confirmed or disconfirmed your early views of love?

We often think of romantic love as something natural and unspoken, something innate rather than learned. But the beliefs we each form regarding romance do not suddenly spring upon us in adolescence as a lightning bolt leaping from a clear sky. Instead, they're forged in our earliest childhood through our observations of others, and then hammered into rough form

and repeatedly reshaped through our firsthand experiences with love. For some of us the belief that emerges is poetic and transcendent. For others it's bitter and hollow. But one truth about romance is inescapable: your view of love powerfully shapes how you communicate in your romantic relationships, how healthy and satisfying your involvements are, and what choices you make in response to relationship challenges.

Chapter Review

Key Terms

Key Concepts

Defining Romantic Relationships

- Although **loving** is sometimes thought of as an intense form of **liking,** the two are very different. You can like someone without loving him or her, and love someone without liking the person.

- When people consider what it means to be in love, they frequently think of **passionate love.** Passionate love is experienced across cultures and ages and is distinct from **companionate love**, although many romantic relationships evolve from passionate to companionate love.

- Many **colors of love** exist – people perceive romantic love and being "in love" in different ways. When both partners in a relationship perceive it as romantic, a **romantic relationship** exists.

Romantic Attraction

- **Social exchange theory** suggests that attraction to others is driven in part by the resources they can offer you. People perceived as offering many benefits and few costs are seen as desirable. For relationships to survive, however, **equity** must exist in the balance of rewards and costs exchanged between partners

- Attraction is strongly influenced by proximity: how frequently you see others and interact with them. This **mere exposure effect** is one reason for the comparative rarity of inter-ethnic romances.

- Most of us find physically appealing people more attractive than physically unappealing people, and we often attribute a host of positive characteristics to them – **the beautiful-is-good effect**. At the same time, we tend to engage in **matching** when it comes to forming long-term romantic relationships.

- Perceived similarity (in interests, beliefs, and values) plays a powerful role in driving attraction, and in general, the **birds-of-a-feather effect** holds true

Relationship Development and Deterioration

- Romantic relationships develop in stages. When coming together, couples commonly go through **initiating** and **experimenting.** During the latter stage couples exchange **small talk.** Although small talk often is disparaged as unimportant, we use it to test whether we want to pursue a more intimate relationship

- Some couples move beyond experimenting to **intensifying** and **integrating.** Few relationships progress to **bonding.**

- As relationships come apart, **differentiating** leads partners to believe that their differences are insurmountable. If they fail to constructively deal with differentiating, they may begin **circumscribing** or even **stagnating.**

- Many relationships end by **avoiding,** although couples who feel they need more "closure" may conduct a **terminating** discussion.

Maintaining Romantic Relationships

- Couples who endure typically use several **relational maintenance** tactics. The most common strategies include treating each other in a positive fashion, working to keep communication open and honest, and providing frequent assurances regarding relationship commitment.

- When faced with severe relational crises, romantic couples use one of four strategies, **voice, loyalty, exit,** or **neglect.** The most effective is voice, the goal being to understand what causes the problem and to negotiate a solution.

The Dark Side of Romantic Relationships

- Couples trying to maintain a long-term romantic relationship face a number of challenges. **Dysfunctional relationship beliefs** lead some people to avoid dealing directly with their problems or cause unrealistic expectations regarding the rewards the relationship provides. Other relationships are challenged by **jealousy.**

- Perhaps the gravest threat to relationship survival is romantic **betrayal.** Two of the most damaging forms of betrayal are sexual infidelity and deception. These cause profound damage because they create a sense of **relational devaluation.**

Key Skills

- What's the single most important ingredient that allows similarity to generate attraction? Discover the answer on pages 342–343.

- Want to know the best—and worst—opening lines for starting a conversation with a stranger? Check out the *Pop Quiz* on page 345.

- How can you communicate in ways that will overcome differentiating? Find the answers on page 352; then complete the *Skills Practice* on page 352.

- What can you do to best deal with a terminating encounter? Review the material on page 354.

- Trying to maintain your romance? Review the tips for using positivity, openness, assurances, social networks, and task and activity sharing described on pages 356–359. Then do the *Skills Practice* on page 359 to discover how to integrate these strategies into your online communication with your partner.

- Facing a relationship crisis? See the suggestions for using the voice strategy on page 360.

- Trying to figure out whether your relationship has a bright enough future to invest further effort into maintaining it? Answer the four questions on page 362 to help you decide.

- How can you overcome dysfunctional beliefs that damage your romantic relationships? Follow the suggestions on pages 362–363.

- Need to control or reduce your jealousy? Check out the strategies on pages 366–367; then complete the *Skills Practice* on page 366.

- Wondering if you tend to betray your romantic partners? Take the *Pop Quiz* on page 367 to test your betrayal potential.

- How can you best deal with betrayal by a romantic partner? Review the discussion on page 372; then work through the *Making Relationship Choices* exercise on pages 370–371.

11

Relationships with Family and Friends

Joanne grew up in an open and supportive family that included her parents and her younger sister Di. "I think my mother had a romantic idea of what family life ought to be," she notes, "and never stopped striving to attain it."[1] One of Joanne's fondest childhood memories is of her mother's laugh. "She had one of the most contagious laughs I've ever heard, though you didn't really hear much—she literally doubled up, apparently unable to draw breath while tears streamed down her face."

When Joanne was 15, her family life changed forever. Her mother was diagnosed with multiple sclerosis, a degenerative nervous-system disease. "I think most people believe, deep down, that their mothers are indestructible; it was a terrible shock to hear that she had an incurable illness." Joanne continued on to college, and after graduating, she went to work in London and began writing a book. In 1990, her mother

---

[1] Information that follows, including quotes, is excerpted from Rowling (2002).

passed away. "It was a terrible time. My father, Di, and I were devastated. I remember feeling as though there was a paving slab pressing down on my chest, a literal pain in my heart."

The heartbreak Joanne felt after her mother's death transformed the images of family in the novel she was writing, titled *Harry Potter and the Philosopher's Stone*. "Harry's feelings about his dead parents became much deeper, much more real." Joanne poured her pain into the manuscript, developing what would become her favorite chapter, "The Mirror of Erised," in which Harry is tormented by the illusory reflection of his dead parents (Rowling, 1997):

A woman standing right behind his reflection was smiling at him. He reached out a hand and felt the air behind him. If she was really there, he'd touch her, but he felt only air—she and the others existed only in the mirror. Then he noticed that she was crying: smiling, but crying at the same time. The tall, thin, black-haired man standing next to her put his arm around her. He wore glasses, and his hair was very untidy. It stuck up at the back, just as Harry's did. Harry was so close to the mirror now that his nose was nearly touching that of his reflection. "Mom?" he whispered. "Dad?" (pp. 208–209)

The pain of losing a parent isn't the only parallel Joanne created between her life and Harry's. Just as Harry eventually finds a new family in his friends, Joanne's emotional survival—and her eventual fame and fortune—largely stemmed from the support offered by her close friend, Fiona Wilson. After her mother's death, Joanne lived on welfare in a rundown apartment in Scotland. Struggling to raise a daughter by herself, she struck up a friendship with Wilson, also a single mother. When Joanne won acceptance into a prestigious teacher training program, she didn't think she could pursue the opportunity because she could not afford childcare. Wilson gave her £4,000 (approximately $7,400). "I broke down and cried when my friend offered it to me. I think we both thought I would never be able to pay it back. She basically said here's a gift to help you."

Wilson's generosity enabled Joanne ("JK") Rowling to earn her degree, though her career as a teacher was soon cut short by the smashing success of her Harry Potter series. More than a quarter *billion* copies of her books have been sold in over 200 countries worldwide and translated into 60 different languages. And Joanne repaid her friend's gift many times over, buying Wilson a house. Yet despite her success, Joanne's thoughts return to her mom: "I miss my mother almost daily, and I feel desperately sad for all she missed. She died before either of her daughters got married, she never met her granddaughter, and I never told her about *Harry Potter*."

For many of us, connections with family and friends form the bedrock of our interpersonal lives. Consider the order in which relationships are formed across our lifespan. We are born or adopted into our families, who care for us from a young age; they are quite literally the first people we see, hear, and touch. From these caregivers, we learn foundational lessons about interpersonal relationships and communication (Fitzpatrick & Badzinski, 1994; Fitzpatrick & Caughlin, 2002). As we progress through childhood, we branch out, forming friendships in school and our community. Only later do we begin dabbling in affairs of the heart, using our experiences with family and friends as an informal guide to exploring the complexities of romance and sexuality. But long before we feel our first romantic yearnings we've already learned to depend on family and friends for support. When romances fail or other life challenges arise, it is our family and friends we fall back on for advice and solace.

Family ties run so deep that we often use kinship as a metaphor to describe closeness in other relationships: "How close are we? We're like *family!*" (Rubin, 1996). But family relationships are also compulsory. As French poet Jacques Delille (1738–1813) once noted, "Fate chooses your relations, you choose your friends." Friendships are indeed voluntary involvements, based on shared beliefs, interests, or other points of similarity. Many of us feel a deep sense of connectedness with our friends. But at the same time, our friendships are more transitory because they lack the structure, obligations, and bonds that tie us to our families.

In this chapter, we look at two types of interpersonal relationships that together play a vital role in our lives—a role that differs markedly from that fulfilled by romantic relationships. You'll learn:

- The defining features of family and the different ways in which families communicate

- Communication strategies to maintain healthy family relationships

- Varied types of friendships you'll experience

- Ways you can communicate so that your friendships survive and thrive

Defining Family

When many of us think of family, iconic TV images fill our heads: the Bradys from *The Brady Bunch,* the Huxtables from *The Cosby Show,* or even *The Simpsons.* Such images depict families in simple, comforting ways: families consist of happily married couples and their biological children, bonded by love. Yet, historically, families have been less about intimacy and more about power and practicality (Hendrick & Hendrick, 1992). People married to forge alliances or pay off personal debts, and women had little or no choice in the matter. Couples had children to continue bloodlines or to produce a pair of much-needed working hands. Indeed, the historical purpose of the family is encoded in the roots of the word itself; *family* comes from the Latin *famulus,* meaning "servant" or "slave."

Of course, families today are more diverse than either history or popular culture reveals. Between 1970 and 2000, the percentage of all American households comprising married couples with biological children declined from 40 percent to just 24 percent (Fields, 2003). During those same decades, the number of single-mother families in the United States grew from 3 million to 10 million, and single-father families grew from 393,000 to 2 million. Rising divorce rates over the past half century have decreased the average size of households as families divide into smaller units and re-form into blended arrangements featuring stepparents and stepchildren. The

● Even the most different families hold certain things in common.

enormous diversity in the contemporary experience of family requires a broad, inclusive definition. **Family** is a group of people who create and maintain a mutual identity, emotional bonds, and communication boundaries through how they interact with each other and with others; who share a common past, present, and future; and who may or may not share a biological heritage (Fitzpatrick & Badzinski, 1994; Turner & West, 1998).

This definition highlights five characteristics that distinguish families from other social groups (Copeland & White, 1991). First, families create a sense of family identity through their interpersonal communication. The way you talk with other family members, the stories you exchange, and even the manner in which members of your family deal with conflict all contribute to a shared sense of what your family is like.

Second, because we forge family relationships during an early and very impressionable period in our lives, these bonds often prove emotionally intense. As author Lillian Rubin (1996) notes, family relationships have "an elemental quality that touches the deepest layers of our inner life and stirs our most primitive emotional responses" (p. 256). Consider the strength of feeling that arises in you when you get into an argument with a parent or sibling, or when you celebrate an important milestone (a graduation, a wedding, a new job) with family members.

Third, families use interpersonal communication to define boundaries, both inside the family and in ways that can distinguish family members from outsiders. As we'll discuss in more detail shortly, some families constrict information that flows out ("Don't you dare talk about our family problems with anyone else"). Some also restrict physical access to the family—for example, by dictating with whom family members can become romantically involved ("No son of mine is going to marry a Protestant!"). Others set few

● No matter who is in them, today's families are some of the most central and formative interpersonal relationships that we have.

such boundaries. For instance, a family may welcome friends and neighbors as unofficial members, such as an "uncle" or "aunt" who isn't really related to your parents. A family may even welcome others' children, such as the kind neighbors across the street whom you think of as your "family away from home."

Fourth, families share a history. Such histories can stretch back for generations and feature family members from a broad array of cultures. These histories often set expectations regarding how family members should behave ("We Ngatas have always been an honest bunch, and we're not about to change that now"). Families also share a common future: they expect to maintain their bonds indefinitely. For better or worse, everything you say and do in the present becomes a part of your family history, shaping future interactions and determining whether your family relationships are healthy or destructive.

And last, family members often share genetic material. This can lead to shared physical characteristics as well as similar personality, outlook on life, mental abilities, and ways of relating to others. For example, some studies suggest that interpersonal inclinations such as shyness and aggressiveness are influenced by genes (Carducci & Zimbardo, 1995).

Types of Family

Despite popular media images, there is currently no "typical" American family. Instead, the characteristics that collectively define family—communication, emotional connection, boundary creation, shared history, and genetic heritage—combine in a variety of ways to create different family types (Turner & West, 1998). The **nuclear family**—a wife, husband, and their biological or adopted children—is one type. Although nuclear families still exist, they represent the minority of families in the United States, and not all nuclear families have stay-at-home moms and working dads.

A **gay** or **lesbian family** consists of two people of the same sex governing a household and serving as parent figures for the biological or adopted children of at least one of them. Between 1.5 to 2 million lesbian and gay families currently live in the United States.

When relatives such as aunts, uncles, parents, children, and grandparents live together in a common household, the result is an **extended family.** By the year 2050, 100 million people in the United States will be over the age of 65, and many of these individuals will be sharing a household with relatives. Numerous Italian American, African American, and Asian American families fall into this category.

In an era in which more than 40 percent of marriages in this country are remarriages for one or both partners (Ganong & Coleman, 1994), the

blended family is a natural result. In this family type, a husband and wife parent at least one child who is not the biological offspring of both adults. Blended families often are called "stepfamilies" or "remarried" families. More than 50 percent of children born throughout the twenty-first century will grow up in blended families (Larson, 1992).

Some couples live together prior to marriage to "test" their compatibility. These **cohabiting couples** consist of two unmarried, romantically involved adults living together in a household, with or without children. In contrast, in a **single-parent family,** only one adult resides in the household, possessing sole responsibility as caregiver for the children.

Communication Patterns in Families

Regardless of the particular type of family you have, its members likely possess beliefs about how they should communicate and interact. These beliefs, and the resulting interpersonal communication, are known as **family communication patterns** (Fitzpatrick & Ritchie, 1994; Ritchie & Fitzpatrick, 1990). Family communication patterns evolve over time, as family members cocreate shared views of appropriate and meaningful family interaction (Koerner & Fitzpatrick, 2004). Family communication patterns arise from two underlying sets of beliefs (Koerner & Fitzpatrick, 1997, 2002, 2004). The first set of beliefs we call **conversation orientation:** the degree of fluidity with

SELF-REFLECTION

What type of family did you grow up with? What makes you collectively a family— the fact that you are biologically related, live in the same household, or share a strong emotional bond? Now think about other people's families. Are there groups that consider themselves families that you don't? If so, why?

SELF-REFLECTION

Does your family have rituals? What part does communication play in enacting these rituals? Which rituals mean the most to you, and why? How does the regular practice of these rituals affect how you feel about your family?

which family members converse and the breadth of topics they discuss. Families with a high conversation orientation communicate regularly with each other—sharing their innermost thoughts and feelings and debating a broad range of ideas and viewpoints. Such families view communication as the principal vehicle for maintaining family bonds.

Studies document that many high conversation families establish and practice *family rituals*—recurring and structured events that help solidify emotional bonds (Baxter & Clark, 1996). For example, shortly after the birth of each of our three sons, my wife and I wrote brief bedtime songs for them. Every night since then, we've sung these songs to each of them as we tuck them in. Despite our decidedly out-of-tune voices, this ritual is an expected part of our nightly routine ("Dad, can you come up and sing your song?"). Other examples of family rituals include sharing a weekly (or nightly) dinner, cooking together, telling bedtime stories, or gathering for a weekend "game night" in which family members play video, computer, or board games (Baxter & Clark, 1996).

In contrast, families with a low conversation orientation view interpersonal communication as something irrelevant and unnecessary for a satisfying, successful family life. Such families interact only infrequently and limit their conversations to a few select topics—weather, daily activities,

current events, and the like. Disclosure of intimate thoughts and feelings between family members is discouraged, as is debate of attitudes and perspectives.

The second set of beliefs that defines family communication patterns is **conformity orientation,** the degree to which families use communication to emphasize similarity or diversity in attitudes, beliefs, and values. High conformity families use their interactions to highlight and enforce uniformity of thought. Their goal is to maintain agreement and avoid any hint of dissent. Such families often are perceived by others as more "traditional," because children are expected to obey parents and other elders, who (in turn) are counted on to make family decisions. Members of these families tend to prioritize family relationships over outside connections such as friendships and romantic involvements. Moreover, they are expected to sacrifice their personal goals for the sake of the family.

Low conformity families communicate in ways that emphasize diversity in attitudes, beliefs, and values, and that encourage members' uniqueness, individuality, and independence. These families typically view outside relationships as equally important to those within the family, and they prioritize individual over family interests and goals. In low conformity families, children contribute to family decision making, and members view the family as a vehicle for individual growth rather than a collective in which members must sacrifice their own interests for the good of the whole.

As communication scholars Ascan Koerner and Mary Anne Fitzpatrick note, when one considers how families align with these two sets of beliefs, four possible family communication patterns emerge (1997, 2002, 2004). Families high in both conversation and conformity are **consensual families.** In such families, members are encouraged to openly share their views with one another as well as debate these beliefs. However, they are expected to steadfastly agree with one another and share a single viewpoint. Some parents in consensual families balance the tension between open communication and the expectation of strict adherence to one viewpoint by routinely encouraging their children to share their thoughts and feelings about important issues ("What do you think we should do?") and then making it clear that only one perspective (the parents') is acceptable. Because of their emphasis on conformity, consensual families perceive conflict as intensely threatening. Consequently, they address conflicts as they occur and seek to resolve them as constructively as possible to preserve family unity.

Families high in conversation but low in conformity are **pluralistic families.** They communicate in open and unconstrained ways, discussing a broad range of topics and exploring them in depth. Pluralistic families enjoy debating the issues of the day, and judge one another's arguments on their merit rather than whether they mesh with other members' attitudes. Because parents in pluralistic families don't feel compelled to wield power over their children, children's contributions to family discussions and decision making are treated as relevant and equally valid. For example, parents in a pluralistic family might ask for their children's opinions regarding a job opportunity ("Should Mom accept the offer from TelCo?") or a family vacation ("Where should we go this year?"), something unlikely to happen in consensual families. Pluralistic families deal directly with conflict, seeking to resolve disputes in productive, mutual-beneficial ways. For this reason, pluralistic family members report the highest rates of conflict resolution of any of these four family types.

Protective families are low on conversation and high on conformity. Parent-child power differences are firmly enforced, and children are expected to quietly obey. Sayings such as "Children should be seen and not heard" and "Children should speak when spoken to" reflect this mind-set. Parents invest little effort in creating opportunities for family discussion and rarely explain their decisions to children. Members of such families avoid conflict because it threatens the conformity they value and because they often lack the skills necessary to manage conflicts constructively.

Families low in both conversation and conformity are **laissez-faire families.** Few emotional bonds exist between their members. Their detachment shows itself in a lack of interaction and a decided disinterest in activities that might foster communication. Similar to parents in pluralistic families, laissez-faire parents believe that children should be independent thinkers and decision makers. But this belief derives from their disinterest in their children's thoughts and decisions. Such parents tend to leave it up to their children to form their own opinions regarding sexual behavior, drug and alcohol usage, and educational achievement. Because members of such families interact infrequently, they rarely get embroiled in conflict. If a disagreement does erupt, they avoid it or (if they feel strongly invested in the issues at stake) they compete to "win" the debate.

Maintaining Family Relationships

The first blizzard roared into De Smet, Dakota Territory, on October 13, 1880, catching residents unawares. In the aftermath, Laura Ingalls Wilder and her family abandoned their homestead, seeking shelter in a small store they owned in town (Wilder, 1940). The move put them nearer to the things critical for their survival: food, coal, and friends. But as the next blizzard descended, their proximity to the town became irrelevant. No one could

POP QUIZ

What Communication Pattern Does Your Family Have?

Place a check mark next to each statement that you agree with. Then read the instructions that follow for determining your family communication pattern.

Conversation Orientation

_____ In my family, we often talk about our plans and hopes for the future.

_____ We frequently talk as a family about the things we have done during the day.

_____ My parents tend to be very open about their emotions.

_____ I really enjoy talking with my parents, even when we disagree.

_____ My parents and I often have long, relaxed conversations about nothing in particular.

_____ In our family, we often discuss our feelings together.

_____ I can tell my parents almost anything.

_____ My parents often ask my opinion when the family is talking about something important.

_____ My parents frequently say things like, "Every member of this family should have some say in decisions."

Conformity Orientation

_____ When anything really important is involved, my parents expect me to obey without question.

_____ In our home, my parents usually have the last word.

_____ My parents feel that it is important that they be the boss.

_____ My parents sometimes become irritated when my views differ from theirs.

_____ If my parents don't approve of a particular behavior, they don't want to know about it.

_____ When I am at home, I am expected to obey my parents' rules.

_____ My parents often say things like, "My ideas are right, and you shouldn't question them."

_____ My parents often say things like, "There are some things that just shouldn't be talked about."

_____ My parents often say things like, "You'll know better when you're older."

Scoring

For each orientation, a total number of check marks of 0–4 indicates "Low" and a total of 5–9 indicates "High." High conversation/high conformity suggests that your family is consensual; high conversation/low conformity, pluralistic; low conversation/high conformity, protective; and low conversation/low conformity, laissez-faire.

Note: This *Pop Quiz* is adapted from the Revised Family Communication Pattern Instrument (Ritchie & Fitzpatrick, 1990).

venture outside without risking death as conditions worsened to zero visibility, −50-degree temperatures, and hurricane-force winds. The blizzards struck again and again until April, holding the entire town hostage. As the storms raged, the Ingalls family retreated to a single room, huddling around their wood stove. By the end of January, they had exhausted their coal and firewood reserves. They had to burn small bundles of hay instead, which they laboriously twisted by hand so the bundles would last longer in the fire. When their food ran out, Laura, her sisters, and her parents took turns grinding seed wheat they had stored for their spring crop. They used a hand-operated coffee grinder to make meal for bread. For weeks, the family of five survived by sharing one small loaf a day.

Although their physical survival was precarious, the Ingalls family maintained themselves emotionally by exchanging assurances of their love for one another, sharing stories of family experiences, and, more than anything else, preserving a positive perspective. For example, when Laura's father decided to brave the blizzard to check on their neighbors, Laura and her sisters—terrified that he would get lost in the storm—stood sobbing at the window. Their mother said, "Now girls, a storm outdoors is no reason for gloom in the house!" (1940, p. 127).

Laura Ingalls Wilder lived to publish the details of her family's ordeal in the book *The Long Winter* (1940). Shortly before her death in 1957, Wilder issued the following statement to her readers, which summarizes the philosophy that had ensured her family's survival (Anderson, 1988):

> Today our way of living and our schools are much different. But the real things haven't changed; they can never change. It is still best to be honest and truthful, to make the most of what we have, to be happy with simple pleasures, and to be cheerful and have courage when things go wrong. (p. 239)

As the story of *The Long Winter* reminds us, and our prior discussion of family definitions and family communication patterns illustrates, the heart of a family is not blood kinship or legal linkages. Rather, it's the quality of communication shared between people who think of themselves as family. And through improving your interpersonal communication skills, you can boost your chances of maintaining healthy and mutually satisfying family relationships.

Successful family communication is challenging, because family relationships have the longest life cycle of any of our interpersonal ties. Family members undergo major changes as they progress through their lives

(Vangelisti, 1993), and the behaviors needed to sustain the family connections must evolve as well (Weigel & Ballard-Reisch, 1999). In the section that follows, we present interpersonal communication practices you can embrace to foster and maintain positive relationships with others in your family—even as your family evolves over time. Specifically, people nurture healthy family bonds through maintaining positive, open, and committed relationships, balancing tensions, creating and sharing family stories, and constructively managing family conflict.

Maintenance Strategies for Families

Many people take their family relationships for granted. Instead of communicating in ways designed to maintain these relationships, people assume that "your family is always there for you" (Vogl-Bauer, 2003). As a consequence, we often treat our family members less favorably than we treat individuals who have no biological or legal connection to us (Vogl-Bauer, 2003). But in order for family relationships to be sustained, they—like all interpersonal involvements—need constant maintenance.

What communication strategies can you employ to forge healthier family relationships? In Chapter 10, you learned several strategies for maintaining romances. Three of these—positivity, openness, and assurances—appear to play an especially important role in nurturing family bonds as well (Vogl-Bauer, 2003). As demonstrated by the Ingalls family communication during the blizzards, *positivity* means communicating with your family members in an upbeat and hopeful fashion. To implement positivity in your family encounters, start doing favors for other family members without being asked, and unexpectedly gift them in little ways that display your caring and emotional support. Invest energy into making each encounter with family members enjoyable. Avoid complaining about family problems that have no solutions; ridiculing family members; and demanding that caregivers, siblings, or other kin give you favored treatment.

Openness in family relationships means behaving toward other family members in ways that are consistent, trustworthy, and ethical. Through openness, you send the signal that other family members can share their feelings and ideas with you without fear of betrayal. Additional ways to practice openness include making time in your schedule to talk with parents, siblings, or children about how they are doing; encouraging them to share their feelings and concerns with you; and offering your perspectives in a cooperative, respectful fashion. It also means avoiding communication practices that undermine family openness, such as betrayal of confidences, refusing to make time for family conversation, reacting defensively when family members share their feelings with you, disparaging family members' viewpoints, and keeping things hidden from your family.

Finally, you can further bolster your family relationships by offering regular *assurances* of how much your family means to you. Let other family members know that you consider your relationship with each of them unique and valuable, and that you are committed to maintaining these bonds well into the future. Use direct affirmation of your feelings ("I love you," "I will always be here for you") as well as indirect messages ("I miss

● Nurturing takes on different forms in different households.

● As in any relationship, conflict is an unavoidable part of family life.

SKILLS PRACTICE

This exercise helps you communicate positivity, openness, and assurances to your family.

❶ Think of a family member with whom you would like to strengthen your bond.

❷ Identify ways you might use positivity, such as surprising this person with a compliment or commending her or him for helping the family.

❸ List ideas for establishing openness—things you can say that will encourage this person to share her or his concerns and that will demonstrate that you're an empathic listener.

❹ Determine how you might use assurances to convey how important this family member is to you.

❺ For your next encounter develop a communication plan that incorporates the best of your ideas.

you" or "I can't wait to be home again so I can spend time with you"). Avoid devaluing family relationships in front of others ("They're *just* my family") and commenting on how other families are superior to yours ("I'd give anything to have other parents").

Remember that you can demonstrate positivity, openness, and assurances just as easily through e-mail, text-messaging, and phone calls as you can through face-to-face communication. Indeed, technology can play an integral role in enabling you to communicate with family members in ways that maintain close ties (Carlson, 1999). With comparatively little effort, you can go online and send your sister or father a virtual card ("Just wanted you to know I was thinking of you!"), text-message your uncle an assurance ("I love you and miss you"), or call your grandmother and offer a message of openness ("I'm always here if you need me"). Unlike face-to-face and phone communication, online communication lets you get in touch with family members at any time (Oravec, 2000).

Dealing with Family Tensions

Within all family relationships, ongoing tensions exist between competing impulses, known as relational dialectics (discussed in Chapter 2). Two dialectics are especially pronounced in families: *autonomy versus connection* and *openness versus protection*. As we establish our own personal and professional identities in the world, each of us must balance our desire for autonomy against the connection that we share with our families and the corresponding expectations and obligations that exist regarding who we "should" be as family members. We also are faced with frequent decisions regarding how openly we should communicate with other family members, as well as how much information about our families we should share with those outside the family unit. Balancing these tensions is challenging. However, you *can* strike a balance—by applying the techniques described below.

Balancing Autonomy and Connection

Even though you may feel intensely connected to your family, you probably also struggle to create your own separate identity. You may enjoy the feeling of intimacy that connectedness brings, while resenting how your family seems blind to your true abilities: "My family refuses to take me seriously because they see me as the family clown," or "My family doesn't respect my ability to make mature decisions because I'm the youngest."

The tension between autonomy and connection in families is especially difficult to manage during adolescence. As children move through their teen years, they begin to assert their independence from parents, and their peers gain influence with them—eventually replacing parents and other family members as the most important shapers of their interpersonal decisions (Golish, 2000). At the same time, if parents and children have forged close relationships before teens begin asserting their autonomy, young people are likely to once again view family as their primary source of social and emotional support when they reach their later teen years (Golish, 2000).

How can you best manage the tension between autonomy and connection in your family? Use three additional relationship maintenance strategies discussed in Chapter 10—sharing activities, sharing tasks, and cultivating social networks. But strike a balance between family relationships and outside involvements for each. Start with sharing activities. As you've seen, developing and implementing special family rituals can help give family members a shared sense of identity and closeness. But sharing such routines *only* with family members (Tuesday-morning coffee and conversation with your sister; Saturday racquetball with your father) can erode the sense of independence you need as an adult. To resolve this tension, establish routines and rituals with romantic partners, friends, and coworkers.

Similarly, balance your dependence on family members to help you carry out everyday tasks (chores, work, errands) with reliance on yourself and other people outside your family. Again, too much dependence on family members in helping you complete tasks—especially those you could accomplish on your own—can erode your self-reliance, self-confidence, and independence (Strauss, 2006).

Finally, examine your social network (including your family), and assess the degree to which family members constitute the closest people in your life. As with shared activities and tasks, a balance between family relationships and outside connections is ideal. If you have few or even no close ties with anyone outside of the family sphere, you may feel intensely dependent on your family and experience a corresponding loss of autonomy. Likewise, having no close ties to any family members can create a sense of independence so extreme that you feel little of that all-important emotional bond with your family.

Balancing Openness and Protection

Families also experience tension between *openness versus protection*. In any close relationship—family bonds included—we want both to share personal information and to protect ourselves from the possible negative consequences of such sharing. In families, the tension between these two needs is even more pronounced. For example, your family may be extremely close, and as a consequence almost anything that you tell one family member quickly becomes common knowledge. This creates a dilemma when you want to share something with only one family member. Do you disclose the information, knowing that within a week's time your entire family will also know it, or do you withhold it?

The balance between openness versus protection is typically defined through **family communication rules**—boundary conditions governing what family members can talk about, how they can discuss such topics, and who should have access to family-relevant information (Turner & West, 1998). In some families, members feel free to talk about any topic, at any time, and in any situation: trivial news about everyday events, weather, politics, television shows, music, religion, sports. In other families, discussion of more sensitive topics such as politics, religion, and international events may be permissible only in certain settings. To illustrate,

FOCUS ON CULTURE

Autonomy and Class: Helicopter Parents

Robyn Lewis home-schooled her sons, but now that they attend college it doesn't mean her involvement in their lives has lessened (ABCnews.go.com, 2005). She creates daily "to do" lists for each, checks their grades and bank accounts online, proofreads their papers, and screens their e-mail. "It's nice to have someone who serves as a secretary mom," says son Brendan. Robyn's response? "I think that's great—a secretary helps keep the boss focused and organized, right?"

In the United States, people have different views of how families should balance autonomy with connection, and these differences often cut along class lines. Middle- and upper-income parents (such as Lewis) are more inclined to view their role as cultivating their children's talents in a highly orchestrated fashion (Lareau, 2003). Organized activities, created and controlled by parents, dominate children's lives. In extreme form, children have little or no autonomy, as parents "hover" over all aspects of their lives like helicopters.

Lower-income parents, however, tend to view their role as allowing their children to mature without adult interference (Lareau, 2003). Children often have more independence in their leisure activities—free to roam their neighborhoods and play with friends, for example—as opposed to participating in scripted "play dates." And when they enter college or the work world, their parents continue to let them develop primarily on their own.

Public elementary and secondary schools in the United States strongly endorse intense connection between parents and children, and they structure their curricula and school-related activities accordingly (Lareau, 2003). But many believe that such intense connectedness does a disservice to children, especially as they mature (Strauss, 2006). For instance, Linda Walter, administrator at Seton Hall University, maintains that "many young adults entering college have the academic skills they need to succeed, but are lacking in self-reliance" (Strauss, 2006).

YOUR TURN

- To what degree did your parents or caregivers emphasize your connection to them as you grew up? How did they encourage your autonomy?

- How has your parents' or caregivers' approach to balancing autonomy and connection influenced their relationship with you now? Are they "helicopters"?

- What are the advantages and disadvantages of the way your parents or caregivers balanced your connection with them and your autonomy?

"I know. But I think I can change him"

your family might be able to talk about religion immediately after attending services together or to debate political issues over dinner, but not want to discuss such matters during breakfast, while watching a DVD, or on the golf course. Still other topics may be permanently excluded from your family discussion altogether: personal sexual history, assault, or abuse; severe legal or financial woes; or extreme health problems. Breaking a family communication rule by forcing discussion of a "forbidden" topic can cause intense emotional discomfort among other family members and may prompt the family to shun the "rule-breaker" (exclude him or her from future family interactions). Keep this in mind before you force discussion of an issue that other family members consider off-limits.

Family communication rules also govern *how* family members talk about topics—including what's considered an acceptable opinion and how deeply family members can explore these opinions. It may be acceptable to talk at any time about the personal lives of your various family members, for instance, but only if your comments are positive. Or it may be permissible to discuss religion after church but only if you espouse a certain viewpoint.

Finally, family communication rules identify the people with whom family members can talk. If your family holds a particular religious or political viewpoint that is at odds with surrounding neighbors' views, you might instruct your children to avoid these topics when conversing with their neighborhood friends. "This stays within the family," you might say, or "Don't talk about this at school." These kinds of rules may be quite fluid. If an outside person proves untrustworthy—he or she violates a confidence—family members may suddenly instruct one another to stop sharing personal information with that individual. Or during a family conflict, your brother might confide in you, then instruct you to "not tell Mom and Dad." After the conflict has been resolved, this same brother might tell you it's now OK for you to discuss the incident with your parents.

Although family communication rules help members know how to balance openness and protection, they also can amplify tension within families as people age. When children grow up, the parent-child relationship shifts from authority based to friendship based (Grotevant & Cooper, 1985). And as this shift occurs, people may feel pressure to change long-standing communication rules. For example, even if your family has never openly discussed severe parental illness, you may feel compelled to talk about this topic if your mother starts displaying early symptoms of Alzheimer's disease. A sibling who was sexually abused may have hidden this experience from family members for years, but after going through therapy, he may feel the need to disclose the incident to his family.

What can you do to improve your family communication rules and, in doing so, bring about a better balance of openness and protection? First, remember that all families identify both approved and taboo conversational topics, certain viewpoints that they want to espouse over others, and people whom they include in and exclude from receiving information about the family. Effective family communication rules aren't "one size fits all." Instead, they should strike the balance between openness and protection that best fits your family. Second, be respectful of the varying opinions and preferences individual family members have regarding openness and protection. Also, keep in mind that if your family communication pattern is low on conversation orientation and high on conformity orientation, any push for a change in communication rules may strike others as a threat to the family.

Finally, if you believe that communication rules should be altered to allow greater openness or increased protection, avoid abrupt, dramatic, and demanding calls for change—"We need to learn how to talk more openly about sex!" Such pronouncements will likely offend family members and put them on the defensive. Instead, identify a single family member who you think might share your views. Discuss your desire for change with him or her, using your competence skills (Chapter 5) and cooperative language (Chapter 7). Ask this person's opinion on the possibility of modifying your family's communication rules, and invite him or her to suggest ideas for implementing the change. If he or she agrees that change is needed, identify an additional family member who might also concur. Then initiate a three-way discussion. Changes in long-standing family communication rules—especially for low conversation, high conformity families—are best accomplished slowly through interactions with one family member at a time.

Sharing Family Stories

When I was growing up, my parents regaled my brother and me with stories of their time together at Pomona College in California. Many of these were funny, like the time my dad and his buddies filled a friend's dorm room from floor to ceiling with wadded-up newspaper while the friend was away for the weekend. But the most poignant was how my dad serenaded my mom from the courtyard of her dorm while she stood on her balcony listening. Forty-five years later, my parents and I visited Pomona. While driving around campus, Mom suddenly shouted "Stop!" and leapt from the car. Dad and I followed her into a well-worn building, only to find her standing in the very courtyard that I had heard described in so many family dinner conversations. Mom stood there, gazing at the balcony where she'd listened to Dad's song more than four decades earlier. "There it is," she whispered, "the spot where your father serenaded me," and her eyes filled with tears.

One of the most important forms of communication that helps maintain family relationships is **family stories,** narrative accounts shared repeatedly

SELF-REFLECTION

What communication rules has your family established for balancing openness versus protection? Given current circumstances in your family, how useful do you think these rules are? Do you think your family should change one or more rules? If so, how would you communicate the need for change to them?

within a family that retell historical events and are meant to bond the family together (Stone, 1988). Such stories provide a sense of shared family identity, establish the mores that govern family life, and provide family members with knowledge of family history that allows them to connect past family experiences with current ones (Stone, 1996).

Family stories take numerous forms. For example, some families (like mine) share *courtship stories* about how the parents fell in love. Courtship stories emphasize the solidity of the parents' relationship, which children find reassuring. But perhaps most important, such stories give children a framework for understanding romantic love. As author Elizabeth Stone (1988) suggests, courtship stories "offer at least one possible way to enter into this intricate dance; they suggest what to feel about love, how to recognize it, and what to do with it" (p. 74). Families also may share *birth stories,* in which members narrate the latter stages of pregnancy, childbirth, and early infancy of a child. Birth stories help children understand how they fit into the family ("You'll always be the baby"), which roles they're expected to play ("First-borns are always so independent!"), and what their parents hope and dream for them ("We knew from the moment you were born that you'd accomplish great things!").

Survival stories relate the coping strategies family members have used to deal with major challenges. Survival in these stories may be physical—as in the accounts that combat soldiers and famine victims tell. Or survival may refer to a family member's ability to prevail by achieving a level of financial stability or other form of success. Survival stories give children the sense that they come from a tough, persevering family, thus preparing them to successfully face their own difficulties in the future.

As is clear from this discussion, the breadth and depth of your family experiences provides you with a rich resource to share with family members in the form of stories, and the creation and telling of such stories can bolster your sense of family identity. But not all shared experiences are ones your family members would like to relive, so exercise caution in relating family stories. To ensure that family stories strengthen, rather than erode, family relationships, select experiences that cast the family and individual members in a positive light and that emphasize unity rather than discord. When sharing stories with children or younger siblings, nieces, and nephews, keep in mind that they will look to your story to provide lessons about values (Stone, 1996). Ask yourself whether the story you'd like to tell will send the message you intend about your family's values.

Stories that cast individual family members in a humorous light require special care. Although such stories may be perfectly appropriate to share, make sure that the "target" family member enjoys and agrees to the telling. For example, you might repeatedly revisit the time your brother brought home an exceptionally strange dating partner to meet the family or recount the day your father accidentally drove the car through the garage wall while miraculously avoiding injury. Avoid sharing stories that breach personal confidences ("John never told any of you what *really* happened, but here it is!") or that make sport of family members in ways they don't enjoy. When in doubt about the appropriateness of a story, simply ask your parent, sibling, or child whether he or she wants you to share the story. If the answer is "no," keep silent.

● Though totem poles serve many functions, one of the most interesting is that they tell stories about a clan's or tribe's history. The animals and designs carved into them symbolize events and the people who played a part in them.

Managing Family Conflict

Like any other human social unit, families experience all manner of conflict. Siblings disagree about whether an aging parent should be placed in a nursing home. Parents want to move the family to another state to take advantage of a great job offer, but the children don't want to leave their neighborhood and school friends. Mothers want their daughters to take over the family business, but the daughters want to pursue different careers. How families manage conflict can powerfully determine whether the relationships within the family grow stronger or begin to disintegrate. Different families deal with conflict in different ways. For example, in some families, yelling at each other until the family messily arrives at a solution is perfectly normal, whereas other families argue only in intense whispers behind closed doors. Regardless of stylistic differences, two things are certain. First, the lessons that we learn about managing conflict from our families will be mirrored in how we deal with conflict in our other interpersonal relationships as adults. Second, maintaining healthy family relationships depends on family members' ability to communicate with each other in ways that constructively manage conflict.

Families have distinct approaches for handling conflict (Wilmot & Hocker, 2001). **Avoidant families** pretend that family disagreements don't exist. When such incidents erupt (as they inevitably do), these families try to squelch further discussion of them without addressing the situation directly. Members may tell each other, "Don't make waves," "You don't want to cause trouble," "You better solve this thing on your own," or "Just walk away and forget about it." In some avoidant families, members rely on destructive indirect communication during times of conflict—including snide comments, sarcasm, sulking, and "the silent treatment."

In **aggressive families,** an attitude of "only the fittest will survive" dominates. Parents teach children to "never back down" and "hold your ground no matter what!" Family members view direct and forceful responses to conflict as an indication of strength. Such families also stress "honesty at all costs." They encourage sharing feelings and showing emotions, even if such sharing proves hurtful or destructive. In addition, aggressive families expect their members to clearly and forcefully articulate and strive to achieve their own desires, even if doing so proves costly to others.

The aggressive approach to managing family conflict can be risky. When a conflict between two family members escalates and is not resolved constructively, the damage spreads beyond the participants. For example, open conflict between husbands and wives in the proximity of their children, known as *interparental conflict*, can set children up for behavioral and emotional problems later. One study found that children growing up in households in which they observed frequent, intense, and negative interparental conflict were significantly more at risk for depression, anxiety, alcohol and substance abuse, and risky sexual behavior (Tschann et al., 2002). They also were substantially more likely to behave aggressively when faced with conflict themselves (Tschann et al., 2002).

Collaborative families also deal with conflict directly and encourage open expression of thoughts and feelings. However, their members temper this openness with concern for one another. If you're part of a collaborative

● In the movie *The Great Santini*, Robert Duvall plays pilot trainer Bull Meechum, a U.S. marine who treats his family with the same aggression as he treats his trainees.

family, for example, you would never receive praise for "telling off" another family member. Collaborative families often establish "official" times (such as mealtimes or family meetings) when members can vent their concerns. They encourage effective listening as well as open interaction between family members. And they view sulking and snide remarks as unacceptable.

A family's conflict approach gives its young members years of informal training regarding the "best" way to handle disputes and disagreements later in life. We each then apply that training in grappling with interpersonal clashes as adults. We also hand these lessons down to our own children. We thus perpetuate both the advantages and disadvantages of the style we've learned.

Inheriting your family's conflict style can also pose challenges in your romantic relationships—in particular, when two partners or spouses come from families with very different styles. For example, suppose your romantic partner grew up in an avoidant family and you grew up in a collaborative family. In this case, painful dynamics may arise as you seek to raise and discuss concerns while your partner steadfastly refuses to respond. And if you have children, they learn confusing and contradictory messages that provide little guidance for how *they* should best manage conflict: Do I avoid and suppress conflict, like Mom? Or do I cooperatively engage it, like Dad?

How can you improve the way in which you manage family conflict? Approach conflicts collaboratively, just as you would do in other interpersonal clashes. Specifically, openly discuss the incompatibility of goals or the competition for resources that has sparked the disagreement. Keep the conversation focused on this source of the trouble, not the character or worth of the individuals involved. Ask the other family member to share his or her view of the situation, and express empathy in response. Be respectful and kind in your communication, avoiding any form of personal attack. In family conflicts, hurling kitchen-sink messages (negative comments that have nothing to do with the current conflict) at the other person becomes especially tempting since you possess a lifetime of knowledge about him or her. Resist this urge, instead keeping the conversation focused on solutions and taking a flexible stance toward the various solutions you and the other person are exploring. Once you've come up with several possible solutions, combine the best parts of them to develop a final one. Evaluate it in terms of its fairness for you, the other person, and additional individuals who might be affected (other immediate family members, relatives, or friends).

Defining Friendship

The movie *Boyz in the Hood* (Singleton & Nicolaides, 1991) launched the career of then 23-year-old writer and director John Singleton, who received two Oscar nominations and won the New York Film Critics Circle Award for Best New Director. The movie depicts the struggle of African American families in south-central Los Angeles to raise their children and maintain healthy family relationships amid gang violence and drug abuse. But at the core of the story is a tale of friendship among three very different boys—Tre, the bright and pacifistic central character, whose father inspires in him a fierce ambition; his best friend Ricky, a talented running back who dreams only of

SELF-REFLECTION

What conflict management approach does your family use—avoidant, aggressive, or collaborative? What are the advantages and disadvantages of that approach? If you would like your family to change its conflict management approach, which family member would you talk to first about this? What might you say?

SKILLS PRACTICE

This exercise helps you to better manage conflict with a family member.

❶ Think about a conflict you're currently experiencing with a family member.

❷ Identify the aspects of collaborative conflict management that you find *most* difficult to apply when communicating with this person. Consider things such as expressing your appreciation for him or her, stressing shared goals, inviting his or her perspective on the conflict, and offering your viewpoints in nonattacking ways.

❸ Think of ways in which you can more effectively integrate these aspects of the collaborative approach into your communication.

❹ Use these ideas during your next encounter with him or her.

playing ball; and Doughboy, Ricky's half brother, an intellectual hedonist who ponders the nature of God while drinking, selling drugs, and dodging drive-by shootings. The friendship of the three endures for years, until Ricky is killed following a dispute with a gang member. In the aftermath, Doughboy and Tre discuss Ricky's death and validate the meaning of their friendship:[2]

> **DOUGHBOY:** I turned on the TV this morning, and they had this show on about living in a violent world. Showed all of these foreign places. I started thinking, either they don't know, they don't show, or they don't care about what's going on in the 'hood. They had all this foreign stuff, but didn't have anything on my brother. I ain't *got* no brother.
>
> **TRE:** Hey Dough...
>
> **DOUGHBOY:** What's up?
>
> **TRE:** You still got one brother left, man.

Like family and romantic bonds, friendships play a crucial role in our lives. They also constitute the most prevalent type of relationship we experience (Blieszner & Adams, 1992). Some friendships endure for decades, during which the friends involved become family, like Doughboy and Tre. Others are formed for convenience, such as the coworker with whom you regularly exchange e-mails while you're both working on a marketing campaign. But all **friendships**—whether casual or close, short- or long-term—are voluntary interpersonal relationships in which the people involved like each other and enjoy each other's company (Fehr, 1996, 2000).

This definition highlights three central aspects of friendships. First, friendships are voluntary. They differ from family relationships because you select your friends. And because friendships are voluntary, the participants must negotiate and maintain the boundaries that define the specific nature of the relationship as it develops (Dainton, Zelley, & Langan, 2003). Second, friendships are rooted in liking. Most of us feel affection and respect for our friends (Rubin, 1973). This liking is fostered through similarity in interests and activities, and through the sharing of self-disclosure that allows friends to build a sense of connection and mutual interdependence. Finally, friendships are enjoyable. Across studies, pleasure in each other's company emerges as the central defining feature of friendships (Hays, 1988).

Friendships differ from other types of interpersonal relationships in several ways. They are easier to break off than are romantic or kin relationships (Fehr, 1996). We're not as emotionally attached to our friends as we are to other intimates, and we're not as emotionally demanding of them. Correspondingly, we're expected to be more loyal to and more willing to help romantic partners and family members than friends (Davis & Todd, 1985). Friends also are less likely than family and romantic partners to share open, public expressions of affection, and they usually spend less of their free time together than do romantic partners (Brehm, Miller, Perlman, & Campbell, 2002). And one of the biggest differences between friendships and family relationships is that friendships tend to be power balanced, whereas many, and perhaps most, family relationships are power imbalanced (parents have power over children; older siblings have power over younger siblings) (Maeda & Ritchie, 2003).

---

[2] Adapted from Singleton and Nicolaides (1991).

"You have the privilege of selecting your friends."

The importance we attribute to our friendships changes throughout our lives. Up through the fourth grade, most children look to their family as their sole source of emotional support (Furman & Simon, 1998). If a child suffers a disappointment at school, has a frightening dream, or just wants to share the events of the day, he or she will turn to family. By the seventh grade, however, young people rely just as much on same-sex friends as they do on family for such support. And by tenth grade, same-sex friends have become the primary providers of emotional support.

This trend reverses in middle adulthood. When people form long-term romantic commitments, their partners become the primary providers of companionship, affection, and support and the importance of friendships begins to wane (Carbery & Buhrmester, 1998). This is especially the case for married men, who before marriage tend to spend most of their time with male friends (Cohen, 1992).

People from different cultures have varied expectations regarding friendships. For example, most Americans believe that friendships don't endure, that you'll naturally lose some friends and gain others over time (Berscheid & Regan, 2005). This belief contrasts sharply with attitudes in other cultures, in which people view friendships as deeply intimate and lasting. As just one example, when asked to identify the closest relationship in their lives, Euro-Americans tend to select romantic partners, whereas Japanese tend to select friendships (Gudykunst & Nishida, 1993).

The Different Forms of Friendship

Like families, friendships take different forms. Yet they all help us to fulfill two primary interpersonal needs: companionship (chances to do fun things together and receive emotional support) and the achievement of practical goals (friends help us deal with problems or everyday tasks) (de Vries, 1996). These needs are not mutually exclusive; many friendships satisfy both.

One of the most important purposes friendships fulfill is enabling people to share life events and activities with others. Compared to family and work relationships, friendship interactions are the least task oriented and tend to revolve around leisure activities such as talking or eating (Argyle & Furnham, 1982). Scholar William Rawlins (1992) describes friendships that focus primarily on sharing time and activities together as **communal friendships.** Communal friends try to get together as often as possible, and they provide encouragement and emotional support to one another during times of need. Importantly, because emotional support is a central aspect of communal friendship, only when both friends fulfill the expectations of support for the relationship does the friendship endure (Burleson & Samter, 1994).

As with other interpersonal relationships, communication technologies such as cell phones, e-mail, and text-messaging have reshaped the way people conduct communal friendships. Thanks to such technologies, you can form such friendships more quickly and with more people than ever before. In the past, people forged communal friendships slowly. They took time to discover the values and interests of their neighbors, coworkers, and acquaintances, and only then began communal friendships with those who shared their values and interests. On the Web, however, people can form virtual

communal friendships very rapidly with a wide range of people whom they may never actually meet face-to-face (Rheingold, 1993).

Moreover, communication technologies have made it possible for communal friends to stay constantly connected with each other. Gone are the days of sitting at home by the phone waiting for a call or watching for a letter to arrive in the mail. For better or worse, you can now e-mail or text-message your friends 24/7 to exchange the latest news in your lives.

We also look to friends for help in achieving practical goals in both our personal and our professional lives. Friends help us study for exams, fix cars, set up computers, and complete professional projects. Friendships in which the parties focus primarily on helping each other achieve practical goals are known as **agentic friendships** (Rawlins, 1992). Agentic friends value sharing time together—but only if they're available and have no other priorities to handle at the moment. They also aren't interested in the emotional interdependence and mutual sharing of personal information that characterize communal friendships. They're available when the need arises, but beyond that, they're uncomfortable with more personal demands or

SELF-REFLECTION

How do you decide whether a potential new friend will be communal, agentic, or both? Do you have more communal friends or agentic? How do you communicate differently with the two types of friends? Which type of friend do you depend on most, day to day? Why?

POP QUIZ

What Kind of Friend Are You?

Think about how you communicate with, relate to, and behave toward your friends. Then check the statements with which you agree and total the number you have marked. Check your score at the bottom.

_____ I strive to always maintain equal give and take in my friendship relationships.

_____ I'm the kind of person my friends can talk with about anything and feel relaxed around.

_____ I think like my friends do and share a similar sense of humor with them.

_____ I don't hold my friends' mistakes against them.

_____ I can be trusted by my friends to keep a secret.

_____ I'm honest with my friends; I don't lie or hold things back.

_____ I can be serious with my friends, and I don't make fun of them when they want to talk about difficult issues.

_____ I'm considerate about my friends' feelings, and I don't do spiteful things.

_____ I can take care of myself, and I have my own ideals and beliefs apart from my friends'.

_____ I respect my friends' needs for privacy.

_____ I encourage my friends when they're up, and I cheer them up when they're down.

_____ I'm generous toward my friends and not self-centered.

_____ I'm fun to be around when I'm with my friends.

_____ I have an upbeat personality and stress the positive side of things when communicating with my friends.

_____ I always keep my promises to friends.

Scoring

These characteristics represent the qualities people associate with close, trustworthy, and dependable friends. If you scored 11–15, you are exceptionally high on these qualities; 6–10, average; 0–5, low.

Note: This _Pop Quiz_ is adapted from Maeda and Ritchie (2003).

● Shakers were a strict Christian sect who proliferated in the mid-nineteenth century. They believed literally in the separation of the sexes, dividing their houses so that men and women had different doors and lived on opposite sides of their communal houses. In contexts such as these, friendship between men and women was improbable.

responsibilities. For example, an agentic friend from work may gladly help you write up a monthly sales report, but she may feel uncomfortable if you ask her for advice about your romantic problems.

Gender and Friendships

In the United States, friendships between women often are stereotyped as communal, whereas friendships between men are presumed to be agentic. Women's friendships supposedly focus only on the joy of companionship, while men's friendships reputedly focus exclusively on accomplishing practical tasks. But male and female same-gender friendships are more similar than they are different (Winstead, Derlaga, & Rose, 1997). Men and women rate the importance of both kinds of friendships equally (Roy, Benenson, & Lilly, 2000), and studies of male friendships in North America have found that companionship is the primary need met by the relationship (Wellman, 1992).

At the same time, Euro-American men, unlike women, learn to avoid direct expressions of affection and intimacy in their friendships with other males. Owing to homophobia, traditional masculine gender roles, and a general reluctance to openly show emotion (among other factors), many American men avoid verbal and nonverbal intimacy in their same-gender friendships, such as disclosing personal feelings and vulnerabilities, touching, and hugging (Bank & Hansford, 2000). But in many other cultures, both men and women look to same-gender friends as their primary source of intimacy. For example, in southern Spain, men and women report feeling more comfortable revealing their deepest thoughts to same-gender friends than to spouses (Brandes, 1987). And traditional Javanese culture holds that marriage should not be too intimate and that a person's most intimate relationship should be with his or her same-gender friends (Williams, 1992).

One of the most radical shifts in relationship patterns over the last few decades has come with the increase in platonic (nonsexual) friendships between men and women in the United States. In the nineteenth century, friendships were almost exclusively same gender, and as recently as the 1970s, cross-gender friendships were still a rarity (Smith-Rosenberg, 1985).

A study of friendship conducted in 1974 found that, on average, men and women had few or no close cross-gender friends (Booth & Hess, 1974). However, by the mid-1980s, 40 percent of men and 30 percent of women reported having close cross-gender friendships (Rubin, 1985). And by the late 1990s, 47 percent of tenth- and twelfth-graders reported having a close friend of the opposite gender (Kuttler, LaGreca, & Prinstein, 1999).

Most cross-gender friendships are not motivated by sexual attraction. One study of such friendships found that 70 percent of men reported motives other than sexual as the basis for their friendships with women (Messman, Canary, & Hause, 1994). A significant number of men and women don't even think about a sexual relationship with their friends. Instead, as researchers Dan Canary and Tara Emmers-Sommer (1997) note, men as well as women "much more commonly value the rewards, supportiveness, and security provided by their friends in lieu of sexual interests" (p. 63).

Despite changing attitudes toward cross-gender friendships, men and women face several challenges in building such relationships (O'Meara, 1989). For one thing, they've learned from early childhood to segregate themselves by gender. In most schools, young boys and girls are placed in separate gym classes, asked to line up separately for class, and instructed to engage in competitions pitting "the boys against the girls" (Thorne, 1986). It's no surprise, then, that young children overwhelmingly prefer friends of the same gender (Reeder, 2003). But as a consequence of this early-life gender segregation, most children enter their teens with only limited experience in building cross-gender friendships. And neither adolescence nor adulthood provides many opportunities for gaining this experience. Think about it: older youth and adult leisure-oriented activities such as competitive sports, community programs, and social organizations (including the Boy Scouts and Girl Scouts) typically are gender segregated (Swain, 1992).

As another challenge, contemporary American society promotes only same-gender friendship and cross-gender coupling as the two most acceptable

relationship options between men and women. So no matter how rigorously a pair of cross-gender friends insists that they're "just friends," their surrounding friends and family members will likely meet these claims with skepticism or even disapproval (Swain, 1992). Many cross-gender friends are subjected to repeated inquiries from important individuals in their lives regarding the true nature of their relationship (Monsour, 1996): "Oh, come on! You expect me to believe that you haven't slept together?" Family members, if they approve of the friendship, often pester such couples to become romantically involved: "You and Pete have so much in common! Why not take things to the next level?" If families disapprove, they encourage termination of the relationship: "I don't want people thinking my daughter is hanging out casually with some guy. Why don't you hang out with other girls instead?" Romantic partners of people involved in cross-gender friendships often vehemently disapprove of such involvements, as both men and women expect their romantic partners to abandon cross-gender friends once they've formed a romantic attachment (Hansen, 1985). Owing to constant disapproval from others and the pressure to justify the relationship, cross-gender friendships are far less stable than same-gender friendships (Berscheid & Regan, 2005).

Friends with Benefits

In the *Seinfeld* episode "The Deal," Jerry and Elaine negotiate a relationship that combines their good friendship with sexual activity (David & Cherones, 1991). As Elaine says, "We just want to take *this* and add *that*." Hoping to forestall problems, they create a set of rules to guide them, including "no phone calls the day after" and "sleeping overnight afterwards is optional." However, the deal quickly sours as they develop expectations that clash with the rules they've established. As their friend George comments, "Where are you living? Are you here? Are you on this planet? It's impossible! It can't be done! Thousands of years, people have been trying to have their cake and eat it too. So all of a sudden the two of you are going to come along and do it. Where do you get the ego!?"

As this *Seinfeld* episode illustrates, sexual attraction does arise between friends. One study found that 87 percent of college women and 93 percent of men reported feeling sexually attracted to a friend at some point in their lives (Asada, Morrison, Hughes, & Fitzpatrick, 2003). Like Jerry and Elaine, some friends deal with sexual attraction by forming a "friends-with-benefits" (FWB) relationship. In **FWB relationships,** the participants engage in sexual activity but not with the purpose of transforming the relationship into a romantic attachment (Hughes, Morrison, & Asada, 2005). FWB relationships appear to be widespread. Studies suggest that around 50 percent of college students have had such a relationship (Afifi & Faulkner, 2000; Mongeau, Ramirez, & Vorrell, 2003).

Those who form FWB relationships do so for two reasons: they welcome the lack of commitment (and all its attendant sacrifices), and they want to satisfy sexual needs (Asada et al., 2003). Both men and women cite these same reasons, contradicting stereotypes that women seek only emotional satisfaction in relationships while men want only sex.

Most partners in an FWB relationship also develop clear rules regarding emotional attachment, communication, and sex in their relationship (Hughes et al., 2005). For example, they commonly strike an agreement not to fall in love. And they establish rules governing the frequency of phone calling, e-mailing, and text-messaging and sex rules regarding safer sex practices, frequency of sex, and sexual exclusivity. But despite these rules, the majority of FWB relationships fail eventually, costing the participants their original friendship as well as the sexual arrangement. What explains this high failure rate? Participants tend to develop romantic feelings despite their best efforts to avoid them, and many decide that the relationship doesn't satisfy them enough emotionally (Hughes et al., 2005).

Maintaining Friendship Relationships

Whether your friendship is communal or agentic (or both), cross-gender or same-gender, "with benefits" or without, the relationship will endure only if you communicate in ways that maintain it. But doing so is hard work. Without the formal ties of blood kinship or marriage to keep them together, friends must constantly cocreate their own relationship definitions and boundaries and determine how best they are maintained.

What specific things do friends do to keep their relationships healthy? Friendships that endure implement maintenance strategies to foster their bond, abide by friendship rules that govern their communication and treatment of each other, and avail themselves of online technologies when their relationship becomes separated by geographic distance.

Maintenance Strategies for Friends

The first strategy friends employ to maintain their relationships is sharing activities: structuring their schedules so that time is provided to share hobbies, interests, and leisure activities. Indeed, many scholars consider sharing

SELF-REFLECTION

Are you currently involved in an FWB relationship? If so, what are its pros and cons? Have you and your friend established rules for the relationship? If so, what are they? And to what degree do you both follow those rules? What path do you expect the relationship to take in the future?

activities *the* most important strategy because friendships (as noted earlier) are largely defined by the partners' enjoyment of each other's company (Fehr, 1996; Messman, Canary, & Hause, 2000). But even more important than the actual sharing of activities is the perception that each friend is willing to make time for the other. Scholar William Rawlins notes that even friends who don't spend much time together can still maintain a satisfying connection as long as each perceives the other as "being there" when needed (Rawlins, 1994).

Of course, most of us have more than one friend simultaneously yet only finite amounts of time available to devote to each. Consequently, we often are put in positions where we have to choose between time and activities shared with one friend versus another. For example, say that two of your closest friends each get tickets to different events for the same night, and they both want to share the evening with you. Whom do you choose, and how do you communicate your decision to the friend not selected? Unfortunately, given the significance that sharing time and activities together plays in defining friendships, your decisions regarding whom you invest your time with will often be perceived by friends as communicating depth of loyalty (Baxter et al., 1997). And in cases where you choose one friend over another, the friend-not-chosen may view your decision as disloyal. To forestall this, draw on your interpersonal communication skills. Express gratitude for the friend's offer, assure him or her that you very much value the relationship, and make concrete plans for getting together another time. For example, "Hey, thanks so much! I would have loved to see the game with you, but I've been trying for months now to check out the new museum exhibit. Want to go to next week's game?"

A second strategy that is essential for friendship maintenance is openness. Openness is important for casual, close, and best friendships, as all friendships are created and maintained through self-disclosure and the discussion of daily life events (Dainton et al., 2003).

Openness in friendships differs little from openness in family and romantic relationships; it means communicating toward your friends in ways that are predictable, trustworthy, and ethical. To foster openness with your friends, routinely make time just to talk—encouraging them to share their thoughts and feelings about various issues, whether online or face-to-face. Equally important, avoid betraying friends—that is, sharing with others personal information they've disclosed to you.

But as with family relationships, balance openness with protection (Dainton et al., 2003). Over time, most friends learn that communication about certain issues, topics, or even people is best avoided in order to protect the relationship and preclude conflict. As a result, friends negotiate communicative boundaries that allow their time together and communication shared to remain positive. Such boundaries can be perfectly healthy as long as both friends agree on them and the issues being avoided aren't central to the survival of the friendship. For example, several years ago a male friend of mine began dating a partner who I thought treated him badly. His boyfriend, whom I'll call "Mike," had a very negative outlook, constantly complained about my friend, and belittled him and their relationship in public. I thought Mike's communication was unethical and borderline abusive. But whenever I expressed my concern, my buddy grew defensive.

SELF-REFLECTION

Think of a good friend. Which conversational topics have you and your friend agreed will be off-limits because discussing them could threaten your bond? Has this avoidance of sensitive subjects helped you maintain the friendship, or has it created too much distance between you?

Mike just had an "edge" to his personality, my friend said, and I "didn't know the real Mike." After several such arguments, we agreed that, for the sake of our friendship, the topic of Mike was off-limits. We both respected this agreement—thereby protecting our friendship—until my friend broke up with Mike. After that, we opened the topic once more to free and detailed discussion.

Abiding by Friendship Rules

Friends can also maintain their relationships through abiding by **friendship rules**—general principles that prescribe appropriate communication and behavior within friendship relationships (Argyle & Henderson, 1984). In an extensive study of friendship maintenance, social psychologists Michael Argyle and Monica Henderson observed 10 friendship rules that people seem to share across cultures. Specifically, adults surveyed in Britain, Italy, Hong Kong, and Japan endorsed these rules, and people from each of these countries described failed friendships as ones that didn't follow them.

1. *Show support.* This rule highlights both the agentic and the communal sides of successful friendships. Within a friendship relationship, you should provide emotional support and offer assistance in times of need, without having to be asked (Burleson & Samter, 1994).

2. *Seek support.* The flip side of the first rule, when you're in a friendship, you should not only deliver support but *seek* support and counsel when needed, disclosing your emotional burdens to your friends. Other than sharing time and activities, mutual self-disclosure serves as the glue that binds friendships together (Dainton et al., 2003).

3. *Respect privacy.* At the same time friends anticipate both support and disclosure, they also recognize that friendships have more restrictive boundaries for sharing personal information than do romantic or family relationships. Recognize this, and avoid pushing your friend to share information that he or she considers too personal and resist sharing information about yourself that's intensely private or irrelevant to your friendship.

4. *Keep confidences.* A critical feature of enduring friendships is trust. When friends share personal information with you, do not betray their confidence by sharing it with others.

5. *Defend your friends.* Part of successful friendships is the feeling that your friends "have your back," so to speak. Likewise, your friends count on you to stand up for them, so defend them in situations where they are being attacked either to their face or behind their back.

6. *Avoid public criticism.* Friends may disagree or even disapprove of each other's behavior on occasion. But airing your grievances publicly in a way that makes your friends look bad will only hurt your friendship. Avoid communication such as questioning a friend's loyalty in front of other friends or commenting on a friend's weight in front of a salesperson.

7. *Make your friends happy.* An essential ingredient to successful friendships is striving to make your friends feel good while you're in their

company. You can do this by communicating with them in a cheerful and optimistic fashion, doing unsolicited favors for them, and buying or making gifts for them.

8. *Manage jealousy*. Unlike long-term romantic relationships, most friendships aren't exclusive. Your close friends likely will have other close friends, perhaps even friends who are more intimate than you. This situation can raise the specter of jealousy. Accept that each of your friends has other good friends as well, and constructively manage any jealousy that arises in you.

9. *Share humor*. Successful friends spend a good deal of their time joking with and teasing each other in affectionate ways. Enjoying a similar sense of humor is an essential aspect of most long-term friendships.

10. *Maintain equity*. In enduring, mutually satisfying friendships, the two people give and get in roughly equitable proportions (Canary & Zelley, 2000; Dainton et al., 2003). Help maintain this equity by conscientiously repaying debts, returning favors, and keeping the exchange of gifts and compliments balanced.

Maintaining Long-Distance Friendships

One of the most intense challenges friends face comes with geographic separation. Upwards of 90 percent of people report having at least one long-distance friendship, and 80 percent report having a close friend who lives far away (Rohlfing, 1990, 1995). Physical separation prevents both communal and agentic friends from adequately satisfying the needs that form the foundation of their relationship. Not surprisingly, geographic separation is the most frequently cited reason for deterioration of friendships (Rohlfing, 1995). This deterioration stems largely from the increased financial burden and logistical difficulty in maintaining the relationship (Aylor, 2003).

Although most friends begin long-distance separations with the intention of seeing each other regularly, they rarely visit solely for the sake of reuniting. Instead, they tend to see each other only when there's some other reason for them to be in the same area. When asked why this is the case, long-distance friends typically report that they don't have the money or time to travel only to visit a friend (Rohlfing, 1995). And when they do visit, these meetings often leave friends feeling empty because their time is divided between other commitments that allow them to reunite (professional conferences; visits with relatives) but don't allow them to spend much time alone together.

Which friendships tend to survive geographic distance, and which lapse? Research suggests that those friendships that survive differ in distinctive ways from those that disintegrate (Rohlfing, 1995). In friendships that survive geographic separation, the two people feel a particularly strong *liking*—that is, affection and respect—for each other. Friendships between individuals who "enjoy knowing each other" and "have great admiration for each other" are most likely to endure.

Friends who overcome separation also accept change as a natural part of life and their relationship. If you get together with a good friend you haven't seen in a long while, you both will likely have changed in terms of profession, attitudes, and appearance. Friends who are comfortable with such changes tend to survive, and friends who want their friend to "always stay the same" don't.

SELF-REFLECTION

Consider the 10 universal rules that successful friends follow. Which of these rules do you abide by in your own friendships? Which do you neglect? How has neglecting some of these rules affected your friendships? If your friendships have suffered, what steps might you take to better follow rules you've previously neglected?

Moreover, friends who survive separation have a strong sense of shared history. In their conversations, they frequently celebrate the past as well as anticipate sharing events in the future. This sense of shared past, present, and future enables them to "pick up where they left off" after being out of touch for a while. Successful long-distance friends thus feel a sense of relationship continuity. Despite the passage of days, weeks, months, and even years without contact, they both perceive their relationship as solid and ongoing.

How can you communicate in ways that foster these qualities in your own long-distance friendships? Use technologies such as cell phones, online chatrooms, e-mail, and text-messaging to regularly communicate with your friends. Focus this communication on activities and interests that you share. Doing this alleviates the feeling of loss that comes with the inability to actually spend time together (Rabby, 1997). It also helps you to "pick up where you left off" when you eventually get together in person again. So, for example, if a friend who now lives far away used to be your daily workout or jogging buddy, send her regular e-mails updating her on your marathon training and inquiring about her performance in local races.

Also use communication technologies to remind your long-distance friends that you still think of them with affection and hold them in high regard. Keep in mind that friendships are rooted in both self-disclosure and liking, so look for opportunities to appropriately express your feelings for your friend. For example, "I miss our Thursday night movie-watching! Have you seen any good films lately?"

In addition, devote some of your communication to fondly recounting events and experiences you have shared in your past, as well as discussing plans for the future. Such exchanges bolster the sense of relational continuity critical to maintaining friendships. To illustrate, "Remember that time we were playing that gig and suddenly the power went out? That was hilarious. Maybe when you're in town again, you can come over and jam with my new band."

Finally, when your long-distance friends go through dramatic life changes—as they inevitably will—use communication technologies to show your support for such changes, even if doing so is painful for you. For instance, a close friend you haven't seen in a while may abandon previously shared religious beliefs, adopt new political viewpoints, or undergo cosmetic surgery that substantially alters his or her looks. In making these and other kinds of significant changes, your friend may look to you for acceptance

SKILLS PRACTICE

This exercise helps you maintain long-distance friendships through online communication.

1 Think of a good friend who lives far away.

2 In your online interactions, focus your message content on interests you share in common, making sure to ask about your friend's continued participation in these things.

3 Send text messages letting your friend know you're thinking of and missing her or him.

4 Craft e-mails that have no purpose other than to fondly recap experiences you've shared in the past.

5 Forward to your friend Web links with ideas for future activities you can share together.

6 When your friend discloses major life changes that she or he is excited about, provide support in the quickest fashion possible, whether by text message, e-mail, phone call, or all three.

Making Relationship Choices

Choosing between Family and Friends

BACKGROUND

If you're like most people, family relationships and friendships form the foundation of your interpersonal life. But when family and friends place competing demands on you, choosing which relationships to honor and how best to communicate your decision is difficult. To see how you would manage such a situation, read the case study and work through the five steps that follow.

1

2

CASE STUDY

You're nearing the end of your last semester in college. Over the last couple of years, you've had four best friends: Jennifer, Colin, Tamika, and Josh. The five of you are really close, and despite a couple of failed "friends-with-benefits" flings, you've all been able to maintain your bond. The Saturday before graduation, Jen calls you up and invites you over. She's acting kind of weird on the phone, so you know something's up.

When you arrive, your friends are all there, waiting for you and looking serious. Jen says, "We've been wanting to talk with you about something for a long time now." You start getting worried, but then she says, "You know how you've always dreamed of a postgraduation tour of Europe but never thought you could afford it? Well, we bought tickets for you; we're all going!" You stand there, stunned. This is something you and your friends only talked about, but you never thought it would actually happen. Yet these generous buddies, who all come from families more affluent than yours, have purchased your airfare as a gift to you. "Come on," says Josh, "you know none of us would have passed Chemistry without your help!" Although you feel somewhat guilty about accepting, you

do—and the five of you begin excitedly discussing plans to depart for London on July 1.

That night, you call your folks to share the good news. Your mother says, "That's fantastic, dear, just as long as you're home for the Fourth of July." When you ask why, your mom tells you that your family is having a huge reunion on the Fourth and that you have to be there. When you tell your mom about the trip dates, she says, "You'll just have to cancel or reschedule. Your duty first and foremost is to your family. This reunion is more important than some trip your friends have cooked up. We expect you to be here!"

You text Jen, and a few minutes later, your cell phone rings. When you tell her about what's happening, she says, "Look, you're always doing everything your family says, right? You got good grades, you chose the right major, and you've even got a job lined up. It's time you did something for yourself. You can see your family anytime. Besides, we already bought your tickets and they're nonrefundable, so it's a done deal. The whole idea of the trip was for us to treat you. Don't you bail on us! If you do, we will *never* forgive you!"

YOUR TURN

While working through the following steps, keep in mind the concepts, skills, and insights you've learned so far in this book, especially this chapter. Also remember: there are no right answers, so think hard about the choice you make! (P.S. Need help? Review the concepts listed below.)

● **Step 1: Reflect on yourself.** What are your thoughts and feelings in this situation, regarding both your friends and your family? What attributions are you making about your family and friends? Are your attributions accurate? Why or why not?

● **Step 2: Reflect on your family and friends.** Using perspective-taking, put yourself in both your family's and your friends' shoes. Consider how they're thinking and feeling. Is one of them right in this situation and the other wrong? Are both of their views valid?

● **Step 3: Identify the optimal outcome.** Think about what's happening now in this situation and what's going to happen. Consider your own feelings as well as those of your family and friends. Given all these factors, what's the best, most constructive relationship outcome possible here? Be sure to consider not just what's best for *you* but what's best for everyone else.

● **Step 4: Locate the roadblocks.** Taking into consideration your own thoughts and feelings, those of your friends and family, and all that has happened in this situation, what factors are keeping you from achieving the optimal outcome you identified in step 3?

● **Step 5: Chart your course.** What will you say to overcome the roadblocks and achieve your optimal relationship outcome?

and support, as a *friend*. A good long-distance friend of mine, Vikram, occupied a job for several years that required a fair degree of professional contact with me, allowing us the opportunity (and excuse) to communicate regularly. Then he accepted a new position with a different company. This new opportunity represented a dramatic professional advancement for him, but it also meant we would have far fewer opportunities to interact once he started the new job. When he broke the news to me, he expected a certain degree of rancor on my part. Instead, I surprised him by expressing my firm support and excitement regarding his decision, even though I knew that, owing to this change, our paths wouldn't cross nearly as often.

The Primacy of Family and Friends

As with romantic relationships, the day-to-day work of maintaining family bonds and friendships isn't especially glamorous. Fate may choose your family, leaving you to select your friends, but both of these relationship types survive only if you invest time and energy into your interpersonal communication. And this communication doesn't have to be complex. A story told to your child or shared with a sibling, gratitude expressed to a parent, an affectionate e-mail sent to a distant friend—all of these simple acts of communication keep your family and friendship bonds alive and thriving.

Yet we often neglect to communicate with family and friends in these ways, in part because such relationships lack the sparkle, excitement, and drama of romances. When we dismiss, look past, or simply take for granted our families and friends, we're like Dorothy in *The Wizard of Oz*—running away from the farm, thinking we'll do just fine on our own.

But life is *not* a skip down the yellow brick road. When we battle metaphorical witches in the form of hardship, disappointment, and even tragedy, it's our family and friends—the scarecrows, tin men, and cowardly lions of our lives—who lock arms with us. They're the ones who help us charge forward, even though we're afraid or discouraged. The truth about our family and friendship relationships stands like the wizard behind the curtain. When you step forward boldly and pull the curtain back, it's revealed. There *is* no place like home.

POSTSCRIPT

We began this chapter with the death of a parent and the gift of a friend. Although the enormity of J. K. Rowling's success is rare, her experiences with family and friends are not. Like Rowling, as you go through your life, you will experience the joy of family life as well as the pain of family conflicts and tragedies. And you'll maintain a constellation of friends—one or more of whom may very well pick you up just when you thought all was lost. These events—tragic and transformational—are human universals, and they remind us of the importance of family and friends in our lives.

What family challenges have you endured, and how did you stay connected to your family while surmounting them? What gifts—of any form—have unexpectedly been given to you by your friends, enabling you to realize dreams you thought were impossible?

J. K. Rowling's story of personal transformation from poverty-stricken single mother

to the most successful writer in history is the stuff of legend. But behind this tale of triumph is a human being who, like many of us, suffered tragic losses and through them learned the true value of family and friendship.

Key Terms

Key Concepts

Defining Family

- Given the diversity in contemporary family structures, scholars define **family** in very inclusive ways. American families come in myriad forms, including **nuclear, gay** or **lesbian, extended, blended, cohabiting couples,** and **single-parent.**

- Regardless of the structure of a family, most families exhibit one of four **family communication patterns,** depending on their degree of **conversation orientation** and **conformity orientation. Consensual, pluralistic, protective,** and **laissez-faire** families have very different communication beliefs and practices that shape the interpersonal relationships among family members.

Maintaining Family Relationships

- One way family members maintain their relationships is by creating **family communication rules** prescribing what topics may be discussed, what opinions should be expressed regarding these topics, and with whom these topics may appropriately be discussed.

- Families also solidify their sense of family identity through sharing **family stories.** Narrative accounts of birth, courtship, and survival bind children, parents, and other relatives together.

- Different families manage conflict in very different ways, often developing one of three approaches: **avoidant, aggressive,** or **collaborative.** Like other forms of interpersonal conflict, disputes between family members are best resolved through the use of collaborative approaches.

Defining Friendship

- Unlike family relationships, **friendships** are voluntary, and the participants generally don't expect them to be as intimate or long lasting as serious romances and family relationships. Depending on the needs being fulfilled, friendships may be primarily **communal** or **agentic.**

- Some people form sexual relationships with their friends, known as friends-with-benefits, or **FWB relationships.** Both men and women enter these relationships to satisfy sexual needs. Most of these relationships fail owing to unanticipated emotional challenges.

Maintaining Friendship Relationships

- One of the greatest challenges friends face is geographic separation. Communication technologies can help such friends overcome distance by interacting regularly and maintaining the sense of shared interests that is critical to the friendship bond.

- Across cultures, people agree on **friendship rules,** the basic principles that underlie the maintenance of successful friendships. Friends who follow these rules are more likely to remain friends than those who don't.

Key Skills

- Want to know your family's communication pattern? Review pages 383–387; then take the *Pop Quiz* on page 387.

- How can you integrate positivity, openness, and assurances into your face-to-face and online family communication and, in doing so, better maintain your family relationships? Check out the suggestions on pages 389–390; then do the *Skills Practice* on page 390.

- What can you do to balance the tension between autonomy and connection in your family relationships? Follow the suggestions on pages 390–391.

- How can you balance openness with protection in your family communication? Revisit the discussion of family communication rules on pages 392–394, as well as the suggestions for modifying these rules on page 394.

- Interested in retelling a family experience as a family story? Before you do, review the suggestions on pages 395–396 for effective and appropriate family storytelling.

- Want to improve the way in which you manage conflict with family members? Follow the recommendations on page 397; then do the *Skills Practice* on page 397.

- What kind of friend are you? Take the *Pop Quiz* on page 401 to find out.

- What's the most important thing for maintaining your friendships? Find out on pages 405–406.

- How can you maintain friendships when you choose to share time with one friend instead of another? Review the suggestions on page 406.

- What can you do to better balance openness and protection in your friendships? See page 406.

- What rules should you follow to maintain healthy friendships? Find the answer on pages 407–408.

- Can a friendship survive geographic separation? Sometimes. Review the suggestions for maintaining long-distance friendships on pages 408–409, 412; then do the *Skills Practice* on page 409.

- What would you do if you had to choose between your family and your friends? Complete the *Making Relationship Choices* exercise on pages 410–411 to find out.

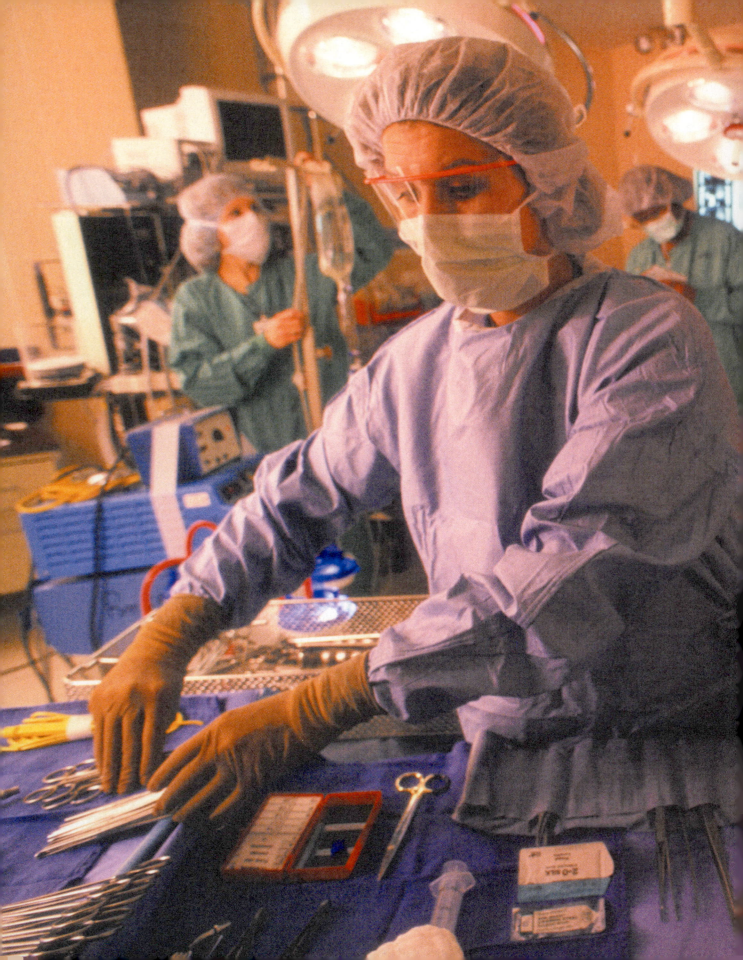

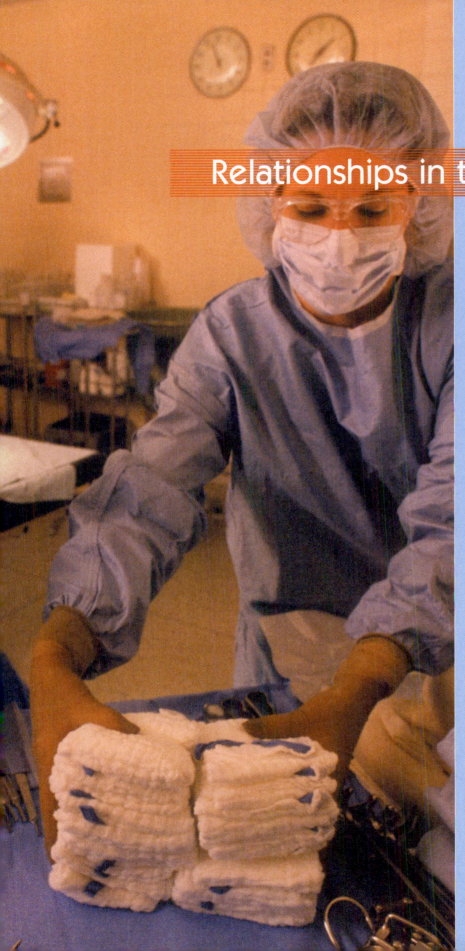

12

Relationships in the Workplace

When Silvia Amaro and Vivian Derr first began working at a California medical office in 1979, neither had any idea that their relationship would endure for more than a quarter century.[1] Silvia was a Latina allergy nurse from south Texas; Vivian, a Euro-American pediatric nurse practitioner from Pennsylvania. Silvia's work responsibilities included assisting physicians, meeting walk-in patients, making phone assessments, and scheduling appointments. Vivian, who was Silvia's supervisor, did all of these tasks plus oversaw the nursing staff. Working together daily, the two quickly made a deal to manage patient visitations by splitting the workload.

Silvia and Vivian's workplace collaboration evolved into a close friendship as the two nurses began sharing personal information with each other. As their friendship deepened, the women's home lives and work

[1] All information and quotes that follow are from V. Derr and S. Amaro (personal communications with author, March and April 2005). Published with permission.

lives became intertwined. Silvia's youngest daughter baby-sat Vivian's son. Vivian gave Silvia's boys sports physicals so Silvia wouldn't have to make time to bring them to a doctor.

After several years, Silvia was promoted to a management position while Vivian was recruited to work at Children's Hospital of Orange County in California. The hospital operated a health van, which traveled throughout the community and provided health care services to underserved and uninsured residents. When the health van's manager resigned, Vivian recruited Silvia for the position. In a reversal of their previous workplace roles, Silvia became Vivian's supervisor. But as Silvia describes, "It didn't make any difference to our friendship."

Silvia was an excellent manager, but at heart she remained an allergy nurse. When the Children's Hospital

started a second van program—a "Breathmobile" providing asthma care for uninsured children—Silvia switched to managing the Breathmobile. She persuaded Vivian to take the reins as health van manager. Today the two women travel to schools and community clinics in the county, giving presentations to parents, teachers, and community members. Their friendship remains steadfast. As Vivian notes, "We can talk on the phone forever. It seems we always have something to run by each other. Our husbands do not understand how we could have so much to say to each other after working side by side all day." Silvia adds, "We always joke about being 'sisters separated at birth.' We tell everyone that!"

The van programs that Silvia and Vivian manage are very successful and so is their enduring and intimate friendship, which has survived stress, power shifts, personal change, and time. For Silvia and Vivian,

as for anyone with a close coworker friendship, the line between work and home life has been blurred. In its place, what has emerged is a union of the personal and the professional that allows these friends to meet their daily work challenges *and* share in each other's private triumphs and troubles. As Vivian describes, "I could not have become the successful manager that I am without Silvia's guidance and support. We are a team. We can work very well apart from each other, but we always come back together when it comes to big decisions. I have never felt anything but love and respect for Silvia." Discussing their relationship separately, Silvia offers a similar sentiment: "We love and respect each other and always bounce big decisions [off] each other, knowing that we can trust what the other person says. We help each other and talk about everything without feeling like we are being judged."

We like to think of our personal and professional lives as separate. Our personal lives consist of "real" relationships with romantic partners, family members, and friends. Our work lives seem to exist in a parallel universe filled with less meaningful interactions.

But this division is a pretense. We spend most of our adult waking hours working and more time interacting with coworkers than with any other type of relationship partner (Sias & Perry, 2004). And our personal and professional identities are fused. When asked "What do you do?" you probably respond with a description of your work. We identify with our work because it provides a sense of purpose and meaning for our lives (Myers, 2002). Consequently, the enjoyment we experience at work can be more personal and profound than we admit. Across industrialized nations, people report higher life satisfaction and healthier family, friendship, and romantic relationships when they feel that their work lives are fulfilling (Myers, 2002).

What makes us happy with our work? Other than the specific activities a job entails, the most important determinants of work satisfaction are the quality of our interpersonal communication in the workplace and the health of our workplace relationships (Albrecht & Bach, 1997). When our workplace communication and relationships are satisfying, we achieve more professionally and feel happier at home. When our workplace communication and relationships slip into dysfunction, on-the-job productivity and relationships outside of the workplace suffer.

In this chapter, we look at interpersonal communication and relationships in the workplace. You'll learn:

- How relationships in the workplace compare with other types of interpersonal relationships

- Tips for building a supportive workplace climate

- Tactics for fostering healthy relationships with peers at work

- Strategies for communicating effectively with supervisors and subordinates

- Suggestions for coping with workplace abuse and harassment

"Interpersonal communication and relationships are an organization's lifeblood."

Defining Workplace Relationships

Whether it's a church, a branch of the military, a corporation, or a nonprofit charity, organizations exist and function because coworkers communicate and form relationships with each other (Contractor & Grant, 1996). All of the information sharing, decision making, and emotional and practical support that occurs through interpersonal communication in the workplace does so in the context of relationships among coworkers (Sias, Krone, & Jablin, 2002). Consequently, interpersonal communication and relationships are an organization's lifeblood.

Any relationship you have with a professional peer, supervisor, subordinate, or mentor can be considered a **workplace relationship,** and such relationships differ along three dimensions: status, intimacy, and choice (Sias & Perry, 2004). Most organizations are structured hierarchically, with people ranked higher or lower than others. Consequently, a defining feature of workplace relationships is the equality or inequality of relationship partners in organizational position and power. Workplace relationships also vary in intimacy. Some remain strictly professional, with the interpersonal communication restricted to work-related concerns. Others, like the relationship between Vivian Derr and Silvia Amaro, become personal through self-disclosure.

Finally, workplace relationships are defined by choice, the degree to which participants willingly engage in them. Although most of us don't get to hand-pick our coworkers, we do choose which coworkers we want to befriend.

Like all interpersonal relationships, workplace relationships provide us with both benefits and costs, although the outcomes associated with workplace relationships are unique. On the plus side, workplace relationships can enhance our professional skills through the insights others provide and increase the speed with which we rise through the organizational hierarchy (Sias & Perry, 2004). They make work more enjoyable, bolster our commitment to the organization, improve morale, and decrease turnover (Sias & Cahill, 1998). On the negative side, close workplace relationships can spawn workplace gossip and cliques (Albrecht & Bach, 1997). They also can add additional stress to our interpersonal lives by forcing us to shoulder not only our own professional burdens but the personal burdens and challenges of our workplace friends.

As we've stressed throughout this book, interpersonal relationships are forged and maintained within the broader milieu of relationship partners' social networks and surrounding ethnic, religious, and socioeconomic class cultures. Workplace relationships are no exception. However, in addition to being shaped by all of the above-mentioned forces, workplace relationships are also strongly defined by each organization's unique culture and interpersonal communication networks. Thus, the first step to understanding how to improve your workplace communication and relationships is to learn how your organization's culture and networks influence those relationships.

The Culture of the Workplace

Like many teens growing up in the United States, I got my first two jobs in chain restaurants—six months at an ice cream parlor and three years at a pizza restaurant. The two workplaces couldn't have been more different. The ice cream parlor had a strict behavior code, and violations were grounds for termination. Workers had to wear buttons saying how "fun" work was, but this was far from the truth. Managers snapped orders at employees and rarely socialized with them outside of the workplace. Because employee turnover was high, few people developed close friendships with coworkers. A siege mentality occupied the restaurant; everyone hunkered down in his or her own workspace. The pizza restaurant was the opposite. Workers socialized after hours, and supervisor-subordinate relationships were friendly. A sense of camaraderie permeated the restaurant, and most employees' closest personal friends were coworkers. Employee turnover was low, and management further encouraged close friendships through outside activities, including a softball team and water-ski parties.

In the same way that different cultures have unique traditions, each workplace possesses a distinctive set of beliefs and practices, known as its **organizational culture** (Katz & Kahn, 1978). An organization's culture derives from three sources, the first of which are norms governing what constitutes appropriate interpersonal communication and relationships (Eisenberg & Goodall, 2004). In each organization, expectations evolve regarding the frequency and tenor of communication. In some organizations,

SELF-REFLECTION

Think of the relationships you have with people at work. What makes them "good" or "bad"? When you compare the benefits and drawbacks of your close workplace relationships, how does this balance sheet affect your feelings about the organization where you work? Your motivation to perform at your best?

● "I had a boss one time who said a wise thing to me. This isn't a pedestrian occurrence in the daily run of things, so I paid attention. 'You can't choose your boss,' he said to me. This idea was expressed with some sadness. He was a President. I was not. But the feeling was something we shared from our relative positions in the cosmos of the Corporation." –Stanley Bing, *Throwing the Elephant*

informality is the norm. For example, you might be encouraged by your supervisor to communicate openly and to challenge his or her ideas, regardless of your place in the hierarchy. In other organizations, people are expected to communicate more formally and to more strictly observe authority.

The second influence on an organization's culture is its workplace artifacts—the objects and structures that define the organization (Schein, 1985). Workplace artifacts include everything from the physical layout of your workspace to dress codes and even motivational items such as hallway posters urging you to always perform at your best.

The third influence on organizational culture is workplace values—the beliefs people share about work performance, dedication to the organization, and coworker relationships. For example, both places I worked for in my youth stressed employee excellence and productivity. But the ice cream parlor discouraged friendships between coworkers, whereas the pizza restaurant encouraged such relationships. Other examples include workplace beliefs regarding corporate responsibility to the environment, commitment to stakeholders (customers, employees, business partners, shareholders, and so forth), and worker integrity and ethical behavior.

When you join an organization, you usually are socialized into its culture (Miller, 1995). Through formal and informal exchanges between new and established coworkers, you discover how you should communicate as well as what's okay or not okay to talk about. You further sense the organization's culture by observing the artifacts you see around you as well as through stated and unstated messages about the organization's values. During my first day as a dishwasher at the ice cream parlor, for example, my trainer (another dishwasher) told me, "People here don't really hang out together; we're all basically in it for the paycheck." My training at the pizza restaurant was conducted by the manager. He encouraged me to stay after work and enjoy free food and drink with my coworkers—an activity he called "new employee training."

Networks in the Workplace

Just as each of us has social networks of acquaintances, friends, and family members linked through communication, workplaces also have systems of communication linkages, known as **organizational networks** (Miller, 1995). Organizational networks are defined by three characteristics: the nature of

SELF-REFLECTION

Think about the culture of an organization you belong to. What norms exist regarding communication? What artifacts bolster these expectations? What values are considered most important for the organization's success? Do you buy into this organizational culture? How does the organizational culture shape your work and your feelings about the organization?

the information that flows through them, the media or channels through which the information flows, and the frequency and number of connections among people in a network, also known as network density.

In each organizational network, the types of information flowing through the network are diverse (Farace, Monge, & Russell, 1977). In some parts of the networks, participants exchange work-related information in the day-to-day process of carrying out their job responsibilities. For instance, people in product development may interact regularly with people in marketing to create the right advertising campaign for a new product. In other parts of the network, participants exchange personal information. The "rumor mill"—by which coworkers pass along gossip and speculate about one another's professional and personal lives—is an example of this.

The second characteristic is the media or channels through which people in workplaces exchange information. These include face-to-face encounters, cell-phone conversations, instant-messaging, and e-mail exchanges. Some networks may be **virtual networks**—groups of coworkers linked solely through e-mail and the Internet. Virtual networks are particularly prevalent in large corporations and in companies where people telecommute (work from home and communicate with coworkers via phone and computer).

Last, networks are defined by their density: how connected on average each member of the network is to other members. In dense networks, every worker knows and regularly interacts with every other network member. By contrast, members of loose networks may have contact with just one or two other members. Density is influenced by a variety of factors, including job requirements (some jobs simply don't allow for much interaction between network members), physical layout of the workspace (whether network members are widely separated or clustered together), and organizational culture (some workplaces encourage frequent interaction; others discourage it). However, two of the strongest factors are familiarity and intimacy; networks in which members have known each other for a long time and are personally close tend to be denser.

Organizational networks come in many different forms. Some are formally defined by the organization—the supervisors to whom you report, the employees you oversee, the peers with whom you collaborate. Others are informal and are created by coworkers themselves. Sometimes **workplace cliques** emerge—dense networks of coworkers who share the same workplace values and broader life attitudes (Jones, 1999). Within any workplace, a number of different cliques may exist: a clique of "slackers" comprising people who do the minimum work necessary, a "fast track" clique of

SKILLS PRACTICE

This exercise helps you assess the strength of your organizational network.

❶ Over three days, track your communication in your organization. Note who you communicate with and whether your communication was about work or not.

❷ Analyze your encounters. How many people did you communicate with? How many encounters were about work? How many were with peers or people higher or lower in the organization's hierarchy?

❸ Consider the people you communicate with. Are they linked to many others in the organization? Are they looked upon favorably?

❹ Consider your analysis. How many people can you count on to provide support? How connected are you to people in positions of power? Given who you communicate with, how are you likely seen by your organization?

ambitious young workers who work extended hours to get ahead, an "old boys" clique of longtime employees who pride themselves on knowing everything about the company, and so forth.

Workplace cliques educate new employees about whom they can trust and which networks they should belong to, helping people to quickly assimilate into the organizational culture. They also provide information about how things work in the organization. For example, when the copier breaks down or you need to get mailroom staff to expedite your shipment, members of a workplace clique can provide you with the assistance you need. But cliques can have disadvantages. For example, they may espouse workplace values contrary to those advocated by the organization. Members of a clique may pride themselves on being "rebels," intentionally flouting authority or disparaging bosses behind their backs. Or worse, they may encourage unethical workplace behavior, such as punching a friend's time card to cover up the fact that the friend is absent.

Regardless of the form that organizational networks take, they are the principal wellsprings from which people get their workplace information. As a consequence, it's vital to keep two things in mind. First, the private is public in the workplace. Because all workplace relationships occur within organizational networks, your communication and behavior *will* serve as material for discussion among network members. Presume that everything you say and do will be shared throughout your organization.

Second, the organizational networks to which you belong can strongly determine the kinds of opportunities—and obstacles—you'll encounter as you advance in your career. For this reason, it's important to build interpersonal ties with coworkers who are both respected and connected. Although you cannot always gain access to the right workplace cliques (especially if they exclude you because of your beliefs, gender, sexual orientation, or ethnicity), you can try to develop interpersonal relationships with organizational insiders, workers who are reputable, knowledgeable, and connected to dense organizational networks. The coworkers you befriend now will strongly determine your experiences in the organization later.

Supportive and Defensive Organizational Climates

Think about an organization with which you're currently involved, as a paid worker, volunteer, or member. How would you describe the overall emotional tone of the place—that is, the way it *feels* to be there? Is it supportive, warm, and welcoming? Detached, cool, and unfriendly? Somewhere in between? This overarching emotional quality of a workplace is known as its **organizational climate.** An organization's climate is the product of all we have just discussed—an organization's culture, its networks, and the interpersonal interaction that occurs within the organization (Kreps, 1990).

As just one person in your organization, you obviously don't have sole control over the climate. Depending on how deeply entrenched are the elements of your organization's culture, networks, and communication that contribute to the climate, you may have little power to change it. Nevertheless, organizational climate is built from the ground up: it is the sum total of individuals' interpersonal behavior in the workplace. Consequently, everything you say and do in your workplace contributes to the climate.

Two types of organizational climate exist (Kreps, 1990). In organizations in which a **defensive climate** dominates, workers describe the workplace environment as unfriendly, rigid, and nonsupportive of their professional and personal needs. Workers in a **supportive climate** describe the workplace as warm, open, and supportive. Although individual organizations' climates vary widely, most fall somewhere between defensive and supportive, depending on how people communicate along six dimensions.

Strategy versus Spontaneity

Imagine you have a supervisor whose every communication seems contrived and calculated. Whenever you express concerns to her, she always responds with the same set phrases, such as "I know just how you feel" and "I'll be sure to take your comments into consideration." You've overheard her using these exact lines with other workers. What kind of climate is she creating?

Part of what distinguishes defensive from supportive climates is the degree to which communication seems strategic versus spontaneous. When coworkers communicate with each other in ways that obviously are rehearsed, they establish a defensive climate. People judge them as phony and pretentious and are less inclined to openly express their own thoughts and feelings. When coworkers communicate in open and honest ways, others view them as authentic and trustworthy, and these perceptions foster a supportive climate.

Dogmatism versus Flexibility

Dogmatism is the tendency to believe that only one perspective, solution, attitude, or belief is correct despite evidence that other possibilities may merit consideration (Ray, 1970). Dogmatic people cling to what they believe no matter what other compelling evidence comes along. They view unquestioned certainty as "strength of character" rather than rigid close-mindedness. People who communicate in a dogmatic fashion in the workplace frame every message as an absolute: "This is the way it's always been done" and

● In the movie *Office Space,* Bill Lumbergh is a supervisor whose strategic communication creates a defensive workplace climate:

BILL LUMBERGH: Hello, Peter. What's happening? Uh, we have sort of a problem here. Yeah, you apparently didn't put one of the new cover sheets on your T.P.S. reports.

PETER GIBBONS: Oh, yeah. I'm sorry about that. I-I forgot.

LUMBERGH: Mm, yeah. You see, we're putting the cover sheets on all T.P.S. reports now before they go out. Did you see the memo about this?

PETER: Yeah. Yeah, yeah, I have the memo right here. I just, uh, forgot. But, uh, it's not shipping out till tomorrow, so there's no problem.

LUMBERGH: Yeah. If you could just go ahead and make sure you do that from now on, that would be great. And, uh, I'll go ahead and make sure you get another copy of that memo. Mm-kay? Bye-bye, Peter.

PETER: Yeah, yeah, no, I have—I have the memo. I've got it. It's right . . .

"What is the emotional tone of your organization—that is, how does it feel to be there?"

"I don't care what the numbers say, I know I'm right!" The result is a defensive climate in which dissent is perceived negatively.

The opposite of dogmatism is flexibility—the willingness to question opinions and decisions and frame statements in conditional terms: "From my perspective, this looks like our best option. What do you see as potential disadvantages?" When people demonstrate flexibility in their interpersonal communication, they view disagreement as constructive rather than adversarial. Contrary opinions are perceived as providing useful alternatives that may ultimately lead to the best possible solutions to problems.

Control versus Collaboration

Think about coworkers whose messages seem designed to get you to do what they want. Even when they're exchanging pleasantries or offering compliments, you still cannot tell if there's an underlying agenda. Now imagine a workplace in which *all* communication is like this. Defensive climates are created when the intention of communication is always to control. The opposite of control is collaboration. Communicating collaboratively means taking others' perspectives into consideration when trying to solve organizational problems ("How do you feel about this?" and "What are your thoughts on this project?").

Evaluation versus Description

Another type of communication that is symptomatic of defensive climates is evaluation—framing complaints about organizational problems in terms of character defects. This may include negative rumormongering ("Can you believe how petty and vindictive John is?") as well as finger-pointing when something goes wrong. For example, when a project misses an important deadline, people immediately cast personal blame: "I can't believe how lazy you are for not finishing this yet!"

People who build supportive workplace climates communicate about such problems using descriptive and objective language: "We're facing a tight schedule with only a week left before the deadline, so we're going to have to push hard to get it done on time."

Detachment versus Empathy

When people seek counsel on pressing problems, they want others to listen supportively and to demonstrate their understanding. In an organization marked by a defensive climate, workers embrace an exaggerated sense of professionalism that excludes all discussion of personal concerns. But coming across as detached, distant, and aloof usually generates hostility and defensiveness, especially in situations in which someone is looking to you for support (Gibb, 1961). People in supportive climates express empathy when listening to others, as discussed in Chapters 3 and 6.

Superiority versus Equality

The final dimension that characterizes organizational climates is superiority versus equality. In defensive climates, the power difference between employees of unequal status is strictly enforced through communication. Supervisors routinely pull rank on employees ("You need to keep in mind who's running the show here!"), and experienced coworkers treat less experienced ones with condescension ("I have a lot more experience than you do"). The result? Morale is eroded as people find themselves and their abilities minimized.

One way to create a more supportive organizational climate is to mitigate power differences and to encourage people to treat one another with respect and appreciation for what each person brings to the organization. Even in relationships where there is a power imbalance, such as the relationships between supervisors and subordinates, coworkers in a supportive climate talk with each other in ways that emphasize shared commitment to a common mission rather than rank and status.

Creating a Supportive Climate

What can you do to help create a supportive workplace climate? As organizational scholar Gary Kreps (1990) notes, given the stress and intensity of many workplaces, it's unlikely that any worker can communicate supportively in every organizational situation. Especially if you're in a position of authority, it's impossible to avoid evaluative, controlling, and strategic communication in your daily activities.

However, the dimensions we explored above suggest six possible tactics for improving workplace climate. These strategies won't necessarily make your climate supportive, but they will help build rather than undermine supportiveness. If you're in a position of authority, you can encourage supportiveness by incorporating these practices into your communication.

First, encourage spontaneity and honesty of expression. Workplace climates are most supportive when people view one another as honest and open.

Second, adopt a flexible mind-set, and communicate this flexibility to others. Examine your decisions, ideas, and viewpoints for errors and weaknesses. Communicate flexibility by avoiding the use of absolutes. Invite input, including critical comments, about your ideas.

Third, collaborate rather than control. Avoid trying to get others to always do exactly what you want them to do. Instead, ask for their ideas and perspectives on possible solutions.

Fourth, describe challenges rather than assign blame. When problems arise at work, talk about them in neutral terms rather than pointing fingers.

Fifth, offer concern rather than professional detachment. When coworkers or employees seek your support on personal dilemmas, demonstrate empathy, respect, and understanding.

And finally, emphasize equality. Avoid pulling rank on people. Especially when you have power over others, it's vital to treat them with respect.

Peer Relationships

Doctors without Borders (known internationally as Médecins sans Frontières, or MSF) is a nonprofit organization that provides medical care to victims of armed conflicts, epidemics, and natural and man-made disasters.[2] Each year volunteers join 25,000 locally hired staff to provide medical aid in more than 70 countries. When conflicts or crises erupt, MSF sends teams of surgeons, anesthesiologists, emergency nurses, and logistics experts into the field to establish operating rooms and clinics, provide basic hygiene assistance, and begin training local medical and support staff. MSF team members eat, sleep, and work together for as long as they're needed. Not surprisingly, given the hostile environments in which they frequently find themselves, MSF team members often form close bonds with one another.

In the time leading up to the Rwandan genocide of 1994, MSF volunteers Jean Nyiligira and Pierre LaPlante weren't just coworkers. They were companions who depended on each other for their very survival. Pierre, a French doctor, and Jean, a Rwandan staff member, toured camps filled with Tutsi and Hutu refugees. Jean served as translator, mechanic, driver, and negotiator for Pierre, frequently using his verbal skills and quick wit at military checkpoints to defuse dangerous tensions.

As this example illustrates, our most meaningful and intimate workplace relationships are those with our **professional peers,** people holding positions of organizational status and power similar to our own. Peers are the most important source of personal and practical support for employees in any type of organization (Rawlins, 1992). And although most of us will never experience the levels of stress and physical threat faced by MSF staff, we recognize the bonds formed between people such as Jean Nyiligira and Pierre LaPlante as akin to the close peer relationships we ourselves develop in the workplace. Our peer relationships are not simply professional; they're often intensely personal.

SELF-REFLECTION

What are the characteristics of your organization's climate? Is your organization's climate supportive, defensive, or somewhere in between? Consider your interpersonal communication in the workplace, including the ways in which you treat your coworkers. How do these interactions affect the climate? What could you do differently to improve your organization's climate?

● In the months before the Hutu-dominated government of Rwanda began systematically killing all Tutsis in the country, Jean Nyiligira and Pierre LaPlante risked their lives to help displaced and diseased Rwandans. Jean was killed in 1994 at the peak of the genocide.

Types of Peer Relationships

Although peer relationships strongly shape the quality of our work lives, not all peer relationships are the same (Fritz & Dillard, 1994; Kram & Isabella, 1985). Information peers are equivalent-status coworkers with whom our communication is limited to work-related content. Information peer relationships typically are created through assignment rather than choice, and as a result, they lack trust and intimacy. Although these relationships are common, especially in large corporations, many people view information peers as less open and less communicatively skilled than collegial or special peers, discussed below (Myers, Knox, Pawlowski, & Ropog, 1999).

Collegial peers are coworkers whom we consider friends. When we communicate with collegial peers, we talk about work and personal issues, and we feel moderate levels of trust and intimacy toward these individuals. Scholars sometimes describe these relationships as "blended" because they incorporate elements of both professional and personal relationships (Bridge & Baxter, 1992). Special peers are equivalent-status coworkers with whom we share very high levels of emotional support, career-related feedback, trust, self-disclosure, and friendship (Sias et al., 2002). The rarest type of relationship, special peers are considered people's best friends in the workplace.

Professional peer relationships can evolve from lesser to greater levels of intimacy over time. The first and most significant relationship transition is from information peer to collegial peer (Sias & Cahill, 1998). Workers who spend extended periods of time together, are placed in proximity with each other, or socialize together outside of the workplace inevitably form stronger bonds with each other. However, sharing time and activities together is not enough to ensure that a coworker relationship will evolve from information to collegial peer. Like personal friendships, perceived similarity in interests, beliefs, and values is what decisively pushes a workplace relationship from acquaintanceship to friendship (Sias & Cahill, 1998).

The evolution of the relationship from information peer to collegial peer is similar for **virtual peers,** coworkers who communicate mainly through phone, e-mail, and other communication technologies. For virtual peers, the progression from information peer to collegial peer hinges on how much time the peers spend interacting and working on shared tasks together. Given the familiarity that many modern workers have with communication technologies and the availability of such technologies in the workplace, it's commonplace for virtual peers to become virtual friends.

The transition from collegial peer to special peer is different, however. Perceived similarity, shared time and tasks, and socializing are all important but are not sufficient to push coworker friendships to the level of best friend (Sias & Cahill, 1998). Instead, the evolution of a coworker friendship to a higher state of intimacy is usually spurred by negative events in partners' personal lives (serious illness, marital discord) or serious work-related problems that require an exceptional level of social support. As demonstrated by the workplace relationship described at the beginning of this chapter, Silvia Amaro and Vivian Derr became special peers in response to personal life challenges each faced.

Maintaining Peer Relationships

Like other interpersonal bonds, peer relationships remain healthy through the energy and effort you and your peers invest in maintenance. One important tactic that helps maintain your peer relationships is positivity, discussed in Chapter 10. A positive perspective and upbeat communication with your peers helps offset the stress and demands everyone faces in the workplace. Practicing positivity in the workplace means communicating with your peers in a cheerful and optimistic fashion and doing unsolicited favors for them.

Openness also plays an important role. Openness means creating feelings of security and trust between you and your peers. You can create such feelings by behaving in predictable, trustworthy, and ethical ways in your relationships with peers. This means following through on your promises, respecting confidences, and demonstrating honesty and integrity in both your personal and your professional behavior.

Two additional tactics will help you maintain your collegial and special peer relationships (Sias et al., 2002). Like assurances given to a romantic partner, assurances given to collegial and special peers help demonstrate your commitment to them. Since choice is what distinguishes close peer relationships from casual ones, a critical part of maintaining these relationships is routinely stressing to your collegial and special peers that your relationships are based on choice rather than professional assignment. This can be accomplished indirectly by inviting peers to join you in activities outside of the workplace, which implies that you consider them friends and not just coworkers. More directly, you can straightforwardly tell collegial and special peers that you think of them primarily as friends.

Second, collegial and special peer relationships grow stronger when the people involved treat one another as whole human beings with unique qualities and do not strictly define each other as just coworkers. Certainly, you'll need to discuss work, but since your relationships with collegial and special peers are blended, remember to also talk about personal topics.

Cross-Sex Peers. Like cross-sex friends in general, cross-sex peers who form workplace friendships often discover that others in their networks view their relationship as sexual rather than platonic (Cleveland, Stockdale, & Murphy, 2000). As a consequence, men and women who form workplace friendships must go to great lengths to publicly defend their relationships as caused solely by proximity and shared tasks (Sias, Smith, & Avdeyeva, 2003). Often, cross-sex peers maintain the boundaries in their relationship by limiting their interactions with each other or by socializing only when both individuals' romantic partners are present.

Workplace Romances. Given how close people can get in the workplace, it's not surprising that romantic feelings occasionally develop between people (Albrecht & Bach, 1997). Despite a popular media focus on salacious affairs between bosses and underlings, 74 percent of people in such relationships report being involved with a peer (Hovick, Meyers, & Timmerman, 2003).

Romantically involved workers are usually perceived by people in their organization as friendly and approachable (Hovick et al., 2003), and they are rarely judged as less productive because of their relationship. Indeed, one study found that only a minority of workers surveyed thought that workplace romances hurt employees' job performance (Dillard, 1987). The majority felt that they made no difference or had beneficial effects. However, the perception of workplace romances is not all positive. Involvement in a romance can create the perception among coworkers that the partners are more interested in each other than in their work, leading to rumors and gossip (Albrecht & Bach, 1997). As a consequence, you can't cultivate a workplace romance without expecting the relationship to become a focus of workplace gossip.

The negative outcomes associated with workplace romances may be more pronounced for women than for men. When such relationships are mixed status—in particular, the woman under the direct supervision of the man—others in the organization often conclude that the woman used the relationship to enhance her career. The resulting workplace gossip can turn especially nasty in such cases (Dillard, 1987). In contrast, men in workplace romances often win their coworkers' admiration (Dillard, 1987).

How can you successfully maintain a workplace romance? First, leave your love at home, so to speak, and communicate with each other in a strictly professional fashion during work hours. When romantic partners maintain a professional demeanor toward each other and communicate with all their coworkers in a consistent and positive fashion, the romance is usually ignored or even encouraged (Buzzanell, 1990).

Second, use e-mail judiciously to maintain your relationship. When used properly, e-mail enables romantic partners to communicate frequently and in a way that maintains professional decorum (Hovick et al., 2003). However, e-mail messages exchanged in the workplace should never contain overly intimate or controversial messages. Although many workers use their business e-mail accounts for personal reasons, it is wise to write e-mails that comply with official policies—no matter who the recipient is. Remember, e-mail is not secure. Anyone with the motivation and know-how can gain access to the messages you and your partner exchange. Be temperate in the content of your e-mails and always consider the consequences should coworkers other than your partner read your messages.

SELF-REFLECTION

If you have had a workplace romance, what were the consequences, benefits, and challenges? How did you and your partner meet these challenges? If you haven't had a workplace romance, what are your perceptions of them? Do you approve or disapprove of workplace romances? How could they affect your organization?

POP QUIZ

Test Your Maintenance of Peer Relationships

Thinking about your collegial and special peer relationships, read the following statements. For each, rate your agreement using a scale of 1 to 7. A rating of 1 means you strongly disagree, 4 means you're neutral, and 7 means you strongly agree. When you're finished, total up your score and interpret it below.

_____ I try to communicate in an upbeat, positive fashion toward my peers.

_____ I try to build my peers up by giving them compliments.

_____ I enjoy doing unsolicited favors for my peers, such as bringing them coffee or lunch or helping them out with work projects.

_____ I strive to communicate in consistent, reliable ways with my peers.

_____ I try to always keep promises I've made to my peers.

_____ If a peer shares something with me in confidence, I honor that confidentiality by not sharing the information with others.

_____ I regularly let my peers know that I consider them not just coworkers but friends.

_____ I do things to convey to my peers that even if we didn't work together, we'd still be friends.

_____ I strive to communicate with my peers in ways that show I value them as unique people rather than just as coworkers.

_____ I try to be there for my peers—willing to talk with them about their personal and work-related concerns.

Scoring

10–29: low maintenance; 30–49: average maintenance; 50–70: high effort.

Note: Items in this *Pop Quiz* are adapted by author from the maintenance scale of Stafford and Canary (1991).

Mixed-Status Relationships

Following the U.S. invasion, soldier John Doe was deployed to Iraq, where he was in regular combat and subsequently received decorations for combat valor.[3] In February 2004, John Doe reenlisted as a member of the Army National Guard's Try One program, which allows veterans to bypass basic training while obtaining military education and using family medical benefits for one year. He re-upped with the assumption that this would be his final year of service. Although he loved his military job, he wanted to spend more time with his family.

On September 4, 2004, John Doe's commanding officer ordered him and the rest of his unit to mobilize for active duty in Iraq for a period that would run at least until April 2006—over two years after his reenlistment period. John Doe felt intensely ambivalent about his superior's order. On the one hand, he recognized that in the military disobeying the lawful order of a superior is a criminal act. But on the other hand, he had enlisted in Try One because it guaranteed him a fixed end date. John Doe felt that 12 years of exemplary military service and a combat tour in Iraq were enough, so after much consideration, he decided to challenge the order of his superior officer. He hired an attorney and filed a lawsuit, naming the Secretary of Defense, Secretary of the Army, and his company commander as defendants. The lawsuit was the first of its kind, and though John Doe eventually failed and was sent back to Iraq, it set off a national controversy regarding the power of military commanders to retain soldiers in their units against their will.

Although it might be tempting to characterize the workplace relationships between military superiors and their subordinates as unusual, most organizations are similarly hierarchical, with some people holding positions of power over others. Relationships between coworkers of different organizational status are called **mixed-status relationships,** and they provide the structural foundation on which most organizations are built (Farace et al., 1977).

Mixed-status relationships take many forms, including officer-subordinate, trainer-trainee, and mentor-protégé. But when most of us think of mixed-status relationships, what leaps to mind are supervisory relationships, ones in which one person outranks and supervises another (Zorn, 1995). Most partners in these relationships are assigned to each other rather than chosen.

Supervisory relationships are less likely than peer relationships to evolve into friendships because of the power imbalance (Zorn, 1995). In most friendships, people downplay any difference in status and emphasize their equality. Supervisors by definition have more power. They direct their subordinates' efforts, evaluate their performance, and make decisions regarding their workers' pay and job security. They may even give orders entailing life-or-death consequences, as in the case of John Doe.

While some supervisors and subordinates can become friends despite the difference in power, many organizations discourage or even forbid friendships between supervisors and their subordinates because it's

---

[3] All information regarding John Doe that follows is excerpted from Davey (2004), Philpott (2004), and Reuters (2004). John Doe's identity has been veiled in the media to protect his anonymity.

assumed that such relationships will impair a supervisor's ability to objectively assess a subordinate's work performance (Zorn, 1995). Research on organizational decision making supports this assumption. Managers are less likely to give negative feedback to employees they like than to those they dislike (Larson, 1984). This occurs for two reasons. First, we are reluctant to give friends who work under us negative feedback because of the relationship consequences that may ensue. For example, our friend may become angry or accuse us of unfairness. Second, as we saw in Chapter 3, our perceptions of others are substantially biased by whether we like them or not. Consequently, if we're in the supervisory position, our affection for a subordinate friend may lead us to judge his or her performance more generously than others.

Managing Up

When John Doe's commanding officer ordered him to deploy, he knew he had no recourse other than legal action. He couldn't just go to his superior and say, "Look, I really want to spend more time with my family, so can you please rescind your order?" Those of us in civilian jobs, however, typically have at least some leverage in getting our bosses to do what we want them to. Persuading superiors to support our work-related needs and wants is achieved through **upward communication**—communication from subordinates to superiors—and is conducted with an eye toward achieving influence (Eisenberg & Goodall, 2004). People feel more satisfied with their work lives when they believe that their supervisors listen and are responsive to their concerns (Eisenberg & Goodall, 2004).

Take a moment to watch the upward communication that members of your organization use with their supervisors. Chances are you'll see a variety of approaches. Some may try ingratiation, trying to gain their supervisor's favor by being unfailingly warm and friendly. Others may play the tactician, behaving in a logical and businesslike manner during every encounter and hoping their overt professionalism will win their supervisor over.

"No, Thursday's out. How about never—is never good for you?"

Organizational communication scholar Eric Eisenberg argues that the most effective form of upward communication is **advocacy** (Eisenberg & Goodall, 2004). Through advocacy, you learn how to read your superior's communication preferences and how to design messages in ways that will be well received by your superior. Advocacy is based on six principles. First, plan before you pitch. Most spontaneous appeals to supervisors ("Can I have a raise?" "Can you sign me up for that software course?") are rejected. To avoid this, take time to craft your request before you pitch it.

Second, know why your supervisor should agree with you. Your supervisor has the power to make decisions, so the burden is on you to present a compelling case. In your message, connect your goals to something your supervisor thinks is important. For example, "If you sign me up for this course, I'll be able to maintain our new database."

Third, tailor your message. Think about successful and unsuccessful attempts to influence your supervisor. Compare the different approaches you and other people have used, and consider their efficacy. Does your supervisor respond more favorably to statistics or to an anecdote? To details or to generalities? Based on your supervisor's preferences, tailor your evidence and appeal accordingly.

Fourth, know your supervisor's knowledge. Many attempts at upward communication fail because subordinates present information at an inappropriate level. For example, they present their request in overly abstract terms, wrongly assuming that their supervisor is familiar with the subject. Or they present their appeal in a simplistic form, inadvertently coming across as condescending. To avoid this, know your supervisor's knowledge of the subject before you broach it. You can find this out by talking to other workers who are familiar with your supervisor.

Fifth, create coalitions before communicating. Most arguments made by one person are unconvincing, particularly when presented by a subordinate to a supervisor. Try to strengthen your argument with support from others in your organization. Remember to present such information as a helpful and personal observation ("Just to make sure I wasn't completely off about the situation, I checked with Joan, Denise, and Erika, and they all agreed") rather than as a threat to your supervisor's authority ("For your information, three other people feel the same way I do!"). And be sure to get approval beforehand from the people whose opinions you plan to cite. Some may not want their viewpoints referenced, and to use their sentiments as support for your arguments without their approval is highly unethical.

And sixth, competently articulate your message. You can plan and tailor a message all you want, but if you're unable to articulate it, your supervisor probably won't take it seriously. Before you talk with your supervisor, revisit the principles of competent messages in Chapter 5 and effective verbal and nonverbal communication described in Chapters 7 and 8 to brush up on your skills.

Communicating with Subordinates

The movie *Harold and Kumar Go to White Castle* tells the story of Harold Lee and Kumar Patel, two friends who encounter bizarre obstacles in their night-long quest for White Castle hamburgers (Leiner, Hurwitz, Schlossberg,

SKILLS PRACTICE

This exercise helps you sharpen your advocacy skills.

❶ Think of a situation in which you might use advocacy to influence someone who has more power than you.

❷ Write down the other person's decision-making and communication preferences.

❸ Create and practice saying messages that embody the principles of advocacy. As you practice, ask yourself if others would be convinced by your messages.

❹ Revisit your situation, but this time, imagine you're talking with people who disagree with you. Generate new messages to counter their objections.

❺ Choose the messages that will best help you advocate in your organization.

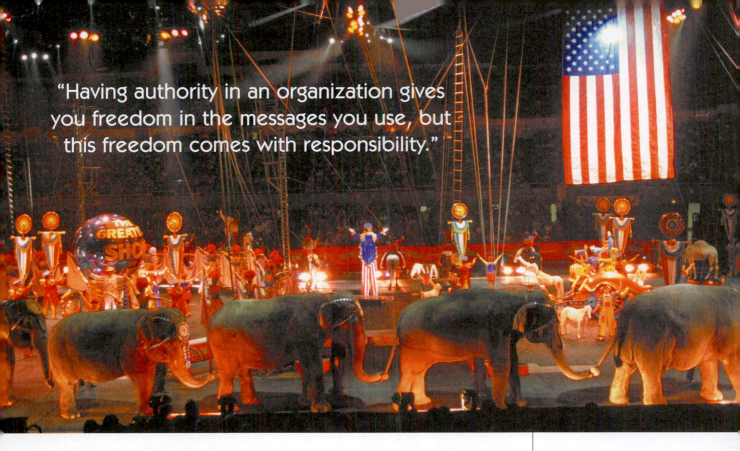

"Having authority in an organization gives you freedom in the messages you use, but this freedom comes with responsibility."

Kahane, & Shapiro, 2004). The film opens with a confrontation between Harold and his supervisor, Billy Carver. It's Friday afternoon, and Billy has been invited by J.D., a fellow supervisor, to a party that night. But Billy has a research report due the following morning for a Saturday meeting with German investors. J.D. encourages Billy to "just get somebody else to do your work for you," so Billy dumps the project on Harold:

BILLY: Harold, I need you to update those models for me.

HAROLD: But Billy, aren't you supposed to . . .

BILLY: I know, but something just came up—I have this meeting with these new clients tonight, and I'm never going to have time to get to those, so that's your responsibility now, big boy.

J.D.: Uh, make sure those are in by nine o'clock sharp tomorrow. With all the downsizing that's been going on around here, we wouldn't want to have to tell Berenson you've been slacking, now would we?

HAROLD: Um, yeah. OK, no problem.

BILLY: Hey, you, have a great weekend, OK buddy. I owe you one—just one.

HAROLD: Thank you.

When you communicate upward, you're typically trying to influence your supervisors. But when you're the supervisor, *you* have the influence. When you present a request or demand to your subordinates—like Billy foisting his report on to Harold—you don't have to worry about using advocacy. You can simply tell them what to do and use whatever language you want. Or can you?

Having formal authority in an organization gives you freedom in the messages you use when interacting with subordinates, known as **downward**

communication. But with this freedom comes responsibility. Although many people in power positions exploit their freedom by abusing or harassing employees (as we'll discuss shortly), what distinguishes effective downward communication is the willingness of empowered people to communicate without relying on their power to appeal to subordinates in positive, empathic, respectful, and open ways.

Effective Downward Communication.   A supervisor's communication sets the tone for his or her subordinates or organization. When a supervisor communicates skillfully, the effects radiate downward; employees are more motivated, more satisfied with their work, and more productive (Eisenberg & Goodall, 2004). But when a supervisor communicates ineffectively, frustration and dissatisfaction build quickly. If you're a manager, you have not only organizational power and status but the power of your interpersonal

FOCUS ON CULTURE

The Model Minority Myth

Karen Chan had worked in the finance department of a midsize retail chain for seven years when a new supervisor was hired. Karen was shocked when he talked about her ethnicity. "My boss would make comments like, 'I can always count on you to get the budget right, because I know Asians are good with numbers.'" Her supervisor's downward communication began to influence the perception of other department heads, who sought Karen's input on complicated financial questions. "I actually majored in English, and when I chose finance as a career, it wasn't because I was a quantitative expert. I knew I had an eye for detail, and I appreciated the foundation finance would provide for a long-term career in business."

Chan decided to confront her boss. She quickly learned that her boss was behaving out of ignorance. "He didn't mean to deliberately hurt me, but I didn't want him to continue doing it. I may want to make a switch to operations or marketing, and my boss's comments were cornering me into a finance career within the firm." They both agreed to communicate about these slips as they occurred.

Many Asian Americans, like Chan, are victims of the model minority myth,

the belief that certain immigrant groups have overcome all the barriers to success and are self-effacing, reliable, hardworking, and technically proficient (Asian American Career Center, n.d.; Hyun, 2005). Writer Jane Hyun of the NAACP encourages workers who feel they are being stereotyped as "model minorities" to discuss the matter directly with their supervisors, much as Karen Chan did (2005). Importantly, you should not try to combat the stereotype by acting irresponsible, loud, or wild. Most employers value workers who are reliable, hardworking, and technically proficient, so you don't want to behave in ways contrary to these attributes.

YOUR TURN

- How does your culture shape your supervisors' downward communication with you?

- What impact does this communication have on your work? On your workplace satisfaction?

- How do the stereotypes you possess shape your downward communication with subordinates?

Note: Information regarding Karen Chan, including quotes, is excerpted from Hyun (2005).

communication to shape the morale and performance of all the workers under you, simply through how you communicate with them.

Effective downward communication can be achieved by observing five principles (Eisenberg & Goodall, 2004). First, routinely and openly emphasize the importance of communication in workplace relationships with subordinates. For example, some supervisors engage in both informal and formal interactions with subordinates—hallway chats, impromptu office visits, weekly status updates, or team meetings. They also clearly and concisely explain instructions, performance expectations, and organizational policies.

Second, listen empathically. Respond positively to your employees' attempts at upward communication rather than perceiving such attempts as a threat to power. Listen to subordinates' suggestions and complaints, and demonstrate a reasonable willingness to take fair and appropriate action in response to what they are saying.

Third, when communicating wants and needs to subordinates, frame these messages as polite requests ("Do you think you could . . .") or persuasive explanations ("Here's why we need to get this done in the next week . . ."). By contrast, ineffective downward communication involves using power to make threats ("Have this done by the end of the week or else") and demands ("Take care of that customer now!").

Fourth, be sensitive to your subordinates' feelings. For instance, if a reprimand is in order, try to make it in private rather than in front of the subordinate's coworkers. Keep such exchanges focused on behaviors that need to change rather than making judgments about the subordinate's character or worth: "John, I noticed that you arrived late to the last three team meetings. I'm worried that late arrivals disrupt the meetings and cause us to spend more time than we have. What ideas do you have for ensuring that you get to meetings on time?"

Last, share relevant information with employees whenever possible. This includes notice of impending organizational changes and explanations about why the changes are coming. For example: "Our company hasn't been meeting its forecasted revenues, so several units, including ours, are being sold to another company. We'll have an opportunity to accept jobs in this company or to move to the company that's acquiring us. As soon as I know more about what this change means for all of us, I'll share that information."

Compliments and Criticism. Two challenges of downward communication are how to effectively praise subordinates and how to constructively criticize them. Offering subordinates praise for their workplace accomplishments fosters a healthy organizational climate. Studies repeatedly show that employees rank "appreciation" and "supervisory recognition" at the top of their lists of factors motivating them to work hard and that feeling unappreciated at work is a leading cause of employee turnover (Forni, 2002).

Complimenting your subordinates is most effectively done when the compliments are focused on a subordinate's work—his or her achievements, expertise, attitude, cooperativeness, and so forth. Avoid compliments about personal matters—like a subordinate's appearance. Regardless of your intention, something as innocuous as complimenting the stylishness of a subordinate's hairstyle or the beauty of his or her skin may make the person

Think about the most effective supervisor you know. Which aspects of this supervisor's communication make him or her so effective? His or her openness? Skill at explaining things? Willingness to listen?

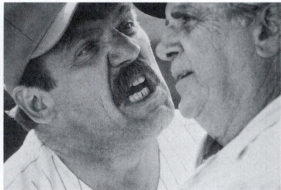

● A supervisor's downward communication shapes the morale and performance of all the workers under her or him.

feel uncomfortable. In some organizations, such compliments can trigger charges of sexual harassment or discrimination.

Also, praise is best presented privately rather than publicly, except in formal contexts such as recognition dinners and award ceremonies. Many supervisors enjoy spontaneously singling out particular employees for praise in front of their coworkers ("Everyone, let's give Samantha a round of applause—she was our unit sales leader again this past month!"). These supervisors incorrectly believe that such praise improves morale, but it can do the opposite. When someone is singled out in front of his or her peers and in a context where such recognition is unexpected, that person's status is elevated. This might be merited, but it could foster resentment and envy among the person's peers and ultimately undermine the organization's climate.

Of course, effectively criticizing subordinates is no easier. Over the years, determining how best to constructively criticize subordinates has been the focus of much managerial musing. But offering constructive criticism isn't as difficult as you might think. Instead, it requires you to draw upon the many skills you have mastered in previous chapters.

Begin by using your knowledge of emotion management from Chapter 4, remaining calm, kind, and understanding throughout the exchange. Open your interaction with positive remarks, and end your comments with similar commendations: "It was obvious you worked really hard on designing that presentation" or "This isn't the end of the world—just something I'd like you to work on for future presentations."

Second, follow the guidelines for rhetorical message design outlined in Chapter 5 and the recommendations for effective verbal communication described in Chapter 7. Informatively, honestly, and clearly identify the issue or behavior that concerns you, describing it neutrally rather than personalizing it or leveling accusations. For example, instead of saying "You clearly don't realize how you came across," say "I think the way you defended our team's work yesterday may not have been the most effective approach." Rather than "You shouldn't have gone in unprepared like that," say, "There seemed to be an expectation in the room of more precise data on projected sales."

Strive to experience and express empathy toward your subordinate through perspective-taking and empathic concern, showing that you understand how he or she may feel: "The same thing has happened to me before" rather than "I would never let something like that happen." Keep in mind how you have felt when receiving criticism from your superiors, and adapt your communication accordingly.

And finally, avoid belaboring the error that has been made, and instead, focus most of your talk time on ideas for avoiding such missteps in the future. Although you have the authority to dictate corrections to them, subordinates respond more favorably when supervisors negotiate solutions with them. Offer your subordinate specific ideas, but frame them as suggestions, asking for their opinion. The goal of constructive criticism is not only to correct the errant behavior but to create a mutual consensus with your subordinate.

Maintaining Mixed-Status Relationships

As we've seen, communicating effectively in mixed-status relationships presents numerous challenges—whether you're trying to influence a superior, praise a subordinate, or provide constructive criticism for an employee whose performance is inadequate. But a broader challenge is maintaining these relationships. Maintaining mixed-status relationships requires you to do two things (Albrecht & Bach, 1997). First, with your supervisor and subordinates, develop and follow communication rules for what's appropriate to talk about as well as when and how to communicate. For example, supervisors who think their subordinates agree with them on how they should communicate tend to rate those subordinates higher on overall performance than subordinates who hold different beliefs about communication (Albrecht & Bach, 1997). Communication rules govern matters such as how often a supervisor and subordinate meet to discuss work projects, whether communications are both formal (weekly status checks) and informal (spontaneous hallway chats), and which channels (e-mail, printed memos, face-to-face conversations) are the most appropriate.

Second, communicate in consistent and reliable ways. This means displaying a stable and professional manner with supervisors and subordinates rather than allowing personal problems or moods to influence your communication. It also means being punctual, following through on appointments and promises, and keeping confidences. Consistency builds trust, an essential component of any interpersonal relationship, and a perception that you're "trustworthy" will feed into other positive perceptions of you as well, including your integrity, openness, and competence (Albrecht & Bach, 1997).

DILBERT: ©Scott Adams/Dist. by United Features Syndicate, Inc.

Of course, these suggestions presume that supervisors and subordinates in your organization are willing to collaborate in maintaining healthy mixed-status relationships. Unfortunately, some people aren't interested in making the effort. They often believe that they're spending enough time and energy cultivating their other interpersonal relationships and shouldn't have to work so hard on workplace relationships. In other cases, they may even intentionally abuse and exploit others in their organization who have lower status and power.

Workplace Abuse

Mixed-status workplace relationships are defined by power imbalance. Such imbalance is a necessary component of organizations because it enables managers to direct others' work and make decisions about resources. At the same time, as the power imbalance between supervisors and subordinates increases, so too does the potential for **workplace abuse**—a person verbally or nonverbally behaving in a hostile way toward another person in the organization (Tepper, 2000). Such abuse doesn't need to involve physical contact; rather, it primarily takes the form of harmful communication and it is mostly done by supervisors toward their subordinates (Sias et al., 2002). Workplace abuse can include making unreasonable demands of people, insulting them privately or publicly, disparaging their ideas and feelings, reminding them of past failures, taking credit for something accomplished by someone else, and being overly critical of people's performance.

Many scholars argue that workplace abuse can cause more damage in an organization than sexual harassment because it's more widespread and tends to go unpunished (Keashly, Trott, & MacLean, 1994). Not surprisingly, victims of workplace abuse feel provoked, frightened, intimidated, or humiliated (Einarsen & Raknes, 1997). They report emotional problems, stress-related illnesses, and substantially less satisfaction with their jobs and lives (Tepper, 2000).

How can you cope with workplace abuse? Some people simply quit and find another job (Bies & Tripp, 1998). Of course, this option is not available to everyone since most people depend on their income for their living and new job opportunities can be limited. Others give in to the abuse, choosing to ignore it or tough it out because the perceived costs of challenging the abusive supervisor are too high. Another option is to use your interpersonal communication skills and to directly confront the abuser (Bies & Tripp, 1998). However, many avoid this tack because of the perceived consequences. For example, if your supervisor is being abusive and you go over your supervisor to someone more highly placed, that person may side with your supervisor.

On the flip side, using your communication skills to challenge workplace abuse can create positive change (Bies & Tripp, 1998). Some supervisors may not realize that they're being abusive. In such cases, directly confronting the person can help make him or her aware of the problem. One study of workplace abuse found that, although the most frequently reported strategy for dealing with abusive supervisors was avoiding or ignoring them, the respondents who confronted their abusers reported improvements in their subsequent interactions (Keashly et al., 1994).

Sexual Harassment

After graduating from college, Leigh-Anne Goins took a job as an office manager before pursuing her dream of going back to school and earning a graduate degree.[4] Her job quickly became a nightmare, as she describes:

> For the first few months my job was wonderful. I was in charge of the office and I was making supervisory decisions. Then my boss's true colors came out. He began coming up behind me and putting his hands on my shoulders, leaning in and talking into my ear. I thought, *no . . . I'm imagining things.* I should have bailed, but I had to pay my rent and I was trying to save money for school. The final straw came when I purchased some brownies and offered one to my boss in addition to my other coworkers. My boss said "no" because he was dieting. I offered one last time, just to be polite, and he responded by covering his mouth like he was going to tell a secret and whispering so that only I could see and hear, "You're my brownie" and licking his lips at me. That was the final straw, being called the office manager's "brownie."

Many people think the problem of sexual harassment in the workplace has been solved. It hasn't. The number of incidences of sexual harassment since the early 1990s has actually climbed, with 12,679 charges of sexual harassment made in 2005 alone (U.S. Equal Employment Opportunity Commission, n.d.). These represent only a small portion of actual instances since the

POP QUIZ

Test Your Perception of Sexual Harassment

Read the following statements and decide if you consider each behavior harmless, uncertain, or severe sexual harassment. Check your perceptions in the key below.

1. Your supervisor touches or pats your private parts.
2. Your supervisor requests sexual favors in exchange for rewards and perks.
3. Your supervisor repeatedly asks you out on a date, even after you make it clear you're not interested.
4. Your supervisor makes sexually suggestive remarks or gestures to you.
5. Your supervisor shows you sexually suggestive visuals.
6. Your supervisor tells you sexually oriented jokes.
7. Your supervisor asks you to run a personal errand.
8. Your supervisor tells sexually explicit jokes in your proximity.
9. Your supervisor touches or pats nonsexual parts of your body.
10. Your supervisor asks you for a date.
11. Your supervisor pays for your meal.
12. Your supervisor helps you with physically demanding work.

Key

Most people rate statements 1–3 severe, 4–7 uncertain, and 8–12 harmless.

Note: Items in this *Pop Quiz* are adapted from Blakely, Blakely, and Moorman (1995).

---

[4] All information regarding the experience of Leigh-Anne Goins is from L-A Goins (personal communication with author, March 2005). Published with permission.

When a Friend Gets Promoted

1

BACKGROUND

Workplace relationships are always challenging to maintain, but when a previous peer is promoted, interpersonal and professional rifts can result. To consider how you might deal with such a situation, read the case study and work through the five steps that follow.

2

CASE STUDY

You became friends with Sean and Janice during new-employee training. Janice is quiet, serious, and responsible. Her life is her work, and she always gives 110 percent. Because of her dedication, she quickly was invited into the company's insider network. She's an incredible worker, but also a truly nice person and always goes out of her way to help you with any job-related problems. You don't socialize much with Janice outside of work, but you really like her. Sean is Janice's opposite. He's outgoing, upbeat, nonchalant, and very funny, and he always brightens your day with a witty observation about life. Sean does what's necessary at work but nothing more. He was quickly embraced by the company's party clique. You consider Sean your best friend at work, and while not a member of his clique, you occasionally party with them.

Unsurprisingly, Janice is promoted, and she is now your and Sean's direct supervisor. Tension quickly escalates between the two because of their disparate workplace values. Janice clearly expects an increase in Sean's productivity, and though you share her work values, you feel caught in the middle. Sean starts constantly com-

plaining to you about Janice, and he still treats her as a peer rather than a superior, even calling her "the Diva" behind her back.

One day, Janice invites you to lunch. After chatting a while, she says, "This is confidential, but I'm telling you this because I admire you as a worker and as a friend. There's going to be a *huge* shake-up soon, including major personnel changes. The company is going in a new direction, one that values excellence in work and dedication to the company. It's not my place to choose your friends, but know this: those who share our values are going to prosper, and those who don't are going to be left behind."

After the lunch, you're shaken. You know what Janice was implying: Sean, his crew, and anyone linked with them—possibly you—are going to be downsized unless they change their work values. You feel terrible. You don't want to lose Sean as a coworker or a friend. But it's obvious that you must distance yourself from Sean and his clique, or you could lose your job. As you're pondering this, Sean walks into your office. "So," he quips, "you and the Diva enjoyed *quite* the long lunch. What's her latest evil scheme?"

YOUR TURN

While working through the following steps, keep in mind the interpersonal communication concepts, skills, and insights you've learned so far in this book, especially this chapter. Also remember: there are no right answers, so think hard about the choice you make! (P.S. Need help? Review the concepts listed below.)

- **Step 1: Reflect on yourself.** What are your thoughts and feelings in this situation? What attributions are you making about Sean, Janice, and the interpersonal communication you experienced? Are your attributions accurate? Why or why not?

- **Step 2: Reflect on your partners.** Using perspective-taking, put yourself in both Sean's and Janice's shoes. Consider how each of them is thinking and feeling. Is one of them right in this situation and the other wrong? Are the views of both valid?

- **Step 3: Identify the optimal outcome.** Think about what's happening now in this situation and what's going to happen. Consider your own feelings as well as those of Sean and Janice and the people around you. Given all these factors, what's the best, most constructive relationship outcome possible here? Be sure to consider not just what's best for *you* but what's best for everyone.

- **Step 4: Locate the roadblocks.** Taking into consideration your own thoughts and feelings, those of Sean and Janice, and all that has happened in this situation, what's preventing you from achieving the optimal outcome you identified in step 3?

- **Step 5: Chart your course.** What can you say and do to overcome the roadblocks and achieve your relationship outcome?

HELPFUL CONCEPTS

Workplace cliques, *423–424*

How networks can impact your career opportunities, *424*

Maintaining peer relationships, *431–432*

Offering constructive criticism, *440–441*

majority of sexual harassment incidents go unreported. Although most people condemn sexual harassment in the workplace, enormous differences exist in perceptions of what constitutes harassment.

Given differences in perception, one way to share a common definition of **sexual harassment** is by looking at the one offered by the U.S. Equal Employment Opportunity Commission (1980):

> Unwelcome sexual advances, requests for sexual favors, and other verbal or physical conduct of a sexual nature constitute sexual harassment when (1) submission to such conduct is made either explicitly or implicitly a term or condition of an individual's employment, (2) submission to or rejection of such conduct by an individual is used as the basis for employment decisions affecting such individual, or (3) such conduct has the intention or effect of unreasonably interfering with an individual's work performance or of creating an intimidating, hostile, or offensive working environment.

This definition suggests that two types of harassment occur in the workplace. The first is quid pro quo harassment—a person in a supervisory position asking for or demanding sexual favors in return for professional advancement or protection from layoffs or other undesirable events (Gerdes, 1999). Much more prevalent than quid pro quo, however, is hostile climate harassment. As Leigh-Anne Goins experienced, hostile climate harassment is sexual behavior intended to disrupt a person's work performance.

Sexual harassment has a devastating effect. Victims of sexual harassment report feeling angry, afraid, and depressed (Cochran, Frazier, & Olson, 1997). Harassment victims are more likely than others to develop substance abuse and other health problems, including weight loss and sleep and stomach disorders (Clair, 1998). Not surprisingly, they also suffer a host of professional problems, including missed work, lower productivity, and ostracism by coworkers who blame them for inviting the harassment (Hickson, Grierson, & Linder, 1991).

The most common way of coping with sexual harassment is to avoid the harasser, ignore the harassment, or interpret the harassment in ways that minimize its seriousness—"It's not a big enough deal to pursue," "He was only flirting," "That's just the way things work here," or "It was all a harmless joke" (Clair, 1993). Some workers confront the harasser, describing his or her actions as inappropriate or threatening or pursuing legal action. Confronting harassers is strongly encouraged as a matter of principle, but the practical consequences can be difficult to manage. In sexual harassment cases, people in the organization often side with the person in the position of authority (Fitzgerald, 1993).

If you are experiencing sexual harassment, remember that fewer than 5 percent of sexual-harassment victims report the problem to an authority (Fitzgerald, 1993). The decision not to report will likely perpetuate the harassment because it can teach harassers that their behavior is okay. The best long-term solution for addressing sexual harassment is to challenge it when it occurs and believe that the harassers deserve to be punished. If you're not sure what to do, contact the EEOC. Go to www.eeoc.gov for detailed information on how to handle such situations, or you can call 1-800-669-4000.

Workplace Relationships and Human Happiness

In his book *The Pursuit of Happiness* (2002), psychologist David Myers comments on the role that workplace relationships play in his life:

> Through our work we identify with a *community*. My sense of community is rooted in the network of supportive friends who surround me on our department team, in the institution whose goals we embrace, and in the profession we call our own. (p. 130)

For many of us, our motivation to work transcends the desire to bring home a paycheck. Although we need the money our jobs provide, we also want to feel that our work is meaningful and important. When asked, "Would you continue working, even if you inherited a huge fortune that made working unnecessary?" three out of four Americans answered "yes" (Eisenberg & Goodall, 1997). And this isn't just an American value: people in nearly every industrialized nation report lower satisfaction with their lives if they're unemployed, regardless of their financial standing (Myers, 2002).

But it's not the work itself that fulfills us; it's the coupling of the professional with the personal, the creation of a coworker community. Day in and day out, we endure work stress and intense demands with those who surround us—our supervisors, subordinates, and peers. These people aren't just coworkers; they can be companions, friends, sometimes even best friends or lovers. When these relationships are healthy, the effects spread to every part of our lives. We're happier in life and more productive on the job. Those around us find us more pleasant to work with, and our organization as a whole thrives. When it comes to workplace relationships, the professional is profoundly personal.

SELF-REFLECTION

Would you continue working if you didn't need to? Why or why not? If you chose not to work, what consequences can you envision for your life? How would not having a job affect your sense of purpose? Your happiness?

POSTSCRIPT

We began this chapter with a narrative of a truly special workplace relationship. Despite differences in backgrounds, personal life challenges, and changes in organizational power and status, Vivian Derr and Silvia Amaro have remained best friends in and out of the workplace for more than a quarter century.

Consider your own work life for a moment. Do you have a coworker you consider your "sibling separated at birth"?

Of your workplace peers and superiors, whom could you count on to help you get through a painful divorce or surmount the challenge of new parenthood? Is there someone you get along with so well that you would recruit him or her to serve as your own supervisor?

Vivian and Silvia's friendship testifies to the primacy of interpersonal relationships in our lives. In a culture in which many of us define our worth largely through our professional

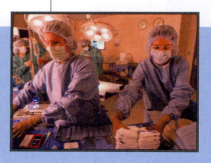

accomplishments—promotions, paychecks, and portfolios—by far the most meaningful accomplishment of all is forging interpersonal relationships that thrive and endure.

Key Terms

Key Concepts

Defining Workplace Relationships

- Our **workplace relationships** are shaped by many forces. Two of the most powerful are **organizational culture** and **organizational networks.** Most workers learn their organization's culture—communication norms, artifacts, and values—during new employee socialization and from interacting with members of various networks.

- Organizational networks are the principal source of workplace information for most employees. Information in networks is exchanged through face-to-face encounters, memos, phone, and e-mail. **Virtual networks** also exist, particularly for workers who telecommute from home.

- When members of networks share common beliefs and personal values, they sometimes form **workplace cliques.** Cliques can provide useful insider information to new employees. Cliques can also be disruptive, particularly when they encourage unethical employee behavior.

Supportive and Defensive Organizational Climates

- The overall emotional tone of your organization, known as the **organizational climate,** can be rigid and cold in a **defensive climate,** open and warm in a **supportive climate,** or somewhere in between. There are several ways you can help foster a supportive climate, including communicating in a collaborative rather than controlling way, empathizing with coworkers' concerns, and emphasizing equality regardless of your rank.

Peer Relationships

- Our closest workplace relationships are with our **professional peers.** Friendships between peers evolve from frequent interaction and common interests. The same is true for **virtual peers.** Peers who become best friends usually are drawn together because of the need for social support in the wake of a personal crisis.

Mixed-Status Relationships

- The primary interpersonal dynamic in **mixed-status relationships** is power. The difference in power between workers and managers makes forming friendships across status lines challenging.

- Much of **upward communication** is designed to gain influence. Although people use different tactics, the most effective is **advocacy,** designing a message that specifically is tailored to the viewpoints of your superior.

- When engaging in **downward communication,** it's important to communicate in positive, empathic, respectful, and open ways.

- The power difference that defines mixed-status relationships sometimes leads to **workplace abuse,** which can cause stress-related illnesses and emotional problems for abused workers. Although many people think **sexual harassment** is on the wane, incidences actually have increased over the last decade.

Key Skills

- What are the pros and cons of workplace cliques? Find the answer on page 424.

- Interested in assessing the strength of your organizational network? Check out the *Skills Practice* on pages 424.

- What are the two most important practical tips to keep in mind about organizational networks? Go to page 424 to find out.

- How can you help build a supportive climate in your workplace? Review the dimensions underlying climate on pages 425–428. Then follow the suggestions on pages 428–429.

- How can you maintain healthy and happy peer relationships? Revisit the suggestions on pages 431–432. Then take the *Pop Quiz* on page 433.

- What can you do to maintain a workplace romance? Check out the recommendations on pages 432–433.

- Interested in enhancing your upward communication? Practice your advocacy skills by revisiting the steps described on pages 435–436. Then do the *Skills Practice* on page 436.

- What are the five most important skills necessary for effective downward communication? Revisit pages 438–439 to find out.

- How can you more effectively praise subordinates? Review the tips for effective compliments on pages 439–440.

- What can you do to make your criticism more constructive? Follow the suggestions on pages 440–441.

- How can you successfully maintain mixed-status relationships? Check out pages 441–442 for the answer.

- Want to enhance your understanding of workplace abuse, as well as how you can better cope with it? Complete the *Skills Practice* on page 442.

- Think you have a firm understanding of sexual harassment? Take the *Pop Quiz* on page 443 to check your perceptions.

- What would you do if two workplace friends put you in a position where you had to choose between your loyalty to each of them? Complete the *Making Relationship Choices* exercise on pages 444–445 to find out.

Glossary

accommodation: (p. 308) A way of handling conflict in which one person sacrifices his or her goals for the goals of another. For example, Louis gives in to Martel over where they should park their cars: "You can have the driveway. I'm tired of arguing about it."

action-oriented listeners: (p. 202) Those who prefer to receive concise, accurate information for decision making—for example, a supervisor who requires brief summaries from department heads and does not want to bat around details in long meetings.

actor-observer effect: (p. 87) A tendency to credit external forces as causes for our behaviors instead of internal factors. For instance, Leon says he snapped at a coworker because she was slow instead of blaming his own impatience.

adaptor: (p. 269) A gesture, often unconsciously made, that serves a physical or psychological purpose. For example, twirling hair while reading, jingling pocket change, and fingering jewelry may be gestures that provide comfort, signal anxiety, or are simply unconscious habits.

advocacy: (p. 436) Communication from a subordinate intended to influence a superior in an organization. For example, you convince your manager to try a new product line.

affect display: (p. 282) A nonverbal behavior that reveals real or pretended emotion, such as a frown, a choked sob, or a smile intended to disguise fear.

agentic friendships: (p. 401) Voluntary relationships focused on achieving specific practical goals, such as those among peers in a study group or colleagues at work.

aggressive families: (p. 396) Families that handle conflict by direct and forceful competition. For example, in Joe's family, standing up for yourself is important even if doing so hurts someone else.

aggressive listening: (p. 209) Also known as *ambushing*. Listening in order to collect information to use against the speaker, such as when a

father encourages his son to describe his ambitions just to ridicule the son's goals.

algebraic impressions: (p. 101) Impressions of others that continually emerge as we add and subtract positive or negative information that we learn about them.

anger: (p. 138) The most intense negative primary emotion, usually triggered by someone or something that seems improper or unfair.

anxious attachment style: (p. 55) The tendency to be overly dependent in an adult relationship that arises if a person learned from his or her childhood caregiver that love is undependable or unpredictable.

appropriateness: (p. 156) A measure of communication competence that indicates how capably a person can match his or her behavior to the expectations or norms of an interpersonal relationship or situation.

artifact: (p. 280) A nonverbal code that represents the way we use objects or personal accessories to express ourselves or influence how others view us. Jewelry, for instance, can indicate economic means, marital status, religious affiliation, style preferences, and taste.

attending: (p. 191) The stage of the listening process in which a listener consciously focuses on received information. For example, you may *hear* a radio but *attend* only when a favorite song comes on.

attention focus: (p. 132) Preventing unwanted emotions by ignoring aspects of an event or encounter that provoke those emotions. For example, you disregard your uncle's snide comments while forcing all your interest on your aunt's conversation.

attributional complexity: (p. 175) An ability to imagine multiple explanations for the behavior of others or to interpret and understand others through perspective-taking and empathy. For example, in spite of Anna's remark, "Well, I guess Raul's mad at you," Justine thinks there could be several reasons why Raul didn't say hello to her.

attributions: (p. 85) Rationales we use to explain interpersonal encounters. For example, Ryan reasons that Jason's quietness in class means that Jason is shy.

avoidance: (p. 306) A way of handling conflict by ignoring the contentious person or topic or by responding with deliberate vagueness. For example, Martel hides behind the newspaper as Louis shouts, "Your car is blocking mine again. How many times do I have to ask you to park it to the side?" See also **skirting; sniping.**

avoidant attachment style: (p. 55) The tendency to avoid intimacy in an adult relationship that arises if a person learned from his or her childhood caregiver that love is hurtful.

avoidant families: (p. 396) Families that handle conflict by ignoring or censoring it. For instance, in Carl's family, people swallow their anger and sulk instead of arguing with each other.

avoiding: (p. 352) A relational stage in which one or both individuals in a couple try to distance themselves from one another physically. For example, Owen changes jobs to have an excuse to travel away from home frequently.

back-channel cues: (p. 193) Responses that nonverbally or verbally signal that a message has been received and understood. For example, saying "Okay, got it" after someone details extensive driving directions.

beautiful-is-good effect: (p. 342) A tendency for physical attractiveness to create the perception of competency and intelligence. For example, a witness is viewed favorably and seems credible because she is good-looking.

betrayal: (p. 367) Intentionally hurting a relational partner with deception, disloyalty, or infidelity.

birds-of-a-feather effect: (p. 342) A tendency to be attracted to others if we perceive them to have levels of physical attractiveness, values, and interests similar to our own.

bizarreness effect: (p. 197) The helpful influence that unusual or odd information has on our ability to remember it. For example, you could associate Robert Phillips's name in your mind with an image of someone wearing a robber's mask and using a Phillips screwdriver to crack a safe.

blended emotions: (p. 122) Two or more primary emotions experienced at the same time. For instance, Melinda feels fear and anger when her daughter is not home after curfew.

blended family: (p. 383) A husband and wife who provide care for one or more children who are not the biological offspring of both adults.

bonding: (p. 349) A relational stage in which an official, public ritual unites two people by the laws or customs of their culture. For example, Ruth marries Owen in her hometown church.

catharsis: (p. 140) Within the field of interpersonal communication, the assumption that open and unrestrained emotional expression is beneficial.

channel: (p. 7) The five sensory avenues (sound, sight, touch, scent, taste) used to transmit information from one person to another. For example, you may apologize by showing someone a sad facial expression, lightly touching his shoulder, and saying, "I'm so sorry."

chronemics: (p. 275) A nonverbal code that represents the ways time is used in interpersonal communication.

chronic hostility: (p. 140) A persistent state of simmering anger or barely suppressed, constant negativity.

circumscribing: (p. 352) A relational stage in which partners avoid talking about topics that produce conflict. For instance, whenever Owen mentions he's interested in changing his job, Ruth becomes upset and changes the subject.

cohabiting couple: (p. 383) Two unmarried adults who are involved romantically and live together with or without children.

collaboration: (p. 312) A way of handling conflict by problem solving so that equal attention is given to both people involved. For example, Martel and Louis brainstorm ways to solve the problem they have with their shared parking area until they come up with an agreeable solution.

collaborative families: (p. 396) Families that handle conflict directly, without hostility. For example, Pamela freely expresses her needs but refrains from belittling her sister.

collectivistic culture: (p. 57) A culture that values the needs and goals of the community or group above an individual's. Because cooperation and group loyalty are important in such a culture, to reflect group belonging, schoolchildren might wear uniforms or a businessperson might keep a personal opinion private rather than disturb the harmony of the group discussion. Contrast **individualistic culture.**

colors of love: (p. 335) A metaphor in which six types of love—agape, eros, ludus, mania, pragma, and storge—are compared to a color wheel.

communal friendships: (p. 400) Voluntary relationships focused on sharing time and activities for pleasure, encouragement, and support.

communication: (p. 6) The process through which people use messages to generate meanings with and across contexts, cultures, channels, and media.

communication accommodation theory: (p. 244) The idea that you can foster a connection and make a favorable impression when you adjust your speech patterns—rate, clarity, and time spent talking—to match the other person's behaviors.

communication apprehension: (p. 166) The fear or nervousness we feel or expect to feel when communicating with others. There are four basic types: context, receiver, temporary, and trait.

communication plans: (p. 167) Mental scripts, composed before communication with others, that include plan actions and plan contingencies. For example, before calling to complain about her telephone bill, Marjorie mentally rehearses how she will explain her problem and what objections she might face. See also **plan actions; plan contingencies.**

communication skills: (pp. 36, 154) Practical, goal-directed behaviors and patterns—such as ways to effectively respond to criticism—that are practiced in interpersonal relationships, based on knowledge of interpersonal communication competence, and aimed at improving the quality of relationships. See also **appropriateness; interpersonal communication competence.**

companionate love: (p. 335) An intense form of liking involving quiet intimacy, emotional investment, and interdependent lives, such as the bond between two best friends.

competition: (p. 309) A way of handling conflict by pursing your own goals in a direct confrontation without concern for the goals of another person. For example, Martel and Louis yell back and forth about whose car should have the driveway parking spot and who should park out front.

complementary relationships: (p. 300) Relationships characterized by an unequal balance of power, such as a marriage in which one spouse is the decision maker.

compromise: (p. 317) An agreeable resolution to a conflict achieved when both people sacrifice some of their goals. For example, though Matt wants to see the sci-fi thriller and Jane wants to see the new animated film, they agree to go to an adventure comedy.

conflict: (p. 296) An interactive communication process shaped by perceptions of resources as limited and goals as incompatible, and by our views of and reactions to the situation.

conformity orientation: (p. 385) The degree to which family members believe they should avoid disagreement and stand unified by the same attitudes, beliefs, and values.

connotative meanings: (p. 229) Subjective or implied associations that words carry beyond their dictionary definitions. For instance, calling someone *slender* suggests something more positive than the words *skinny* or *scrawny* do, though all three words mean "underweight." Contrast **denotative meanings.**

consensual families: (p. 386) Families characterized by high levels of conformity and conversation orientation. For example, Dan's parents encourage their son to be open but also expect him to maintain family unity through agreement or obedience.

constitutive rules: (p. 222) Guidelines about what words mean according to a particular language's vocabulary. For instance, "pencil" is *Bleistift* in German and *matita* in Italian.

content-oriented listeners: (p. 203) Those who prefer factual information, detail, and intellectual stimulation from messages—for example, a supervisor who reviews the success of a fund-raising event by requesting data analyzing the effectiveness of her team's publicity campaign instead of asking to hear about team members' experiences.

context: (p. 7) The situation in which communication occurs. Context includes the physical locations, backgrounds, genders, ages, moods, and relationships of the communicators, as well as the time of day.

control messages: (p. 169) Defensive responses that use counterattack or going on the offensive to deflect criticism—for instance, saying, "Are you through? Good, because I've heard just about enough and now you're going to listen to me."

conventional messages: (p. 162) Communicating to emphasize rules and responsibilities to control the behavior of others—for example, saying, "You're late again today and were late twice last week. You know the rules about tardiness."

conversation orientation: (p. 383) The degree to which family members believe unrestrained communication and emotion-sharing are important.

Cooperative Principle: (p. 238) The idea that meaningful verbal messages are informative, truthful, understandable, and tied to the topic of discussion. For example, listening closely to your friend's problem with a coworker and then responding with support would demonstrate the

Cooperative Principle; interrupting your friend to brag about your new laptop would not.

cooperative verbal communication: (p. 238) Speaking in a clear, inclusive, and responsible way.

culture: (pp. 29, 57) A learned set of values, beliefs, and behaviors shared by a large group of people. Culture affects what it means to be an American as well as a woman.

cumulative annoyance: (p. 306) A buildup of suppressed irritations and accumulated frustration that grows to a flash point. For example, Martel's anger about where Louis parks his car is a reaction to several other incidents when Louis was inconsiderate.

deactivation: (p. 133) Preventing unwanted emotions by systematically desensitizing oneself to emotional experience. For example, Josh insulates himself with numbness after his wife's death.

deception: (p. 246) Deliberately providing false information or intentionally omitting important details in order to mislead.

defensive climate: (p. 425) A workplace atmosphere that is unfriendly, judgmental, discouraging, or inflexible. Contrast **supportive climate.**

defensive communication: (p. 169) Reactions to perceived criticism, or to hurt, that can be hostile. For instance, when Stacy asks Lena to slow down her driving, Lena snaps back, "I'm not going that fast. If you don't like the way I drive, ride with someone else." See also **control messages; dogmatic messages; indifference messages; superiority messages.**

demand-withdraw pattern: (p. 320) A way of handling conflicts that is linked to gender roles. For example, a man retreats in response to a woman confronting him.

denotative meanings: (p. 229) The dictionary definitions of a word. For example, the noun *iron* has several denotative meanings: it can signify an appliance, a golf club, an element or metal, and a gun. Contrast **connotative meanings.**

dialects: (p. 224) Language variations unique to particular regions or groups; they may include differences in vocabulary, grammar, and pronunciation. For example, in various regions of the United States, carbonated beverages are called *soda, pop,* or *coke.*

differentiating: (p. 352) A relational stage in which a couple experiences tension over individual differences in goals or interests. For example, Ruth and Owen argue over whose family they are going to visit for Thanksgiving and how little time he has spent helping her redecorate the house.

dirty secrets: (p. 310) Truthful but destructive messages used deliberately to hurt someone during a conflict. For example, Judith tells her sister, "That boy you like—Craig? I heard him tell Elaine you laugh like a horse."

display rules: (p. 127) Cultural norms guiding appropriate ways to manage and communicate emotions. For example, customary ways to show grief range from stoic reserve to open weeping to exaggerated wailing.

dogmatic messages: (p. 169) Defensive responses that refuse to recognize other viewpoints as valid, such as saying, "I know I'm right, no matter what you say."

dominance: (p. 285) An exertion of power or influence over another person. It may occur through nonverbal behavior as in crowding into a person's intimate zone threateningly, staring someone down, or keeping another person waiting.

domination: (p. 316) One person persuading another to abandon his or her goals to resolve a conflict. For example, Jane wants to see the new animated film, but Matt refuses. So she tells Matt that his choice, a sci-fi film, is fine.

downward communication: (pp. 437–38) Messages that travel in an organization from a superior to subordinates. For example, the CEO of the company calls the regional managers together for a strategy session. Contrast **upward communication.**

dyadic: (p. 20) Communication involving only two people.

dysfunctional relationship beliefs: (p. 362) False ideas about romantic relationships that yield destructive outcomes, such as believing that if your partner sincerely loves you, he or she will automatically understand how you think.

eavesdropping: (p. 208) Intentionally listening in on private conversations.

effectiveness: (p. 156) The ability to communicate in order to present oneself well, to accomplish practical goals, and to foster interpersonal connections.

embarrassment: (p. 59) A feeling of awkwardness or humiliation that comes when we lose face, failing to present ourselves publicly as we wish, as when we make a social blunder. See also **face.**

emblem: (p. 269) A gesture that symbolizes a specific verbal meaning within a given culture, such as the "thumbs up" or the "V" for victory sign. The meaning of such gestures may change dramatically from culture to culture, varying from humorous to obscene.

emotion: (p. 119) An intense reaction that indicates how we interpret the event, our physiological arousal, the way we label the experience, and how we manage our communication of that reaction.

emotional contagion: (p. 121) The spreading of emotion from person to person, such as anger running through a mob or the infectiousness of a baby's laughter.

emotional intelligence: (p. 130) The ability to accurately interpret and handle your own emotions and the emotions of others in order to communicate constructively.

emotion management: (p. 131) Efforts to control which emotions you experience, when you have them, and how you choose to express them.

emotion-sharing: (p. 120) Disclosing emotions to others. For instance, Al tells Ron how angry he is with a coworker.

empathy: (p. 106) Understanding of another person's perspective and awareness of his or her feelings. For instance, Gill doesn't agree with Mike's protest against the new policies at work, but he can see why Mike was worried and angry.

encounter avoidance: (p. 132) Preventing unwanted emotions by keeping away from situations or people likely to provoke them. For example, Jessica infuriates Roxanne, so Roxanne moves out of their shared apartment.

encounter structuring: (p. 132) Preventing unwanted emotions by avoiding discussion of difficult topics or personal areas of contention. For instance, Natalie and Julie avoid talking about living expenses because Natalie is jealous of Julie's income.

environment: (p. 280) A nonverbal code that represents the ways fixed and semifixed features in our surroundings affect our communication. For example, a casino's exciting sounds, lights, and absence of windows or clocks encourage patrons to linger.

equity: (p. 340) A sense of balance in a relationship; fairness evident in the give-and-take between partners.

escalation: (p. 310) A dramatic rise in emotional intensity and increasing hostility during conflict, such as teasing that inflates to a heated exchange of insults.

ethics: (pp. 28, 158) A code of moral principles that guide respectful, honest behavior toward others. Ethical communication is free of racist or sexist remarks.

ethnocentrism: (p. 174) The attitude that your own culture's ways are superior to those of all other cultures; the view that your culture represents the standard by which all other cultures are measured. For example, Americans, accustomed to lining up, who consider cultures that don't use waiting lines as disorganized are displaying ethnocentrism. Contrast **world-mindedness.**

exit strategy: (p. 361) An active, destructive approach a couple uses to handle a relational problem. One or both individuals may leave or threaten to leave the relationship. For example, Paul tells Nathan that if he doesn't stop running up their credit cards he'll leave and make sure all the debts will be in Nathan's name.

experimenting: (p. 345) A relational stage in which two people become acquainted by sharing factual information about themselves and making light conversation or small talk. For instance, after Ruth is introduced to Owen, they talk about their jobs and where they went to school, and they discover they both like jazz.

expertise currency: (p. 302) Power that comes from possessing specialized skills or knowledge that is valuable to others, such as knowing CPR if someone stops breathing.

expressive messages: (p. 162) Disclosing personal thoughts and feelings that in some instances are inappropriate and ineffective. For example, calmly saying, "I'm angry because you're late again," or snarling, "You're late again and I'm fed up with your whiney excuses."

extended family: (p. 382) A group of people who are related to one another—such as aunts, uncles, cousins, or grandparents—and live in the same household.

face: (p. 59) The self we allow others to see; the aspects of ourselves we choose to present publicly. For instance, you dress up and speak carefully for an important social occasion, though in private you're very casual.

family: (p. 381) A group of people who communicate to create and share a mutual identity, emotional bond, common history, heritage, and boundaries for interaction.

family communication patterns: (p. 383) Beliefs about the role communication should play in family life and the interactions that result from those beliefs. Among families there are variations in how much or little conversation and conformity are expected in a family. See also **conformity orientation; conversation orientation.**

family communication rules: (pp. 383, 392) The guidelines a family establishes about what topics family members may discuss, how they should speak about them, and to whom they may talk about certain topics. For instance, Melinda knows that she can ask her parents about her grandfather but cannot speak of him to her aunt, who is deeply resentful of him.

family stories: (p. 394) Anecdotes of family events retold to bond family members. For example, Katie's mother often recounts how Katie was born on the day of a crippling blizzard.

feedback: (pp. 16, 193) Verbal and nonverbal messages that a receiver uses to respond to a sender, such as a frown or saying, "I disagree." See also **interactive communication model.**

feelings: (p. 122) Brief emotional reactions resulting in limited arousal, such as the fleeting nostalgia you experience hearing a familiar song.

fields of experience: (p. 17) Life experiences, attitudes, values, and beliefs that a communicator brings to an interaction and that shape how messages are sent and received. For example, when Frank thinks of family, he imagines many relatives, including grandparents and cousins, but Noelle's sense of family is limited to her parents and stepbrother. See also **interactive communication model.**

flaming: (p. 177) Online verbal aggression. For example, in a nasty e-mail, Robert writes to his co-worker Matt, calling him an "egotistical fathead" and ridiculing his project as "moronic nonsense."

friendship rules: (p. 407) Guidelines for appropriate communication and behavior within friendships, such as keeping a confidence and showing support.

friendships: (p. 398) Voluntary relationships between people who like and enjoy being with each other.

friendship-warmth touch: (p. 272) A touch used to convey regard, affection, or camaraderie, such as an arm across another's shoulders, a victory slap between teammates, or playful jostling between friends.

functional-professional touch: (p. 272) A touch used to accomplish a task, such as a physical therapist positioning a client's arm or a dancer gripping his partner's waist for a lift.

fundamental attribution error: (p. 86) A mistake made by assigning the cause of someone's behavior to his or her personality rather than to outside forces. For instance, Sheila blamed Mark's flash of anger on a bad temper instead of unusual stress at work.

FWB relationships (friends with benefits): (p. 404) Friendships negotiated to include sexual activity without a commitment to deeper emotional bonds.

gay or lesbian family: (p. 382) A group consisting of two people of the same sex who serve as parents for the biological children of one of the adults.

gender: (pp. 31, 52) The composite of social, psychological, and cultural attributes that characterize us as male or female.

Gestalt: (p. 99) All-encompassing positive or negative first impression we receive from others. See also **halo effect; horn effect.**

grief: (p. 141) Intense sadness that follows a substantial loss. For instance, Beth grieves for the loss of her marriage now that her divorce is final.

halo effect: (p. 101) A tendency to interpret anything another person says or does in a favorable light because that person made a positive first impression.

haptics: (p. 272) A nonverbal code that represents messages conveyed through touch. See also **friendship-warmth touch; functional-professional touch; love-intimacy touch; sexual-arousal touch; social-polite touch.**

hearing: (p. 188) The sensory process of taking in and interpreting sound.

high-context culture: (p. 225) A culture that relies more on the context of a conversation than on the words themselves for meaning. For example, after asking to purchase two theater tickets, a Japanese person might hear, "Sorry, very difficult," and immediately understand this as a subtle, indirect response meaning, "I am embarrassed that I can't provide you what you wish, but the performance is sold out." Contrast **low-context culture.**

high self-monitors: (p. 156) People who see themselves as others see them and can adapt their behavior appropriately. For example, Leon becomes aware he's been preoccupied and silent during the group discussion, so he apologizes and leans forward to listen more attentively. Contrast **low self-monitors.**

honesty: (p. 67) Truthful communication, without exaggeration or omission of relevant information. Failing to tell someone something can be as dishonest as an outright lie.

horn effect: (p. 101) A tendency to interpret anything another person says or does in a negative light because that person made an unfavorable first impression.

I-It: (p. 21) A type of perception and communication that occurs when you treat others as though they are objects and distance yourself from them—for example, when you dismiss someone by saying, "I don't have time for your stupid questions. Figure it out yourself."

"I" language: (p. 242) Communication that uses the pronoun "I" in sentence construction to take responsibility for what is said and to avoid creating an accusatory message—for example, "I'm frustrated because I think I'm doing more than you are on this project" instead of "You're really underperforming on this project." See also **"we" language; "you" language.**

illustrator: (p. 269) A gesture used to demonstrate or emphasize an accompanying verbal message. For example, a fisherman holds his hands apart to show the size of his catch, or someone points emphatically at a door while saying "Leave!"

immediacy: (p. 269) An interest that is communicated nonverbally so that a person seems especially alert or attentive to you.

impersonal communication: (p. 21) Messages that have insignificant impact on our thoughts, emotions, behaviors, or relationships, such as commenting about the television schedule or passing someone and saying "How's it going?" without looking up.

implicit personality theories: (p. 96) Presumptions we make about the personalities of others by generalizing from limited knowledge of a few of their traits. For instance, Bradley assumes that Will is a disorganized procrastinator because of Will's casual, friendly manner.

indifference messages: (p. 169) Defensive responses to criticism that suggest apathy and a lack of concern, such as saying, "So what? Say whatever you want, I couldn't care less."

individualistic culture: (p. 57) A culture that values individuality over group goals. For instance, in the United States, self-reliance, self-expression, and personal achievement are prized. Schoolchildren are taught be outspoken and to challenge opinions, and they dress to reflect their individual tastes and interests. Contrast **collectivistic culture.**

ingroupers: (p. 90) People you consider fundamentally similar to yourself because of their interests, affiliations, or backgrounds. Contrast **outgroupers.**

initiating: (p. 345) A relational stage in which two people meet and form their first impressions of one another. For instance, Owen introduces himself in an e-mail to Ruth after reading her profile in an online dating site, and she responds with her telephone number.

instrumental goals: (p. 24) Practical goals you want to achieve or tasks you want to accomplish

through a particular interpersonal encounter, such as asking for driving directions or about ingredients in a recipe.

integrating: (p. 347) A relational stage in which two people become a couple and begin to share an identity. For example, Ruth and Owen share an apartment together and spend time with one another's families.

integrative agreements: (p. 317) Conflict resolution achieved when both people collaborate to meet all of their goals. For example, because Matt and Jane can't agree on what film to see, they decide they'd both be happier going to a comedy club.

intensifying: (p. 347) A relational stage characterized by deeper self-disclosures, more commitment and trust, stronger feelings, and signs of affection and intimacy between two people. For example, Owen and Ruth have been dating for more than a year and talk with excitement about a future together.

interaction: (p. 7) A series of messages exchanged between people, such as a chain of e-mails or the discussion that takes place during a job interview.

interactive communication model: (p. 16) A depiction of communication messages that are exchanged back and forth between a sender and a receiver and are influenced by the fields of experience of both communicators. For example, two people send coded instant messages to each other.

intercultural competence: (p. 172) The ability to communicate with people from different backgrounds in ways that are ethical, appropriate, and effective.

interpersonal communication: (p. 20) A dynamic form of communication between two (or more) people in which the messages exchanged significantly influence their thoughts, emotions, behaviors, and relationships.

interpersonal communication competence: (pp. 36, 154) The ability to communicate appropriately, effectively, and ethically in a consistent way.

interpersonal impressions: (p. 98) Ideas about who people are and how we feel about them. For instance, when Sarah and Georgia met, Georgia thought Sarah's quietness meant that Sarah was unfriendly and conceited.

interpersonal relationships: (p. 36) Emotional, intellectual, and/or physical involvements between people that are formed through communication.

interpretation: (p. 84) The stage of perception in which we assign our own meaning to sensory data we have selected. For instance, Randy thinks a man running down the sidewalk hurries because he is late, but Shondra infers that the man is chasing someone.

intimacy: (p. 284) An emotional bonding or connection between individuals that generally includes higher levels of nonverbal involvement. Those who are more intimate share more time, touch more, and are more comfortable with each other in intimate space.

intimacy currency: (p. 302) Power that comes from a close relationship. For example, you can easily persuade a close friend to change her mind because she is fond of you.

intimate space: (p. 273) The narrowest proxemic zone. It ranges from 0 to 18 inches of space between communicators—touching distance.

intrapersonal communication: (p. 20) Communication involving only one person, such as talking to yourself.

I-Thou: (p. 21) A type of perception and communication that has the effect of bonding us with others, such as seeking connections with others, seeing things from others' points of view, and treating others as unique individuals.

jealousy: (p. 366) A hurt, resentful, or hostile reaction when a valued relationship seems threatened. For instance, Tyler is jealous when his girlfriend, Mary, flirts with Scott.

Jefferson strategy: (p. 140) Using a deliberate time delay to reduce your anger before you respond to a triggering event. For instance, Jon counts to 10 before he reacts to his young daughter's naughty behavior.

kinesics: (p. 266) A nonverbal code that represents messages communicated in facial expressions, posture, body movements, gestures, and eye contact.

kitchen-sinking: (p. 298) A response to a conflict in which one person uses any and all complaints to attack the other. For example, although Mary and Pat are arguing about the budget, Mary adds, "I'm sick of the mess you left in the garage and these papers all over the family room."

laissez-faire families: (p. 386) Families characterized by low levels of conformity and conversation orientation. For example, Samantha's parents prefer limited communication and encourage their daughter to make her own choices and decisions.

liking: (p. 332) A feeling of fondness, respect, and warmth typical of friendship.

linear communication model: (p. 16) A depiction of communication messages that flow one way from a sender to a receiver, such as when a person sends an e-mail or a radio announcer broadcasts the news.

linguistic determinism: (p. 231) The view that the language we use determines and limits the way we think about and perceive the world.

linguistic relativity: (p. 232) The theory that languages create variations in the ways cultures perceive the world. For example, the Navajo word for "yellow" can refer to a point on a compass or to a time of day.

listening: (p. 188) The five-stage process of receiving, attending to, understanding, responding to, and recalling messages.

listening functions: (p. 199) The five general purposes that listening serves: to analyze, to appreciate, to comprehend, to discern, and to support.

listening style: (p. 202) An individual's pattern of listening behaviors and preferences. See also **action-oriented listeners; content-oriented listeners; people-oriented listeners; time-oriented listeners.**

loneliness: (p. 167) Feelings of social isolation and lack of companionship.

long-term memory: (p. 193) A set of information stored in the part of the mind where knowledge such as your mailing address is permanently held.

looking-glass self: (p. 46) Sociologist Charles Horton Cooley's metaphor for how our self-concepts come from our impressions of what others think of us. For example, a young girl who believes others consider her poor in sports formulates an image of herself as uncoordinated even though she is a good dancer.

love-intimacy touch: (p. 272) A touch indicating deep emotional feeling, such as two romantic partners holding hands or two close friends embracing.

loving: (p. 333) An intense emotional commitment based on intimacy, caring, and attachment; a sense of union deeper than liking.

low-context culture: (p. 225) A culture that relies on words themselves, rather than on the conversational situation or subtle hints or implied meaning, to convey meaning. In the United States, for example, we prefer directness and clarity rather than what we view as vague hints. Contrast **high-context culture.**

low self-monitors: (p. 156) People who do not realize their behavior is inappropriate or resist adapting their behavior because it doesn't feel authentic. For instance, Amanda continues telling long stories about herself without realizing her listeners find her boring. Contrast **high self-monitors.**

loyalty strategy: (p. 360) A passive, constructive approach to a relational problem in which a couple relies on time rather than on open discussion to solve the problem. For instance, Paul and Nathan know they have problems with their bills but believe that in a few months they'll spend more carefully and correct the budget.

lurking: (p. 180) Observing the communication of others online without participating in order to get a sense of the group.

mask: (p. 59) The public, exterior self we use to disguise our true emotion or identity—for example, putting on a happy face when you are sad or pretending to be confident while inside you feel shy or anxious.

matching: (p. 342) A tendency to be attracted to others whom we perceive to be at our own level of attractiveness. For example, Michael dates Jennifer because she is pretty but not unapproachably gorgeous.

media: (p. 7) Tools used to communicate, including everything from newspapers, blackboards, and photographs to computers, cell phones, and television.

mental bracketing: (p. 192) An intentional refocusing of attention that allows you to avoid preoccupation while listening—for example, by consciously dismissing your worries about an upcoming exam in order to focus on a customer's request at work.

mere exposure effect: (p. 341) A positive result that comes from repeated interaction with another person. For example, the more June sees of Tom, the more attracted to him she becomes.

message: (p. 7) A unit of communication, such as waving to someone or saying "hello."

meta-communication: (p. 26) Verbal or nonverbal communication about communication messages that conveys how the messages should be interpreted.

misrepresentation: (p. 246) Giving faulty or inaccurate information unintentionally; to misspeak without meaning to be false or confusing. For example, a newscaster mistakenly reports an inaccurate statistic.

misunderstanding: (p. 247) Confusion resulting from the misinterpretation of a message. For example, your request to be ready at eight o'clock might be interpreted to mean 8 p.m. when you really mean 8 a.m.

mixed message: (p. 262) Communication characterized by a contradiction between a verbal and nonverbal message, such as saying, "I'm so happy for you," in a sarcastic tone of voice.

mixed-status relationships: (p. 434) Associations between people at different levels of power and status in an organization, such as a manager and a sales clerk.

mnemonics: (p. 197) Devices that help you memorize information. For example, the mnemonic *Roy G. Biv* is commonly used to recall the order of the seven colors in the spectrum.

moods: (p. 123) Low-intensity states of mind lasting longer than emotions. For example, Martin generally feels cheerful, and Robin is usually grumpy.

M-time (monochronemic time): (p. 275) A cultural orientation toward time, viewing it as an important resource and valuing punctuality and schedules. In the United States, for instance, appointments are important; Americans stand in line to be served one at a time and to maintain efficiency. Contrast **P-time (polychronemic time).**

naming: (p. 233) Assigning words to represent people, objects, places, and ideas.

narcissistic listening: (p. 212) A self-centered approach to listening. The listener encourages conversation centered on his or her own interests. For example, Neil acts bored while Jack describes a recent ski trip, interrupting Jack and switching the topic to his own recent car purchase.

negativity effect: (p. 100) A tendency to view negative information as a more accurate representation of a person's character than positive information.

neglect strategy: (p. 361) A passive, destructive approach a couple uses to handle a relational problem. The individuals may avoid each other, not speak, or complain about the problem without offering solutions. For example, when credit card bills arrive in the mail, Paul tears them open and rants about his and Nathan's climbing debts, and Nathan finds excuses to be out of the house.

noise: (p. 16) Environmental interference that inhibits a message on the way to its destination. For instance, a student is distracted from her instructor's message by hallway noise, a flickering light, and someone's strong perfume.

nonverbal communication: (p. 260) An intentional or unintentional transmission of meaning without language, made through the eight nonverbal codes.

nonverbal communication codes: (p. 265) Eight categories used to organize nonverbal behaviors: artifacts, chronemics, environment, haptics, kinesics, physical appearance, proxemics, and vocalics.

nuclear family: (p. 382) A father, mother, and their biological children.

online communication: (p. 31) Interaction through Internet-connected technology such as e-mail, text- or instant-messaging, chatrooms, multiuser discussions, listservs and other mailing lists, and Usenet newsgroups.

online disinhibition: (p. 177) A tendency to self-disclose personal information more freely online than in person. For example, in e-mails, Shannon finds herself confiding in Paul about her previous marriage much more readily than she ever does when they are face-to-face.

organization: (p. 83) The stage of perception in which we mentally structure selected sensory data into meaningful patterns.

organizational climate: (p. 425) The predominant emotional atmosphere of a workplace environment. For example, employees might say their organization feels warm, frenetic, unfriendly, or serene.

organizational culture: (p. 421) A distinct set of workplace traditions, values, and practices.

organizational networks: (p. 422) Communication links among an organization's members, such as the nature, frequency, and ways information is exchanged. For example, you have weekly face-to-face status meetings with your boss or receive daily reminder e-mails from an assistant.

outgroupers: (p. 90) People you consider fundamentally different from you because of their interests, affiliations, or backgrounds. Contrast **ingroupers.**

paraphrasing: (p. 194) An active listening response that summarizes or restates a message. For example, after listening to a friend, Marlene says, "So what you're saying is that you'd love a different job but can't face moving again."

passion: (p. 136) A blend of joy and surprise that may also include excitement, amazement, and sexual attraction.

passionate love: (p. 333) A state of intense emotional longing, sexual desire, and idealization of the one loved.

people-oriented listeners: (p. 203) Those who encourage rapport-building, sharing emotions, and empathy. For example, Carl enjoys Elaine's descriptions of the triumphs and difficulties she's had learning to snowboard.

perception: (p. 82) The process of selecting, organizing, and interpreting information received by our senses.

perception-checking: (p. 107) A five-step method for testing impressions of others to avoid errors in judgment. It involves checking your punctuation, knowledge, attributions, perceptual influences, and impressions.

personal currency: (p. 302) Power that comes from characteristics that others admire in you, such as having a reputation for being the life of the party or the most beautiful person in the room.

personal idioms: (p. 223) Personal ways of speaking unique to a particular relationship, such as pet names or private phrases with special meaning. For example, Uncle Henry was known for his practical jokes; now, years after his death, family members still refer to a practical joke as "pulling a Henry."

personality: (p. 95) Traits that guide the typical ways an individual thinks, feels, and acts.

personal space: (p. 273) The proxemic zone that ranges from 18 inches to 4 feet of space between communicators. It is the spatial separation most often used in the United States for friendly conversation.

physical appearance: (p. 278) A nonverbal code that represents the effects of body type, clothing, hairstyle, and physical features on communication.

plan actions: (p. 167) Mentally preparing for a communication situation by thinking through how you will act and what you might say. For instance, although Justine is nervous about her first parent-teacher conference, she plans to greet each parent warmly, and she prepares notes about each student's progress to stay on track.

plan contingencies: (p. 167) Mentally anticipating alternative ways a conversation might go; thinking through what the other person might say and how you would respond. For instance, to be prepared for whatever might come up, Jacob tried out various scenarios in his mind about what questions he might be asked during a job interview.

pluralistic families: (p. 386) Families characterized by low levels of conformity and high levels of conversation orientation. For example, Julie's parents encourage her to express herself freely, and when conflicts arise, they collaborate with her to resolve them.

positivity bias: (p. 100) A tendency for first impressions of others to be more positive than negative.

power: (pp. 269, 299) An ability to influence or control events and people. It may be communicated verbally and through each of the eight nonverbal codes.

power currency: (p. 301) The ways in which power is held, exchanged, or exerted interpersonally. See also **expertise currency; intimacy currency; personal currency; resource currency.**

power-distance: (p. 303) The gap in a culture between individuals with power and those with little influence. For example, in some cultures, well-defined class distinctions limit interaction across class lines, but other cultures downplay status and privilege to foster a spirit of equality.

primacy effect: (p. 100) A tendency to place extra importance on the first information we receive about a person. For example, as soon as Laurie hears Martin's Australian accent, she is enchanted.

primary emotions: (p. 121) Six emotions that are displayed uniquely and are consistent across cultures: anger, disgust, fear, joy, sadness, and surprise.

professional peers: (p. 429) People who hold jobs at the same level of power and status.

protective families: (p. 386) Families characterized by high levels of conformity and low levels of conversation orientation. For example, Brian's parents expect their son to be respectful, and they discourage family discussions.

provocateurs: (p. 209) Aggressive listeners who bait and attack others in online communication. For example, a group member stirs up trouble in a chatroom by criticizing the study group leader and then humiliates other respondents.

proxemics: (p. 273) A nonverbal code that represents the physical distance between communicators. See also **intimate space; personal space; public space; social space.**

pseudo-conflict: (p. 307) A mistaken perception that a conflict exists when it doesn't. For example, Barbara thinks Anne is angry with her because Anne hasn't spoken to her all evening, but Anne is actually worried about a report from her physician.

pseudo-listening: (p. 208) Pretending to listen while preoccupied or bored.

P-time (polychronemic time): (p. 277) A cultural orientation toward time, viewing it loosely and fluidly and valuing human relationships over strict schedules and efficiency. In Mexico, for instance, punctuality may be sacrificed to savor a conversation. Contrast **M-time (monochronemic time).**

public space: (p. 273) The widest proxemic zone. It ranges outward from 12 feet and is most appropriate in public speaking settings.

punctuation: (p. 83) Sequencing information by cause and effect. For example, Bobby claims his sister started the backseat argument, but she insists that he poked her first.

reappraisal: (p. 133) Managing difficult and unavoidable emotions constructively by changing your thinking before a triggering event occurs. For instance, though previously fearful of giving a speech, Luke reduces his anxiety by repeating positive affirmations and getting excited about the chance to share what he knows.

recalling: (p. 196) The stage of the listening process in which a listener is able to remember information received.

receiver: (p. 16) The individual for whom a message is intended or to whom it is delivered.

receiving: (p. 188) The stage of the listening process in which a listener takes in information by seeing and hearing. For example, the listener hears words spoken while reading facial expressions and gestures.

regulative rules: (p. 222) Language guidelines that govern spelling and grammar as well as conversational usage. For example, we know how to respond correctly to a greeting, and we know that cursing in public is inappropriate.

regulator: (p. 269) A gesture used to control the flow of communication, signal turn-taking, or include or exclude someone—for example, averting eye contact to avoid someone or zipping up book bags as a class to signal to a professor that the lecture should end.

relational devaluation: (p. 368) The pain and disappointment that come with the realization that your partner doesn't love and respect you as you expected. For example, Billie is deeply hurt to discover that Jake is also dating Sharon and lying about it.

relational dialectics: (p. 67) Opposing tensions that exist in interpersonal relationships, such as the tension between wishing to be completely honest with a partner yet not wanting to be hurtful.

relational maintenance: (p. 355) Efforts that partners make to continue their relationship satisfactorily. They may show devotion by making time to talk, spend time together, and offer help or support to one another.

relationship goals: (p. 24) Goals of building, maintaining, or destroying relationships with others through interpersonal communication, such as when Valencia compliments Carl's taste in music to encourage his attentions.

resource currency: (p. 301) Power that comes from controlling material items others want or need, such as money, food, cars, or toys.

responding: (p. 193) The stage of the listening process in which a listener indicates nonverbally or verbally, such as by nodding or murmuring agreement, whether a message has been received, attended to, and understood.

rhetorical messages: (p. 162) Responses intended to resolve problems nonjudgmentally, to build consensus, and to convey respect and empathy—for example, saying, "I'm sorry you've been having trouble arriving on time. Let's figure out what we can do so that this doesn't happen again."

romantic relationship: (p. 336) A connection two people choose to share that is perceived romantically by both. For instance, Louise is in love with Robert, and Robert returns her affections.

salience: (p. 83) The degree to which sensory data attracts attention because of its importance, as when you see a loved face in a crowd; because of its vividness, as when you hear a sudden shout; or by being unexpected, as when you come home to a new furniture arrangement.

schemata: (p. 84) Mental patterns we use to interpret and make information familiar. When Charlie describes his home as "retro," Amanda visualizes it before she even sees it.

secure attachment style: (p. 55) The tendency to feel a sense of safety and trust in an adult relationship that arises if a person learned from his or her childhood caregiver that love is reliable and good.

seeing: (p. 188) The sensory process of taking in and interpreting visual images.

selection: (p. 82) The stage of perception in which we narrow our attention, focusing on specific sensory data. For example, though surrounded by sights, sounds, and smells in the restaurant, Boyd focuses on calculating the tip.

selective listening: (p. 207) Listening that captures only parts of a message and dismisses the rest. For example, Rhonda lists three telephone messages left for her business partner Jenna and reminds Jenna about a problem with a product supplier and an afternoon appointment. Jenna listens and responds only to the news of one of the telephone messages, the call from a man she met last week and is interested in.

self: (p. 44) The total picture of who one is, including self-awareness, self-concept, and self-esteem.

self-awareness: (p. 44) The capacity to see ourselves as others see us. For example, at a party you realize that your jokes aren't appreciated.

self-concept: (p. 46) An overall idea of who you are based on your values and beliefs. For instance, Jack describes himself as a Baptist, a downhill skier, quick-tempered, generally optimistic, and an average student.

self-disclosure: (p. 69) Open communication of private information about yourself to others. For example, you tell someone your childhood nickname or your deepest fears.

self-discrepancy theory: (p. 48) The idea that your self-esteem results from comparing who you are to what you and others wish you were. For example, you expected to be brilliant during a job interview but realize you were nervous and tongue-tied.

self-esteem: (p. 47) Your feelings about your self-worth; how you value the image you hold of yourself. For example, Jill felt low about herself after skiing poorly on a run that her friends managed easily.

self-fulfilling prophecies: (p. 46) Expectations that make an outcome more likely to occur. The expectations may be positive or negative. For example, a woman who worried that she would do poorly in a job interview fumbles her responses, and a tennis player who imagines a successful match plays magnificently.

self-presentation goals: (p. 24) Goals of showing yourself to others, through interpersonal communication, as you wish to be perceived, such as when Valencia stifles her frustration because she wants to be seen as cooperative.

self-serving bias: (p. 87) A biased tendency to credit ourselves instead of external factors for our success. For instance, Ruth attributes the success of a project to her leadership qualities rather than to the dedicated efforts of her team.

sender: (p. 16) The individual who generates, packages, and delivers a message.

separation: (p. 316) A sudden withdrawal of one person from a situation that serves to resolve a conflict in the short term. For example, you walk away from an argument to cool off, or you angrily retreat to your room.

sexual-arousal touch: (p. 272) An intentional touch designed to arouse sexually.

sexual harassment: (p. 446) Unwelcome sexual advances, physical contact, or requests that render a workplace offensive or intimidating.

sexual orientation: (p. 31) Enduring emotional or physical attraction to others that ranges from exclusive heterosexuality to exclusive homosexuality and includes various forms of bisexuality.

short-term memory: (p. 192) A set of information, such as where you last placed your keys or parked the car, stored in the part of the mind where it is temporarily held.

shyness: (p. 167) The tendency to be timid, be reserved, and talk less in the presence of others.

single-parent family: (p. 383) A household in which one adult has the sole responsibility to be the children's caregiver.

skirting: (p. 306) A way of avoiding conflict by shifting the topic or making light of the issue. For example, Martel tries to evade Louis's criticism about where Martel parked his car by teasing, "I did you a favor. You walked twenty extra steps. Exercise is good for you."

small talk: (p. 346) Light, usually factual, conversation shared by people as they become acquainted or casually interact with one another, such as talk about the weather or a recent sports event.

sniping: (p. 306) A way of avoiding conflict by attacking with a hostile verbal jab and cutting off any opportunity for the other person to respond, such as when Martel answers Louis's criticism about where he parked his car by insulting Louis and stomping out the door.

social comparison: (p. 44) Evaluating how your idea of yourself measures up to your impressions of others. For example, you might subtly check out how others are dressed at a party or how they scored on an exam to see if you compare favorably.

social exchange theory: (p. 339) A way of comparing the benefits a relationship offers and the costs required to maintain it with your expectations of what relationships should be like and what you believe you deserve. For example, Meredith thinks Leonard is perfect for her because he is much more attentive and affectionate than her previous boyfriends and seems so easy to please.

social network currency: (p. 302) Power that comes with personal connections that others consider important, such as being on a first-name basis with a sports celebrity.

social penetration theory: (p. 64) Altman and Taylor's psychological model representing layers of information that you reveal about yourself, ranging from basic facts on the outside to the most private feelings and values at the core.

social-polite touch: (p. 272) A touch, such as a handshake, used to demonstrate social norms or culturally expected behaviors.

social science: (p. 12) The scientific study of human mental, behavioral, and relational actions.

social space: (p. 273) The proxemic zone that ranges from 4 to 12 feet of space between communicators. It is the spatial separation most often used in the United States for conversations between acquaintances and strangers.

speech acts: (p. 235) The conversational actions performed with words, such as the question "Is the antique clock in your window for sale?" and the reply "Yes, let me get it out to show you."

stagnating: (p. 352) A relational stage in which communication between partners becomes ritualized and empty. For instance, day after day, Owen and Ruth speak only to ask if a bill has been paid or what is on television, without really listening to one another's answers.

stereotyping: (p. 102) Categorizing people into social groups to make simplistic and general judgments about them, such as assuming everyone from a small town is friendly and city people are not.

structural improvements: (p. 317) Beneficial changes that occur when an intense conflict is managed collaboratively and the partners redefine their expectations productively.

submissiveness: (p. 285) A nonverbal behavior, such as a shrinking posture and lowered eye gaze, that indicates giving up control or allowing others power.

sudden-death statements: (p. 310) Messages, communicated at the height of a conflict, that sound final or unconditional, such as "It's over. I never want to see you again."

superiority messages: (p. 169) Defensive responses that claim higher ground or to be above criticism—for example, saying, "I think I know just a little more than you do about this" or "Who do you think you're talking to? No one speaks to me like that."

supportive climate: (p. 425) A workplace atmosphere that is supportive, warm, collaborative, and friendly. Contrast **defensive climate.**

supportive communication: (p. 143) Sharing messages that express emotional support and offer help, such as telling a person of your sympathy, listening to someone without judging, or offering to deliver a meal to a grieving friend.

suppression: (p. 131) Managing emotion by squelching its accompanying thoughts or by censoring outward displays. For example, Amanda stifles her anger, knowing it will kill her chances of receiving a good tip.

symbols: (p. 222) Socially agreed-upon representations of things, ideas, and events. For example, the letters of the alphabet are symbols for specific sounds in English.

symmetrical relationships: (p. 300) Relationships characterized by an equal balance of power, such as a business partnership in which the partners co-own their company.

terminating: (p. 354) A relational stage in which one or both partners end a relationship. For instance, Ruth asks Owen for a divorce once she realizes their marriage has deteriorated beyond salvation.

territoriality: (p. 275) A nonverbal behavior of claiming and defining physical space, such as spreading personal stuff to claim the entire library table or routinely using the same parking slot at work.

time-oriented listeners: (p. 202) Those who prefer brief, concise messages to save time—for example, a supervisor who says, "I'm busy Robert. Ten words or less, what do you want?"

transactional communication model: (p. 17) A depiction of communication messages that pass between communicators simultaneously. For example, a salesperson who watches his customer's facial expression while describing a product is sending and receiving messages at the same time.

trolling: (p. 177) Unethically provoking others in online communication by intentionally posting hostile messages.

Uncertainty Reduction Theory: (p. 88) A theory explaining our inclination to try to predict events, to anticipate them, or to explain behaviors in order to become comfortable in unfamiliar settings. For example, before agreeing to date Rob, Cheryl asks mutual friends about him.

understanding: (p. 192) The stage of the listening process in which a listener assigns meaning to a message. For example, you may hear and attend to a lecture well enough to take accurate notes yet make no sense of the material.

upward communication: (p. 435) Messages that travel in an organization from a subordinate to a superior. For instance, a clerk notifies the department manager that inventory needs to be reordered. Contrast **downward communication.**

venting: (p. 132) An explosive expression of positive or negative emotion, such as shrieking in happiness when a player scores or storming into an office to rage at an employee.

verbal aggression: (p. 170) Hostile, sometimes profane, remarks that attack the appearance, behavior, or character of others—for example, calling someone names or ridiculing what someone is wearing.

verbal communication: (p. 221) The sharing of spoken or written language between people.

virtual networks: (p. 423) Communication links between members of an organization made through e-mail or the Internet.

virtual peers: (p. 430) Coworkers who communicate with one another by means of electronic technologies such as the telephone, fax messages, and e-mail.

vocalics: (p. 270) A nonverbal code that represents vocal characteristics such as volume, pitch, rate, voice quality, vocalized sounds, and silence. For instance, a pause might signal discomfort, create tension, or be used to heighten drama. A change in pitch turns a statement into a question.

voice strategy: (p. 360) An active, constructive approach that both individuals in a couple use to handle a relational problem by talking it through together. For example, Nathan and Paul brainstorm ways to trim their monthly bills until they are both satisfied with a manageable budget.

"we" language: (p. 242) Communication that uses the pronoun *we* in sentence construction to be inclusive and strengthen a sense of connection—for example, "We need to decide what color to paint the living room" instead of "I need you to tell me what color paint you want for the living room." See also **"I" language; "you" language.**

workplace abuse: (p. 442) Verbal or nonverbal hostility directed at a person at work; it may consist of insults, unreasonable demands, or claims of credit for someone else's work.

workplace cliques: (p. 423) Circles of coworkers who share common perspectives about life and values in the workplace.

workplace relationships: (p. 420) Connections with others, such as your supervisor, coworkers, and subordinates, in a professional setting.

world-mindedness: (p. 173) The ability to practice and demonstrate acceptance and civility toward other cultural beliefs and customs; the ability to avoid judgment and faulty assumptions by being open-minded and respectful and by resisting ethnocentric attitudes. Contrast **ethnocentrism.**

"you" language: (p. 242) Communication that states or implies the pronoun *you* as the focus of attention in a sentence that comes across as accusatory or provokes a defensive reaction—such as "You haven't done your share of the work on this project." Contrast **"I" language; "we" language.**

References

ABCnews.go.com. (2005, October 21). Do "helicopter Moms" do more harm than good? *"Hovering mothering" has become common on college campuses.* Retrieved April 10, 2006, from http://abcnews.go.com/2020/Health/story?id=1237868&page=1

Adamson, A., & Jenson, V. (Directors). (2001). *Shrek* [Motion picture]. United States: DreamWorks SKG.

Adorno, T. W., Frenkel-Brunswik, E., Levinson, D. J., & Sanford, R. N. (1950). *The authoritarian personality.* New York: Harper Books.

Afifi, W. A., & Faulkner, S. L. (2000). On being "just friends": The frequency and impact of sexual activity in cross-sex friendships. *Journal of Social and Personal Relationships, 17,* 205–222.

Ainsworth, M. D. S., Blehar, M. C., Waters, E., & Wall, S. (1978). *Patterns of attachment: A psychological study of the strange situation.* Hillsdale, NJ: Erlbaum.

Akers, C. W. (1980). *Abigail Adams: An American woman.* Boston: Little, Brown.

Albrecht, T. L., & Bach, B. W. (1997). *Communication in complex organizations: A relational approach.* Fort Worth, TX: Harcourt Brace.

Alexander, J. F. (1973). Defensive and supportive communications in normal and deviant families. *Journal of Consulting and Clinical Psychology, 40,* 223–231.

Alexie, S. (1993). *The Lone Ranger and Tonto fistfight in heaven.* New York: HarperCollins.

Allport, G. W. (1954). *The nature of prejudice.* Cambridge, MA: Addison-Wesley.

Altman, I., & Taylor, D. A. (1973). *Social penetration: The development of interpersonal relationships.* New York: Holt, Rinehart & Winston.

American Idol. (n.d.). Retrieved February 26, 2006, from http://www.idolonfox.com

Andersen, P. A. (1997). Cues of culture: The basis of intercultural differences in nonverbal communication. In L. A. Samovar & R. E. Porter (Eds.), *Intercultural communication: A reader* (8th ed., pp. 244–255). Belmont, CA: Wadsworth.

Andersen, P. A. (1999). *Nonverbal communication: Forms and functions.* Mountain View, CA: Mayfield.

Andersen, P. A., Lustig, M. W., & Andersen, J. F. (1990). Changes in latitude, changes in attitude: The relationship between climate and interpersonal communication predispositions. *Communication Quarterly, 38,* 291–311.

Anderson, N. H. (1981). *Foundations of information integration theory.* Orlando, FL: Academic Press.

Anderson, W. T. (1988). *A Little House sampler.* Lincoln: University of Nebraska Press.

Andrews, C. (2005, December 14). Capitol spruce is Christmas tree, state senate says. *Lansing State Journal.*

APA Online. (n.d.). *Just the facts about sexual orientation and youth: A primer for principals, educators, and school personnel.* Retrieved June 19, 2006, from http://www.apa.org/pi/lgbc/publications/justthefacts.html

Archer, J. (2000). Sex differences in aggression between heterosexual partners: A meta-analytic review. *Psychological Bulletin, 126,* 651–680.

Argyle, M. (1969). *Social interaction.* New York: Atherton Press.

Argyle, M., & Furnham, A. (1982). The ecology of relationships: Choice of situations as a function of relationship. *British Journal of Social Psychology, 21,* 259–262.

Argyle, M., & Henderson, M. (1984). The rules of friendship. *Journal of Social and Personal Relationships, 1,* 211–237.

Argyle, M., & Lu, L. (1990). Happiness and social skills. *Personality and Individual Differences, 11,* 1255–1261.

Aries, E. (1996). *Men and women in interaction: Reconsidering the differences.* New York: Oxford University Press.

Asada, K. J. K., Morrison, K., Hughes, M., & Fitzpatrick, S. (2003, May). *Is that what friends are for? Understanding the motivations, barriers, and emotions associated with friends with benefits relationships.* Paper presented at the annual meeting of the International Communication Association, San Diego, CA.

Asch, S. E. (1946). Forming impressions of personality. *Journal of Abnormal and Social Psychology, 41,* 258–290.

Asian American Career Center. (n.d.). *Goldsea career success.* Retrieved June 13, 2006, from http://goldsea.com/Career/career.html

Asimov, N. (1997, January 19). Opening Pandora's box: The Oakland school board member principally responsible for the controversial resolution on Ebonics reflects on several weeks of turmoil. *The San Francisco Chronicle.*

Attner, P. (1982, December 14). Recent dearth of touchdowns concerns Gibbs. *The Washington Post.*

Atwood, M. (1985). *The handmaid's tale.* New York: Fawcett Crest.

Austen, J. (1995). *Sense and sensibility.* New York: Penguin Books. (Original work published 1811)

Aylor, B. A. (2003). Maintaining long-distance relationships. In D. J. Canary & M. Dainton (Eds.), *Maintaining relationships through communication: Relational, contextual, and cultural variations* (pp. 127–139). Mahwah, NJ: Erlbaum.

Baber, R. E. (1939). *Marriage and family.* New York: McGraw-Hill.

Baldwin-Avery, P., McCornack, S. A., & Pickett, M. (1992, May). *The role of women's decision-making in date rape and sexual misunderstandings: A new look at an old argument.* Paper presented at the annual meeting of the International Communication Association, Miami, FL.

Ballaster, R. (1995). Introduction. In J. Austen, *Sense and sensibility* (pp. vii–xxv). New York: Penguin Books.

Bank, B. J., & Hansford, S. L. (2000). Gender and friendship: Why are men's best same-sex friendships less intimate and supportive? *Personal Relationships, 7,* 63–78.

Baptiste, D. A., Jr. (1990). Therapeutic strategies with black-Hispanic families: Identity problems of a neglected minority. *Journal of Family Psychotherapy, 1,* 15–38.

Barker, L. L. (1971). *Listening behavior.* Englewood Cliffs, NJ: Prentice-Hall.

Barnes, S. B. (2001). *Online connections: Internet interpersonal relationships.* Cresskill, NJ: Hampton Press.

Barnes, S. B. (2003). *Computer-mediated communication: Human-to-human communication across the Internet.* Boston: Allyn and Bacon.

Barnett, O. W., Miller-Perrin, C. L., & Perrin, R. D. (1997). *Family violence across the life-span: An introduction.* Thousand Oaks, CA: Sage.

Barnlund, D. C. (1975). *Private and public self in Japan and the United States.* Tokyo: Simul Press.

Bateson, G. (1958). *Naven: A survey of the problems suggested by a composite picture of the culture of a New Guinea tribe drawn from three points of view* (2nd ed). Stanford, CA: Stanford University Press.

Baxter, L. A. (1988). A dialectical perspective on communication strategies in relationship development. In S. Duck (Ed.), *Handbook of personal relationships: Theory, research, and interventions* (pp. 257–273). Chichester, England: Wiley.

Baxter, L. A. (1990). Dialectical contradictions in relationship development. *Journal of Social and Personal Relationships, 7,* 69–88.

Baxter, L. A., & Clark, C. L. (1996). Perceptions of family communication patterns and the enactment of family rituals. *Western Journal of Communication, 60,* 254–268.

Baxter, L. A., Mazanec, M., Nicholson, J., Pittman, G., Smith, K., & West, L. (1997). Everyday loyalties and betrayals in personal relationships. *Journal of Social and Personal Relationships, 14,* 655–678.

Baxter, L. A., & Montgomery, B. M. (1996). *Relating: Dialogues and dialectics.* New York: Guilford Press.

Baxter, L. A., Wilmot, W. W., Simmons, C. A., and Swartz, A. (1993). Ways of doing conflict: A folk taxonomy of conflict events in personal relationships. In P. J. Kalbfleisch (Ed.), *Interpersonal communication: Evolving interpersonal relationships* (pp. 89–108). Hillsdale, NJ: Erlbaum.

Beach, W. A. (2002). Between dad and son: Initiating, delivering, and assimilating bad cancer news. *Health Communication, 14,* 271–298.

Bell, R. A., Buerkel-Rothfuss, N. L., & Gore, K. E. (1987). Did you bring the yarmulke for the cabbage patch kid? The idiomatic communication of young lovers. *Human Communication Research, 14,* 47–67.

Bellafante, G. (2005, August 23). Courtship ideas of South Asians get a U.S. touch. *New York Times,* pp. A1, A13.

Bennett, S. H. (2003). *Radical pacifism: The War Resisters League and Gandhian nonviolence in America, 1915–1963.* Syracuse, NY: Syracuse University Press.

Benoit, P. J., & Benoit, W. E. (1990). To argue or not to argue. In R. Trapp & J. Schuetz (Eds.), *Perspectives on argumentation: Essays in honor of Wayne Brockriede* (pp. 55–72). Prospect Heights, IL: Waveland Press.

Berger, C. R. (1987). Communicating under uncertainty. In M. E. Roloff & G. R. Miller (Eds.), *Interpersonal processes* (pp. 39–62). Newbury Park, CA: Sage.

Berger, C. R., & Bell, R. A. (1988). Plans and the initiation of social relationships. *Human Communication Research, 15,* 221.

Berger, C. R., & Bradac, J. J. (1982). *Language and social knowledge: Uncertainty in interpersonal relations.* London: Edward Arnold.

Berger, C. R., & Calabrese, R. J. (1975). Some explorations in initial interaction and beyond: Toward a developmental theory of interpersonal communication. *Human Communication Research, 1,* 99–112.

Berkowitz, L., & Harmon-Jones, E. (2004). Toward an understanding of the determinants of anger. *Emotion, 4,* 107–130.

Berscheid, E. (2002). Emotion. In H. H. Kelley et al. (Eds.), *Close relationships* (2nd ed., pp. 110–168). Clinton Corners, NY: Percheron Press.

Berscheid, E., & Ammazzalorso, H. (2001). Emotional experience in close relationships. In G. J. O. Fletcher & M. S. Clark (Eds.), *Blackwell handbook of social psychology: Vol. 2. Interpersonal processes* (pp. 309–330). Malden, MA: Blackwell.

Berscheid, E., & Peplau, L. A. (2002). The emerging science of relationships. In H. H. Kelley et al. (Eds.), *Close relationships* (pp. 1–19). Clinton Corners, NY: Percheron Press.

Berscheid, E., & Regan, P. (2005). *The psychology of interpersonal relationships.* Upper Saddle River, NJ: Pearson Education.

Berscheid, E., & Walster, E. (1978). *Interpersonal attraction* (2nd ed.). Reading, MA: Addison-Wesley.

Bevan, T., Simmons, R. (Producers), Hornby, H., DeVincentis, D. V., Pink, S., Cusack, J., Rosenberg, S. (Writers), & Frears, S. (Director). (2000). *High fidelity* [Motion picture]. United States: Working Title Films.

Bianconi, L. (2002). *Culture and identity: Issues of authenticity in another value system.* Paper presented at the XII Sietar-EU Conference, Vienna.

Bies, R. J., & Tripp, T. M. (1998). Two faces of the powerless: Coping with tyranny in organizations. In R. M. Kramer & M. A. Neale (Eds.), *Power and influence in organizations* (pp. 203–219). Thousand Oaks, CA: Sage.

Bing, Stanley. (2002). *Throwing the elephant: Zen and the art of managing up.* New York: Harper Business.

Birdwhistell, R. L. (1952). *Introduction to kinesics: An annotation system for analysis of body motion and gesture.* Washington, DC: U.S. Department of State, Foreign Service Institute; Ann Arbor, MI: University Microfilms.

Birdwhistell, R. L. (1955). Background to kinesics. *Etc., 13,* 10–18.

Birdwhistell, R. L. (1970). *Kinesics and context: Essays on body motion communication*. Philadelphia: University of Pennsylvania Press.

Blakely, G. L., Blakely, E. H., & Moorman, R. H. (1995). The relationship between gender, personal experience, and perceptions of sexual harassment in the workplace. *Employee Responsibilities and Rights Journal, 8,* 263–274.

Blieszner, R., & Adams, R. G. (1992). *Adult friendship*. Newbury Park, CA: Sage.

Bochner, S., & Hesketh, B. (1994). Power distance, individualism/collectivism, and job related attitudes in a culturally diverse work group. *Journal of Cross-Cultural Psychology, 25,* 233–257.

Bodenhausen, G. V., Macrae, C. N., & Sherman, J. W. (1999). On the dialectics of discrimination: Dual processes in social stereotyping. In S. Chaiken & Y. Trope (Eds.), *Dual process theories in social psychology* (pp. 271–290). New York: Guilford Press.

Bodhi, B., & Nanamoli, B. (1995). *The middle length discourse of the Buddha: A translation of the Majjhima Nikaya*. Somerville, MA: Wisdom Publications.

Booth, A., & Hess, E. (1974). Cross-sex friendship. *Journal of Marriage and the Family, 36,* 38–46.

Bornstein, R. F. (1989). Exposure and affect: Overview and meta-analysis of research, 1968–1987. *Psychological Bulletin, 106,* 265–289.

Bowlby, J. (1969). *Attachment and loss: Vol. 1. Attachment*. New York: Basic Books.

Boylan, P. (2001). Accommodation through a transformation of consciousness. In K. Koch & T. Muggin (Eds.), *Globalization, foreign languages, and intercultural learning*. Proceedings of the first SIETAR-UK Conference. South Bank University, London.

Brandes, S. (1987). Sex roles and anthropological research in rural Andalusia. *Women's Studies, 13,* 357–372.

Bregman, A., Golin, S. (Producers), Gondry, M. (Director), & Kaufman, C. (Writer). (2004). *Eternal sunshine of the spotless mind* [Motion picture]. United States: Focus Features.

Brehm, S. S., Miller, R. S., Perlman, D., & Campbell, S. M. (2002). *Intimate relationships* (3rd ed.). Boston: McGraw-Hill.

Brend, R. (1975). Male-female intonation patterns in American English. In B. Thorne & N. Henley (Eds.), *Language and sex: Difference and dominance* (pp. 84–87). Rowley, MA: Newbury House.

Brewer, M. B. (1993). Social identity, distinctiveness, and in-group homogeneity. *Social Cognition, 11,* 150–164.

Brewer, M. B. (1999). The psychology of prejudice: Ingroup love or outgroup hate? *Journal of Social Issues, 55,* 429–444.

Brewer, M. B., & Campbell, D. T. (1976). *Ethnocentrism and intergroup attitudes: East African evidence*. Beverly Hills, CA: Sage.

Bridge, K., & Baxter, L. A. (1992). Blended relationships: Friends as work associates. *Western Journal of Communication, 56,* 200–225.

Brody, L. R., & Hall, J. A. (2000). Gender, emotion, and expression. In M. Lewis & J. M. Haviland (Eds.), *Handbook of emotions* (2nd ed., pp. 338–349). New York: Guilford Press.

Brontë, E. (1995). *Wuthering heights*. Oxford: Oxford University Press. (Original work published 1848)

Brookhiser, R. (2003, April). Close up: The mind of George W. Bush. *The Atlantic Monthly Online*. Retrieved February 26, 2006, from http://www.theatlantic.com/doc/prem/200304/brookhiser

Brown, R. (1965). *Social psychology*. New York: Free Press.

Bruner, J., & Taguiri, R. (1954). The perception of people. In G. Lindzey (Ed.), *Handbook of social psychology* (Vol. 1, pp. 601–633). Cambridge, MA: Addison-Wesley.

Buber, M. (1965). *The knowledge of man: A philosophy of the interhuman*. New York: Harper & Row.

Buber, M. (1970). *I and thou*. New York: Scribner. (Original work published 1936)

Bulfinch, T. (1985). *The golden age of myth and legend*. London: Bracken Books. (Original work published 1855)

Burgoon, J. K., Buller, D. B., & Woodall, W. G. (1996). *Nonverbal communication: The unspoken dialogue* (2nd ed.). New York: McGraw-Hill.

Burgoon, J. K., & Dunbar, N. E. (2000). An interactionist perspective on dominance-submission: Interpersonal dominance as a dynamic, situationally contingent social skill. *Communication Monographs, 67,* 96–121.

Burgoon, J. K., & Hoobler, G. D. (2002). Nonverbal signals. In M. L. Knapp & J. A. Daly (Eds.), *Handbook of interpersonal communication* (3rd ed., pp. 240–299). Thousand Oaks, CA: Sage.

Burgoon, M. (1995). A kinder, gentler discipline: Feeling good about being mediocre. In B. R. Burleson (Ed.), *Communication yearbook 18* (pp. 464–479). Thousand Oaks, CA: Sage.

Buriel, R., & De Ment, T. (1997). Immigration and sociocultural change in Mexican, Chinese, and Vietnamese American families. In A. Booth, A. C. Crouter, & N. Landale (Eds.), *Immigration and the family: Research and policy on U.S. immigrants* (pp. 165–200). Mahwah, NJ: Erlbaum.

Burleson, B. R., & MacGeorge, E. L. (2002). Supportive communication. In M. L. Knapp & J. A. Daly (Eds.), *Handbook of interpersonal communication* (pp. 374–422). Thousand Oaks, CA: Sage.

Burleson, B. R., Metts, S., & Kirch, M. W. (2000). Communication in close relationships. In C. Hendrick & S. S. Hendrick (Eds.), *Close relationships: A sourcebook* (pp. 244–258). Thousand Oaks, CA: Sage.

Burleson, B. R., & Samter, W. (1994). A social skills approach to relationship maintenance: How individual differences in communication skills affect the achievement of relationship functions. In D. J. Canary & L. Stafford (Eds.), *Communication and relational maintenance* (pp. 61–90). New York: Academic Press.

Bush, V. D., Rose, G. M., Gilbert, F., & Ingram, T. N. (2001). Managing culturally diverse buyer-seller relationships: The role of intercultural disposition and adaptive selling in developing intercultural communication competence. *Journal of the Academy of Marketing Sciences, 29,* 391–404.

Bushman, B. J., & Baumeister, R. F. (1998). Threatened egotism, narcissism, self-esteem, and direct and displaced aggression: Does self-love or self-hate lead to violence? *Journal of Personality and Social Psychology, 75,* 219–229.

Buss, A. H. (1984). A conception of shyness. In J. A. Daly & J. C. McCroskey (Eds.), *Avoiding communication: Shyness, reticence, and communication apprehension* (pp. 39–50). Beverly Hills, CA: Sage.

Buss, D. M., Larsen, R. J., Westen, D., & Semmelroth, J. (1992). Sex differences in jealousy: Evolution, physiology, and psychology. *Psychological Science, 3,* 251–255.

Buss, D. M., Shackelford, T. K., Kirkpatrick, L. A., Choe, J. C., Lim, H. K., Hasegawa, M., et al. (1999). Jealousy and the nature of beliefs about infidelity: Tests of competing hypotheses about sex differences in the United States, Korea, and Japan. *Personal Relationships, 6,* 125–150.

Butterfield, L. H., Friedlander, M., & Kline, M-J. (1975). *The book of Abigail and John: Selected letters of the Adams family, 1762–1784.* Cambridge, MA: Harvard University Press.

Buunk, B. P., Angleitner, A., Oubaid, V., & Buss, D. M. (1996). Sex differences in jealousy in evolutionary and cultural perspective: Tests from the Netherlands, Germany, and the United States. *Psychological Science, 7,* 359–363.

Buzzanell, P. (1990, November). *Managing workplace romance.* Paper presented at the annual meeting of the Speech Communication Association, Chicago.

Cacioppo, J. T., Klein, D. J., Berntson, G. G., & Hatfield, E. (1993). The psychophysiology of emotion. In M. Lewis & J. M. Haviland (Eds.), *Handbook of emotions* (pp. 119–142). New York: Guilford Press.

Cahn, D. (1992). *Conflict in intimate relationships.* New York: Guilford Press.

California Department of Education. (n.d.). *Cesar E. Chavez.* Retrieved February 25, 2006, from http:// chavez.cde.ca.gov

Campbell, R. G., & Babrow, A. S. (2004). The role of empathy in responses to persuasive risk communication: Overcoming resistance to HIV prevention messages. *Health Communication, 16,* 159–182.

Canary, D. J., & Cupach, W. R. (1988). Relational and episodic characteristics associated with conflict tactics. *Journal of Social and Personal Relationships, 5,* 305–322.

Canary, D. J., Cupach, W. R., & Messman, S. J. (1995). *Relationship conflict: Conflict in parent-child, friendship, and romantic relationships.* Thousand Oaks, CA: Sage.

Canary, D. J., Emmers-Sommer, T. M., & Faulkner, S. (1997). *Sex and gender differences in personal relationships.* New York: Guilford Press.

Canary, D. J., & Hause, K. S. (1993). Is there any reason to research sex differences in communication? *Communication Quarterly, 41,* 129–144.

Canary, D. J., & Spitzberg, B. H. (1989). A model of the perceived competence of conflict tactics. *Human Communication Research, 15,* 630–649.

Canary, D. J., & Stafford, L. (1992). Relational maintenance strategies and equity in marriage. *Communication Monographs, 59,* 243–267.

Canary, D. J., & Stafford, L. (1994). Maintaining relationships through strategic and routine interaction. In D. J. Canary & L. Stafford (Eds.), *Communication and relational maintenance* (pp. 3–22). San Diego: Academic Press.

Canary, D. J., & Zelley, E. (2000). Current research programs on relational maintenance behaviors. In Michael E. Roloff (Ed.), *Communication yearbook 23* (pp. 305–339).

Cappella, J. N. (1987). Interpersonal communication: Definitions and fundamental questions. In C. R. Berger & S. H. Chaffee (Eds.), *Handbook of communication science* (pp. 184–237). Newbury Park, CA: Sage.

Carbery, J., & Buhrmester, D. (1998). Friendship and need fulfillment during three phases of young adulthood. *Journal of Social and Personal Relationships, 15,* 393–409.

Carducci, B. J., & Zimbardo, P. G. (1995, November/ December). Are you shy? *Psychology Today, 28,* 34–41.

Carlson, C. J. (1999). The influence of technology on families: An Asian perspective. *Family Journal, 7,* 231–236.

Carlson, J. G., & Hatfield, E. (1992). *Psychology of emotion.* Orlando, FL: Harcourt Brace Jovanovich.

Carney, D. R., Hall, J. A., & Smith LeBeau, L. S. (2005). Beliefs about the nonverbal expression of social power. *Journal of Nonverbal Behavior, 29,* 105–123.

Carton, J. S., Kessler, E. A., & Pape, C. L. (1999). Nonverbal decoding skills and relationship well-being in adults. *Journal of Nonverbal Behavior, 23,* 91–100.

Caughlin, J. P., & Vangelisti, A. L. (1999). Desire for change in one's partner as a predictor of the demand/withdraw pattern of marital communication. *Communication Monographs, 66,* 66–89.

Caughlin, J. P., & Vangelisti, A. L. (2000). An individual difference explanation of why married couples engage in demand/withdraw patterns of conflict. *Journal of Social and Personal Relationships, 17,* 523–551.

Cerpas, N. (2002). Variation in the display and experience of love between college Latino and non-Latino heterosexual romantic couples. *Ronald E. McNair Scholarship research report.* University of California, Berkeley.

Chadha, G. (Director/Writer/Producer). (2002). *Bend it like Beckham* [Motion picture]. United Kingdom: Warner Brothers.

Chaffee, S. H., & Berger, C. R. (1987). What communication scientists do. In C. R. Berger & S. H. Chaffee (Eds.), *Handbook of communication science* (pp. 99–122). Newbury Park, CA: Sage.

Chaplin, T. M., Cole, P. M., & Zahn-Waxler, C. (2005). Parental socialization of emotion expression: Gender differences and relations to child adjustment. *Emotion, 5,* 80–88.

Chapman, B. (2004). Remembering Rwanda. *Dispatches: MSF Canada newsletter, 6,* 1–3.

Chelune, G. J., Sultan, F. E., & Williams, C. L. (1980). Loneliness, self-disclosure, and interpersonal effectiveness. *Journal of Counseling Psychology, 27,* 462–468.

Chen, G.-M., & Chung, J. (1997). The "Five Asian Dragons": Management behaviors and organization communication. In L. A. Samovar & R. E. Porter (Eds.), *Intercultural communication: A reader* (pp. 317–328). Belmont, CA: Wadsworth.

Chen, G.-M., & Starosta, W. J. (1998). *Foundation of intercultural communication.* Boston: Allyn and Bacon.

Chesebro, J. L. (1999). The relationship between listening styles and conversational sensitivity. *Communication Research Reports, 16,* 233–238.

Chung, J. H., Des Roches, C. M., Meunier, J., & Eavey, R. D. (2005). Evaluation of noise-induced hearing loss in young people using a web-based survey technique. *Pediatrics, 115,* 861–867.

Clair, R. P. (1993). The use of framing devices to sequester organizational narratives: Hegemony and harassment. *Communication Monographs, 60,* 113–136.

Clair, R. P. (1998). *Organizing silence.* Albany: State University of New York Press.

Clark, R. A., & Delia, J. (1979). Topoi and rhetorical competence. *Quarterly Journal of Speech, 65,* 187–206.

Clarke, M. L. (1953). *Rhetoric at Rome: A historical survey.* London: Cohen and West.

Cleveland, J. N., Stockdale, M., & Murphy, K. R. (2000). *Women and men in organizations: Sex and gender issues at work.* Mahwah, NJ: Erlbaum.

Cline, A. (2006). *Southern Baptists and the role of women: Wives must submit to their husbands.* Retrieved April 9, 2006, from http://atheism.about. com/od/baptistssouthernbaptists/a/baptistwomen.htm

Cochran, C. C., Frazier, P. A., & Olson, A. M. (1997). Predictors of responses to unwanted sexual attention. *Psychology of Women Quarterly, 21,* 207–226.

Cody, M. J., & McLaughlin, M. L. (1990). Interpersonal accounting. In H. Giles & P. Robinson (Eds.), *Handbook of language and social psychology* (pp. 227–255). London: Wiley.

Cohen, T. F. (1992). Men's families, men's friends: A structural analysis of constraints on men's social ties. In P. M. Nardi (Ed.), *Men's friendships: Vol. 2. Research on men and masculinities* (pp. 115–131). Newbury Park, CA: Sage.

Cole, M., & Cole, S. R. (1989). *The development of children.* New York: Freeman.

Contractor, N. S., & Grant, S. (1996). The emergence of shared interpretations in organizations: A self-organizing systems perspective. In J. H. Watt & C. A. VanLear (Eds.), *Dynamic patterns in communication processes* (pp. 215–230). Thousand Oaks, CA: Sage.

Cooley, C. H. (1902). *Human nature and the social order.* New York: Scribner.

Copeland, A. P., & White, K. M. (1991). *Studying families.* Newbury Park, CA: Sage.

Costanzo, F. S., Markel, N. N., & Costanzo, R. R. (1969). Voice quality profile and perceived emotion. *Journal of Counseling Psychology, 16,* 267–270.

Couch, L. L., Jones, W. H., & Moore, D. S. (1999). Buffering the effects of betrayal: The role of apology, forgiveness, and commitment. In J. M. Adams & W. H. Jones (Eds.), *Handbook of interpersonal commitment and relationship stability* (pp. 451–469). New York: Kluwer Academic/Plenum.

Coupland, N., Giles, H., & Wiemann, J. M. (Eds.). (1991). *Miscommunication and problematic talk.* Newbury Park, CA: Sage.

Covarrubias, P. (2000). Of endearment and other terms of address: A Mexican perspective. In M. W. Lustig & J. Koestner (Eds.), *Among us: Essays on identity, belonging, and intercultural competence* (pp. 9–17). New York: Longman.

Crane, D., & Kauffman, M. (Creators). (1998). *Friends* [Television series]. New York: NBC.

Crider, D. M., Willits, F. K., & Kanagy, C. L. (1991). Rurality and well-being during the middle years of life. *Social Indicators, 24,* 253–268.

Cross, S. E., & Madson, L. (1997). Models of the self: Self-construals and gender. *Psychological Bulletin, 122,* 5–37.

Cunningham, M. (1988). Does happiness mean friendliness? Induced mood and heterosexual self-disclosure. *Personality and Social Psychology Bulletin, 14,* 283–297.

Cupach, W. R., & Canary, D. J. (1997). *Competence in interpersonal conflict.* New York: McGraw-Hill.

Custudio, J. (2002). The divine Ms. C.H.O.: Margaret Cho on her new stand-up movie, Lea Delaria, Joan Rivers, and the meaning of gay pride. Retrieved February 24, 2006, from www.montrealmirror.com/ARCHIVES/2002/080102/divers7.html

Cutler, H. C., & His Holiness the Dalai Lama. (1998). *The art of happiness: A handbook for living.* New York: Riverhead Books.

Dainton, M., & Stafford, L. (1993). Routine maintenance behaviors: A comparison of relationship type, partner similarity and sex differences. *Journal of Social and Personal Relationships, 10,* 255–271.

Dainton, M., Zelley, E., & Langan, E. (2003). Maintaining friendships throughout the lifespan. In D. J. Canary & M. Dainton (Eds.), *Maintaining relationships through communication: Relational, contextual, and cultural variations* (pp. 79–102). Mahwah, NJ: Erlbaum.

Daly, J. (1975). *Listening and interpersonal evaluations.* Paper presented at the annual meeting of the Central States Speech Association, Kansas City, MO.

Daly, J. A., & McCroskey, J. C. (Eds.). (1984). *Avoiding communication: Shyness, reticence, and communication apprehension.* Beverly Hills, CA: Sage.

Daly, J. A., McCroskey, J. C., Ayres, J., Hopf, T., & Ayres, D. M. (Eds.). (2004). *Avoiding communication: Shyness, reticence, and communication apprehension* (3rd ed.). Cresskill, NJ: Hampton Press.

Daly, J. A., & Stafford, L. (1984). Correlates and consequences of social-communicative anxiety. In J. A. Daly & J. C. McCroskey (Eds.), *Avoiding communication: Shyness, reticence, and communication apprehension* (pp. 125–143). Beverly Hills, CA: Sage.

Dash, J. (2001). *The world at her fingertips: The story of Helen Keller.* New York: Scholastic Press.

Davey, M. (2004, December 6). 8 soldiers sue over Army's stop-loss policy. *The New York Times* [online]. Retrieved April 1, 2006, from http://www.nytimes.com/2004/12/06/national/06soldiers.html?ex=1260075600&%

David, L. (Writer), & Cherones, T. (Director). (1991). The deal [Television series episode]. In L. David (Producer), *Seinfeld.* New York: National Broadcasting Company.

David, L. (Writer), & Cherones, T. (Director). (1992). The pitch [Television series episode]. In T. Kaiser (Producer), *Seinfeld.* New York: NBC.

Davies, M., Stankov, L., & Roberts, R. D. (1998). Emotional intelligence: In search of an elusive construct. *Journal of Personality and Social Psychology, 75,* 989–1015.

Davis, K. E., & Todd, M. L. (1985). Assessing friendship: Prototypes, paradigm cases, and relationship description. In S. Duck & D. Perlman (Eds.), *Understanding personal relationships: An interdisciplinary approach* (pp. 17–38). London: Sage.

Davis, M. H. (1994). *Empathy: A social psychological approach.* Madison, WI: Brown and Benchmark.

Deaf President Now. (n.d.). Retrieved February 26, 2006, from http://en.wikipedia.org/wiki/Deaf_President_Now

Delgado-Gaitan, C. (1993). Parenting in two generations of Mexican American families. *International Journal of Behavioral Development, 16,* 409–427.

Delia, J. G. (1972). Dialects and the effects of stereotypes on interpersonal attraction and cognitive processes in impression formation. *Quarterly Journal of Speech, 58,* 285–297.

Delia, J. G. (1987). Communication research: A history. In C. R. Berger & S. H. Chaffee (Eds.), *Handbook of communication science* (pp. 20–98). Newbury Park, CA: Sage.

Demme, J. (Director), Tally, T. (Writer), & Bozman, R. (Producer). (1991). *The silence of the lambs* [Motion picture]. United States: Orion Pictures.

Dermer, M., & Thiel, D. L. (1975). When beauty may fail. *Journal of Personality and Social Psychology, 31,* 1168–1176.

Deutsch, F. M. (1990). Status, sex, and smiling: The effect of role on smiling in men and women. *Personality and Social Psychology Bulletin, 16,* 531–540.

Devine, P. G. (1989). Stereotypes and prejudice: Their automatic and controlled components. *Journal of Personality and Social Psychology, 56,* 5–18.

de Vries, B. (1996). The understanding of friendship: An adult life course perspective. In C. Magai & S. McFadden (Eds.), *Handbook of emotion, aging, and the life course* (pp. 249–268). New York: Academic Press.

Diggs R. C., & Stafford, L. (1998). Maintaining marital relationships: A comparison between African-American and European American married individuals. In V. J. Duncan (Ed.), *Towards achieving Maat* (pp. 192–292). Dubuque, IA: Kendall/Hunt.

Dillard, J. (1987). Close relationships at work: Perceptions of the motives and performance of relational participants. *Journal of Social and Personal Relationships, 4,* 179–193.

Dindia, K. (1987). The effects of sex of subject and sex of partner on interruptions. *Human Communication Research, 13,* 345–371.

Dindia, K., & Allen, M. (1992). Sex differences in self-disclosure: A meta-analysis. *Psychological Bulletin, 112,* 106–124.

Dindia, K., & Canary, D. J. (1993). Definitions and theoretical perspectives on maintaining relationships. *Journal of Social and Personal Relationships, 10,* 163–173.

Donohue, W. A., & Kolt, R. (1992). *Managing interpersonal conflict.* Newbury Park, CA: Sage.

Dreyer, A. S., Dreyer, C. A., & Davis, J. E. (1987). Individuality and mutuality in the language of families of field-dependent and field-independent children. *Journal of Genetic Psychology, 148,* 105–117.

Duan, C., & Hill, C. E. (1996). The current state of empathy research. *Journal of Counseling Psychology, 43,* 261–274.

Duck, S. (1994). *Meaningful relationships: Talking, sense, and relating.* Newbury Park, CA: Sage.

Duck, S., & Wood, J. T. (1995). For better, for worse, for richer, for poorer: The rough and the smooth of relationships. In S. Duck & J. T. Wood (Eds.), *Confronting relationship challenges* (pp. 1–21). Thousand Oaks, CA: Sage.

Dues, M., & Brown, M. (2004). *Boxing Plato's shadow: An introduction to the study of human communication.* Boston: McGraw-Hill.

Duncan, S., Jr., & Fiske, D. W. (1977). *Face-to-face interaction: Research, methods, and theory.* New York: Wiley.

Eagly, A. H., Ashmore, R. D., Makhijani, M. G., & Longo, L. C. (1991). What is beautiful is good, but. . . . : A meta-analytic review of research on the physical attractiveness stereotype. *Psychological Bulletin, 110,* 109–128.

Ebbeson, E., Duncan, B., & Konecni, V. (1975). Effects of content of verbal aggression on future verbal aggression: A field experiment. *Journal of Experimental Social Psychology, 11,* 192–204.

Einarsen, S., & Raknes, B. I. (1997). Harassment in the workplace and the victimization of men. *Violence and Victims, 12,* 247–263.

Eisenberg, E. M., & Goodall, H. L. (1997). *Organizational communication Balancing creativity and constraint* (2nd ed.). New York. St. Martin's Press.

Eisenberg, E. M., & Goodall, H. L., Jr. (2004). *Organizational communication: Balancing creativity and constraint* (4th ed.). Boston: Bedford/St. Martin's.

Ekman, P. (1972). Universals and cultural differences in facial expressions of emotion. In J. R. Cole (Ed.), *Nebraska Symposium on Motivation, Vol. 19* (pp. 207–283). Lincoln: University of Nebraska Press.

Ekman, P. (1976). Movements with precise meanings. *Journal of Communication, 26,* 14–26.

Ekman, P. (1999). Basic emotions. In T. Dalgleish & M. Power (Eds.), *Handbook of cognition and emotion* (pp. 45–60). Sussex, UK: Wiley.

Ekman, P., & Friesen, W. V. (1969). The repertoire of nonverbal behavior: Categories, origins, usage, and coding. *Semiotica, 1,* 49–98.

Ellis, D. G. (1999). *From language to communication.* Mahwah, NJ: Erlbaum.

Englehardt, E. E. (2001). Introduction to ethics in interpersonal communication. In E. E. Englehardt (Ed.), *Ethical issues in interpersonal communication: Friends, intimates, sexuality, marriage, and family.* Orlando, FL: Harcourt College.

The English language: Words borrowed from other languages. (n.d.). Retrieved February 27, 2006 from http://www.krysstal.com/borrow.html

Esquivel, L. (1992). *Like water for chocolate.* New York: Doubleday.

Farace, R. V., Monge, P. R., & Russell, H. M. (1977). *Communicating and organizing.* Reading, MA: Addison-Wesley.

Feeney, J. A., & Noller, P. (1990). Attachment style as a predictor of adult romantic relationships. *Journal of Personality and Social Psychology, 58,* 281–291.

Fehr, B. (1996). *Friendship processes.* Thousand Oaks, CA: Sage.

Fehr, B. (2000). The life cycle of friendship. In C. Hendrick & S. S. Hendrick (Eds.), *Close relationships: A sourcebook* (pp. 71–82). Thousand Oaks, CA: Sage.

Feingold, A. (1988). Matching for attractiveness in romantic partners and same-sex friends: A meta-analysis and theoretical critique. *Psychological Bulletin, 104,* 226–235.

Felmlee, D. H. (2001). No couple is an island: A social network perspective on dyadic stability. *Social Forces, 79,* 1259–1287.

Fenigstein, A., Scheier, M. F., & Buss, A. H. (1975). Public and private self-consciousness: Assessment and theory. *Journal of Consulting and Clinical Psychology, 43,* 522–527.

Festinger, L., Riecken, H. W., & Schachter, S. (1956). *When prophecy fails: A social and psychological study of a modern group that predicted the destruction of the world.* New York: Harper Torchbooks.

Fiedler, K., Pampe, H., & Scherf, U. (1986). Mood and memory for tightly organized social information. *European Journal of Social Psychology, 16,* 149–165.

Field, A. E., Cheung, L., Wolf, A. M., Herzog, D. B., Gortmaker, S. L., & Colditz, G. A. (1999). Exposure to the mass media and weight concerns among girls. *Pediatrics, 103,* 36.

Fielding, H. (2001). *Bridget Jones's diary.* New York: Penguin Books. (Original work published 1996)

Fields, J. (2003). Current population reports: Children's living arrangements and characteristics, March 2002. *U.S. Census Bureau. P20-547.* Retrieved April 1, 2006, from http://www.census.gov/prod/2003pubs/p20-547.pdf

Fischer, A. H., Rodriguez Mosquera, P. M., van Vianen, A. E. M., & Manstead, A. S. R. (2004). Gender and culture differences in emotion. *Emotion, 4,* 87–94.

Fisher, B. A. (1983). Differential effects of sexual composition and interactional context on interaction patterns in dyads. *Human Communication Research, 9,* 225–238.

Fisher, J. D., Rytting, M., & Heslin, R. (1976). Hands touching hands: Affective and evaluative effects of an interpersonal touch. *Sociometry, 39,* 416–421.

Fishman, P. (1977). Interactional shitwork. *Heresies: A feminist publication on arts and politics, 2,* 99–101.

Fiske, S. T., & Taylor, S. E. (1991). *Social cognition* (2nd ed.). New York: McGraw-Hill.

Fitzgerald, L. F. (1993). Sexual harassment: A research analysis and agenda for the 1990s. *Journal of Vocational Behavior, 42,* 5–27.

Fitzpatrick, M. A. (1988). Between husbands and wives: Communication in marriage. Newbury Park, CA: Sage.

Fitzpatrick, M. A., & Badzinski, D. M. (1994). All in the family: Interpersonal communication in kin relationships. In M. L. Knapp & G. R. Miller (Eds.), *Handbook of interpersonal communication* (2nd ed., pp. 726–771). Thousand Oaks, CA: Sage.

Fitzpatrick, M. A., & Caughlin, J. P. (2002). Interpersonal communication in family relationships. In M. L. Knapp & J. A. Daly (Eds.), *Handbook of interpersonal communication* (pp. 726–778). Thousand Oaks, CA: Sage.

Fitzpatrick, M. A., Jandt, F. E., Myrick, F. L., & Edgar, T. (1994). Gay and lesbian couple relationships. In R. J. Ringer (Ed.), *Queer words, queer images: Communication and the (re)construction of homosexuality* (pp. 265–277). New York: New York University Press.

Fitzpatrick, M. A., & Ritchie, L. D. (1994). Communication schemata within the family: Multiple perspectives on family interaction. *Human Communication Research, 20,* 275–301.

Fletcher, G. J. O., & Simpson, J. A. (2000). Ideal standards in close relationships: Their structure and functions. *Current Directions in Psychological Science, 9,* 102–105.

Floyd, K. (1999). All touches are not created equal: Effects of form and duration on observers' interpretations of an embrace. *Journal of Nonverbal Behavior, 23,* 283–299.

Floyd, K., & Burgoon, J. K. (1999). Reacting to nonverbal expressions of liking: A test of interaction adaptation theory. *Communication Monographs, 66,* 219–239.

Floyd, K., & Morman, M. T. (1999). The measurement of affectionate communication. *Communication Quarterly, 46,* 144–162.

Forgas, J. P., & Bower, G. H. (1987). Mood effects on person perception judgments. *Journal of Personality and Social Psychology, 53,* 53–60.

Forni, P. M. (2002). *Choosing civility: The twenty-five rules of considerate conduct.* New York: St. Martin's Griffin.

Fortenberry, J. H., Maclean, J., Morris, P., & O'Connell, M. (1978). Mode of dress as a perceptual cue to deference. *Journal of Social Psychology, 104,* 139–140.

Foss, S. K., Foss, K. A., & Trapp, R. (1991). *Contemporary perspectives in rhetoric* (2nd ed.). Prospect Heights, IL: Waveland Press.

Fox, K. R. (1992). Physical education and development of self-esteem in children. In N. Armstrong (Ed.), *New directions in physical education: II. Towards a national curriculum* (pp. 33–54). Champaign, IL: Human Kinetics.

Fox, K. R. (1997). The physical self and processes in self-esteem development. In K. Fox (Ed.), *The physical self* (pp. 111–139). Champaign, IL: Human Kinetics.

Fox, S. A. (2000). The uses and abuses of computer-mediated communication for people with disabilities. In D. O. Braithwaite & T. L. Thompson (Eds.), *Handbook of communication and people with disabilities: Research and application* (pp. 319–336). Mahwah, NJ: Erlbaum.

Frank, R. H. (2000). *Luxury fever: Money and happiness in an era of excess.* Princeton, NJ: Princeton University Press.

Frederikse, M. E., Lu, A., Aylward, E., Barta, P., & Pearlson, G. (1999). Sex differences in the inferior parietal lobule. *Cerebral Cortex, 9,* 896–901.

Freides, D. (1974). Human information processing and sensory modality: Cross-modal functions, information complexity, memory, and deficit. *Psychological Bulletin, 81,* 284–310.

Frijda, N. H. (2005). Emotion experience. *Cognition and emotion, 19,* 473–497.

Fritz, J. H., & Dillard, J. P. (1994, November). *The importance of peer relationships in organizational socialization.* Paper presented at the annual meeting of the Speech Communication Association, New Orleans.

Fuendeling, J. M. (1998). Affect regulation as a stylistic process within adult attachment. *Journal of Social and Personal Relationships, 15,* 291–322.

Furger, R. (1996). I'm okay, you're online. *PC World, 14,* 310–312.

Furman, W., & Simon, V. A. (1998). Advice from youth: Some lessons from the study of adolescent relationships. *Journal of Social and Personal Relationships, 15,* 723–739.

Furr, R. M., & Funder, D. C. (1998). A multimodal analysis of personal negativity. *Journal of Personality and Social Psychology, 74,* 1580–1591.

Gaines, S. O., Jr., & Agnew, C. R. (2003). Relationship maintenance in intercultural couples: An interdependence analysis. In D. J. Canary & M. Dainton (Eds.), *Maintaining relationships through communication: Relational, contextual, and cultural variations* (pp. 231–253). Mahwah, NJ: Erlbaum.

Gaines, S. O., Jr., Chalfin, J., Kim, M., & Taing, P. (1998). Communicating prejudice in personal relationships. In M. L. Hecht (Ed.), *Communicating prejudice* (pp. 163–186). Thousand Oaks, CA: Sage.

Ganong, L. H., & Coleman, M. (1994). *Remarried family relationships.* Thousand Oaks, CA: Sage.

Garcia, P., & Geisler, J. (1988). Sex and age/grade differences in adolescents' self-disclosure. *Perceptual and Motor Skills, 67,* 427–432.

Gerdes, L. I. (1999). *Sexual harassment: Current controversies.* San Diego, CA: Greenhaven.

Gettings, J. (2005). *Civil disobedience: Black medalists raise fists for civil rights movement.* Retrieved February 24, 2006, from www.infoplease.com/spot/mm-mexicocity.html

Gibb, J. R. (1961). Defensive communication. *Journal of Communication, 11,* 141–148.

Gibson, B., & Sachau, D. (2000). Sandbagging as a self-presentational style: Claiming to be less than you are. *Personality and Social Psychology Bulletin, 26,* 56–70.

Gifford, R., Ng, C. F., & Wilkinson, M. (1985). Nonverbal cues in the employment interview: Links between applicant qualities and interviewer judgments. *Journal of Applied Psychology, 70,* 729–736.

Giles, H., Coupland, N., & Coupland, J. (Eds.). (1991). *Contexts of accommodation: Developments in applied linguistics.* Cambridge, England: Cambridge University Press.

Giles, H., & Street, R. L. (1994). Communicator characteristics and behavior. In M. L. Knapp & G. R. Miller (Eds.), *Handbook of interpersonal communication* (2nd ed., pp. 103–161). Beverly Hills, CA: Sage.

Gist, Y. J., & Hetzel, L. I. (2004). *We the people: Aging in the United States.* Retrieved February 25, 2006, from www.census.gov/prod/2004pubs/censr-19.pdf

Glaser, B. G., & Strauss, A. L. (1967). *The discovery of grounded theory: Strategies for qualitative research.* Chicago: Aldine.

Gleason, L. B. (1989). *The development of language.* Columbus, OH: Merrill.

Goetz, J., & LeCompte, M. (1981). Ethnographic research and the problem of data reduction. *Anthropology and Education Quarterly, 12,* 51–70.

Goffman, E. (1955). On facework: An analysis of ritual elements in social interaction. *Psychiatry, 18,* 319–345.

Goffman, E. (1959). *The presentation of self in everyday life.* Garden City, NY: Doubleday Anchor Books.

Goffman, E. (1979). Footing. *Semiotica, 25,* 124–147.

Goldstein, T. (2001). I'm not white: Anti-racist teacher education for white early childhood educators. *Contemporary Issues in Early Childhood, 2,* 3–13.

Golish, T. D. (2000). Changes in closeness between adult children and their parents: A turning point analysis. *Communication Reports, 13,* 79–97.

Goodwin, C. (1981). *Conversational organization: Interaction between speakers and hearers.* New York: Academic Press.

Gottman, J. M. (1979). *Marital interaction: Experimental investigations.* New York: Academic Press.

Gottman, J. M. (1994). *What predicts divorce? The relationship between marital processes and marital outcomes.* Hillsdale, NJ: Erlbaum.

Gottman, J. M., Coan, J., Carrere, S., & Swanson, C. (1998). Predicting marital happiness and stability from newlywed interactions. *Journal of Marriage and the Family, 60,* 5–22.

Gottman, J. M., & Levenson, R. W. (2000). The timing of divorce: Predicting when a couple will divorce over a 14-year period. *Journal of Marriage and Family, 62,* 737–745.

Grammer, K., & Thornhill, R. (1994). Human facial attractiveness and sexual selection: The role of averageness and symmetry. *Journal of Comparative Psychology, 108,* 233–242.

Gravois, J. (2005). When the student can't understand the instructor, who's to blame? *The Chronicle of Higher Education, 51,* Issue 31, A10.

Grice, H. P. (1989). *Studies in the way of words.* Cambridge, MA: Harvard University Press.

Gross, J. J. (1998). The emerging field of emotion regulation: An integrative review. *Review of General Psychology, 2,* 271–299.

Gross, J. J., & John, O. P. (2002). Wise emotion regulation. In L. Feldman Barrett & P. Salovey (Eds.), *The wisdom in feeling: Psychological processes in emotional intelligence* (pp. 297–319). New York: Guilford Press.

Gross, J. J., Richards, J. M., & John, O. P. (2006, in press). Emotion regulation in everyday life. In D. K. Snyder, J. A. Simpson, & J. N. Hughes (Eds.), *Emotion regulation in couples and families: Pathways to dysfunction and health.* Washington, DC: American Psychological Association.

Grotevant, H. D., & Cooper, C. R. (1985). Patterns of interaction in family relationships and the development of identity exploration on adolescence. *Child Development, 56,* 415–428.

Gudykunst, W. B., & Kim, Y. Y. (2003). *Communicating with strangers: An approach to intercultural communication* (4th ed.). New York: McGraw-Hill.

Gudykunst, W. B., & Nishida, T. (1993). Closeness in interpersonal relationships in Japan and the United States. *Research in Social Psychology, 8,* 85–97.

Guerin, B. (1999). Children's intergroup attribution bias for liked and disliked peers. *Journal of Social Psychology, 139,* 583–589.

Guerrero, L. K., & Andersen, P. A. (1998). Jealousy experience and expression in romantic relationships. In P. A. Andersen & L. K. Guerrero (Eds.), *Handbook of communication and emotion* (pp. 155–188). San Diego, CA: Academic Press.

Gumperz, J. J., & Levinson, S. C. (Eds.). (1996). *Rethinking linguistic relativity.* New York: Cambridge University Press.

Haas, S. M., & Stafford, L. (1998). An initial examination of maintenance behaviors in gay and lesbian relationships. *Journal of Social and Personal Relationships, 15,* 846–855.

Haider, M. (1972). Neuropsychology of attention, expectation, and vigilance. In C. H. Weaver (Ed.), *Human listening: Processes and behavior.* Indianapolis, IN: Bobbs-Merrill.

Hall, E. T. (1959). *The silent language.* Garden City, NY: Doubleday.

Hall, E. T. (1966). A system of the notation of proxemic behavior. *American Anthropologist, 65,* 1003–1026.

Hall, E. T. (1976). *Beyond culture.* Garden City, NY: Anchor.

Hall, E. T. (1981). *The silent language.* New York: Anchor/Doubleday.

Hall, E. T. (1983). *The dance of life: The other dimension of time.* New York: Doubleday.

Hall, E. T. (1997a). Context and meaning. In L. A. Samovar & R. E. Porter (Eds.), *Intercultural communication: A reader* (pp. 45–53). Belmont, CA: Wadsworth.

Hall, E. T. (1997b). Monochronic and polychronic time. In L. A. Samovar & R. E. Porter (Eds.), *Intercultural communication: A reader* (8th ed., pp. 277–284). Belmont, CA: Wadsworth.

Hall, E. T., & Hall, M. R. (1987). *Understanding cultural differences.* Yarmouth, ME: Intercultural Press.

Hall, J. A. (1984). *Nonverbal sex differences: Communication accuracy and expressive style.* Baltimore: Johns Hopkins University Press.

Hall, J. A. (1998). How big are nonverbal sex differences? The case of smiling and sensitivity to nonverbal cues. In D. J. Canary & K. Dindia (Eds.), *Sex differences and similarities in communication: Critical essays and empirical investigations of sex and gender in interaction* (pp. 155–178). Mahwah, NJ: Erlbaum.

Hall, J. A., Carter, J. D., & Horgan, T. G. (2000). Gender differences in nonverbal communication of emotion. In A. H. Fischer (Ed.), *Gender and emotion: Social psychological perspectives* (pp. 97–117). Cambridge, England: Cambridge University Press.

Hammer, M. R., Bennett, M. J., & Wiseman, R. (2003). Measuring intercultural sensitivity: The intercultural development inventory. *International Journal of Intercultural Relations, 27,* 421–443.

Hansen, G. L. (1985). Dating jealously among college students. *Sex Roles 12,* 713–721.

Harms, L. S. (1961). Listener judgments of status cues in speech. *Quarterly Journal of Speech, 47,* 164–168.

Harrison, K. (2001). Ourselves, our bodies: Thin-ideal media, self-discrepancies, and eating-disorder symptoms in adolescents. *Journal of Social and Clinical Psychology, 20,* 289–323.

Hatfield, E. (1983). Equity theory and research: An overview. In H. H. Blumberg, A. P. Hare, V. Kent, & M. Davies (Eds.), *Small groups and social interaction* (Vol. 2, pp. 401–412). Chichester, England: Wiley.

Hatfield, E., & Rapson, R. L. (1987). Passionate love: New directions in research. In W. H. Jones & D. Perlman (Eds.), *Advances in personal relationships* (Vol. 1, pp. 109–139). London: Jessica Kingsley.

Hatfield, E. E., & Sprecher, S. (1986). *Mirror, mirror . . . the importance of looks in everyday life.* Albany: State University of New York Press.

Hatfield, E., Traupmann, J., & Sprecher, S. (1984). Older women's perceptions of their intimate relationships. *Journal of Social and Clinical Psychology, 2,* 108–124.

Hatfield, E., Traupmann, J., Sprecher, S., Utne, M., & Hay, M. (1985). Equity in close relationships. In W. Ickes (Ed.), *Compatible and incompatible relationships* (pp. 91–171). New York: Springer-Verlag.

Hathaway, S. R., & McKinley, J. C. (1942). *Minnesota Multiphasic Personality Inventory.* Minneapolis: University of Minnesota Press.

Hays, R. B. (1988). Friendship. In S. Duck (Ed.), *Handbook of personal relationships: Theory, research, and interventions* (pp. 391–408). Chichester, England: Wiley.

Hazan, C., & Shaver, P. R. (1987). Romantic love conceptualized as an attachment process. *Journal of Personality and Social Psychology, 52,* 511–524.

Heider, F. (1958). *The psychology of interpersonal relations.* New York: Wiley.

Hendrick, C., & Hendrick, S. S. (1988). Lovers wear rose colored glasses. *Journal of Social and Personal Relationships, 5,* 161–183.

Hendrick, S. S., & Hendrick, C. (1992). *Romantic love.* Thousands Oaks, CA: Sage.

Heritage, J. C., & Watson, D. R. (1979). Formulations as conversational objectives. In G. Pathas (Ed.), *Everyday language: Studies in ethnomethodology.* New York: Irvington.

Heslin, R. (1974, May). *Steps toward a taxonomy of touching.* Paper presented at the annual meeting of the Midwestern Psychological Association, Chicago.

Hess, J. (Director/Writer), Hess, J. (Writer), Coon, J., Wyatt, C., & Covel, S. (Producers). (2004). *Napolean Dynamite* [Motion picture]. United States: Fox Searchlight/Paramount.

Hickson, M., III, Grierson, R. D., & Linder, B. C. (1991). A communication perspective on sexual harassment: Affiliative nonverbal behaviors in asynchronous relationships. *Communication Quarterly, 39,* 111–118.

Higgins, E. T. (1987). Self-discrepancy: A theory relating self and affect. *Psychological Review, 94,* 319–340.

Higgins, E. T. (1989). Continuities and discontinuities in self-regulatory and self-evaluative processes: A developmental theory relating self and affect. *Journal of Personality, 57,* 407–444.

Hill, C. T., Rubin, Z., & Peplau, L. A. (1976). Breakups before marriage: The end of 103 affairs. *Journal of Social Issues, 32,* 147–168.

Hinton, S. E. (1967). *The outsiders.* New York: Dell.

Hodgins, H. S., & Belch, C. (2000). Interparental violence and nonverbal abilities. *Journal of Nonverbal Behavior, 24,* 3–24.

Hofstede, G. (1991). *Cultures and organizations.* London: McGraw-Hill.

Hofstede, G. (1998). I, we, they. In J. N. Martin, T. K. Nakayama, & L. A. Flores (Eds.), *Readings in cultural contexts* (pp. 345–357). Mountain View, CA: Mayfield.

Hofstede, G. (2001). *Culture's consequences* (2nd ed.). Thousand Oaks, CA: Sage.

Honeycutt, J. M. (1999). Typological differences in predicting marital happiness from oral history behaviors and imagined interactions. *Communication Monographs, 66,* 276–291.

Horne, C. F. (1917). *The sacred books and early literature of the east: Vol. II. Egypt.* New York: Parke, Austin, & Lipscomb.

Hovick, S. R. A., Meyers, R. A., & Timmerman, C. E. (2003). E-mail communication in workplace romantic relationships. *Communication Studies, 54,* 468–480.

Howard, P. E. N., Rainie, L., & Jones, S. (2001, November). Days and nights on the Internet: The impact of a diffusing technology. *American Behavioral Scientist, 45,* 383–405.

Hughes, M., Morrison, K., & Asada, K. J. K. (2005). What's love got to do with it? Exploring the impact of maintenance rules, love attitudes, and network support on friends with benefits relationships. *Western Journal of Speech Communication, 69,* 49–66.

Hurley, D. (2005, April 19). Divorce rate: It's not as high as you think. *New York Times,* p. F7.

Hyde, J. S., & Linn, M. C. (1988). Gender differences in verbal ability: A meta-analysis. *Psychological Bulletin, 104,* 53–69.

Hyun, J. (2005). *Breaking the bamboo ceiling: Career strategies for Asians.* New York: HarperCollins.

Imahori, T. T. (2005, May). *De-individualizing intercultural communication studies: Relational and contextual foci.* Paper presented at the annual meeting of the International Communication Association, New York.

Infante, D. A., Chandler, T. A., & Rudd, J. E. (1989). Test of an argumentative skill deficiency model of interspousal violence. *Communication Monographs, 56,* 163–177.

Infante, D. A., Myers, S. A., & Burkel, R. A. (1994). Argument and verbal aggression in constructive and destructive family and organizational disagreements. *Western Journal of Communication, 58,* 73–84.

Infante, D. A., & Wigley, C. J. (1986). Verbal aggressiveness: An interpersonal model and measure. *Communication Monographs, 53,* 61–69.

Jackson, D. C., Malmstadt, J. R., Larson, C. L., & Davidson, R. J. (2000). Suppression and enhancement of emotional responses to unpleasant pictures. *Psychophysiology, 37,* 515–522.

Jacobs, S. (1994). Language and interpersonal communication. In M. L. Knapp & G. R. Miller (Eds.), *Handbook of interpersonal communication* (2nd ed., pp. 199–228). Thousand Oaks, CA: Sage.

Jacobs, S., Dawson, E. J., & Brashers, D. (1996). Information manipulation theory: A replication and assessment. *Communication Monographs, 63,* 70–82.

Jacobson, N. S. (1990). Contributions from psychology to an understanding of marriage. In F. D. Fincham & T. N. Bradbury (Eds.), *The psychology of marriage* (pp. 258–275). New York: Guilford Press.

Jankowiak, W. R., & Fischer, E. F. (1992). A cross-cultural perspective on romantic love. *Ethnology, 31,* 149–155.

Jespersen, O. (1922). *Language: Its nature, development and origin.* New York: Allen & Unwin.

Jimmy Carter The Playboy Interview. (1976). Retrieved February 24, 2006, from www.arts.mcgill.ca/programs/history/faculty/TROYWEB/Courseweb/JimmyCarterThePlayboyInterview.htm

John, O. P. (1990). The "Big Five" factor taxonomy: Dimensions of personality in the natural language and in questionnaires. In L. A. Pervin (Ed.), *Handbook of personality: Theory and research* (pp. 66–100). New York: Guilford Press.

John, O. P., & Gross, J. J. (2004). Healthy and unhealthy emotion regulation: Personality processes, individual differences, and lifespan development. *Journal of Personality, 72,* 1301–1334.

Joinson, A. N. (2001, March-April). Self-disclosure in computer-mediated communication: The role of self-awareness and visual anonymity. *European Journal of Social Psychology, 31,* 177–192.

Jones, D. C., Vigfusdottir, T. H., & Lee, Y. (2004). Body image and the appearance culture among adolescent girls and boys: An examination of friends' conversations, peer criticism, appearance magazines, and the internalization of appearance ideals. *Journal of Adolescent Research, 19,* 323–339.

Jones, S. E., & LeBaron, C. D. (2002). Research on the relationship between verbal and nonverbal communication: Emerging integrations. *Journal of Communication, 52,* 499–521.

Jones, T. E. (1999). *If it's broken, you can fix it: Overcoming dysfunction in the workplace.* New York: AMACOM Books.

Jones, W. H., & Burdette, M. P. (1994). Betrayal in relationships. In A. L. Weber & J. H. Harvey (Eds.), *Perspectives on close relationships* (pp. 243–262). Boston: Allyn and Bacon.

Jourard, S. M. (1964). *The transparent self.* New York: Van Nostrand Reinhold.

Kagawa, N., & McCornack, S. A. (2004, November). *Collectivistic Americans and individualistic Japanese: A cross-cultural comparison of parental understanding.* Paper presented at the annual meeting of the National Communication Association, Chicago.

Kaharit, K., Zachau, G., Eklof, M., Sandsjo, L., & Moller, C. (2003). Assessment of hearing and hearing disorders in rock/jazz musicians. *International Journal of Audiology, 42,* 279–288.

Kahneman, D. (1973). *Attention and effort.* Englewood Cliffs, NJ: Prentice-Hall.

Katz, D., & Kahn, R. (1978). *The social psychology of organizations* (2nd ed.). New York: Wiley.

Katz, J. (1983). A theory of qualitative methodology. In R. M. Emerson (Ed.), *Contemporary field research: A collection of readings* (pp. 127–148). Prospect Heights, IL: Waveland Press.

Katz, J., & Farrow, S. (2000). Discrepant self-views and young women's sexual and emotional adjustment. *Sex Roles, 42,* 781–805.

Keashly, L., Trott, V., & MacLean, L. M. (1994). Abusive behavior in the workplace: A preliminary investigation. *Violence and Victims, 9,* 341–357.

Keesing, R. M. (1974). Theories of culture. *Annual Review of Anthropology, 3,* 73–97.

Kellermann, K. (1989). The negativity effect in interaction: It's all in your point of view. *Human Communication Research, 16,* 147–183.

Kellermann, K. (1991). The conversation MOP: Progression through scenes in discourse. *Human Communication Research, 17,* 385–414.

Kellermann, K., & Reynolds, R. (1990). When ignorance is bliss: The role of motivation to reduce uncertainty in uncertainty reduction theory. *Human Communication Research, 17,* 5–75.

Kelley, H. H., & Thibaut, J. W. (1978). *Interpersonal relations: A theory of interdependence.* New York: Wiley.

Kelly, A. E., & McKillop, K. J. (1996). Consequences of revealing personal secrets. *Psychological Bulletin, 120,* 450–465.

Kemper, S., Ferrell, P., Harden, T., Finter-Urczyk, A., & Billington, C. (1998). Use of elderspeak by young and older adults to impaired and unimpaired listeners. *Aging, Neuropsychology, and Cognition, 5,* 43–55.

Kemper, S., & Harden, T. (1999). Experimentally disentangling what's beneficial about elderspeak from what's not. *Psychology and Aging, 14,* 656–670.

Kennedy, G. A. (1999). *Classical rhetoric and its Christian and secular tradition from ancient to modern times.* Chapel Hill: University of North Carolina Press.

Kephart, W. (1967). Some correlates of romantic love. *Journal of Marriage and the Family, 29,* 470–479.

King, P. (1989, September 18). Inside the NFL. *Sports Illustrated, 71,* Issue 12, p. 20.

King, S. K. (2001). *Territoriality.* Retrieved March 5, 2006, from http://www.huna.org/html/territor.html

Klein, R. C. A. (1998). Conflict and violence in the family: Cross-disciplinary issues. In R. C. A. Klein (Ed.), *Multidisciplinary perspectives on family violence* (pp. 1–13). New York: Routledge.

Kleinke, C. L., Meeker, F. B., & Staneski, R. A. (1986). Preference for opening lines: Comparing ratings by men and women. *Sex Roles, 15,* 585–600.

Klinetob, N. A., & Smith, D. A. (1996). Demand-withdraw communication in marital interaction: Tests of interspousal contingency and gender role hypotheses. *Journal of Marriage and Family, 58,* 945–958.

Klopf, D. W. (2001). *Intercultural encounters: The fundamentals of intercultural communication* (5th ed.). Englewood, CO: Morton.

Knapp, M. L., Daly, J. A., Albada, K. F., & Miller, G. R. (2002). Background and current trends in the study of interpersonal communication. In M. L. Knapp & J. A. Daly (Eds.), *Handbook of interpersonal communication* (3rd ed., pp. 3–20). Thousand Oaks, CA: Sage.

Knapp, M. L., & Hall, J. A. (2002). *Nonverbal communication in human interaction* (5th ed.). Belmont, CA: Wadsworth/Thomson Learning.

Knapp, M. L., & Vangelisti, A. L. (2000). *Interpersonal communication and human relationships* (4th ed.). Boston: Allyn and Bacon.

Koerner, A. F., & Fitzpatrick, M. A. (1997). Family type and conflict: The impact of conversation orientation and conformity orientation on conflict in the family. *Communication Studies, 48,* 59–75.

Koerner, A. F., & Fitzpatrick, M. A. (2002). Toward a theory of family communication. *Communication Theory, 12,* 70–91.

Koerner, A. F., & Fitzpatrick, M. A. (2004). Communication in intact families. In A. Vangelisti (Ed.), *Handbook of family communication* (pp. 177–195). Mahwah, NJ: Erlbaum.

Kostiuk, L. M., & Fouts, G. T. (2002). Understanding of emotions and emotion regulation in adolescent females with conduct problems: A qualitative analysis. *The Qualitative Report, 7,* 1–10.

Kowner, R. (1996). Facial asymmetry and attractiveness judgments in developmental perspective. *Journal of Experimental Psychology: Human Perception and Performance, 22,* 662–675.

Kozan, M., & Ergin, C. (1998). Preference for third-party help in conflict management in the United States and Turkey. *Journal of Cross-Cultural Psychology, 29,* 525–539.

Kram, K. E., & Isabella, L. A. (1985). Mentoring alternatives: The role of peer relationships in career development. *Academy of Management Journal, 28,* 110–132.

Kramarae, C. (1981). *Women and men speaking: Frameworks for analysis.* Rowley, MA: Newbury House.

Krause, J. (2001). *Properties of naturally produced clear speech at normal rates and implications for intelligibility enhancement.* Unpublished doctoral dissertation, Massachusetts Institute of Technology, Cambridge, MA.

Kreider, R. M. (2005). *Number, timing, and duration of marriages and divorces: 2001.* Washington, DC: U.S. Census Bureau.

Kreps, G. L. (1990). *Organizational communication.* New York: Longman.

Kubany, E. S., Richard, D. C., Bauer, G. B., & Muraoka, M. Y. (1992). Impact of assertive and accusatory communication of distress and anger: A verbal component analysis. *Aggressive Behavior, 18,* 337–347.

Kudoh, T., & Matsumoto, D. (1985). Cross-cultural examination of the semantic dimensions of body postures. *Journal of Personality and Social Psychology, 48,* 1440–1446.

Kuhn, J. L. (2001). Toward an ecological humanistic psychology. *Journal of Humanistic Psychology, 41,* 9–24.

Kuttler, A. F., LaGreca, A. M., & Prinstein, M. J. (1999). Friendship qualities and social-emotional functioning of adolescents with close, cross-sex friends. *Journal of Research on Adolescence, 9,* 339–366.

Langdridge, D., & Butt, T. (2004). The fundamental attribution error: A phenomenological critique. *British Journal of Social Psychology, 43,* 357–369.

Lareau, A. (2003). *Unequal childhoods: Class, race, and family life.* Berkeley: University of California Press.

Larsen, R. J., & Ketelaar, T. (1991). Personality and susceptibility to positive and negative emotional states. *Journal of Personality and Social Psychology, 61,* 132–140.

Larson, J. (1992). Understanding step families. *American Demographics, 14,* 36–40.

Larson, J. R. (1984). The performance feedback process: A preliminary model. *Organizational Behavior and Human Performance, 33,* 42–76.

Lasswell, H. D. (1927). *Propaganda technique in the world war.* New York: Knopf.

Lasswell, H. D. (1948). The structure and function of communication in society. In L. Bryson (Ed.), *The communication of ideas* (pp. 32–51). New York: Harper & Row.

Lea, M., & Spears, R. (1992). Paralanguage and social perception in computer-mediated communication. *Journal of Organizational Computing, 2,* 321–341.

Leary, M. R. (2001). Toward a conceptualization of interpersonal rejection. In M. R. Leary (Ed.), *Interpersonal rejection* (pp. 3–20). New York: Oxford University Press.

Lee, J. A. (1973). *The colors of love: An exploration of the ways of loving.* Don Mills, Ontario: New Press.

Leiner, D. (Director), Hurwitz, J. (Writer), Schlossberg, H. (Writer), Kahane, N. (Producer), & Shapiro, G. (Producer). (2004). *Harold and Kumar go to White Castle* [Motion picture]. United States: New Line Cinema.

Lemerise, E. A., & Dodge, K. A. (1993). The development of anger and hostile interactions. In M. Lewis and J. M. Haviland (Eds.), *Handbook of emotions* (pp. 537–546). New York: Guilford Press.

Levin, P. H. (1987). *Abigail Adams: A biography.* New York: St. Martin's Press.

Levine, T. R., McCornack, S. A., & Baldwin Avery, P. (1992). Sex differences in emotional reactions to discovered deception. *Communication Quarterly, 40,* 289–296.

Levinson, S. C. (1985). *Pragmatics.* Cambridge, England: Cambridge University Press.

Lilley, R. (2005, December 9). Trouble in paradise: Villagers flee as Vanuatu volcano spews gas. *Associated Press.*

Lippa, R. A. (2002). *Gender, nature, and nurture.* Mahwah, NJ: Erlbaum.

Lippmann, W. (1922). *Public opinion.* New York: Harcourt, Brace.

Loehlin, J. C., McCrae, R. R., Costa, P. T., Jr., & John, O. P. (1998). Heritabilities of common and measure-specific components of the Big Five personality factors. *Journal of Research in Personality, 32,* 431–453.

Loftus, E. F. (1979). *Eyewitness testimony.* Cambridge, MA: Harvard University Press.

Lopes, P. N., Salovey, P., Cote, S., & Beers, M. (2005). Emotion regulation abilities and the quality of social interaction. *Emotion, 5,* 113–118.

Luft, J. (1970) *Group processes: An introduction to group dynamics* (2nd ed.). Palo Alto, CA: National Press Books.

Lustig, M. W., & Koester, J. (2006). *Intercultural competence: Interpersonal communication across cultures* (5th ed.). Boston: Allyn and Bacon.

Lyons, J., McLeod, E., Moore, D., Todd, J., Todd, S. (Producers), Roach, J. (Director), Myers, M. (Writer/Producer), & McCullers, M. (Writer). (1999). *Austin Powers: The spy who shagged me* [Motion picture]. United States: New Line.

Lyons, M. J., Plante, A., Kamachi, M., Akamatsu, S., Campbell, R., & Coleman, M. (2000, August). *The Noh mask effect: Culture and view dependent facial expression perception.* Proceedings of the eleventh conference of the International Society for Research on Emotion, Quebec City.

MacCulloch, J. A. (1911). *The religion of the ancient Celts.* Edinburgh, Scotland: T.&T. Clark.

MacEwan, G. (1969). *Tatanga Mani, walking buffalo of the Stonies.* Edmonton, Alberta, Canada: Hurtig.

Macrae, C. N., & Bodenhausen, G. V. (2001). Social cognition: Categorical person perception. *British Journal of Psychology, 92,* 239–255.

Maeda, E., & Ritchie, L. D. (2003). The concept of Shinyuu in Japan: A replication of and comparison to Cole and Bradac's study on U.S. friendship. *Journal of Social and Personal Relationships, 20,* 579–598.

Malandro, L. A., & Barker, L. L. (1983). *Nonverbal communication.* Reading, MA: Addison-Wesley.

Malcolm X. (1964). *Personal letter.* Retrieved March 23, 2006, from http://en.wikisource.org/wiki/Letter_from_Malcolm_X

Manusov, V., & Hegde, R. (1993). Communicative outcomes of stereotype-based expectancies: An observational student of cross-cultural dyads. *Communication Quarterly, 41,* 338–354.

Marks, G., Miller, N., & Maruyama, G. (1981). Effects of targets' physical attractiveness on assumptions of similarity. *Journal of Personality and Social Psychology, 41,* 198–206.

Martin, J. N., Flores, L. A., & Nakayama, T. K. (1998). Ethical issues in intercultural communication. In J. N. Martin, T. K. Nakayama, & L. A. Flores (Eds.), *Readings in cultural contexts* (pp. 455–462). Mountain View, CA: Mayfield.

Martin, J. N., & Nakayama, T. K. (1997). *Intercultural communication in contexts.* Mountain View, CA: Mayfield.

Marzano, R. J., & Arredondo, D. E. (1996). *Tactics for thinking.* Aurora, CO: Mid Continent Regional Educational Laboratory.

Marzano, R. J., Arredondo, D. E., & Brandt, R. S. (1987). *Tactics for thinking: Instructional report.* Alexandria, VA: Association for Supervision and Curriculum Development.

Mashek, D. J., & Aron, A. (2004). *Handbook of closeness and intimacy.* Mahwah, NJ: Erlbaum.

Maslow, A. H. (1943). A theory of human motivation. *Psychological Review, 50,* 370–396.

Maslow, A. H. (1970). *Motivation and personality* (2nd ed.). New York: Harper & Row.

Matlin, M., & Stang, D. (1978). *The Pollyanna principle: Selectivity in language, memory, and thought.* Cambridge, MA: Schenkman.

Mauss, I. B., Levenson, R. W., McCarter, L., Wilhelm, F. H., & Gross, J. J. (2005). The tie that binds: Coherence among emotion experience, behavior, and physiology. *Emotion, 5,* 175–190.

Mayer, J. D., & Salovey, P. (1997). What is emotional intelligence? In P. Salovey & J. D. Sluyter (Eds.), *Emotional development and emotional intelligence* (pp. 3–31). New York: Basic Books.

McCornack, S. A. (1992). Information manipulation theory. *Communication Monographs, 59,* 1–16.

McCornack, S. A. (1997). The generation of deceptive messages: Laying the groundwork for a viable theory of interpersonal deception. In J. O. Greene (Ed.), *Message production: Advances in communication theory* (pp. 91–126). Mahwah, NJ: Erlbaum.

McCornack, S. A. (2004, November). *Message design logics: Is there really any such thing?* Paper presented at the annual meeting of the National Communication Association, Chicago.

McCornack, S. A., & Husband, R. (1986, May). *The evolution of a long-term organizational conflict: A design logic approach.* Paper presented at the annual meeting of the International Communication Association, Chicago.

McCornack, S. A., & Levine, T. R. (1990). When lies are uncovered: Emotional and relational outcomes of discovered deception. *Communication Monographs, 57,* 119–138.

McCrae, R. R. (2001). Trait psychology and culture. *Journal of Personality, 69,* 819–846.

McCrae, R. R., & Costa, P. T., Jr. (1996). Toward a new generation of personality theories: Theoretical contexts for the five-factor model. In J. S. Wiggins (Ed.), *The five-factor model of personality: Theoretical perspectives* (pp. 51–87). New York: Guilford Press.

McCrae, R. R., & Costa, P. T., Jr. (1997). Personality trait structure as a human universal. *American Psychologist, 52,* 509–516.

McCrae, R. R., & Costa, P. T., Jr. (2001). A five-factor theory of personality. In L. A. Pervin and O. P. John (Eds.), *Handbook of personality: Theory and research* (2nd ed., pp. 139–153). New York: Guilford Press.

McCrae, R. R., Costa, P. T., Jr., Ostendorf, F., Angleitner, A., Hrebickova, M., Avia, M. D., et al. (2000). Nature over nurture: Temperament, personality, and life span development. *Journal of Personality and Social Psychology, 78,* 173–186.

McCroskey, J. C., & Richmond, V. P. (1987). Willingness to communicate. In J. C. McCroskey & J. A. Daly (Eds.), *Personality and interpersonal communication* (pp. 129–156). Beverly Hills, CA: Sage.

McCroskey, J. C., & Richmond, V. P. (1991). Willingness to communicate: A cognitive view. In M. Booth-Butterfield (Ed.), *Communication, cognition, and anxiety* (pp. 19–37). Beverly Hills, CA: Sage.

McCullough, D. (2001). *John Adams.* New York: Simon & Schuster.

McIntosh, P. (1999). White privilege: Unpacking the invisible knapsack. In E. Lee, D. Menkart, & M. Okazawa-Rey (Eds.), *Beyond heroes and holidays: A practical guide to K–12 anti-racist, multicultural education and staff development* (pp. 79–82). Washington, DC: Network of Educators on the Americas.

McLaughlin, M. L., & Cody, M. J. (1982). Awkward silences: Behavioral antecedents and consequences of the conversational lapse. *Human Communication Research, 8,* 299–316.

Mead, G. H. (1934). *Mind, self, and society.* Chicago: University of Chicago Press.

Mehrabian, A. (1972). *Nonverbal communication.* Chicago: Aldine.

Mehrabian, A., & Wiener, M. (1967). Decoding of inconsistent communications. *Journal of Personality and Social Psychology, 6,* 109–114.

Mercer, J. (1998, March 20). An unusual reunion at Gallaudet: 10 years after push for "Deaf President Now." *The Chronicle of Higher Education.*

Messman, S. J., Canary, D. J., & Hause, K. S. (1994, February). *Motives, strategies, and equity in the maintenance of opposite-sex friendships.* Paper presented at the Western States Communication Association convention, San Jose, CA.

Messman, S. J., Canary, D. J. & Hause, K. S. (2000). Motives to remain platonic, equity, and the use of maintenance strategies in opposite-sex friendships. *Journal of Social and Personal Relationships, 17,* 67–94.

Metts, S., & Chronis, H. (1986, May). *Relational deception: An exploratory analysis.* Paper presented at the annual meeting of the International Communication Association, Chicago.

Metts, S., & Cupach, W. R. (1990). The influence of romantic beliefs and problem-solving responses on satisfaction in romantic relationships. *Human Communication Research, 17,* 170–185.

Metts, S., & Planalp, S. (2002). Emotional communication. In M. L. Knapp & J. A. Daly (Eds.), *Handbook of interpersonal communication* (pp. 339–373). Thousand Oaks, CA: Sage.

Michalos, A. C. (1991). *Global report on student well-being: Vol. 1. Life satisfaction and happiness.* New York: Springer-Verlag.

Michaud, S. G., & Aynesworth, H. (1989). *The only living witness: A true account of homicidal insanity.* New York: Signet.

Mickelson, K. D., Kessler, R. C., & Shaver, P. R. (1997). Adult attachment in a nationally representative sample. *Journal of Personality and Social Psychology, 73,* 1092–1106.

Mies, M. (1991). *Patriarchy and accumulation on a world scale: Women in the international division of labor.* London: Zed Books.

Miller, G. R., & Steinberg, M. (1975). *Between people: A new analysis of interpersonal communication.* Chicago: Science Research Associates.

Miller, H., & Arnold, J. (2001). Breaking away from grounded identity: Women academics on the web. *CyberPsychology and Behavior, 4,* 95–108.

Miller, K. (1995). *Organizational communication: Approaches and processes.* Belmont, CA: Wadsworth.

Miller, L. C., Berg, J. H., & Archer, R. L. (1983). Openers: Individuals who elicit intimate self-disclosure. *Journal of Personality and Social Psychology, 44,* 1234–1244.

Miller, L. C., Cody, M. L., & McLaughlin, M. L. (1994). Situations and goals as fundamental constructs in interpersonal communication research. In M. L. Knapp & G. R. Miller (Eds.), *Handbook of interpersonal communication* (2nd ed., pp. 162–198). Beverly Hills, CA: Sage.

Millman, J. (1999, August 10). *Brilliant careers: Fred Rogers.* Retrieved February 26, 2006, from http://www.salon.com/people/bc/1999/08/10/rogers/

Mister Rogers. (n.d.) Retrieved February 26, 2006, from http://www.tvacres.com/child_mrrogers.htm

Mitchell, M. (1936). *Gone with the wind.* New York: Macmillan.

Mongeau, P. A., Hale, J. L., & Alles, M. (1994). An experimental investigation of accounts and attributions following sexual infidelity. *Communication Monographs, 61,* 326–344.

Mongeau, P. A., Ramirez, A., & Vorrell, M. (2003, February). *Friends with benefits: Initial explorations of sexual, non-romantic relationships.* Paper presented at the annual meeting of the Western Communication Association, Salt Lake City, UT.

Monsour, M. (1996). Communication and cross-sex friendships across the life-cycle: A review of the literature. In B. Burleson (Ed.), *Communication yearbook 20* (pp. 375–414). Thousand Oaks, CA: Sage.

Montagu, M. F. A. (1971). *Touching: The human significance of the skin.* New York: Columbia University Press.

MTV.com. (n.d.). *The Real World: New York.* Retrieved March 25, 2006, from http://www.mtv.com/onair/dyn/realworld-season1/series.jhtml

Mulac, A., Bradac, J. J., & Mann, S. K. (1985). Male/female language differences and attributional consequences in children's television. *Human Communication Research, 11,* 481–506.

Mulac, A., Incontro, C. R., & James, M. R. (1985). Comparison of the gender-linked language effect and sex role stereotypes. *Journal of Personality and Social Psychology, 49,* 1098–1109.

Myers, D. G. (2002). *The pursuit of happiness: Discovering the pathway to fulfillment, well-being, and enduring personal joy.* New York: HarperCollins.

Myers, S. A., Knox, R. L., Pawlowski, D. R., & Ropog, B. L. (1999). Perceived communication openness and functional communication skills among organizational peers. *Communication Reports, 12,* 71–83.

National Communication Association. (1999). *NCA credo for ethical communication.* Retrieved February 25, 2006, from www.natcom.org/nca/Template2.asp?bid=514.

National Communication Association. (2002, October). *Communication research: Profile of a discipline.* Presentation made to the National Research Council. Retrieved June 19, 2006, from http://www.natcom.org/nca/ Template2.asp?bid=1345

National Communication Association. (2003). *Pathways to careers in communication. What is communication?* Retrieved June 19, 2006, from http://www.natcom.org/nca/Template2.asp?bid=398

Neimeyer, R. A., & Mitchell, K. A. (1988). Similarity and attraction: A longitudinal study. *Journal of Social and Personal Relationships, 5,* 131–148.

Neulip, J. W., & McCroskey, J. C. (1997). The development of a U.S. and generalized ethnocentrism scale. *Communication Research Reports, 14,* 385–398.

Ng, S. H. (1998). Social psychology in an aging world: Ageism and intergenerational relations. *Asian Journal of Social Psychology, 1,* 99–116.

Nishiyama, K. (1971). Interpersonal persuasion in a vertical society. *Speech Monographs, 38,* 148–154.

Nofsinger, R. E. (1999). *Everyday conversation.* Prospect Heights, IL: Waveland Press.

O'Connor, B. P., & Rigby, H. (1996). Perceptions of baby talk, frequency of receiving baby talk, and self-esteem among community and nursing home residents. *Psychology and Aging, 11,* 147–154.

O'Connor, S. (1987). *The lion and the cobra* [LP record]. London: Ensign Records.

Ohbuchi, K., & Sato, K. (1994). Children's reactions to mitigating accounts: Apologies, excuses, and intentionality of harm. *Journal of Social Psychology, 134,* 5–17.

Ohbuchi, K-I., & Tedeschi, J. T. (1997). Multiple goals and tactical behaviors in social conflicts. *Journal of Applied Social Psychology, 27,* 2177–2199.

O'Keefe, B. J. (1988). The logic of message design. *Communication Monographs, 55,* 80–103.

O'Keefe, B. J., & Lambert, B. L. (1989, November). *Effects of message design logic on the communication of intention.* Paper presented at the annual meeting of the Speech Communication Association, San Francisco.

O'Keefe, B. J., & Lambert, B. L. (1995). Managing the flow of ideas: A local management approach to message design. In B. R. Burleson (Ed.), *Communication yearbook 18* (pp. 54–82). Thousand Oaks, CA: Sage.

O'Keefe, B. J., & McCornack, S. A. (1987). Message design logic and message goal structure: Effects on perceptions of message quality in regulative communication situation. *Human Communication Research, 14,* 68–92.

O'Leary, K. D., & Vivian, D. (1990). Physical aggression in marriage. In F. D. Fincham & T. N. Bradbury (Eds.), *The psychology of marriage: Basic issues and applications* (pp. 323–348). New York: Guilford Press.

O'Meara, J. D. (1989). Cross-sex friendship: Four basic challenges of an ignored relationship. *Sex Roles, 21,* 525–543.

O'Neil, W. (1997). If Ebonics isn't a language, then tell me, what is? *Rethinking Schools Online, 12.* Retrieved February 27, 2006, from http://www.rethinkingschools.org/archive/12_01/eboneil.shtml

Oravec, J. (2000). Internet and computer technology hazards: Perspectives for family counseling. *British Journal of Guidance and Counselling, 28,* 309–324.

Orbe, M. P., & Warren, K. T. (2000). Different standpoints, different realities: Race, gender, and perceptions of intercultural conflict. *Communication Quarterly, 48,* 51–57.

Palmer, M. T., & Simmons, K. B. (1995). Communicating intentions through nonverbal behaviors: Conscious and nonconscious encoding of liking. *Human Communication Research, 22,* 128–160.

Park, H. S., Levine, T. R., McCornack, S. A.,Morrison, K., & Ferrara, M. (2002). How people really detect lies. *Communication Monographs, 69,* 144–157.

Parker, S., Mitchell, R., & Boccia, M. (1995). *Self-awareness in animals and humans: Developmental perspectives.* New York: Cambridge University Press.

Parkinson, B., Totterdell, P., Briner, R. B., & Reynolds, S. (1996). *Changing moods: The psychology of mood and mood regulation.* London: Longman.

Parks, M. R. (1994). Communicative competence and interpersonal control. In M. L. Knapp & G. R. Miller (Eds.), *Handbook of interpersonal communication* (2nd ed., pp. 589–620). Beverly Hills, CA: Sage.

Parks, M. R. (1996). Making friends in cyberspace. *Journal of Communication, 46,* 80–97.

Parks, M. R., & Adelman, M. B. (1983). Communication networks and the development of romantic relationships: An expansion of uncertainty reduction theory. *Human Communication Research, 10,* 55–79.

Parks, M. R., & Floyd, K. (1996). Making friends in cyberspace. *Journal of Communication, 46,* 80–97.

Parks, M. R., & Roberts, L. D. (1998). "Making MOOsic": The development of personal relationships online and a comparison to their off-line counterparts. *Journal of Social and Personal Relationships, 15,* 517–537.

Parry, W. (2002). *Tell us something we don't already know: Metal god Rob Halford on life after coming out*. Retrieved February 24, 2006, from www.gaypeopleschronicle.com/stories02/02aug23.htm.

Pasch, L. A., Bradbury, T. N., & Davila, J. (1997). Gender, negative affectivity, and observed social support behavior in marital interaction. *Personal Relationships, 4,* 361–378.

Patterson, M. L. (1983). *Nonverbal behavior: A functional perspective*. New York: Springer-Verlag.

Patterson, M. L. (1988). Functions of nonverbal behavior in close relationships. In S. W. Duck (Ed.) *Handbook of personal relationships* (pp. 41–56). New York: Wiley.

Patterson, M. L. (1995). A parallel process model of nonverbal communication. *Journal of Nonverbal Behavior, 19,* 3–29.

Payne, M. J., & Sabourin, T. C. (1990). Argumentative skill deficiency and its relationship to quality of marriage. *Communication Research Reports, 7,* 121–124.

Pennebaker, J. W. (1997). *Opening up: The healing power of expressing emotions*. New York: Guilford Press.

Pennsylvania Dutch Country Welcome Center. (n.d.). *The Amish: FAQs*. Retrieved March 18, 2006, from http://www.padutch.com/atafaq.shtml

Peplau, L. A., & Spalding, L. R. (2000). The close relationships of lesbians, gay men and bisexuals. In C. Hendrick & S. S. Hendrick (Eds.), *Close relationships: A sourcebook* (pp. 111–123). Thousand Oaks, CA: Sage.

Perry, T., & Delpit, L. (1998). *The real Ebonics debate: Power, language, and the education of African-American children*. Boston: Beacon Press.

Pervin, L. A. (1993). Affect and personality. In M. Lewis & J. M. Haviland (Eds.), *Handbook of emotions* (pp. 301–311). New York: Guilford Press.

Peterson, D. R. (2002). Conflict. In H. H. Kelley et al. (Eds.), *Close Relationships* (2nd ed., pp. 360–396). Clinton Corners, NY: Percheron Press.

Petronio, S. (1991). Communication boundary management: A theoretical model of managing disclosure of private information between marital couples. *Communication Theory, 1,* 311–335.

Petronio, S. (2000). The boundaries of privacy: Praxis of everyday life. In S. Petronio (Ed.), *Balancing the secrets of private disclosures* (pp. 37–49). Mahwah, NJ: Erlbaum.

Pfeiffer, S. M., & Wong, P. T. P. (1989). Multidimensional jealousy. *Journal of Social and Personal Relationships, 6,* 181–196.

Philpott, T. (2004, October). Stop stop loss. *Today's officer*. Retrieved April 2, 2006, from http://www.moaa.org/todaysofficer/columnists/Philpott/Stop.asp

Piaget, J. (1926). *Language and thought of the child* (M. Gabain, Trans.). London: Routledge & Kegan Paul.

Planalp, S., & Honeycutt, J. M. (1985). Events that increase uncertainty in personal relationships. *Human Communication Research, 11,* 593–604.

Plutchik, R. (1980). *Emotions: A psycho-evolutionary synthesis*. New York: Harper & Row.

Plutchik, R. (1993). Emotions and their vicissitudes: Emotions and psychopathology. In M. Lewis & J. M. Haviland (Eds.), *Handbook of emotions* (pp. 53–66). New York: Guilford Press.

Pomerantz, A. (1990). On the validity and generalizability of conversation analytic methods: Conversation analytic claims. *Communication Monographs, 57,* 231–235.

Popper, K. (2004). *The logic of scientific discovery*. New York: Routledge. (Original work published 1934)

Pruitt, D. G., & Carnevale, P. J. (1993). *Negotiation in social conflict*. Monterey, CA: Brooks-Cole.

Rabby, M. K. (1997, November). *Maintaining relationships via electronic mail*. Paper presented at the annual meeting of the National Communication Association, Chicago.

Rabby, M. K., & Walther, J. B. (2003). Computer-mediated communication effects on relationship formation and maintenance. In D. J. Canary & M. Dainton (Eds.), *Maintaining relationships through communication: Relational, contextual, and cultural variations* (pp. 141–162). Mahwah, NJ: Erlbaum.

Rahim, M. A., & Mager, N. R. (1995). Confirmatory factor analysis of the styles of handling interpersonal conflict: First-order factor model and its invariance across groups. *Journal of Applied Psychology, 80,* 122–132.

Raines, R. S., Hechtman, S. B., & Rosenthal, R. (1990). Nonverbal behavior and gender as determinants of physical attractiveness. *Journal of Nonverbal Behavior, 14,* 253–267.

Rainey, V. P. (2000, December). The potential for miscommunication using email as a source of communications. *Transactions of the Society for Design and Process Science, 4,* 21–43.

Rawlins, W. K. (1992). *Friendship matters: Communication, dialectics, and the life course*. New York: Aldine de Gruyter.

Rawlins, W. K. (1994). Being there and growing apart: Sustaining friendships during adulthood. In D. J. Canary & L. Stafford (Eds.), *Communication and relational maintenance* (pp. 275–294). New York: Academic Press.

Ray, J. J. (1970). The development and validation of a balanced dogmatism scale. *Australian Journal of Psychology, 22,* 253–260.

Ray, J. J. (1972). A new balanced F scale, and its relation to social class. *Australian Psychologist, 7,* 155–166.

Reeder, H. M. (2003). The effect of gender role orientation on same- and cross-sex friendship formation. *Sex Roles, 49,* 143–152.

Regan, P. C., Kocan, E. R., & Whitlock, T. (1998). Ain't love grand: A prototype analysis of the concept of romantic love. *Journal of Social and Personal Relationships, 15,* 411–420.

Regional vocabularies of American English. (n.d.). Retrieved February 27, 2006, from http://en.wikipedia.org/wiki/Regional_vocabularies_of_American_English

Register, L. M., & Henley, T. B. (1992). The phenomenology of intimacy. *Journal of Social and Personal Relationships, 9,* 467–481.

Reik, T. (1972). *A psychologist looks at love*. New York: Lancer.

Reuters. (2004, August 18). Army guardsman sues to get out. *The Washington Post* [online]. Retrieved April 1, 2006, from http://www.washingtonpost.com/wp-dyn/articles/A9535-2004 Aug17.html

Rheingold, H. (1993). *The virtual community: Homesteading on the electronic frontier*. New York: Addison-Wesley.

Richards, J. M., Butler, E. A., & Gross, J. J. (2003). Emotion regulation in romantic relationships: The cognitive consequences of concealing feelings. *Journal of Social and Personal Relationships, 20,* 599–620.

Ridge, R. D., & Berscheid, E. (1989, May). *On loving and being in love: A necessary distinction.* Paper presented at the annual convention of the Midwestern Psychological Association, Chicago.

Rintel, E. S., & Pittam, J. (1997). Strangers in a strange land: Interaction management on Internet relay chat. *Human Communication Research, 23,* 507–534.

Ritchie, L. D., & Fitzpatrick, M. A. (1990). Family communication patterns: Measuring interpersonal perceptions of interpersonal relationships. *Communication Research, 17,* 52–544.

Robinson, W. S. (1951). The logical structure of analytic induction. *American Sociological Review, 16,* 812–818.

Roethlisberger, F. J., & Dickson, W. J. (1939). *Management and the worker.* Cambridge, MA: Harvard University Press.

Rohlfing, M. E. (1990, November). *Communicating long-distance friendship.* Paper presented at the annual convention of the Speech Communication Association, Chicago.

Rohlfing, M. E. (1995). Doesn't anybody stay in one place anymore? An exploration of the under-studied phenomenon of long-distance relationships. In J. T. Wood & S. Duck (Eds.), *Under-studied relationships: Off the beaten track* (pp. 173–196). Thousand Oaks, CA: Sage.

Roloff, M. E., & Soule, K. P. (2002). Interpersonal conflict: A review. In M. L. Knapp & J. A. Daly (Eds.), *Handbook of interpersonal communication* (3rd ed., pp. 475–528). Thousand Oaks, CA: Sage.

Rosenburg, M. (1965). *Society and the adolescent self-image.* Princeton, NJ: Princeton University Press.

Rosencranz, M. L. (1965). Sociological and psychological approaches to clothing research. *Journal of Home Economics, 57,* 26–29.

Rosenfeld, H. M. (1987). Conversational control functions of nonverbal behavior. In A.W. Siegman & S. Feldstein (Eds.), *Nonverbal behavior and communication* (2nd ed., pp. 563–602). Hillsdale, NJ: Erlbaum.

Rothbart, M. K., Ahadi, S. A., & Evans, D. E. (2000). Temperament and personality: Origins and outcomes. *Journal of Personality and Social Psychology, 78,* 122–135.

Rowatt, W. D., Cunningham, M. R., & Druen, P. B. (1998). Deception to get a date. *Personality and Social Psychology Bulletin, 24,* 1228–1242.

Rowling, J. K. (1997). *Harry Potter and the sorcerer's stone.* New York: Scholastic Press.

Rowling, J. K. (2002). I miss my mother so much. *InsideMS, 20,* 1–7.

Roy, R., Benenson, J. F., & Lilly, F. (2000). Beyond intimacy: Conceptualizing sex differences in same-sex friendships. *The Journal of Psychology, 134,* 93–101.

Rubin, L. (1985). *Just friends.* New York: Harper & Row.

Rubin, L. B. (1996). Reflections on friendship. In K. M. Galvin & P. J. Cooper (Eds.), *Making connections: Readings in relational communication* (pp. 254–257). Los Angeles: Roxbury.

Rubin, Z. (1973). *Liking and loving: An invitation to social psychology.* New York: Holt, Rinehart & Winston.

Rusbult, C. E. (1987). Responses to dissatisfaction in close relationships: The exit-voice-loyalty-neglect model. In D. Perlman & S. Duck (Eds.), *Intimate relationships: Development, dynamics, and deterioration* (pp. 209–237). Newbury Park, CA: Sage.

Russell, D., Peplau, L. A., & Cutrona, C. E. (1980). The revised UCLA loneliness scale: Concurrent and discriminant validity evidence. *Journal of Personality and Social Psychology, 39,* 472–480.

Saarni, C. (1993). Socialization of emotion. In M. Lewis & J. M. Haviland (Eds.), *Handbook of emotions* (pp. 435–446). New York: Guilford Press.

Sabourin, T. C., Infante, D. A., & Rudd, J. E. (1993). Verbal aggression in marriages: A comparison of violent, distressed but nonviolent, and nondistressed couples. *Human Communication Research, 20,* 245–267.

Salovey, P., Mayer, J. D., & Caruso, D. (2002). The positive psychology of emotional intelligence. In C. R. Snyder & S. J. Lopez (Eds.), *The handbook of positive psychology* (pp. 159–171). New York: Oxford University Press.

Salovey, P., & Rodin, J. (1988). Coping with envy and jealousy. *Journal of Social and Clinical Psychology, 7,* 15–33.

Sapir, E. (1929). The status of linguistics as a science. *Language, 5,* 207–214.

Sarason, B. R., Pierce, G. R., & Sarason, I. G. (1990). Social support: The sense of acceptance and the role of relationships. In B. R. Sarason, I. G. Sarason, & G. R. Pierce (Eds.), *Social support: An interactional view* (pp. 97–128). New York: Wiley.

Savicki, V., Kelley, M., & Oesterreich, E. (1999). Judgments of gender in computer-mediated communication. *Computers in Human Behavior, 15,* 185–194.

Schein, E. H. (1985). *Organizational culture and leadership.* San Francisco: Jossey-Bass.

Scherer, K. R. (1974). Acoustic concomitants of emotional dimensions: Judging affect from synthesized tone sequences. In S. Weitz (Ed.), *Nonverbal communication: Readings with commentary* (pp. 105–111). New York: Oxford University Press.

Scherer, K. R. (2001). Appraisal considered as a process of multilevel sequential checking. In K. R. Scherer, A. Schorr, & T. Johnstone (Eds.), *Appraisal processes in emotion* (pp. 92–120). Oxford, England: Oxford University Press.

Schlaepfer, T. E., Harris, G. J., Tien, A. Y., Peng, L., Lee, S., & Pearlson, G. D. (1995). Structural differences in the cerebral cortex of healthy female and male subjects: A magnetic resonance imaging study. *Psychiatry Research, 61,* 129–135.

Schramm, W. (Ed.). (1954). *The process and effects of mass communication.* Urbana: University of Illinois Press.

Schultz, H. (Creator & Executive Producer). (2003). *Extreme makeovers* [Television series]. New York: ABC.

Schutz, A. (1999). It was your fault! Self-serving biases in autobiographical accounts of conflicts in married couples. *Journal of Social and Personal Relationships, 16,* 193–208.

Searle, J. (1965). What is a speech act? In Max Black (Ed.), *Philosophy in America* (pp. 221–239). Ithaca, NY: Cornell University Press.

Searle, J. A. (1969). *Speech acts.* Cambridge; England: Cambridge University Press.

Searle, J. A. (1976). The classification of illocutionary acts. *Language in Society, 5,* 1–24.

Seta, J. J., & Seta, C. E. (1993). Stereotypes and the generation of compensatory and noncompensatory expectancies of group members. *Personality and Social Psychology Bulletin, 19,* 722–731.

Shackelford, T. K., & Buss, D. M. (1997). Anticipation of marital dissolution as a consequence of spousal infidelity. *Journal of Social and Personal Relationships, 14,* 793–808.

Shah, M. B., King, S., & Patel, A. S. (2004). Intercultural disposition and communication competence of future pharmacists. *American Journal of Pharmaceutical Education, 69,* 1–11.

Shannon, C. E., & Weaver, W. (1949). *The mathematical theory of communication.* Urbana: University of Illinois Press.

Shaver, P. R., Wu, S., & Schwartz, J. C. (1992). Cross-cultural similarities and differences in emotion and its representation. In M. S. Clark (Ed.), *Emotion* (pp. 175–212). Newbury Park, CA: Sage.

Shedletsky, L. J., & Aitken, J. E. (2004). *Human communication on the Internet.* Boston: Pearson Education/Allyn and Bacon.

Shweder, R. A. (1993). The cultural psychology of the emotions. In M. Lewis & J. M. Haviland (Eds.), *Handbook of emotions* (pp. 417–431). New York: Guilford Press.

Sias, P. M., & Cahill, D. J. (1998). From co-workers to friends: The development of peer friendships in the workplace. *Western Journal of Communication, 62,* 273–300.

Sias, P. M., Krone, K. J., & Jablin, F. M. (2002). An ecological systems perspective on workplace relationships. In M. L. Knapp & J. A. Daly (Eds.), *Handbook of interpersonal communication* (pp. 615–642). Thousand Oaks, CA: Sage.

Sias, P. M., & Perry, T. (2004). Disengaging from workplace relationships: A research note. *Human Communication Research, 30,* 589–602.

Sias, P. M., Smith, G., & Avdeyeva, T. (2003). Sex and sex composition similarities and differences in workplace friendship development. *Communication Studies, 54,* 322–337.

Sillars, A. L. (1980). Attributions and communication in roommate conflicts. *Communication Monographs, 47,* 180–200.

Sillars, A. L., Folwell, A. L., Hill, K. C., Maki, B. K., Hurst, A. P., & Casano, R. A. (1994). Marital communication and the persistence of misunderstanding. *Journal of Social and Personal Relationships, 11,* 611–617.

Sillars, A. L., Pike, G. R., Jones, T. S., & Murphy, M. A. (1984). Communication and understanding in marriage. *Human Communication Research, 10,* 317–350.

Sillars, A. L., Roberts, L. J., Leonard, K. E., & Dun, T. (2000). Cognition during marital conflict: The relationship of thought and talk. *Journal of Social and Personal Relationships, 17,* 479–502.

Sillars, A. L., & Wilmot, W. W. (1994). Communication strategies in conflict and mediation. In J. Wiemann & J. Daly (Eds.), *Communicating strategically: Strategies in interpersonal communication* (pp. 163–190). Hillsdale, NJ: Erlbaum.

Silvera, D. H., Krull, D. S., & Sassler, M. A. (2002). Typhoid Pollyanna: The effect of category valence on retrieval order of positive and negative category members. *European Journal of Cognitive Psychology, 14,* 227–236.

Silversides, B. V. (1994). *The face pullers: Photographing native Canadians, 1871–1939.* Saskatoon, Saskatchewan: Fifth House.

Simmel, G. (1950). *The sociology of Georg Simmel* (K. H. Wolff, Ed. and Trans.). New York: Free Press. (Original work published 1908)

Simpson, J. A., Rholes, W. S., & Nelligan, J. S. (1992). Support seeking and support giving within couples in an anxiety-provoking situation: The role of attachment styles. *Journal of Personality and Social Psychology, 62,* 434–446.

Singleton, J. (Writer/Director), & Nicolaides, S. (Producer). (1991). *Boyz in the hood* [Motion picture]. United States: Columbia Pictures.

Smith, B. L., Lasswell, H. D., & Casey, R. D. (1946). *Propaganda, communication, and public opinion.* Princeton, NJ: Princeton University Press.

Smith, C. A., & Kirby, L. D. (2004). Appraisal as a pervasive determinant of anger. *Emotion, 4,* 133–138.

Smith, G., & Anderson, K. J. (2005). Students' ratings of professors: The teaching style contingency for Latino/a professors. *Journal of Latinos and Education, 4,* 115–136.

Smith-Rosenberg, C. (1985). *Disorderly conduct: Visions of gender in Victorian America.* New York: Knopf.

Snyder, M. (1974). Self-monitoring of expressive behavior. *Journal of Personality and Social Psychology, 30,* 526–537.

Soto, J. A., Levenson, R. W., & Ebling, R. (2005). Cultures of moderation and expression: Emotional experience, behavior, and physiology in Chinese Americans and Mexican Americans. *Emotion, 5,* 154–165.

Soukup, C. (1999). The gendered interactional patterns of computer-mediated chatrooms: A criticial ethnographic study. *Information Society, 15,* 169–176.

Spears, R., Postmes, T., Lea, M., & Watt, S. E. (2001). A SIDE view of social influence. In J. P. Forgas & K. D. Williams (Eds.), *Social influence: Direct and indirect processes* (pp. 331–350). Philadelphia: Psychology Press–Taylor and Francis Group.

Spender, D. (1984). Defining reality: A powerful tool. In C. Kramarae, M. Schultz, & W. O'Barr (Eds.), *Language and power* (pp. 195–205). Beverly Hills, CA: Sage.

Spender, D. (1990). *Man made language.* London: Pandora Press.

Spitzberg, B. (1997). A model of intercultural communication competence. In L. A. Samovar & R. E. Porter (Eds.), *Intercultural communication: A reader* (pp. 379–391). Belmont, CA: Wadsworth.

Spitzberg, B. H., & Cupach, W. R. (1984). *Interpersonal communication competence.* Beverly Hills, CA: Sage.

Spitzberg, B. H., & Cupach, W. R. (2002). Interpersonal skills. In M. L. Knapp & J. A. Daly (Eds.), *Handbook of interpersonal communication* (3rd ed., pp. 564–611). Thousand Oaks, CA: Sage.

Sprecher, S. (1986). The relation between equity and emotions in close relationships. *Social Psychology Bulletin, 49,* 309–321.

Sprecher, S. (2001). A comparison of emotional consequences of and changes in equity over time using global and domain-specific measures of equity. *Journal of Social and Personal Relationships, 18,* 477–501.

Sprecher, S., & Metts, S. (1989). Development of the romantic beliefs scale and examination of the effects of gender and gender-role orientation. *Journal of Social and Personal Relationships, 6,* 387–411.

Sprecher, S., & Regan, P. C. (1998). Passionate and companionate love in courting and young married couples. *Sociological Inquiry, 68,* 163–185.

Stafford, L. (2003). Maintaining romantic relationships: A summary and analysis of one research program. In D. J. Canary & M. Dainton (Eds.), *Maintaining relationships through communication: Relational, contextual, and cultural variations* (pp. 51–77). Mahwah, NJ: Erlbaum.

Stafford, L., & Canary, D. J. (1991). Maintenance strategies and romantic relationship type, gender, and relational characteristics. *Journal of Social and Personal Relationships, 8,* 217–242.

Stafford, L., Dainton, M., & Haas, S. (2000). Measuring routine and strategic relational maintenance: Scale revision, sex versus gender roles, and the prediction of relational characteristics. *Communication Monographs, 67,* 306–323.

Stiff, J. B., Dillard, J. P., Somera, L., Kim, H., & Sleight, C. (1988). Empathy, communication, and prosocial behavior. *Communication Monographs, 55,* 198–213.

Stimson, E. (1998, March). *The real Mister Rogers: This Presbyterian minister is as genuinely nice in person as he is on TV.* Retrieved February 26, 2006, from http://www.pcusa.org/today/archive/features/feat9803a.htm

Stone, E. (1988). *Black sheep and kissing cousins: How our family stories shape us.* New York: Penguin Books.

Stone, E. (1996). Family ground rules. In K. M. Galvin & P. Cooper (Eds.), *Making connections: Readings in relational communication* (pp. 59–67). Los Angeles: Roxbury.

Strauss, V. (2006, March 21). Putting parents in their place: Outside class. *The Washington Post,* p. A08.

Streek, J. (1980). Speech acts in interaction: A critique of Searle. *Discourse Processes, 3,* 133–154.

Streek, J. (1993). Gesture as communication I: Its coordination with gaze and speech. *Communication Monographs, 60,* 275–299.

Streek, J. (2002). Culture, meaning, and interpersonal communication. In M. L. Knapp & J. A. Daly (Eds.), *Handbook of interpersonal communication* (pp. 300–336). Thousand Oaks, CA: Sage.

Suler, J. R. (2004). The online disinhibition effect. *CyberPsychology and Behavior, 7,* 321–326.

Sumner, W. G. (1906). *Folkways.* Boston: Ginn.

Sunnafrank, M. (1991). Interpersonal attraction and attitude similarity: A communication-based assessment. In J. A. Andersen (Ed.), *Communication yearbook 14* (pp. 451–483). Newbury Park, CA: Sage.

Surra, C. A., & Longstreth, M. (1990). Similarity of outcomes, interdependence, and conflict in dating relationships. *Journal of Personality and Social Psychology, 59,* 501–516.

Surra, C., & Hughes, D. (1997). Commitment processes in accounts of the development of pre-marital relationships. *Journal of Marriage and the Family, 59,* 5–21.

Susana. (2004, November 1). *Sharing thoughts and memories of Cesar E. Chavez.* Message posted to www.colapublib.org/chavez/memories.html

Swain, S. O. (1992). Men's friendships with women: Intimacy, sexual boundaries, and the informant role. In P. M. Nardi (Ed.). *Men's friendships: Vol. 2. Research on men and masculinities* (pp. 153–172). Newbury Park, CA: Sage.

Tan, A. (2003). Mother tongue. In R. Bass & J. Young (Eds.), *Beyond borders: A cultural reader.* Boston: Houghton Mifflin.

Tannen, D. (1990). *You just don't understand: Women and men in conversation.* New York: Morrow.

Tardy, C. H. (2000). Self-disclosure and health: Revising Sidney Jourard's hypothesis. In S. Petronio (Ed.), *Balancing the secrets of private disclosures* (pp. 111–122). Mahwah, NJ: Erlbaum.

Tardy, C., & Dindia, K. (1997). Self-disclosure. In O. Hargie (Ed.), *The handbook of communication skills.* London: Routledge.

Tavris, C. (1989). *Anger: The misunderstood emotion.* New York: Touchstone Press.

Tepper, B. J. (2000). Consequences of abusive supervision. *Academy of Management Journal, 43,* 178–190.

Thayer, R. E., Newman, J. R., & McClain, T. M. (1994). Self-regulation of mood: Strategies for changing a bad mood, raising energy, and reducing tension. *Journal of Personality and Social Psychology, 67,* 910–925.

Thomas, L. T., & Levine, T. R. (1994). Disentangling listening and verbal recall: Related but separate constructs? *Human Communication Research, 21,* 103–127.

Thompson, J. K., Heinberg, L. J., Altabe, M., & Tantleff-Dunn, S. (1999). *Exacting beauty: Theory, assessment, and treatment of body image disturbances.* Washington, DC: American Psychological Association.

Thorne, B. (1986). Boys and girls together . . . but mostly apart: Gender arrangements in elementary schools. In W. Hartup & Z. Rubin (Eds.), *Relationships and development* (pp. 167–184). Hillsdale, NJ: Erlbaum.

Tidwell, L. C., & Walther, J. B. (2002). Computer-mediated communication effects on disclosure, impressions, and interpersonal evaluations: Getting to know one another a bit at a time. *Human Communication Research, 28,* 317–348.

Ting-Toomey, S. (1985). Toward a theory of conflict and culture. In W. B. Gudykunst, L. P. Stewart, & S. Ting-Toomey (Eds.), *Communication, culture, and organizational processes* (pp. 71–86). Beverly Hills, CA: Sage.

Ting-Toomey, S. (1997). Managing intercultural conflicts effectively. In L. A. Samovar & R. E. Porter (Eds.), *Intercultural communication: A reader* (pp. 392–403). Belmont, CA: Wadsworth.

Ting-Toomey, S. (1999). *Communicating across cultures.* New York: Guilford Press.

Tippett, M. (1994). The face pullers. [Review of the book *The face pullers*]. *Canadian Historical Review, 75,* 1–4.

Tjaden, P., & Thoennes, N. (1999). *Extent, nature, and consequences of intimate partner violence: Findings from the*

National Violence Against Women Survey. Washington, DC: National Institute of Justice/Centers for Disease Control and Prevention.

Todd, J., Todd, S. (Producers), & Nolan, C. (Writer/Director). (2000). *Memento* [Motion picture]. United States: Newmarket Films.

Tolkien, J. R. R. (1973). *The two towers*. New York: Ballantine Books. (Original work published 1954)

Triandis, H. C. (1995). *Individualism and collectivism*. Boulder, CO: Westview Press.

Tsai, J. L., & Levenson, R. W. (1997). Cultural influences of emotional responding: Chinese American and European American dating couples during interpersonal conflict. *Journal of Cross-Cultural Psychology, 28*, 600–625.

Tschann, J. M., Flores, E., Marin, B. V., Pasch, L. A., Baisch, E. M., & Wibbelsman, C. J. (2002). Interparental conflict and risk behaviors among Mexican American adolescents: A cognitive-emotional model. *Journal of Abnormal Child Psychology, 30*, 373–385.

Turkle, S. (1995). *Life on the screen: Identity in the age of the Internet*. New York: Simon & Schuster.

Turner, L. H., & West, R. (1998). *Perspectives on family communication*. Mountain View, CA: Mayfield.

Turner, R. E., Edgley, C., & Olmstead, G. (1975). Information control in conversations: Honesty is not always the best policy. *Kansas Journal of Sociology, 11*, 69–89.

Ty Cobb. (n.d.). Retrieved February 25, 2006, from http://en .wikipedia.org/wiki/Ty_Cobb

United Nations Inter-Agency Network on Women and Gender Equality. (2002, March). *Gender equality and the millennium development goals (MDG): Assessing progress in achieving gender equality*. Washington, DC: Author.

U.S. Department of Labor. (1991). *Skills and new economy*. Washington, DC: U.S. Government Printing Office.

U.S. Equal Employment Opportunity Commission. (n.d.). *Sexual harassment charges: 1992–2005*. Retrieved March 31, 2006, from http://www.eeoc.gov/ stats/harass.html

U.S. Equal Employment Opportunity Commission. (1980). Guidelines on discrimination because of sex. *Federal Register, 45*, 74676–74677.

Vallacher, R. R., Nowak, A., Froehlich, M., & Rockloff, M. (2002). The dynamics of self-evaluation. *Personality and Social Psychology Review, 6*, 370–379.

Van Rooijen, L. (1973). Talking about the bright side: Pleasantness of the referent as a determinant of communication accuracy. *European Journal of Social Psychology, 3*, 473–478.

Vangelisti, A. (1993). Communication in the family: The influence of time, relational prototypes, and irrationality. *Communication Monographs, 60*, 42–54.

Vangelisti, A. L. (2002). Interpersonal processes in romantic relationships. In M. L. Knapp and J. A. Daly (Eds.), *Handbook of interpersonal communication* (pp. 643–679). Thousand Oaks, CA: Sage.

Vogl-Bauer, S. (2003). Maintaining family relationships. In D. J. Canary, & M. Dainton (Eds.), *Maintaining relationships through communication: Relational, contextual, and cultural variations* (pp. 31–50). Mahwah, NJ: Erlbaum.

Waldron, H. B., Turner, C. W., Alexander, J. F., & Barton, C. (1993). Coding defensive and supportive communications:

Discriminant validity and subcategory convergence. *Journal of Family Psychology, 7*, 197–203.

Walker, A. (1992). *The color purple*. New York: Harcourt. (Original work published 1982)

Wallace, P. (1999). *The psychology of the Internet*. Cambridge, England: Cambridge University Press.

Walther, J. B., & Parks, M. R. (2002). Cues filtered out, cues filtered in: Computer-mediated communication and relationships. In M. L. Knapp & J. A. Daly (Eds.), *Handbook of interpersonal communication* (3rd ed., pp. 529–563). Thousand Oaks, CA: Sage.

Waterman, A. (1984). *The psychology of individualism*. New York: Praeger.

A watershed moment: Deaf President Now. (n.d.). Retrieved February 26, 2006, from Gallaudet University Web site: www.gallaudet.edu/x228.xml

Watson, K. W., Barker, L. L., & Weaver, J. B., III. (1995). The listening styles profile (LSP-16): Development and validation of an instrument to assess four listening styles. *International Journal of Listening, 9*, 1–13.

Watzlawick, P., Beavin, J. H., & Jackson, D. D. (1967). *Pragmatics of human communication: A study of interactional patterns, pathologies, and paradoxes*. New York: Norton.

Webster's New World College Dictionary (3rd Ed.). (1997). New York: Macmillan.

Weigel, D. J., & Ballard-Reisch, D. S. (1999). The influence of marital duration on the use of relationship maintenance behaviors. *Communication Reports, 12*, 59–69.

Weinberg, N., Schmale, J. D., Uken, J., & Wessel, K. (1995). Computer-mediated support groups. *Social Work with Groups, 17*, 43–55.

Weir, P. (Writer/Director), Williamson, D. (Writer), & Lovell, P. (Producer). (1981). *Gallipoli* [Motion picture]. Australia: South Australian Film Corporation.

Weiss, H. M., Suckow, K., & Cropanzano, R. (1999). Effects of justice conditions on discrete emotions. *Journal of Applied Psychology, 84*, 786–794.

Wellman, B. (1992). Men in networks: Private communities, domestic friendships. In P. M. Nardi (Ed.), *Men's friendships: Vol. 2. Research on men and masculinities* (pp. 74–114). Newbury Park, CA: Sage.

Wells, G. L., Lindsay, R. C. L., & Tousignant, J. P. (1980). Effects of expert psychological advice on human performance in judging the validity of eyewitness testimony. *Law and Human Behavior, 4*, 275–285.

Wheeless, L. R. (1978). A follow-up study of the relationships among trust, disclosure, and interpersonal solidarity. *Human Communication Research, 4*, 143–145.

White, G. L. (1980). Physical attractiveness and courtship progress. *Journal of Personality and Social Psychology, 39*, 660–668.

Whorf, B. L. (1952). *Collected papers on metalinguistics*. Washington, DC: Department of State, Foreign Service Institute.

Wiederman, M. W., & Kendall, E. (1999). Evolution, sex, and jealousy: Investigation with a sample from Sweden. *Evolution and Human Behavior, 20*, 121–128.

Wiemann, J. M. (1977). Explication and test of a model of communicative competence. *Human Communication Research, 3*, 195–213.

Wilder, L. I. (1940). *The long winter.* New York: HarperCollins.

Wilkins, B. M., & Andersen, P. A. (1991). Gender differences and similarities in management communication: A meta-analysis. *Management Communication Quarterly, 5,* 6–35.

Williams, K., Kemper, S., & Hummert, M. (2003). Improving nursing home communication: An intervention to reduce elderspeak. *The Gerontologist, 43,* 242–247.

Williams, W. L. (1992). The relationship between male-male friendship and male-female marriage: American Indian and Asian comparisons. In P. M. Nardi (Ed.), *Men's friendships: Vol. 2. Research on men and masculinities* (pp. 186–200). Newbury Park, CA: Sage.

Wilmot, W. W., & Hocker, J. L. (2001). *Interpersonal conflict* (6th ed.). Boston: McGraw-Hill.

Wilson, T. D. (2002). *Strangers to ourselves: Discovering the adaptive unconscious.* Cambridge, MA: Harvard University Press.

Winstead, B. A., Derlaga, V. J., & Rose, S. (1997). *Gender and close relationships.* Thousand Oaks, CA: Sage.

Winterson, J. (1993). *Written on the body.* New York: Knopf.

Wolvin, A. D. (1987). *Culture as a listening variable.* Paper presented at the summer conference of the International Listening Association, Toronto, Canada.

Wolvin, A., & Coakley, C. G. (1996). *Listening.* Madison, WI: Brown & Benchmark.

Wood, J. T. (1998). *But I thought you meant . . .: Misunderstandings in human communication.* Mountain View, CA: Mayfield.

Wood, W., Rhodes, N., & Whelan, M. (1989). Sex differences in positive well-being: A consideration of emotional style and marital status. *Psychological Bulletin, 106,* 249–264.

Worthen, J. B., Garcia-Rivas, G., Green, C. R., & Vidos, R. A. (2000). Tests of a cognitive-resource-allocation account of the bizarreness effect. *Journal of General Psychology, 127,* 117–144.

Wright, K. B. (2000). Perceptions of online support providers: An examination of perceived homophily, source credibility, communication and social support within online support groups. *Communication Quarterly, 48,* 44–59.

Wu, D. Y. H., & Tseng, W. (1985). Introduction: The characteristics of Chinese culture. In W. Tseng & D. Y. H. Wu (Eds.), *Chinese culture and mental health* (pp. 3–13). Orlando, FL: Academic Press.

Yum, Y-O., & Canary, D. J. (2003). Maintaining relationships in Korea and the United States: Features of Korean culture that affect relational maintenance beliefs and behaviors. In D. J. Canary & M. Dainton (Eds.), *Maintaining relationships through communication: Relational, contextual, and cultural variations* (pp. 277–296). Mahwah, NJ: Erlbaum.

Zahn-Waxler, C. (2001). The development of empathy, guilt, and internalization of distress: Implications for gender differences in internalizing and externalizing problems. In R. Davidson (Ed.), *Anxiety, depression, and emotion: Wisconsin symposium on emotion, Vol. 1* (pp. 222–265). New York: Oxford University Press.

Znaniecki, F. (1934). *The method of sociology.* New York: Farrar & Rinehart.

Zorn, T. E. (1995). Bosses and buddies: Constructing and performing simultaneously hierarchical and close friendship relationships. In J. T. Wood & S. Duck (Eds.), *Understudied relationships: Off the beaten track* (pp. 122–147). Thousand Oaks, CA: Sage.

Zuckerman, M., Hodgins, H., & Miyake, K. (1990). The vocal attractiveness paradigm: Replication and elaboration. *Journal of Nonverbal Behavior, 14,* 97–112.

Zuckerman, M., Miyake, K., & Hodgins, H. S. (1991). Cross-channel effects of vocal and physical attractiveness and their implications for interpersonal perception. *Journal of Personality and Social Psychology, 60,* 545–554.

Credits

Text Credits

Sherman Alexie, excerpt from *The Lone Ranger and Tonto Fistfight in Heaven*. Copyright © 1993 by Sherman Alexie. Reprinted with the permission of Grove/Atlantic, Inc.

Li-Young Lee, "Eating Together" from *Rose*. Copyright © 1986 by Li-Young Lee. Reprinted with the permission of BOA Editions, Ltd., www.BOAEditions.org.

Amy Tan, "Mother Tongue." Copyright © 1990 by Amy Tan. First appeared in *The Threepenny Review*. Reprinted by permission of the author and the Sandra Dijkstra Literary Agency.

Art Credits

Inside Front Cover (by row) **1,** © Ed Bock/CO; **2,** © Andrew Fox/Alamy; **5,** Nick Vedros/agefotostock; **6,** © Brand X Pictures/Alamy; **10,** © Simon Marcus/CO; **11,** Creatas/Jupiter Images; **xxi,** (top) Alex Mares Manton/GI; (bot.) © Yuri-Gripas/Reuters/CO; **xxii,** (top) Todd Bigelow/Aurora/GI; (cent.) Jonathan Ferrey/GI; (bot.) © Digital Art/CO; **xxiii,** (top) © 20th Century Fox/PF; (cent.) Justin Guariglia/NGS/GI; (bot.) Wallack Kirkland/GI; **xxiv,** (top) Arthur Schatz/Time & Life Pictures/GI; (cent.) © Richard Kalvar/Magnum Photos; (bot.) © Jean Gaumy/Magnum Photos; **xxv,** (top) AP-WW; (cent.) WARNER BROS/The Kobal Collection; (bot.) AP-WW; **xxvi,** (top) © Royalty-Free/CO; (cent.) NYT Pictures/George Tames; (bot.) Stuart Franklin/Magnum Photos; **xxvii,** (top) © Karen Kasmauski/CO; (cent.) © Keith Dannemiller/CO; (bot.) Chris Bale/GI; **xxviii,** (top) Ian Berry/Magnum Photos; (cent.) © Adrian Dennis/epa/CO; (bot.) David Frazier/PhotoEdit; **xxix,** (top) Michael Newman/PhotoEdit; (cent.) AP-WW; (bot.) AP-WW. **2, 3, 4,** (all) © Royalty-Free/CO; **6,** Buena Vista Pictures/PF; **7,** Tony Savino/The Image Works; **8,** (l.) © Yuri-Gripas/Reuters/CO; (cent.) AP-WW; (r.) © UNHCR /handout/ Reuters/CO; **9,** (l.) © Shannon Stapleton/Reuters/CO; (r.) © Brant Ward/San Francisco Chronicle/CO; **10,** (l.) Giraudon/ Art Resource, NY; (cent.) Aristotle and Plato: detail from the School of Athens in the Stanza della Segnatura, 1510–11 (fresco) (detail of 472), Raphael (Raffaello Sanzio of Urbino) (1483–1520) Vatican Museums and Galleries, Vatican City, Italy, The Bridgeman Art Library; (r.) © British Library, London, UK/The Bridgeman Art Library; **11,** (l.) © Royal Asiatic Society, London, UK/The Bridgeman Art Library; (r.) Courtesy of the IISH Stefan R. Landsberger Collection; **14,** © Hekimian Julien/CO-Sy; **15,** Paramount/PF; **19,** NASA/Roger Ressmeyer/CO; **20,** Bruce Davidson/Magnum Photos; **21,** AP-WW; **22,** © David Young-Wolff/PhotoEdit; **23,** © Bettmann/CO; **24,** © Steve McCurry/ Magnum Photos; **25,** © Roger Ressmeyer/CO; **26,** © Arthur Klonsky/CO; © Roger Ressmeyer/CO; **27,** Bill Ray/Time & Life Pictures/GI; **28,** Pierre-Franck Colombier/AFP/GI; **29,** (r.) Patrick Zachmann/Magnum Photos; (l.) Howard Sochurek/Time & Life Pictures/GI; **31,** (top) Carl De Keyzer/Magnum; (bot.) Kelvin Murray/GI; **32,** Alex Mares Manton/GI; **33,** From Cartoonbank.com. All rights reserved; **36,** Eugene Richards/ Magnum Photos; **37,** (top) Steve McCurry/Magnum; (bot.) © Royalty-Free/CO; **44,** (top) Wildlife Conservation Society; (bot.) STONE SOUP © 1996 Jan Eliot. Reprinted with permission of UNIVERSAL PRESS SYNDICATE. All rights reserved; **45,** © Gabe Palmer/CO; **47,** Nina Leen/Time & Life Pictures/GI; **48,** © Randy Faris/CO; **49,** (top) Jonathan Ferrey/GI; (bot.) Munish Sharma/Reuters/Landov; **52,** (top) Nancy Honey/GI; (cent.) Caroline Penn/Panos Pictures; (bot.) Todd Bigelow/Aurora/ GI; **53,** Allan Grant/Time & Life Pictures/GI; **54,** (top) Dilbert: © Scott Adams/Dist. by United Feature Syndicate, Inc.; (bot. l.) West Rock/GI; (bot. cent.) Jordan Coonrad; (bot. r.) Allan Seiden/Pacificstock.com; **55,** (l.) Bob Thomas/GI; (cent.) © Paul A. Souders/CO; (r.) Seth Goldfarb/GI; **56,** John Dominis/Time & Life Pictures/GI; **58,** © Contographer ®/CO; **62,** BOONDOCKS © 2005 Aaron McGruder. Dist. by UNIVERSAL PRESS SYNDICATE. Reprinted with permission. All rights reserved; **63,** DREAMWORKS LLC/The Kobal Collection; **65,** Carol Kohen/GI; **69,** BREVITY: © Guy & Rodd/Dist. by United Feature Syndicate, Inc.; **70,** © Ariel Skelley/CO; **78, 79, 80** (all) © Digital Art/CO; **85,** (l.) © Royalty-Free/CO; (l. cent.) Tom Schierlitz/ GI; (r. cent.) © Royalty-Free/CO; (r.) © Royalty-Free/CO; **87,** © Chapman/The Image Works; **88,** (top) © David Alan Harvey/ Magnum Photos; (cent.) Martin Parr/Magnum Photos; (bot.) David R. Frazier/The Image Works; **90,** © ArenaPal/Topham/ The Image Works; **91,** University of California, Irvine; **97,** (all) Yale Joel/Time & Life Pictures/GI; **98,** The Enigma, 1898, from 'L'Estampe Moderne', published Paris 1897–99 (color litho) by Bellery-Defonaines, Henri Jules Ferdinand (1867–1910); **99,** © Bettmann/CO; **100,** © Copyright The Trustees of The British Museum; **104,** Photo by Chi Modu/diverseimages/GI; **106,** (l.) AP/Wide World Photos; (r.) © Bettmann/CO; **107,** NON SEQUITUR ©1997 Wiley Miller. Dist. By UNIVERSAL PRESS SYNDICATE. Reprinted with permission. All rights reserved; **111,** © Digital Art/CO; **114, 115, 116,** (all) Columbia/ The Kobal Collection; **118,** © 20th Century Fox/PF; **120,** AP-WW; **122,** (l.) Alfred Eisenstaedt/Time & Life Pictures/GI; (cent.) Ferdinando Scianna/Magnum Photos; (r.) Photodisc/GI; **123,** (l.) Photodisc/Getty Images; (cent.) Richard Kalvar/Magnum Photos; (r.) Bruce Davidson/Magnum Photos; **125,** (both) © Jeff Greenberg/PhotoEdit; **126,** Gilles Peress/Magnum Photos; **127,** BIG TOP © 2003 Harrell. Dist. By UNIVERSAL PRESS SYNDICATE. Reprinted with permission. All rights reserved; **128,** (l.) Study of a Woman Weeping (black chalk on paper) by Carpeaux, Jean-Baptiste (1827–75) Private Collection/Agnew's, London, UK/The Bridgeman Art Library; (r.) Study of a man shouting (charcoal on paper) by Buonarroti, Michelangelo (1475–1564); **131,** © The New Yorker Collection 2003 Bruce Eric Kaplan from cartoonbank.com. All Rights Reserved; **132,** AP-WW; **133,** Rod Morata/GI; **137,** John Dominis/Time & Life Pictures/GI; **138,** (l.) © Richard Schulman/CO; (cent.) Phil Schermeister/GI; (r.) Justin Guariglia/NGS/GI; **141,** © Arko Datta/Reuters/CO; **146,** Wallack Kirkland/GI; **147,** Royalty-Free/CO; **150, 151, 152,** (all) Arthur Schatz/Time & Life Pictures/ GI; **154,** © New Line Cinema/PF, NY, **155,** © Harry Benson;

Roger-Viollet/The Image Works; **421,** Michael Cogliantry/GI; **422,** (l.) © National Aeronautics & Space Administration/SSPL/Image Works; (cent.) Michael Newman/PhotoEdit; (r.) © Bruno Barbey/ Magnum Photos client; **423,** (l.) AP-WW; (cent.) Anne-Marie Weber/GI; (r.) Australia Picture Library/Index Stock Imagery; **424,** AP-WW; **425,** © 20th Century-Fox/PF; **426,** Horace Bristol/Time & Life Pictures/GI; **427,** © Jack Kurtz/The Image Works; **429,** © Patrick Robert/Sygma/CO; **431,** © J. Wenk/Columbia Pictures/ ZUMA/CO; **432,** (top) NBC/PF; (bot.) © A. Snyder/Photex/ zefa/CO; **435,** (l.) © The New Yorker Collection 1993 Robert Mankoff from cartoonbank.com. All Rights Reserved; (r.) © ABC Photographer: Danny Feld/PF; **437,** Michael Newman/PhotoEdit; **440,** (l.) James Hardy/GI; (r.) Bruce Ayres/GI; **441,** DILBERT: © Scott Adams/Dist. by United Features Syndicate, Inc.; **447,** David Joel/GI.

Name Index

Butt, T., 86, 87
Butterfield, L. H., 338
Buunk, B. P., 368
Buzzanell, P., 433

Cacioppo, J. T., 119
Cahill, D. J., 421, 430
Cahn, D., 297
Calabrese, R. J., 88, 342
Campbell, D. T., 91
Campbell, R. G., 105, 267
Campbell, S. M., 338, 342, 398
Canary, Dan, 31, 52, 93, 159, 243, 297,
    312, 340, 355, 356, 403, 406,
    408, 433
Cappella, J. N., 17
Carbery, J., 400
Carducci, B. J., 167, 382
Carlos, John, 55–57
Carlson, C. J., 390
Carlson, J. G., 138
Carnevale, P. J., 317
Carney, D. R., 285
Carrere, S., 237
Carter, J. D., 92, 263
Carter, Jimmy, 69
Carton, J. S., 259
Caruso, D., 130
Casano, R. A., 249
Casey, R. D., 12
Caughlin, J. P., 297, 320, 379
Cerpas, N., 335
Chadha, G., 118
Chaffee, S. H., 13
Chalfin, J., 341
Chan, Karen, 438
Chandler, T. A., 209
Chaplin, T. M., 129
Chapman, B., 429
Chastain, Brandi, 281
Chavez, Cesar, 151–52, 181
Chelune, G. J., 167
Chen, G.-M., 172, 174, 205, 224, 244,
    264, 265, 275
Cherones, T., 155, 404
Chesebro, J. L., 187, 202, 204
Cheung, L., 50
Chilon of Sparta, 44
Cho, Margaret, 50
Choe, J. C., 368
Chronis, H., 247
Chung, J., 205
Chung, J. H., 189
Cicero, 10
Clair, R. P., 446
Clark, C. L., 384
Clark, M. L., 10

Clark, R. A., 24
Cleveland, J. N., 103, 432
Cline, A., 300
Clinton, William Jefferson, 202, 246
Coakley, C. G., 188, 193, 197
Coan, J., 237
Cobb, Tyrus "Ty," 164–65, 170
Cochran, C. C., 446
Cody, M. J., 61, 194, 195
Cody, M. L., 156
Cohen, T. F., 400
Colditz, G. A., 50
Cole, M., 219
Cole, P. M., 129
Cole, S. R., 219
Coleman, M., 267, 382
Contractor, N. S., 420
Cook, Toni, 217–18, 225, 253
Cooley, Charles Horton, 46
Coon, J., 320
Cooper, C. R., 393
Copeland, A. P., 381
Costa, P. T., 52, 95
Costanzo, F. S., 282
Costanzo, R. R., 282
Cote, S., 129, 131
Couch, L. L., 367
Coupland, N., 244
Coupland, J., 244
Covarrubias, Patricia, 88
Covel, S., 320
Cowell, Simon, 199, 200
Cranch, Richard, 338
Crane, D., 270
Crider, D. M., 124
Cropanzano, R., 139
Cropsey, Alan, 233
Cross, S. E., 54
Cruise, Tom, 130, 132
Cunningham, M., 59, 124
Cupach, W. R., 36, 94, 153, 154, 158,
    159, 297, 312, 361, 362, 363
Cupach, William R., 331
Cusack, J., 228
Custudio, J., 50
Cutler, H. C., 49
Cutrona, C. E., 167

Dainton, M., 237, 355, 356, 398, 406,
    407, 408
Dalai Lama, 49
Daly, J. A., 10, 11, 30, 166, 167, 194
Dash, J., 22
Datta, Arko, 141
Davey, M., 434
David, L., 155, 404
Davidson, R. J., 133

Davies, M., 130
Davila, J., 237
Davis, J. E., 242
Davis, K. E., 398
Davis, M. H., 106
Dawson, E. J., 239
De Ment, T., 127
de Vries, B., 400
Delgado-Gaitan, C., 300
Delia, J. G., 11, 12, 24
Delia, Jesse G., 224
Delille, Jacques, 379
Delpit, L., 217, 218
Demme, J., 265
Derlaga, V. J., 402
Dermer, M., 342
Derr, Vivian, 417–18
Des Roches, C. M., 189
Deutsch, F. M., 263
DeVicentis, D. V., 228
Devine, P. G., 103
Dickson, W. J., 11
Diggs, R. C., 355
Dillard, J., 106, 107, 430, 432, 433
Dindia, Kathryn, 69, 71, 243, 355
Dodge, K. A., 138
Donohue, W. A., 295, 299
Dreyer, A. S., 242
Dreyer, C. A., 242
Druen, P. B., 59
Duan, C., 106
Duck, Steve, 32, 237
Dues, M., 10
Dun, T., 314
Dunbar, N. E., 285
Duncan, B., 140
Duncan, S., Jr., 193

Eagly, A. H., 342
Eavey, R. D., 189
Ebbeson, E., 140
Ebling, R., 127, 128
Edgar, T., 338
Edgley, C., 68
Einarsen, S., 442
Eisenberg, E. M., 421, 435, 436, 438,
    439, 447
Eisenhower, Dwight D., 93
Eklof, M., 189
Ekman, P., 121, 260, 269
Elizabeth I, 93
Ellis, D. G., 221
Emmers-Sommer, Tara, 31, 52, 93, 403
Englehardt, E. E., 159
Ergin, C., 321
Esquivel, Laura, 333–34
Evans, D. E., 52

Subject Index

abuse, workplace, 442–43, 446
accommodation, 308–9
action-oriented listeners, 202, 203
actions, performing, 234–35
actions, plan, 167
actor-observer effects, 87
adaptors, 269
advocacy, 476
affect displays, 282
affection, 332
agentic friendships, 401–2
aggression, verbal
    and aggressive listening, 209
    and interpersonal competence,
        170–71
aggressive families, 396
aggressive listening, 209, 212
aging, 160
agreeableness
    defined, 96
    and emotion management, 129
algebraic impressions, 101–2
ambiguity, 261
American Idol (television program),
        199, 200
analyze, listening to, 200
anger
    and defensiveness, 170
    as primary emotion, 138–41
annoyance, cumulative, 306–7
anthropology, 11, 12
apologies, 60–61
appreciate, listening to, 200
apprehension, communication, 166–69
appropriateness
    and intercultural competence, 172–73
    and interpersonal competence,
        155–56
argumentation, 8
arranged marriages, 350
artifacts, 265, 280
assurances
    and family relationships, 389–90
    and professional peers, 432
    and romantic partners, 357–58
attachment, in romantic
        relationships, 333
attachment styles, 54–55
    anxious attachment style, 55
    avoidant attachment style, 55
    secure attachment style, 55

attending, 191–92
attention focus, 132–33
attraction, romantic, 338–43
attractiveness, physical, 342
attributional complexity, 175–76
attributions, 110
    and defensiveness, 170
    defined, 85–87
    halo and horn effects, 102
    and perception-checking, 107
audience analysis, 8
*Austin Powers: The Spy Who Shagged
        Me* (film), 244–45
autonomy
    versus connection, 68
    and family relationships, 390–91
avoidance, 306
avoidant families, 396
avoiding, 352

back-channel cues, 193
Ballets Africains, Les, 298–99
beautiful-is-good effect, 342
behavioral jealousy, 366
Bend It like Beckham (film), 118
betrayal, 367–72
Big Five personality traits
    defined, 95, 96
    and emotions, 129–30
birds-of-a-feather effect, 342–43
birth stories, 395
bizarreness effect, 197
Black English, 218
blended emotions, 122
blended families, 383
body movements, 265–70, 283
bonding stage, 349–50
Boyz in the Hood (film), 397–98
Brady Bunch, The (television
        program), 380
brain
    gender differences in, 91
    language activity in, 220
Bridget Jones's Diary (Fielding), 176
business studies, 11

capitalization, 270
caring, 333
catharsis, 140

change, personal, 363
channels, communication
    defined, 7
    and nonverbal communication,
        260–61
chronemics, 265, 275–78
circumscribing, 352
clarifying, 195
clarity, 241
climate, organizational, 425–29
cliques, workplace, 423–24
clothing, 279
cognitive jealousy, 366
cohabiting couples, 383
collaboration
    in conflict management, 310–14
    workplace, 427
collaborative families, 396–97
collectivistic cultures
    communication goals in, 173
    conflict approaches in, 321, 324
    defined, 57–58
    listening styles in, 204–5
collegial peers, 430
Color Purple, The (Walker), 234
colors of love, 335
communal friendships, 400
communication
    academic study of, 8–9, 12
    defined, 6–7, 18–22
    goals, 22–24
    historical perspective, 9–12
    issues, 29–32
    nonverbal, 260
    principles, 25–29
    process models, 14–18
    skills, defined, 36, 154
communication accommodation
        theory, 244
Como agua para chocolate (Esquivel),
        333–34
companionate love, 335
competence, communication
    characteristics of, 155–59
    defined, 36, 154
    and online communication, 176–81
    types of messages, 159–64
    See also incompetence,
        communication
competition, 309–10
complementary relationships, 300

compliments, 439–40
comprehend, listening to, 199
compromise, 317
conflict
  approaches to
    accommodation, 308–9
    avoidance, 306–9
    collaboration, 310–13
    competition, 309–10
  contexts for
    close relationships, 297–98
    families, 396–97
    romantic relationships, 360–61
    workplace, 442–43, 446
  defined, 296–97
  external variables
    culture, 321–24
    gender, 320–21
    power, 298–305
  formal study of, 11
  resolutions, 315–19
  and violence, 314–15
conformity orientation, 385–86
connection, 390–91
connotative meanings, 229–30
conscientiousness, 96
consensual families, 386
constitutive rules, 222, 226–27
contagion, emotional, 121
content information, 25
content-oriented listeners, 203
context
  and communication, 7
  and communication
    apprehension, 166
  and culture, 225
contingencies, plan, 167
control, workplace, 427
controlled tests, 14
control messages, 169
conventional messages, 160–62
conversation
  defined, 236
  and nonverbal communication, 283
  orientation, 383–85
conversational scripts, 240
Cooperative Principle, 238–39
cooperative verbal communication,
    237–44
correction, 68
Cosby Show, The (television
    program), 380
courtship stories, 395
"Credo for Ethical Communication"
    (National Communication
    Association), 158
crises, 360–61
criticism, 440–41

cross-sex peers, 432
culture
  and communication
    cooperative verbal
      communication, 243–44
    language, 224–25
    listening style, 205
    nonverbal communication, 264–65
    views of interpersonal
      communication, 29–30
  defined, 29, 57
  and interpersonal relationships
    conflict, 321–24
    friendship, 400, 402
    power, 302–4
    self-disclosure, 70–71
  organizational, 421–24
  and personal experience
    emotion, 127–28
    happiness, 124
    passionate love, 334–35
    perception, 90–91
    personal space, 264, 275
    self, 55–58

deactivation, 133
deception
  defined, 246–47
  in romantic relationships,
    368, 372
defensiveness
  with competitive conflict
    management, 310
  defined, 169–70
  and organizational climate, 425–28
demand-withdrawal pattern, 320–21
denotative meanings, 229
density, network, 423
description, 428
destructive communication, 32, 33
detachment, 428
dialectics, relational
  within families, 390–92
  forms of, 67–69
dialects, 223–24
differentiating, 352
dirty secrets, 310
disagreement, 362–63
discern, listening to, 200
disinhibition, online, 177
display rules, 127–28
Doctors without Borders, 429
dogmatic messages, 169
dogmatism in the workplace, 425–27
dominance, social, 285
domination, in conflict resolution,
    316–17

downward communication, 436–41
dyads, 20
dynamic communication, 20, 27–28
dysfunctional relationship beliefs,
    362–66

"Eating Together" (Lee), 141
eavesdropping, 207–8
EEOC (Equal Employment
    Opportunity Commission), 446
effective communication
  and intercultural competence, 173
  and interpersonal competence,
    156–57
elderspeak, 160
embarrassment, 59–60
emblems, 269
emoticons, 120
emotional intelligence, 139
emotional jealousy, 366
emotions
  within close relationships, 135–36
    anger, 138–41
    grief, 141–43
    passion, 136–38
  contributing factors, 127–30
  defined, 119–21
  displays of, 282
  versus feelings and moods, 122–25
  management of, 130–35, 144–45
  sharing of, 120–21
  types of, 121–22
empathy
  formal study of, 11
  and perception of others, 105–6
  and supportive organizational
    climates, 428
encounter avoidance, 132, 170
encounter structuring, 132, 170
environment, communicating through,
    265, 280–81
Equal Employment Opportunity
    Commission (EEOC), 446
equality, workplace, 428
equity in relationships, 340
escalation, 310
*Eternal Sunshine of the Spotless Mind,
    The* (film), 354–55
ethics
  and communication effectiveness,
    157–59
  defined, 28–29
  historical perspective, 10
  and intercultural competence, 173
  and perception, 110–11
  and power, 300–301
ethnocentrism, 174–75

evaluation, 427
evolution of language, 226–27
exit strategy, 361
experimenting stage, 345–47
expertise currency, 302
expressive messages, 160–62
extended families, 382
external attributions, 86, 102, 107, 110
extraversion, 96, 129
Extreme Makeovers (television program), 278
eye contact, 263
  and culture, 264–65
  managing interactions with, 283
  as nonverbal communication code, 268–69

face, losing, 59–60
facial expressions, 263, 266–68
families
  communication patterns in, 383–87
  conflict in, 396–97
  defining, 380–82
  maintenance strategies, 389–94
  rituals in, 385
  and self, 54–55
  sharing stories in, 394–95
  types of, 382–83
feedback
  and active listening, 193–94
  in interactive communication model, 16–17
feelings, 122–23
fields of experience, 17
fixed features, 281
flaming, 13, 177
flexibility, 425–27
Friends (television program), 270
friendships
  cross-gender, 403
  defining, 397–400
  forms of, 400–402
  and gender, 402–4
  maintaining, 405–9, 412
  rules for, 407–8
  sexual activity within, 404–5
friendship-warmth touch, 272
friends-with-benefits (FWB) relationships, 404–5
functional-professional touch, 272
fundamental attribution errors, 86–87
FWB (friends-with-benefits) relationships, 404–5

Gallipoli (film), 14–15
gay families, 382

gender
  and communication
    cooperative verbal communication, 243
    listening style, 205
    nonverbal communication, 262–64, 285
    online communication, 62
  defined, 31
  and interpersonal relationships
    conflict, 320–21
    friendships, 402–4
    power, 304–5
    self-disclosure, 71, 74
  and personal experience
    emotion, 128–29
    passionate love, 334
    perception, 91–94
    self, 52–54
    socialization, 52
  and society
    perceived differences, 363
    physical appearance, 279
    stereotyping, 103
Gestalts, 99–101
gestures, 269–70
goals, interpersonal, 22–24, 156–57
Gone with the Wind (Mitchell), 318–19
Great Santini, The (film), 396
grief, 141–43

halo effect, 101, 102
Handmaid's Tale, The (Atwood), 268
happiness, 124
haptics, 265, 272–73, 283, 284
Harold and Kumar Go to White Castle (film), 436–37
Harry Potter and the Philosopher's Stone (Rowling), 378
hearing, 188–89
helicopter parents, 392
hierarchy of needs, 23
high-context cultures, 225
High Fidelity (film), 228–30
high self-monitors, 156, 157
honesty, 67–68, 239
horn effect, 101, 102
hostile climate harassment, 446
hostility, chronic
  and aggressive listening, 209
  self-test for, 131
  and suppression of anger, 140
hypothesis testing, 14

idioms, personal, 223
I-It relationships, 21

"I" language, 241–42
illustrators, 269
immediacy, 269
impersonal communication, 21–22
implicit personality theories, 96–98
impressions, interpersonal, 98–105
incompetence, communication
  communication apprehension, 166–69
  defensiveness, 169–70
  of Ty Cobb, 164–65
indifference messages, 169
individualistic cultures
  conflict approaches in, 321, 324
  defined, 57–58
  group decision making in, 173
  and listening style, 204–5
infidelity, sexual, 368
information peers, 430
informativeness, 239
ingroupers, 90
initiating stage, 345
instructors, foreign-born, 171–72
instrumental goals
  in collective and individualistic cultures, 173
  and communication effectiveness, 156–57
  defined, 24
integrating stage, 347
integrative agreements, 317
intelligence, emotional, 130–31
intensifying stage, 347
intentional communication, 26–27
interactions, 7, 11
interactive communication model, 16–17
intercultural competence, 171–76
internal attributions, 86, 102, 107, 110
internet communication. *See* online communication
interparental conflict, 396
interpersonal communication, defined, 20
interpersonal communication competence, defined, 154
interpersonal relationships, 36
interpreting information, 84–88
intimacy
  and nonverbal communication, 284–85
  and personal space, 273
  as power currency, 302
  in romantic relationships, 333
intrapersonal communication, 20
irreversibility, 27
italics, 272
I-Thou relationships, 21

jealousy, 366–67
Jefferson strategy, 140–41, 170
Jerry McGuire (film), 244–45
Johari Window, 65–67

kinesics, 265–70, 283
kitchen-sink messages
    and cumulative annoyance, 306–7
    defined, 298
    and family conflict, 397

laissez-faire families, 386–87
language. *See* verbal communication
lesbian families, 382
Like Water for Chocolate (Esquivel),
    333–34
liking, 332–33
linear communication model, 16
linguistic determinism, 231
linguistic relativity, 232–33
Lion and the Cobra, The (O'Connor),
    262, 263
listening
    functions of, 199–201
    ineffective, 206–9
    process, 188–93
    Ptah Hotep on, 10
    styles of, 201–5
loneliness, 167–69
long-distance friendships, 408–9, 412
long-term conflict outcomes, 318
long-term memory, 193
Long Winter, The (Wilder), 388
looking-glass self, 45
loudness, vocal, 270, 283
love-intimacy touch, 272
loving, 332–33
low-context cultures, 225
low self-monitors, 156, 157
loyalty strategy, 360–61
lurking, 180

managers. *See* mixed-status
    relationships
marriages, arranged, 350
masks
    of Japanese Noh theater, 267
    and public self-presentation, 59
mass communication studies, 8
matching, 342
meaning
    and nonverbal communication,
        261–62, 281–82
    and verbal communication, 228–30
Médecins sans Frontières (MSF), 429

media, 7, 8
Memento (film), 192
memory, 192–93
mental bracketing, 192
mere exposure effect, 341
messages
    and defensive communication,
        169–70
    defined, 7
    types of, 159–64
meta-communication, 26
mind-reading, 363
mispresentation, 246–47
misunderstandings, 247–49, 252
mixed messages, 262
mixed-status relationships, 434–35
    downward communication, 436–41
    maintenance of, 441–42
    upward communication, 435–36
    and workplace abuse, 442–43, 446
mnemonics, 197
model minority myth, 438
moods, 123–25
"Mother Tongue" (Tan), 220–21
MSF (Médecins sans Frontières), 429
M-time, 275–78

naming, 232–33
Napoleon Dynamite (film), 320
narcissistic listening, 212
needs, hierarchy of, 23
negativity effect, 100–101
neglect strategy, 361
networks, organizational, 422–24
neuroticism, 96, 129
New York Yankees, 280
Noh masks, 267
noise, communication, 16
noise pollution, 189
nonverbal communication
    codes for (*see* nonverbal
        communication codes)
    defined, 260
    functions, 281–85
    managing, 288–89
    principles, 260–65
    study of, 12
nonverbal communication codes, 256
    artifacts (objects), 280
    body movements (kinesics), 265–70
    chronemics (time), 275–78
    environment, 280–81
    haptics (touch), 272–73
    physical appearance, 278–79
    proxemics (personal space),
        273–75
    vocalics, 265, 270–72

novelty, 68–69
nuclear families, 382

Oakland school board incident,
    217–18, 225, 253
objects, communicating
    through, 280
Office Space (film), 425
online communication, 31
    communication style
        linearity of, 16
        self-disclosure, 71
        self-presentation, 61–62
        use of punctuation, 270
    groups
        discussion groups, 13
        support groups, 142–43
        virtual networks, 423
    negative aspects
        competitive conflict resolution, 309
        deception, 246–47
        flaming, 13
        lurking, 180
        provocateurs, 209
        trolling, 177
    relationships
        communal friendships, 26–27
        communication competence,
            176–81
        professional peers, 430
opening lines, 345
openness
    in family relationships, 384, 390
    in friendships, 406–7
    as personality trait, 96
    with professional peers, 431
    versus protection, 67–68
    and relational maintenance, 356–57
Oprah (television program), 130, 132
organizational communication
    climate, 425–29
    culture, 421–24
    networks, 422–24
organization of perceptions, 83–84
ought self, 48
outgroupers, 90
Outsiders, The (Hinton), 94–95

pacifism, radical, 308
paraphrasing, 194–95
passion, romantic, 136–38, 333–35
peers, professional, 429–33
people-oriented listeners, 203
perception
    checking, 107, 110
    improving, 105–10

influences on, 89–96
interpersonal impressions, 98–105
as process, 82–88
personal currency, 302
personality
  and emotion, 129–30
  and perception, 94–97
personal space, 264, 265, 273–75
physical appearance
  and attractiveness, 342
  as nonverbal communication code,
    265, 278–80
pitch, voice
  and affect displays, 282
  as nonverbal communication code,
    270–71
  and self-presentation, 283
plans, communication, 167
pluralistic families, 386
political science, 11
political speeches, 8
Pollyanna (Porter), 100
positive feedback, 193–94
positivity
  with family members, 389
  with professional peers, 431
  with romantic partners, 356
positivity bias, 100
power
  characteristics, 299–301
  and conflict, 298–99
  and culture, 302–4
  currencies, 301–2
  and gender, 304–5
  and posture, 269–70
power-distance, 302–4
Pragmatics of Human Communication
    (Watzlawick et al.), 12
praise, 439–40
predictability, 68–69
presentation of self, 58–62
primacy effect, 100–101
primary emotions, 121
process, communication as, 7, 12
professional peers, 429–33
protection, 67–68
protective families, 386, 390, 391–92
provocateurs, 209
proxemics, 265, 273–75
proximity
  as nonverbal communication code,
    265, 273–75
  and romantic attraction, 341–42
pseudo-conflict, 307
pseudo-listening, 208–9
psychology, 11
P-time, 277–78
public space, 273

public speaking, 10
punctuation, 83–84, 107
Punnovada Sutta, 308

qualitative research, 13–14
quantitative research, 14
quid pro quo harassment, 446

Rabbit Romeo (cartoon), 329
race/ethnicity
  and cultural identity, 55–57
  perceptions of, 92
  and stereotyping, 103
radical pacifism, 308
Real World, The (television program),
    293–94, 309, 325
reappraisal, 133–34, 170
recalling, 196–98
receiving
  and communication
    apprehension, 166
  in linear communication model, 16
  and perception, 188–91
regulative rules, 222–23, 227
regulators, 269, 283
relational devaluation, 368
relational dialectics, 390–92
relational goals
  in collectivistic and individualistic
    cultures, 173
  and communication effectiveness,
    156–57
  types of, 24
relational maintenance, 355–59
relationship information, 25–26
relationships, managing, 237
relevance, 240–41
reprimands, 440–41
research methods
  development of, 11–12
  quantitative and qualitative
    approaches, 13–14
resource currency, 301–2
resources, 339–40
respect, 300, 333
responding, 193–95
rhetoric, 8, 10
rhetorical messages, 160–64
rituals, family, 384
romantic relationships
  attraction, 338–43
  challenges to, 362–68, 372
  crises, 360–61
  decisions concerning, 361–62
  defining, 332–38
  elements of, 336–38

maintenance strategies, 355–59
stages of development, 344–49
stages of dissolution, 350–54
in the workplace, 432–33
Romeo and Juliet (Shakespeare),
    329–30, 362, 373
rules
  constitutive and regulative, 222–23
  for family communication, 392–94
  for friendships, 407–8
  and nonverbal communication, 261

salience, 83
Sapir-Whorf hypothesis, 231–33
schemata, 84, 107
screen names, 62
seeing, 188
Seinfeld (television program), 155, 404
selection of information, 82–83
selective ignoring, 367
selective listening, 207
self
  components of, 44–47
  presentation of, 58–62
  and relationships, 63–69
  sources of, 52–58
self-awareness, 44–46
self-bolstering, 366–67
self-concept, 45–46
self-disclosure, 69–74
self-discrepancy theory, 48
self-esteem, 47–51
self-fulfilling prophecies, 46–47
self-monitoring, 156, 157
self-presentation, 24
  in collectivistic and individualistic
    cultures, 173
  and communication effectiveness,
    156–57
  and nonverbal communication,
    282–83
self-presentation goals, 24
self-reliance, 366
self-serving bias, 87–88
semi-fixed features, 281
senders, 16
seniors, 160
Sense and Sensibility (Austen),
    115–16, 131, 132, 147
separation, 316
SEP (Standard English Proficiency)
    program, 218, 225
September 11, 2001, terrorist attacks,
    125–27
sexual activity, expectations
    concerning, 363
sexual-arousal touch, 272

sexual desire, 335
sexual harassment, 443, 446
sexual infidelity, 368
sexual orientation, 31
sharing
    activities, 358, 405–6
    tasks, 358–59
short-term conflict resolutions,
    316–17
short-term memory, 192–93
Shrek (film), 63
shyness, 167–69
Silence of the Lambs, The (film),
    265–66
similarity, 342–43
Simpsons, The (television program),
    380
single-parent families, 383
skirting, 306
Slow Food Movement, 278
small talk, 346
sniping, 306
social comparison, 44–45
social exchange theory, 339
social networks
    as power currency, 302
    and romantic partners, 359–60
social penetration theory, 64–65
social-polite touch, 272
social psychology, 10–11
social science, 11–12
social space, 273
sociology, 11
Southern Baptist Convention, 300
Special Operations School, 174
special peers, 430
speech acts, 235
speech and rhetorical studies, 8
speeches, political, 8
speech rate, 271
spontaneous communication, 425
stagnating, 352
Standard English Proficiency (SEP)
    program, 218, 225
stereotyping, 102–5
stories, family, 394–95
strategic communication, 425
structural improvements, 317
submissiveness, 285

subordinates. *See* mixed-status
    relationships
sudden-death statements, 310
superiority and organizational
    climate, 428
superiority messages, 169
supervisors. *See* mixed-status
    relationships
support
    listening to, 199–200
    and organizational climate, 425–29
support groups, 142
supportive communication, 143
suppression, 131–32, 140
survival stories, 395
symbols, 222
symmetrical relationships, 300
symmetry, facial, 278–79

telecommunication studies, 8–9
temporary communication
    apprehension, 166
tensions, family, 390
terminating, 354
territoriality, 275
theory, development of, 13–14
thought and language, 230–33
time, communicating through, 265,
    275–78
time-oriented listeners, 202–3
tone, vocal, 271–72
*Tonto and the Lone Ranger Fistfight in
    Heaven* (Alexie), 135
touch, communicating through, 265,
    272–73, 283, 284
trait communication apprehension, 166
transactional communication model,
    17–18
trolling, 177, 180
Two Towers, The (Tolkien), 154

uncertainty reduction theory, 88–89
understanding, 192–93
unintentional communication, 26–27
United States Air Force, 174
unsolvable conflicts, 318–19
upward communication, 435–36

venting, 131–32, 140
verbal aggression
    and aggressive listening, 209
    and interpersonal incompetence,
        170–71
verbal communication
    characteristics, 220–27
    cooperative, 237–44
    functions, 227
        conversation, 236
        managing relationships, 237
        naming, 233
        performing actions, 234–35
        shaping thought, 230–33
        sharing meaning, 228–30
    and gender, 93–94
    and nonverbal communication, 262
violence, 314–15
virtual networks, 423
virtual peers, 430
virtual vocalics, 270, 272
vocalics
    and affect displays, 282
    as nonverbal communication code,
        265, 270–72
voice strategy, 360

"we" language, 242
West Side Story (musical), 329
When Prophecy Fails (Keech), 92
White Privilege (McIntosh), 92
word choice, 10
workplace relationships
    abuse in, 442–43, 446
    and cliques, 423–24
    defining, 420–21
    and organizational climate, 425–29
    and organizational culture, 421–24
    with professional peers, 429–33
    See also mixed-status relationships
World Cup, 281
world-mindedness, 173–75
Written on the Body (Winterson), 284
Wuthering Heights (Brontë), 207

"you" language, 241–42